BERG/Unesco

D1646743

World social science information dire(

Répertoires mondiaux d'information en sciences sociales

Repertorios mundiales de información sobre las ciencias sociales

World
social science
information directories

A series based on the output of the DARE Data Bank of the Unesco Social and Human Sciences Documentation Centre

Répertoires mondiaux
d'information
en sciences sociales

Collection ayant pour source la Banque de données DARE du Centre de documentation en sciences sociales et humaines de l'Unesco

Repertorios mundiales
de información
sobre las ciencias sociales

Colección basada en la producción del Banco de Datos DARE del Centro de Documentación de Ciencias Sociales y Humanas de la Unesco

1988

Selective inventory of social science information and documentation services
Third edition

Prepared by the Unesco Social and
Human Sciences Documentation Centre

Inventaire sélectif des services d'information et de documentation en sciences sociales
Troisième édition

Préparé par le Centre de documentation
en sciences sociales et humaines de
l'Unesco

Inventario selectivo de servicios de información y documentación en ciencias sociales
Tercera edición

Preparado por el Centro de
Documentación de Ciencias Sociales y
Humanas de la Unesco

BERG/Unesco

Published in 1988 by Berg Publishers Limited and the United Nations Educational, Scientific and Cultural Organization. Printed in Great Britain by Billings of Worcester

Publié en 1988 par Berg Publishers Limited et l'Organisation des Nations Unies pour l'éducation, la science et la culture. Imprimé par Billings of Worcester, Royaume-Uni

Publicado en 1988 por Berg Publishers Limited y la Organización de las Naciones Unidas para la Educación, la Ciencia y la Cultura. Impreso por Billings of Worcester, Reino Unido

© Unesco 1988

The paperback edition of this book is distributed exclusively by UNESCO, Paris
ISBN 92-3-002575-5

Unesco
7 place de Fontenoy, 75700 Paris, France

The cloth edition is distributed by Berg Publishers Limited
ISBN 0-85496-270-0

Berg Publishers Limited
77 Morrell Avenue, Oxford OX4 1NQ, UK
175 Fifth Avenue/Room 400, New York, NY 10010, USA
Nordalbingerweg 14, 2000 Hamburg 61, FRG

British Library Cataloguing in Publication Data

Selective inventory of social science information and documentation services. – 3rd ed. – (World social science information directories).
1. Social sciences. Documentation services
I. Unesco. *Social and Human Sciences Documentation Centre* II. Inventaire sélectif des services d'information et de documentation en sciences sociales III. Series
025'.063

ISBN 0-85496-270-0 cloth

Library of Congress Cataloging-in-Publication data applied for

Contents

Table des matières

Indice

Preface

This inventory is produced from Unesco's DARE Data Bank and based on replies obtained from a widely distributed questionnaire. It is intended to provide details of the major social science information services.

The term *information service*, as used here, applies to any body whose principal function is to provide information or data, in one form or another, to those working in the field of the social sciences. Such bodies are, by and large, involved in documentation: they give access either to documents as such (printed matter, cartographic materials, audio-visual supports) or to information pertaining to those documents (bibliographical searches, analyses, syntheses). They go by different names. Some are libraries, but those have been included only if, as well as specializing in the social sciences, they also provide additional services such as, for example, publishing, producing bibliographies, compiling information bulletins, etc. Others are called documentation centres, information services or reference bureaux, while finally there are those bodies which, though their activity is not based on documents as such, furnish primary data. Depending on their nature, these services may be called data banks, data archives or data libraries, and owe their existence to the rapid advances made in the field of computer science.

All such bodies are listed in the Inventory, provided that they do not confine themselves solely to meeting the needs of their own staff or the staff of the organization to which they are attached. We have accordingly omitted the many services belonging either to private firms or governmental bodies which gather and process data for their own use.

In order to qualify for inclusion in the Inventory, the services must be equipped to perform the various functions expected of them; this is the second criterion for inclusion. Thus, they must have permanent staff and information sources.

This criterion of structure should not be confused with that of size: an efficient service can be developed by a very small staff carrying out specific activities. On the other hand, a world inventory cannot attempt to provide an exhaustive list of services down to the smallest units; that can be done only by national inventories.

In deciding on which services to include, we were guided by a criterion of minimum size which varied, however, with the extent of the field covered. Thus, organizations providing highly specialized services have been included, irrespective of number of staff.

The services selected for inclusion vary considerably in character. They may be autonomous bodies or, for that matter, departments or branches of research, or educational institutions of a national government or of an international organization.

A service is regarded as autonomous if it has its own staff and provides specific facilities. It need not even have a name and may be simply known as the *information service* of a particular institution.

In some instances, entries have been made for large university libraries in countries where they are the richest national source of social science documentary information. As to what constitutes the *social sciences*, the customary Unesco definition has been applied, but with a certain degree of flexibility so as to include the subject matter which each country regards as connected with the social sciences. In this respect, national conceptions sometimes differ, and we felt that it would be useful to reflect this diversity, since the object of a world inventory is to make known the situation that has developed in each country in response to the policies of the responsible national bodies.

This is the third edition of the Inventory. It is based on the content of the DARE data bank at Unesco, supplemented by replies obtained from a widely distributed questionnaire. The present edition contains a total of 894 information services, nearly double the number in its predecessor, and covers 38 additional countries. In order to provide more information, two additional indexes have been included, namely the Geographical coverage index and the Data bases index.

Although the data in the Inventory have been repeatedly checked, errors and omissions may still exist. All modifications and additions should be entered on the questionnaire at the end of this Inventory and sent to Unesco at the following address:

Social and Human Sciences
Documentation Centre
Unesco
7 Place de Fontenoy
75700 PARIS
France

Préface

Le présent inventaire a été composé à partir de la Banque de données DARE de l'Unesco sur la base des réponses obtenues à un questionnaire ayant fait l'objet d'une large distribution. Son objet est de fournir des renseignements précis sur les principaux services d'information relevant des sciences sociales.

Les *services d'information* sont tous les organismes ayant pour fonction principale de fournir, sous une forme quelconque, de l'information ou des données à des publics travaillant dans le domaine des sciences sociales. Ces organismes sont en majorité documentaires; ils donnent accès soit aux documents eux-mêmes (documents écrits, matériaux cartographiques, supports audiovisuels, etc.), soit à des informations renvoyant à ces documents (références bibliographiques, analyses, synthèses, etc.). Ils sont désignés par des noms divers. Certains sont des bibliothèques: elles ont été retenues si elles sont spécialisées en sciences sociales et si elles ne se contentent pas de conserver et de communiquer leurs fonds de documents, mais offrent d'autres services comme des publications documentaires, des recherches bibliographiques, des bulletins d'information courante, etc. D'autres organismes portent des noms comme centres de documentation, services d'information, bureaux de référence, etc. D'autres enfin, n'ont pas comme base de leur activité des documents proprement dits, mais fournissent des données primaires. Suivant leurs caractéristiques, ces services portent des noms divers: banques de données, archives de données, bibliothèques de données, et n'ont pu se constituer que grâce aux progrès rapides de l'informatique.

Ces services ont été retenus dans cet inventaire à condition qu'ils soient mis à la disposition d'un certain public et ne se contentent pas de fournir des informations à leur propre personnel ou au personnel de l'établissement dont ils dépendent. Nous avons donc éliminé un grand nombre d'organismes appartenant aussi bien à des entreprises privées qu'à des administrations gouvernementales qui rassemblent et traitent des données pour leur usage exclusif.

Un autre autre critère de sélection est la nécessité pour les organismes considérés d'être structurés d'une façon qui leur permette d'exécuter les diverses tâches nécessaires. Ils doivent donc posséder une infrastructure permanente.

Ce critère de la structure ne se confond pas avec celui de la dimension: des services efficaces peuvent être constitués par une toute petite équipe, dont les membres effectuent une série déterminée de tâches diverses. Mais il n'est pas question ici de donner un inventaire exhaustif de tous les services existants, si petits soient-ils: cet objectif ne peut être atteint que par des inventaires nationaux. Nous avons utilisé pour la sélection un critère de dimension minimale, qui n'est d'ailleurs pas uniforme mais varie suivant l'ampleur du domaine scientifique couvert. Ainsi, des organismes offrant des services trés spécialisés ont eté inclus sans tenir compte du nombre de leurs effectifs.

Au surplus, les services retenus sont de statuts très divers. Ils peuvent être des organismes autonomes aussi bien que des départements ou des branches d'un établissement de recherche ou d'enseignement, d'un ministère ou d'une administration ou encore d'une organisation internationale. L'existence autonome d'un service se reconnaît à ce qu'il dispose d'un personnel propre et fournit sous son nom des produits spécifiques. Il peut même ne pas avoir de nom parfaitement caractérisé, et s'appeler seulement *service d'information* de tel établissement.

On a retenu quelques grandes bibliothèques universitaires, dans les pays où elles constituent en même temps la source nationale la plus riche en information documentaire pour les sciences sociales. Les *sciences sociales* elles-mêmes ont été définies comme le fait habituellement l'Unesco. Mais cette définition a été appliquée de façon souple, de manière à couvrir les matières qui, dans chaque pays, sont considérées comme relevant des sciences sociales. Les conceptions nationales à cet égard sont parfois différentes les unes des autres. Nous avons estimé utile de refléter cette diversité, puisque le but d'un inventaire mondial est de faire connaître la situation existant dans chaque pays, telle que l'ont modelée les organismes nationaux responsables.

Il s'agit ici de la troisième édition de ce répertoire. Il a été établi à partir de la Banque de Données DARE de l'Unesco augmentée des réponses à un questionnaire qui a fait l'objet d'une large distribution. Cette édition comprend un total de 894 services d'information, près du double de la précédente édition, et couvre 38 pays supplémentaires. Afin de présenter une information plus détaillée, deux index ont été ajoutés. Il s'agit de l'Index des domaines géographiques couverts et de l'Index des bases de données.

Malgré des vérifications répétées, une publication de cette nature ne peut être exempte d'erreurs ou d'inexactitudes. L'Unesco serait reconnaissante aux utilisateurs de bien vouloir, en répondant au questionnaire publié en annexe, envoyer toutes corrections ou informations complémentaires à l'adresse suivante:

Unesco
Centre de documentation en sciences
sociales et humaines
7 Place de Fontenoy
75700 PARIS
France

Prefacio

Este inventario ha sido preparado partiendo del Banco de datos DARE de la Unesco, en base a las respuestas obtenidas a un cuestionario ampliamente distribuído. Su finalidad es proporcionar informaciones precisas sobre los principales servicios de información en materia de ciencias sociales.

Se designa acquí como *servicios de información* a todos los organismos cuya función principal es suministrar, bajo cualquier forma, informaciones o datos a quienes trabajan en la esfera de las ciencias sociales. Estos organismos están, en su mayoría, relacionados con la documentación; permiten el acceso, ya sea a los documentos mismos (material y escritos cartográficos, apoyos audiovisuales, etc.), como a las informaciones que remiten a dichos documentos (referencias bibliográficas, análisis, síntesis, etc.). Dichos servicios se designan con diversos nombres. Algunos de ellos son bibliotecas; se las ha incluido en el inventario cuando se especializan en ciencias sociales y no se limitan a conservar y a comunicar sus existencias de documentos, sino que ofrecen además otros servicios como publicaciones documentales, investigaciones bibliográficas, boletines de información de actualidad, etc. Otros organismos llevan nombres tales como centros de documentación, servicios de información, oficinas de consulta, etc.

Por último, otros no tienen como base de su actividad los documentos propiamente dichos, sino que proporcionan datos primarios. Según sus características, estos servicios se llaman de diferentes maneras: bancos de datos, archivos de datos, bibliotecas de datos, y se han podido establecer gracias a los progresos rápidos de la informática. Dichas entidades se han registrado en el inventario cuando prestan servicios al publico y no se limitan a suministrar información a su propio personal o al personal del establecimiento del cual dependen. De ahí que se haya eliminado un gran número de organismos pertenecientes tanto a empresas privadas como a oficinas gubernamentales que compilan y tratan datos exclusivamente para su propio uso.

Otro criterio de selección es la necesidad que tienen los organismos considerados, de ser estructurados de tal manera que puedan ejecutar las diversas tareas necesarias, vale decir que deben poseer una infraestructura permanente.

Este criterio de la estructura no debe confundirse con el de la dimensión: hay servicios eficaces que pueden contar con un personal muy reducido, cuyos miembros efectúan una serie determinada de tareas diversas. Pero aquí no se trata de hacer un inventario exhaustivo de todos los servicios existentes, incluso de los más pequeños, ya que este objetivo sólo se puede lograr en los inventarios nacionales. Hemos utilizado, para hacer la selección, un criterio de dimensión mínima, que por otra parte, no es uniforme sino variable, según la amplitud del campo científico abarcado. Así pues, se han incluído algunos organismos que ofrecen servicios muy especializados sin considerar su capacidad en materia de personal.

Además, los servicios que hemos incluído tienen estatutos muy diversos. Puede tratarse de organismos autónomos, como también de departamentos o filiales de un establecimiento de investigación o de enseñanza, de un ministerio o de una administración, o de una organización internacional. La existencia autónoma de un servicio, se reconoce por el hecho de disponer de un personal propio y de suministrar productos específicos bajo su nombre. Puede, incluso, no tener un nombre perfectamente caracterizado y llamarse simplemente *servicio de información* de tal o cual establecimiento.

Se han registrado algunas grandes bibliotecas universitarias en los países donde ellas constituyen al mismo tiempo la fuente nacional más rica en materia de información documental para las ciencias sociales. Se ha trabajado sobre la base de la definición habitual de *ciencias sociales* de la Unesco. Pero esta definición se ha aplicado de manera flexible para englobar las materias que, en cada país, se consideran como pertenecientes a las ciencias sociales. Los conceptos

nacionales a este respecto difieren a veces de un país a otro. Consideramos útil reflejar esta diversidad, porque la finalidad de un inventario mundial es difundir la situación de cada país, tal como la han modelado los organismos nacionales responsables.

Se presenta ahora la tercera edición del repertorio. Ha sido establecido a partir del Banco de datos DARE de la Unesco, al cual se añadieron las respuestas a un cuestionario que fue ampliamente distribuído. Esta edición incluye un total de 894 servicios de información, es desir, casi el doble de la edición anterior, y abarca 38 países más. Con el fin de presentar una información más detallada se agregaron dos índices; se trata del Indice de los ámbitos geográficos de los servicios y del Indice de bases de datos.

A pesar de las repetidas verificaciones realizadas en el curso de su preparación, una obra como la presente puede no estar exenta de errores o de inexactitudes. Por ello la Unesco estará muy agradecida con aquellos usuarios que, valiéndose del cuestionario incluído en el Anexo, tengan a bien hacerle llegar las correcciones necesarias, así como informaciones complementarias, a la siguiente dirección:

Unesco
Centro de documentación en
ciencias sociales y humanas
7 Place de Fontenoy
75700 PARIS
France

Field Codes

Official name of service
Synonymous name(s) and acronym(s)
Parent organization
Address and cable address
Created
Head of service
Size of staff: professional; other; total
Scope and type of service: international
    or national; public or private; profit or
    non-profit
Systems & networks attached to
Material(s) describing the service
Working language(s)
Subject coverage
Geographical coverage
Data being processed and size
Data processing method(s): manual;
    partially computerized; computerized
Hardware used
Software used
Storage media: traditional shelving of
    publications; fiches; tapes; discs;
    microfiches; CD-ROM
Type of activity: data collection; data
    analysis; distribution of information;
    scientific research and
    methodological activities in the field
    of social science information and
    documentation; training of social
    science information and
    documentation personnel;
    publication

Periodicals published
Documentary or bibliographical
    publications
Clientele
Access to service
Type & description of services provided

Codage par zone

Codificación por áreas

Nom officiel du service
Autre(s) nom(s) officiel(s) et sigle(s)
Organisation mère
Adresse postale et télégraphique
Créé en
Directeur actuel
Effectif: professionnel; autre; total
Champ d'action et type du service:
    international ou national; public ou
    privé; à but lucratif ou sans but
    lucratif
Appartenance à un système ou réseau
Publication(s) décrivant le service
Langue(s) de travail
Sujet(s) traité(s)
Domaine(s) géographique(s)
Données traitées et volume
Méthodes de traitement des données:
    manuelle; partiellement automatisée;
    par ordinateur
Matériel informatique
Logiciel
Stockage des données: collection de
    publications sur rayonnages; fiches;
    bandes ou disques magnétiques;
    microfiches; CD-ROM
Type d'activité: collecte de données;
    analyse de données; distribution
    d'information; activités de recherche
    scientifique et méthodologique dans
    le domaine de l'information et de la
    documentation en sciences sociales;
    formation de personnel pour
    l'information et la documentation en
    sciences sociales; publication

Nombre oficial del servicio
Otro(s) nombre(s) oficial(es) y siglas(s)
Organización matriz
Dirección postal y telegráfica
Fundado en
Director actual
Cantidad de personal: profesional; otro;
    total
Ambito y typo de servicio: internacional
    o nacional; publica o privado; con o
    sin fin lucrativo
Vinculación a un sistema o red
Publicacion(es) que describe(n) al
    servicio
Idioma(s) de trabajo
Temas tratados
Zonas geográficas
Datos tratados y volumen
Método de tratamiento de datos:
    manual; parcialmente automatizado;
    por ordenador
Equipo de computación
Sistemas de programación
Almacenamiento de datos: colocación
    en estantes; fichas; cintas magnéticas
    o discos magnéticos; microfichas;
    CD-ROM
Tipo de actividad: acopio de datos;
    análisis de datos; distribución de
    información; actividades de
    investigación científica y
    metodológica en el ámbito de las
    ciencias sociales; formación de
    personal para la información y la
    documentación en ciencias sociales;
    publicación

Périodiques publiés

Publications documentaires ou
   bibliographiques

Utilisateurs

Conditions de service

Type et description des services offerts

Publicaciones periódicas publicadas

Publicaciones documentales o
   bibliográficas

Usuarios

Acceso al servicio

Tipo y descripción de los servicios que se
   ofrecen

INDEX OF COUNTRIES/INDEX DES PAYS/INDICE DE PAISES

SECTION I - INDEX OF INFORMATION SERVICES AND ACRONYMS WITH INDICATION OF HOST
COUNTRY OF THE SERVICE

A

A. N. Sinha Institute of Social Studies, Library
    INDIA *394*
Aarhus Graduate School of Management and Modern Languages, Library
    DENMARK *258*
ABI/INFORM
    U. S. A. *759*
ABS, Central Information Service
    AUSTRALIA *116*
Academia de Humanismo Cristiano, Grupo de Investigaciones Agrarias, Biblioteca y
    Centro de Documentación
    CHILE *214*
Academia de Ştiinţe Sociale şi Politicé, Centrul de Informare şi Documentare
    ROMANIA *640*
Academia de Ştiinţe Sociale şi Politice, Oficiul de informare Documentare in
    Stiinţele Sociale şi Politice
    ROMANIA *641*
Academia de Ştiinte Sociales şi Politice, Oficiul de Informare-Documentare
    ROMANIA *642*
Academia Nacional de la Historia, Biblioteca
    ARGENTINA *89*
Academic Library "Dr. Nicolas Mikhov"
    BULGARIA *173*
Academy of Economics in Cracow, Library
    POLAND *610*
Academy of Economics in Poznan, Main Library
    POLAND *611*
Academy of Educational Development, Clearinghouse on Development Communication
    U. S. A. *760*
Academy of Sciences of the Byelorussian Soviet Socialist Republic, Department of
    Scientific Information in Social Sciences
    BYELORUSSIAN SSR *178*
Academy of Sciences of the German Democratic Republic, Centre for Social Science
    Information
    GERMAN DEMOCRATIC REPUBLIC *340*
The Academy of Sciences of the Kazakh SSR, Section of Scientific Information
    U. S. S. R. *868*
The Academy of Sciences of the Kirgiz SSR, Institute of Scientific Information in
    Social Sciences
    U. S. S. R. *869*
Academy of Social and Political Science, Office for Documentary Information
    ROMANIA *642*
Academy of Social and Political Sciences, Office of Information and Documentation in
    Social and Political Sciences
    ROMANIA *641*
Academy of Social Sciences, Scientific Information Centre and Library
    POLAND *613*
ACCIS
    SWITZERLAND *1*
Addis Ababa University, Institute of Ethiopian Studies, Information Service
    ETHIOPIA *276*
ADIPA
    MALAYSIA *10*

1

Administrative Research Institute, Documentation Centre
    ARGENTINA *111*
ADPSS
    ITALY *461*
Advisory and Information Services Division, United Nations Centre on Transnational
    Corporations
    U. S. A. *67*
Advisory Committee for the Co-ordination of Information Systems
    SWITZERLAND *1*
AE WR
    POLAND *609*
AEK
    POLAND *610*
AES
    SWITZERLAND *694*
AFB
    GERMANY (FEDERAL REPUBLIC) *342*
African Institute for Economic and Social Development, Documentation Centre
    COTE D'IVOIRE *240*
African Institute for Economic Development and Planning
    SENEGAL *2*
African Studies Centre, Library and Documentation Department
    NETHERLANDS *537*
African Training and Research Centre for Women
    ETHIOPIA *3*
African Training and Research Centre in Administration for Development, Division of
    Documentation
    MOROCCO *4*
Afrika Studie-en Dokumentatiecentrum
    BELGIUM *144*
Afrika-Studiecentrum, Afdeling Bibliotheek en Documentatie
    NETHERLANDS *537*
Agence Canadienne de Développement International, Centre d'Information sur le
    Développement
    CANADA *183*
Agency for International Development, Center for Development Information and
    Evaluation
    U. S. A. *761*
AGRODATA
    PERU *589*
AIAS Library
    AUSTRALIA *117*
Aichi Prefectural Labour Centre, Labour Reference Library
    JAPAN *474*
Aichiken Kinro Kaikan Rodo Tosyo Siryoshitu
    JAPAN *474*
AID/CDIE
    U. S. A. *761*
AIDO
    IRAQ *6*
Ain-Shams University, Center of Childhood Studies
    EGYPT *268*
AISC
    GERMANY (FEDERAL REPUBLIC) *341*
AIU Library and Documentation Centre
    INDIA *397*
AIUTA
    BELGIUM *141*

2

ANPAT, Association Nationale pour la Prévention des Accidents du Travail
BELGIUM *149*
Anthropological Survey of India
INDIA *396*
APAIS
AUSTRALIA *126*
APCCI, Service de Documentation
FRANCE *286*
APDC, LDC
MALAYSIA *7*
Arab Industrial Development Organization, Documentation, Publication and Scientific
Computation Division
IRAQ *6*
Arab League Education, Cultural and Scientific Organization, Department of
Documentation and Information
TUNISIA *5*
Aragon Foundation Information Services
ARGENTINA *100*
Arbeitskreis für Internationale Wissenschaftskommunikation
GERMANY (FEDERAL REPUBLIC) *341*
Arbeitsstelle Friedensforschung Bonn
GERMANY (FEDERAL REPUBLIC) *342*
Arbetarrörelsens Arkiv och Bibliothek
SWEDEN *673*
Arbetslivscentrum, Aramis
SWEDEN *674*
Archives Culturelles du Sénégal
SENEGAL *646*
Archives Economiques Suisses
SWITZERLAND *694*
Archives of Business and Labour
AUSTRALIA *119*
Archivio Dati e Programmi per le Scienze Sociali
ITALY *461*
Archivio Disarmo, Centro di Documentazione sulla Pace sul Disarmo
ITALY *462*
ARCSS
EGYPT *270*
Arquivo Histórico de Moçambique
MOZAMBIQUE *535*
The Arthur and Elizabeth Schlesinger Library on the History of Women in America
U. S. A. *820*
ASDOC
BELGIUM *144*
Asian and Pacific Development Centre, Library and Documentation Centre
MALAYSIA *7*
Asian Center Library
PHILIPPINES *603*
Asian Centre/GIIS
SWITZERLAND *689*
Asian Mass Communication Research and Information Centre, Documentation Unit
SINGAPORE (REPUBLIC) *8*
Asmara University, Institute of African Studies, Library
ETHIOPIA *277*
Asociación Latinoamericana de Instituciones Financieras de Desarrollo, Centro de
Documentación
PERU *9*
Asociación Nacional de Industriales, Biblioteca, Centro de Documentación e

4

B

B. C. Roy Memorial Library
INDIA *412*
B I
U. S. A. *768*
Balch Institute for Ethnic Studies, Library
U. S. A. *766*
Banaras Hindu University, Centre for the Study of Nepal, Library with Documentation Services
INDIA *398*
Banco Central de Reserva de el Salvador, Biblioteca "Luis Alfaro Duran"
EL SALVADOR *274*
Banco Central de Reserva del Perú, Centro de Información y Documentación
PERU *587*
Banco de la Nación Argentina, Biblioteca Manuel Belgrano
ARGENTINA *90*
Banco de la Nación Centro de Información y Documentación
PERU *588*
Bandaranaike Centre for International Studies
SRI LANKA *662*
Bandaranaike Centre for International Studies, Library
SRI LANKA *662*
Bangladesh Institute of Development Studies, Library
BANGLADESH *136*
Bangladesh Institute of International and Strategic Studies, Library
BANGLADESH *137*
Bangladesh Management Development Centre, Library
BANGLADESH *138*
Banque d'Information Politique et d'Actualité
FRANCE *312*
J. V. Barry Memorial Library, Australian Institute of Criminology
AUSTRALIA *122*
Base Social Research, Education and Communication, Documentation Center
PARAGUAY *586*
BASE-ISEC, CD
PARAGUAY *586*
Basler Mission, Bibliothek
SWITZERLAND *688*
Basler Mission, Library
SWITZERLAND *688*
Basque Government, Department of Presidence, Basque Institute of Public Administration, Archive, Library and Documentation Central Service
SPAIN *656*
BDIC
FRANCE *288*
BDL
CANADA *209*
BEBR
U. S. A. *838*
Benjamin Franklin Library
MEXICO *513*
BfZ
GERMANY (FEDERAL REPUBLIC) *343*
Bhandarkar Oriental Research Institute, Library
INDIA *399*
BIBL/ILO
SWITZERLAND *48*

6

Bibliographic Information on Southeast Asia
   AUSTRALIA *128*
Biblioteca Benjamin Franklin
   MEXICO *513*
Biblioteca Central "Dr. Roberto Repetto"
   ARGENTINA *91*
Biblioteca de Humanidades, Universidad Nacional del Sur, Departamento de Humanidades

   ARGENTINA *114*
Biblioteca del Poder Legislativo
   URUGUAY *752*
Biblioteca Isidro Fabela
   MEXICO *533*
Biblioteca "José Artigas", Junta de Vecinos de Montevideo
   URUGUAY *755*
Biblioteca Lorenzo Mendoza
   VENEZUELA *884*
Biblioteca Manuel Belgrano
   ARGENTINA *90*
Biblioteca Nacional de Antropología e Historia
   MEXICO *514*
Biblioteca Regional del Caribe
   PUERTO RICO *631*
Biblioteca "Rogelio Calabrese"
   ARGENTINA *92*
Biblioteek voor Hedendaagse Dokumentatie
   BELGIUM *142*
Biblioteka SGPS
   POLAND *628*
Biblioteka Uniwersytecka w Warszawie
   POLAND *629*
Bibliotheek, Universiteit Antwerpen, College voor de Ontwikkelingslanden
   BELGIUM *153*
Bibliotheek Van Beide Instellingen
   NETHERLANDS *553*
Bibliotheek van het Vredespaleis
   NETHERLANDS *538*
Bibliothek für Zeitgeschichte
   GERMANY (FEDERAL REPUBLIC) *343*
Bibliothèque de Documentation Internationale Contemporaine et Musée des Deux Guerres
   Mondiales
   FRANCE *288*
Bibliothèque "Dr. Nicolas Mikhov"
   BULGARIA *173*
Bibliothèque Fonds Quetelet
   BELGIUM *143*
Bibliothèque Léon Graulich
   BELGIUM *152*
Bidhan Chandra Roy Memorial Library
   INDIA *412*
BIDOC-SOZA
   NETHERLANDS *550*
BIDS, Library
   BANGLADESH *136*
BIISS, Library
   BANGLADESH *137*
BIM/MIC
   UNITED KINGDOM *719*

BIPA
    FRANCE *312*
BISA
    AUSTRALIA *128*
BLPES
    UNITED KINGDOM *721*
BLS
    U. S. A. *863*
BMDC, Library
    BANGLADESH *138*
BOI Industry Documentation Service
    PHILIPPINES *596*
Bolivia-Instituto Nacional de Estadistica
    BOLIVIA *155*
Bolivia-National Institute of Statistics
    BOLIVIA *155*
Boreal Institute for Northern Studies, Library
    CANADA *201*
BPA
    GERMANY (FEDERAL REPUBLIC) *363*
Brigham Young University, Social Science Division Library
    U. S. A. *767*
The British Council, Library
    SINGAPORE (REPUBLIC) *651*
British Institute of Management, Management Information Centre
    UNITED KINGDOM *719*
British Library, Business Information Service
    UNITED KINGDOM *720*
British Library of Political and Economic Science
    UNITED KINGDOM *721*
Brookings Institution, Social Science Computation Centre and Library
    U. S. A. *768*
Bulgarian Academy of Sciences Scientific Information Centre for Natural, Mathematical and Social Sciences
    BULGARIA *167*
Bundeskanzleramt, Administrative Bibliothek und Österreichische Rechtsdokumentation
    AUSTRIA *129*
Bundeskrimimalamt, Computergestuetzes Dokumentationssystem für Literatur
    GERMANY (FEDERAL REPUBLIC) *344*
Bundesministerium der Justiz, Juristisches Informationssystem für die Bundesrepublik Deutschland
    GERMANY (FEDERAL REPUBLIC) *345*
BUP-CENDI
    PERU *594*
Bureau for Research, Documentation and Monitoring of the Directorate of Criminal Affairs
    ITALY *469*
Bureau International du Travail, Centre International d'Informations de Securité et d'Hygiène du Travail
    SWITZERLAND *50*
Bureau International du Travail, Service des Politiques Rurales de l'Emploi
    SWITZERLAND *51*
Business Information Service, British Library
    UNITED KINGDOM *720*
BUW
    POLAND *629*

C

CAFRAD, Division de la Documentation
  MOROCCO *4*
California Institute of International Studies, World Affairs Report
  U. S. A. *769*
California State Law Library
  U. S. A. *770*
Canadian Council on Social Development, Library
  CANADA *182*
Canadian International Development Agency, Development Information Centre
  CANADA *183*
Canadian Social Science Data Archive, Institute for Social Research, York University

  CANADA *212*
Canadian Socio-Economic Information Management System
  CANADA *184*
CANSIM
  CANADA *184*
CARDI Literature Service
  TRINIDAD AND TOBAGO *708*
CARFF
  ETHIOPIA *3*
Caribbean Agricultural Research and Development Institute, Literature Service
  TRINIDAD AND TOBAGO *708*
Caribbean Documentation Centre
  TRINIDAD AND TOBAGO *32*
Caribbean Regional Library
  PUERTO RICO *631*
Carleton University, Social Science Data Archive
  CANADA *185*
CAS
  CZECHOSLOVAKIA *245*
Case Western Reserve University, Applied Social Sciences Library
  U. S. A. *771*
Catalyst Information Center
  U. S. A. *772*
Catholic Academy of Theology in Warsaw, Library
  POLAND *612*
Catholic University of Nijmegen, Third World Center
  NETHERLANDS *547*
Catholic University of Puerto Rico, Law School, Mons. Juan Fremiot Torres Oliver Law
  Library
  PUERTO RICO *634*
CBAE
  UNITED KINGDOM *724*
CBER, University of Alabama
  U. S. A. *830*
CBI
  BULGARIA *166*
CBS
  POLAND *615*
CCSD Library
  CANADA *182*
CDI/NPD
  SRI LANKA *665*
CDIP
  BENIN *154*

9

CDJC
    FRANCE *297*
CDN
    TUNISIA *711*
CDTM
    FRANCE *299*
CEA, Unidad de Información
    CUBA *242*
CEACS
    JAPAN *13*
CECOM
    POLAND *614*
CEDAF
    BELGIUM *144*
CEDAM
    FRANCE *290*
CEDDU
    MEXICO *515*
CEDEJ
    EGYPT *271*
CEDES, Biblioteca
    ARGENTINA *93*
CEDESC
    COSTA RICA *17*
CEDE-UNIANDES, Biblioteca
    COLOMBIA *233*
CEDHAL
    BRAZIL *164*
CEDIAS-Musée Social
    FRANCE *293*
CEDIME
    ECUADOR *265*
CEDIPAZ
    COSTA RICA *18*
CEDISAM
    VENEZUELA *883*
CEDO
    COLOMBIA *83*
CEDOCAL
    FRANCE *338*
CEDOC-FLACSO/Chile
    CHILE *218*
CEDOH
    HONDURAS *381*
CEDS
    BELGIUM *145*
CEDUCEE
    FRANCE *291*
CEFOD-Documentation
    CHAD *213*
CEGET, Centre de Documentation
    FRANCE *294*
CEIL-CONICET, Biblioteca
    ARGENTINA *11*
CEIL-CONICET, Library
    ARGENTINA *11*
CELADE / DOCPAL
    CHILE *20*

JAPAN   *487*
Center for Studies and Training in Development, Documentation
    CHAD   *213*
Center for the Study of the State and the Society, Library
    ARGENTINA   *93*
Center of Scientific Information in Social Sciences at the Presidium of the Academy
of Sciences of the Uzbek SSR
    U. S. S. R.   *879*
Center of Studies on America, Information Unit
    CUBA   *242*
Center za Proucevanje Sodelovanja z Dezelami v Razvoju, Specialna
Knjizbuca/Dokumentacijsko-Informacijska Sluzba
    YUGOSLAVIA   *887*
Central American Socioeconomic Documentation Centre
    COSTA RICA   *17*
Central American University "José Simeón Cañas", Library
    EL SALVADOR   *275*
Central Archive for Empirical Social Research
    GERMANY (FEDERAL REPUBLIC)   *368*
Central Bureau of Statistics, the Library
    NORWAY   *579*
Central Economic Library, Bratislava
    CZECHOSLOVAKIA   *254*
Central European Mass Communication Research Documentation Centre
    POLAND   *614*
Central Institute of Statistics, Data Base
    ITALY   *466*
Central Library "Dr. Roberto Repetto" of the Supreme Court of Justice
    ARGENTINA   *91*
Central Library of Economic Sciences
    CZECHOSLOVAKIA   *255*
Central Library of Labour and Social Security
    POLAND   *616*
Central School of Planning and Statistics Library, Central Economic Library
    POLAND   *628*
Central Statistical Library
    POLAND   *615*
Central Statistical Office, Library and Documentation Service
    HUNGARY   *384*
Central Statistical Office, Library on Statistics
    FINLAND   *284*
Centralförbundet för Alkohol- och Narkotikaupplysning, Bibliotek och IoD-central
    SWEDEN   *675*
Centralna Biblioteka Statystyczna
    POLAND   *615*
Centre against Apartheid: Publicity, Assistance, Promotion of International Action
Branch
    U. S. A.   *72*
Centre Asiatique/IUHEI
    SWITZERLAND   *689*
Centre d'Ethnologie Française/Musée des Arts et Traditions Populaires
    FRANCE   *289*
Centre d'Etude et de Documentation sur l'Afrique Noire et Madagascar
    FRANCE   *290*
Centre d'Etude et de Documentation sur l'URSS, la Chine et l'Europe de l'Est
    FRANCE   *291*
Centre d'Etudes Africaines, Laboratoire de Sociologie et Géographie Africaines,
Bibliothèque

Centre de Recherches, d'Etudes et de Documentation sur les Institutions et la
  Legislation Africaine
  SENEGAL *650*
Centre de Recherches et d'Etudes sur les Sociétés Méditerranéennes, Service de
  Documentation
  FRANCE *302*
Centre de Recherches et de Documentation du Sénégal
  SENEGAL *647*
Centre de Recherches et de Documentation sur la Chine Contemporaine
  FRANCE *303*
Centre de Recherches pour le Développement International, Bibliothèque
  CANADA *190*
Centre des Droits de l'Homme, Services d'Information
  FRANCE *337*
Centre des Hautes Etudes Touristiques
  FRANCE *304*
Centre des Nations Unies pour les Etablissements Humains, Division de l'Information
  KENYA *65*
Centre Européen pour les Loisirs et l'Education
  CZECHOSLOVAKIA *33*
Centre for African and Asian Studies, Documentation and Exchange Service
  BRAZIL *158*
Centre for African Studies and Documentation
  BELGIUM *144*
Centre for Development Information
  SRI LANKA *665*
Centre for Development Studies Library
  INDIA *400*
Centre for Documentation on Refugees
  SWITZERLAND *78*
The Centre for East Asian Cultural Studies
  JAPAN *13*
Centre for Latin American Information, Documentation and Analysis
  VENEZUELA *881*
Centre for Management Development, Library for Management Studies
  NIGERIA *568*
Centre for Middle Eastern and Islamic Studies Documentation Unit
  UNITED KINGDOM *722*
Centre for Policy Research, Library
  INDIA *401*
Centre for Research and Development
  INDIA *402*
Centre for Research, Documentation and University Exchange
  KENYA *501*
Centre for Resource Management
  NEW ZEALAND *566*
Centre for Social Research and Documentation
  BELGIUM *145*
Centre for Social Science Information of the German Democratic Republic Academy of
  Sciences
  GERMAN DEMOCRATIC REPUBLIC *340*
Centre for Strategic and International Studies, Library
  INDONESIA *447*
Centre for Studies in Social Sciences, Calcutta, Library
  INDIA *403*
Centre for the Coordination of Social Science Research and Documentation in Africa
  South of Sahara
  ZAIRE *12*

Centre for the Study and Research on Labour of the National Council of Scientific and
    Technological Research
    ARGENTINA *11*
Centre for the Study of Developing Societies, Data Unit
    INDIA *404*
Centre for the Study of Nepal, Library with Documentation Services, Banaras Hindu
    University
    INDIA *398*
Centre for Urban and Environmental Research and Development, Documentation and
    Information Section for Urban and Environmental Problems
    INDONESIA *451*
Centre for Urban and Regional Studies
    ARGENTINA *95*
Centre International d'Information pour la Terminologie
    AUSTRIA *46*
Centre international d'Information sur les Sources de l'Histoire Balkanique et
    Méditerranéenne
    BULGARIA *172*
Centre International de Documentation Parlementaire
    SWITZERLAND *43*
Centre International de l'Enfance, Service de Documentation
    FRANCE *14*
Centre International de Recherches sur le Bilinguisme
    CANADA *199*
Centre International des Civilisations Bantu
    GABON *339*
Centre Ivoirien de Recherches Economiques et Sociales, Bibliothèque
    COTE D'IVOIRE *239*
Centre Latinoaméricain sur la Jeunesse, Bibliothèque
    URUGUAY *22*
Centre National de Documentation
    MOROCCO *534*
Centre National de Documentation Economique
    ALGERIA *85*
Centre National de Documentation Scientifique et Technique
    SENEGAL *648*
Centre National de Documentation "Sécurité et Hygiène"
    BELGIUM *149*
Centre National de la Recherche Appliquée au Développement Rural, Centre de
    Documentation pour la Recherche Agricole
    MADAGASCAR *508*
Centre National de la Recherche Scientifique et Technique, Direction de l'Information
    Scientifique et Technique
    BURKINA-FASO *176*
Centre National de la Recherche Scientifique, Réseau Documentaire Amérique Latine
    FRANCE *305*
Centre of Bibliographic Documentation on Criminal Law and Procedure
    ITALY *463*
Centre of Bibliographic Information
    BULGARIA *166*
Centre of Research, Study and Documentation on the African Establishments and
    Legislation
    SENEGAL *650*
Centre of Scientific Information in Social Sciences of the Academy of Sciences of the
    Armenian SSR
    U. S. S. R. *873*
Centre of Scientific Information in Social Sciences of the Academy of Sciences of the
    Azerbaijan Soviet Socialist Republic

U. S. S. R. *874*
Centre of Scientific Information in Social Sciences of the Academy of Sciences of the Latvian SSR
U. S. S. R. *877*
Centre of Scientific Information in Social Sciences of the Academy of Sciences of the Lithuanian SSR
U. S. S. R. *878*
Centre of Scientific Information in Social Sciences of the Estonian Academy of Sciences
U. S. S. R. *875*
Centre of Scientific Information in Social Sciences of the Georgian Academy of Sciences
U. S. S. R. *876*
The Centre on Integrated Rural Development for Asia and the Pacific
BANGLADESH *15*
Centre on Rural Documentation
INDIA *434*
Centre Régional Arabe pour la Recherche et la Documentation en Sciences Sociales
EGYPT *270*
Centre Régional de Documentation sur les Traditions Orales et pour le Développement des Langues Africaines
CAMEROON (UNITED REPUBLIC) *16*
Centro de Documentación "Antonio Carrillo Flores"
MEXICO *517*
Centro de Documentación de Honduras
HONDURAS *381*
Centro de Documentación de "Vector"
CHILE *215*
Centro de Documentación e Información de los Movimientos Sociales del Ecuador
ECUADOR *265*
Centro de Documentación e Información sobre Areas Marginales y Municipalismo, Fundación para el Desarrollo de la Comunidad y Fomento Municipal
VENEZUELA *883*
Centro de Documentación Económica y Social de Centroamerica
COSTA RICA *17*
Centro de Documentación Español de la Comunicación
SPAIN *655*
Centro de Documentación Europea
SPAIN *661*
Centro de Documentación para América Latina y el Caribe, Instituto Latinoamericano de la Comunicación Educativa
MEXICO *523*
Centro de Documentación para las Comunicaciones, Universidad Autónoma de Bucaramanga, Facultad de Comunicación Social
COLOMBIA *231*
Centro de Documentación "Rafael M. Salas"
COLOMBIA *235*
Centro de Estudios de Estado y Sociedad, Biblioteca
ARGENTINA *93*
Centro de Estudios de Población, Biblioteca
ARGENTINA *94*
Centro de Estudios del Desarrollo, Biblioteca, Universidad Central de Venezuela
VENEZUELA *885*
Centro de Estudios del Desarrollo Económico, Biblioteca
COLOMBIA *233*
Centro de Estudios Demográficos y de Desarrollo Urbano
MEXICO *515*
Centro de Estudios Latinoamericanos, Centro de Documentación

PANAMA *583*

Centro de Estudios sobre America, Unidad de Información
CUBA *242*

Centro de Estudios Urbanos y Regionales
ARGENTINA *95*

Centro de Estudos Afro-Asiáticos, Serviço de Documentação e' Intercâmbio
BRAZIL *158*

Centro de Estudos de Demografia Histórica de América Latina, Universidade de São Paulo
BRAZIL *164*

Centro de Información Científica y Humanistica
MEXICO *528*

Centro de Información, Documentación y Analisis Latinoamericano
VENEZUELA *881*

Centro de Información, Investigación y Documentación del Uruguay
URUGUAY *753*

Centro de Información y Documentación del Banco de la Nación
PERU *588*

Centro de Informaciones y Estudios del Uruguay, Centro de Documentación
URUGUAY *754*

Centro de Investigaciones en Ciencias Sociales, Departamento de Información para el Desarrollo Social
VENEZUELA *882*

Centro de Investigaciones Interdisciplinarias en Humanidades, Departamento de Información y Documentación
MEXICO *529*

Centro de Investigaciones para el Desarrollo Integral, Centro de Documentación "Rafael M. Salas"
COLOMBIA *235*

Centro de Investigaciones Regionales "Dr. Hideyo Noguchi", Unidad de Apoyo a la Investigación Científica
MEXICO *527*

Centro de Perfeccionamiento Experimentación e Investigaciones Pedagógicas, Sistema Nacional de Información Educacional, RED Documental
CHILE *216*

Centro di Documentazione Bibliografica in Materia di Diritto e Procedura Penale
ITALY *463*

Centro di Recerca e Documentazione Febbraio '74
ITALY *464*

Centro Internacional de Documentación e Información para la Paz
COSTA RICA *18*

Centro Internacional de Estudios Superiores de Comunicación para America Latina, Centro de Documentación
ECUADOR *266*

Centro Internacional de Investigaciones para el Desarrollo, Oficina Regional para la América Latina y et Caribe, Biblioteca
COLOMBIA *19*

Centro Internazionale di Documentazine e Studi Sociologici sui Problemi del Lavoro
ITALY *470*

Centro Internazionale di Studi e Documentazione sulle Comunità Europee
ITALY *465*

Centro Latinoamericano de Demografia, Sistema de Documentación sobre Población de América Latina
CHILE *20*

Centro Latinoamericano de Documentación Económica y Social
CHILE *21*

Centro Latinoamericano sobre Juventud, Biblioteca
URUGUAY *22*

17

Copenhagen School of Economics and Business Administration, Library
   DENMARK *259*
Cornell Institute of Social and Economic Research, Data Service
   U. S. A. *779*
Cornell University, Cornell Institute for Social and Economic Research, Data Service

   U. S. A. *779*
Corte Suprema, Biblioteca de Derecho
   PUERTO RICO *632*
COSEBI
   MEXICO *533*
Council of Europe, Documentation Centre for Education in Europe
   FRANCE *28*
CPDS
   PARAGUAY *585*
CPEIP, SINIE, RED Documental
   CHILE *216*
CPFH, Library Information Program
   U. S. A. *777*
CPR Library
   INDIA *401*
CPSDVR
   YUGOSLAVIA *887*
CPUR
   U. S. A. *786*
CRDCC
   FRANCE *303*
CRDI Bibliothèque
   CANADA *190*
CRDS
   SENEGAL *647*
CRED, Library
   U. S. A. *845*
CREDILA
   SENEGAL *650*
CREDU
   KENYA *501*
CRIDSSH
   ALGERIA *86*
CSARU, University Library
   ALGERIA *87*
CSDS, Data Unit
   INDIA *404*
CSEAS
   JAPAN *487*
CSI, Knihovna
   CZECHOSLOVAKIA *244*
CSIS Library
   INDONESIA *447*
Cultural and Social Anthropology Research Unit, University Library
   ALGERIA *87*
Cultural Archives of Senegal
   SENEGAL *646*
Curaçao Department of Education, Library
   NETHERLANDS ANTILLES *536*
CYRC
   PHILIPPINES *597*
Czechoslovak Academy of Sciences, Institute for Philosophy and Sociology, Centre for

22

BERLIN (WEST) *371*
Deutsches Jugendinstitut, Abteilung Dokumentation und Information
GERMANY (FEDERAL REPUBLIC) *348*
Deutsches Übersee-Institut, Übersee-Dokumentation
GERMANY (FEDERAL REPUBLIC) *349*
Development Information Network on South Asia
SRI LANKA *663*
Development Studies and Research Centre
SUDAN *672*
DEVINSA
SRI LANKA *663*
Devlet Planlama Teşkilati, Dokumantasyon Servisi
TURKEY *714*
DFD
FRANCE *29*
DHIP
FRANCE *310*
DHL
U. S. A. *68*
Direction de la Documentation Française, Bibliothèque
FRANCE *311*
DIS
U. S. A. *70*
Disarmament Information Branch, United Nations Department of Disarmament Affairs
U. S. A. *69*
Documentatiebureau voor Oosteuropees Recht
NETHERLANDS *555*
Documentatiecentrum Jeugdvoorzieningen
NETHERLANDS *539*
Documentation and Information Center on Ecuador's Social Movements
ECUADOR *265*
Documentation Center for Urban Studies
AUSTRIA *132*
Documentation Centre Child Care
NETHERLANDS *539*
Documentation Centre for Education in Europe
FRANCE *28*
Documentation Centre for Science Policy
SWITZERLAND *690*
La Documentation Française, Banque d'Information Politique et d'Actualité
FRANCE *312*
Documentation Française, Centre d'Information et de Documentation Internationale Contemporaine
FRANCE *313*
Documentation Office for East European Law
NETHERLANDS *555*
Dokumentationsstelle für Wissenschaftspolitik
SWITZERLAND *690*
DPLS
U. S. A. *858*
DRI
U. S. A. *780*
DSE/ZD
GERMANY (FEDERAL REPUBLIC) *346*
DSRC
SUDAN *672*
DUH/NORAD, Library
NORWAY *578*

24

Dutch Centre for Documentation of Legal History and Lexiconography, Library
    NETHERLANDS *552*
E3m
    SWITZERLAND *695*

E

East-West Center, Institute of Culture and Communication, Resources Materials
    Collection
    U. S. A. *782*
ECA Population Division, Information Service
    ETHIOPIA *74*
ECLAC/CARISPLAN
    TRINIDAD AND TOBAGO *32*
ECLAC/ILPES Joint Library
    CHILE *23*
ECLE
    CZECHOSLOVAKIA *33*
Ecole Nationale d'Administration Publique
    CANADA *197*
ECONIMFORM
    HUNGARY *388*
Economic and Social Commission for Asia and the Pacific Library
    THAILAND *30*
Economic and Social Commission for Asia and the Pacific, Population Information
    Section of the Population Division
    THAILAND *31*
Economic and Social Council, Library and Documentation
    FRANCE *309*
Economic and Social Planning Institute, Processing Center for Economic Development
    BRAZIL *161*
Economic and Social Research Council Data Archive
    UNITED KINGDOM *725*
Economic Commission for Africa, Population Division, Information Service
    ETHIOPIA *74*
Economic Commission for Latin America and the Caribbean, Caribbean Information
    System/Economic and Social Planning
    TRINIDAD AND TOBAGO *32*
Economic Council of Canada, Library
    CANADA *187*
Economic Development Information Network
    U. S. A. *792*
ECPR - ᐁIS
    NORWAY *34*
EDICLINE Economic Documentation and Information Centre Ltd.
    UNITED KINGDOM *726*
Educational Research Centre, King Saud University
    SAUDI ARABIA *644*
Educational Resources Information Center Clearinghouse for Social Studies/Social
    Science Education
    U. S. A. *783*
Eduskunnan Kirjasto/Riksdagsbiblioteket
    FINLAND *279*
EIC, Bibliothèque
    CANADA *188*
EIC, Library
    CANADA *188*
EIPA, Library

NETHERLANDS 36
Ekonomický Ústav Csav, Útvar Vedeckých Informaci
    CZECHOSLOVAKIA 245
El Colegio de México, Biblioteca "Daniel Cosio Villegas", Sección de Información y
    Selección
    MEXICO 518
El Colegio de Michoacán, Biblioteca
    MEXICO 519
Emploi et Immigration Canada, Bibliothèque
    CANADA 188
Employment and Immigration Canada, Library
    CANADA 188
Erasmus Universiteit Rotterdam, SRM-Documentation Centre
    NETHERLANDS 540
Erasmus University Rotterdam, Social Research Methodology Documentation Centre
    NETHERLANDS 540
ERIC/ChESS
    U. S. A. 783
ESCAP Library
    THAILAND 30
ESCAP/POPIN
    THAILAND 31
Escuela de Administración de Negocios Para Graduados, Centro de Documentación
    PERU 590
Escuela Nacional de Estudios Profesionales Acatlán, Centro de Información y
    Documentación
    MEXICO 530
Escuela Superior de Administración Pública, Biblioteca
    PERU 592
Escuela Universitaria de Psicologia, Biblioteca
    URUGUAY 756
ESCWA Library
    IRAQ 73
ESRC Data Archive
    UNITED KINGDOM 725
Ethnikon Kentron Kinonikon Erevnon
    GREECE 375
Ethnographical Museum, Library
    HUNGARY 390
Ethnographical Museum of Sweden, Library
    SWEDEN 677
Etnografiska Museet, Library
    SWEDEN 677
EUI, Library
    ITALY 37
EUP, Biblioteca
    URUGUAY 756
European Centre for Leisure and Education
    CZECHOSLOVAKIA 33
European Community Information Service, Library
    U. S. A. 784
European Consortium for Political Research, Data Information Service
    NORWAY 34
European Foundation for the Improvement of Living and Working Conditions, Library an
    Information Service
    IRELAND 35
European Institute of Public Administration, Library
    NETHERLANDS 36

26

European University Institute, Library
    ITALY 37
Expansion Industrielle Régionale, Centre de Documentation Gouvernemental
    CANADA 194

F

Facultad de Filosofía, Humanidades y Artes, Universidad Nacional San Juan, Biblioteca
    Dr. Juan José Nissen
    ARGENTINA 115
Facultad de Filosofía y Letras, Universidad Nacional de Cuyo, Biblioteca
    ARGENTINA 110
Facultad Latinoamericana de Ciencias Sociales Costa Rica, Centro de Documentación
    COSTA RICA 38
Facultad Latinoamericana de Ciencias Sociales-Programa Bolivia, Biblioteca
    BOLIVIA 156
Facultad Latinoamericana de Ciencias Sociales-Programa Buenos Aires
    ARGENTINA 98
Facultad Latinoamericana de Ciencias Sociales-Programa de Santiago, Chile, Centro de
    Documentación
    CHILE 218
Facultad Latinoamericana de Ciencias Sociales-Sede Academia México, Biblioteca
    MEXICO 520
Family Resources Database
    U. S. A. 807
FAO/ESH, Reference Unit
    ITALY 39
Fawcett Library, City of London Polytechnic
    UNITED KINGDOM 723
FCRB, Centro de Documentação
    BRAZIL 159
Federal Chancellery, Administrative Library and Austrian Law Documentation
    AUSTRIA 129
Federal Council of Investments, Documentation Center
    ARGENTINA 97
Federal Ministry of Justice, Legal Information System for the Federal Republic of
    Germany
    GERMANY (FEDERAL REPUBLIC) 345
Federal Press and Information Office
    GERMANY (FEDERAL REPUBLIC) 363
Federal Statistical Office, Library-Documentation-Archives Services
    GERMANY (FEDERAL REPUBLIC) 364
Federal University of Acre, Ruy Alberto da Costa Lins Central Library
    BRAZIL 165
Fédération Internationale pour le Planning Familial, Bibliothèque
    UNITED KINGDOM 53
Femenina University of the Sacred Heart, Library
    PERU 595
FF/IBF
    GERMANY (FEDERAL REPUBLIC) 350
FhG IRB
    GERMANY (FEDERAL REPUBLIC) 352
FIEL, Biblioteca
    ARGENTINA 99
FIIA, Library
    FINLAND 285
The Finnish Institute of International Affairs, Library
    FINLAND 285

FISE/UNICEF
FRANCE *308*
FJBAC Biblioteca
MEXICO *521*
FLACSO
COSTA RICA *38*
FLACSO, Programa Buenos Aires
ARGENTINA *98*
FLACSO-Programa Bolivia, Library
BOLIVIA *156*
FLACSO-Sede Academia México, Biblioteca
MEXICO *520*
Florida Joint Legislative Management Committee, Division of Legislative Library
Services
U. S. A. *785*
FOFIFA, Centre de Documentation pour la Recherche Agricole
MADAGASCAR *508*
Folketingets Bibliotek og Oplysningstjeneste
DENMARK *257*
Fondation Nationale de Gérontologie, Centre de Documentation Vieillissement et
Vieillesse
FRANCE *314*
Fondation Nationale des Sciences Politiques, Services de Documentation
FRANCE *315*
Fondo Colombiano de Investigaciones Cientificas y Proyectos Especiales "Francisco
Jose de Caldas", Biblioteca y División de la Documentación
COLOMBIA *229*
Fonds des Nations Unies pour les Activités en Matière de Population, Bibliothèque
U. S. A. *77*
Food and Agriculture Organization of the United Nations, Human Resources,
Institutions and Agrarian Reform Division, Reference Unit
ITALY *39*
Footscray Institute of Technology, Library
AUSTRALIA *124*
Forschungsinstitut für Friedenspolitik, Informationsbüro
GERMANY (FEDERAL REPUBLIC) *350*
Forschungsinstitut für internationale Politik und Sicherheit, Stiftung Wissenschaft
und Politik. Bibliothek und Dokumentation
GERMANY (FEDERAL REPUBLIC) *351*
Foundation for Community Development and Municipal Improvement, Centre for
Documentation and Information for Squatter Settlements and Municipal Affairs
VENEZUELA *883*
Fovárosi Szabó Ervin Könyvtár Szociológiai Dokumentációs Osztály
HUNGARY *382*
Fraunhofer Society, Information Centre for Regional Planning and Building
Construction
GERMANY (FEDERAL REPUBLIC) *352*
Fraunhofer-Gesellschaft, Informationszentrum Raum und Bau
GERMANY (FEDERAL REPUBLIC) *352*
FRD
U. S. A. *807*
Free University of Berlin, Information Centre for Politics and Mass Communication
BERLIN (WEST) *372*
Freie Universität Berlin, Informationszentrum Politik und Massenkommunikation
BERLIN (WEST) *372*
French Senate, Parliamentary Documentation and Information Printing Service
FRANCE *332*
Fundação Case de Rui Barbosa, Centro de Documentação

BRAZIL *159*
Fundação SEADE
BRAZIL *160*
Fundação Sistema Estadual de Análise de Dados, Central de Dados e Referências
BRAZIL *160*
Fundación de Investigaciones Económicas Latinoamericanas, Biblioteca
ARGENTINA *99*
Fundación Javier Barros Sierra, Biblioteca
MEXICO *521*
Fundación José María Aragón, Servicios de Información
ARGENTINA *100*
Fundación para el Desarrollo de la Comunidad y Fomento Municipal, Centro de Documentación e Información sobre Areas Marginales y Municipalismo
VENEZUELA *883*

G

GAMA
FRANCE *336*
Gandhi Peace Foundation
INDIA *405*
GBI
GERMANY (FEDERAL REPUBLIC) *353*
GBL
U. S. S. R. *871*
GBP
POLAND *616*
Geo Abstracts Ltd.
UNITED KINGDOM *727*
Geografisch Instituut, Bibliotheek
NETHERLANDS *541*
Geographical Institute, Library
NETHERLANDS *541*
Georgia State University, Center for Public and Urban Research
U. S. A. *786*
German Archives of Books in Munich
GERMANY (FEDERAL REPUBLIC) *347*
German Foundation for International Development, Documentation Centre
GERMANY (FEDERAL REPUBLIC) *346*
German Historical Institute Paris
FRANCE *310*
German Institute of Urban Affairs, Information and Documentation Division
BERLIN (WEST) *371*
German Overseas Institute, Overseas Documentation
GERMANY (FEDERAL REPUBLIC) *349*
German Youth Institute, Department of Documentation and Information
GERMANY (FEDERAL REPUBLIC) *348*
Gesellschaft für Betriebswirtschaftliche Information mbH
GERMANY (FEDERAL REPUBLIC) *353*
Ghana Institute of Management and Public Administration, Library and Documentation Centre
GHANA *373*
Giannini Foundation of Agriculture Economics, Library
U. S. A. *787*
GIMPA Library and Documentation Centre
GHANA *373*
GIPA, Library
INDIA *407*

Global Information Network
    U. S. A. *788*
Główna Biblioteka Pracy i Zabezpieczenia Społecznego
    POLAND *616*
Gobierno Vasco, Departamento de Presidencia, Instituto Vasco de Administración
    Pública, Servicio Central de Archivo, Biblioteca y Documentación
    SPAIN *656*
Gokhale Institute of Politics and Economics, Library
    INDIA *406*
Gokhale Institute of Public Affairs, Library
    INDIA *407*
Gosudarstvennaja Ordena Lenina Biblioteka SSSR Imeni V.I. Lenina
    U. S. S. R. *871*
Gosudarstvennaya Publichnaya Istoricheskaya Biblioteka Ministerstva Kultury RSFSR
    U. S. S. R. *872*
Göteborgs Universitet, Språkdata
    SWEDEN *678*
Greco 26 - CNRS
    FRANCE *305*
Groupe d'Analyse Macroéconomique Appliquée
    FRANCE *336*
Gujarat Vidyapith Granthalaya, Bibliographical and Documentation Service
    INDIA *408*

H

Habitat Information Division
    KENYA *65*
Handelehøjskolens Aarhus, Biblioteket
    DENMARK *258*
Handelshögskolans Bibliotek i Stockholm
    SWEDEN *679*
Handelshøjskolens Bibliotek, Kobenhavn
    DENMARK *259*
Harry S. Truman Research Institute for the Advancement of Peace, Library and
    Documentation Center
    ISRAEL *458*
Harvard University, Center for Population Studies Library
    U. S. A. *789*
Harvard University, Tozzer Library
    U. S. A. *790*
Haut Commissariat des Nations Unies pour les Réfugiés, Centre de Documentation sur
    les Réfugiés
    SWITZERLAND *78*
Hawaii State, Legislative Reference Bureau, Library
    U. S. A. *791*
Hebrew University of Jerusalem, Harry S. Truman Research Institute for the
    Advancement of Peace, Library and Documentation Center
    ISRAEL *458*
The Hebrew University of Jerusalem, Social Sciences Data Archive
    ISRAEL *459*
Helsingin Kauppakorkeakoulun Kirjasto
    FINLAND *280*
Helsingin Yliopiston Kehitysmaainstituttin Kirjasto
    FINLAND *281*
Helsingin Yliopiston Valtiotieteellissen Tiedekunnan Kirjasto
    FINLAND *282*
Helsinki School of Economics Library

HWWA-Institute of Economic Research - Hamburg, Information Centre
    GERMANY (FEDERAL REPUBLIC) *354*
I3m
    SWITZERLAND *695*

I

I Z
    GERMANY (FEDERAL REPUBLIC) *356*
IAB, Informationsdienste
    GERMANY (FEDERAL REPUBLIC) *357*
IAMSEA
    RWANDA *643*
IARS, Information Library
    EGYPT *272*
IAS, Library
    ETHIOPIA *277*
    THAILAND *700*
IBERCOMNET
    SPAIN *655*
Iberoamerican Institute
    JAPAN *500*
IBISCUS Association, Information System on Developing Countries
    FRANCE *287*
IBRC/EDIN
    U. S. A. *792*
ICBF, Biblioteca
    COLOMBIA *230*
ICC
    FRANCE *14*
ICPE Information and Library Service
    YUGOSLAVIA *890*
ICPSR
    U. S. A. *846*
ICRB
    CANADA *199*
ICRIER, Documentation Centre
    INDIA *409*
ICSSD
    FRANCE *44*
ICTED
    FRANCE *27*
Idayu Foundation, Library
    INDONESIA *454*
IDEP
    SENEGAL *2*
IDOC Documentation Service
    ITALY *45*
IDPM, Library
    UNITED KINGDOM *749*
IDRC Library
    CANADA *190*
IDRC/Latin America Regional Office
    COLOMBIA *19*
IDS Library
    UNITED KINGDOM *750*
IDSA Library, Documentation and Information Service
    INDIA *419*

de Documentation et d'Information
CZECHOSLOVAKIA *252*

Institut du Sahel, Programme de Réseau Sahélien de Documentation et d'Information Scientifiques et Techniques
MALI *512*

Institut Ekonomskih Nauka Biblioteka
YUGOSLAVIA *888*

Institut Européen d'Administration Publique, Bibliothèque
NETHERLANDS *36*

Institut Européen Interuniversitaire de l'Action Sociale
BELGIUM *42*

Institut Fondamental d'Afrique Noire - Cheikh Anta Diop, Bibliothèque
SENEGAL *649*

Institut Français d'Etudes Andines, Bibliothèque
PERU *591*

Institut für Arbeitsmarkt-und Berufsforschung der Bundesanstalt für Arbeit, Informationsdienste
GERMANY (FEDERAL REPUBLIC) *357*

Institut für Auslandsbeziehungen, Bibliothek
GERMANY (FEDERAL REPUBLIC) *358*

Institut für Höhere Studien und Wissenschaftliche Forschung, Bibliothek
AUSTRIA *130*

Institut für Weltwirtschaft an der Universität Kiel, Bibliothek
GERMANY (FEDERAL REPUBLIC) *366*

Institut für Wissenschaftliche Zusammenarbeit mit Entwicklungsländern
GERMANY (FEDERAL REPUBLIC) *359*

Institut Haïtien de Statistiques et d'Informatique
HAITI *380*

Institut Historique Allemand de Paris
FRANCE *310*

Institut International des Sciences Administratives, Bibliothèque
BELGIUM *47*

Institut National de la Recherche Agronomique - Station d'Economie et de Sociologie Rurales, Service de Documentation
FRANCE *322*

Institut National de la Statistique et des Etudes Economiques, Division "Documentation"
FRANCE *323*

Institut National de la Statistique et des Etudes Economiques, Observatoire Economique de Paris
FRANCE *330*

Institut National pour la Formation et la Recherche en Education, Centre de Documentation et d'Information Pédagogiques
BENIN *154*

Institut Panafricain pour le Développment/Afrique Centrale Francophone, Centre de Documentation
CAMEROON (UNITED REPUBLIC) *180*

Institut po Naukite za Darzavata i Pravoto, Sluzba za Naucna Informacija i Dokumentacija Kam
BULGARIA *169*

Institut po Sociologija, Otdel za Naucna Informacija i Dokumentacija
BULGARIA *170*

Institut Québécois de Recherche sur la Culture
CANADA *189*

Institut Universitaire d'Etudes du Développement, Bibliothèque et Centre de Documentation
SWITZERLAND *692*

Institut Universitaire Européen, Bibliothèque

ITALY   37
nstitut za Medjunarodnu Politiku i Privredu, Centar Za Naučnu Informaciju i
Dokumentaciju, Beograd
YUGOSLAVIA   889
nstitut za Mezdunarodni Otnosenija i Socialisticeska Integracija, Naucen
Informacionen Centar
BULGARIA   171
nstitute for Advanced Studies, Library
AUSTRIA   130
he Institute for Czech Language, Department of Scientific Information
CZECHOSLOVAKIA   251
nstitute for Defence Studies and Analyses, Library, Documentation and Information
Service
INDIA   419
nstitute for Development Policy and Management Library, University of Manchester
UNITED KINGDOM   749
nstitute for Development Studies
INDONESIA   449
nstitute for Economic and Social Research, Education and Information Library
INDONESIA   448
nstitute for Economics, Market Research and Informatics
HUNGARY   383
nstitute for Foreign Cultural Relations Library
GERMANY (FEDERAL REPUBLIC)   358
nstitute for Information and Documentation in Social Sciences and Humanities
SPAIN   658
nstitute for International Law
NETHERLANDS   560
nstitute for International Relations and Socialist Integration, Scientific
Information Centre
BULGARIA   171
nstitute for International Studies
NETHERLANDS   543
nstitute for Policy Research, Southwest Ohio Regional Data Center, University of
Cincinnati
U. S. A.   836
nstitute for Population and Social Research, Data Collection and Processing Unit
THAILAND   701
nstitute for Scientific Cooperation
GERMANY (FEDERAL REPUBLIC)   359
nstitute for Scientific Information
U. S. A.   793
nstitute for Social and Economic Change, Library
INDIA   420
nstitute for Social Inquiry
U. S. A.   837
nstitute for the Study of Drug Dependence, Library and Information Service
UNITED KINGDOM   729
nstitute for World Economics of the Hungarian Academy of Sciences
HUNGARY   387
nstitute of Advanced Latin American Studies, Library and Documentation Centre
FRANCE   321
nstitute of Advanced Legal Studies, Library
UNITED KINGDOM   730
nstitute of Advanced Studies, Research School of Pacific Studies
AUSTRALIA   120
nstitute of African Studies, Library
ETHIOPIA   277

Institute of Arab Research and Studies, Library
    EGYPT *272*
Institute of Asian Studies, Library
    THAILAND *700*
Institute of Constitutional and Parliamentary Studies, Library
    INDIA *421*
Institute of Contemporary History and Wiener Library
    UNITED KINGDOM *731*
Institute of Culture and Communication, Resources Materials Collection
    U. S. A. *782*
Institute of Czechoslovak and World History, Department of Scientific Information
    CZECHOSLOVAKIA *250*
Institute of Developing Economies, Library and Statistical Research Department
    JAPAN *480*
Institute of Development Studies, Library
    UNITED KINGDOM *750*
Institute of Development Studies, Library and Documentation Centre
    SWITZERLAND *692*
Institute of Economic Growth Library
    INDIA *422*
The Institute of Economic Research, Library
    JAPAN *475*
Institute of Economic Sciences Library
    YUGOSLAVIA *888*
Institute of Economics at the Hungarian Academy of Sciences, Library and
    Documentation
    HUNGARY *389*
Institute of Economics, Bulgarian Academy of Sciences, Department of Scientific and
    Statistical Economic Information and Library
    BULGARIA *168*
Institute of Economics of the Polish Academy of Sciences, Library
    POLAND *619*
Institute of Economics, Scientific Information Section
    CZECHOSLOVAKIA *245*
Institute of Ethiopian Studies, Information Service
    ETHIOPIA *276*
Institute of Geography and Spatial Organization of the Polish Academy of Sciences
    POLAND *618*
Institute of Government Studies Library, University of California at Berkeley
    U. S. A. *831*
Institute of Human Sciences, Library, Documentation and Publications Service
    CAMEROON (UNITED REPUBLIC) *179*
Institute of Iberoamerican Cooperation, Hispanic Library
    SPAIN *657*
Institute of International Politics and Economics, Information and Documentation
    Centre, Belgrade
    YUGOSLAVIA *889*
Institute of International Studies, Library
    CHILE *219*
Institute of Labor and Industrial Relations Library
    U. S. A. *842*
Institute of Labour Market and Occupational Research of the Federal Employment
    Agency, Information Service
    GERMANY (FEDERAL REPUBLIC) *357*
Institute of Latin American Studies, Library
    SWEDEN *684*
    UNITED KINGDOM *744*
Institute of Law, Czechoslovak Academy of Sciences, Documentation and Information

FRANCE 27

International Development Research Centre, Latin America and the Caribbean Regional
Office, Library
    COLOMBIA 19

International Development Research Centre, Library
    CANADA 190

International Documentation and Communication Center, Documentation Service
    ITALY 45

International Economic Data Bank
    AUSTRALIA 125

International Information and Documentation Center in Barcelona
    SPAIN 654

International Information Centre and Archives for the Women's Movement
    NETHERLANDS 544

International Information Centre for Terminology
    AUSTRIA 46

International Information Centre on Sources of Balkan and Mediterranean History
    BULGARIA 172

International Institute for Population Sciences, Library
    INDIA 424

International Institute of Administrative Sciences, Library
    BELGIUM 47

International Institute of Social History
    NETHERLANDS 545

International Labour Office, Central Library and Documentation Branch
    SWITZERLAND 48

International Labour Office, Clearing-House on Conditions of Work
    SWITZERLAND 49

International Labour Office, International Occupational Safety and Health Information
Centre
    SWITZERLAND 50

International Labour Office, Regional Employment Programme for Latin America and the
Caribbean
    CHILE 220

International Labour Office, Rural Employment Policies Branch, Documentation Centre
    SWITZERLAND 51

International Management Development Seminars
    JAPAN 493

International Monetary Fund, Economic Information System
    U. S. A. 52

International Peace Research Institute, Oslo, Library
    NORWAY 572

International Planned Parenthood Federation, Library
    UNITED KINGDOM 53

International Statistical Institute, Research Centre Dynamic Data Base
    NETHERLANDS 54

International Statistical Research Centre
    NETHERLANDS 546

International Trade Centre UNCTAD/GATT, Trade Information Service
    SWITZERLAND 55

Inter-University Consortium for Political and Social Research
    U. S. A. 846

Inter-University European Institute on Social Welfare
    BELGIUM 42

Investigaciones Sociales, Educación y Comunicaciones, Centro de Documentación
    PARAGUAY 586

Iowa Social Science Institute, University of Iowa
    U. S. A. 843

ITESM, Biblioteca
    MEXICO *525*
IUED, Bibliothèque et Centre de Documentation
    SWITZERLAND *692*
IUPERJ
    BRAZIL *162*
IZ
    POLAND *623*

J

Jamaica Information Service, Library
    JAMAICA *471*
The Japan Institute of Labour, Labour Reference Library
    JAPAN *488*
Jawaharlal Nehru University, New Delhi, Library
    INDIA *425*
JIS
    JAMAICA *471*
The Johns Hopkins University, Population Information Program
    U. S. A. *794*
Junta de Vecinos de Montevideo, Biblioteca "José Artigas"
    URUGUAY *755*
JURIS
    GERMANY (FEDERAL REPUBLIC) *345*
Juristisches Informationssystem für die Bundesrepublik Deutschland
    GERMANY (FEDERAL REPUBLIC) *345*

K

The "K. Marx" Higher Institute of Economics, Information Centre and Library
    BULGARIA *174*
Kammer für Arbeiter und Angestellte für Wien, Sozialwissenschaftliche
    Studienbibliothek
    AUSTRIA *131*
Karl Marx University of Economic Sciences, Central Library
    HUNGARY *388*
Karol Acadiecki Academy of Economics in Katowice, Main Library
    POLAND *608*
Karve Institute of Social Service
    INDIA *426*
Katholieke Universiteit Nijmegen, Derde Wereld Centrum
    NETHERLANDS *547*
KDZ
    AUSTRIA *132*
Keidanren Library
    JAPAN *481*
Keidanren Toshokan
    JAPAN *481*
Keio Gijuku Daigaku Mita Joho Senta
    JAPAN *482*
Keio University Mita Library and Information Center
    JAPAN *482*
Keizai Kenkyusho Shiryoshitsu
    JAPAN *475*
Keizakenkyujo, Nippon Keizai Tokei Bunken Senta
    JAPAN *477*
Kenya Institute of Administration, Library

44

L

Labor Relations and Research Center Library, University of Massachusetts
  U. S. A. *844*
Laboratoire d'Information et de Documentation en Géographie
  FRANCE *324*
Laboratoire de Psychologie Sociale, Service de Documentation
  FRANCE *335*
LAIS, Library
  SWEDEN *684*
LARRDIS
  INDIA *438*
Latin America Social Sciences, Documentation Area
  ARGENTINA *26*
Latin American Association of Development Financing Institutions, Documentation
  Centre
  PERU *9*
Latin American Centre for Economic and Social Documentation
  CHILE *21*
Latin American Centre on Youth, Library
  URUGUAY *22*
Latin American Demographic Centre, Latin American Population Documentation System
  CHILE *20*
Latin American Faculty of Social Sciences, Bolivia, Library
  BOLIVIA *156*
Latin American Faculty of Social Sciences, Buenos Aires Program
  ARGENTINA *98*
Latin American Faculty of Social Sciences, Chile, Documentation Centre
  CHILE *218*
Latin American Faculty of Social Sciences Costa Rica, Documentation Centre
  COSTA RICA *38*
Latin American Faculty of Social Sciences, Library
  MEXICO *520*
Laval University, International Centre for Research on Bilingualism
  CANADA *199*
Law in the Service of Man, Library
  ISRAEL *457*
Law Library, Louisiana State University
  U. S. A. *797*
Law Library, University of Georgia
  U. S. A. *839*
Law/Social Science Reference Service
  U. S. A. *809*
League of Arab States Documentation and Information Center
  TUNISIA *57*
Learned Information Ltd.
  UNITED KINGDOM *733*
Legal Information System for the Federal Republic of Germany
  GERMANY (FEDERAL REPUBLIC) *345*
Legislative Reference Bureau Library, State of Hawaii
  U. S. A. *791*
Lembaga Penelitian Pendidikan dan Penerangan Ekonomi dan Sosial, Perpustakaan
  INDONESIA *448*
Lembaza Studi Pembangunan
  INDONESIA *449*
LEPPES
  INDONESIA *448*
Liaisons Sociales

46

47

UGANDA 717
Makerere University, Makerere Institute of Social Research Library
  UGANDA 717
Management Development Institute, Library
  INDIA 429
Management Information Centre
  UNITED KINGDOM 719
Manuel Belgrano Library
  ARGENTINA 90
Marga Institute, Documentation Centre
  SRI LANKA 664
Markaz al-Maaloumat al Ihsaaiah wa al-Tawthiq al-Tarbawi
  SAUDI ARABIA 645
Marx Károly Közgazdaságtudományi Egyetem Központi Könyvtára
  HUNGARY 388
Max Planck Institute for Comparative Public Law and International Law, Library
  GERMANY (FEDERAL REPUBLIC) 360
Max-Planck-Institut für Ausländisches Öffentliches Recht und Völkerrecht, Bibliothek

  GERMANY (FEDERAL REPUBLIC) 360
Max-Planck-Institut für Ausländisches und Internationales Patent-, Urheber- und
  Wettbewerbsrecht, Bibliothek
  GERMANY (FEDERAL REPUBLIC) 361
Max-Planck-Institute for Foreign and International Patent, Copyright and Competition
  Law, Library
  GERMANY (FEDERAL REPUBLIC) 361
MDC
  U. S. A. 798
MDI Library
  INDIA 429
Mead Data Central, Inc.
  U. S. A. 798
Merlin Gerin - Information Department
  FRANCE 326
Merlin Gerin - Service Documentation
  FRANCE 326
Merriam Center Library
  U. S. A. 799
Metropolitan Ervin Szabo Library, Budapest, Sociology Department
  HUNGARY 382
Mezdunaroden Informacionen Centar po Balkanistika
  BULGARIA 172
MIC
  UNITED KINGDOM 719
The Michael Somare Library
  PAPUA NEW GUINEA 584
Michigan State University, Africana Library
  U. S. A. 800
Michigan State University, Sahel Documentation Center
  U. S. A. 801
MIDS
  INDIA 427
Milli Prodüktivite Merkezi Egitim ve Yayin Şubesi
  TURKEY 715
Mindanao Development Studies Center, Library
  PHILIPPINES 607
Ministère de l'Economie et des Finances, Service Autonome de la Documentation, des
  Archives et des Publications

48

COTE D'IVOIRE *241*
Ministère de l'Equipement, du Logement, de l'Aménagement du Territoire et des
Transports, Service Technique de l'Urbanisme, Centre de Documentation
FRANCE *327*
Ministère de la Coopération, Centre de Documentation
FRANCE *328*
Ministère de la Recherche Scientifique et Technologique pour le Développement, Centre
d'Information et de Documentation Scientifique et Technique
MADAGASCAR *509*
Ministère des Affaires Etrangères, du Commerce Extérieur et de la Coopération au
Développement, Bibliothèque Africaine
BELGIUM *147*
Ministerie van Sociale Zaken, Bibliotheek en Documentatie
NETHERLANDS *550*
Ministério da Fazenda, Biblioteca
BRAZIL *163*
Ministerio de Educación, Centro de Documentación y Biblioteca
NICARAGUA *567*
Ministry of Education, Centre for Statistical Data and Educational Documentation
(Data Center)
SAUDI ARABIA *645*
Ministry of Education, Library and Documentation Centre
NICARAGUA *567*
Ministry of Finance and Planning, Centre for Development Information
SRI LANKA *665*
Ministry of Finance, Library
BRAZIL *163*
Ministry of Foreign Affairs, Foreign Trade and Cooperation, African Library
BELGIUM *147*
Ministry of Foreign Affairs, Library "José Ma. Lafragua"
MEXICO *526*
Ministry of Human Resource Development, Department of Culture, Central Secretariat
Library
INDIA *430*
Ministry of Planning, Development and Training, National Documentation Centre
GRENADA *376*
Ministry of Scientific and Technological Research for Development, Scientific and
Technical Information and Documentation Centre
MADAGASCAR *509*
Ministry of Social Affairs, Library and Documentation Service
NETHERLANDS *550*
MISR Library
UGANDA *717*
Mita Library and Information Center
JAPAN *482*
MLA
U. S. A. *802*
Modern Language Association of America
U. S. A. *802*
Mons. Juan Fremiot Torres Oliver Law Library, Catholic University of Puerto Rico
PUERTO RICO *634*
Monterey Institute of International Studies, William Tell Coleman Library
U. S. A. *803*
MPM
TURKEY *715*
MRSTD, CIDST
MADAGASCAR *509*
Mta Közgazdaságtudományi Intézete, Könyvtár és Dokumentáció

HUNGARY *389*
Musée de l'Homme, Bibliothèque
FRANCE *329*
Musée Royal de l'Afrique Centrale, Bibliothèque et Service de Documentation Africaine
‐BELGIUM *148*

N

NARESA
SRI LANKA *667*
NASA Industrial Applications Center
U. S. A. *852*
NASSDOC
INDIA *435*
Nationaal Documentatie Centrum "Veiligheid en Hygiëne", Studie en Documentatie
BELGIUM *149*
National Academy of History, Library
ARGENTINA *89*
National Anthropological Archives
U. S. A. *804*
National Association of Social Workers, Social Work Research and Abstracts
U. S. A. *805*
National Center for Computer Crime Data
U. S. A. *806*
National Centre of Applied Research to Research Development, Documentation Centre f **Agricultural Research**
MADAGASCAR *508*
The National Centre of Economic Information and Documentation
ALGERIA *85*
National Centre of Historical Documentation and Research
ANGOLA *88*
National Centre of Social Research
GREECE *375*
National Children's Bureau, Information and Library Service
UNITED KINGDOM *735*
National Collegiate Software Clearinghouse, NCSU
U. S. A. *812*
National Commission on the Role of Filipino Women, Clearinghouse and Information Center on Women
PHILIPPINES *598*
National Council for Research, National Documentation Centre
SUDAN *669*
National Council of Applied Economic Research, Documentation Service
INDIA *431*
National Council on Family Relations, Family Resources Database
U. S. A. *807*
National Diet Library, Indexing Division, Serials Department
JAPAN *485*
National Documentation Centre
MOROCCO *534*
SUDAN *670*
TUNISIA *711*
National Documentation Centre for Health and Family Welfare
INDIA *432*
National Documentation Centre, Grenada
GRENADA *376*
National Economic and Development Authority, Library

Section
NETHERLANDS *554*
Netherlands Institute of Human Rights
NETHERLANDS *559*
New School for Social Research, Raymond Fogelman Library
U. S. A. *808*
New York State Education Department, Law/Social Science Reference Service
U. S. A. *809*
New York University, Elmer Holmes Babst Library, Tamiment Library
U. S. A. *810*
New Zealand Department of Statistics, Information Sciences Division
NEW ZEALAND *563*
New Zealand Institute of Economic Research, Library
NEW ZEALAND *564*
NIAS
INDIA *436*
NIBR Biblioteket
NORWAY *575*
NIDA, Library and Information Center
THAILAND *702*
Nigerian Institute of International Affairs, Library and Documentation Services
NIGERIA *569*
Nigerian Institute of Social and Economic Research, Library
NIGERIA *570*
Nihon Rodokyokai, Rodo Toshokan
JAPAN *488*
Nikkei Economic Electronic Databank System
JAPAN *489*
Nikkei Telecom Japan News and Retrieval
JAPAN *489*
Nippon Keizai Tokei Bunken Senta
JAPAN *477*
NIR
BOTSWANA *157*
NIRD, Library
INDIA *434*
NISER Library
NIGERIA *570*
NISSO, Afdeling Bibliotheek and Documentatie
NETHERLANDS *554*
NISSO, Library and Documentation Section
NETHERLANDS *554*
NNSR
U. S. A. *811*
NNSR Machine Readable Branch, Special Archives Division
U. S. A. *811*
NOMOS DATAPOOL/EDICLINE
UNITED KINGDOM *726*
Nomura Research Institute, Japan Economic and Business Data Base
JAPAN *490*
NORC, Library
U. S. A. *835*
Nordic Documentation Center for Mass Communication Research
DENMARK *261*
Nordic Documentation Center for Mass Communication Research, Sweden
SWEDEN *687*
NORDICOM
DENMARK *261*

NORDICOM, Sweden
    SWEDEN *687*
Nordisk Dokumentationscentral for Massekommunikations-Forskning
    DENMARK *261*
Nordiska Afrikainstitutets Bibliotek
    SWEDEN *680*
Norsk Institutt for by- og Regionforskning, Biblioteket
    NORWAY *575*
Norsk Samfunnsvitenskapelig Datajeneste
    NORWAY *576*
Norsk Utenrikspolitisk Institutt, Biblioteket
    NORWAY *577*
North Carolina State University, College of Humanities and Social Sciences, Nationa
    Collegiate Software Clearinghouse
    U. S. A. *812*
Northern Illinois University, Clearinghouse For Sociological Literature
    U. S. A. *813*
Northwestern University, International Comparative Political Parties Project
    U. S. A. *814*
Norwegian Computing Centre for the Humanities
    NORWAY *573*
Norwegian Institute for Urban and Regional Research, Library
    NORWAY *575*
Norwegian Institute of International Affairs, Library
    NORWAY *577*
Norwegian Research Council for Science and the Humanities, Information and
    Documentation Service for On-Going Research in the Social Sciences and the
    Humanities
    NORWAY *574*
Norwegian Social Science Data Services
    NORWAY *576*
NPA Documentation Centre
    JAMAICA *472*
NPC Library
    EGYPT *273*
NRI/E, Japan Economic and Business Data Bank
    JAPAN *490*
NSD
    NORWAY *576*
NUPI, Library
    NORWAY *577*
NYB, Information Services
    UNITED KINGDOM *736*
NZSTATS Information Sciences Division
    NEW ZEALAND *563*

O

OAS, Colombus Memorial Library
    U. S. A. *58*
Observatoire Economique de Paris, Institut National de la Statistique et des Etude:
    Economiques
    FRANCE *330*
Odense Universitet, Dansk Data Arkiv
    DENMARK *262*
Odense University, Danish Data Archives
    DENMARK *262*
ODEPLAN, Biblioteca

54

Orientální Ústav Csav, Stredisko Vedeckých Informací
   CZECHOSLOVAKIA   246
Országgyülési Könyvtár
   HUNGARY   391
Országos Müszaki Információs Közpointés Könyvtar
   HUNGARY   392
Országos Vezetóképzó Központ, Tudományos Tájékoztató Szolgálat
   HUNGARY   393
Osaka Chamber of Commerce and Industry Library
   JAPAN   492
Osaka Keizai Daigaku Tosmokan
   JAPAN   491
Osaka Shoko Kaigisho Shoko-Toshokan
   JAPAN   492
Osaka University of Economics, Library
   JAPAN   491
Oskar Lange Academy of Economics in WrocJaw, Main Library
   POLAND   609
Osmania University, Regional Centre for Urban and Environmental Studies
   INDIA   437
Ośrodek Informacji Naukowej, Polskiej Akademii Nauk, Biblioteka
   POLAND   624
Österreichische Forschungsstiftung für Entwicklungshilfe, Dokumentation
   AUSTRIA   133
Oú Csav, Svi
   CZECHOSLOVAKIA   246
Oulu University Library
   FINLAND   283
Oulun Yliopiston Kirjasto
   FINLAND   283
Overseas Development Institute Library
   UNITED KINGDOM   737
OVK TTSZ
   HUNGARY   393

P

Pacific Information Centre
   FIJI   278
PADIS
   ETHIOPIA   59
PAIS
   U. S. A.   819
Pakistan Institute of Development Economics, Library and Documentation Centre
   PAKISTAN   581
Pan African Documentation and Information System
   ETHIOPIA   59
Panafrican Institute for Development, Documentation Centre
   CAMEROON (UNITED REPUBLIC)   180
Paris Chamber of Trade and Industry, Documentation Centre
   FRANCE   307
Parlement du Canada, Bibliothèque du Parlement, Service d'Information et de
   référence
   CANADA   192
Parliament Library and Reference, Research, Documentation and Information Service
   INDIA   438
Parliament of Canada, Library of Parliament, Information and Reference Branch
   CANADA   192

Parliamentary and Law Library
ARGENTINA *101*
Paul B. Sheatsley Library
U. S. A. *835*
PCF-MI
PHILIPPINES *601*
Peace Palace Library
NETHERLANDS *538*
Peace Research Centre
INDIA *439*
Peace Research Centre, University of Nijmegen
NETHERLANDS *561*
Peace Research Information Unit Bonn
GERMANY (FEDERAL REPUBLIC) *342*
Peace Research Institute - Dundas
CANADA *193*
Permanent InterState Committee for Drought Control in the Sahel, Documentation and Information Service
BURKINA-FASO *177*
Permanent Secretariat of the General Treaty for the Economic Integration of Central America, Information and Documentation Centre
GUATEMALA *377*
Peruvian Center of Social Studies, Agrarian Documentation Center
PERU *589*
Philippine Social Science Council, Library
PHILIPPINES *600*
Philipps University, Foreign Language Research Information Center
GERMANY (FEDERAL REPUBLIC) *362*
Philipps-Universität, Marburg, Informationszentrum für Fremdsprachenforschung
GERMANY (FEDERAL REPUBLIC) *362*
PIDE Library and Documentation Section
PAKISTAN *581*
PIIE, Biblioteca
CHILE *222*
The Planning Exchange
UNITED KINGDOM *738*
PNUD Biblioteca
ECUADOR *267*
PNUD Library
ECUADOR *267*
POLIS
UNITED KINGDOM *728*
Polish Academy of Sciences Kórnik, Library
POLAND *625*
Polish Institute of International Affairs, Department for Scientific Information and the Library
POLAND *626*
Polska Amademia Nauk, Biblioteka Kórnicka
POLAND *625*
Polski Instytut Spraw Międzynarodowych, Zakład Informachi Naukowej i Biblioteka
POLAND *626*
POPIN
U. S. A. *71*
POPIN-Africa
ETHIOPIA *74*
Population Center Foundation, Management of Information Unit
PHILIPPINES *601*
Population Council, Office of Communications

U. S. A. *60*
Population Information Network, United Nations
    U. S. A. *71*
Population Reference Bureau, Decision Demographics
    U. S. A. *815*
Poznan Society of Friends of Arts and Sciences, Library
    POLAND *627*
Poznańskiego Towarztstwa Przyjacioł Nauk, Biblioteka
    POLAND *627*
PPK-PH
    INDONESIA *450*
PPPPL-DKI Jakarta, DOCINFO
    INDONESIA *451*
PREALC
    CHILE *220*
Predicasts
    U. S. A. *816*
Présidence de la République, Direction Générale de la Banque de Données
    MADAGASCAR *510*
Presidencia de la Nación, Secretaría de Planificación, Departamento Biblioteca
    ARGENTINA *106*
Presidencia de la Republica, Oficina de Planificación Nacional, Biblioteca
    CHILE *221*
Presidency of the Nation, Planning Secretariat, Library Department
    ARGENTINA *106*
Press und Informationsamt der Bundesregierung
    GERMANY (FEDERAL REPUBLIC) *363*
PRI-D
    CANADA *193*
Princeton University, Office of Population Research
    U. S. A. *817*
PRIO, Library
    NORWAY *572*
Programa de las Naciones Unidas para el Desarrollo, Biblioteca
    ECUADOR *267*
Programa Interdisciplinario de Investigaciones en Educación, Biblioteca
    CHILE *222*
Programa Regional del Empleo para América Latina y El Caribe, Oficina Internaciona
del Trabajo
    CHILE *220*
Programme de Réseau Sahélien de Documentation et d'Information Scientifiques et
Techniques
    MALI *512*
Project SHARE
    U. S. A. *861*
PSPO
    BELGIUM *151*
PSSC Library
    PHILIPPINES *600*
Psychological Abstracts Information Services
    U. S. A. *818*
Psychological Institute of Czechoslovak Academy of Sciences, Information Centre
    CZECHOSLOVAKIA *247*
Psychologický Ústav CSAV, Stredisko Vedeckých Informací
    CZECHOSLOVAKIA *247*
PsycINFO
    U. S. A. *818*
PTPN/BIBL

POLAND *627*
Public Administration National Institute, Library and Publications Department
ARGENTINA *104*
Public Affairs Information Service, Inc.
U. S. A. *819*
Pusat Pelayanan Keadilan dan Pengabdian Hukum
INDONESIA *450*
Pusat Penelitian dan Pengembangan Perkotaan dan Lingkungan, Bagian Dokumentasi dan Informasi
INDONESIA *451*
Pusat Penelitian Unika Atma Jaya, Perpustakaan
INDONESIA *452*

R

R C
YUGOSLAVIA *891*
Radcliffe College, Arthur and Elizabeth Schlesinger Library on the History of Women in America
U. S. A. *820*
RCCDC, Special Library/Documentation-Information Service
YUGOSLAVIA *887*
Real Instituto de Antropologia y Linguistica
NETHERLANDS *549*
Referalni Centar za Naucne Informacije
YUGOSLAVIA *891*
Referral Center for Scientific Informations
YUGOSLAVIA *891*
Refugee Documentation Center
GERMANY (FEDERAL REPUBLIC) *369*
Regional Centre for Urban and Environmental Studies, Osmania University
INDIA *437*
Regional Industrial Expansion, Government Documentation Centre
CANADA *194*
Regional Information Network on Arab Women, Social Research Center
EGYPT *269*
Representation of the Commission of the European Communities in Turkey
TURKEY *713*
RESADOC
MALI *512*
RESAGRI
FRANCE *331*
Research and Documentation Centre Women and Autonomy
NETHERLANDS *556*
Research and Information System for the Non-Aligned and other Developing Countries, Documentation Centre and Data Archives
INDIA *440*
Research Centre for Cooperation with Developing Countries, Special Library/Documentation-Information Service
YUGOSLAVIA *887*
Research Centre for Women's Studies, Reference Service and Documentation Centre
INDIA *442*
Research Institute for Economics and Business Administration, Library
JAPAN *483*
Research Institute for International Politics and Security, Science and Politics Foundation. Library and Documentation Service
GERMANY (FEDERAL REPUBLIC) *351*
Research Institute for Peace Policy, Information Office

GERMANY (FEDERAL REPUBLIC) *350*
The Research Libraries, the New York Public Library, Economic and Public Affairs Division
U. S. A. *821*
Research Library on African Affairs
GHANA *374*
Research School of Pacific Studies, Australian National University
AUSTRALIA *120*
Réseau de Documentation en Economie Agricole
FRANCE *331*
RIEBA, Library
JAPAN *483*
RIIA, Library
UNITED KINGDOM *739*
Rijksuniversiteit Leiden, Documentatiebureau voor Oosteuropees Recht
NETHERLANDS *555*
Rijksuniversiteit Leiden, Onderzoek en Dokumentatie Centrum Vrouwen en Autonomie
NETHERLANDS *556*
Riksdagsbiblioteket
SWEDEN *681*
RILA
NETHERLANDS *549*
RIPS, Library
GHANA *79*
The Rockefeller University, Rockefeller Archive Center
U. S. A. *822*
Roper Center for Public Opinion Research
U. S. A. *837*
Roskilde Universitetsbibliotek
DENMARK *263*
Roskilde University Centre
DENMARK *263*
Roskilde University Library
DENMARK *263*
Royal Institute of International Affairs, Library
UNITED KINGDOM *739*
Royal Institute of International Affairs, Press Library
UNITED KINGDOM *740*
Royal Institute of Linguistics and Anthropology
NETHERLANDS *549*
The Royal Library
DENMARK *260*
Royal Museum of Central Africa, Library and African Documentation Service
BELGIUM *148*
The Royal Norwegian Ministry of Development Cooperation, Library
NORWAY *578*
Royal Tropical Institute, Department of Information and Documentation
NETHERLANDS *548*
RPD/NIROV
NETHERLANDS *553*
RSFSR/GPIB
U. S. S. R. *872*
RSPACS
AUSTRALIA *120*
RUB
DENMARK *263*
RUC
DENMARK *263*

MALAYSIA *511*

Service Autonome de la Documentation, des Archives et des Publications
COTE D'IVOIRE *241*

Service d'Information Tiers-Monde
SWITZERLAND *695*

Service Ecole Tiers-Monde
SWITZERLAND *695*

Shakai Kagaku Kenkyusho, Tokyo Daigaku
JAPAN *495*

Shri Ram Centre for Industrial Relations and Human Resources
INDIA *441*

SIAS, Library and Information Centre
DENMARK *61*

SIC-PAS
POLAND *624*

SICSS
U. S. S. R. *878*

SIECA/CDI
GUATEMALA *377*

SIL Cameroun
CAMEROON (UNITED REPUBLIC) *181*

SIM
NETHERLANDS *559*

SIRLS
CANADA *210*

SISBI
ARGENTINA *109*

Slavic Research Center
JAPAN *478*

Sleský Ústav
CZECHOSLOVAKIA *248*

Slezský Ústav CSAV, Stredisko Vedeckých Infomaci
CZECHOSLOVAKIA *248*

SLIDA
SRI LANKA *668*

The Slovak Academy of Sciences, Central Library Information Centre
CZECHOSLOVAKIA *249*

Slovenskej Akaémie Vied, Ústredná Kniznica Informacné Centrum
CZECHOSLOVAKIA *249*

SNDT Women's University, Research Centre for Women's Studies, Reference Service and
Documentation Centre
INDIA *442*

Sociaal-Wetenschappelijk Informatie-en Documentatiecentrum
NETHERLANDS *557*

Social Research Center, Regional Information Network on Arab Women, American
University in Cairo
EGYPT *269*

Social Research Institute
THAILAND *697*

Social Research Methodology Documentation Centre
NETHERLANDS *540*

Social Science Computer Research Institute, University of Pittsburgh
U. S. A. *853*

Social Science Computing Laboratory, University of Western Ontario
CANADA *211*

Social Science Data and Programs Archive
ITALY *461*

Social Science Data Archives

INDIA *443*
SRIA
U. S. A. *848*
SRM-Documentation Centre
NETHERLANDS *540*
SSA
SWITZERLAND *693*
SSCL
CANADA *211*
SSCRI
U.`S. A. *853*
SSD
SWEDEN *685*
SSDA
AUSTRALIA *121*
CANADA *185*
ISRAEL *459*
SSDL
U. S. A. *850*
SSEES, Library
UNITED KINGDOM *747*
SSRC Library, Punjab
PAKISTAN *582*
SSRFC
NEW ZEALAND *565*
Stanford University, The Hoover Institution on War, Revolution and Peace, Library an
Archives
U. S. A. *827*
State and University Library of Arhus
DENMARK *264*
State Data Analysis System Foundation, São Paulo
BRAZIL *160*
State Data Program
U. S. A. *833*
State Planning Organization, Documentation Service
TURKEY *714*
State Planning Secretariat
GUYANA *379*
State Public Historical Library of the Ministry of Culture of the RSFSR
U. S. S. R. *872*
State University of New York at Albany, Graduate Library for Public Affairs and
Policy
U. S. A. *828*
Statens Psykologisk-Pedagogiska Bibliotek
SWEDEN *682*
Statistics Canada, Library
CANADA *195*
Statistics Sweden, Library
SWEDEN *683*
Statistique Canada, Library
CANADA *195*
Statistisches Bundesamt, Abt. Bibliothek-Documentation-Archiv
GERMANY (FEDERAL REPUBLIC) *364*
Statistisk Sentralbyrås Bibliotek
NORWAY *579*
Statistiska Centralbyråns Bibliotek
SWEDEN *683*
Statsbiblioteket Århus

TECS
    INDIA *444*
Tenri Central Library
    JAPAN *494*
Tenri University, Tenri Central Library
    JAPAN *494*
Thai Khadi Research Institute
    THAILAND *705*
Thailand Information Center, Academic Resource Center
    THAILAND *699*
Thammasat University, Thai Khadi Research Institute
    THAILAND *705*
Third World Information Service
    SWITZERLAND *695*
Third World School Service
    SWITZERLAND *695*
TIC
    THAILAND *699*
Tilastokeskus/Tilastokirjasto
    FINLAND *284*
TMC Asser Instituut voor Internationaal en Europees Recht
    NETHERLANDS *560*
The Tokyo Chamber of Commerce and Industry, Commercial and Industrial Library
    JAPAN *499*
Tokyo Daigaku Shakai Kagaku Kenkyusho
    JAPAN *495*
Tokyo Daigaku Toyobunka Kenkyujo
    JAPAN *496*
The Tokyo Institute for Municipal Research, Municipal Reference Library
    JAPAN *498*
Tokyo Keizai University Library
    JAPAN *497*
Tokyo Keizaidaigaku Toshokan
    JAPAN *497*
Tokyo Shisei Chosakai, Shisei Semmon Toshokan
    JAPAN *498*
Tokyo Shoko Kaigisho Shoko Toshokan
    JAPAN *499*
Tribal Research Institute, Library
    THAILAND *706*
Trier University, Center for Psychological Information and Documentation
    GERMANY (FEDERAL REPUBLIC) *367*
Tsentr Nauchnoi Informatsii po Obshchestvennym Naukam Akademii Nauk Armyanskoi SSR
    U. S. S. R. *873*
Tsentr Nauchnoi Informatsii po Obshchestvennym Naukam Akademii Nauk Azerbaijanskoi
    SSR
    U. S. S. R. *874*
Tsentr Nauchnoi Informatsii po Obshchestvennym Naukam Akademii Nauk Estonskoi SSR
    U. S. S. R. *875*
Tsentr Nauchnoi Informatsii po Obshchestvennym Naukam Akademii Nauk Gruzinskoi SSR
    U. S. S. R. *876*
Tsentr Nauchnoi Informatsii po Obshchestvennym Naukam Akademii Nauk Latviiskoi SSR
    U. S. S. R. *877*
Tsentr Nauchnoi Informatsii po Obshchestvennym Naukam pri Otdelenii Obshchestvennykh
    Nauk Akademii Nauk Litovskoi SSR
    U. S. S. R. *878*
Tsentr Nauchnoi Informatsii po Obshchestvennym Naukam pri Presidiume Akademii Nauk
    Uzbekskoi SSR

67

UNCTC
  U. S. A. *67*
UN/DIS
  U. S. A. *70*
UN-ECLAC/CARISPLAN
  TRINIDAD AND TOBAGO *32*
UNESCO Centre de Documentation des Sciences Sociales et Humaines
  FRANCE *76*
UNESCO Oficina Regional de Cultura para América Latina y el Caribe, Centro de Documentación
  CUBA *75*
UNESCO Regional Office for Culture in Latin America and the Caribbean, Documentation Centre
  CUBA *75*
UNESCO Social and Human Sciences Documentation Centre
  FRANCE *76*
UNESCWA, Library
  IRAQ *73*
UNHCR/CDR
  SWITZERLAND *78*
UNIDI, IIS
  COSTA RICA *238*
UNIDI, Institute of Social Research
  COSTA RICA *238*
UNIN/IDD
  ZAMBIA *894*
Unit Penyelidekan Sosioekonomi
  MALAYSIA *511*
Unité de Recherche en Anthropologie Sociale et Culturelle, Bibliothèque Universitaire
  ALGERIA *87*
United Nations Association of Norway, Data and Information Services
  NORWAY *580*
United Nations Centre for Human Settlements, Information Division
  KENYA *65*
United Nations Centre for Regional Development, Information Exchange and Publications Programme
  JAPAN *66*
United Nations Centre on Transnational Corporations, Advisory and Information Services Division
  U. S. A. *67*
United Nations, Dag Hammarskjold Library
  U. S. A. *68*
United Nations, Department for Disarmament Affairs, Disarmament Information Branch
  U. S. A. *69*
United Nations, Department of International Economic and Social Affairs, Development Information System
  U. S. A. *70*
United Nations, Department of International Economic and Social Affairs, Population Information Network
  U. S. A. *71*
United Nations, Department of Political and Security Council Affairs, Centre against Apartheid: Publicity, Assistance, Promotion of International Action Branch
  U. S. A. *72*
United Nations Economic and Social Commission for Western Asia, Library and Documentation Section
  IRAQ *73*
United Nations Economic Commission for Africa, Population Division, Information

URUGUAY 757

Universidad de la República, Facultad de Derecho y Ciencias Sociales, Departamento de Documentación y Biblioteca
URUGUAY 758

Universidad de Los Andes, Facultad de Economía, Centro de Estudios del Desarrollo Económico, Biblioteca
COLOMBIA 233

Universidad de Puerto Rico, Colegio Universitario de Cayey, Biblioteca
PUERTO RICO 635

Universidad de Puerto Rico, Escuela de Derecho, Biblioteca
PUERTO RICO 636

Universidad de Puerto Rico Sistema de Bibliotecas, Río Piedras Campus
PUERTO RICO 637

Universidad de San Buenaventura, Biblioteca
COLOMBIA 234

Universidad de San Carlos de Guatemala, Biblioteca Central
GUATEMALA 378

Universidad del Pacífico, Biblioteca-Centro de Documentación e Información
PERU 594

Universidad EAFIT, Consejo de Documentación e Intercambio de Casos
COLOMBIA 83

Universidad Femenina del Sagrado Corázon, Biblioteca
PERU 595

Universidad Interamericana de Puerto Rico, Instituto de Investigación, Centro de Documentación de la Mujer
PUERTO RICO 638

Universidad Nacional Autónoma de México, Centro de Información Científica y Humanística
MEXICO 528

Universidad Nacional Autónoma de Mexico, Centro de Investigaciones Interdisciplinarias en Humanidades, Departamento de Información y Documentación

MEXICO 529

Universidad Nacional Autonoma de Mexico, Escuela Nacional de Estudios Profesionales Acatlán, Centro de Información y Documentación
MEXICO 530

Universidad Nacional Autónoma de México, Facultad de Ciencias Políticas y Sociales, Centro de Documentación
MEXICO 531

Universidad Nacional Autonóma de México, Instituto de Investigaciones Sociales, Biblioteca
MEXICO 532

Universidad Nacional de Cuyo, Facultad de Filosofía y Letras, Biblioteca
ARGENTINA 110

Universidad Nacional de la Plata, Instituto de Investigaciones Administrativas, Centro de Documentación
ARGENTINA 111

Universidad Nacional de Lomas de Zamora, Facultad de Ciencias Sociales, Biblioteca
ARGENTINA 112

Universidad Nacional de Rosario, Faculdad de Ciencias Económicas, Biblioteca
ARGENTINA 113

Universidad Nacional del Sur, Departamento de Humanidades, Biblioteca de Humanidades

ARGENTINA 114

Universidad Nacional San Juan, Facultad de Filosofía, Humanidades y Artes, Biblioteca Dr. Juan José Nissen
ARGENTINA 115

Universidad National Autónoma de Mexico, Coordinación de Servicios Bibliotecarios

MEXICO 533
niversidad Pontificia Bolivariana, Centro de Investigaciones para el Desarrollo
Integral, Centro de Documentación "Rafael M. Salas"
COLOMBIA 235
niversidad Sofia, Instituto Iberoamericano
JAPAN 500
niversidade de São Paulo, Centro de Estudos de Demografia Histórica da América
Latina
BRAZIL 164
niversidade Eduardo Mondlane, Arquivo Histórico de Moçambique
MOZAMBIQUE 535
niversidade Federal do Acre, Biblioteca Central Ruy Alberto da Costa Lins
BRAZIL 165
niversità di Bologna, Dipartimento di Sociologia, Centro Internazionale di
Documentazione e Studi Sociologici sui Problemi del Lavoro
ITALY 470
niversität Düsseldorf, Forschungsabteilung für Philosophischen Information und
Dokumentation
GERMANY (FEDERAL REPUBLIC) 365
niversität Kiel, Institut für Weltwirtschaft, Bibliothek
GERMANY (FEDERAL REPUBLIC) 366
niversität Trier, Zentralstelle für Psychologische Information und Dokumentation
GERMANY (FEDERAL REPUBLIC) 367
niversität zu Köln, Zentralarchiv für Empirische Sozialforschung
GERMANY (FEDERAL REPUBLIC) 368
niversité Catholique de Louvain, Faculté des Sciences Economiques, Sociales et
Politiques, Bibliothèque
BELGIUM 151
niversité d'Anvers, Collège pour les Pays en voie de Développement, Bibliothèque
BELGIUM 153
niversité d'Oran, Centre de Recherche et d'Information Documentaire en Sciences
Sociales et Humaines
ALGERIA 86
niversité d'Oran, Unité de Recherche en Anthropologie Sociale et Culturelle,
Bibliothèque Universitaire
ALGERIA 87
niversité d'Ottawa, Bibliothèque Morisset (Sciences Sociales et Humaines)
CANADA 206
niversité de Benin, Unité de Recherche Démographique, Centre de Documentation
TOGO 707
niversité de Dakar, Faculté des Sciences Juridiques et Economiques, Centre de
Recherches, d'Etudes et de Documentation sur les Institutions et la Législation
Africaine
SENEGAL 650
niversité de Kinshasa, Centre Interdisciplinaire d'Etudes et de Documentation
Politiques, Service de Documentation et des Publications
ZAIRE 893
niversité de Liège, Faculté de Droit, d'Economie et de Sciences Sociales,
Bibliothèque Léon Graulich
BELGIUM 152
niversité de Montpellier, Institut de Recherches et d'Etudes pour le Traitement de
l'Information Juridique
FRANCE 334
niversité de Montréal, Bibliothèque des Lettres et des Sciences Humaines
CANADA 196
niversité de Paris VII, Laboratoire de Psychologie Sociale, Service de
Documentation
FRANCE 335

University of California at Berkeley, Giannini Foundation of Agricultural Economics,
Library
    U. S. A. 787
University of California, Berkeley, Institute of Governmental Studies, Library
    U. S. A. 831
University of California, Public Policy Research Organization, Data Management and
Analysis
    U. S. A. 832
University of California, State Data Program
    U. S. A. 833
University of Canterbury, Centre for Resource Management
    NEW ZEALAND 566
University of Canterbury, CRM
    NEW ZEALAND 566
University of Chicago, Far Eastern Library
    U. S. A. 834
University of Chicago, National Opinion Research Center, Paul B. Sheatsley Library
    U. S. A. 835
University of Chile, Center for the Study of Jewish Culture
    CHILE 223
University of Chile, Political Science Institute, Library
    CHILE 224
University of Cincinnati, Institute for Policy Research, Southwest Ohio Regional Data
Center
    U. S. A. 836
University of Cologne, Central Archive for Empirical Social Research
    GERMANY (FEDERAL REPUBLIC) 368
University of Connecticut, Institute for Social Inquiry, Roper Center for Public
Opinion Research
    U. S. A. 837
University of Costa Rica, Eugenio Fonseca Tortos Library
    COSTA RICA 237
University of Delhi, Department of Social Work, Documentation Centre
    INDIA 445
University of Dhaka, Institute of Statistical Research and Training, Library
    BANGLADESH 139
University of Dundee, European Documentation Centre, Law Library
    UNITED KINGDOM 742
University of Durban-Westville, Documentation Centre
    SOUTH AFRICA 653
University of Düsseldorf, Research Division for Philosophy Information and
Documentation, Philosophy Information Service
    GERMANY (FEDERAL REPUBLIC) 365
University of Florida, College of Business Administration, Bureau of Economic and
Business Research
    U. S. A. 838
University of Georgia, School of Law, Law Library
    U. S. A. 839
University of Göteborg, Department of Political Science, Nordic Documentation Center
for Mass Communication Research
    SWEDEN 687
University of Göteborg, Språkdata
    SWEDEN 678
University of Helsinki, Institute of Development Studies, Library
    FINLAND 281
University of Helsinki, Social Science Library
    FINLAND 282
University of Idaho, Social Sciences Library

U. S. A. *840*
University of Illinois at Urbana-Champaign, Education and Social Science Library
U. S. A. *841*
University of Illinois, Institute of Labor and Industrial Relations Library
U. S. A. *842*
University of Indonesia, Center for Justice and the Rule of Law
INDONESIA *450*
University of Indonesia, Faculty of Economics, The Demographic Institute, Library
INDONESIA *453*
University of Iowa, Iowa Social Science Institute
U. S. A. *843*
University of Khartoum, Faculty of Economic and Social Studies, Development Studies and Research Centre
SUDAN *672*
University of Kiel, Institute of World Economics, Library
GERMANY (FEDERAL REPUBLIC) *366*
University of Leeds, African Studies Unit
UNITED KINGDOM *743*
University of Leiden, Documentation Office for East European Law
NETHERLANDS *555*
University of Leiden, Research and Documentation Centre Women and Autonomy
NETHERLANDS *556*
University of London, Institute of Latin American Studies, Library
UNITED KINGDOM *744*
University of London, Institute on Commonwealth Studies, Library
UNITED KINGDOM *745*
University of London, School of Oriental and African Studies, Library
UNITED KINGDOM *746*
University of London, School of Slavonic and East European Studies, Library
UNITED KINGDOM *747*
University of London, Warburg Institute, Library
UNITED KINGDOM *748*
University of Manchester, Institute for Development Policy and Management, Library
UNITED KINGDOM *749*
University of Manitoba, Elizabeth Dafoe Library
CANADA *205*
University of Massachusetts, Labor Relations and Research Center, Library
U. S. A. *844*
University of Michigan, Center for Research on Economic Development, Library
U. S. A. *845*
University of Michigan, Institute for Social Research, Inter-university Consortium for Political and Social Research
U. S. A. *846*
University of Minnesota, Drug Information Services
U. S. A. *847*
University of Montreal, Humanities and Social Sciences Library
CANADA *196*
University of New Hampshire, State and Regional Indicators Archive
U. S. A. *848*
University of New South Wales, Social Welfare Research Centre
AUSTRALIA *127*
University of Nijmegen, Peace Research Centre
NETHERLANDS *561*
University of North Carolina at Chapel Hill, the Center for Early Adolescence, Information Services Division
U. S. A. *849*
University of North Carolina, Institute for Research in Social Science, Social Science Data Library

U. S. A. *850*
University of Oran, Cultural and Social Anthropology Research Unit, University
Library
ALGERIA *87*
University of Ottawa, Morisset Library (Humanities and Social Sciences)
CANADA *206*
University of Papua New Guinea, the Michael Somare Library
PAPUA NEW GUINEA *584*
University of Pittsburgh, Economics Library
U. S. A. *851*
University of Pittsburgh, NASA Industrial Applications Center
U. S. A. *852*
University of Pittsburgh, Social Science Computer Research Institute
U. S. A. *853*
University of Puerto Rico, School of Law, Library
PUERTO RICO *636*
University of Puerto Rico, University College of Cayey, Library
PUERTO RICO *635*
University of Puerto Rio, Rio Piedras Campus, Libraries System
PUERTO RICO *637*
University of Qatar Documentation and Humanities Research Centre
QATAR *639*
University of South Dakota, School of Business, Business Research Bureau
U. S. A. *854*
University of St. Gallen for Business Administration, Economics and Social Sciences
SWITZERLAND *691*
University of Stockholm, Institute of Latin American Studies, Library
SWEDEN *684*
University of Sussex, Institute of Development Studies, Library
UNITED KINGDOM *750*
University of Sydney, Bibliographic Information on Southeast Asia
AUSTRALIA *128*
University of Tennessee, Knoxville, College of Business Administration, Center for
Business and Economic Research
U. S. A. *855*
University of Texas at Austin, Linguistics Research Center
U. S. A. *856*
University of the Philippines, Asian Center Library
PHILIPPINES *603*
University of the Philippines, Institute of Mass Communication
PHILIPPINES *604*
University of the Philippines, School of Economics, Library
PHILIPPINES *605*
University of the Philippines, School of Urban and Regional Planning
PHILIPPINES *606*
University of the Punjab, Social Sciences Research Centre, Library
PAKISTAN *582*
University of the Republic, Faculty of Social Sciences and Law, Library and
Documentation Department
URUGUAY *758*
University of the Republic, School of Economic and Administrative Sciences, Institute
of Administration, Library
URUGUAY *757*
University of the South Pacific, Pacific Information Centre
FIJI *278*
University of the West Indies, Institute of Social and Economic Research,
Documentation and Data Centre
JAMAICA *473*

University of Tokyo, Institute of Oriental Culture
    JAPAN 496
University of Tokyo, Institute of Social Science
    JAPAN 495
University of Toronto, Victoria University Library
    CANADA 207
University of Warwick, Library
    UNITED KINGDOM 751
University of Waterloo, Dana Porter Library
    CANADA 208
University of Waterloo, Leisure Studies Data Bank
    CANADA 209
University of Waterloo, Specialized Information Retrieval and Library Services
    CANADA 210
University of West Indies, Faculty of Law Library
    BARBADOS 140
University of Western Ontario, Social Science Computing Laboratory
    CANADA 211
University of Wisconsin, Madison, Center for Demography and Ecology, Library
    U. S. A. 857
University of Wisconsin-Madison, Data and Program Library Serivce
    U. S. A. 858
Univerza Edvarda Kardelja v Ljubljani, Osrednja Druzboslovna Knjiznica Jozeta
    Goricarja, Specializirani Indoc Center za Druzboslovje
    YUGOSLAVIA 892
Uniwersytet Warszawski, Biblioteka
    POLAND 629
Uniwersytet Warszawski, Połaczone Biblioteki: Instytutu Filozofii i Socjologii pan
    Oraz Wydziału Filozofii i Socjologii UW
    POLAND 630
UNLZ, Facultad de Ciencias Sociales, Biblioteca
    ARGENTINA 112
UNRISD, Reference Centre
    SWITZERLAND 80
UNSDRI, Information Service
    ITALY 81
UP-IMC
    PHILIPPINES 604
UPSE
    MALAYSIA 511
URASC, Bibliothèque Universitaire
    ALGERIA 87
Urban Institute Library
    U. S. A. 859
U.S. Department of Commerce, Bureau of the Census, Library
    U. S. A. 860
U.S. Department of Health and Human Services, Project SHARE
    U. S. A. 861
U.S. Department of Housing and Urban Development, HUD USER
    U. S. A. 862
U.S. Department of Labor, Bureau of Labor Statistics
    U. S. A. 863
Ústav Ceskoslovenských a Svetových Dejin Csav, Oddeleni vedeckých Informací
    CZECHOSLOVAKIA 250
Ústav pro Jazyk Ceský Csav, Útvar Vedeckých Informací
    CZECHOSLOVAKIA 251
Ustav Státu a Práva CSAV, Útvar Vedeckých Informací
    CZECHOSLOVAKIA 252

Ustredi Vedeckých Informaci Ceskoslovenské Akademie Ved, Záklasni Knihovna
CZECHOSLOVAKIA 253
Ústredná Ekonomická Kniznica
CZECHOSLOVAKIA 254
Ústredni Ekonomická Knihovna
CZECHOSLOVAKIA 255
ÚVI EÚ CSAV
CZECHOSLOVAKIA 245

V

V. I. Lenin State Library of the USSR
U. S. S. R. 871
"Vector" Center of Economic and Social Studies, Documentation Centre
CHILE 215
VFSI "D. A. Cenov", Svistov, Naucna Biblioteka "Akademik Dr. Nicolas Mihov"
BULGARIA 173
VGBIL
U. S. S. R. 880
Victoria University Library, University of Toronto
CANADA 207
Vien Kinh Te The Gioi, Phong Thong Tin Tu Lieu
VIET-NAM (SOCIALIST REPUBLIC) 886
Vienna Chamber of Labour, Social Sciences Library
AUSTRIA 131
Vienna Institute for Comparative Economic Studies, Information Services
AUSTRIA 134
Viss Institut po Ikonomika "K. Marx", Informacionen Centar S Biblioteka
BULGARIA 174
Vsesojuznaja Gosudarstvennaja Biblioteka Inostrannoj Literatury
U. S. S. R. 880

W

Walter P. Reuther Library of Labor and Urban Affairs
U. S. A. 864
Warburg Institute Library
UNITED KINGDOM 748
The Warsaw University Library
POLAND 629
Warsaw University, United Libraries of: Institute of Philosophy and Sociology of the
Polish Academy of Sciences, Department of Social Sciences
POLAND 630
Wayne State University, Walter P. Reuther Library of Labor and Urban Affairs
U. S. A. 864
Wen Xian Qing Bao Zhong Xin
CHINA (PEOPLE'S REPUBLIC) 225
The Western Institute, Library
POLAND 623
Wiener Institut für Internationale Wirtschaftsvergleiche, Informationszentrum
AUSTRIA 134
The H. W. Wilson Company, Wilsonline
U. S. A. 865
Wilsonline
U. S. A. 865
Wirtschaftsuniversität Wien, Sozialwissenschaftliche Informationsstelle
AUSTRIA 135
World Affairs Report

U. S. A. _769_
World Bank, International Economic Department, Socio-Economic Data Division
U. S. A. _84_

X

Xavier Labour Relations Institute, Library
INDIA _446_
Xavier University, Mindanao Development Studies Center, Library
PHILIPPINES _607_
XLRI, Library
INDIA _446_

Y

Yale University, Human Relations Area Files
U. S. A. _866_
Yayasan Idayu, Perpustakaan
INDONESIA _454_
YMCA Historical Library
U. S. A. _867_
York University, Institute for Social Research, Canadian Social Science Data Archiv

CANADA _212_
Young Men's Christian Associations of the United States of America, Historical
Library
U. S. A. _867_

Z

ZDWF
GERMANY (FEDERAL REPUBLIC) _369_
Zentralarchiv für Empirische Sozialforschung
GERMANY (FEDERAL REPUBLIC) _368_
Zentralbibliothek der Wirtschaftswissenschaften in der Bundesrepublik Deutschland
GERMANY (FEDERAL REPUBLIC) _366_
Zentrale Dokumentationsstelle der Freien Wohlfahrtspflege für Flüchtlinge
GERMANY (FEDERAL REPUBLIC) _369_
Zentrum für gesellschaftswissenschaftliche Information, Akademie der Wissenschaften
der DDR
GERMAN DEMOCRATIC REPUBLIC _340_
Zentrum für Historische Sozialforschung
GERMANY (FEDERAL REPUBLIC) _370_
ZHSF
GERMANY (FEDERAL REPUBLIC) _370_
ZK-UVI CSAV
CZECHOSLOVAKIA _253_
ZPID
GERMANY (FEDERAL REPUBLIC) _367_

International & Regional / Internacional & Regional

1 - ADVISORY COMMITTEE FOR THE CO-ORDINATION OF INFORMATION SYSTEMS

SYNONYMOUS NAMES: ACCIS;
Comité Consultatif pour la Coordination des Systèmes d'Information;
Comite Consultivo para la Coordinación de Sistemas de Información
ADDRESS: Palais des Nations,
16, avenue J. Trembley,
Petit-Sacconex,
1211 Geneva 10,
SWITZERLAND
TEL: (22) 988591 - TELEX: 289696
CREATED: 1983   *HEAD:* Mr. J. Lemoine, Chairman
Ms. C. Walker, Executive Secretary
SIZE OF STAFF: Professional: 4   Other: 3   Total: 7
TYPE OF SERVICE: international; non-profit
MATERIALS DESCRIBING THE SERVICE: - ACCIS: What it is, what it does, 1987 (brochure)
WORKING LANGUAGE(S): English
SUBJECT COVERAGE: social sciences
GEOGRAPHICAL COVERAGE: global
DATA BEING PROCESSED AND SIZE: computerized data on UN data bases, serials and
information sources
DATA PROCESSING METHODS: computerized
HARDWARE USED: IBM PC/AT
SOFTWARE USED: CDS/Micro ISIS
STORAGE MEDIA: discs
TYPE OF ACTIVITY: data collection; data analysis; distribution of information;
publication
PERIODICALS PUBLISHED:
- ACCIS Newsletter, 6 p.a.
PUBLICATIONS: - ACCIS guide to United Nations information sources on food and
agriculture, 1987
- ACCIS guide to United Nations information sources on the environment, 1988
- Directory of United Nations databases and information systems, 1985
- Register of United Nations serial publications, 1988
- UN register of development activities, 1988
ACCESS TO SERVICE: services open to specific categories of users, free of charge
TYPE & DESCRIPTION OF SERVICES PROVIDED: Provides library services, on-line services
from own data base DUNDIS - ECHO Service, and information on magnetic tapes.

2 - AFRICAN INSTITUTE FOR ECONOMIC DEVELOPMENT AND PLANNING

SYNONYMOUS NAMES: Institut Africain de Développement Economique et de Planification;
IDEP
PARENT ORGANIZATION: United Nations Economic Commission for Africa
ADDRESS: United Nations Economic Commission for Africa,
B.P. 3186,
Dakar,
SENEGAL
TEL: 22.10.20 - TELEX: 579 IDEP SG
CABLE: IDEP
CREATED: 1964   *HEAD:* Prof. E. Montasser, Director
SIZE OF STAFF: Professional: 9

TYPE OF SERVICE: international; public; non-profit
SYSTEMS & NETWORKS ATTACHED TO: United Nations Specialized Agencies
SUBJECT COVERAGE: social sciences; administrative sciences; demography; economics
GEOGRAPHICAL COVERAGE: Africa
DATA PROCESSING METHODS: manual; computerized
HARDWARE USED: IBM 36/5360
SOFTWARE USED: FORTRAN, FLSTAT, SLMATH
STORAGE MEDIA: traditional shelving of publications; tapes; discs
TYPE OF ACTIVITY: data collection; data analysis; distribution of information;
    publication
CLIENTELE: government officials
ACCESS TO SERVICE: services open to specific categories of users, free of charge
TYPE & DESCRIPTION OF SERVICES PROVIDED: Provides library services, bibliographic and
    quantitative data searches of information using its own data base, ECA Data
    Base.

3 - AFRICAN TRAINING AND RESEARCH CENTRE FOR WOMEN

SYNONYMOUS NAMES: ATRCW;
    CARFF
PARENT ORGANIZATION: United Nations Economic Commission for Africa
ADDRESS: P.O. Box 3001,
    Addis Ababa,
    ETHIOPIA
    CABLE: ECA ADDIS - TELEX: 21029 ECA
CREATED: 1975   HEAD: Ms. M. Tadesse, Chief
SIZE OF STAFF: Professional: 1   Total: 1
TYPE OF SERVICE: International
WORKING LANGUAGE(S): English; French
SUBJECT COVERAGE: social sciences; women; women and development
GEOGRAPHICAL COVERAGE: Africa
DATA BEING PROCESSED AND SIZE: 5,000 documentation items
DATA PROCESSING METHODS: partially computerized
HARDWARE USED: Hewlett Packard Series II
SOFTWARE USED: MINISIS
STORAGE MEDIA: traditional shelving of publications, fiches, tapes, microfiches
TYPE OF ACTIVITY: data collection; publication
ACCESS TO SERVICE: services open to specific categories of users, free of charge
TYPE & DESCRIPTION OF SERVICES PROVIDED: Provides bibliographies and research
    services on women and development.

4 - AFRICAN TRAINING AND RESEARCH CENTRE IN ADMINISTRATION FOR DEVELOPMENT, DIVISION OF DOCUMENTATION

SYNONYMOUS NAMES: CAFRAD, Division de la Documentation
ADDRESS: Pavillon International,
    Boulevard Mohammed V,
    B.P. 310,
    Tanger,

MOROCCO
TEL: 36430 - TELEX: 33664 M
CABLE: CAFRAD
CREATED: 1964   HEAD: M. Lelo, Library Chief
SIZE OF STAFF: Professional: 3   Other: 4   Total: 7
TYPE OF SERVICE: international; non-profit
SYSTEMS & NETWORKS ATTACHED TO: African Network of Administrative Information (ANAI)
MATERIALS DESCRIBING THE SERVICE: - CAFRAD 1988 activities (leaflet)
WORKING LANGUAGE(S): English; French; Arabic
SUBJECT COVERAGE: administrative sciences; social sciences
GEOGRAPHICAL COVERAGE: Africa
DATA BEING PROCESSED AND SIZE: 20,860 books; 700 periodicals
DATA PROCESSING METHODS: manual
STORAGE MEDIA: traditional shelving of publications; fiches
TYPE OF ACTIVITY: data collection; distribution of information; data analysis;
        publication
PERIODICALS PUBLISHED: - African Administrative Studies, 2 p.a.
        - CAFRAD News, 4 p.a.
        - Administrative Information Sources, 4 p.a.
        - ANAI Newsletter
PUBLICATIONS: - Bibliographies and collections of articles published by CAFRAD
        - CAFRAD thesaurus
        - African network of administrative information index
        - African administrative studies index
        - Bibliography on rural development and local administration
        - African abstracts on rural development
CLIENTELE: professors, researchers, planners
ACCESS TO SERVICE: services open to specific categories of users
TYPE & DESCRIPTION OF SERVICES PROVIDED: Provides library services, bibliographic
        searches of information, photocopies, microforms and translation of
        documents upon request.

5 - ALECSO, IDARAT AL-TAWTHIQ WAL-MALOUMAT

SYNONYMOUS NAMES: Arab League Education, Cultural and Scientific Organization,
        Department of Documentation and Information
ADDRESS: P.O. Box 1120,
        Avenue Mohamed V,
        Tunis,
        TUNISIA
        TEL: 784-466 - TELEX: 13825
CREATED: 1970   HEAD: M. T. Khafagy,
TYPE OF SERVICE: international; public; non-profit
SUBJECT COVERAGE: social sciences; education; culture
GEOGRAPHICAL COVERAGE: Arab countries
DATA BEING PROCESSED AND SIZE: 5,000 books
DATA PROCESSING METHODS: computerized
CLIENTELE: researchers
ACCESS TO SERVICE: open to specific categories of users, free of charge

6 - ARAB INDUSTRIAL DEVELOPMENT ORGANIZATION, DOCUMENTATION, PUBLICATION AND SCIENTIFIC COMPUTATION DIVISION

SYNONYMOUS NAMES: AIDO
ADDRESS: P.O. Box 3156,
Al-Saadoon Street,
Baghdad,
IRAQ
TEL: 718 287 03
CREATED: 1978
TYPE OF SERVICE: international; public; non-profit
SYSTEMS & NETWORKS ATTACHED TO: Arab Information Network (Arab Infonet)
SUBJECT COVERAGE: economics; industrial development; economic planning
GEOGRAPHICAL COVERAGE: Arab countries
TYPE & DESCRIPTION OF SERVICES PROVIDED: Library services, provision of microforms, provision of files of bibliographical references and statistical data, query-answer service, retrospective bibliographic searches, selective dissemination of information, consultancy and training, terminology control

7 - ASIAN AND PACIFIC DEVELOPMENT CENTRE, LIBRARY AND DOCUMENTATION CENTRE

SYNONYMOUS NAMES: APDC, LDC
ADDRESS: Pesiaran Duta,
P.O. Box 12224,
Kuala Lumpur,
MALAYSIA
TEL: (03) 254-8088 - TELEX: MA 30676 APDEC
CABLE: APDECEN, Kuala Lumpur
CREATED: 1980   *HEAD:* Ms. S. R. Shamsudin, Librarian
SIZE OF STAFF: Professional: 2   Other: 3   Total: 5
TYPE OF SERVICE: international; public; non-profit
MATERIALS DESCRIBING THE SERVICE: - Library and Documentation Centre (brochure), 198
WORKING LANGUAGE(S): English
SUBJECT COVERAGE: social sciences; development; economic planning; rural development management; public enterprises; trade; industry; women and development
GEOGRAPHICAL COVERAGE: Asia; Pacific area
DATA BEING PROCESSED AND SIZE: 31,000 books; 450 periodicals; 300 newsletters/bulletin titles; 6,744 pamphlets; 1,051 microfiches
DATA PROCESSING METHODS: partially computerized
HARDWARE USED: Olivetti PC M24
SOFTWARE USED: CDS-ISIS
STORAGE MEDIA: traditional shelving of publications
TYPE OF ACTIVITY: data collection; data analysis; publication
PERIODICALS PUBLISHED:
- Recent Additions, 6 p.a. since 1984
PUBLICATIONS: - Checklist of periodicals, 1986
- Taxation patterns and policies in South-East countries: a bibliography, 1985
- Publications on population programme management: a bibliography, 1985
- South Pacific: a bibliography, 1985
- Civil service in Asia: a bibliography, 1986

- Rural industries: a bibliography, 1986
- Rural energy planning: a bibliogrpahy, 1987

CLIENTELE: government officers, researchers
ACCESS TO SERVICE: open to specific categories of users, free of charge
TYPE & DESCRIPTION OF SERVICES PROVIDED: Provides library services, bibliographic searches, selective dissemination of information, microforms and photocopies.

8 - ASIAN MASS COMMUNICATION RESEARCH AND INFORMATION CENTRE, DOCUMENTATION UNIT

SYNONYMOUS NAMES: AMIC Documentation Unit
ADDRESS: 39 Newton Road,
Singapore 1130,
SINGAPORE (REPUBLIC)
TEL: 2515106 - TELEX: AMICSI RS 55524
CABLE: AMICINFO
CREATED: 1971   *HEAD:* Ms. E. Bong, Programme Specialist
SIZE OF STAFF: Professional: 1   Other: 2   Total: 3
TYPE OF SERVICE: international; public; non-profit
SYSTEMS & NETWORKS ATTACHED TO: COMNET
WORKING LANGUAGE(S): English
SUBJECT COVERAGE: mass communication; social sciences
GEOGRAPHICAL COVERAGE: Asia; Pacific Area
DATA BEING PROCESSED AND SIZE: 12,000 documentation items: books (1,000 p.a.); periodicals (3,000 issues p.a.); seminars/articles (50 p.a.)
DATA PROCESSING METHODS: partially computerized
HARDWARE USED: HP Micro 3000; IBM PC/XT; IBM compatible AT; MacIntosh Plus; RadioShact TRS-80 II
SOFTWARE USED: MINISIS
STORAGE MEDIA: traditional shelving of publications, fiches, tapes
TYPE OF ACTIVITY: data collection; data analysis; distribution of information; publication; SSID scientific and methodological activities
PERIODICALS PUBLISHED: - Mass Com Periodicals Literature Index (MCPL), 6 p.a.
- Accessions List, 4 p.a.
- Communication Bibliography Series, irr.
- Amicinfo and Documentation Lists in Media Asia, 4 p.a.
PUBLICATIONS: - Directory of mass communication institutions in Asia, 1986
CLIENTELE: researchers (100 p.a.)
ACCESS TO SERVICE: open to specific categories of users, free of charge
TYPE & DESCRIPTION OF SERVICES PROVIDED: Provides library services, bibliographic and literature abstracts searches, selective dissemination of information, microfilms and photocopies.

9 - ASOCIACIÓN LATINOAMERICANA DE INSTITUCIONES FINANCIERAS DE DESARROLLO, CENTRO DE DOCUMENTACIÓN

SYNONYMOUS NAMES: ALIDE/CEDOM;
Latin American Association of Development Financing Institutions, Documentation Centre

ADDRESS: Paseo de la República 3211,
San Isidro - Apartado Postal 3988,
Lima 1,
PERU
TEL: 422400 - TELEX: 21037PE
CABLE: ALIDE, Lima
CREATED: 1974   *HEAD:* A. Ciurlizza Mellon, Chief
SIZE OF STAFF: Professional: 6   Other: 2   Total: 8
TYPE OF SERVICE: international; private; non-profit
SYSTEMS & NETWORKS ATTACHED TO: The Information Network of ALIDE - RIALIDE
MATERIALS DESCRIBING THE SERVICE: - Brochure
WORKING LANGUAGE(S): Spanish; English; Portuguese
SUBJECT COVERAGE: economics; finance; development banking
GEOGRAPHICAL COVERAGE: Latin America; Caribbean area
DATA BEING PROCESSED AND SIZE: 16,000 books and articles, etc.
DATA PROCESSING METHODS: partially computerized
HARDWARE USED: IBM PC-AT
SOFTWARE USED: DBase III; CDS/ISIS
STORAGE MEDIA: traditional shelving of publications, fiches, discs
TYPE OF ACTIVITY: data collection; publication
PERIODICALS PUBLISHED:
- Resúmenes Informativos, 6 p.a.
PUBLICATIONS: - Directorio latinoamericano de instituciones financieras de
desarrollo, 1985
- Fuentes de financiamiento internacional para proyectos de América Latina
el Caribe, 1985
- Repertorio de oportunidades de capacitación para la Banca de desarrollo d
America Latina 1986-1987, 1986
CLIENTELE: members of ALIDE (174)
ACCESS TO SERVICE: open to all users, some paid services
TYPE & DESCRIPTION OF SERVICES PROVIDED: Provides library services, bibliographic,
literature and quantiative data searches, selective dissemination of
information, production of information on magnetic tape and photocopies.

10 - ASSOCIATION OF DEVELOPMENT RESEARCH AND TRAINING INSTITUTES OF ASIA AND THE PACIFIC, DEVELOPMENT INFORMATION CLEARING HOUSE AND REFERRAL SERVICE

SYNONYMOUS NAMES: ADIPA;
Association des Instituts de Recherche et de Formation en Matière de
Développement pour l'Asie et le Pacifique
ADDRESS: c/o Asian and Pacific Development Centre,
Periaran Duta,
P.O. Box 12224,
50770 Kuala Lumpur,
MALAYSIA
TEL: 03-2548088 - TELEX: MA30676 APDEC
CABLE: APDECEN KUALA LUMPUR
CREATED: 1973   *HEAD:* Mrs. A. How,
SIZE OF STAFF: Professional: 2
TYPE OF SERVICE: international; regional; non-profit
SYSTEMS & NETWORKS ATTACHED TO: Inter-Regional Coordinating Committee of Development

Associations (ICCDA)
MATERIALS DESCRIBING THE SERVICE: - ADIPA general information handbook
    - ADIPA (brochure)
WORKING LANGUAGE(S): English
SUBJECT COVERAGE: social sciences; development
GEOGRAPHICAL COVERAGE: Asia; Pacific area
DATA PROCESSING METHODS: computerized
HARDWARE USED: IBM/XT; IBM compatible
SOFTWARE USED: CDS/ISIS
STORAGE MEDIA: traditional shelving of publications; tapes; discs
TYPE OF ACTIVITY: data collection; distribution of information; SSID scientific and
    methodological activities; SSID training; publication
PERIODICALS PUBLISHED:
    - ADIPA Newsletter
PUBLICATIONS: - Register of development expertise in Asia-Pacific, 1987
CLIENTELE: member institutions (more than 150)
ACCESS TO SERVICE: services open to specific categories of users
TYPE & DESCRIPTION OF SERVICES PROVIDED: Provides library services and selective
    dissemination of information. Is also building up data bases on on-going and
    recently completed projects on socio-economic development and profiles of
    institutions of development, and development experts.

11 - CEIL-CONICET, BIBLIOTECA

SYNONYMOUS NAMES: CEIL-CONICET, Library;
    Centre for the Study and Research on Labour of the National Council of
    Scientific and Technological Research
PARENT ORGANIZATION: Consejo Nacional de Investigaciones Cientificas y Tecnicas
ADDRESS: Corrientes 2470, 4 piso, oficina "17",
    1046 Buenos Aires,
    ARGENTINA
    TEL: 48-7440
CREATED: 1971   *HEAD:* Prof. A. C. Guerrero, Director
SIZE OF STAFF: Total: 1
TYPE OF SERVICE: national; public; non-profit
SYSTEMS & NETWORKS ATTACHED TO: Red Nacional de Ciencias Sociales (REDICSA);
    PLANINDEX - Argentina; Catalogo Colectivo de Bibliotecas Empresarias
    (CACOBE)
WORKING LANGUAGE(S): Spanish
SUBJECT COVERAGE: administrative sciences; labour
GEOGRAPHICAL COVERAGE: Argentina; global
DATA BEING PROCESSED AND SIZE: 8,300 books; 560 periodicals
DATA PROCESSING METHODS: manual; partially computerized
HARDWARE USED: PC - XT IBM
SOFTWARE USED: MICRO-ISIS Unesco
STORAGE MEDIA: fiches; magnetic discs
TYPE OF ACTIVITY: data analysis; distribution of information; SSID training
PERIODICALS PUBLISHED:
    - Boletin Bibliografico de Biblioteca
    - Boletin sobre Condiciones de Trabajo
PUBLICATIONS: - Catálogo sobre temas específicos

CLIENTELE: researchers, students
ACCESS TO SERVICE: services open to specific categories of users, free of charge
TYPE & DESCRIPTION OF SERVICES PROVIDED: Provides current library services as well
information on magnetic tapes on discs. Has its own data base: LISU.
Photocopying service if requested.

12 - CENTRE DE COORDINATION DES RECHERCHES ET DE DOCUMENTATION EN SCIENCES SOCIALES DESSERVANT L'AFRIQUE SUB-SAHARIENNE, DOCUMENTATION DE RÉFÉRENCE EN SCIENCES SOCIALES

SYNONYMOUS NAMES: CERDAS;
Centre for the Coordination of Social Science Research and Documentation in
Africa South of Sahara
ADDRESS: B.P. 836,
Kinshasa XI,
ZAIRE
TEL: 27003 - TELEX: 21216 ZR
CREATED: 1974   *HEAD:* Mr. D. Lapika, Director
SIZE OF STAFF: Professional: 3
TYPE OF SERVICE: international; public; non-profit
MATERIALS DESCRIBING THE SERVICE: - Le Cerdas a 10 ans, 1987
WORKING LANGUAGE(S): French; English
SUBJECT COVERAGE: social sciences; demography; economics; law; political science;
social anthropology; cultural anthropology; sociology
GEOGRAPHICAL COVERAGE: Africa South of the Sahara
DATA BEING PROCESSED AND SIZE: 600 books; 50 periodicals
DATA PROCESSING METHODS: manual
STORAGE MEDIA: traditional shelving of publications; microfilms; microfiches
TYPE OF ACTIVITY: data collection; data analysis; publication
PERIODICALS PUBLISHED:
- CERDAS Liaison. Bulletin d'Information Trimestiel, 4 p.a.
- Accession List
PUBLICATIONS: - Catalogue général des auteurs et matières
- Catalogues des documents divers
- Répertoire des institutions en sciences sociales, 1987
- Sciences sociales en Afrique/Social Sciences in Africa, 1982
CLIENTELE: researchers, university staff
ACCESS TO SERVICE: open to all users, free of charge
TYPE & DESCRIPTION OF SERVICES PROVIDED: Provides library services and photocopies.

13 - THE CENTRE FOR EAST ASIAN CULTURAL STUDIES

SYNONYMOUS NAMES: CEACS
PARENT ORGANIZATION: Toko Bunko (Oriental Library)
ADDRESS: c/o The Toyo Bunko,
Honkomagome 2-chome, 28-21,
Bunkyo-ku,
Tokyo 113,
JAPAN

TEL: 03-942-0121
CABLE: TOKYO: TOYOBUNKO
CREATED: 1961   *HEAD:* H. Kitamura, Director
TYPE OF SERVICE: international; private; non-profit
WORKING LANGUAGE(S): Japanese; English
SUBJECT COVERAGE: social sciences; history; linguistics; social anthropology;
    cultural anthropology; sociology
GEOGRAPHICAL COVERAGE: Asia
DATA BEING PROCESSED AND SIZE: periodicals; reports; on-going research; pamphlets
DATA PROCESSING METHODS: manual
STORAGE MEDIA: traditional shelving of publications
TYPE OF ACTIVITY: data collection; publication
PERIODICALS PUBLISHED: - East Asian Cultural Studies, p.a.
PUBLICATIONS: - Asian studies in Japan, 1973-1983, 1987
    - Survey of Central Asian Studies in Japan, 1868-1980, 1987
    - Historic cities of Asia, 1986
    - Recent archaeological discoveries in Asia, 1987
    - Collection of materials in Asian languages
CLIENTELE: researchers and research institutions of Asian studies
ACCESS TO SERVICE: services open to researchers only, free of charge
TYPE & DESCRIPTION OF SERVICES PROVIDED: Provides bibliographic and literature
    abstract searches.

14 - CENTRE INTERNATIONAL DE L'ENFANCE, SERVICE DE DOCUMENTATION

SYNONYMOUS NAMES: CIE;
    International Children's Centre, Documentation Service;
    ICC
ADDRESS: Château de Longchamp,
    Carrefour de Longchamp,
    Bois de Boulogne,
    75016 Paris,
    FRANCE
    TEL: (1) 45.20.79.92 - TELEX: CIENFAN 648 379 F
    CABLE: CENTRENFANCE-PARIS
CREATED: 1950   *HEAD:* Ms. A. Parrical, Chief of the Service
SIZE OF STAFF: Professional: 10   Other: 5   Total: 15
TYPE OF SERVICE: international; public; non-profit
SYSTEMS & NETWORKS ATTACHED TO: RESHUS (CNRS); RESADOC (Réseau documentaire
    intersahélien); BIREME (Réseau latino-américain d'information sur la santé)
MATERIALS DESCRIBING THE SERVICE: - Le Centre International de l'Enfance: notes et
    études documentaires, 3 Dec. 1979, La documentation française, Paris, 31 p.
WORKING LANGUAGE(S): French; English; Spanish
SUBJECT COVERAGE: psychology; sociology; social welfare; education; public health;
    children; adolescents
GEOGRAPHICAL COVERAGE: global
DATA BEING PROCESSED AND SIZE: 12,000-15,000 books; 500 periodicals; reports
DATA PROCESSING METHODS: computerized
HARDWARE USED: Hewlett Packard
SOFTWARE USED: MINISIS
STORAGE MEDIA: traditional shelving of publications, fiches, magnetic discs

TYPE OF ACTIVITY: data collection; data analysis; publication; distribution of
information; SSID training
PERIODICALS PUBLISHED: - L'Enfant en milieu tropical, 6 p.a.
- Bibliographical Bulletin (nutrition, vaccination, diarrheas)
CLIENTELE: 17,000 p.a.
ACCESS TO SERVICE: open to all users, against payment
TYPE & DESCRIPTION OF SERVICES PROVIDED: Provides library services, bibliographies,
retrospective bibliographic searches using its own data base "BIRD"
containing 70,000 references on all issues related to children and
adolescents including health problems, and available through G CAM serveur.
Also provides searches on other data bases such as: PASCAL, MEDLINE, Reshus
FRANCIS and IBISCUS accessed through DATASTAR, G CAM and QUESTEL, selective
dissemination of information and production of information on magnetic
tapes.

15 - THE CENTRE ON INTEGRATED RURAL DEVELOPMENT FOR ASIA AND THE PACIFIC

SYNONYMOUS NAMES: CIRDAP
ADDRESS: Chameli House,
17, Topkhana Road,
GPO Box 2883,
Dhaka,
BANGLADESH
TEL: 238751 - TELEX: 642333 CIRDAP BJ
CABLE: CIRDAP DHAKA
CREATED: 1979   *HEAD:* Mr. A. T. M. Shamsul Haque, Director
TYPE OF SERVICE: international; non-profit
MATERIALS DESCRIBING THE SERVICE: - CIRDAP Documentation and Information (brochure)
WORKING LANGUAGE(S): English
SUBJECT COVERAGE: rural development; agriculture
GEOGRAPHICAL COVERAGE: Asia; Pacific area
DATA BEING PROCESSED AND SIZE: 13,000 books and documents; 340 periodicals
DATA PROCESSING METHODS: partially computerized
TYPE OF ACTIVITY: data analysis; distribution of information; publication
PERIODICALS PUBLISHED:
- CIRDAP Newsletter, 4 p.a.
- CIRDAP Report, 1 p.a.
PUBLICATIONS: - A Directory of rural development institutions/agencies in CIRDAP
member countries, 1982
- Regional bibliography (series)
CLIENTELE: researchers, academics, administrators, students
ACCESS TO SERVICE: services open to specific categories of users, free of charge
TYPE & DESCRIPTION OF SERVICES PROVIDED: Provides library service, bibliographic
searches of information, selective dissemination of information and
microforms.

16 - CENTRE RÉGIONAL DE DOCUMENTATION SUR LES TRADITIONS ORALES ET POUR LE DÉVELOPPEMENT DES LANGUES AFRICAINES

SYNONYMOUS NAMES: CERDOTOLA
ADDRESS: B. P. 479,
    Yaounde,
    CAMEROON (UNITED REPUBLIC)
    TEL: 23.05.46
CREATED: 1977   *HEAD:* Soundjock-Soundjock, Executive-Secretary
SIZE OF STAFF: Professional: 7   Other: 3   Total: 10
TYPE OF SERVICE: international; public; non-profit
WORKING LANGUAGE(S): French
SUBJECT COVERAGE: sociology; cultural anthropology; social anthropology; history;
    culture; linguistics; oral tradition; music
GEOGRAPHICAL COVERAGE: Central Africa
TYPE OF ACTIVITY: research; documentation; publication
PERIODICALS PUBLISHED:
    - Bulletin de Liaison
PUBLICATIONS: - ALAC: structures et méthodes
    - ALAC: inventaires préliminaires: Cameroun (LACAM), Burundi (ALZ) et Zaire
    (ALZ)
    - LETAC: Cameroun, Centrafrique, Zaïre et Tchad
    - Le Feu et l'étoile
    - Introduction critique à la littérature orale d'Afrique centrale

17 - CENTRO DE DOCUMENTACIÓN ECONÓMICA Y SOCIAL DE CENTROAMERICA

SYNONYMOUS NAMES: CEDESC;
    Central American Socioeconomic Documentation Centre
PARENT ORGANIZATION: Confederación Universitaria Centroamericana, CSUCA
ADDRESS: Apartado 37-2060,
    Ciudad Universitaria "Rodrigo Facio",
    San José,
    COSTA RICA
    TEL: 25-27-44 - TELEX: 3011 COSUCA CR
    CABLE: COSUCA
CREATED: 1978   *HEAD:* A. M. Lungo, Director
SIZE OF STAFF: Professional: 2
TYPE OF SERVICE: international; non-profit
MATERIALS DESCRIBING THE SERVICE: - Documentación Socioeconómica Centroamericana,
    1984, Report
WORKING LANGUAGE(S): Spanish; English; French
SUBJECT COVERAGE: social sciences; political science; sociology; education; economics
GEOGRAPHICAL COVERAGE: Central America
DATA BEING PROCESSED AND SIZE: 2,000 books; 700 periodicals; 4,000 official reports
DATA PROCESSING METHODS: partially computerized
HARDWARE USED: NORTH STAR DIMENSION
SOFTWARE USED: MICROISIS
STORAGE MEDIA: traditional shelving of publications; microfiches, tapes and discs
TYPE OF ACTIVITY: data collection; data analysis; SSID scientific and methodological
    activities; SSID training

CLIENTELE: researchers, university teachers, post-graduate students
ACCESS TO SERVICE: open to specific categories of users, free of charge
TYPE & DESCRIPTION OF SERVICES PROVIDED: Provides library services, literature
abstract and bibliographic searches of information. Provision of photocopie
and translation of documents upon request.

18 - CENTRO INTERNACIONAL DE DOCUMENTACIÓN E INFORMACIÓN PARA LA PAZ

SYNONYMOUS NAMES: CEDIPAZ;
The International Centre of Documentation and Information for Peace
PARENT ORGANIZATION: Universidad Para la Paz de Naciones Unidas
ADDRESS: P.O. Box 199-1250,
Orcazú,
San José,
COSTA RICA
TEL: 49.10.72
CABLE: 2331 MACAZE
CREATED: 1979   *HEAD:* Ms. O. M. Rodríguez Blanco, Librarian
SIZE OF STAFF: Professional: 1   Total: 1
TYPE OF SERVICE: international; public
WORKING LANGUAGE(S): English; Spanish; French
SUBJECT COVERAGE: Social sciences; peace
GEOGRAPHICAL COVERAGE: global
DATA BEING PROCESSED AND SIZE: books, documents, periodical publications
DATA PROCESSING METHODS: manual
TYPE OF ACTIVITY: data collection; data analysis
CLIENTELE: 80 visitors per month
ACCESS TO SERVICE: services open to specific categories of users

19 - CENTRO INTERNACIONAL DE INVESTIGACIONES PARA EL DESARROLLO, OFICINA REGIONAL PARA LA AMÉRICA LATINA Y ET CARIBE, BIBLIOTECA

SYNONYMOUS NAMES: CIID/Oficina Regional para la América Latina y el Caribe,
Biblioteca;
International Development Research Centre, Latin America and the Caribbean
Regional Office, Library;
IDRC/Latin America Regional Office
PARENT ORGANIZATION: International Development Research Centre, Ottawa, Ontario,
Canada
ADDRESS: Apartado Aéreo 53016,
Bogotá D.E.,
COLOMBIA
TEL: 255.86.00 - TELEX: 45366
CABLE: RECENTRE
CREATED: 1974   *HEAD:* V. G. Isaza, Librarian
SIZE OF STAFF: Professional: 1   Other: 1   Total: 2
TYPE OF SERVICE: international
SYSTEMS & NETWORKS ATTACHED TO: BIBLIOTECA CIID
WORKING LANGUAGE(S): Spanish; English; French

SUBJECT COVERAGE: social sciences; administrative sciences; education; demography; geography
GEOGRAPHICAL COVERAGE: Latin America; Caribbean area
DATA BEING PROCESSED AND SIZE: 2,350 books; 6,000 documents; 215 seminars; 500 articles
DATA PROCESSING METHODS: manual; partially computerized
HARDWARE USED: IBM/XT
SOFTWARE USED: CDS/ISIS
STORAGE MEDIA: microfiches, traditional shelving of publications
TYPE OF ACTIVITY: data collection; publication
ACCESS TO SERVICE: services open to specific categories of users, free of charge
TYPE & DESCRIPTION OF SERVICES PROVIDED: Provides retrospective bibliographies and question-answer service.

20 - CENTRO LATINOAMERICANO DE DEMOGRAFÍA, SISTEMA DE DOCUMENTACIÓN SOBRE POBLACIÓN DE AMÉRICA LATINA

SYNONYMOUS NAMES: CELADE / DOCPAL;
Latin American Demographic Centre, Latin American Population Documentation System
PARENT ORGANIZATION: UN Economic Commission for Latin America
ADDRESS: CELADE,
Casilla 91,
Alonso de Córdoba 3107,
Santiago,
CHILE
TEL: 283206
CABLE: UNATIONS
CREATED: 1976   HEAD: B. Johnson de Vodanovic,
SIZE OF STAFF: Professional: 1   Other: 2   Total: 3
TYPE OF SERVICE: international; public; non-profit
SYSTEMS & NETWORKS ATTACHED TO: POPIN (Population Information Network of the United Nations)
WORKING LANGUAGE(S): Spanish
SUBJECT COVERAGE: demography; social sciences; sociology
GEOGRAPHICAL COVERAGE: Latin America; Caribbean Area
DATA BEING PROCESSED AND SIZE: 27,000 documentation items
DATA PROCESSING METHODS: computerized
HARDWARE USED: IBM 370/3031
SOFTWARE USED: CDS/ISIS; CELENTRY for data entry
PERIODICALS PUBLISHED:
    - DOCPAL (Latin American Population Abstracts), 2 p.a.
CLIENTELE: researchers, institutions and general public
ACCESS TO SERVICE: open to all users, free of charge
TYPE & DESCRIPTION OF SERVICES PROVIDED: Provides library services, photocopies and retrospective bibliographic on-line searches.

21 - CENTRO LATINOAMERICANO DE DOCUMENTACIÓN ECONÓMICA Y SOCIAL

SYNONYMOUS NAMES: CLADES;
    Latin American Centre for Economic and Social Documentation
PARENT ORGANIZATION: Economic Commission for Latin America and the Caribbean (ECLAC
ADDRESS: Avenida Dag Hammarskjold s/n,
    Casilla 179-D,
    Santiago de Chile,
    CHILE
    TEL: 48.50.51 - TELEX: 240077
    CABLE: UNATIONS
CREATED: 1971   *HEAD:* C. Evangelista, Director
SIZE OF STAFF: Professional: 10   Other: 4   Total: 14
TYPE OF SERVICE: international; public; non-profit
SYSTEMS & NETWORKS ATTACHED TO: Development Sciences Information System, (DEVSIS);
    and Information System for Planning (INFOPLAN)
MATERIALS DESCRIBING THE SERVICE: - Información básica sobre el Centro
    Latinoamericano de Documentación Económica y Social (CLADES) de la Comisión
    Económica para América Latina, Santiago, CEPAL, 1977, 5 p.
    - CLADES: its role and function, Ibid., September 1977, 14 p.
SUBJECT COVERAGE: economics; social sciences; sociology; information science
GEOGRAPHICAL COVERAGE: Latin America; Caribbean Area
DATA BEING PROCESSED AND SIZE: 10,000 books and documents; 127 periodicals; 10,000
    entries on economic and social planning
DATA PROCESSING METHODS: manual; computerized
HARDWARE USED: IBM 4341; IBM PC/XT
SOFTWARE USED: CDS/ISIS; CDS/MicroISIS
TYPE OF ACTIVITY: data collection; distribution of information; SSID training;
    publication
PERIODICALS PUBLISHED: - PLANINDEX Abstracts
    - Informativo Terminológico
    - Informativo INFOPLAN
PUBLICATIONS: - INFOPLAN: temas especiales del desarrollo
    - INFOLAC: Lineamientos de un programam regional para el fortalecimiento de
    la cooperación entre Redes y Sistemas Nacionales de Información en America
    Latina y el Caribe
    - services open to specific categories of users, free of charge
CLIENTELE: researchers, specialists on planning, decision-makers
ACCESS TO SERVICE: services open to specific categories of users, free of charge
TYPE & DESCRIPTION OF SERVICES PROVIDED: Provides library services, query-answer
    service, photocopies, selective dissemination of information and referral
    service. Data bases available include: Bibliography on Thesauri and Related
    Tools; CLADES Information and Documentation; Documents on Planning Generated
    in Latin America and the Caribbean.

22 - CENTRO LATINOAMERICANO SOBRE JUVENTUD, BIBLIOTECA

SYNONYMOUS NAMES: CELAJU, Biblioteca;
    Latin American Centre on Youth, Library;
    Centre Latinoaméricain sur la Jeunesse, Bibliothèque
ADDRESS: Germán Barbato 1358,

Apto 602,
Montevideo,
URUGUAY
TEL: 90.11.49
CREATED: 1986   *HEAD:* B. Dabezies, Head
SIZE OF STAFF: Professional: 2   Other: 1   Total: 3
TYPE OF SERVICE: international; private; non-profit
MATERIALS DESCRIBING THE SERVICE: - Information bulletin ENCUENTRO
    - ENCUENTRO
WORKING LANGUAGE(S): Spanish; English; French
SUBJECT COVERAGE: social sciences; sociology; social welfare; political science; law; demography; youth
GEOGRAPHICAL COVERAGE: Latin America; Caribbean area
DATA BEING PROCESSED AND SIZE: 3,000 books; 120 periodicals publications; 500 reports; 400 on-going researches; 150 seminars; 60 courses; 50 specialized bibliographies
DATA PROCESSING METHODS: manual
STORAGE MEDIA: traditional shelving of publications, fiches
TYPE OF ACTIVITY: data collection; data analysis; distribution of information; SSID scientific and methodological activities; SSID training; publication
PERIODICALS PUBLISHED: - Latino-Americana sobre la Juventud
    - Encuentro, 6 p.a.
PUBLICATIONS: - Guías bibliográficas sobre temas específicos
    - Estudios (series)
    - Bibliografías sobre Juventud (Series)
    - Directorio de instancias de juventud
    - Rodríguez, E., Juventud, paz y democracia en América del Sur
CLIENTELE: governmental organizations, research and documentation centres, youth organizations
ACCESS TO SERVICE: services open to all users, free of charge
TYPE & DESCRIPTION OF SERVICES PROVIDED: Provides library services, bibliographic, literature abstract and quantitative data searches of information and selective dissemination of information, with on-line services and access to data bases CEPAL, DGEYC, CINTERFOR, "Equipos Consultores Asociados". Photocopying and translating facilities are also available.

23 - CEPAL/ILPES, BIBLIOTECA CONJUNTA

SYNONYMOUS NAMES: ECLAC/ILPES Joint Library
PARENT ORGANIZATION: United Nations, Economic Commission for Latin America and the Caribbean
ADDRESS: A. Dag Hammarskjold,
    Casilla 179-D,
    Santiago,
    CHILE
    TEL: 485051 - TELEX: 340295 (Transradio) 441054 (ITT) 240077 (Chile)
    CABLE: UNATIONS
CREATED: 1948   *HEAD:* Mr. J. Beza, Chief Librarian
SIZE OF STAFF: Professional: 6   Other: 3   Total: 9
TYPE OF SERVICE: international; public; non-profit
SYSTEMS & NETWORKS ATTACHED TO: ECLAC Bibliographic Information System

MATERIALS DESCRIBING THE SERVICE: - Guía del usuario, 1971
    - Cómo usar los catálogos de la Biblioteca CEPAL/ILPES: guía para el usuar
    (E/CEPAL/LIB/15, 1977)
    - Biblioteca CEPAL-ILPES. Santiago, Chile 1980 leaflet
WORKING LANGUAGE(S): Spanish
SUBJECT COVERAGE: economics; social sciences
GEOGRAPHICAL COVERAGE: global; Latin America; Central America; Caribbean area
DATA BEING PROCESSED AND SIZE: 41,500 books and pamphlets; 110,700 printed and
    mimeographed documents of the United Nations; 2,760 serial titles
DATA PROCESSING METHODS: partially computerized
HARDWARE USED: IBM
SOFTWARE USED: ISIS
STORAGE MEDIA: traditional shelving of publications, fiches; tapes; disks;
    microfiches
TYPE OF ACTIVITY: data collection; data analysis; publication
PERIODICALS PUBLISHED:
    - Boletín Mensual
    - Indice de Revistas Académicas Recibidas, 54 p.a.
    - Selección de Documentos de las Naciones Unidas recibidos en la Biblioteca
    27 p.a.
PUBLICATIONS: - Indice de anuarios que se reciben regularmente en la Biblioteca
    - Indice de revistas que se reciben regularmente en la Biblioteca
    - CEPALINDEX, 1 p.a.
    - Bibliografía sobre recesión económica, 1985
    - Bibliografía sobre estilos de desarrollo, 1982
    - Bibliografía sobre deuda externa 1970-1983, 1984
    - Bibliografía seleccionada sobre productividad, 1985
    - Bibliografía sobre política social, 1985
CLIENTELE: university staff and students, members of UN offices
ACCESS TO SERVICE: open to all users, free of charge
TYPE & DESCRIPTION OF SERVICES PROVIDED: Provides library services, on-line
    bibliographic searches using its own data base: BIBLOS. Also provides
    selective dissemination of information.

24 - CODESRIA DOCUMENTATION AND INFORMATION CENTRE

SYNONYMOUS NAMES: CODICE;
    CODESRIA, Centre de Documentation et d'Information
ADDRESS: B.P. 3304,
    Dakar,
    SENEGAL
    TEL: 23.02.11 - TELEX: 3339 CODES SG
CREATED: 1983   *HEAD:* Mrs. W. N. Wagacha, Director
SIZE OF STAFF: Professional: 2
TYPE OF SERVICE: international; private; non-profit
SYSTEMS & NETWORKS ATTACHED TO: Inter-Regional Coordinating Committee of Development
    Associations (ICCDA)
MATERIALS DESCRIBING THE SERVICE: - brochure
WORKING LANGUAGE(S): English; French
SUBJECT COVERAGE: economics; social sciences; political science; psychology;
    education; sociology; development

GEOGRAPHICAL COVERAGE: Africa; developing countries
DATA BEING PROCESSED AND SIZE: 2,000 books; 250 conference proceedings; 300
    periodicals; 3000 reports and documents
DATA PROCESSING METHODS: computerized
HARDWARE USED: IBM/XT
SOFTWARE USED: Micro CDS/ISIS
TYPE OF ACTIVITY: data collection; data analysis; SSID training; publication
PUBLICATIONS: - Index of Africa social science periodical articles
CLIENTELE: university researchers and professors, policy makers
TYPE & DESCRIPTION OF SERVICES PROVIDED: Provides current awareness and retrospective
    bibliographic searches, selective dissemination of information, microfiches
    and photocopies.

25 - COMMISSION OF THE EUROPEAN COMMUNITIES, CENTRAL LIBRARY

SYNONYMOUS NAMES: Commission des Communautés Européennes, Bibliothèque Centrale
ADDRESS: Rue de la Loi, 200,
    B-1040 Brussels,
    BELGIUM
    TEL: (02) 235.11.11
    CABLE: COMEUR Brussels
CREATED: 1958   *HEAD:* Mr. E. Gaskell, Head
SIZE OF STAFF: Professional: 21   Other: 32   Total: 53
TYPE OF SERVICE: international
MATERIALS DESCRIBING THE SERVICE: - The Library and documentation services of the
    Commission in European Communities Information, ed. M. Hopkins, London:
    Mansell, 1985, pp. 91-101
WORKING LANGUAGE(S): French; English; German; Dutch; Italian; Danish; Greek; Spanish;
    Portuguese
SUBJECT COVERAGE: social sciences; law; economics; statistics; linguistics; political
    science; administrative sciences; information science
GEOGRAPHICAL COVERAGE: Western Europe; Northern Europe; Southern Europe
DATA BEING PROCESSED AND SIZE: 300,000 books; 3,500 periodicals
DATA PROCESSING METHODS: computerized
HARDWARE USED: Siemens 7.760
SOFTWARE USED: System BS 2000; retrieval: GOLEM
STORAGE MEDIA: traditional shelving of publications, microfiches, magnetic tapes,
    discs
TYPE OF ACTIVITY: data collection; distribution of information; publication
PERIODICALS PUBLISHED: - Publications and Documents of the European Communities, 1
    p.a.
    - Recent Publications on the European Communities, monthly
CLIENTELE: officials of the Commission and other Community institutions, approved
    external visitors (65,000 visitors and 30,000 telephone enquiries p.a.)
ACCESS TO SERVICE: services open to officials and specific categories of external
    users
TYPE & DESCRIPTION OF SERVICES PROVIDED: Provides library services and bibliographic
    searches, on-line services using its own data bases "ECLAS" (Library),
    "SCAD" (Documentation Service), "CELEX", "CRONOS" among other
    Commission data bases.

26 - CONSEJO LATINOAMERICANO DE CIENCIAS SOCIALES, ARÉA DOCUMENTACIÓN

SYNONYMOUS NAMES: CLACSO, Aréa Documentación;
    Latin America Social Sciences, Documentation Area
ADDRESS: Callao 875 - 3 piso E/F,
    1023 Capital Federal,
    ARGENTINA
CREATED: 1984   *HEAD:* Ms S. Maggioli, Head
SIZE OF STAFF: Professional: 2   Total: 2
TYPE OF SERVICE: private; non-profit
SYSTEMS & NETWORKS ATTACHED TO: Inter-Regional Coordinating Committee of Development
    Associations (ICCDA); Red de Información en Ciencias Sociales de Argentina
    (REDICSA)
WORKING LANGUAGE(S): Spanish
SUBJECT COVERAGE: social sciences
GEOGRAPHICAL COVERAGE: Latin America; Central America; Caribbean area
DATA BEING PROCESSED AND SIZE: 1,000 on-going research
DATA PROCESSING METHODS: manual; computerized
HARDWARE USED: IBM PC/XT
SOFTWARE USED: MICRO ISIS (UNESCO)
STORAGE MEDIA: Traditional shelving of publications; fiches; diskettes
TYPE OF ACTIVITY: data collection; data analysis; distribution of information
CLIENTELE: Researchers and scholars
ACCESS TO SERVICE: Services open to specific categories of users, free of charge
TYPE & DESCRIPTION OF SERVICES PROVIDED: Provides library services, searches of
    information, on-line services from its own data bases: PRO, on-going
    research in member institutes; CATA - CATRE, publications in member
    institutes and provision of photocopies.

27 - COOPÉRATION INTERNATIONALE EN MATIÈRE DE DOCUMENTATION SUR L'ECONOMIE DES TRANSPORTS

SYNONYMOUS NAMES: CIDET;
    International Co-operation in Transport Economics Documentation;
    ICTED
PARENT ORGANIZATION: Conférence Européenne des Ministres des Transports
ADDRESS: 19, rue de Franqueville,
    75775 Paris Cedex 16,
    FRANCE
    TEL: (1) 45.24.82.00 - TELEX: 611040
CREATED: 1972   *HEAD:* Mrs. P. Coquand, Head of Documentation Centre
SIZE OF STAFF: Professional: 3
TYPE OF SERVICE: international; public; non-profit
MATERIALS DESCRIBING THE SERVICE: - ICTED information, special issue, May 1983
WORKING LANGUAGE(S): French; English; German
SUBJECT COVERAGE: economics; transport
GEOGRAPHICAL COVERAGE: Austria; Belgium; Denmark; Finland; France; Germany (Federal
    Republic); Greece; Ireland; Italy; Luxembourg; Netherlands; Norway;
    Portugal; Spain; Sweden; Switzerland; Turkey; United Kingdom; Yugoslavia
DATA BEING PROCESSED AND SIZE: 4,000 books; 16,000 articles; reports; studies; on-
    going research; theses

ATA PROCESSING METHODS: computerized
ARDWARE USED: B6800
OFTWARE USED: Autodoc/Esaquest
TORAGE MEDIA: discpack and microfiche editions
YPE OF ACTIVITY: data analysis; publication
ERIODICALS PUBLISHED: - Research in Transport Economics, 1 p.a.
UBLICATIONS: - Bibliographies
         - List of periodicals abstracted
         - Statistical yearbooks in transport
         - List of descriptors in transport economics
LIENTELE: central and local administrations, universities, international
         organisations, private firms, etc.
YPE & DESCRIPTION OF SERVICES PROVIDED: Provides bibliographies, information on
         research in progress and microfiches on subscription. Own data base
         "TRANSDOC" is available through ESA/IRS.

6 - COUNCIL OF EUROPE, DOCUMENTATION CENTRE FOR EDUCATION IN EUROPE

YNONYMOUS NAMES: Conseil de l'Europe, Centre de Documentation pour l'Education en
         Europe
ARENT ORGANIZATION: Council of Europe
DDRESS: B.P. 431 R6,
         67006 Strasbourg Cedex,
         FRANCE
         TEL: 88.61.49.61 - TELEX: Strasbourg 870-943
         CABLE: EUROPA
REATED: 1962   *HEAD:* W. F. Barrett,
IZE OF STAFF: Professional: 3   Other: 2   Total: 5
YPE OF SERVICE: international; public; non-profit
ORKING LANGUAGE(S): French; English
UBJECT COVERAGE: education
EOGRAPHICAL COVERAGE: Europe
ATA BEING PROCESSED AND SIZE: 21,000 books (1,000 p.a.); 400 periodicals; printed
         documents of the Council of Europe concerning education
ATA PROCESSING METHODS: manual
YPE OF ACTIVITY: documentation; publication
ERIODICALS PUBLISHED: - News Letter/Faits Nouveaux, 5 p.a.
         - List of acquisitions, irr.
UBLICATIONS: - Educational developments in the United Kingdom, 1982-87
LIENTELE: members of the Council of Europe and all interested persons in comparative
         education
CCESS TO SERVICE: open to all users, free of charge
YPE & DESCRIPTION OF SERVICES PROVIDED: Provides library and query answering
         services from data base: "European Documentation and Information System for
         Education (EUDISED)". Also provides bibliographic, literature abstracts,
         selective dissemination of information, microforms and photocopies.

International & Regional / Internacional & Regional

29 - DATA FOR DEVELOPMENT INTERNATIONAL ASSOCIATION

SYNONYMOUS NAMES: DFD
ADDRESS: 122, avenue de Hambourg,
13008 Marseille,
FRANCE
TEL: 91.73.90.18 - TELEX: 430258 INFOSYS - TELEFAX: (91) 730138
CABLE: DAFODEL, MARSEILLE
CREATED: 1973   *HEAD:* Mr. J. Salmona, Director General
TYPE OF SERVICE: international; private; non-profit
SYSTEMS & NETWORKS ATTACHED TO: Government Data Network (GDN)
MATERIALS DESCRIBING THE SERVICE: - Data gathering and organisation at central leve
- Data use for planning at national level
- Data organisation and use at local level
WORKING LANGUAGE(S): French; English
SUBJECT COVERAGE: administrative sciences; public administration; development
planning
GEOGRAPHICAL COVERAGE: global
DATA PROCESSING METHODS: computerized
TYPE OF ACTIVITY: SSID training; SSID scientific and methodological activities
PERIODICALS PUBLISHED:
- DFD Newsletter
- DFD News Bulletin
PUBLICATIONS: - Information systems in public administration, 1981
CLIENTELE: Individuals and organizations
ACCESS TO SERVICE: services open to members. Membership fee for individuals is SW
Fr.50 per annum, and SW Fr.300 for institutions. All candidates for
membership are submitted for the Board's approval which is given on the
basis of the candidate's expertise and involvement in information systems
and in public administration
TYPE & DESCRIPTION OF SERVICES PROVIDED: Has developed an approach to the integrate
planning and development of government information systems (both
quantitative and non quantitative) which takes into consideration the
information gaps and attempt to optimise the allocation of available
information resources. Also provides bibliographical references from its
data base.

30 - ECONOMIC AND SOCIAL COMMISSION FOR ASIA AND THE PACIFIC LIBRARY

SYNONYMOUS NAMES: ESCAP Library
PARENT ORGANIZATION: United Nations Economic and Social Council
ADDRESS: United Nations Building,
Rajadamnern Avenue,
Bangkok 10200,
THAILAND
TEL: (02) 2829161-200 - TELEX: 82392 ESCAP TH
CABLE: ESCAP THAILAND
CREATED: 1947   *HEAD:* Mr. N. P. Cummins, Chief
SIZE OF STAFF: Professional: 2   Other: 17   Total: 19
TYPE OF SERVICE: international
WORKING LANGUAGE(S): English; French

98

UBJECT COVERAGE: demography; economics; social welfare; sociology; socio-economic
   development; development planning; agricultural development; industrial
   development; human settlements; transport; transnational corporations; women
EOGRAPHICAL COVERAGE: Asia; Pacific area
ATA BEING PROCESSED AND SIZE: 200,000 monographs; 4,000 serials; 4,000 journal
   articles; 50,000 documents
ATA PROCESSING METHODS: computerized
ARDWARE USED: NEC 350
OFTWARE USED: IRS 4 (Information Retrieval System)
TORAGE MEDIA: tapes, magnetic discs
YPE OF ACTIVITY: data collection; data analysis; publication
ERIODICALS PUBLISHED: - Asian Bibliography, 2 p.a.
   - Rural Development: a Select Biliography, 1 p.a.
   - ESCAP Documents and Publications, 1 p.a.
   - EBIS Register of Serials, 2 p.a.
LIENTELE: government officials, researchers and delegates
CCESS TO SERVICE: services open to specific categories of users, free of charge
YPE & DESCRIPTION OF SERVICES PROVIDED: Provides reference, bibliographic,
   information retrieval and current awareness services, and selective
   dissemination of information.

**1 - ECONOMIC AND SOCIAL COMMISSION FOR ASIA AND THE PACIFIC, POPULATION INFORMATION
SECTION OF THE POPULATION DIVISION**

YNONYMOUS NAMES: ESCAP/POPIN
ARENT ORGANIZATION: United Nations Economic and Social Commission for Asia and the
   Pacific
DDRESS: The United Nations Building,
   Rajadamnern Avenue,
   Bangkok 10200,
   THAILAND
   TEL: 282-9161 - TELEX: 82392 ESCAP TH
   CABLE: ESCAP Bangkok 10200
REATED: 1969   *HEAD:* Mr. F. J. Burian,
IZE OF STAFF: Professional: 7   Other: 15   Total: 22
YPE OF SERVICE: international; public; non-profit
YSTEMS & NETWORKS ATTACHED TO: Population Information System (POPIN)
ATERIALS DESCRIBING THE SERVICE: - Brochure
ORKING LANGUAGE(S): English; French; Chinese
UBJECT COVERAGE: demography; social sciences; mass communication; population
EOGRAPHICAL COVERAGE: Asia; Pacific area
ATA BEING PROCESSED AND SIZE: 1,500 books; 430 periodicals; 1,000 brochures; 8,000
   conference documents; 20,000 microfiches
ATA PROCESSING METHODS: computerized
ARDWARE USED: NEC 350
OFTWARE USED: IRS-4 Data Management Package
TORAGE MEDIA: traditional shelving of publications; fiches; tapes; discs;
   microfiches
YPE OF ACTIVITY: data collection; data analysis; distribution of information;
   publication; SSID scientific and methodological activities; SSID training;
   technical and advisory services

PERIODICALS PUBLISHED: - APPJ (Asian-Pacific Population Journal), 4 p.a.
- Adopt (Asian-Pacific and worldwide documents on population topics), 12 p.a.
- Population Headlines, 12 p.a.
- Population Research Leads, 3 p.a.
PUBLICATIONS: - Catalogue of ESCAP population publications
- Inventory of local family planning programme experiences in countries of the ESCAP region
CLIENTELE: ESCAP member countries, UN agencies staff
ACCESS TO SERVICE: services open to specific categories of users, free of charge
TYPE & DESCRIPTION OF SERVICES PROVIDED: Provides computerized literature searches from EBIS/POPFILE and external data bases on request, reference and referr services, responses to enquiries and query answering service.

32 - ECONOMIC COMMISSION FOR LATIN AMERICA AND THE CARIBBEAN, CARIBBEAN INFORMATION SYSTEM/ECONOMIC AND SOCIAL PLANNING

SYNONYMOUS NAMES: ECLAC/CARISPLAN;
Commission Economique pour l'Amérique Latine et les Caraïbes, Système d'Information des Caraïbes/Planification Economique et Sociale
PARENT ORGANIZATION: United Nations
ADDRESS: ECLAC Subregional Headquarters for the Caribbean,
Caribbean Documentation Centre,
P.O. Box 1113,
2 Frederick Street, Salvatori Bldg.,
Port-of-Spain,
TRINIDAD AND TOBAGO
TEL: (62) 35595 - TELEX: 394
CABLE: ECLA PORT-OF-SPAIN
CREATED: 1979   *HEAD:* W. Primus, Project-Coordinator
SIZE OF STAFF: Professional: 4   Other: 6   Total: 10
TYPE OF SERVICE: international; public; non-profit
SYSTEMS & NETWORKS ATTACHED TO: Latin American Planning Information Network (INFOPLAN)
MATERIALS DESCRIBING THE SERVICE: - Caribbean Information System, a brochure in 3 parts
- The Caribbean Information System for Economic and Social Planning
- Caribbean Documentation Centre
- CARISPLAN Database user guide
SUBJECT COVERAGE: social sciences; administrative sciences; demography; economics; education; political science; sociology; technology transfer; development
GEOGRAPHICAL COVERAGE: Caribbean area
DATA BEING PROCESSED AND SIZE: data base of 15,000 records consisting of documents, reports, books and archives
DATA PROCESSING METHODS: computerized
HARDWARE USED: HP 32449A 3000/37 mini computer with 2 Mb CPU; HP 7933 404 MB Hard Disk
SOFTWARE USED: MINISIS
STORAGE MEDIA: traditional shelving of publications; fiches; tapes; discs; microfiches
TYPE OF ACTIVITY: distribution of information; SSID scientific and methodological

activities; SSID training; publication
ERIODICALS PUBLISHED: - CARISPLAN Abstracts
   - Current Awareness Bulletin
LIENTELE: technical personnel of government departments, researchers, policy-makers,
   post-graduate students
CCESS TO SERVICE: services open to specific categories of users, free of charge
YPE & DESCRIPTION OF SERVICES PROVIDED: Provides library services, bibliographic and
   literature abstract searches, selective dissemination of information,
   microforms, photocopies, and production of bibliograhic information on
   magnetic tapes. Also provides on-line services using own data base including
   15,000 entries, as well as external data bases such as "US Claims,
   ENVIROLINE, UNESCO, WORLD REPORTER" available through DIALOG, IDRC (Ottawa)
   and DATASOLVE.

B - EUROPEAN CENTRE FOR LEISURE AND EDUCATION

YNONYMOUS NAMES: ECLE;
   Centre Européen pour les Loisirs et l'Education
ARENT ORGANIZATION: Institute for Philosophy and Sociology of the Czechoslovak
   Academy of Sciences
DDRESS: Jilská 1,
   CS-110 00 Prague 1,
   CZECHOSLOVAKIA
   TEL: 24-58-46
REATED: 1968   HEAD: Prof. Dr. J. Pátek, Director
ZE OF STAFF: Professional: 3   Other: 1   Total: 4
PE OF SERVICE: international; public; non-profit
STEMS & NETWORKS ATTACHED TO: Co-operative Education Abstracting Service (CEAS)
ATERIALS DESCRIBING THE SERVICE: - ECLE information brochure, Prague, 1970, 16 p.
BJECT COVERAGE: sociology; adult education
OGRAPHICAL COVERAGE: Europe
ATA BEING PROCESSED AND SIZE: books
ATA PROCESSING METHODS: manual
RIODICALS PUBLISHED:
   - MAE news
BLICATIONS: - Selected bibliographies on specialized items
   - Index of society and leisure, Vol. I-IV, 1969-72, 1974, Vol. V-VIII, 1973-
   1976
   - List of publications (1969-1974), 1975
   - Working papers (series)
IENTELE: research institutes, universities, specialized libraries
CESS TO SERVICE: open to specific categories of users
PE & DESCRIPTION OF SERVICES PROVIDED: Provides library services and annotated
   bibliographies and bibliographic surveys on different problems, information
   on adult education system in European countries and on progress of the
   International Project Organization and Structure of Adult Education in
   Europe.

34 - EUROPEAN CONSORTIUM FOR POLITICAL RESEARCH, DATA INFORMATION SERVICE

SYNONYMOUS NAMES: ECPR - DIS
ADDRESS: c/o Norwegian Social Science Data Services (NSD),
         Hans Holmboesgt. 22,
         N-5007 Bergen,
         NORWAY
         TEL: 05-212117
CREATED: 1970   HEAD: Prof. S. Kuhnce, Head
SIZE OF STAFF: Professional: 3   Other: 1   Total: 4
TYPE OF SERVICE: international; public; non-profit
SUBJECT COVERAGE: political science; social sciences
GEOGRAPHICAL COVERAGE: Western Europe
TYPE OF ACTIVITY: distribution of information; publication
PERIODICALS PUBLISHED:
         - European Political Data Newsletter, 4 p.a.

35 - EUROPEAN FOUNDATION FOR THE IMPROVEMENT OF LIVING AND WORKING CONDITIONS,
     LIBRARY AND INFORMATION SERVICE

ADDRESS: Loughlinstown House,
         Shankill,
         County Dublin,
         IRELAND
         TEL: (01) 826888 - TELEX: 30726 EURF-EI
CREATED: 1975   HEAD: N. Wood, Head of Section
SIZE OF STAFF: Professional: 3   Other: 3   Total: 6
TYPE OF SERVICE: international; non-profit
MATERIALS DESCRIBING THE SERVICE: - brochure
WORKING LANGUAGE(S): 9 official languages of the EEC
SUBJECT COVERAGE: social sciences; administrative sciences; economics; law; social
         anthropology; cultural anthropology; social welfare; sociology; working
         conditions; living conditions
GEOGRAPHICAL COVERAGE: EEC countries
DATA BEING PROCESSED AND SIZE: 8,000 books; 250 journals; 1,000 research reports
DATA PROCESSING METHODS: manual
STORAGE MEDIA: traditional shelving of publications, microfiches
TYPE OF ACTIVITY: data collection; data analysis; publication; distribution of
         information; SSID scientific and methodological activities
PERIODICALS PUBLISHED:
         - EF News
PUBLICATIONS: - Catalogue of publications
         - Subject guide to Foundation reports published in the English language
CLIENTELE: open to all bona fide researchers (European)
ACCESS TO SERVICE: for internal users and specific category of users, free of charge
TYPE & DESCRIPTION OF SERVICES PROVIDED: Bibliographic and literature searches
         provided, on-line services using DIMDI, EURIS, ESA, TELESYSTEMS QUESTEL;
         selective dissemination of information, provision of microforms and
         photocopies. Relevant data bases available for searching including: Labor
         CIS, ENREP, Social Scisearch, Acompline, Sigle.

36 - EUROPEAN INSTITUTE OF PUBLIC ADMINISTRATION, LIBRARY

SYNONYMOUS NAMES: EIPA, Library;
Institut Européen d'Administration Publique, Bibliothèque
ADDRESS: 0. L. Vrouweplein 22,
NL-6211 HE Maastricht,
NETHERLANDS
TEL: 043-296222
CREATED: 1981   *HEAD:* Mr. H. Chevrolet, Head Librarian
TYPE OF SERVICE: international; public; private; profit; non-profit
SUBJECT COVERAGE: administrative sciences; public administration; political science;
public management; law; economics; European politics
GEOGRAPHICAL COVERAGE: EEC countries (Western Europe)
DATA BEING PROCESSED AND SIZE: 6,500 books; 200 periodicals
DATA PROCESSING METHODS: computerized
STORAGE MEDIA: traditional shelving of publications
TYPE OF ACTIVITY: data collection; data analysis; publication
CLIENTELE: governments, researchers, public executives
ACCESS TO SERVICE: open to the public for reference purposes only
TYPE & DESCRIPTION OF SERVICES PROVIDED: Provides library services, inter-library
loans, selective dissemination of information, photocopies, on-line searches
of own data base and external data bases in Europe and the USA (i.e. CELEX
and SCAD).

37 - EUROPEAN UNIVERSITY INSTITUTE, LIBRARY

SYNONYMOUS NAMES: EUI, Library;
Institut Universitaire Européen, Bibliothèque;
Instituto Universitario Europeo, Biblioteca
PARENT ORGANIZATION: European University Institute
ADDRESS: Via dei Roccettini, 5,
50016 San Domenico di Fiesole,
ITALY
TEL: 055/477931 - TELEX: 571528 IUE
CABLE: UNIVEUR
CREATED: 1975   *HEAD:* W. Dehennin, Librarian
SIZE OF STAFF: Professional: 16   Other: 8   Total: 24
TYPE OF SERVICE: international; public; non-profit
MATERIALS DESCRIBING THE SERVICE: - European University Institute annual report
SUBJECT COVERAGE: political science; economics; history; law; social sciences
GEOGRAPHICAL COVERAGE: Western Europe - EEC countries
DATA BEING PROCESSED AND SIZE: 150,000 books; 3,000 periodicals; 100,000 microcopies
DATA PROCESSING METHODS: computerized
SOFTWARE USED: GEAC
STORAGE MEDIA: traditional shelving of publications; tapes; microfiches
TYPE OF ACTIVITY: data collection
PERIODICALS PUBLISHED:
- List of Documents for Exchange
CLIENTELE: researchers (PhD students, fellows, academic staff)
ACCESS TO SERVICE: services open to specific categories of users, free of charge
TYPE & DESCRIPTION OF SERVICES PROVIDED: Provides library services, bibliographic

searches in its own catalogue and others such as Social Scisearch,
Historical Abstracts, Economic Abstracts International, Celex, Francis, PA
and Dissertation Abstracts. Also provides selective dissemination of
information, current awareness display of abstract journals and
bibliographic bulletins, and photocopies.

38 - FACULTAD LATINOAMERICANA DE CIENCIAS SOCIALES COSTA RICA, CENTRO DE DOCUMENTACIÓN

SYNONYMOUS NAMES: FLACSO;
    Latin American Faculty of Social Sciences Costa Rica, Documentation Centre
ADDRESS: Secretariat General,
    P.O. Box 5429,
    1000 San José,
    COSTA RICA
    TEL: 53-18-11 - TELEX: 2846 FLACSOCR
    CABLE: FLACSOCR
CREATED: 1981   *HEAD:* Ms. C. Arguedas, Head
SIZE OF STAFF: Professional: 1   Other: 1   Total: 2
TYPE OF SERVICE: international; public; non-profit
WORKING LANGUAGE(S): Spanish; English; French
SUBJECT COVERAGE: social sciences; economics; political science; sociology
GEOGRAPHICAL COVERAGE: Latin America; Caribbean area; Central America
DATA BEING PROCESSED AND SIZE: 3,700 books; 2,000 articles; 65 seminar proceedings
DATA PROCESSING METHODS: manual
STORAGE MEDIA: fiches
TYPE OF ACTIVITY: data collection; data analysis; SSID scientific and methodologica
    activities; publication
PERIODICALS PUBLISHED:
    - Boletín Bibliográfico
PUBLICATIONS: - Bibliografía general y seleccionada de referencia sobre integració
    - Bibliografía general y seleccionada de referencia sobre teoría y aspecto
    económicos, políticos y sociales de América Latina y América Central
    - Bibliografía general de referencia sobre les Comunidades Europeas (CEE)
    - Bibliografía analizada y seleccionada del Centro de Documentación
CLIENTELE: researchers and students (approx. 800 p.a.)
ACCESS TO SERVICE: services open to specific categories of users, free of charge
TYPE & DESCRIPTION OF SERVICES PROVIDED: Provides library services and bibliograph
    and literature searches.

39 - FOOD AND AGRICULTURE ORGANIZATION OF THE UNITED NATIONS, HUMAN RESOURCES, INSTITUTIONS AND AGRARIAN REFORM DIVISION, REFERENCE UNIT

SYNONYMOUS NAMES: FAO/ESH, Reference Unit
PARENT ORGANIZATION: United Nations
ADDRESS: Via delle Terme di Caracalla,
    00100 Rome,
    ITALY
    TEL: 57971 - TELEX: 610181 FAO I

CABLE: FOODAGRI Rome
REATED: 1986   HEAD: Mrs. .H. Meliczek, Agrarian Reform and Rural Development
                Officer
IZE OF STAFF: Professional: 1   Other: 1   Total: 2
YPE OF SERVICE: international; non-profit
UBJECT COVERAGE: demography; rural development; human resources; women in
          agriculture; agrarian reform; agricultural education
EOGRAPHICAL COVERAGE: global
ATA BEING PROCESSED AND SIZE: books; articles; reports; seminars; training courses;
          research results
ATA PROCESSING METHODS: partially computerized
ARDWARE USED: IBM 3083 BX with MVS/SP 1.8; 3,380 disk drives; 3,420 tape units
OFTWARE USED: CDS/ISIS
TORAGE MEDIA: traditional shelving of publications; microfiches
YPE OF ACTIVITY: distribution of information
ERIODICALS PUBLISHED:
          - ESHD Accessions List
UBLICATIONS: - Bibliography of FAO documentation on rural development 1980-1984
LIENTELE: researchers from other UN agencies and FAO member countries
CCESS TO SERVICE: services open to specific categories of users, free of charge
YPE & DESCRIPTION OF SERVICES PROVIDED: Provides library services, bibliographic
          searches of information, on-line services using its own data base "ESHD".
          Photocopies can be obtained upon request.

O - HUMAN RIGHTS INFORMATION AND DOCUMENTATION SYSTEM

YNONYMOUS NAMES: HURIDOCS
DDRESS: c/o HBC,
        Grenseveien 99,
        N-0663 Olso,
        NORWAY
        TEL: (2) 653965 - TELEX: 79744 hbc n (for huridocs) - TELEFAX: (2) 644857
REATED: 1984   HEAD: K. Rupesinghe, Chairman
                H. Thoolen, Secretary
IZE OF STAFF: Professional: 1   Other: 1   Total: 2
YPE OF SERVICE: international; public; non-profit
ATERIALS DESCRIBING THE SERVICE: - brochure
ORKING LANGUAGE(S): English; French; Spanish
UBJECT COVERAGE: law; political science; human rights; civil and political rights;
          economic, social and cultural rights
EOGRAPHICAL COVERAGE: global
ATA PROCESSING METHODS: computerized
YPE OF ACTIVITY: data collection; data analysis; distribution of information; SSID
          training; publication; conference-organization
ERIODICALS PUBLISHED:
          - HURIDOCS News
UBLICATIONS: - Bibliography of publications from NGOs concerned with human rights
          1970-1981, 1982
          - Knabe, F., Human rights terminology, 1982
          - Knabe, F., Draft human rights thesaurus, 1982
          - Encuesta sobre la disponibilidad de información y documentación de

derechos humanos en America Latina y el Caribe, 1983
- N.G.O. publications on human rights 1970-1981, 1982
- Directory of human rights information and documentation facilities in the
field of human rights in Western Europe, 1982
- Inaugural Conference final report, 1982
- Stormorken, B., Huridocs standard formats for the recording and exchange
of information on human rights, 1985
- Report of human rights information technology seminar, 1985
- Knabe, F. (ed.), Report of the joint conference on communication,
development and human rights, 1986
- Bibsys: a database system for handling bibliographic data on
microcomputers, 1986
ACCESS TO SERVICE: open to all users, free of charge
TYPE & DESCRIPTION OF SERVICES PROVIDED: Global network of non-governmental
organizations and integrated information system and service whose purpose
to facilitate the identification, location and free flow of public human
rights information through the establishment of basic tools, the developme
of new standards, the teaching on information handling techniques, advisor
services on information handling systems and softwares, and coordination
among the different documentation centres.

41 - HUMAN RIGHTS INTERNET

SYNONYMOUS NAMES: HRI
ADDRESS: Harvard Law School,
          Pound Hall, Room 401,
          Cambridge,
          Massachusetts 02138,
          U. S. A.
          TEL: (617) 495-9924 - TELEX: 5106014536
          CABLE: INTERNET
CREATED: 1976   *HEAD:* Ms. L. S. Wiseberg, Executive Director
SIZE OF STAFF: Professional: 4   Total: 4
TYPE OF SERVICE: international; private; non-profit
MATERIALS DESCRIBING THE SERVICE: - HRI leaflet
WORKING LANGUAGE(S): English; French; Spanish
SUBJECT COVERAGE: law; human rights; social sciences; education; political science
GEOGRAPHICAL COVERAGE: global
DATA BEING PROCESSED AND SIZE: books, articles, journals, reports (2,000 p.a.)
DATA PROCESSING METHODS: computerized
HARDWARE USED: Fortune Computer, UNIX-Based
SOFTWARE USED: BRS micro/search
STORAGE MEDIA: microfiches
TYPE OF ACTIVITY: data collection; data analysis; distribution of information;
          publication; SSID training
PERIODICALS PUBLISHED: - Human Rights Internet Reporter, 4 p.a.
PUBLICATIONS: - Human rights directory: Western Europe, 1982
          - Human rights directory: Eastern Europe, 1987
          - Human rights directory: North America, 1984
          - Human rights documents updated through 1983, 1986
          - Human rights directory: Latin America, 1988

- Access to justice: the struggle for human rights in Southeast Asia, 1985
- Teaching human rights, 1981

CLIENTELE: researchers, lawyers, human rights organizations, journalists, policy-makers

ACCESS TO SERVICE: services open to all users, some paid services

TYPE & DESCRIPTION OF SERVICES PROVIDED: International communications network and clearinghouse on human rights covering 200 organizations and individuals. Provides library services, bibliographic and literature searches on its own "full-text" database containing the citations and articles found in the Human Rights Internet Reporter and directories; also provides microfiches and copies of original documents.

42 - INSTITUT EUROPÉEN INTERUNIVERSITAIRE DE L'ACTION SOCIALE

SYNONYMOUS NAMES: IEIAS;
        Inter-University European Institute on Social Welfare
ADDRESS: 179, rue du Débarcadère,
        B-6001 Marcinelle,
        BELGIUM
        TEL: 71-36.62.73
        CABLE: INEIASSOC
CREATED: 1970   *HEAD:* Mr. P. Rozen, Secretary-General
                Mr. S. Mayence, Director General
SIZE OF STAFF: Professional: 3   Other: 1   Total: 4
TYPE OF SERVICE: international; private; non-profit
MATERIALS DESCRIBING THE SERVICE: - printed notice
SUBJECT COVERAGE: social welfare; community development; social sciences
GEOGRAPHICAL COVERAGE: Western Europe
DATA BEING PROCESSED AND SIZE: 12,000 books; 600 periodicals; 500 theses
DATA PROCESSING METHODS: computerized
TYPE OF ACTIVITY: data collection; data analysis; publication
PERIODICALS PUBLISHED:
        - Accession List, 4 p.a.
PUBLICATIONS: - Bibliographies on specific subjects
CLIENTELE: social workers
ACCESS TO SERVICE: open to all users, free of charge
TYPE & DESCRIPTION OF SERVICES PROVIDED: Provides reference services and photocopies. This Centre administers also the "European Regional Clearing Housing for Community Work" (C.H.) since 1976.

43 - INTERNATIONAL CENTRE FOR PARLIAMENTARY DOCUMENTATION

SYNONYMOUS NAMES: Centre International de Documentation Parlementaire;
        CIDP
PARENT ORGANIZATION: Inter-Parliamentary Union
ADDRESS: Place du Petit-Saconnex,
        Case Postale 438,
        1211 Geneva 19,
        SWITZERLAND

TEL: (022) 34.41.50 - TELEX: 289784
CABLE: INTERPARLEMENT-GENEVE
CREATED: 1965   *HEAD:* P. S. J. Dawe, Director
SIZE OF STAFF: Professional: 3   Other: 1   Total: 4
TYPE OF SERVICE: international; public; non-profit
MATERIALS DESCRIBING THE SERVICE: - Printed notice (available in English and French
WORKING LANGUAGE(S): English; French
SUBJECT COVERAGE: law; government; constitutional law; political science;
        parliamentary system; elections
GEOGRAPHICAL COVERAGE: global
DATA BEING PROCESSED AND SIZE: 7,000 books; 135 periodicals; reports; texts of laws
        material concerning the institution of Parliament, constitutions, and othe
DATA PROCESSING METHODS: manual
STORAGE MEDIA: traditional shelving of publications
TYPE OF ACTIVITY: data collection; publication; conference-organization
PERIODICALS PUBLISHED:
        - Chronicle of Parliamentary Elections and Development, 1 p.a.
        - Inter-Parliamentary Bulletin, 4 p.a.
PUBLICATIONS: - World directory of parliaments, 1987
        - World-wide bibliography on parliaments (1983-1985), 1986
        - Distribution of seats by sex in parliamentary assemblies, 1985
        - Parliaments of the world, a comparative reference compendium, 1986
CLIENTELE: students, researchers, experts
ACCESS TO SERVICE: open to all users, free of charge
TYPE & DESCRIPTION OF SERVICES PROVIDED: Collects information on the composition,
        organization and functioning of national parliaments. Deals with
        constitutional law and law pertaining to parliaments, and elections.
        Provides library services, bibliographies, photocopies and microforms of
        documents, documentary dossiers and selective dissemination of information

44 - INTERNATIONAL COMMITTEE FOR SOCIAL SCIENCE INFORMATION AND DOCUMENTATION

SYNONYMOUS NAMES: ICSSD;
        Comité International pour l'Information et la Documentation en Sciences
        Sociales;
        CIDSS
ADDRESS: 27, rue Saint Guillaume,
        75341 Paris Cedex 07,
        FRANCE
        TEL: (1) 45.49.50.50 - TELEX: F.201002 scipol
CREATED: 1950   *HEAD:* Mr. J. Meyriat, Secretary General
SIZE OF STAFF: Professional: 4   Other: 4   Total: 8
TYPE OF SERVICE: international; private; non-profit
MATERIALS DESCRIBING THE SERVICE: - The International Committee for Social Science
        Information and Documentation. A brief presentation, in SSID liaison
        bulletin 1981 no. 2
WORKING LANGUAGE(S): English; French
SUBJECT COVERAGE: social sciences
GEOGRAPHICAL COVERAGE: global
DATA PROCESSING METHODS: partially computerized
HARDWARE USED: GEAC; IBM PC; APPLE II

OFTWARE USED: own software
TORAGE MEDIA: tapes; discs
YPE OF ACTIVITY: data collection; data analysis; distribution of information; SSID
scientific and methodological activities; publication
ERIODICALS PUBLISHED: - International Bibliography of the Social Sciences (4 vols:
sociology, political science, economics, social and cultural anthropology),
1 p.a. since 1951
- Annual Report
LIENTELE: the world social science community
CCESS TO SERVICE: open to all users, especially institutions, free of charge
YPE & DESCRIPTION OF SERVICES PROVIDED: As an operational body the Committee has a
coordinating function for national and regional social science information
institutions, a consultative function towards Unesco and other international
organizations, a policy-making function in the field of SSID, a normative
function in cooperation with ISO and other specialized bodies. Provides
searches of information using own data base IBSS (International Bibliography
of the Social Sciences) and selective dissemination of information.

5 - INTERNATIONAL DOCUMENTATION AND COMMUNICATION CENTER, DOCUMENTATION SERVICE

YNONYMOUS NAMES: IDOC Documentation Service
DDRESS: Via S. Maria dell'Anima 30,
00186 Rome,
ITALY
TEL: (39-6) 65.68.332
REATED: 1965   *HEAD:* Mr. H. Hunke, Secretary General
IZE OF STAFF: Professional: 5
YPE OF SERVICE: international; private; non-profit
ORKING LANGUAGE(S): English; Italian
UBJECT COVERAGE: political science; social sciences; social anthropology; social
welfare; religion; society; social change; development; transnational
corporations; new world information order, impact of new technology; human
rights; racial discrimination; sex discrimination
EOGRAPHICAL COVERAGE: global
ATA BEING PROCESSED AND SIZE: 51,000 publications and unpublished material
(conference papers and reports, mimeographed sheets, etc.)
ATA PROCESSING METHODS: computerized
ARDWARE USED: TELEVIDEO
OFTWARE USED: SUPERFILE FYI 2000
TORAGE MEDIA: traditional shelving of publications
YPE OF ACTIVITY: distribution of information; SSID training; publication
ERIODICALS PUBLISHED: - IDOC Internazionale, 6 p.a. (in English)
- Emergenze, 6 p.a. (in Italian)
- IDOC Monthly Documentation Bulletin
LIENTELE: scholars, journalists, researchers, church and development personnel,
action groups (150 p.a.), non-governmental organizations
CCESS TO SERVICE: services open to all users, free of charge
YPE & DESCRIPTION OF SERVICES PROVIDED: Provides bibliographic and literature
abstract searches, on-line services using own data base, selective
dissemination of information, enquiry services, interpretative services and
photocopy service of important documents.

46 - INTERNATIONAL INFORMATION CENTRE FOR TERMINOLOGY

SYNONYMOUS NAMES: INFOTERM;
Centre International d'Information pour la Terminologie;
Austrian Standards Institute
PARENT ORGANIZATION: Österreichisches Normungsinstitut (ÖN)
ADDRESS: Heinestr. 38,
Postfach 130,
A-1021 Vienna 2,
AUSTRIA
TEL: (0222) 26.75.35 - TELEX: 115960 onorma
CABLE: AUSTRIANORM
CREATED: 1971   *HEAD:* C. Galinski, Director
SIZE OF STAFF: Professional: 4   Other: 3   Total: 7
TYPE OF SERVICE: international; public; non-profit
SYSTEMS & NETWORKS ATTACHED TO: Related to TermNet and Unesco/GIP/UNISIST
MATERIALS DESCRIBING THE SERVICE: - Infoterm, International Information Centre for
Terminology. Ten years of activities 1971-1981. Wien, ON, 1982
WORKING LANGUAGE(S): English; German; French
SUBJECT COVERAGE: information science; linguistics; terminology
GEOGRAPHICAL COVERAGE: global
DATA BEING PROCESSED AND SIZE: 15,000 articles; books, standards (500 p.a.)
DATA PROCESSING METHODS: manual; partially computerized
TYPE OF ACTIVITY: data collection; data analysis; distribution of information;
publication
PERIODICALS PUBLISHED: - StandarTerm
- Infoterm Newsletter
- TermNet News
- Biblioterm
PUBLICATIONS: - Infoterm series, 8 vols.
- Terminological data banks. Proceedings of the First International
Conference convened in Vienna, April 2-3, 1979, 1980
- Theoretical and methodological problems of terminology, 1981
- Rondeau, G.; Felber, H. (eds.), Textes choisis de terminologie, vol. 1,
1981
- Terminologies for the eighties, 1982
- Felber, H.; Krommer-Benz, M.; Manu, A., International bibliography of
standardized vocabularies/Bibliographie internationale de vocabulaire
normalisés/Internationale Bibliographie der Normvorterbücher. Munchen, New
York, London, Paris, K-G. Saur Verlag, 2nd ed. 1979, XXIV-540 p.
CLIENTELE: subject specialists, language mediators, documentalists
ACCESS TO SERVICE: services open to all users, free of charge
TYPE & DESCRIPTION OF SERVICES PROVIDED: Acts as a clearing house, referral agency
and analysis centre for the theory, utilization and documentation of
terminology within the international network for terminological activities
(TermNet). Provides library services, information searches, selective
dissemination of information, information on magnetic tapes or discs,
microforms and photocopies.

7 - INTERNATIONAL INSTITUTE OF ADMINISTRATIVE SCIENCES, LIBRARY

SYNONYMOUS NAMES: IIAS, Library;
Institut International des Sciences Administratives, Bibliothèque;
IISA, Bibliothèque
ADDRESS: 1, rue Defacqz,
B-1050 Brussels,
BELGIUM
TEL: (02) 538.91.65 - TELEX: 65933 iisa b
CABLE: INTERADMIN
HEAD: Mr. F. Balsinhas Covas, Head
TYPE OF SERVICE: private; non-profit
SUBJECT COVERAGE: administrative sciences
DATA BEING PROCESSED AND SIZE: 10,000 books; 7,000 documents
DATA PROCESSING METHODS: partially computerized
HARDWARE USED: Sanyo micro-computer MS-DOS
SOFTWARE USED: Microquestel
STORAGE MEDIA: discs
TYPE OF ACTIVITY: research; documentation; research promotion; conference-
organization; publication
PERIODICALS PUBLISHED: - Sélection Bibliographique Internationale de Sciences
Administratives (SBISA), 6 p.a.
ACCESS TO SERVICE: open to administrative science specialists
TYPE & DESCRIPTION OF SERVICES PROVIDED: Provides library services, bibliographic and
literature abstracts searches.

8 - INTERNATIONAL LABOUR OFFICE, CENTRAL LIBRARY AND DOCUMENTATION BRANCH

SYNONYMOUS NAMES: BIBL/ILO;
ILO Library
ADDRESS: 4, route des Morillons,
CH-1211 Geneva 22,
SWITZERLAND
TEL: (41.22) 99.86.75 - TELEX: 22.271 BIT CH
CABLE: INTERLAB GENEVE
CREATED: 1919   *HEAD:* K. Wild, Chief
SIZE OF STAFF: Professional: 14   Other: 16   Total: 30
TYPE OF SERVICE: international; public; non-profit
SYSTEMS & NETWORKS ATTACHED TO: ARAMIS (Swedish Centre for Workday Life); ESA-IRS
(European Space Agency); HRIN (Human Resource Information Network); Pergamon
ORBIT Infoline
MATERIALS DESCRIBING THE SERVICE: - ILO Library: a brief introduction, 1987
- La Bibliothèque du BIT, 1987
- La Biblioteca de la OIT, 1987
WORKING LANGUAGE(S): English; French; Spanish
SUBJECT COVERAGE: economics; social sciences; administrative sciences; demography;
law; political science; social welfare; statistics; labour; employment
GEOGRAPHICAL COVERAGE: global
DATA BEING PROCESSED AND SIZE: 1,000,000 documents; 7,500 periodicals; 200 abstract
journals; 40,000 microcopies
DATA PROCESSING METHODS: computerized

HARDWARE USED: Hewlett-Packard 3000 68
SOFTWARE USED: MINISIS
STORAGE MEDIA: traditional shelving of publications; fiches; tapes; discs;
     microfiches
PERIODICALS PUBLISHED:
     - International Labour Documentation. Abstracting Bulletin, 12 p.a.
     - Register of Periodicals in the ILO Library, microfiche, 2 p.a.
PUBLICATIONS: - ILO thesaurus: labour, employment and training terminology, 1985
     - Library catalogue, (microfiche): 1965-1977; 1978-1987
     - ILO publications and documents, (microfiche), 1919-1987
CLIENTELE: ILO officials, government, employers' and workers' representatives, and
     researchers
ACCESS TO SERVICE: services open to specific categories of users
TYPE & DESCRIPTION OF SERVICES PROVIDED: Provides library services, bibliographic on
     line searching using its own data base LABORDOC including 150,000
     bibliographical items, selective dissemination of information mainly on
     employment, labour relations and labour law. Its general catalogue is also
     available through DIALOG; ESA-IRS, ESRIN, Frascati, Italy; Pergamon ORBIT
     Infoline and other information hosts. Also provides information on magnetic
     tapes, microfilms, microforms and photocopies.

49 - INTERNATIONAL LABOUR OFFICE, CLEARING-HOUSE ON CONDITIONS OF WORK

SYNONYMOUS NAMES: ILO, Clearing-House on Conditions of Work
ADDRESS: 4, route des Morillons,
     CH-1211 Geneva 22,
     SWITZERLAND
     TEL: 99.70.78 - TELEX: 22.271 BIT CH
CREATED: 1979   HEAD: Mrs. M. Jankanish, Information Officer
SIZE OF STAFF: Professional: 1   Other: 1   Total: 2
TYPE OF SERVICE: international; public
MATERIALS DESCRIBING THE SERVICE: - IOB newsletter (Geneva), Volume 5, Number 5,
     November 1982
WORKING LANGUAGE(S): English
SUBJECT COVERAGE: labour; working conditions; quality of life
GEOGRAPHICAL COVERAGE: global
DATA BEING PROCESSED AND SIZE: books; articles; on-going research; conference report
DATA PROCESSING METHODS: computerized
HARDWARE USED: Hewlett-Packard 3000 model mini-computer
SOFTWARE USED: MINISIS software package
TYPE OF ACTIVITY: data collection; data analysis; publication; SSID scientific and
     methodological activities
PERIODICALS PUBLISHED: - Conditions of Work Digest
PUBLICATIONS: - Conditions of work: research in progress, 1987
          - Conditions of work and quality of working life: a directory of
          institutions, 1986
ACCESS TO SERVICE: open to all users
TYPE & DESCRIPTION OF SERVICES PROVIDED: Provides bibliographic searches of
     information.

O - INTERNATIONAL LABOUR OFFICE, INTERNATIONAL OCCUPATIONAL SAFETY AND HEALTH INFORMATION CENTRE

NONYMOUS NAMES: ILO/CIS;
Bureau International du Travail, Centre International d'Informations de
Securité et d'Hygiène du Travail
DDRESS: 4, route des Morillons,
CH-1211 Geneva 22,
SWITZERLAND
TEL: (41.22) 99.67.40 - TELEX: 22.271 BIT CH - TELEFAX: (22) 988685
CABLE: CISINTERLAB
REATED: 1959   *HEAD:* J. Takala, Head
IZE OF STAFF: Professional: 7   Other: 11   Total: 18
YPE OF SERVICE: international; public; non-profit
YSTEMS & NETWORKS ATTACHED TO: CIS National Centres
UBJECT COVERAGE: social welfare; labour; psychology; sociology; law; economics;
sociology of work; labour management relations; health
EOGRAPHICAL COVERAGE: global
ATA BEING PROCESSED AND SIZE: 40,000 books, periodicals, films, microforms, laws,
standards, reports and others
ATA PROCESSING METHODS: computerized
ARDWARE USED: HP 3000
OFTWARE USED: MINISIS
YPE OF ACTIVITY: distribution of information; publication
ERIODICALS PUBLISHED: - List of Periodicals Abstracted, irr. since 1965
- CIS Information Sheets/Notes documentaires du CIS, irr.
- Safety and Health at Work; ILO-CIS Bulletin/Sécurité et Santé du Travail,
Bulletin BIT-CIS, 6 p.a. since 1987
UBLICATIONS: - CIS thesaurus, 1976
- CIS bibliographies: different series of bibliographies on special subjects
LIENTELE: subscribers of printed products; subscribers on-line service; subscribers
to CD-ROM database (compact disc-read only memory)
CCESS TO SERVICE: subscription service open to all
YPE & DESCRIPTION OF SERVICES PROVIDED: Provides bibliographic on-line searching
using its own system "CIS data base" including 30,000 items in the fields
of occupational safety and health, sociology of work, labour administration
and labour management relations. Provision of information on magnetic tapes
and microfilms. Its general catalogue is also available through
TELESYSTEMES-QUESTEL, Paris, France; ESA-IRS, ESRIN, Frascati, Italy; CCOTTS
Hamilton (Ont.) Canada, National Board of Occupational Safety and Health,
Sweden.

1 - INTERNATIONAL LABOUR OFFICE, RURAL EMPLOYMENT POLICIES BRANCH, DOCUMENTATION CENTRE

YNONYMOUS NAMES: ILO-EMP/RU;
Organización Internacional del Trabajo, Servicio de las Politicas Rurales
del Empleo;
Bureau International du Travail, Service des Politiques Rurales de l'Emploi;
Oficina Internacional del Trabajo, Servicio de las Politicas Rurales del
Empleo

ADDRESS: Employment and Development Department,
4, route des Morillons,
CH-1211 Geneva 22,
SWITZERLAND
TEL: 966111 - TELEX: 22271 BIT CH
CABLE: INTERLAB Geneva
CREATED: 1973   HEAD: Ms. E. Schaad, Documentalist
S. Radwan, Chief
SIZE OF STAFF: Professional: 11   Other: 7   Total: 18
TYPE OF SERVICE: international
SYSTEMS & NETWORKS ATTACHED TO: International Labour Information Systems (ILIS)
WORKING LANGUAGE(S): English; French; Spanish; German; Portuguese
SUBJECT COVERAGE: social sciences; economics; social anthropology; social welfare;
sociology; role of rural women; participation in rural development; rural
population; employment; rural migration; agricultural policy; labour market;
refugees
GEOGRAPHICAL COVERAGE: developing countries; global
DATA BEING PROCESSED AND SIZE: books, articles, reports
DATA PROCESSING METHODS: computerized
HARDWARE USED: Hewlett Packard 3000
SOFTWARE USED: Minisis
STORAGE MEDIA: traditional shelving of publications
TYPE OF ACTIVITY: data collection; data analysis; distribution of information
PUBLICATIONS: - The Challenge of rural poverty: a progress report on research and
technical co-operation concerning rural employment, agrarian institutions
and policies, 1985
CLIENTELE: researchers, university students
ACCESS TO SERVICE: services open to all users, free of charge
TYPE & DESCRIPTION OF SERVICES PROVIDED: Provides library services, bibliographic
searches of information, on-line services, information on magnetic tapes,
discs (through LABORDOC or microforms) and photocopies. Has its own data
base EMPRU and has access to LABORDOC through ARAMIS, ESA-IRS, HRIM and
ORBIT data bases.

52 - INTERNATIONAL MONETARY FUND, ECONOMIC INFORMATION SYSTEM

ADDRESS: Bureau of Statistics,
700 Nineteenth St. N.W.,
Washington, D.C. 20431,
U. S. A.
TEL: (202) 623-7000 - TELEX: (RCA) 248331 IMF UR
CABLE: INTERFUND WASHINGTON
CREATED: 1986   HEAD: Mr. W. Dannemann, Director, Bureau of Statistics
SIZE OF STAFF: Professional: 73   Other: 43   Total: 116
TYPE OF SERVICE: international; public; non-profit
WORKING LANGUAGE(S): English
SUBJECT COVERAGE: economics; statistics
GEOGRAPHICAL COVERAGE: global, with regional breakdowns and individual country
presentation
DATA PROCESSING METHODS: computerized
HARDWARE USED: IBM 3081-KX (mainframe) with local area network (LAN) to IMF staff

OFTWARE USED: DBMS Model 204
TORAGE MEDIA: traditional shelving of publications; magnetic tapes
YPE OF ACTIVITY: data collection; distribution of information; publication
ERIODICALS PUBLISHED: - Government Finance Statistics Yearbook
- International Financial Statistics
- Balance of Payments Statistics
- Direction of Trade Statistics
CCESS TO SERVICE: free of charge, some services against payment
YPE & DESCRIPTION OF SERVICES PROVIDED: Provides library services and distributes
200,000 paper documents and 6,000 magnetic tapes per year.

3 - INTERNATIONAL PLANNED PARENTHOOD FEDERATION, LIBRARY

YNONYMOUS NAMES: IPPF, Library;
Fédération Internationale pour le Planning Familial, Bibliothèque
DDRESS: Regent's College,
Inner Circle,
Regent's Park,
London NW1 4NS,
UNITED KINGDOM
TEL: (01) 486 0741 - TELEX: 919573 IPEPEE G
CABLE: IPEPEE London
REATED: 1964   *HEAD:* R. Ward, Librarian
IZE OF STAFF: Professional: 1   Other: 1   Total: 2
YPE OF SERVICE: international; private; non-profit
ATERIALS DESCRIBING THE SERVICE: - Visitor's guide, rev. ed., 1982, 25 p. mimeo
ORKING LANGUAGE(S): English; French; Spanish
UBJECT COVERAGE: demography; family planning
EOGRAPHICAL COVERAGE: global
ATA BEING PROCESSED AND SIZE: 5,000 books (1,000 p.a.); 200 journals (20 p.a.);
2,000 files (1,000 p.a.); 5,000 microfiches (250 p.a.); 1,000 audiovisuals
(50 p.a.)
ATA PROCESSING METHODS: manual
TORAGE MEDIA: traditional shelving of publications
ERIODICALS PUBLISHED:
- IPPF cooperative information service (ICIS, acquisition list), 4 p.a.
UBLICATIONS: - Special bibliographies
- Population and family planning classification, London, 1975, 106 p.
(available also in French and Spanish)
LIENTELE: family planning workers
CCESS TO SERVICE: open to all users, free of charge
YPE & DESCRIPTION OF SERVICES PROVIDED: Provides library services, photocopies and
access to bibliographical files.

4 - INTERNATIONAL STATISTICAL INSTITUTE, RESEARCH CENTRE DYNAMIC DATA BASE

YNONYMOUS NAMES: ISIRC/DDB
DDRESS: 428 Prinses Beatrixlaan,
P.O. Box 950,

2270 AZ Voorburg,
NETHERLANDS
TEL: (3170) 694341 - TELEX: 32260 isi nl
CABLE: STATIST VOORBURG
CREATED: 1983   *HEAD:* Prof. D. Finney, Director
SIZE OF STAFF: Professional:˙6   Other: 5   Total: 11
TYPE OF SERVICE: international; public; non-profit
WORKING LANGUAGE(S): English; French
SUBJECT COVERAGE: demography; statistics; fertility; socio-economic development;
      family planning; marriage; status of women; mortality; surveys; methodology
GEOGRAPHICAL COVERAGE: developing countries; developed countries; global
DATA BEING PROCESSED AND SIZE: demographic data sets, World Fertility Survey (approx
      250 data sets); tabulations, reports, research, etc
DATA PROCESSING METHODS: computerized
HARDWARE USED: Hewlett Packard 3000 series 42 system; PC; IBM AT
SOFTWARE USED: research software (Fortran, Cobol programs), SPSS (a.o. CLUSTERS)
STORAGE MEDIA: tapes, diskettes, microfiches
TYPE OF ACTIVITY: data collection; data analysis; publication; SSID scientific and
      methodological activities; SSID training; distribution of information
PERIODICALS PUBLISHED:
    - Dynamic data base brochure (Newsletter)
    - Dynamic data base catalogue, 1987
CLIENTELE: researchers, universities, experts, World Bank, several UN organizations
ACCESS TO SERVICE: services open to specific categories of users, (reimbursement of
      postage and handling charge)
TYPE & DESCRIPTION OF SERVICES PROVIDED: Dynamic Data Base specializes in demograph
      analysis and contains a central archive of computerized survey data of
      national coverage. Also provides survey processing software, free advice or
      methodology and analyses on request. Services include quantitative data
      searches, selective dissemination of information, production of information
      on magnetic tapes and photocopies.

55 - INTERNATIONAL TRADE CENTRE UNCTAD/GATT, TRADE INFORMATION SERVICE

ADDRESS: Palais des Nations,
      CH-1211 Geneva 10,
      SWITZERLAND
      TEL: 34-60-21 - TELEX: 289052 ITC-CH
CREATED: 1968   *HEAD:* Y. Mori, Chief
SIZE OF STAFF: Professional: 7   Other: 17   Total: 24
TYPE OF SERVICE: international; public; non-profit
MATERIALS DESCRIBING THE SERVICE: - ITC activities and services in trade information
SUBJECT COVERAGE: economics; international trade
GEOGRAPHICAL COVERAGE: global
DATA BEING PROCESSED AND SIZE: 5,000 books; 800 periodicals; 400 reports; 1,500 file
      in the information file system; 2 data bases
DATA PROCESSING METHODS: partially computerized
HARDWARE USED: ICC mainframe computer Geneva (IBM 3090 processor)
SOFTWARE USED: INQUIRE, MARK IV, SAS, DIALOG
STORAGE MEDIA: traditional shelving of publications, files, microfiches (possible
      downloading on diskettes and copy on magnetic tape)

YPE OF ACTIVITY: data collection; data analysis; distribution of information;
   publication
UBLICATIONS: - International trade documentation; annotated list of publications
   received by the ITC
   - ITC Core list: basic documentation for trade information, 1982
   - Thesaurus of international trade terms, 1982
   - Annotated bibliography of product serials
LIENTELE: ITC professional staff, international organizations, administrative
   officers, researchers, developing country organizations, businessmen
CCESS TO SERVICE: services open to specific categories of users, free of charge,
   some services charged
YPE & DESCRIPTION OF SERVICES PROVIDED: Provides library services, selective
   dissemination of information, information on magnetic tapes or discs,
   microforms and photocopies. On-line services with their main data bases in
   trade information: TRADERS (ITC company profiles), COMTRADE (UNSO trade
   statistics), TPO (ITC directory of trade promotion organizations). Also has
   access to external databases including Data-Star, Dialog, Echo, ESA/IRS, G-
   CAM, IP Sharp, Infoline, Orbit, Questel, EDS, through ICC.

6 - ISIS WOMEN'S INTERNATIONAL CROSS-CULTURAL EXCHANGE INFO-DOC CENTRE

SYNONYMOUS NAMES: ISIS-WICCE
ADDRESS: ISIS Switzerland,
   P.O. Box 2471,
   CH-1211 Geneva 2,
   SWITZERLAND
   TEL: 022/33.67.46
CREATED: 1975
SIZE OF STAFF: Total: 15
TYPE OF SERVICE: international; non-profit
MATERIALS DESCRIBING THE SERVICE: - Brochure
WORKING LANGUAGE(S): English
SUBJECT COVERAGE: sociology; social sciences; women
GEOGRAPHICAL COVERAGE: global
DATA PROCESSING METHODS: manual
STORAGE MEDIA: traditional shelving of publications; fiches
TYPE OF ACTIVITY: data collection; data analysis; publication; SSID training
PERIODICALS PUBLISHED: - Revista Isis Internacional de las Mujeres, 2 p.a., since
   1984
   - Boletín de la Red de Salud de las Mujeres Latinoamericanas y del Caribe
PUBLICATIONS: - Resource guide on women and development, 1982
   - Mujeres y medios de comunicación: Asia y el Pacífico, 1984
   - La Guia de Isis Internacional sobre recursos audio-visuales para las
   mujeres, 1985
   - Wells, T.; Foo Gaik Sim, Hasta que tengamos nostros. La mujeres como
   consumidoras, 1987
   - Mujeres en el desarrollo: una guia de recursos para la organización y la
   acción
   - Crecer juntas: mujeres, feminismo y educación popular, América Latina y el
   Caribe, 1987
   - Base de datos mujer/Women's database, 1988

ACCESS TO SERVICE: open to all users, paid services
TYPE & DESCRIPTION OF SERVICES PROVIDED: Provides library reference services,
     annotated bibliographies on women, resources on specific topics or countrie
     and documentation packages on specific themes. ISIS Italy: Via San Saba 5,
     Interno 1, 00153 Rome, Italy. ISIS Chile: Casilla 2067, Correo Central,
     Santiago, Chile, Tel: 490271.

57 - LEAGUE OF ARAB STATES DOCUMENTATION AND INFORMATION CENTER

SYNONYMOUS NAMES: ALDOC
ADDRESS: 37, Khereddine Pacha Street,
     Tunis,
     TUNISIA
     TEL: 890-100
HEAD: Mrs. F. Zahawi, Director
SIZE OF STAFF: Total: 68
TYPE OF SERVICE: international; non-profit
MATERIALS DESCRIBING THE SERVICE: - ALDOC brochure
          - Library guide
WORKING LANGUAGE(S): Arabic
SUBJECT COVERAGE: social sciences; administrative sciences; demography; economics;
          education; law; political science; social welfare
GEOGRAPHICAL COVERAGE: Arab countries
DATA BEING PROCESSED AND SIZE: 21,000 books; 1,600 periodicals; UN documents; press
          clippings; audiovisual materials
DATA PROCESSING METHODS: computerized
HARDWARE USED: MP 3000, III + 48
SOFTWARE USED: MINISIS
STORAGE MEDIA: fiches; tapes; discs; microfiches
TYPE OF ACTIVITY: distribution of information; SSID training; publication
PERIODICALS PUBLISHED: - Contents of Periodicals, 12 p.a.
          - Quarterly Specialized Bibliography Fahras, 3 p.a.
          - New Accessions, 12 p.a.
          - Aris-Net Newsletter, 12 p.a.
CLIENTELE: Arab and international organizations, researchers, students
ACCESS TO SERVICE: services open to all users, free of charge
TYPE & DESCRIPTION OF SERVICES PROVIDED: Provides library services, searches of
     information, selective dissemination of information, magnetic tapes,
     microforms and photocopies. Also provides on-line services using own data
     base "ALIF" as well as external data bases, DIALOG, ESA/IRS, DATASOLVE and
     WORLD REPORTER.

58 - ORGANIZATION OF AMERICAN STATES, COLOMBUS MEMORIAL LIBRARY

SYNONYMOUS NAMES: OAS, Colombus Memorial Library
ADDRESS: 17th Street and Constitution Avenue, NW,
     Washington, D.C. 20006-4499,
     U. S. A.
     TEL: (202) 458-6040

CREATED: 1890   HEAD: Mr. T. L. Welch, Director
SIZE OF STAFF: Professional: 11   Other: 11   Total: 22
TYPE OF SERVICE: international; public; non-profit
SUBJECT COVERAGE: social sciences; demography; economics; education; geography;
        history; law; political science; law; human rights
GEOGRAPHICAL COVERAGE: Latin America; Caribbean area
DATA BEING PROCESSED AND SIZE: 525,000 books and pamphlets, 3,000 periodicals and
        serials; 45,000 photographs, 3,500 maps; 30,000 microforms
DATA PROCESSING METHODS: partially computerized
STORAGE MEDIA: magnetic tapes
TYPE OF ACTIVITY: distribution of information; publication
PUBLICATIONS: - Hall, G. K., Index to Latin American periodical literature 1929-1960,
        1961-1965, Boston, Mass., 1962, 8 vols.; Suppl. 1967, 2 vols.
        - Hall, G. K., Index to Latin American periodicals, Boston, Mass., Vol. 1,
        1961; Vol. 2, 1962
        - Current bibliographical information
        - Hipólito Unanue bibliographical series
CLIENTELE: researchers in the field covered by the library (20,000 p.a.)
ACCESS TO SERVICE: open to all users, free of charge
TYPE & DESCRIPTION OF SERVICES PROVIDED: Provides library services, provision of
        files of bibliographic references, of microforms (OAS official records and
        documentation of the IAC on human rights) and photocopies against payment.
        The library has also access to DIALOG and OCLC data bases.

59 - PAN AFRICAN DOCUMENTATION AND INFORMATION SYSTEM

SYNONYMOUS NAMES: PADIS
PARENT ORGANIZATION: United Nations Economic Commission for Africa
ADDRESS: UNECA/PADIS,
        P.O. Box 3001,
        Addis Ababa,
        ETHIOPIA
        TEL: 158553 - TELEX: 21029 ET
        CABLE: ECA, Addis Ababa
CREATED: 1980   HEAD: D. E. Benzine, Director
SIZE OF STAFF: Professional: 13   Other: 17   Total: 30
TYPE OF SERVICE: international; non-profit
MATERIALS DESCRIBING THE SERVICE: - What is PADIS?, brochure, 1987
WORKING LANGUAGE(S): English; French; Arabic
SUBJECT COVERAGE: social sciences; administrative sciences; demography; economics;
        social welfare; socio-economic development
GEOGRAPHICAL COVERAGE: Africa
DATA BEING PROCESSED AND SIZE: approx. 8,000 entries in PAD-DEV data base; 160,000
        time series entries in PADIS-STAT; 6,000 entries in African Experts TCDC
        data base
DATA PROCESSING METHODS: computerized
HARDWARE USED: HP 3000/58
SOFTWARE USED: MINISIS
STORAGE MEDIA: traditional shelving of publications; discs; tapes; microfiches
TYPE OF ACTIVITY: data collection; data analysis; distribution of information; SSID
        training; publication

PERIODICALS PUBLISHED: - Devindex Africa, 4 p.a.
- African Statistical Yearbook, 1 p.a.
- PADIS Newsletter, 4 p.a.
PUBLICATIONS: - Directory of African experts
CLIENTELE: ECA member states, particularly government ministries of planning and development, universities and research institutions
TYPE & DESCRIPTION OF SERVICES PROVIDED: Provides bibliographic, literature abstract and quantitative data searches, on-line interrogation of own data bases (PA DEV, PADIS-COM, PADIS-TCDC, PADIS-INST, PADIS-PROM, PADIS-STAT), and external data bases (UNDIS, ACCIS, AGRIS, LABORDOC, DEVSIS-Canada and UNIDO). Also provides selective dissemination of information, information o magnetic tapes, microforms, photocopies and a question-answering service.

60 - POPULATION COUNCIL, OFFICE OF COMMUNICATIONS

ADDRESS: One Dag Hammarskjöld Plaza,
New York,
N.Y. 10017,
U. S. A.
TEL: (212) 644-1300 - TELEX: 234722 POCO UR
CABLE: POPCOUNCIL NEW YORK
CREATED: 1952   *HEAD:* Ms. E. Churchill, Head
TYPE OF SERVICE: international; private; non-profit
MATERIALS DESCRIBING THE SERVICE: - The Population Council annual report
WORKING LANGUAGE(S): English; Spanish; French
SUBJECT COVERAGE: social sciences; demography; economics; political science; social anthropology; cultural anthropology; social welfare; sociology; demography; population problems; population increase; family planning; birth control; rural development; health
GEOGRAPHICAL COVERAGE: Developing countries; Europe; North America
DATA BEING PROCESSED AND SIZE: articles, reports, seminars, press releases
DATA PROCESSING METHODS: manual; computerized
HARDWARE USED: IBM PC XT
TYPE OF ACTIVITY: data analysis; distribution of information; SSID scientific and methodological activities; SSID training; publication
PERIODICALS PUBLISHED: - Population and Development Review, 4p.a.
- Studies in Family Planning, 6 p.a.
- NORPLANT Worldwide, 3 p.a.
- Alternatives/Alternativas, 2 p.a.
PUBLICATIONS: - Handbook for family planning operations research design, 1986
- Population factors in development planning in the Middle East, 1986
CLIENTELE: population professionals and non-specialists
ACCESS TO SERVICE: services open to specific categories of users
TYPE & DESCRIPTION OF SERVICES PROVIDED: Provides library information and technical services, searches of information from the automated bibliographic retrieva system and selective dissemination of information. Microforms, photocopies and translation facilities are also available. Has developed a software package: "FIVFIV/SINSIN" for the projects on the socioeconomic variables and "TARGET" for fertility decline projections, both intended for use on microcomputers.

51 - SCANDINAVIAN INSTITUTE OF ASIAN STUDIES, LIBRARY AND INFORMATION CENTER

SYNONYMOUS NAMES: SIAS, Library and Information Centre
ADDRESS: Njalsgade 80,
      DK-2300 Copenhagen S,
      DENMARK
      CABLE: SIASNOR
CREATED: 1967   *HEAD:* Mr. K. R. Haellquist, Head
SIZE OF STAFF: Professional: 3
TYPE OF SERVICE: international; public; non-profit
SUBJECT COVERAGE: social sciences; humanities
GEOGRAPHICAL COVERAGE: East Asia; Southeast Asia
TYPE OF ACTIVITY: distribution of information; SSID scientific and methodological
    activities; publication
PERIODICALS PUBLISHED: - Asia Yearbook
                - Asia Handbook
PUBLICATIONS: - Balser, H., Subject catalog of the library, 3rd supplement, 1987
          - Balser, H., Cumulative list of periodicals, 1985
CLIENTELE: faculties, institutions, training colleges, media
ACCESS TO SERVICE: services open to all users, free of charge
TYPE & DESCRIPTION OF SERVICES PROVIDED: Provides library services, information on
    researches and research projects, and photocopies.

52 - SOUTH PACIFIC COMMISSION, LIBRARY

SYNONYMOUS NAMES: SPC Library
PARENT ORGANIZATION: South Pacific Commission
ADDRESS: B.P. D5,
      Nouméa Cedex,
      NEW CALEDONIA
      TEL: 26.20.00 - TELEX: 3139 NM - TELEFAX: (687) 263818
      SOUTHPACOM NOUMEA
CREATED: 1947   *HEAD:* Ms. K. Berg, Librarian
SIZE OF STAFF: Professional: 2   Other: 2   Total: 4
TYPE OF SERVICE: international
MATERIALS DESCRIBING THE SERVICE: - The South Pacific Commission: history, aims and
    activities. 10th ed. Noumea: SPC, 1987
WORKING LANGUAGE(S): English; French
SUBJECT COVERAGE: demography; economics; environment; women; youth; health;
    agriculture; development; statistics; fisheries, media
GEOGRAPHICAL COVERAGE: Pacific area
CLIENTELE: researchers
ACCESS TO SERVICE: open to specific categories of users
TYPE & DESCRIPTION OF SERVICES PROVIDED: Provides library services, bibliographic
    searches and selective dissemination. Also provides on-line services using
    other data base accessed through Dialog.

63 - SPECIAL UNIT FOR TECHNICAL CO-OPERATION AMONG DEVELOPING COUNTRIES, INQUIRY SERVICES

SYNONYMOUS NAMES: TCDC/INRES;
        INRES/UNDP
PARENT ORGANIZATION: UNDP
ADDRESS: UNDP,
        1 United Nations Plaza, Room FF1248,
        New York,
        N. Y. 10017,
        U. S. A.
        TEL: (212) 906 5734
        CABLE: UNDEVPRO, New York
CREATED: 1974   *HEAD:* Mr. J. Van Eyndhoven, Principal Information Services Office
SIZE OF STAFF: Professional: 2   Other: 1   Total: 3
TYPE OF SERVICE: international; public; non-profit
WORKING LANGUAGE(S): English; Spanish; French
SUBJECT COVERAGE: social sciences; scientific cooperation; development; technology
GEOGRAPHICAL COVERAGE: Developing Countries
DATA BEING PROCESSED AND SIZE: 3,200 INRES registration forms
DATA PROCESSING METHODS: computerized
HARDWARE USED: IBM-3081 Computer INQUIRE data base
SOFTWARE USED: Infodata Inquire
STORAGE MEDIA: discs; tapes
TYPE OF ACTIVITY: data collection; distribution of information
CLIENTELE: users in developing countries and organizations of UN system (100 p. month)
ACCESS TO SERVICE: open to all users, free of charge
TYPE & DESCRIPTION OF SERVICES PROVIDED: INRES is an information referral service c
        "capacities of developing countries to assist others in technical cooperation".

64 - SURVEY RESEARCH CONSULTANTS INTERNATIONAL INC., WORLD DATA DISTRIBUTORS

ADDRESS: 156 Bulkley Street,
        P.O. Box No. 25,
        Williamstown,
        Massachusetts 01267,
        U. S. A.
        TEL: (413) 458-4414, 458-5338 - TELEX: 951-443
        CABLE: SRCINC
CREATED: 1977   *HEAD:* Mr. P. K. Hastings,
SIZE OF STAFF: Professional: 4   Other: 10   Total: 14
TYPE OF SERVICE: international; profit
SUBJECT COVERAGE: social sciences; political science; sociology
GEOGRAPHICAL COVERAGE: global
DATA BEING PROCESSED AND SIZE: Public opinion survey data (100)
DATA PROCESSING METHODS: computerized
HARDWARE USED: CDC, CYBER-74
SOFTWARE USED: SPSS-X
STORAGE MEDIA: tapes, discs

YPE OF ACTIVITY: data collection; data analysis
ERIODICALS PUBLISHED: - World Opinion Update, 12 p.a.
  - Williamstown, survey research consultants international, 1 p.a.
UBLICATIONS: - Index to international public opinion
LIENTELE: teachers, students, researchers, government officials and businessmen
CCESS TO SERVICE: open to all users, against payment
YPE & DESCRIPTION OF SERVICES PROVIDED: Offers on-line quantitative data search
  services. Also provides selective dissemination of information.

5 - UNITED NATIONS CENTRE FOR HUMAN SETTLEMENTS, INFORMATION DIVISION

YNONYMOUS NAMES: UNCHS (Habitat), Information Division;
  Centre des Nations Unies pour les Etablissements Humains, Division de
  l'Information
DDRESS: P.O. Box 30030,
  Nairobi,
  KENYA
  TEL: 333930 - TELEX: 22996
  CABLE: UN HABITAT
REATED: 1978   *HEAD:* Mr. J. Darshan,
IZE OF STAFF: Professional: 7   Other: 8   Total: 15
YPE OF SERVICE: international; public; non-profit
ATERIALS DESCRIBING THE SERVICE: - United Nations Centre for Human Settlements
  (Habitat), what it is, what it does, how it works (leaflet)
ORKING LANGUAGE(S): English; French; Spanish
UBJECT COVERAGE: human settlements
EOGRAPHICAL COVERAGE: developing countries
ATA BEING PROCESSED AND SIZE: 1,400 books; 170 periodicals; 11,300 documents; 2,570
  microfiches
ATA PROCESSING METHODS: partially computerized
ARDWARE USED: IBM XT compatible
OFTWARE USED: Micro CDS/ISIS
YPE OF ACTIVITY: distribution of information; SSID training; SSID scientific and
  methodological activities
ERIODICALS PUBLISHED:
  - Library Bulletin
UBLICATIONS: - Trilingual thesaurus in the field of human settlements
LIENTELE: educational and training institutions; governmental agencies; professional
  groups; non-governmental agencies (approx. 660 reference requests)
CCESS TO SERVICE: services open to specific categories of users, free of charge
YPE & DESCRIPTION OF SERVICES PROVIDED: Provides library services, bibliographic
  searches of information, on-line services using its own data bases: "HSLIB"
  and "HABIDOC", selective dissemination of information, films, audiovisual
  and printed materials, and photocopies. Also assists governments in the
  establishment of modern information handling techniques.

66 - UNITED NATIONS CENTRE FOR REGIONAL DEVELOPMENT, INFORMATION EXCHANGE AND PUBLICATIONS PROGRAMME

SYNONYMOUS NAMES: UNCRD, Information Exchange and Publications Programme
ADDRESS: Nagono 1-47-1,
　　　　　　Nakamura-ku,
　　　　　　Nagoya 450,
　　　　　　JAPAN
　　　　　　TEL: (052) 561-9377 - TELEX: J59620 UNCENTRE
　　　　　　CABLE: UNCENTRE Nagoya
CREATED: 1971
TYPE OF SERVICE: international
WORKING LANGUAGE(S): English; Japanese
SUBJECT COVERAGE: administrative sciences; economics; education; geography; social
　　　　welfare; sociology; regional development
GEOGRAPHICAL COVERAGE: Developing countries; Asia; Pacific area; Middle East; Latin
　　　　America; Caribbean area; Africa
DATA BEING PROCESSED AND SIZE: books (11,000 English and 3,000 Japanese); periodica
　　　　(350 English and 20 Japanese); basic texts; country studies; reference
　　　　books; government documents; maps
DATA PROCESSING METHODS: partially computerized
HARDWARE USED: NEC PC9801 VM
SOFTWARE USED: dBASE III
STORAGE MEDIA: traditional shelving of publications; discs
TYPE OF ACTIVITY: data collection; data analysis; distribution of information;
　　　　publication
PERIODICALS PUBLISHED:
　　　　- UNCRD Newsletter, 2 p.a.
　　　　- UNCRD Bulletin, 1 p.a.
PUBLICATIONS: - Country bibliographies
CLIENTELE: 5 to 10 users per day
ACCESS TO SERVICE: services open to specific categories of users, free of charge
TYPE & DESCRIPTION OF SERVICES PROVIDED: Provides library services, bibliographic
　　　　searches of information and photocopies.

67 - UNITED NATIONS CENTRE ON TRANSNATIONAL CORPORATIONS, ADVISORY AND INFORMATION SERVICES DIVISION

SYNONYMOUS NAMES: UNCTC
ADDRESS: New York,
　　　　　　N. Y. 10017,
　　　　　　U. S. A.
　　　　　　TEL: (212) 754-3176 - TELEX: UNCTNC 661062
　　　　　　CABLE: UNATIONS New York
CREATED: 1974　　　*HEAD:* Mr. S. K. B. Asante, Director
SIZE OF STAFF: Professional: 16　　　Other: 15　　　Total: 31
TYPE OF SERVICE: international
MATERIALS DESCRIBING THE SERVICE: - Users guide to the Information System on
　　　　Transnational Corporations: a technical paper, 1980
SUBJECT COVERAGE: administrative sciences; economics; law; political science;
　　　　transnational corporations; international business; international economic

relations; foreign direct investment; national development; economic growth; technology transfer
EOGRAPHICAL COVERAGE: global; developing countries
ATA PROCESSING METHODS: partially computerized
OFTWARE USED: INQUIRE; DBase III and Lotus 1-2-3
TORAGE MEDIA: traditional shelving of publications; tapes; discs; microfiches
YPE OF ACTIVITY: data collection; data analysis; distribution of information; SSID training
ERIODICALS PUBLISHED:
- CTC Reporter, 2 p.a.
UBLICATIONS: - UNCTC current studies (series)
- List of company directories and summary of their contents, 1983
- UNCTC bibliography 1974-1987, 1988
LIENTELE: officials of governments and intergovernmental organizations, trade union and business organizations, academic and research institutions
CCESS TO SERVICE: services open to specific categories of users, free of charge
YPE & DESCRIPTION OF SERVICES PROVIDED: Provides library services, bibliographic and quantitative data searches of information, selective dissemination of information, information on magnetic tapes and discs. Maintains its own data bases, "Bibliography on Transnational Corporations, Contracts and Agreements with Transnational Corporations and Corporate Database on Transnational Corporation", and has access to other data bases through DIALOG, DOW JONES, ORBIT, DUN & BROADSTREET. Also provides assistance in developing countries for the setting up of reference libraries on TNCs installation of computer systems and training of staff to operate them.

8 - UNITED NATIONS, DAG HAMMARSKJOLD LIBRARY

YNONYMOUS NAMES: DHL
DDRESS: United Nations Headquarters,
New York,
NY 10017,
U. S. A.
TEL: (212) 963-1234 - TELEX: 232422
CABLE: UNATIONS NEWYORK
REATED: 1945   *HEAD:* Mr. L. Khitrov,
IZE OF STAFF: Professional: 65   Other: 87   Total: 152
YPE OF SERVICE: international
UBJECT COVERAGE: political science; economics; international law; international relations; history and activities of the United Nations
EOGRAPHICAL COVERAGE: global
ATA BEING PROCESSED AND SIZE: 380,000 books; 15,000 periodicals; newspapers; maps
ATA PROCESSING METHODS: computerized
ARDWARE USED: IBM 3081 K
OFTWARE USED: INQUIRE
TORAGE MEDIA: traditional shelving of publications; microfiches
YPE OF ACTIVITY: data collection; data analysis; distribution of information; publication
ERIODICALS PUBLISHED:
- Current bibliographical information, 12 p.a.
- Acquisitions List, 4 p.a.

PUBLICATIONS: - UNDOC: current index
- Index to proceedings of General Assembly, Economic and Social Council, Security Council and Trusteeship Council
CLIENTELE: members of the UN Secretariat and permanent missions to the UN
ACCESS TO SERVICE: services open to specific categories of users, free of charge
TYPE & DESCRIPTION OF SERVICES PROVIDED: Provides library services, interlibrary loans, bibliographic searches of information, on-line services using its data base "UNBIS". Has also access to other data bases through DIALOG and NEXIS. Also provides selective dissemination of information, microforms a photocopies upon request.

69 - UNITED NATIONS, DEPARTMENT FOR DISARMAMENT AFFAIRS, DISARMAMENT INFORMATION BRANCH

SYNONYMOUS NAMES: DDA
ADDRESS: New York,
N. Y. 10017,
U. S. A.
TEL: (212) 963-5938 - TELEX: 62450 UNATIONS NYK
CABLE: UNATIONS NETWORK
CREATED: 1983
SIZE OF STAFF: Professional: 13   Other: 8   Total: 21
TYPE OF SERVICE: international
SYSTEMS & NETWORKS ATTACHED TO: UN Computer System
MATERIALS DESCRIBING THE SERVICE: - UN disarmament machinery - Fact Sheet No. 35
WORKING LANGUAGE(S): English
SUBJECT COVERAGE: economics; political science; disarmament
GEOGRAPHICAL COVERAGE: global
DATA BEING PROCESSED AND SIZE: books; articles; reports; on-going research; seminar training courses
DATA PROCESSING METHODS: computerized
HARDWARE USED: IBM 3272
SOFTWARE USED: Inquiere PQ-1; UNBIS; Mark IV
STORAGE MEDIA: traditional shelving of publications; fiches; tapes; discs; microfiches
TYPE OF ACTIVITY: data collection; data analysis; distribution of information; SSI scientific and methodological activities
CLIENTELE: 159 member states, research institutes, scholars
ACCESS TO SERVICE: services open to specific categories of users
TYPE & DESCRIPTION OF SERVICES PROVIDED: Provides library services, bibliographic search of information, on-line services, selective dissemination of information and photocopies.

70 - UNITED NATIONS, DEPARTMENT OF INTERNATIONAL ECONOMIC AND SOCIAL AFFAIRS, DEVELOPMENT INFORMATION SYSTEM

SYNONYMOUS NAMES: UN/DIS
ADDRESS: Room DC2-1772,
New York,

N. Y. 10017,
U. S. A.
TEL: (212) 963.4839
CABLE: UNATIONS NEW YORK
CREATED: 1978   *HEAD:* Ms. L. N. Mutter, Officer-in-Charge
SIZE OF STAFF: Professional: 3   Other: 2   Total: 5
TYPE OF SERVICE: international; public; non-profit
MATERIALS DESCRIBING THE SERVICE: - The Development Information System of DIESA, brochure
WORKING LANGUAGE(S): English
SUBJECT COVERAGE: social sciences; economics; demography; social welfare; administrative sciences; criminology; natural resources; energy; transport; transnational corporations; statistics; information management; finance; industry; population; family planning; women; youth; crime; socio-economic development
GEOGRAPHICAL COVERAGE: global
DATA BEING PROCESSED AND SIZE: 11,000 unpublished reports
DATA PROCESSING METHODS: computerized
HARDWARE USED: Hewlett Packard 3000 ser. 30; minicomputer
SOFTWARE USED: MINISIS
STORAGE MEDIA: tapes; disks; microfiches
TYPE OF ACTIVITY: data collection; data analysis; publication
PERIODICALS PUBLISHED:
    - Development information abstracts, 6 p.a.
PUBLICATIONS: - Catalogue with abstracts of studies in the field of transport, 1983
    - Macro thesaurus for information processing in the field of economic and social development, 1985
CLIENTELE: government officials and UN officers
ACCESS TO SERVICE: services open to all users, free of charge
TYPE & DESCRIPTION OF SERVICES PROVIDED: Computerized bibliographic information storage and on-line retrieval system providing retrospective bibliographic searches, selective dissemination of information; also provides documents in hardcopy and distribution of copies of DIS data base on tape .

71 - UNITED NATIONS, DEPARTMENT OF INTERNATIONAL ECONOMIC AND SOCIAL AFFAIRS, POPULATION INFORMATION NETWORK

SYNONYMOUS NAMES: POPIN
PARENT ORGANIZATION: United Nations
ADDRESS: Population Division,
    United Nations Headquarters,
    New York,
    NT 10017,
    U. S. A.
    Tel: (212) 963-3186 - TELEX: 232 422
    CABLE: UNATIONS NEW YORK
SIZE OF STAFF: Professional: 2   Other: 1   Total: 3
TYPE OF SERVICE: international; non-profit
MATERIALS DESCRIBING THE SERVICE: - Popin brochure
SUBJECT COVERAGE: demography; economics; population; population policy; migration; urbanization; family planning; fertility; mortality; projections;

environment; development
GEOGRAPHICAL COVERAGE: global
DATA PROCESSING METHODS: manual
STORAGE MEDIA: traditional shelving of publications
TYPE OF ACTIVITY: data collection; distribution of information
PERIODICALS PUBLISHED:
    - POPIN Bulletin
PUBLICATIONS: - Guide to the computerization of population documentation storage and
    retrieval systems
    - Guide to selecting a classification scheme for a population information
    centre
    - Guide to networking for population information centres
    - POPIN thesaurus: population multilingual thesaurus
TYPE & DESCRIPTION OF SERVICES PROVIDED: Provides library services, bibliographic
    searches of information and selective dissemination of information.

72 - UNITED NATIONS, DEPARTMENT OF POLITICAL AND SECURITY COUNCIL AFFAIRS, CENTRE AGAINST APARTHEID: PUBLICITY, ASSISTANCE, PROMOTION OF INTERNATIONAL ACTION BRANCH

ADDRESS: New York,
    N.Y. 10017,
    U. S. A.
    TEL: 963-5315 - TELEX: 62450-82731
    CABLE: UNATIONS NEWYORK
CREATED: 1967   HEAD: Mr. A. Abrous, Chief
SIZE OF STAFF: Professional: 8   Other: 6   Total: 14
TYPE OF SERVICE: international; non-profit
MATERIALS DESCRIBING THE SERVICE: - United Nations Centre against Apartheid, New
    York, 1986 (brochure)
WORKING LANGUAGE(S): English; French
SUBJECT COVERAGE: political science; law; apartheid; racial discrimination; human
    rights; political prisoners; nuclear weapons;
GEOGRAPHICAL COVERAGE: global
DATA BEING PROCESSED AND SIZE: notes and documents, press releases, information
    notes, seminar and conference reports, studies, leaflets, pamphlets, slide
    posters
DATA PROCESSING METHODS: manual
TYPE OF ACTIVITY: data collection; data analysis; publication
PERIODICALS PUBLISHED:
    - News Digest
    - Notes and Documents, Regular Series/Special Issues
    - Information Note
PUBLICATIONS: - Consolidated list of documents and publications indexes (1983-1986)
CLIENTELE: governments, medias, anti-apartheid movements, non-governmental
    organizations
ACCESS TO SERVICE: services open to specific categories of users, free of charge
TYPE & DESCRIPTION OF SERVICES PROVIDED: Depositary library of United Nations
    providing selective dissemination of information.

73 - UNITED NATIONS ECONOMIC AND SOCIAL COMMISSION FOR WESTERN ASIA, LIBRARY AND DOCUMENTATION SECTION

SYNONYMOUS NAMES: UNESCWA, Library
ADDRESS: Division of Administration,
P.O. Box 27,
Airport Road,
Baghdad,
IRAQ
TEL: 556-9400 - TELEX: 213303 UNECWA IK
CABLE: UNATIONS, ECWA
CREATED: 1962   *HEAD:* R. C. Bordcosh, Chief
SIZE OF STAFF: Professional: 1   Other: 6   Total: 7
TYPE OF SERVICE: international
SYSTEMS & NETWORKS ATTACHED TO: United Nations (UN)
MATERIALS DESCRIBING THE SERVICE: - UNESCWA - Library user's guide
WORKING LANGUAGE(S): Arabic; English; French
SUBJECT COVERAGE: social sciences; demography; economics; social welfare; sociology;
statistics; agriculture; industry; natural resources
GEOGRAPHICAL COVERAGE: Bahrain; Democratic Yemen; Egypt; Iraq; Jordan; Kuwait;
Lebanon; Oman; Qatar; Saudi Arabia; Syrian Arab Republic; United Arab
Emirates; Yemen; Palestine Liberation Organization
DATA BEING PROCESSED AND SIZE: 10,000 documentation items
DATA PROCESSING METHODS: computerized
SOFTWARE USED: CDS/Micro ISIS
STORAGE MEDIA: traditional shelving of publications; microfiches
TYPE OF ACTIVITY: data collection; data analysis; distribution of information; SSID
scientific and methodological activities; SSID training
PERIODICALS PUBLISHED:
- Table of Contents of Periodicals Received at ESCWA Library
- Acquisition List - ESCWA Library
PUBLICATIONS: - Special bibliography series: women
CLIENTELE: government officials, university professors, students, researchers, UN
experts (1,300)
ACCESS TO SERVICE: services open to specific categories of users, free of charge
TYPE & DESCRIPTION OF SERVICES PROVIDED: Provides library services, bibliographic
searches, selective dissemination of information, photocopies.

74 - UNITED NATIONS ECONOMIC COMMISSION FOR AFRICA, POPULATION DIVISION, INFORMATION SERVICE

SYNONYMOUS NAMES: POPIN-Africa
ADDRESS: P.O. Box 3001,
Addis Ababa,
ETHIOPIA
TEL: 44.72.00
CABLE: ECA, Addis Ababa
CREATED: 1984   *HEAD:* Mr. A. Bahri, Chief, Population Division
SIZE OF STAFF: Professional: 3   Other: 4   Total: 7
TYPE OF SERVICE: international; non-profit
SYSTEMS & NETWORKS ATTACHED TO: POPIN Global

WORKING LANGUAGE(S): English; French
SUBJECT COVERAGE: demography; economics; education; law; sociology; population; social sciences
GEOGRAPHICAL COVERAGE: all 50 ECA member states; Africa
DATA BEING PROCESSED AND SIZE: books; periodicals; reports; seminars
DATA PROCESSING METHODS: computerized
HARDWARE USED: HP 3000
SOFTWARE USED: MINISIS
TYPE OF ACTIVITY: data collection; data analysis; distribution of information; SSIC scientific and methodological activities; publication
PERIODICALS PUBLISHED:
  - African Population Newsletter, 2 p.a.
PUBLICATIONS: - POPINDEX-Africa
  - African directory of demographers
  - African population studies series
CLIENTELE: researchers, planners, demographers
ACCESS TO SERVICE: services open to all users, free of charge
TYPE & DESCRIPTION OF SERVICES PROVIDED: Provides library services, bibliographic, literature abstract and quantitative data searches, on-line searches using own data base "POPIN", selective dissemination of information, production of information on magnetic tapes and photocopies.

75 - UNITED NATIONS EDUCATIONAL, SCIENTIFIC AND CULTURAL ORGANIZATION, REGIONAL OFFICE FOR CULTURE IN LATIN AMERICA AND THE CARIBBEAN, DOCUMENTATION CENTRE

SYNONYMOUS NAMES: Organización de las Naciones Unidades para la Educación, la Ciencia y la Cultura, Oficina Regional de Cultura para América Latina y el Caribe, Centro de Documentación;
UNESCO Regional Office for Culture in Latin America and the Caribbean, Documentation Centre;
UNESCO Oficina Regional de Cultura para América Latina y el Caribe, Centro de Documentación
ADDRESS: Calzada 551,
  Vedado,
  Apartado 4158,
  La Habana - 4,
  CUBA
  TEL: 32-7741 - TELEX: 512154 UNESCO CU
  CABLE: UNESCO-HABANA
CREATED: 1978   *HEAD:* Mrs. Y. Arencibia Huidobro, Librarian
SIZE OF STAFF: Professional: 3   Other: 1   Total: 4
SYSTEMS & NETWORKS ATTACHED TO: Unesco Integrated Documentation Network
MATERIALS DESCRIBING THE SERVICE: - Brochure
SUBJECT COVERAGE: social sciences; humanities; cultural development; culture; histo
GEOGRAPHICAL COVERAGE: Latin America; Caribbean Area
DATA BEING PROCESSED AND SIZE: 10,000 documentation items
DATA PROCESSING METHODS: manual; partially computerized
HARDWARE USED: IBM PC-XT
SOFTWARE USED: MICRO-ISIS
STORAGE MEDIA: traditional shelving of publications
PERIODICALS PUBLISHED:

- Informaciones Trimestrales, 4 p.a.
- Accession List
PUBLICATIONS: - Elementos para una bibliografía sobre folklore, cultura, y educación permanente en América latina
- Las Ciencias sociales en el proceso de desarrollo de la América latina y Africa, 1978
- Comunidad idiomática entre Hispanoamérica y España en el lapso colonial, 1980
- Función histórica de los elementos ibéricos en el desarrollo de las culturas latinoamericanas, 1980
- Movimientos migratorios en América latina y el Caribe. Bibliografía, 1981
- El Caribe. Bibliografía, 1982
CLIENTELE: university researchers, teachers, experts
ACCESS TO SERVICE: open to specific categories of users, free of charge
TYPE & DESCRIPTION OF SERVICES PROVIDED: Provides library services and bibliographies using its own data base "INFO". Its purpose is to promote cultural development and to disseminate Latin American culture and history.

76 - UNITED NATIONS EDUCATIONAL, SCIENTIFIC AND CULTURAL ORGANIZATION, SOCIAL AND HUMAN SCIENCES DOCUMENTATION CENTRE ·

SYNONYMOUS NAMES: UNESCO Social and Human Sciences Documentation Centre;
Organisation des Nations Unies pour l'Education, la Science et la Culture, Centre de Documentation des Sciences Sociales et Humaines;
UNESCO Centre de Documentation des Sciences Sociales et Humaines
ADDRESS: 7, place Fontenoy,
75700 Paris,
FRANCE
TEL: (1) 45.68.38.06 - TELEX: 270602, 204461
CABLE: UNESCO, PARIS
CREATED: 1975
SIZE OF STAFF: Total: 4
TYPE OF SERVICE: international; public; non-profit
SYSTEMS & NETWORKS ATTACHED TO: Unesco's Computerized Documentation System
MATERIALS DESCRIBING THE SERVICE: - DARE, Unesco computerized data retrieval system for documentation in the social sciences. Reports and papers in the social sciences, No. 27, 1972
- DARE information management system, a condensed system description (computer design version 2). Reports and papers in the social sciences, No. 31, 1975
SUBJECT COVERAGE: social sciences
GEOGRAPHICAL COVERAGE: global
DATA BEING PROCESSED AND SIZE: data on social science institutions, specialists, research projects, periodicals, information services and information courses
DATA PROCESSING METHODS: computerized
HARDWARE USED: IBM 3083
SOFTWARE USED: CDS/ISIS, WYLBUR
TYPE OF ACTIVITY: data collection; data analysis; distribution of information; SSID scientific and methodological activities; publication
PERIODICALS PUBLISHED:
- Information Note

PUBLICATIONS: - World list of social science periodicals, 1986
- World directory of social science institutions, 1985
- Selective inventory of information services, 1985
- World directory of peace research and training institutions, 1988
- Directory of social science information courses, 1988
- World directory of human rights teaching and research institutions, 1988
CLIENTELE: scholars and institutions in Member States, international organizations
ACCESS TO SERVICE: open to all users, free of charge
TYPE & DESCRIPTION OF SERVICES PROVIDED: Provides current awareness services, selective printouts of data from its own data base "DARE", referral and liaison service.

77 - UNITED NATIONS FUND FOR POPULATION ACTIVITIES, LIBRARY

SYNONYMOUS NAMES: Fonds des Nations Unies pour les Activités en Matière de Population, Bibliothèque
ADDRESS: 220 E. 42nd Street, Room DN-170,
New York,
N.Y. 10017,
U. S. A.
TEL: (212) 850-5809 - TELEX: 422031, 422 038 - TELEFAX: 212-370-0201
CREATED: 1969   *HEAD:* A. Green, Chief, Library and Population Information Service Unit
SIZE OF STAFF: Professional: 2   Other: 1   Total: 3
SUBJECT COVERAGE: demography; social welfare; economics; sociology; population; family planning; maternal and child health
GEOGRAPHICAL COVERAGE: global
DATA BEING PROCESSED AND SIZE: books, articles, reports, on-going research, seminar training courses, audio-visual materials; (approx. 4,000 in all)
DATA PROCESSING METHODS: partially computerized
HARDWARE USED: PC
SOFTWARE USED: MICRO-ISIS, DATA TREK
STORAGE MEDIA: traditional shelving of publications
TYPE OF ACTIVITY: distribution of information
CLIENTELE: specialists and the general public
ACCESS TO SERVICE: open to all users
TYPE & DESCRIPTION OF SERVICES PROVIDED: Provides library services, bibliographic a literature abstract searches of information, selective dissemination of information with on-line services using own data base "Library Catalog". Has also access to external data bases MEDLINE/POPLINE, DIALOG, NEXUS through TELEMET. Photocopies can be provided upon request.

78 - UNITED NATIONS HIGH COMMISSIONER FOR REFUGEES, CENTRE FOR DOCUMENTATION ON REFUGEES

SYNONYMOUS NAMES: UNHCR/CDR;
Haut Commissariat des Nations Unies pour les Réfugiés, Centre de Documentation sur les Réfugiés
ADDRESS: Case Postale 2500,

CH-1211 Geneva 2 Dépot,
SWITZERLAND
TEL: 398111 - TELEX: 27492 UNHCR CH
CABLE: HICOMREF Geneva
REATED: 1987   *HEAD:* Mr. J. Thoolen, Chief
IZE OF STAFF: Professional: 4   Other: 4   Total: 8
YPE OF SERVICE: international; public; non-profit
YSTEMS & NETWORKS ATTACHED TO: UNHCR
ATERIALS DESCRIBING THE SERVICE: - Information paper
ORKING LANGUAGE(S): English; French; Spanish
UBJECT COVERAGE: social welfare; education; law; political science; refugees
EOGRAPHICAL COVERAGE: global
ATA BEING PROCESSED AND SIZE: monographs, reports, articles
ATA PROCESSING METHODS: computerized
OFTWARE USED: INQUIRE
TORAGE MEDIA: traditional shelving of publications, microfiches
YPE OF ACTIVITY: data collection; data analysis; distribution of information;
      publication
ERIODICALS PUBLISHED:
      - Refugee Abstracts, 4 p.a.
UBLICATIONS: - Bibliography on refugee women, 1985
      - Bibliography on refugee children, 1987
      - International bibliography of refugee literature, 1985
LIENTELE: 2,200 users requesting information p.a.
CCESS TO SERVICE: services open to specific categories of users, free of charge
YPE & DESCRIPTION OF SERVICES PROVIDED: Provides question answering services,
      bibliographic and literature abstract searches of information using its own
      data base "Refugee Abstracts" and photocopies against payment.

79 - UNITED NATIONS REGIONAL INSTITUTE FOR POPULATION STUDIES, LIBRARY

YNONYMOUS NAMES: RIPS, Library
ARENT ORGANIZATION: Economic Commission for Africa (ECA)
DDRESS: University of Ghana,
      P.O. Box 96,
      Legon,
      GHANA
      TEL: 774070 - TELEX: 2164 RIPS GH
      CABLE: RIPS, ACCRA
REATED: 1972
IZE OF STAFF: Total: 35
YPE OF SERVICE: international; public; non-profit
YSTEMS & NETWORKS ATTACHED TO: Economic Commission for Africa (ECA)
ORKING LANGUAGE(S): English
UBJECT COVERAGE: social sciences; demography; economics; cultural anthropology;
      sociology
EOGRAPHICAL COVERAGE: English speaking Africa
ATA BEING PROCESSED AND SIZE: African censuses and surveys since the 1960s; World
      Fertility Survey data for African countries
ATA PROCESSING METHODS: computerized
ARDWARE USED: WANG VS 80

SOFTWARE USED: SCSS, MCA, MINITAB
STORAGE MEDIA: tapes, discs, microfiches
TYPE OF ACTIVITY: data collection; data analysis; distribution of information; SSID
    scientific and methodological activities; SSID training; publication
PERIODICALS PUBLISHED:
    - RIPS Newsletter
PUBLICATIONS: - Monograph series
    - Occasional paper series
    - Working paper series
    - Bibliographic series
CLIENTELE: national statistics offices; census bureaus; universities; research
    centres
ACCESS TO SERVICE: services open to all users, free of charge
TYPE & DESCRIPTION OF SERVICES PROVIDED: Provides library services, bibliographic,
    literature abstract and quantitative data searches of information, selecti
    dissemination of information and photocopies.

80 - UNITED NATIONS RESEARCH INSTITUTE FOR SOCIAL DEVELOPMENT, REFERENCE CENTRE

SYNONYMOUS NAMES: UNRISD, Reference Centre
PARENT ORGANIZATION: United Nations
ADDRESS: Palais des Nations,
        CH-1211 Geneva,
        SWITZERLAND
        TEL: 98 84 00 - TELEX: 28.96.96
        CABLE: UNATIONS, Geneva
CREATED: 1963   HEAD: Ms. F. Jaffré,
SIZE OF STAFF: Professional: 1
TYPE OF SERVICE: international; public; non-profit
SYSTEMS & NETWORKS ATTACHED TO: UM Library's network, Geneva
WORKING LANGUAGE(S): English; French; Spanish
SUBJECT COVERAGE: social sciences; economics; political science; social anthropolog
    sociology; social development
GEOGRAPHICAL COVERAGE: global
DATA BEING PROCESSED AND SIZE: 2,000 books, 200 periodicals, seminars; UNRISD books
    on sale
DATA PROCESSING METHODS: manual; computerized
HARDWARE USED: ICC Computer, Geneva; IBM 370/158 Model J
SOFTWARE USED: own and ICC software
STORAGE MEDIA: traditional shelving of publications
TYPE OF ACTIVITY: data collection; distribution of information; publication
PERIODICALS PUBLISHED:
    - Research notes
CLIENTELE: students, universities, research institutes, U.N. organizations
ACCESS TO SERVICE: open to all users, free of charge
TYPE & DESCRIPTION OF SERVICES PROVIDED: Provides library services, bibliographic a
    quantitative data searches of information, selective dissemination of
    information, information on magnetic tapes or discs and photocopies.

81 - UNITED NATIONS SOCIAL DEFENCE RESEARCH INSTITUTE, INFORMATION SERVICE

SYNONYMOUS NAMES: UNSDRI, Information Service;
Institut de Recherche des Nations Unies sur la Défense Sociale, Service de Documentation
ADDRESS: Via Giulia 52,
00186 Rome,
ITALY
TEL: 6877437 - TELEX: 610181 FAO I UNSDRI
CABLE: UNSDRI 00186 Rome
CREATED: 1968   *HEAD:* Ms. M. E. Andreotti, Librarian
SIZE OF STAFF: Professional: 1   Other: 2   Total: 3
TYPE OF SERVICE: international; public; non-profit
SUBJECT COVERAGE: law; criminology; sociology
GEOGRAPHICAL COVERAGE: global
DATA BEING PROCESSED AND SIZE: 35,000 books; periodicals; UN and Council of Europe documents
DATA PROCESSING METHODS: manual
STORAGE MEDIA: traditional shelving of publications, microfiches
TYPE OF ACTIVITY: distribution of information
CLIENTELE: researchers, university teachers, government officials (100 p.a.)
ACCESS TO SERVICE: services open to specific categories of users, free of charge
TYPE & DESCRIPTION OF SERVICES PROVIDED: Provides library services, bibliographic searches of information and selective dissemination of information.

82 - THE UNITED NATIONS UNIVERSITY, LIBRARY SERVICES UNIT

ADDRESS: Toho Seimei Building, 28th floor,
15-1, Shibuya 2-chome,
Shibuya-ku,
Tokyo 150,
JAPAN
TEL: (03) 499-2811 - TELEX: J25442 UNATUNIV - TELEFAX: 03-499-2828
CABLE: UNATUNIV TOKYO
CREATED: 1973   *HEAD:* Dr. F. Schindeler, Director of Dissemination
SIZE OF STAFF: Total: 2
TYPE OF SERVICE: international; public; non-profit
MATERIALS DESCRIBING THE SERVICE: - Directory of United Nations Information Systems (IOB)
WORKING LANGUAGE(S): English
SUBJECT COVERAGE: social sciences; social anthropology; cultural anthropology; political science; sociology; development; welfare
GEOGRAPHICAL COVERAGE: global
DATA BEING PROCESSED AND SIZE: 10,000 books and reports; 350 periodicals; selected UN and UN system documents
DATA PROCESSING METHODS: computerized
HARDWARE USED: FACOM-M-200 through time sharing service
SOFTWARE USED: FAIRS
STORAGE MEDIA: traditional shelving of publications; microfiches
TYPE OF ACTIVITY: data collection; distribution of information; publication
PERIODICALS PUBLISHED:

- List of New Library Acquisitions
PUBLICATIONS: - Indexes
CLIENTELE: UNU Network
ACCESS TO SERVICE: services open to specific categories of users
TYPE & DESCRIPTION OF SERVICES PROVIDED: Provides library services, bibliographic
   searches, surveys, reference and delivery services and on-line services
   using own database "UNU Library Catalogue" as well as external databases
   such as DIALOG and "Nichigai ASSIST".

83 - UNIVERSIDAD EAFIT, CONSEJO DE DOCUMENTACIÓN E INTERCAMBIO DE CASOS

SYNONYMOUS NAMES: CEDO
PARENT ORGANIZATION: Consejo Latinoamericano de Escuelas de Administración (CLADEA)
ADDRESS: Carrera 49 no. 7Sur-50,
   Apartado Aéreo 3300,
   Medellín,
   Antioquia,
   COLOMBIA
   TEL: 2660500
CREATED: 1973   *HEAD:* M. I. Restrepo de Sánchez, Director
SIZE OF STAFF: Professional: 1   Other: 1   Total: 2
TYPE OF SERVICE: international; non-profit
WORKING LANGUAGE(S): Spanish
SUBJECT COVERAGE: administrative sciences; economics
GEOGRAPHICAL COVERAGE: Latin America
DATA BEING PROCESSED AND SIZE: 1,500 cases and technical notes
DATA PROCESSING METHODS: computerized
HARDWARE USED: NAS/AS/5-3
SOFTWARE USED: Total, SAS
TYPE OF ACTIVITY: data analysis; distribution of information; publication
PERIODICALS PUBLISHED:
   - Annual Bibliography
   - Current Awareness
CLIENTELE: teachers and researchers
ACCESS TO SERVICE: open to specific categories of users, paid services
TYPE & DESCRIPTION OF SERVICES PROVIDED: Main activities include the compilation of
   an annual bibliography of cases furnished by CLADEA members. Also provides
   literature abstract services, on-line service using own database, selective
   dissemination of information and photocopies.

84 - WORLD BANK, INTERNATIONAL ECONOMIC DEPARTMENT, SOCIO-ECONOMIC DATA DIVISION

ADDRESS: 1818 H Street, N.W.,
   Washington, DC 20433,
   U. S. A.
   TEL: 477-1234 - TELEX: RCA 248423
   CABLE: INTBAFRAD Washington
HEAD: Mr. J. O'Connor, Chief
TYPE OF SERVICE: international

SUBJECT COVERAGE: demography; economics; education; socio-economic indicators
DATA PROCESSING METHODS: computerized
HARDWARE USED: IBM 3090; IBM PC AT/XT
SOFTWARE USED: LOTUS; DBASE III; EXPRESS/M2O4
STORAGE MEDIA: hard discs; back-up tapes
TYPE OF ACTIVITY: data collection; data analysis; distribution of information;
        publication
PUBLICATIONS: - World tables
ACCESS TO SERVICE: services open to specific categories of users
TYPE & DESCRIPTION OF SERVICES PROVIDED: Provides selective dissemination of
        information and production of information on magnetic tapes or discs from
        the "Bank Economic and Social Database" (BEDS), and IEC working files.

Algeria / Algérie / Argelia

85 - CENTRE NATIONAL DE DOCUMENTATION ECONOMIQUE

SYNONYMOUS NAMES: CNIDE;
        The National Centre of Economic Information and Documentation
PARENT ORGANIZATION: Ministère de la Planification et de l'Aménagement du Territoire
ADDRESS: Chemin Ibn Badis El Mouiz,
        El Biar,
        Algiers,
        ALGERIA
        TEL: 78.03.23 - Telex: 52.560 DZ
CREATED: 1981   *HEAD:* A. Tahar, Director-General
SIZE OF STAFF: Professional: 6   Other: 29   Total: 35
TYPE OF SERVICE: national; public; non-profit
SYSTEMS & NETWORKS ATTACHED TO: AGRIS, Infoterra
WORKING LANGUAGE(S): French
SUBJECT COVERAGE: economics; demography
GEOGRAPHICAL COVERAGE: Algeria; Northern Africa; Mediterranean Area
DATA BEING PROCESSED AND SIZE: economic studies, regulations
DATA PROCESSING METHODS: manual
STORAGE MEDIA: traditional shelving of publications, microfiches
TYPE OF ACTIVITY: publication
PUBLICATIONS: - Catalogue des études en dépôt légal au Ministère de la Planification
        et de l'Aménagement du Territoire
        - Catalogue des textes réglementaires organisant l'économie algérienne de
        1962 à 1983
CLIENTELE: planners, researchers, students
ACCESS TO SERVICE: open to all users, free of charge
TYPE & DESCRIPTION OF SERVICES PROVIDED: Provides catalogues and files.

86 - UNIVERSITÉ D'ORAN, CENTRE DE RECHERCHE ET D'INFORMATION DOCUMENTAIRE EN SCIENCES SOCIALES ET HUMAINES

SYNONYMOUS NAMES: CRIDSSH
ADDRESS: 87-89, rue Larbi Ben M'Hidi,
        Oran,

ALGERIA
TEL: 39-70-50
CREATED: 1979   *HEAD:* M. N. Mahieddin, Director
SIZE OF STAFF: Professional: 2   Other: 9   Total: 11
TYPE OF SERVICE: national; public; non-profit
WORKING LANGUAGE(S): Arabic; French; English
SUBJECT COVERAGE: social sciences; economics; history; law; linguistics; psychology
GEOGRAPHICAL COVERAGE: Algeria; Africa; Middle East; Islamic countries; North
    America; Europe
DATA BEING PROCESSED AND SIZE: 16,000 book and theses; 1,000 periodicals
DATA PROCESSING METHODS: manual
STORAGE MEDIA: traditional shelving of publications
TYPE OF ACTIVITY: data collection; publication
PERIODICALS PUBLISHED: - Cahiers du CRIDSSH
    - Etudes et Documents (séries histoire, géographie, droit)
    - Matériaux Bibliographiques
    - Documents de Travail du CRIDSSH
    - Chronique Législative
PUBLICATIONS: - Elaidi, A.; Taleb, M., Lexique économique et social (Français/Arabe)
    1982
CLIENTELE: students, teachers, researchers
ACCESS TO SERVICE: open to specific categories of users, free of charge
TYPE & DESCRIPTION OF SERVICES PROVIDED: Provides library services, assistance to
    research, exchange of publications.

**87 - UNIVERSITÉ D'ORAN, UNITÉ DE RECHERCHE EN ANTHROPOLOGIE SOCIALE ET CULTURELLE,
BIBLIOTHÈQUE UNIVERSITAIRE**

SYNONYMOUS NAMES: URASC, Bibliothèque Universitaire;
    University of Oran, Cultural and Social Anthropology Research Unit,
    University Library;
    CSARU, University Library
PARENT ORGANIZATION: Ministère de l'Enseignement Supérieur
ADDRESS: Ex CERDRO,
    B.P. 1524,
    Es-Senia,
    Oran,
    ALGERIA
    TEL: 34-01-25
CREATED: 1985   *HEAD:* Mr. F. Bentabet,
SIZE OF STAFF: Professional: 3   Other: 5   Total: 8
TYPE OF SERVICE: national; public; non-profit
MATERIALS DESCRIBING THE SERVICE: - Les Actes de l'URASC, annuaire 1985, 1986
    - Qu'est-ce que l'URASC? brochure d'information, 1985
WORKING LANGUAGE(S): Arabic; French
SUBJECT COVERAGE: social anthropology; cultural anthropology; social sciences
GEOGRAPHICAL COVERAGE: Algeria; Maghreb, Northern Africa; Arab countries; Africa
DATA PROCESSING METHODS: manual
TYPE OF ACTIVITY: distribution of information; publication
CLIENTELE: researchers
ACCESS TO SERVICE: services open to specific categories of users, free of charge

YPE & DESCRIPTION OF SERVICES PROVIDED: Provides library services.

Angola

8 - CENTRO NACIONAL DE DOCUMENTAÇÃO E INVESTIGAÇÃO HISTÓRICA

YNONYMOUS NAMES: National Centre of Historical Documentation and Research
ARENT ORGANIZATION: Secretaria de Estado da cultura
DDRESS: CP 1267-C,
        Rua Pedro Félix Machado 49,
        Luanda,
        ANGOLA
        TEL: 334410 - TELEX: 4129
REATED: 1977   *HEAD:* Ms. A. da Fonseca Ferreira, Director
IZE OF STAFF: Total: 9
YPE OF SERVICE: national; public; non-profit
ATERIALS DESCRIBING THE SERVICE: - Centro Nacional de Documentação e Investigação
        Historica da Secretaria de Estado da Cultura
ORKING LANGUAGE(S): Portuguese
UBJECT COVERAGE: history; cultural anthropology; social sciences
EOGRAPHICAL COVERAGE: Central Africa; Southern Africa
ATA BEING PROCESSED AND SIZE: books; articles; reports; training courses
ATA PROCESSING METHODS: manual
TORAGE MEDIA: traditional shelving of publications; fiches; microfilms
YPE OF ACTIVITY: data collection; distribution of information; SSID scientific and
        methodological activities; SSID training; publication
ERIODICALS PUBLISHED:
        - Accession Lists
        - Guia de Informação documental
LIENTELE: teachers, students
CCESS TO SERVICE: services open to all users, free of charge
YPE & DESCRIPTION OF SERVICES PROVIDED: Provides library services, bibliographic and
        quantitative data searches and selective dissemination of information.

Argentina / Argentine / Argentina

39 - ACADEMIA NACIONAL DE LA HISTORIA, BIBLIOTECA

SYNONYMOUS NAMES: National Academy of History, Library
ADDRESS: Balcarce 139,
        1064 Buenos Aires,
        ARGENTINA
        TEL: 331-4633
CREATED: 1893   *HEAD:* Mrs. G. G. Barcala de Moyano, Head Librarian
SIZE OF STAFF: Total: 2
TYPE OF SERVICE: national; public; non-profit
MATERIALS DESCRIBING THE SERVICE: - Breve reseña (brochure)
WORKING LANGUAGE(S): Spanish
SUBJECT COVERAGE: social sciences; history
GEOGRAPHICAL COVERAGE: Argentina; Europe; Latin America
DATA BEING PROCESSED AND SIZE: 50,000 books, periodicals and reports

Argentina / Argentine / Argentina

DATA PROCESSING METHODS: partially computerized
HARDWARE USED: IBM-PC Modelo "A"
SOFTWARE USED: MICRO-ISIS Unesco
STORAGE MEDIA: traditional shelving of publications, fiches, discs
TYPE OF ACTIVITY: data collection; data analysis; distribution of information; SSID
     scientific and methodological activities; publication
PERIODICALS PUBLISHED: - Investigaciones y Ensayos, 2 p.a.
     - Indice General de Todos los Trabajos Publicados
     - Boletin de la Academia Nacional de la Historia, 1 p.a.
CLIENTELE: academics, researchers, students (2,500 persons p.a.)
ACCESS TO SERVICE: services open to all users, free of charge
TYPE & DESCRIPTION OF SERVICES PROVIDED: Library services include bibliographic and
     literature searches as well as selective dissemination of information and
     provision of photocopies.

90 - BANCO DE LA NACIÓN ARGENTINA, BIBLIOTECA MANUEL BELGRANO

PARENT ORGANIZATION: Banco de la Nación Argentina
ADDRESS: Bartolome Mitre 326,
     Buenos Aires 1036,
     ARGENTINA
     TEL: 34-4041
CREATED: 1946   HEAD: Mr. N. Sidero, Director
SIZE OF STAFF: Professional: 3
TYPE OF SERVICE: national; private; non-profit
WORKING LANGUAGE(S): Spanish
SUBJECT COVERAGE: economics; law; administrative sciences; agriculture; finance
GEOGRAPHICAL COVERAGE: global
DATA BEING PROCESSED AND SIZE: 8,000 books; 65 periodicals
DATA PROCESSING METHODS: manual
STORAGE MEDIA: traditional shelving of publications; fiches
TYPE OF ACTIVITY: data collection; distribution of information
CLIENTELE: civil servants, teachers, researchers
ACCESS TO SERVICE: services open to specific categories of users, free of charge
TYPE & DESCRIPTION OF SERVICES PROVIDED: Provides library services, searches of
     information and selective dissemination of information.

91 - BIBLIOTECA CENTRAL "DR. ROBERTO REPETTO"

SYNONYMOUS NAMES: Central Library "Dr. Roberto Repetto" of the Supreme Court of
     Justice
PARENT ORGANIZATION: Corte Suprema de Justicia de la Nación
ADDRESS: Talcahuano 550 - 7 piso,
     1013 Buenos Aires,
     ARGENTINA
     TEL: 40.9167
CREATED: 1950   HEAD: Mrs. A. M. Agüero de Franco, Librarian
SIZE OF STAFF: Professional: 3   Other: 17   Total: 20
TYPE OF SERVICE: public; non-profit

WORKING LANGUAGE(S): Spanish
SUBJECT COVERAGE: law; political science
GEOGRAPHICAL COVERAGE: Argentina
DATA BEING PROCESSED AND SIZE: 25,000 books; 500 periodicals
DATA PROCESSING METHODS: manual
TYPE OF ACTIVITY: data collection; distribution of information
CLIENTELE: members of the judicial power, lawyers and legal students
ACCESS TO SERVICE: services open to all users, free of charge
TYPE & DESCRIPTION OF SERVICES PROVIDED: Provides library services, bibliographic
        searches and photocopies.

2 - BIBLIOTECA "ROGELIO CALABRESE"

PARENT ORGANIZATION: Colegio de Graduados en Ciencias Económicas
ADDRESS: Viamonte 1582 Subsuelo,
        1055 Buenos Aires,
        ARGENTINA
        TEL: 49-3397 (int. 53)
CREATED: 1918   HEAD: Mrs. E. Díaz, Head
SIZE OF STAFF: Professional: 3   Other: 5   Total: 8
TYPE OF SERVICE: national; public; non-profit
WORKING LANGUAGE(S): Spanish
SUBJECT COVERAGE: administrative sciences; economics; law; sociology
GEOGRAPHICAL COVERAGE: Argentina
DATA BEING PROCESSED AND SIZE: 24,000 books; 400 periodicals
DATA PROCESSING METHODS: manual
TYPE OF ACTIVITY: distribution of information; publication
PERIODICALS PUBLISHED:
        - Boletín de Económicas, 12 p.a.
        - Jornadas Tributarias. Trabajo, 12 p.a.
        - Jornada Nacional de Sistemas de Información Trabajos, 12 p.a.
CLIENTELE: experts, students
ACCESS TO SERVICE: open to all users
TYPE & DESCRIPTION OF SERVICES PROVIDED: Provides library services and bibliographic
        searches of information.

3 - CENTRO DE ESTUDIOS DE ESTADO Y SOCIEDAD, BIBLIOTECA

SYNONYMOUS NAMES: CEDES, Biblioteca;
        Center for the Study of the State and the Society, Library
ADDRESS: Pueyrredón 510 - piso 7,
        1032 Buenos Aires,
        ARGENTINA
        TEL: 961/2496
CREATED: 1975   HEAD: Mrs. L. Plate, Librarian
SIZE OF STAFF: Total: 1
TYPE OF SERVICE: private; non-profit
SYSTEMS & NETWORKS ATTACHED TO: Sistema de Información para la Planificación
        (INFOPLAN)

WORKING LANGUAGE(S): Spanish
SUBJECT COVERAGE: economics; history; political science; sociology
GEOGRAPHICAL COVERAGE: Latin America; Argentina
DATA BEING PROCESSED AND SIZE: 7,000 books and reports; 230 periodicals
DATA PROCESSING METHODS: manual
STORAGE MEDIA: fiches
TYPE OF ACTIVITY: data collection; data analysis; distribution of information;
        publication
PERIODICALS PUBLISHED:
        - Accession lists
CLIENTELE: researchers
ACCESS TO SERVICE: services open to specific categories of users, free of charge
TYPE & DESCRIPTION OF SERVICES PROVIDED: Provides library services, bibliographic
        searches of information and photocopies. Catalogues available from INFOPLA
        DOCPAL, CEPAL, CLAD.

94 - CENTRO DE ESTUDIOS DE POBLACIÓN, BIBLIOTECA

SYNONYMOUS NAMES: CENEP, Biblioteca;
        CENEP, Library
ADDRESS: Casilla 4397, Correo Central,
        1000 Buenos Aires,
        ARGENTINA
        TEL: 961-0309
CREATED: 1974   *HEAD:* Mrs. E. Linares, Head Librarian
SIZE OF STAFF: Professional: 1   Other: 1   Total: 2
TYPE OF SERVICE: non-profit
WORKING LANGUAGE(S): Spanish
SUBJECT COVERAGE: demography; population; surveys
GEOGRAPHICAL COVERAGE: global; Argentina
DATA BEING PROCESSED AND SIZE: 9,500 books and on-going research; 140 periodicals
DATA PROCESSING METHODS: manual
STORAGE MEDIA: traditional shelving of publications
TYPE OF ACTIVITY: distribution of information; publication
PERIODICALS PUBLISHED:
        - Boletín de Accesión
CLIENTELE: researchers, students, experts
ACCESS TO SERVICE: services open to all users, free of charge
TYPE & DESCRIPTION OF SERVICES PROVIDED: Provides library services, interlibrary
        loans, bibliographic and quantitative data searches of information. Deals
        with population in general with special emphasis on Argentina.

95 - CENTRO DE ESTUDIOS URBANOS Y REGIONALES

SYNONYMOUS NAMES: CEUR;
        Centre for Urban and Regional Studies
ADDRESS: Av. Corrientes 2835 7 piso, Cuerpo "A",
        1193 Buenos Aires,
        ARGENTINA

REATED: 1961   *HEAD:* Mr. P. Gutman, Director
YPE OF SERVICE: non-profit
ORKING LANGUAGE(S): Spanish
UBJECT COVERAGE: social sciences; economics; demography; sociology; political
        science; geography; human settlements; regional development; environment;
        development; population
EOGRAPHICAL COVERAGE: Argentina; Latin America
ATA BEING PROCESSED AND SIZE: 3,000 books; 1,000 periodicals
ATA PROCESSING METHODS: manual
TORAGE MEDIA: traditional shelving of publications
YPE OF ACTIVITY: distribution of information; SSID scientific and methodological
        activities; SSID training
ERIODICALS PUBLISHED: - Cuadernos del CEUR
        - CEUR Bulletin
LIENTELE: faculties, experts
CCESS TO SERVICE: open to all users
YPE & DESCRIPTION OF SERVICES PROVIDED: Provides library services and selective
     . dissemination of information.

6 - CENTRO LINCOLN

YNONYMOUS NAMES: Lincoln Centre, United States Information Service
ARENT ORGANIZATION: Servicio Informativo y Cultural de los Estados Unidos de América
DDRESS: Florida 935,
        1005 Buenos Aires,
        ARGENTINA
        TEL: 311-7148
REATED: 1950   *HEAD:* Mr. R. V. Cagnoli, Director
IZE OF STAFF: Professional: 7   Other: 10   Total: 17
YPE OF SERVICE: national; public; non-profit
ATERIALS DESCRIBING THE SERVICE: - Guia del Centro Lincoln
ORKING LANGUAGE(S): English; Spanish
UBJECT COVERAGE: social sciences
EOGRAPHICAL COVERAGE: Argentina
ATA BEING PROCESSED AND SIZE: 17,900 books; 300 periodicals; 2,400 pamphlets; VCRs,
        cassettes and records
ATA PROCESSING METHODS: manual; partially computerized
ARDWARE USED: IBM PC 1 - Hardisk 10 MB Modems
OFTWARE USED: LOGICAT, Crosstalk, Pro-Search, Card catalog, BIBLINK, PRO-CITE,
        MULTIMATE, DBASE III, LOTUS 1-2-3 - custom made (for membership file)
TORAGE MEDIA: traditional shelving of publications; microfiches; microfilms; discs
YPE OF ACTIVITY: distribution of information
LIENTELE: professionals, university professors and students, government officials
        and congressmen, general public (450 visitors a day)
CCESS TO SERVICE: services open to all users, free of charge
YPE & DESCRIPTION OF SERVICES PROVIDED: Library services include bibliographic and
        literature searches, selective dissemination of information, on-line
        services and photocopies.

97 - CONSEJO FEDERAL DE INVERSIONES, DIRECCIÓN DE INFORMACIÓN, AREA CENTRO DE DOCUMENTACIÓN

SYNONYMOUS NAMES: Federal Council of Investments, Documentation Center
ADDRESS: San Martin 871,
Buenos Aires (1004),
ARGENTINA
TEL: 313-2200 - TELEX: 21180 CFI AR
CREATED: 1964   *HEAD:* Ms N. J. de Pivetta, Director
SIZE OF STAFF: Professional: 6   Other: 3   Total: 9
TYPE OF SERVICE: national; public; non-profit
WORKING LANGUAGE(S): Spanish
SUBJECT COVERAGE: social sciences; socio-economic development
GEOGRAPHICAL COVERAGE: Argentina
DATA BEING PROCESSED AND SIZE: 20,000 books; 700 periodicals
DATA PROCESSING METHODS: manual; partially computerized
HARDWARE USED: Data General Eclipse 330
STORAGE MEDIA: traditional shelving of publications
TYPE OF ACTIVITY: data collection; data analysis; distribution of information
PERIODICALS PUBLISHED:
- Bibliographic Information, 6 p.a.
PUBLICATIONS: - Catalogue of CFI publications, 1983-85, 2 vol.
CLIENTELE: researchers (30 per day)
ACCESS TO SERVICE: open to specific categories of users, free of charge
TYPE & DESCRIPTION OF SERVICES PROVIDED: Provides library services, bibliographic an
literature abstracts, searches of information, photocopies and translations
upon request.

98 - FACULTAD LATINOAMERICANA DE CIENCIAS SOCIALES-PROGRAMA BUENOS AIRES

SYNONYMOUS NAMES: FLACSO, Programa Buenos Aires;
Latin American Faculty of Social Sciences, Buenos Aires Program
ADDRESS: Federico Lacroze 2097,
Casilla 145 SUC 26,
1426 Buenos Aires,
ARGENTINA
TEL: 771.09.78 - TELEX: 18937 FLACS AR
CABLE: FLACSOBUE
CREATED: 1974   *HEAD:* Mr. G. Cosse, Director
SIZE OF STAFF: Professional: 1   Other: 1   Total: 2
TYPE OF SERVICE: international; public; non-profit
SYSTEMS & NETWORKS ATTACHED TO: Red de Información en Ciencias Sociales Argentina
(REDISCA)
WORKING LANGUAGE(S): Spanish
SUBJECT COVERAGE: social sciences; education; economics
GEOGRAPHICAL COVERAGE: Latin America
DATA BEING PROCESSED AND SIZE: 4,500 books; 500 periodicals; 15,000 documents
DATA PROCESSING METHODS: manual
TYPE OF ACTIVITY: data collection; data analysis; distribution of information;
publication
PERIODICALS PUBLISHED: - América Latina Internacional, 4 p.a.

- Documentos e Informes de Investigación
PUBLICATIONS: - Catálogo
CLIENTELE: Students, researchers
ACCESS TO SERVICE: services open to all users, free of charge
TYPE & DESCRIPTION OF SERVICES PROVIDED: Provides library services and bibliographic
        searches.

99 - FUNDACIÓN DE INVESTIGACIONES ECONÓMICAS LATINOAMERICANAS, BIBLIOTECA

SYNONYMOUS NAMES: FIEL, Biblioteca
ADDRESS: Esmeralda 320 - 4 Piso,
        1343 Buenos Aires,
        ARGENTINA
        TEL: 35-1733/9270
CREATED: 1964   *HEAD:* Ms. L. Silberleib, Library Director
SIZE OF STAFF: Other: 1 ` Total: 1
TYPE OF SERVICE: public; non-profit
SYSTEMS & NETWORKS ATTACHED TO: Members of the Red de Bibliotecas de Ciencias
        Sociales de Argentina and the INFOPLAN network
WORKING LANGUAGE(S): Spanish
SUBJECT COVERAGE: economics
GEOGRAPHICAL COVERAGE: Argentina; Latin America
DATA BEING PROCESSED AND SIZE: 5,000 books; 150 periodicals; seminars, courses, etc.
DATA PROCESSING METHODS: manual
STORAGE MEDIA: data collection; distribution of information
PERIODICALS PUBLISHED: - Indicadores de Coyuntura, 12 p.a.
CLIENTELE: experts, students, professors
ACCESS TO SERVICE: services open to all users, free of charge
TYPE & DESCRIPTION OF SERVICES PROVIDED: Provides bibliographic and literature
        searches, selective dissemination of information and photocopies.

00 - FUNDACIÓN JOSÉ MARÍA ARAGÓN, SERVICIOS DE INFORMACIÓN

SYNONYMOUS NAMES: Aragon Foundation Information Services
ADDRESS: Cordoba 1345, 9 piso,
        1055 Buenos Aires,
        ARGENTINA
        TEL: 42-9831
CREATED: 1970   *HEAD:* Mrs. D. Babini, Director
SIZE OF STAFF: Professional: 6   Other: 3   Total: 9
TYPE OF SERVICE: private; non-profit
SYSTEMS & NETWORKS ATTACHED TO: Red de Información sobre Ciencias Sociales (REDICSA);
        INTERPHIL
WORKING LANGUAGE(S): Spanish
SUBJECT COVERAGE: social sciences; postgraduate education
GEOGRAPHICAL COVERAGE: global
DATA BEING PROCESSED AND SIZE: 3,000 university catalogues and international courses;
        800 reference books; 500 reports
DATA PROCESSING METHODS: computerized

Argentina / Argentine / Argentina

HARDWARE USED: IBM, PC-AT and EPSON
SOFTWARE USED: MICRO ISIS, LOTUS, DB III, MULTIMATE
TYPE OF ACTIVITY: data collection; data analysis; distribution of information;
    publication
PERIODICALS PUBLISHED:
    - Informes Mensuales sobre Becas y Cursos
    - Bibliografía Argentina de Ciencias Sociales, 1 p.a.
PUBLICATIONS: - Directorio de fundaciones Argentinas, 1979, suppl. 1982
CLIENTELE: students, researchers, decision-makers (6,000 enquiries per year)
ACCESS TO SERVICE: services open to all users free of charge, exceptionally against
    payment
TYPE & DESCRIPTION OF SERVICES PROVIDED: Provides library services, bibliographic
    searches, selective dissemination of information, production of informatic
    on magnetic tapes and photocopies. Has its own data bases, BECAS,
    FUNDACIONES, BACS, including data on postgraduate training opportunities,
    courses and fellowships.

101 - HONORABLE LEGISLATURA DE BUENOS AIRES, BIBLIOTECA

SYNONYMOUS NAMES: Parliamentary and Law Library
ADDRESS: Casilla de Correo 101,
    1900 La Plata,
    ARGENTINA
    TEL: 21.00.81
HEAD: Ms. M. A. Nápoli de Poloni, Director
SIZE OF STAFF: Total: 48
TYPE OF SERVICE: national; public; non-profit
WORKING LANGUAGE(S): Spanish; French; English
SUBJECT COVERAGE: law; political science; social sciences; administrative sciences
    demography; economics; education; geography; history; sociology
GEOGRAPHICAL COVERAGE: Argentina
DATA BEING PROCESSED AND SIZE: 50,000 books; 2,500 periodicals
DATA PROCESSING METHODS: manual
TYPE OF ACTIVITY: data collection; data analysis; SSID training
CLIENTELE: lawyers, university students, researchers (10,500 users p.a.)
ACCESS TO SERVICE: services open to all users
TYPE & DESCRIPTION OF SERVICES PROVIDED: Provides library services, bibliographic
    searches, photocopies and translation of documents upon request.

102 - INSTITUTO NACIONAL DE ANTROPOLOGÍA, BIBLIOTECA

SYNONYMOUS NAMES: National Institute of Anthropology, Library
PARENT ORGANIZATION: Dirección Nacional de Antropología y Folklore, Secretaria de
    Cultura de la Nación
ADDRESS: 3 de Febrero 1370/78,
    1426 Buenos Aires,
    ARGENTINA
    TEL: 784-5482
CREATED: 1943   HEAD: Ms. E. Borgogno, Chief of Library

SIZE OF STAFF: Professional: 3
TYPE OF SERVICE: national; public; non-profit
WORKING LANGUAGE(S): Spanish
SUBJECT COVERAGE: social anthropology; cultural anthropology; folklore; archaeology; linguistics; ethnology
GEOGRAPHICAL COVERAGE: Argentina
DATA BEING PROCESSED AND SIZE: 12,000 books; 1,580 periodicals
DATA PROCESSING METHODS: manual
STORAGE MEDIA: traditional shelving of publications; fiches
TYPE OF ACTIVITY: data collection; distribution of information; publication
PERIODICALS PUBLISHED: - Cuadernos del Instituto Nacional de Antropologia
    - Indice de Publicaciones Periódicas de Antropología
PUBLICATIONS: - Specialized anthropological bibliography
CLIENTELE: researchers and students
ACCESS TO SERVICE: open to specific categories of users, free of charge
TYPE & DESCRIPTION OF SERVICES PROVIDED: Provides library services, bibliographic and literature searches, selective dissemination of information, production of information on magnetic tapes and photocopies.

03 - INSTITUTO NACIONAL DE ESTADÍSTICA Y CENSOS, BIBLIOTECA

SYNONYMOUS NAMES: INDEC, Biblioteca;
    National Institute of Statistics and Census, Library
PARENT ORGANIZATION: Secretaría de Planificación
ADDRESS: Hipólito Yrigoyen 250, Piso 2, Of. 1209,
    (1210) Buenos Aires,
    ARGENTINA
    TEL: 34-6411
CREATED: 1968   *HEAD:* Mr. L. A. Beccaria,
SIZE OF STAFF: Professional: 3   Other: 5   Total: 8
TYPE OF SERVICE: national; public; non-profit
WORKING LANGUAGE(S): Spanish
SUBJECT COVERAGE: social sciences; demography; statistics; surveys
GEOGRAPHICAL COVERAGE: Argentina
DATA PROCESSING METHODS: computerized
HARDWARE USED: IBM PCXT
SOFTWARE USED: MINI-MICRO CDS ISIS
TYPE OF ACTIVITY: data analysis
PERIODICALS PUBLISHED: - Estadistica Mensual
        - Anuario Estadístico de la República Argentina. Comercio Exterior
        - Boletin Estadistico Trimestral
        - Estudios INDEC
        - Metodologias INDEC
        - Recopilaciones INDEC
CLIENTELE: researchers, students, experts (200 p. month)
ACCESS TO SERVICE: services open to all users, free of charge
TYPE & DESCRIPTION OF SERVICES PROVIDED: Provides library services and bibliographic searches of information.

104 - INSTITUTO NACIONAL DE LA ADMINISTRACIÓN PÚBLICA, DEPARTAMENTO BIBLIOTECA Y PUBLICACIONES

SYNONYMOUS NAMES: Public Administration National Institute, Library and Publication Department
ADDRESS: Av. Roque Sáenz Peña 501, 8 piso,
1035 Buenos Aires,
ARGENTINA
TEL: 331-5514
CREATED: 1973   *HEAD:* A. E. Moran, Chief of Library Department
SIZE OF STAFF: Professional: 4   Other: 13   Total: 17
TYPE OF SERVICE: international; public; non-profit
SYSTEMS & NETWORKS ATTACHED TO: Planindex; Redicsa; Red Centro Latinoamericano Administración para el Desarrollo
WORKING LANGUAGE(S): Spanish
SUBJECT COVERAGE: administrative sciences; political science; social sciences; sociology
GEOGRAPHICAL COVERAGE: Argentina
DATA BEING PROCESSED AND SIZE: 20,000 books; 300 periodicals
DATA PROCESSING METHODS: manual
TYPE OF ACTIVITY: data collection; data analysis; publication
PERIODICALS PUBLISHED:
        - Boletín Informativo
        - Boletines bibliográficos
CLIENTELE: civil servants, researchers, professors and students
ACCESS TO SERVICE: open to all users, free of charge
TYPE & DESCRIPTION OF SERVICES PROVIDED: Provides library services, bibliographies, research, photocopies and microforms.

105 - INSTITUTO NACIONAL DE LA ADMINISTRACIÓN PÚBLICA, DIRECCIÓN GENERAL DE DOCUMENTACIÓN E INFORMACIÓN

SYNONYMOUS NAMES: National Institute of Public Administration, Data and Information General Direction
PARENT ORGANIZATION: Secretaría de la Función Pública, Presidencia de la Nación Argentina
ADDRESS: Avenida Roque Saenz Peña 501, 8 Piso,
1035 Buenos Aires,
ARGENTINA
TEL: 33.5514-5515
CREATED: 1973   *HEAD:* Mr. A. E. Moran, Director
SIZE OF STAFF: Professional: 8   Other: 10   Total: 18
TYPE OF SERVICE: public; national; non-profit
SYSTEMS & NETWORKS ATTACHED TO: Red Latinoamerica de Documentatión e Información sobre Administración Pública ; Red de Información sobre Ciencias Sociales (REDICSA) ; Red de Documentatión e Información sobre Planificación (PLANINDEX)
WORKING LANGUAGE(S): Spanish
SUBJECT COVERAGE: administrative sciences; public administration; economics; education; law; political science; sociology
GEOGRAPHICAL COVERAGE: Argentina; Latin America

ATA BEING PROCESSED AND SIZE: 20,000 books and documents; 260 titles of periodicals
ATA PROCESSING METHODS: partially computerized
ARDWARE USED: IBM PC (compatible TC)
OFTWARE USED: MICRO/ISIS
TORAGE MEDIA: traditional shelving of publications; microfilms; discs
YPE OF ACTIVITY: data collection; data analysis; distribution of information; publication
ERIODICALS PUBLISHED:
  - Novedades Bibliográficas, 12 p.a.
UBLICATIONS: - Recursos humanos (series)
  - Tecnologias de gestión (series)
  - Normativa de la administración pública (series)
  - Reorganización de la administración pública (series)
  - Relación Estado-usuarios (series)
  - Documentación e información (series)
LIENTELE: civil servants, researchers, teachers, students related to public administration, general public
CCESS TO SERVICE: library loans for internal users. Services free of charge for external users, but restricted to library consultations
YPE & DESCRIPTION OF SERVICES PROVIDED: Provides library services, bibliographic and literature abstracts searches of information, selective dissemination of information, microforms and photocopies.

06 - PRESIDENCIA DE LA NACIÓN, SECRETARÍA DE PLANIFICACIÓN, DEPARTAMENTO BIBLIOTECA

YNONYMOUS NAMES: Presidency of the Nation, Planning Secretariat, Library Department
DDRESS: Hipólito Yrigoyen 250,
  8 piso, of. 801 c,
  1310 Buenos Aires,
  ARGENTINA
REATED: 1963   *HEAD:* Prof. A. Garcia Acosta, Library Coordinator
IZE OF STAFF: Professional: 4   Other: 7   Total: 11
YPE OF SERVICE: national; public; non-profit
ORKING LANGUAGE(S): Spanish
UBJECT COVERAGE: economics; social welfare; economic planning; social planning; project evaluation
EOGRAPHICAL COVERAGE: global; Argentina
ATA BEING PROCESSED AND SIZE: 25,000 books; 1,000 periodicals; 5,000 other printed documents
ATA PROCESSING METHODS: manual
TORAGE MEDIA: traditional shelving of publications; fiches
YPE OF ACTIVITY: distribution of information; SSID scientific and methodological activities; SSID training; publication
ERIODICALS PUBLISHED:
  - Boletin Bibliográfico, irr.
UBLICATIONS: - Bibliografias especializadas
  - Catálogo de publicaciones de la institución
LIENTELE: postgraduate students, public and private enterprises (600 users a month)
CCESS TO SERVICE: open to all users
YPE & DESCRIPTION OF SERVICES PROVIDED: Provides library services, bibliographic and quantitative data searches, selective dissemination of information,

provision of photocopies and translation of documents upon request.

107 - SECRETARÍA DE PLANIFICACIÓN, CENTRO DE DOCUMENTACIÓN Y BIBLIOTECA

SYNONYMOUS NAMES: Department of Planning, Documentation and Library Center
PARENT ORGANIZATION: Presidencia de la Naciona, Secretaria de Planificación
ADDRESS: Hipólito Yirigoyen 250, Piso 8,
      C. P. 1310,
      Buenos Aires,
      ARGENTINA
      TEL: 331-1121
CREATED: 1962   *HEAD:* Prof. A. García Acosta, Director
SIZE OF STAFF: Professional: 7   Other: 5   Total: 12
TYPE OF SERVICE: public
SYSTEMS & NETWORKS ATTACHED TO: Red Información en Ciencias Sociales; Catálogo
    Colectivo de Bibliotecas Económicas, REDNAPLAN/ARGENTINA/CEPAL/CLADES/CHI
WORKING LANGUAGE(S): Spanish
SUBJECT COVERAGE: economics; social welfare
GEOGRAPHICAL COVERAGE: global
DATA BEING PROCESSED AND SIZE: 40,000 documentation items
DATA PROCESSING METHODS: manual
TYPE OF ACTIVITY: data collection; distribution of information; SSID scientific an
    methodological activities; SSID training
PERIODICALS PUBLISHED:
    - Boletín Bibliografico
CLIENTELE: consultants, researchers, graduate students (approx. 50 per day)
ACCESS TO SERVICE: services open to all users, free of charge
TYPE & DESCRIPTION OF SERVICES PROVIDED: Provides library services, bibliographic
    literature abstract searches, selective dissemination of information,
    microforms, photocopies and translation of documents upon request. Also
    provides on-line services using external data bases available through
    DIALOG.

108 - UNIVERSIDAD DE BELGRANO, DIRECCIÓN DE BIBLIOTECAS

SYNONYMOUS NAMES: University of Belgrano, Library Department
ADDRESS: Teodoro Garcia 2090,
      C. P. 1426,
      1426 Buenos Aires,
      ARGENTINA
      TEL: 771-8485 - TELEX: 18658 FUBEL
CREATED: 1964   *HEAD:* Ms. M.-L. E. Gomez, Director
SIZE OF STAFF: Professional: 5   Other: 13   Total: 18
TYPE OF SERVICE: private; non-profit
WORKING LANGUAGE(S): Spanish
SUBJECT COVERAGE: social sciences; agriculture; architecture; systems analysis
GEOGRAPHICAL COVERAGE: Argentina
DATA BEING PROCESSED AND SIZE: 70,000 documentation items
DATA PROCESSING METHODS: partially computerized

SOFTWARE USED: MICRO-ISIS
TYPE OF ACTIVITY: data collection; data analysis; distribution of information; SSID
   scientific and methodological activities; SSID training
PERIODICALS PUBLISHED: - Ideas en Ciencias Sociales
   - Ideas en Arte y Technologia
PUBLICATIONS: - Libros de la editorial de Belgrano
CLIENTELE: graduate students, university professors
ACCESS TO SERVICE: services open to specific categories of users, free of charge
TYPE & DESCRIPTION OF SERVICES PROVIDED: Provides library services, bibliographic,
   literature abstract and quantitative data searches, and photocopies. Also
   provides on-line services using external data bases available through
   DIALOG.

109 - UNIVERSIDAD DE BUENOS AIRES, SISTEMA DE BIBLIOTECAS Y DE INFORMACIÓN

SYNONYMOUS NAMES: SISBI;
   University of Buenos Aires, Libraries and Information System
PARENT ORGANIZATION: Universidad de Buenos Aires
ADDRESS: Azcuenaga 280,
   1029 Buenos Aires,
   ARGENTINA
   TEL: 47-6060 - TELEX: 18694 IBUBA AR
CREATED: 1985   *HEAD:* Prof. G. Luvecce, Director-General
SIZE OF STAFF: Professional: 8   Other: 2   Total: 10
TYPE OF SERVICE: public; non-profit
SYSTEMS & NETWORKS ATTACHED TO: Red Nacional de Bibliotecas Universitarias (RENBU)
MATERIALS DESCRIBING THE SERVICE: - RENBU informativo: Red Nacional de Bibliotecas
   Universitarias
WORKING LANGUAGE(S): Spanish
SUBJECT COVERAGE: social sciences
GEOGRAPHICAL COVERAGE: Argentina
DATA PROCESSING METHODS: manual; partially computerized
HARDWARE USED: PC IBM XT
SOFTWARE USED: MICRO CDS/ISIS; MACRO CDS/ISIS
TYPE OF ACTIVITY: data collection; data analysis; distribution of information; SSID
   scientific and methodological activities; SSID training
CLIENTELE: teachers, researchers, students
ACCESS TO SERVICE: open to all users
TYPE & DESCRIPTION OF SERVICES PROVIDED: Provides library services and bibliographic
   searches of information.

110 - UNIVERSIDAD NACIONAL DE CUYO, FACULTAD DE FILOSOFÍA Y LETRAS, BIBLIOTECA

SYNONYMOUS NAMES: National University of Cuyo, Faculty of Philosophy and Letters,
   Library
ADDRESS: C.C. 345,
   5500 Mendoza - Rca.,
   ARGENTINA
   TEL: 230506

Argentina / Argentine / Argentina

CREATED: 1970   HEAD: Mrs. S. Martínez Puig, Director
SIZE OF STAFF: Total: 25
TYPE OF SERVICE: national; public; non-profit
SUBJECT COVERAGE: social sciences; demography; education; geography; history;
        linguistics; philosophy; social anthropology; sociology
DATA BEING PROCESSED AND SIZE: 120,000 books
DATA PROCESSING METHODS: manual
TYPE OF ACTIVITY: distribution of information; publication
PERIODICALS PUBLISHED: - Adjuntamos Lista de Canje
        - Anales de Arqueología y Etnología
        - Anales Lingüística
        - Cuadernos de Sociología
        - Cuyo Anuario de Historia del Pensamiento Argentino
        - Philosophia, 1 p.a.
        - Revista de Estudios Clásicos, 1 p.a.
        - Revista de Historia Americana y Argentina, 1 p.a.
        - Revista de Lenguas Extranjeras, 1 p.a.
        - Revista de Literaturas Modernas, 1 p.a.
        - Boletín de Estudios Geográficos
        - Boletín de Literaturas Comparadas
ACCESS TO SERVICE: services open to specific categories of users, free of charge
TYPE & DESCRIPTION OF SERVICES PROVIDED: Provides library services.

111 - UNIVERSIDAD NACIONAL DE LA PLATA, INSTITUTO DE INVESTIGACIONES ADMINISTRATIV
      CENTRO DE DOCUMENTACIÓN

SYNONYMOUS NAMES: National University of La Plata, Administrative Research Institu
        Documentation Centre
PARENT ORGANIZATION: Facultad de Ciencias Económicas
ADDRESS: 48.6 y 7. 4to. Piso. Of. 411,
        Casilla de Correo 376,
        1900 La Plata,
        ARGENTINA
        TEL: (021) 43985 - TELEX: BULAP-AR-31151
CREATED: 1979   HEAD: Lic. H. Clavo, Director
SIZE OF STAFF: Professional: 1   Other: 1   Total: 2
TYPE OF SERVICE: national; public; non-profit
WORKING LANGUAGE(S): Spanish
SUBJECT COVERAGE: administrative sciences; law
GEOGRAPHICAL COVERAGE: Argentina
DATA BEING PROCESSED AND SIZE: books, articles, reports, on-going research
DATA PROCESSING METHODS: manual
STORAGE MEDIA: fiches
TYPE OF ACTIVITY: data collection; data analysis; publication
PERIODICALS PUBLISHED: - Sección "documentación" de la Revista de ciencias
        administrativas
CLIENTELE: researchers, teachers, students (300 p.a.)
ACCESS TO SERVICE: open to specific categories of users, free of charge
TYPE & DESCRIPTION OF SERVICES PROVIDED: Provides library services, bibliographies
        surveys, selective dissemination of information including individual
        profiles and provision of documents.

12 - UNIVERSIDAD NACIONAL DE LOMAS DE ZAMORA, FACULTAD DE CIENCIAS SOCIALES, BIBLIOTECA

YNONYMOUS NAMES: National University of Lomas de Zamora, Faculty of Social Sciences, Library;
UNLZ, Facultad de Ciencias Sociales, Biblioteca
DDRESS: Juan XXIIII y Camino de Cintura,
Casillo de Correos 95,
1832 Lomas de Zamora,
ARGENTINA
TEL: 243.7040
REATED: 1986   *HEAD:* Mr. A. Martín Roman, Librarian
IZE OF STAFF: Total: 2
YPE OF SERVICE: public; national; non-profit
'ORKING LANGUAGE(S): Spanish
UBJECT COVERAGE: social sciences; administrative sciences; education; history; linguistics; philosophy; political science; psychology; social anthropology; cultural anthropology; social welfare; sociology
EOGRAPHICAL COVERAGE: Argentina
ATA PROCESSING METHODS: manual
ARDWARE USED: IBM XT
TORAGE MEDIA: traditional shelving of publications; fiches; tapes; microfiches
YPE OF ACTIVITY: data collection; data analysis; distribution of information; SSID scientific and methodological activities; publication
ERIODICALS PUBLISHED:
- Boletín Informativo, 6 p.a.
UBLICATIONS: - Cuadernos de Ciencias de la Educación, no.1 y 2, 1987
LIENTELE: students, teachers, graduates, employees (approx. 700 users p.a.)
CCESS TO SERVICE: services open to all users, free of charge
YPE & DESCRIPTION OF SERVICES PROVIDED: Provides literature abstract, searches of information, selective dissemination of information and photocopies upon request.

13 - UNIVERSIDAD NACIONAL DE ROSARIO, FACULDAD DE CIENCIAS ECONÓMICAS, BIBLIOTECA

YNONYMOUS NAMES: National University of Rosario, Faculty of Economic Sciences, Library
DDRESS: 3 de Febrero 2160,
2000 Rosario, Santa Fe,
ARGENTINA
TEL: 212287
REATED: 1905   *HEAD:* Mr. O. M. López, Director
IZE OF STAFF: Professional: 1
YPE OF SERVICE: national; public; non-profit
ORKING LANGUAGE(S): Spanish
UBJECT COVERAGE: economics; social sciences; administrative sciences; demography; political science
EOGRAPHICAL COVERAGE: Argentina
ATA BEING PROCESSED AND SIZE: 99,750 books and reports
ATA PROCESSING METHODS: manual
YPE OF ACTIVITY: distribution of information; publication

Argentina / Argentine / Argentina

PERIODICALS PUBLISHED:
- Boletín de Obras
- Síntesis Bibliográfica de Publicaciones Periódicas
- Aportes Bibliográficos
CLIENTELE: students, professors
ACCESS TO SERVICE: services open to all users
TYPE & DESCRIPTION OF SERVICES PROVIDED: Provides library services.

114 - UNIVERSIDAD NACIONAL DEL SUR, DEPARTAMENTO DE HUMANIDADES, BIBLIOTECA DE HUMANIDADES

SYNONYMOUS NAMES: National University of South Argentina, Humanities Department, Library
ADDRESS: Calle 12 de Octubre y Perú,
8000 Bahía Blanca,
ARGENTINA
CREATED: 1956   *HEAD:* Mrs. A. Auliel de Villa,
SIZE OF STAFF: Professional: 2   Other: 1   Total: 3
TYPE OF SERVICE: national; non-profit
SYSTEMS & NETWORKS ATTACHED TO: Junta de Bibliotecas Universitarias Argentina (JUBIUNA)
SUBJECT COVERAGE: humanities; history; linguistics; philosophy; psychology; social anthropology; cultural anthropology; sociology
GEOGRAPHICAL COVERAGE: Argentina
DATA BEING PROCESSED AND SIZE: 20,000 books; 1,750 periodicals
DATA PROCESSING METHODS: manual
STORAGE MEDIA: traditional shelving of publications, cassettes, microfiches
TYPE OF ACTIVITY: distribution of information; publication
PERIODICALS PUBLISHED:
- Acquisition List
CLIENTELE: professors, researchers, students
ACCESS TO SERVICE: services open to specific categories of users, free of charge
TYPE & DESCRIPTION OF SERVICES PROVIDED: Provides library services and bibliographi searches of information.

115 - UNIVERSIDAD NACIONAL SAN JUAN, FACULTAD DE FILOSOFÍA, HUMANIDADES Y ARTES, BIBLIOTECA DR. JUAN JOSÉ NISSEN

SYNONYMOUS NAMES: National University of San Juan, Faculty of Philosophy, Humanit and Arts
ADDRESS: Avenida Ignacio de la Roza 235 (West),
5400 San Juan,
ARGENTINA
TEL: 228577
CREATED: 1973   *HEAD:* A. C. Daneri de Correa,
SIZE OF STAFF: Professional: 6   Other: 6   Total: 12
TYPE OF SERVICE: international; public
MATERIALS DESCRIBING THE SERVICE: - Conoce usted la Biblioteca? Universidad Nacion de San Juan, 1983

UBJECT COVERAGE: social sciences; education; geography; history; linguistics
EOGRAPHICAL COVERAGE: Argentina
YPE OF ACTIVITY: distribution of information; publication
ERIODICALS PUBLISHED:
- Boletin Informativo
YPE & DESCRIPTION OF SERVICES PROVIDED: Provides library services, selective
dissemination of information and photocopies upon request.

16 - AUSTRALIAN BUREAU OF STATISTICS, INFORMATION SERVICES

YNONYMOUS NAMES: ABS, Central Information Service
DDRESS: P.O. Box 10,
Belconnen A.C.T. 2616,
AUSTRALIA
TEL: (062) 527 911 - TELEX: 62020
REATED.: 1980   HEAD: M. J. Sattler, Director, Information Services
IZE OF STAFF: Professional: 44   Other: 43   Total: 87
YPE OF SERVICE: national; public; non-profit
YSTEMS & NETWORKS ATTACHED TO: ABN (Australian Bibliographic Network)
ATERIALS DESCRIBING THE SERVICE: - Australian Bureau of Statistics, Annual report
- AUSSTATS data guide, 1987
ORKING LANGUAGE(S): English
UBJECT COVERAGE: statistics; demography; economics; socio-economic indicators;
population; housing; employment; income; trade; welfare; crime
EOGRAPHICAL COVERAGE: Australia
ATA BEING PROCESSED AND SIZE: statistical data
ATA PROCESSING METHODS: computerized
ARDWARE USED: FACOM M 382
OFTWARE USED: programs developed by ABS
TORAGE MEDIA: traditional shelving of publications, magnetic tapes, microfiches,
discs
YPE OF ACTIVITY: data collection; data analysis; distribution of information;
publication
UBLICATIONS: - Australia and state year books (series)
- Census of population and housing information papers (series)
- Technical papers (series)
- Estimates of population, population projections, vital statistics,
migration (series)
- Labour force, employment conditions, consumer income, and expenditure
(series)
LIENTELE: government, private enterprises, academics, private individuals,
international organizations (28,000 inquiries in 1986)
CCESS TO SERVICE: open to all users free of charge, some paid services
YPE & DESCRIPTION OF SERVICES PROVIDED: Publishes 1,650 publications p.a., and
provides library services, searches of information for secondary analysis,
selective dissemination of information, AUSSTATS on-line service using
CSIRONET (CSIRO's public access computer network). Also provides information
on VIATEL (a national video text service). Relevant data bases available
include TRACCS (trade statistics) and CENSUS (population census statistics).
Includes a microfiche service (260,000 copies dispatched p.a.) and a

magnetic tape service (1,300 copies released p.a.). Photocopies are
available upon request.

117 - AUSTRALIAN INSTITUTE OF ABORIGINAL STUDIES, LIBRARY

SYNONYMOUS NAMES: AIAS Library
ADDRESS: P.O. Box 553,
      Canberra, ACT 2601,
      AUSTRALIA
      TEL: (062) 461111 - TELEX: ABINST - FAX: (062)461125
CREATED: 1964   *HEAD:* Mr. W. Dix, Principal
TYPE OF SERVICE: public; non-profit
WORKING LANGUAGE(S): English
SUBJECT COVERAGE: social sciences; aboriginal studies; indigenous populations
GEOGRAPHICAL COVERAGE: Australia
DATA BEING PROCESSED AND SIZE: 21,000 books; 11,500 pamphlets; 15,000 sound tapes
      200,000 prints and colour slides; 270,000 meters of film
DATA PROCESSING METHODS: partially computerized
SOFTWARE USED: Unix, Corporate Retriever
STORAGE MEDIA: traditional shelving of publications; fiches; tapes; disks; films;
      video, etc.
TYPE OF ACTIVITY: data collection; data analysis; distribution of information; SSI
      scientific and methodological activities; SSID training; publication
PERIODICALS PUBLISHED: - Australian Aboriginal Studies, 2 p.a.
      - Australian Aborigines in the News, microfiche, 2 p.a.
      - Newsletter
      - Annual Bibliography
CLIENTELE: students, researchers
ACCESS TO SERVICE: services open to all users, free of charge
TYPE & DESCRIPTION OF SERVICES PROVIDED: Provides library services, bibliographic
      searches of information, selective dissemination of information, informa
      on magnetic tapes or discs and photocopies.

118 - AUSTRALIAN INSTITUTE OF FAMILY STUDIES, FAMILY INFORMATION CENTRE

ADDRESS: 300 Queen Street,
      Melbourne,
      Victoria 3000,
      AUSTRALIA
      TEL: (03) 608.6888
CREATED: 1983   *HEAD:* Ms. M. Davis, Head
SIZE OF STAFF: Total: 3
TYPE OF SERVICE: national; public; non-profit
SYSTEMS & NETWORKS ATTACHED TO: AUSTRALIS (Network of CSIRO)
MATERIALS DESCRIBING THE SERVICE: - Family database (brochure)
      - Family database: a national register of Australian family studies
      research, 1986
      - Family user's guide, 1987
WORKING LANGUAGE(S): English

BJECT COVERAGE: family; law; social welfare; social law; economic law; marriage;
         divorce; rights of the child
OGRAPHICAL COVERAGE: Australia
TA BEING PROCESSED AND SIZE: 6,000 bibliographical references
TA PROCESSING METHODS: computerized
FTWARE USED: STAIRS
ORAGE MEDIA: magnetic tapes
PE OF ACTIVITY: distribution of information; publication
RIODICALS PUBLISHED:
         - Australian Institute of Family Studies Newsletter
         - Family Database Annual
BLICATIONS: - Family thesaurus, 1987
CESS TO SERVICE: paid services open to all users
PE & DESCRIPTION OF SERVICES PROVIDED: Provides library services, interlibrary loan
         service, and on-line bibliographies from its own database "Family
         Database".

9 - AUSTRALIAN NATIONAL UNIVERSITY, ARCHIVES OF BUSINESS AND LABOUR

DRESS: Research School of the Social Sciences,
         G.P.O. Box 4,
         Canberra ACT 2601,
         AUSTRALIA
         TEL: 062-492219 - TELEX: AA62694 SOPAC
         CABLE: NATUNIV CANBERRA
AD: Mr. M. J. Saclier, Archives Officer
ZE OF STAFF: Professional: 6   Other: 2   Total: 8
PE OF SERVICE: national; public; non-profit
RKING LANGUAGE(S): English
BJECT COVERAGE: administrative sciences; economics; labour; trade unions
OGRAPHICAL COVERAGE: Australia
TA BEING PROCESSED AND SIZE: archival collections of Australian companies and trade
         unions (5 linear shelf kilometres)
PE OF ACTIVITY: data collection; publication
RIODICALS PUBLISHED:
         - Ablative (Archives Bulletin)
BLICATIONS: - List of holdings
CESS TO SERVICE: services open to researchers
PE & DESCRIPTION OF SERVICES PROVIDED: Provides reference services, searches of
         information and photocopies.

20 - AUSTRALIAN NATIONAL UNIVERSITY, INSTITUTE OF ADVANCED STUDIES, RESEARCH SCHOOL
         OF PACIFIC STUDIES

NONYMOUS NAMES: RSPACS
DRESS: GPO Box 4,
         Canberra,
         ACT 2601,
         AUSTRALIA

157

TEL: 062-49 2221 - TELEX: AA 62694 SOPAC
CABLE: NATUNIV Canberra
CREATED: 1947   HEAD: Prof. R. G. Ward, Director
TYPE OF SERVICE: national; public; non-profit
MATERIALS DESCRIBING THE SERVICE: - Annual report
WORKING LANGUAGE(S): English
SUBJECT COVERAGE: social sciences
GEOGRAPHICAL COVERAGE: Asia; Pacific area
DATA PROCESSING METHODS: computerized
TYPE OF ACTIVITY: data collection; data analysis
ACCESS TO SERVICE: services open to specific categories of users, some paid service
TYPE & DESCRIPTION OF SERVICES PROVIDED: Provides bibliographic and quantitative da
      searches and on-line searches of own data bases "International Economic
      Data Bank" (statistical), "Livelihood Strategies, Java" (numerical),
      "Land Records Malaysia" (numerical) and "Land Use Malaysia" (numerical).

121 - AUSTRALIAN NATIONAL UNIVERSITY, SOCIAL SCIENCE DATA ARCHIVES

SYNONYMOUS NAMES: SSDA
PARENT ORGANIZATION: Research School of Social Sciences
ADDRESS: G.P.O. Box 4,
      Canberra 2601,
      AUSTRALIA
      TEL: 61-62-494400 - TELEX: 62694 SOPAC AA62694
      CABLE: NATUNIV, Canberra
CREATED: 1982   HEAD: Dr. R. G. Jones, Head
SIZE OF STAFF: Professional: 5   Other: 1   Total: 6
TYPE OF SERVICE: national; public; non-profit
SYSTEMS & NETWORKS ATTACHED TO: Australian Consortium for Social and Political
      Research Inc. (ACSPRI)
MATERIALS DESCRIBING THE SERVICE: - SSDA brochure
      - ACSPRI brochure
WORKING LANGUAGE(S): English
SUBJECT COVERAGE: social sciences
GEOGRAPHICAL COVERAGE: Australia
DATA BEING PROCESSED AND SIZE: 550 computer-readable data files and documentation;
      public opinion polls; Australian census
DATA PROCESSING METHODS: computerized
HARDWARE USED: DEC-10, VAX
SOFTWARE USED: system and in-house programs
STORAGE MEDIA: magnetic tapes, discs
TYPE OF ACTIVITY: data collection; data analysis; distribution of information; SSID
      training; publication
PERIODICALS PUBLISHED:
      - ACSPRI Newsletter
      - SSDA Bulletin
PUBLICATIONS: - User's guide to machine readable data files
      - Drug use in Australia: a directory of survey research projects
      - Inventory of Australian surveys
      - Australian social surveys: journal extracts 1974-1978
      - SSDA catalogue, 1987

IENTELE: social science researchers, teachers and students (100 p.a.)
CESS TO SERVICE: open to specific categories of users, paid services
PE & DESCRIPTION OF SERVICES PROVIDED: Provides quantitative data searches from
        academic, government, private business and opinion polls in the social
        sciences relating to social, political and economic affairs, information on
        magnetic tapes, photocopies and selective dissemination of information.

2 - J. V. BARRY MEMORIAL LIBRARY, AUSTRALIAN INSTITUTE OF CRIMINOLOGY

RENT ORGANIZATION: Australian Institute of Criminology
DRESS: P.O. Box 28,
        Woden, ACT 2606,
        AUSTRALIA
        TEL: (062) 833833 - TELEX: AA61340 - TELEFAX: (062) 833843
EATED: 1975   *HEAD:* Mr. J. Myrtle, Librarian
ZE OF STAFF: Professional: 2   Other: 1   Total: 3
PE OF SERVICE: national; public; non-profit
STEMS & NETWORKS ATTACHED TO: AUSINET (ACI computer services)
TERIALS DESCRIBING THE SERVICE: - CINCH, the Australian criminology database, 1988
        (leaflet)
        - CINCH database user guide
BJECT COVERAGE: law; criminology; criminal law; criminal justice; victimology
OGRAPHICAL COVERAGE: Australia
TA BEING PROCESSED AND SIZE: journals; books; conference proceedings; reports;
        thesis; on-going research
TA PROCESSING METHODS: computerized
FTWARE USED: STAIRS
PE OF ACTIVITY: distribution of information
RIODICALS PUBLISHED:
        - Information Bulletin of Australian Criminology
BLICATIONS: - Ittis, J. (ed.), Fifth seminar for librarians in the criminal justice
        system, 1987
IENTELE: criminologists, students, researchers, social workers, lawyers,
        psychologists
CESS TO SERVICE: open to all users
PE & DESCRIPTION OF SERVICES PROVIDED: Provides library and information services,
        bibliographic and literature abstract searches of information, on-line
        services using its own data base "CINCH" (containing 16,700 records and
        updated quarterly) and access to other data bases. Also provides selective
        dissemination of information, information on magnetic tapes or discs and
        photocopies.

23 - CLEARING-HOUSE ON MIGRATION ISSUES

YNONYMOUS NAMES: CHOMI
ARENT ORGANIZATION: Ecumenical Migration Centre
DDRESS: 133 Church Street,
        Richmond 3121,
        Victoria,

AUSTRALIA
TEL: (03) 428 4948
HEAD: Ms. R. Singer, Coordinator
SIZE OF STAFF: Professional: 2   Other: 2   Total: 4
TYPE OF SERVICE: international; non-profit
WORKING LANGUAGE(S): English
SUBJECT COVERAGE: sociology; migration; immigration; racial discrimination; ethnic
        groups; culture; education; refugees
GEOGRAPHICAL COVERAGE: Australia, global
DATA BEING PROCESSED AND SIZE: 40,000 books and reports; 250 periodicals
DATA PROCESSING METHODS: partially computerized
HARDWARE USED: IBM compatible
SOFTWARE USED: DBASE III and HURIDOCS
STORAGE MEDIA: traditional shelving of publications
TYPE OF ACTIVITY: data collection; distribution of information; SSID training;
        publication
PERIODICALS PUBLISHED: - CHOMI DAS: a Quarterly Documentation and Abstracts Service
        - Migration Action
PUBLICATIONS: - Mail order catalogue 1987-88
CLIENTELE: students, academics, teachers, researchers, clergy, medical professional
        legal professionals, government bodies, community agencies (5,000 p.a.)
ACCESS TO SERVICE: services open to all users free of charge
TYPE & DESCRIPTION OF SERVICES PROVIDED: Provides library services, bibliographic
        searches, selective dissemination of information and photocopies.

124 - FOOTSCRAY INSTITUTE OF TECHNOLOGY, LIBRARY

ADDRESS: P.O. Box 64,
        Footscray,
        Victoria 3011,
        AUSTRALIA
        TEL: 61 (3) 688-4544 - TELEX: 36596 FITLEX AA
CREATED: 1982   *HEAD:* Ms. L. Giles-Peters, Coordinator
SIZE OF STAFF: Professional: 2   Other: 1   Total: 3
TYPE OF SERVICE: national; non-profit
WORKING LANGUAGE(S): English
SUBJECT COVERAGE: sociology; leisure; tourism; sport
DATA BEING PROCESSED AND SIZE: books; articles; reports; audiovisual materials
DATA PROCESSING METHODS: computerized
HARDWARE USED: Honeywell DP 58/44
SOFTWARE USED: Cobol Text Editor
STORAGE MEDIA: tapes; discs
TYPE OF ACTIVITY: data collection; publication
PERIODICALS PUBLISHED: - Australian Leisure Index
PUBLICATIONS: - Australian leisure bibliography, 1983
        - Australian tourism index 1982-1986, 1987
CLIENTELE: researchers, recreation professionals, students, travel industry
ACCESS TO SERVICE: open to all users
TYPE & DESCRIPTION OF SERVICES PROVIDED: Provides on-line services using its own dat
        base "Australian Leisure Index" containing 16,000 citations with abstracts
        and available through CSIRO AUSTRALIS.

25 - INTERNATIONAL ECONOMIC DATA BANK

SYNONYMOUS NAMES: IEDB
PARENT ORGANIZATION: National Centre for Development Studies/Australia-Japan Research
        Centre, Australian National University
ADDRESS: J.G. Crawford Building,
        Australian National University,
        GPO Box 4,
        Canberra,
        ACT 2601,
        AUSTRALIA
        TEL: (062) 49 3065 - TELEX: AA 62694 SOPAC
        CABLE: NATUNIV, Canberra
CREATED: 1982   *HEAD:* Ms. P. R. Phillips, Manager
SIZE OF STAFF: Professional: 4   Other: 1   Total: 5
TYPE OF SERVICE: national; public; non-profit
WORKING LANGUAGE(S): English
SUBJECT COVERAGE: economics
GEOGRAPHICAL COVERAGE: global
DATA PROCESSING METHODS: computerized
HARDWARE USED: Facom M360R
SOFTWARE USED: SAS
STORAGE MEDIA: magnetic tapes and discs
TYPE OF ACTIVITY: data analysis
CLIENTELE: academics and government departments (60 per day)
ACCESS TO SERVICE: services open to specific categories of users, free of charge
TYPE & DESCRIPTION OF SERVICES PROVIDED: Provides quantitative data searches,
        selective dissemination of information and information on magnetic tapes or
        discs.

26 - NATIONAL LIBRARY OF AUSTRALIA, AUSTRALIAN PUBLIC AFFAIRS INFORMATION SERVICE

SYNONYMOUS NAMES: APAIS
ADDRESS: Parkes Place,
        Canberra,
        ACT 2600,
        AUSTRALIA
        TEL: (062) 621111 - TELEX: 62100 - TELEFAX: (062) 571703
        CABLE: NATLIBAUST Canberra
CREATED: 1978   *HEAD:* Mr. R. Jordan, Editor
SIZE OF STAFF: Professional: 6   Other: 2   Total: 8
TYPE OF SERVICE: international; public; non-profit
SYSTEMS & NETWORKS ATTACHED TO: AUSINET (ACI Computer Services, Melbourne, Victoria,
        Australia); OZLINE (National Library of Australia, Canberra A.C.T.
        Australia)
MATERIALS DESCRIBING THE SERVICE: - APAIS (publicity brochure), 7 pages, 1987
        - Kenny, J. A., Australian Public Affairs Information Service in Australian
        Library Journal, 1974, pages 372-374
WORKING LANGUAGE(S): English
SUBJECT COVERAGE: social sciences; economics; political science; humanities
GEOGRAPHICAL COVERAGE: Australia

DATA BEING PROCESSED AND SIZE: 125,000 bibliographical references of Australian periodicals and publications; foreign publications on Australian subject matters

DATA PROCESSING METHODS: computerized

HARDWARE USED: IBM 3081

SOFTWARE USED: Library software package (British Library) with local modifications

STORAGE MEDIA: tapes

TYPE OF ACTIVITY: data collection; publication

PERIODICALS PUBLISHED: - APAIS, 11 p.a.

PUBLICATIONS: - APAIS Australian public affairs information service
    - APAIS thesaurus

CLIENTELE: librarians, researchers, scholars

ACCESS TO SERVICE: services open to all users, against payment ($75.00 per connect hour)

TYPE & DESCRIPTION OF SERVICES PROVIDED: Current subject index to Australian periodical and newspaper articles, scholarly journals, conference papers and books. This database is available in printed form and online from the National Library's computer network and from AUSINET. Items indexed in APAIS are located in the National Library and may be obtained from the Loan Service. Also provides photocopies.

127 - UNIVERSITY OF NEW SOUTH WALES, SOCIAL WELFARE RESEARCH CENTRE

PARENT ORGANIZATION: Commonwealth Department of Social Security

ADDRESS: P.O. Box 1,
    Kensington 2033,
    NSW,
    AUSTRALIA
    TEL: (02) 6975150

CREATED: 1980   *HEAD:* Dr. P. Saunders, Director

TYPE OF SERVICE: international; public; non-profit

WORKING LANGUAGE(S): English

SUBJECT COVERAGE: social welfare

GEOGRAPHICAL COVERAGE: Australia

DATA BEING PROCESSED AND SIZE: books; reports; on-going research; seminars

DATA PROCESSING METHODS: computerized   -

HARDWARE USED: Olivetti M24 PCs with hard discs; NEC 3550; Hitachi

SOFTWARE USED: Dbase III; BASIC; Lotus 123; WORD; Crosstalk; SPSS PC; Kermit

STORAGE MEDIA: traditional shelving of publications; tapes; microfiches

TYPE OF ACTIVITY: data collection; data analysis; distribution of information; SSID scientific and methodological activities; publication

ACCESS TO SERVICE: services open to specific categories of users, free of charge

TYPE & DESCRIPTION OF SERVICES PROVIDED: Provides library services, bibliographic, literature abstract and quantitative data searches, on-line services using external data bases of the Australian Bureau of Statistics.

28 - UNIVERSITY OF SYDNEY, BIBLIOGRAPHIC INFORMATION ON SOUTHEAST ASIA

NONYMOUS NAMES: BISA
DDRESS: Sydney,
NSW 2006,
AUSTRALIA
TEL: (02) 692-2222 - TELEX: AA 20056 (FISHLIB) - TELEFAX: (02) 692 4203
CABLE: UNIVSYD
REATED: 1981   *HEAD:* Ms. H. Jarvis, Director
IZE OF STAFF: Other: 3
YPE OF SERVICE: national; non-profit
YSTEMS & NETWORKS ATTACHED TO: ABN - Australian Bibliographic Network
ATERIALS DESCRIBING THE SERVICE: - BISA: an Australian database on Southeast Asia,
1984, leaflet
- BISA and its implications and benefits for librarians in developing
countries, 1983
ORKING LANGUAGE(S): English
UBJECT COVERAGE: economics; government; agriculture; history; religion; social
sciences
EOGRAPHICAL COVERAGE: Southeast Asia; Indonesia; Malaysia; Singapore (Republic);
Philippines; Thailand; Brunei; Viet-Nam (Socialist Republic)
ATA BEING PROCESSED AND SIZE: 20,000 books and documents; 15,000 indexed articles
ATA PROCESSING METHODS: partially computerized
ARDWARE USED: IBM mainframe, IBM AT, Olivetti M-24 microcomputers
OFTWARE USED: BIBLIUS (in-house system), CDS/ISIS (micro), Inmagic, DBASE III,
Wordstar
TORAGE MEDIA: tapes, diskettes, discs, microfiches, cards
YPE OF ACTIVITY: data collection; data analysis; publication; distribution of
information; SSID scientific and methodological activities; SSID training
UBLICATIONS: - BISA catalogue on microfiche
- Zachri, R. (ed.), Crime in Indonesia: an index to selected articles from
Tempo 1981-1985, 1986
- Aguirre, V. V., ASEAN law: a select bibliography, 1986
- Zakiah Aman, S., Trade and industry in Malaysia: a subject index to select
reference sources 1985-1985, 1986
- Sangtada, R., Isan, (Northeast Thailand): a select bibliography, 1986
- Widyawan, R., Modern Indonesian drama: a select bibliography, 1986
- Hoong Khen, Y., Malaysian government names: an authority list, 1986
- Lee, V. C., Index to Philippine book reviews 1972-1982, 1987
- Kaur, M., Portuguese Eurasians in Malaysia: a subject approach, 1987
- Thongyoi, D., Lannathai (Northern Thailand): a select bibliography, 1987
- Lee, M. S., Singaporean education in perspective: a select bibliography,
1987
- Fabito, C. D., Philippine liberation theology: an index to selected
materials, 1987
LIENTELE: general Australian community, especially academic, government,
researchers, education sectors
CCESS TO SERVICE: services open to all users, some paid services, some free of
charge
YPE & DESCRIPTION OF SERVICES PROVIDED: Provides library services, on-line
bibliographic and literature searches using its own database BISA (including
20,000 references) available on ABN Australian Bibliographic Network. It
reflects principally the holdings of 4 major libraries (University of

Sydney, Monash University, Australian National University and the National Library of Australia). Also provides information on magnetic tapes, microforms and consultancy.

129 - BUNDESKANZLERAMT, ADMINISTRATIVE BIBLIOTHEK UND ÖSTERREICHISCHE RECHTSDOKUMENTATION

SYNONYMOUS NAMES: Federal Chancellery, Administrative Library and Austrian Law Documentation
ADDRESS: Herrengasse 23,
      1010 Vienna,
      AUSTRIA
      TEL: (0222) 53115/2646
CREATED: 1849   *HEAD:* Prof. Dr. O. A. Simmler, Director
SIZE OF STAFF: Professional: 8   Other: 15   Total: 23
TYPE OF SERVICE: international; public; private
WORKING LANGUAGE(S): German
SUBJECT COVERAGE: administrative sciences; law; demography; economics; history; law; political science; social welfare; social sciences; information science
GEOGRAPHICAL COVERAGE: Austria
TYPE OF ACTIVITY: data collection; distribution of information
PUBLICATIONS: - Index zum österreichischen Reichs-, Staats- und Bundesgesetzblatt
ACCESS TO SERVICE: services open to specific categories of users, free of charge
TYPE & DESCRIPTION OF SERVICES PROVIDED: Provides library services, bibliographic and literature abstract searches of information, and restricted microforms and photocopies.

130 - INSTITUT FÜR HÖHERE STUDIEN UND WISSENSCHAFTLICHE FORSCHUNG, BIBLIOTHEK

SYNONYMOUS NAMES: Institute for Advanced Studies, Library
ADDRESS: Stumpergasse 56,
      A-1060 Vienna,
      AUSTRIA
      TEL: (0222) 59991
      CABLE: TRANSACADEMIA
HEAD: Prof. H. Seidel, Director
SIZE OF STAFF: Total: 2
TYPE OF SERVICE: private; non-profit
SUBJECT COVERAGE: economics; sociology; political science; administrative sciences
DATA BEING PROCESSED AND SIZE: 25,000 books: 400 social science periodicals; statistical material; research reports
DATA PROCESSING METHODS: computerized
HARDWARE USED: UNIVAC 1100/81
TYPE OF ACTIVITY: data collection; data analysis; publication
CLIENTELE: scholars and scientific workers
TYPE & DESCRIPTION OF SERVICES PROVIDED: Provides library services.

131 - KAMMER FÜR ARBEITER UND ANGESTELLTE FÜR WIEN, SOZIALWISSENSCHAFTLICHE STUDIENBIBLIOTHEK

SYNONYMOUS NAMES: Vienna Chamber of Labour, Social Sciences Library
ADDRESS: Prinz-Eugen-Strasse, 20-22,
   Postfach 534,
   A1040 Vienna,
   AUSTRIA
   TEL: (0222) 65 37 65 - TELEX: 1690
CREATED: 1921   *HEAD:* Mr. J. Vass,
SIZE OF STAFF: Professional: 10   Other: 10   Total: 20
TYPE OF SERVICE: national; private; non-profit
MATERIALS DESCRIBING THE SERVICE: - Sozialwissenschaftliche Studienbibliothek:
   Bestand, Kataloge, Benützung, 1982 (Guide)
SUBJECT COVERAGE: social sciences; social policy; labour problems; economics;
   political problems; social welfare
GEOGRAPHICAL COVERAGE: global
DATA BEING PROCESSED AND SIZE: 240,000 books and 1,100 periodicals
DATA PROCESSING METHODS: manual; partially computerized
HARDWARE USED: IBM
SOFTWARE USED: BIBOS
STORAGE MEDIA: traditional shelving of publications; tapes; microfiches
TYPE OF ACTIVITY: distribution of information; publication
PERIODICALS PUBLISHED:
   - Zeitschriftenschau, 6 p.a.
CLIENTELE: 4,500 users p.a.   .
ACCESS TO SERVICE: open to all users, free of charge
TYPE & DESCRIPTION OF SERVICES PROVIDED: Library services, selective dissemination of
   information, on-line services, bibliographic and literature searches,
   provision of photocopies.

132 - KOMMUNALWISSENSCHAFTLICHES DOKUMENTATIONSZENTRUM

SYNONYMOUS NAMES: KDZ;
   Documentation Center for Urban Studies
ADDRESS: Mariahilferstrasse 136,
   A-1150 Vienna,
   AUSTRIA
   TEL: (0222) 837512
CREATED: 1969   *HEAD:* H. Bauer, Director
SIZE OF STAFF: Professional: 8   Other: 4   Total: 12
TYPE OF SERVICE: public; non-profit
MATERIALS DESCRIBING THE SERVICE: - Bauer, H; Ortuer, H., Wissenschaftliche Beratung
   für Gemeinden, in Zurick in die Zukunft, 1987
WORKING LANGUAGE(S): German
SUBJECT COVERAGE: administrative sciences; economics; political science; social
   welfare; local government; public finance; public administration; public
   law; urban planning; housing; health; transport; social service
GEOGRAPHICAL COVERAGE: Austria; Germany (Federal Republic); Switzerland
DATA BEING PROCESSED AND SIZE: 47,000 items including books, articles, pamphlets and
   reports

DATA PROCESSING METHODS: manual; computerized
TYPE OF ACTIVITY: data collection; data analysis; distribution of information;
      publication
PERIODICALS PUBLISHED: - KDZ-Literaturrundschau, 4 p.a.
CLIENTELE: students, politicans, members of local authorities
ACCESS TO SERVICE: services open to all users, free of charge
TYPE & DESCRIPTION OF SERVICES PROVIDED: Provides library services, selective
      dissemination of information and bibliographies.

133 - ÖSTERREICHISCHE FORSCHUNGSSTIFTUNG FÜR ENTWICKLUNGSHILFE, DOKUMENTATION

SYNONYMOUS NAMES: ÖFSE, Dokumentation;
      Austrian Foundation for Development Research, Documentation
ADDRESS: Türkenstrasse 3,
      A-1090 Vienna,
      AUSTRIA
      CABLE: DEVELFOUND-VIENNA
CREATED: 1967   *HEAD:* Dr. G. Kramer, Head
SIZE OF STAFF: Professional: 5
TYPE OF SERVICE: national; private; non-profit
WORKING LANGUAGE(S): German
SUBJECT COVERAGE: social sciences; economics; education; history; political science;
      sociology; development
GEOGRAPHICAL COVERAGE: Africa; Asia; Latin America
DATA BEING PROCESSED AND SIZE: books; articles
DATA PROCESSING METHODS: manual
TYPE OF ACTIVITY: data collection; distribution of information; publication
PERIODICALS PUBLISHED: - Ausgewählte Neue Literatur zur Entwicklungspolitik
     - Österreichische Entwicklungspolitik
CLIENTELE: students, researchers, development administrators, NGOs (4,000 p.a.)
ACCESS TO SERVICE: services open to all users, free of charge
TYPE & DESCRIPTION OF SERVICES PROVIDED: Provides library services, bibliographic and
      literature searches, selective dissemination of information and photocopies.

134 - WIENER INSTITUT FÜR INTERNATIONALE WIRTSCHAFTSVERGLEICHE, INFORMATIONSZENTRUM

SYNONYMOUS NAMES: Vienna Institute for Comparative Economic Studies, Information
      Services
ADDRESS: Postfach 87,
      A-1103 Vienna,
      AUSTRIA
      TEL: (222) 78260179
CREATED: 1984   *HEAD:* Mr. P. Havlik, Database Administrator
SIZE OF STAFF: Professional: 5
TYPE OF SERVICE: international; public; non-profit
SYSTEMS & NETWORKS ATTACHED TO: I. P. SHARP (Timesharing Services)
WORKING LANGUAGE(S): English
SUBJECT COVERAGE: economics
GEOGRAPHICAL COVERAGE: Eastern Europe; Yugoslavia; USSR

DATA BEING PROCESSED AND SIZE: more than 50 periodicals and government statistics
DATA PROCESSING METHODS: computerized
HARDWARE USED: IBM-PC
SOFTWARE USED: MAGIC
STORAGE MEDIA: tapes, discs
TYPE OF ACTIVITY: data collection; data analysis; distribution of information; SSID scientific and methodological activities; publication
PERIODICALS PUBLISHED:
   - COMECON DATA
   - COMECON FOREIGN TRADE DATA
CLIENTELE: research community, banks
ACCESS TO SERVICE: services open to specific categories of users, against payment
TYPE & DESCRIPTION OF SERVICES PROVIDED: Provides library services, bibliographic and quantitative data searches using its own data base (Eastern Bloc Countries Economic Data Base), research analysis, on-line services, selective dissemination of information and information on magnetic tapes or discs.

35 - WIRTSCHAFTSUNIVERSITÄT WIEN, SOZIALWISSENSCHAFTLICHE INFORMATIONSSTELLE

SYNONYMOUS NAMES: SOWIS;
   Social Science Information Centre
PARENT ORGANIZATION: Universitätsbibliothek, Wirtschatsuniversität Wien/University Library University of Economics in Vienna
ADDRESS: Augasse 6,
   A-1090 Vienna,
   AUSTRIA
   TEL: 34.05.25
CREATED: 1984   *HEAD:* Dr. B. Schmeikal,
SIZE OF STAFF: Professional: 2   Other: 1   Total: 3
TYPE OF SERVICE: national; public; non-profit
MATERIALS DESCRIBING THE SERVICE: - Brochure
WORKING LANGUAGE(S): German
SUBJECT COVERAGE: social sciences; economics
DATA BEING PROCESSED AND SIZE: research reports, on-going research, grey literature; information on institutions and researchers
DATA PROCESSING METHODS: computerized
HARDWARE USED: IBM PCAT
SOFTWARE USED: IV + V
STORAGE MEDIA: traditional shelving of publications, discs
TYPE OF ACTIVITY: data collection; data analysis; distribution of information; publication
PERIODICALS PUBLISHED:
   - Themendokumentation
CLIENTELE: researchers
ACCESS TO SERVICE: services open to all users, free of charge for members of academic institutions
TYPE & DESCRIPTION OF SERVICES PROVIDED: Provides library services, bibliographic and literature searches, on-line search on IDAS data base and outside data bases including DIALOG, STN, QUESTEL, INKA, DATASTAR and FIZ-TECHNIK. Also provides selective dissemination of information and photocopies.

Bangladesh

136 - BANGLADESH INSTITUTE OF DEVELOPMENT STUDIES, LIBRARY

SYNONYMOUS NAMES: BIDS, Library
ADDRESS: E-17 Agargaon,
        Sher-e-Banglanagar,
        Dhaka-1207,
        G.P.O. Box 3854,
        BANGLADESH
        TEL: 313536
        CABLE: BIDECON
CREATED: 1957   *HEAD:* S. Haque, Chief Librarian
SIZE OF STAFF: Professional: 7   Other: 8   Total: 15
TYPE OF SERVICE: international; national; public; non-profit
SYSTEMS & NETWORKS ATTACHED TO: Development Information Network on South Asia
        (DEVINSA), a DEVSIS oriented regional information network
WORKING LANGUAGE(S): English; Bengali
SUBJECT COVERAGE: social sciences; economics; agriculture; rural development;
        population; industry; human resources
GEOGRAPHICAL COVERAGE: Bangladesh; developed countries; developing countries
DATA BEING PROCESSED AND SIZE: 100,000 documentation items
DATA PROCESSING METHODS: manual
TYPE OF ACTIVITY: data collection; data analysis; distribution of information; SSID
        scientific and methodological activities; publication
PUBLICATIONS: - Rural development studies: a select bibliography
        - Rural development of Bangladesh: a select bibliography
        - Union catalogue of current periodicals of major libraries in Dhaka
        - Catalogue of government publications (Pakistan): a list of BIDS library
        holdings
        - A Select bibliography on green revolution
        - A Select bibliography on spatial distribution: rural and urban
        - Bangladesh industry studies: a select bibliography
        - Bangladesh agricultural economics: a select bibliography
CLIENTELE: researchers, policy makers, planners, administrators, university teaching
        staff, high officials of Foreign Missions and NGOS (100 per day)
ACCESS TO SERVICE: open to all users, free of charge
TYPE & DESCRIPTION OF SERVICES PROVIDED: Provides library services, bibliographic,
        literature abstract and quantitative data searches of information using own
        data base, selective dissemination of information and photocopies.

137 - BANGLADESH INSTITUTE OF INTERNATIONAL AND STRATEGIC STUDIES, LIBRARY

SYNONYMOUS NAMES: BIISS, Library
ADDRESS: /46 Elephant Road,
        Dhaka,
        BANGLADESH
        TEL: 40.62.45
SIZE OF STAFF: Professional: 3
TYPE OF SERVICE: public
SUBJECT COVERAGE: demography; economics; geography; history; law; philosophy;

international relations
GEOGRAPHICAL COVERAGE: South Asia; Southeast Asia
DATA BEING PROCESSED AND SIZE: 6,000 books; 7,000 periodicals; 50 reports; on-going
research
DATA PROCESSING METHODS: manual
TYPE OF ACTIVITY: data collection; data analysis; distribution of information;
publication
CLIENTELE: researchers
ACCESS TO SERVICE: services open to specific categories of users
TYPE & DESCRIPTION OF SERVICES PROVIDED: Provides library services, searches of
information and photocopies.

138 - BANGLADESH MANAGEMENT DEVELOPMENT CENTRE, LIBRARY

SYNONYMOUS NAMES: BMDC, Library
PARENT ORGANIZATION: Ministry of Industries
ADDRESS: 4, Sobhanbag,
Mirpur Road,
Dhaka 1207,
BANGLADESH
TEL: 325086-90
CABLE: MANAGEMENT
CREATED: 1961   HEAD: Mr. M. Hossain, Director General
SIZE OF STAFF: Professional:˙45
TYPE OF SERVICE: national; public
WORKING LANGUAGE(S): Bangla; English
SUBJECT COVERAGE: administrative sciences; management
GEOGRAPHICAL COVERAGE: global
DATA BEING PROCESSED AND SIZE: 12,000 books; 80 periodicals
DATA PROCESSING METHODS: manual
TYPE OF ACTIVITY: distribution of information; SSID training
PERIODICALS PUBLISHED: - Management Development Quarterly
- Annual Programme
- Annual Report
CLIENTELE: academics, trainers, researchers, trainees, university students (40 per
- day)
ACCESS TO SERVICE: services open to all users
TYPE & DESCRIPTION OF SERVICES PROVIDED: Provides library services, literature
abstract searches, selective dissemination of information, photocopies and
translation of documents.

139 - UNIVERSITY OF DHAKA, INSTITUTE OF STATISTICAL RESEARCH AND TRAINING, LIBRARY

SYNONYMOUS NAMES: ISRT
ADDRESS: Dhaka 1000,
BANGLADESH
TEL: 501298; 503811
CREATED: 1964   HEAD: Dr. Md. Humayn Kabir, Director
SIZE OF STAFF: Professional: 17   Other: 20   Total: 47

TYPE OF SERVICE: national; public; non-profit
MATERIALS DESCRIBING THE SERVICE: - Brochure
WORKING LANGUAGE(S): English; Bangla
SUBJECT COVERAGE: statistics
GEOGRAPHICAL COVERAGE: Bangladesh
DATA BEING PROCESSED AND SIZE: 10,250 books and periodicals; 500 reports
DATA PROCESSING METHODS: partially computerized
HARDWARE USED: IBM 5280
TYPE OF ACTIVITY: data collection; data analysis; distribution of information; SSID
        scientific and methodological activities; SSID training; publication
PERIODICALS PUBLISHED: - Jouranl of Statistical Research, bi-annual
        - Rural Demography, bi-annual
CLIENTELE: teachers, students, researchers
ACCESS TO SERVICE: services open to specific categories of users, free of charge
TYPE & DESCRIPTION OF SERVICES PROVIDED: Provides library services, bibliographic,
        literature abstract and quantitative data searches, on-line services using
        own data bases and outside data bases, selective dissemination of
        information and photocopies.

Barbados / Barbade / Barbados

140 - UNIVERSITY OF WEST INDIES, FACULTY OF LAW LIBRARY

ADDRESS: Cave Hill Campus,
        P.O. Box 64,
        Cave Hill,
        BARBADOS
        TEL: 02191 - TELEX: WB 2257
        CABLE: UNIVADOS
CREATED: 1970   *HEAD:* Mr. J. Dyrud,
SIZE OF STAFF: Professional: 4   Other: 12   Total: 16
TYPE OF SERVICE: international
MATERIALS DESCRIBING THE SERVICE: - Guide to the Faculty of Law Library
SUBJECT COVERAGE: law; political science; sociology
GEOGRAPHICAL COVERAGE: Caribbean area
DATA BEING PROCESSED AND SIZE: 60,000 volumes of law reports, legal periodicals,
        monographs, pamphlets and treaties
DATA PROCESSING METHODS: manual
STORAGE MEDIA: traditional shelving of publications
TYPE OF ACTIVITY: distribution of information; publication
PERIODICALS PUBLISHED:
        - Accessions List
PUBLICATIONS: - WILIP indexes (West Indian Legislation Project)
        - ibliographies (on specific topics)
CLIENTELE: students, researchers and legal practitioners
ACCESS TO SERVICE: services open to specific categories of users
TYPE & DESCRIPTION OF SERVICES PROVIDED: Provides library services, bibliographic
        searches using external data base "LEXIS", selective dissemination of
        information, and photocopies.

Belgium / Belgique / Bélgica

141 - ASSOCIATION INTERNATIONALE DES UNIVERSITÉS DU 3ÈME AGE, BUREAU DE DOCUMENTATION

SYNONYMOUS NAMES: AIUTA
ADDRESS: rue du Débarcadère, 179,
        6001 Marcinelle,
        BELGIUM
        TEL: 071/43.20.70
CREATED: 1981   HEAD: Mr. S. Mayence, President of the Scientific Council of AIUTA
SIZE OF STAFF: Professional: 1   Other: 1   Total: 2
TYPE OF SERVICE: international; private; non-profit
WORKING LANGUAGE(S): French
SUBJECT COVERAGE: social welfare; sociology; gerontology; old age
GEOGRAPHICAL COVERAGE: Europe; North America; South America; Africa
DATA BEING PROCESSED AND SIZE: 650 books per year; articles from 630 journals
DATA PROCESSING METHODS: computerized
HARDWARE USED: IBM
STORAGE MEDIA: tapes, discs
TYPE OF ACTIVITY: data collection; publication
PERIODICALS PUBLISHED: - Yearbook
ACCESS TO SERVICE: open to specific categories of users, free of charge
TYPE & DESCRIPTION OF SERVICES PROVIDED: Provides bibliographies and research.

142 - BIBLIOTEEK VOOR HEDENDAAGSE DOKUMENTATIE

SYNONYMOUS NAMES: Library on Contemporary Documentation
ADDRESS: Parklaan 2,
        2700 Sint Niklaas Waas,
        BELGIUM
        TEL: (03) 776-5063
CREATED: 1964   HEAD: Mr. Y. van Garsse.
TYPE OF SERVICE: international
WORKING LANGUAGE(S): English; French
SUBJECT COVERAGE: social sciences; administrative sciences; economics; political
        science
GEOGRAPHICAL COVERAGE: global
DATA PROCESSING METHODS: manual; partially computerized
HARDWARE USED: IBM
SOFTWARE USED: own
STORAGE MEDIA: traditional shelving of publications; fiches; tapes; microfiches
TYPE OF ACTIVITY: data collection; distribution of information
PERIODICALS PUBLISHED:
        - Monthly Bulletin
ACCESS TO SERVICE: services open to specific categories of users
TYPE & DESCRIPTION OF SERVICES PROVIDED: Provides library services, bibliographic,
        literature abstract and quantitative data searches, selective dissemination
        of information, microforms and photocopies.

Belgium / Belgique / Bélgica

143 - BIBLIOTHÈQUE FONDS QUETELET

PARENT ORGANIZATION: Ministère des Affaires Economiques/Ministry of Economic Affai
ADDRESS: 6, rue de l'Industrie,
      B-1040 Brussels,
      BELGIUM
      TEL: 02/512.79.50 - TELEX: 21062 Mineco B
CREATED: 1831   *HEAD:* Mr. G. de Saedeleer, Head Librarian
SIZE OF STAFF: Professional: 10   Other: 25   Total: 35
SYSTEMS & NETWORKS ATTACHED TO: DCS, EURONET
SUBJECT COVERAGE: economics; social sciences; demography; law; sociology; statisti
      administrative sciences
DATA BEING PROCESSED AND SIZE: 120,000 books; 7,000 periodicals
DATA PROCESSING METHODS: computerized
HARDWARE USED: IBM
SOFTWARE USED: STAIRS
TYPE OF ACTIVITY: data collection; data analysis
ACCESS TO SERVICE: open to all users, some paid services
TYPE & DESCRIPTION OF SERVICES PROVIDED: Provides library services, bibliographic,
      literature and survey data searches using their own data base "QLIB"
      including 190,000 items covering the field of economics. Also provides
      selective dissemination of information and photocopies.

144 - CENTRE D'ETUDES ET DE DOCUMENTATION AFRICAINES

SYNONYMOUS NAMES: CEDAF;
      Afrika Studie-en Dokumentatiecentrum;
      ASDOC;
      Centre for African Studies and Documentation
ADDRESS: 7, place Royale,
      B-1000 Brussels,
      BELGIUM
      TEL: 512.92.12
CREATED: 1970   *HEAD:* B. Verhaegen, Co-Director
                      F. Reyntjens, Co-Director
SIZE OF STAFF: Professional: 1   Other: 2   Total: 3
TYPE OF SERVICE: national; private; non-profit
WORKING LANGUAGE(S): French
SUBJECT COVERAGE: economics; political science; social sciences
GEOGRAPHICAL COVERAGE: Africa
DATA BEING PROCESSED AND SIZE: 4,000 books; 400 theses; 6,000 articles and documen
DATA PROCESSING METHODS: Manual; computerized
STORAGE MEDIA: traditional shelving of publications, microfiches
TYPE OF ACTIVITY: data collection; data analysis; publication
PERIODICALS PUBLISHED: - Cahiers du CEDAF-ASDOC Studies
        - Bulletin Bibliographique - Bibliografische Berichten
CLIENTELE: researchers, students (1,000 p.a.)
ACCESS TO SERVICE: services open to all users, free of charge
TYPE & DESCRIPTION OF SERVICES PROVIDED: Provides library services.

45 - CENTRE D'ETUDES ET DE DOCUMENTATION SOCIALES

SYNONYMOUS NAMES: CEDS;
        Centre for Social Research and Documentation
ADDRESS: 30, rue des Augustins,
        4000 Liège,
        BELGIUM
        TEL: (041)23.38.04
CREATED: 1946   *HEAD:* M. F. Natalis-Wera,
SIZE OF STAFF: Professional: 6   Other: 1   Total: 7
TYPE OF SERVICE: national; private; non-profit
SYSTEMS & NETWORKS ATTACHED TO: Fédération des Centres d'Etudes et de Documentation
        Sociales
MATERIALS DESCRIBING THE SERVICE: - Activités du Centre d'Etudes et de Documentation
        Sociales (brochure)
WORKING LANGUAGE(S): French
SUBJECT COVERAGE: social sciences; social law; social welfare; social work
GEOGRAPHICAL COVERAGE: Belgium
DATA BEING PROCESSED AND SIZE: 2,600 books; 200 periodicals; 6 abstract journals
DATA PROCESSING METHODS: computerized
HARDWARE USED: IBM PC 256K
SOFTWARE USED: DBASE III
STORAGE MEDIA: discs
TYPE OF ACTIVITY: data collection; data analysis; distribution of information;
        publication
PERIODICALS PUBLISHED:
        - Pêle-Mêle, 4 p.a.
CLIENTELE: social workers, teachers, students
ACCESS TO SERVICE: open to all users, free of charge
TYPE & DESCRIPTION OF SERVICES PROVIDED: Provides library services and literature
        data searches.

**46 - CENTRE DE DOCUMENTATION ET D'INFORMATION INTERUNIVERSITAIRE EN SCIENCES
        SOCIALES**

SYNONYMOUS NAMES: CENDIS ASBL
PARENT ORGANIZATION: Université Libre de Bruxelles-Université Catholique de Louvain
ADDRESS: 1, place Montesquieu-Bte 18,
        B-1348 Louvain-la-Neuve,
        BELGIUM
        TEL: 010/41.81.81
CREATED: 1982   *HEAD:* P. Feldheim, President
                Mr. P. Laurent, Director
SIZE OF STAFF: Professional: 4   Other: 1   Total: 5
TYPE OF SERVICE: national
SUBJECT COVERAGE: social sciences; economics; education; sociology; labour; social
        law
DATA BEING PROCESSED AND SIZE: 3,000 documents on employment
DATA PROCESSING METHODS: computerized
HARDWARE USED: PRIME computer
SOFTWARE USED: ADLIB of LMR

STORAGE MEDIA: discs
TYPE OF ACTIVITY: data collection; data analysis; publication
ACCESS TO SERVICE: services open to all users, some paid services
TYPE & DESCRIPTION OF SERVICES PROVIDED: Services provided by the Centre include
    library services for reference use only, selective dissemination of
    information, production of information on magnetic tapes and bibliographi
    literature and quantitative data searches from own statistical data base,
    "SIGEDA" (containing 3,000 socio-economic variables aggregated by country
    and from a bibliographic data base. Other address: Institut de Sociologie
    44 avenue Jeanne, 1050 Brussels.

147 - MINISTÈRE DES AFFAIRES ETRANGÈRES, DU COMMERCE EXTÉRIEUR ET DE LA COOPÉRATIO AU DÉVELOPPEMENT, BIBLIOTHÈQUE AFRICAINE

SYNONYMOUS NAMES: Ministry of Foreign Affairs, Foreign Trade and Cooperation, Afri
    Library
ADDRESS: Place Royale 7,
    1000 Bruxelles,
    BELGIUM
    TEL: (02) 511.5870
CREATED: 1885   HEAD: international; public; non-profit,
SIZE OF STAFF: Total: 6
SYSTEMS & NETWORKS ATTACHED TO: BELINDIS
SUBJECT COVERAGE: social sciences
GEOGRAPHICAL COVERAGE: Africa
DATA BEING PROCESSED AND SIZE: books, articles, reports, seminars
DATA PROCESSING METHODS: computerized
HARDWARE USED: ITT
SOFTWARE USED: STAIRS
STORAGE MEDIA: traditional shelving of periodicals; fiches; microfiches
TYPE OF ACTIVITY: data collection; data analysis; distribution of information;
    publication
CLIENTELE: university professors, university students, researchers
ACCESS TO SERVICE: services open to all users, free of charge
TYPE & DESCRIPTION OF SERVICES PROVIDED: Provides library services, bibliographic,
    literature abstract searches, selective dissemination of information and
    photocopies .

148 - MUSÉE ROYAL DE L'AFRIQUE CENTRALE, BIBLIOTHÈQUE ET SERVICE DE DOCUMENTATION AFRICAINE

SYNONYMOUS NAMES: Royal Museum of Central Africa, Library and African Documentatio
    Service
PARENT ORGANIZATION: Ministerie van Opvoeding/Ministère de l'Education Nationale
ADDRESS: Steenweg op Leuven 13,
    B-1980 Tervuren,
    BELGIUM
    TEL: (02) 767 5401
CREATED: 1897   HEAD: Mr. M. d'Hertefelt, Head of Department

SIZE OF STAFF: Professional: 3
TYPE OF SERVICE: public; national; non-profit
WORKING LANGUAGE(S): Dutch; French
SUBJECT COVERAGE: social anthropology; cultural anthropology; history; archaeology; linguistics; social sciences; African literature; natural sciences
GEOGRAPHICAL COVERAGE: Africa south of the Sahara and other tropical areas
DATA BEING PROCESSED AND SIZE: 80,000 books; 1,900 periodicals
DATA PROCESSING METHODS: manual
TYPE OF ACTIVITY: data collection; data analysis; distribution of information
PERIODICALS PUBLISHED: - Bibliographie de l'Afrique Sud-saharienne
CLIENTELE: students, scientists (310 p.a.)
ACCESS TO SERVICE: services open to all users, free of charge
TYPE & DESCRIPTION OF SERVICES PROVIDED: Provides library services, bibliographic searches of information and photocopies.

149 - NATIONAAL DOCUMENTATIE CENTRUM "VEILIGHEID EN HYGIËNE", STUDIE EN DOCUMENTATIE

SYNONYMOUS NAMES: Centre National de Documentation "Sécurité et Hygiène"; ANPAT, Association Nationale pour la Prévention des Accidents du Travail
PARENT ORGANIZATION: Nationale Vereniging tot Voorkoming van Arbeidsongevallen (NVVA)/Association Nationale pour la Prévention des Accidents du Travail (ANPAT)
ADDRESS: NVVA - ANPAT,
        Gachardstr. 88, Bus 4,
        B-1050 Brussels,
        BELGIUM
        TEL: (02) 648.03.37 - TELEFAX: (02) 648.68.67
CREATED: 1951   *HEAD:* Mr. H. de Lange, Director, Studies and Documentation Service
SIZE OF STAFF: Professional: 3   Other: 4   Total: 7
TYPE OF SERVICE: national; private; non-profit
SYSTEMS & NETWORKS ATTACHED TO: Centre International de Sécurité (CIS)
WORKING LANGUAGE(S): French; Dutch
SUBJECT COVERAGE: social welfare; working conditions; health
GEOGRAPHICAL COVERAGE: Belgium
DATA BEING PROCESSED AND SIZE: 7,000 books; 150 periodicals; 2,900 CIS microcopies
DATA PROCESSING METHODS: partially computerized
HARDWARE USED: Microcomputer
SOFTWARE USED: Dbase III
STORAGE MEDIA: traditional shelving of publications; CD-ROM; microfiches
TYPE OF ACTIVITY: data analysis; distribution of information
PERIODICALS PUBLISHED: - Promosafe, 6 p.a.
        - Operatie Veiligheid/Objectif Prevention, 10 p.a.
PUBLICATIONS: - Technical fiches and documents on dangerous products
        - Syllabus "Sécurité et Hygiène"
        - Le corps au travail (physiologie humaine du milieu de travail)
        - Actes du Colloque international 1986 sur les affiches de sécurité
CLIENTELE: security officers, firms, insurance companies, teachers, ministries, general public (around 2,650 visitors p.a.)
ACCESS TO SERVICE: services open to all users (against payment for non-affiliated members)

TYPE & DESCRIPTION OF SERVICES PROVIDED: Provides library services, bibliographic searches of information, selective dissemination of information, on-line services and photocopies. Holds a CD-ROM collection of various data bases related to occupational health and safety: CDOSH including CISDOC, HSE Lin NIOSHTIC, and CHEM-BANK including RTECS, CHRIS, OHMTADS. Subscription to these CD-ROM discs can be made through ANPAT.

150 - SYSTÈME BIBLIOGRAPHIQUE ET DOCUMENTAIRE RELATIF À L'IMMIGRATION

SYNONYMOUS NAMES: Sybidi
ADDRESS: rue P.E. Janson, 13,
        B-1050 Brussels,
        BELGIUM
        TEL: 02-537.19.71
CREATED: 1982   *HEAD:* Mr. F. Dassetto, Coordinator
TYPE OF SERVICE: international; private; non-profit
SYSTEMS & NETWORKS ATTACHED TO: EURYDICE
WORKING LANGUAGE(S): French
SUBJECT COVERAGE: social sciences; political science; psychology; social welfare;
        sociology; statistics; linguistics; law; immigration
GEOGRAPHICAL COVERAGE: Belgium
DATA BEING PROCESSED AND SIZE: 400 documentation items
DATA PROCESSING METHODS: partially computerized
HARDWARE USED: IBM 360
SOFTWARE USED: software of the Université Catholique de Louvain
STORAGE MEDIA: discs
TYPE OF ACTIVITY: data analysis; publication
PERIODICALS PUBLISHED: - Sybidi Périodique, 2 p.a.
PUBLICATIONS: - Sybidi Documents
ACCESS TO SERVICE: paid services
TYPE & DESCRIPTION OF SERVICES PROVIDED: Network of correspondents analysing (220) periodicals, research results, theses and reports. Provides bibliographies

151 - UNIVERSITÉ CATHOLIQUE DE LOUVAIN, FACULTÉ DES SCIENCES ECONOMIQUES, SOCIALES POLITIQUES, BIBLIOTHÈQUE

SYNONYMOUS NAMES: PSPO
ADDRESS: place Montesquieu, 1,
        B-1348 Louvain-La-Neuve,
        BELGIUM
        TEL: 10/41.81.81
HEAD: L. d'Arras d'Haudrecy, Librarian
SIZE OF STAFF: Professional: 1   Other: 8   Total: 9
TYPE OF SERVICE: national; public
WORKING LANGUAGE(S): French
SUBJECT COVERAGE: social sciences; administrative sciences; demography; economics;
        political science; social anthropology; cultural anthropology; social
        welfare; sociology
DATA BEING PROCESSED AND SIZE: 5,000 books p.a.; 10,000 articles p.a.

DATA PROCESSING METHODS: computerized
HARDWARE USED: IBM 370; MDS; IBM PC
STORAGE MEDIA: microfiches
TYPE OF ACTIVITY: data collection; publication
CLIENTELE: 4,300 readers
ACCESS TO SERVICE: open to all users, free of charge
TYPE & DESCRIPTION OF SERVICES PROVIDED: Provides library services and bibliographies
        from its own computerized data base and other data bases through Lockheed,
        SDC and Euronet.

152 - UNIVERSITÉ DE LIÈGE, FACULTÉ DE DROIT, D'ECONOMIE ET DE SCIENCES SOCIALES, BIBLIOTHÈQUE LÉON GRAULICH

ADDRESS: Faculté de Droit,
        Université de Liège,
        place du XX Août, 7,
        4000 Liège,
        BELGIUM
CREATED: 1929   *HEAD:* Prof. P. Graulich,
SIZE OF STAFF: Total: 9
TYPE OF SERVICE: national; public; non-profit
WORKING LANGUAGE(S): French
SUBJECT COVERAGE: law; economics; social sciences
GEOGRAPHICAL COVERAGE: Belgium
DATA BEING PROCESSED AND SIZE: 4,000 books p.a.
DATA PROCESSING METHODS: computerized
HARDWARE USED: IBM
TYPE OF ACTIVITY: data collection; data analysis; publication
PERIODICALS PUBLISHED: - Annales de la Faculté de Droit
PUBLICATIONS: - Répertoire des périodiques, 1981
        - Catalogues alphabétique et systématique
CLIENTELE: professors, students, lawyers, notaries
ACCESS TO SERVICE: open to all users, free of charge
TYPE & DESCRIPTION OF SERVICES PROVIDED: Provides traditional and computerized
        library services.

153 - UNIVERSITEIT ANTWERPEN COLLEGE VOOR DE ONTWIKKELINGSLANDEN, BIBLIOTHEEK

SYNONYMOUS NAMES: Université d'Anvers, Collège pour les Pays en voie de
        Développement, Bibliothèque;
        University of Antwerp, College for Developing Countries, Library;
        RUCA
ADDRESS: Middelheimlaan 1,
        B-2020 Antwerpen,
        BELGIUM
        TEL: (03) 218-0663 - TELEX: 33362 RUCABI
CREATED: 1965   *HEAD:* Ms. F. Martens, Librarian
SIZE OF STAFF: Professional: 2
TYPE OF SERVICE: national; public; non-profit

MATERIALS DESCRIBING THE SERVICE: - Guide des usagers (Univ. d'Anvers - RUCA)
WORKING LANGUAGE(S): Dutch; French; English
SUBJECT COVERAGE: economics; social sciences; political science; sociology;
   education; geography; administrative sciences; demography; rural
   development; public finance; development planning; tourism
GEOGRAPHICAL COVERAGE: developing countries
DATA BEING PROCESSED AND SIZE: 7,500 books; 200 periodicals; 650 master theses
DATA PROCESSING METHODS: partially computerized
HARDWARE USED: DIGITAL DEC PDP
SOFTWARE USED: VUBIS II
STORAGE MEDIA: traditional shelving of publications; terminals
TYPE OF ACTIVITY: distribution of information; SSID scientific and methodological
   activities; publication
PERIODICALS PUBLISHED:
    - Acquisitions of the Antwerp University Libraries
    - ALA: Africa, Latin America, Asia, irr.
    - List of Periodicals
CLIENTELE: students, staff, researchers and general public
ACCESS TO SERVICE: services open to all users
TYPE & DESCRIPTION OF SERVICES PROVIDED: Provides library services, bibliographic
   information searches, selective dissemination of information, and
   photocopies. Also provides on-line services using own data bases.

154 - INSTITUT NATIONAL POUR LA FORMATION ET LA RECHERCHE EN EDUCATION, CENTRE DE DOCUMENTATION ET D'INFORMATION PÉDAGOGIQUES

SYNONYMOUS NAMES: CDIP;
   National Institute for Training and Research in Education, Instructional
   Documentation and Information Centre
ADDRESS: rue de l'Inspection,
   B.P. 437,
   Porto-Novo,
   BENIN
   TEL: 21-34-86
CREATED: 1972 *HEAD:* E. Aigbede, Head
SIZE OF STAFF: Professional: 7 Other: 37 Total: 44
TYPE OF SERVICE: national; public; non-profit
WORKING LANGUAGE(S): French
SUBJECT COVERAGE: social sciences; education
GEOGRAPHICAL COVERAGE: French speaking Africa; USA; Canada; Brazil; Mexico; Chile;
   Saudi Arabia; India; Viet-nam (Socialist Republic); Japan; Europe
DATA PROCESSING METHODS: manual
STORAGE MEDIA: traditional shelving of publications
TYPE OF ACTIVITY: data collection; SSID scientific and methodological activities;
   SSID training; publication
PERIODICALS PUBLISHED: - L'Education Béninoise
    - Bulletin Signalétique d'Articles de Revues
    - Bulletin de Liaison
PUBLICATIONS: - Catalogue des rapports, mémoires et thèses
CLIENTELE: teachers, students, educational staff (approx. 22,000 users)

CCESS TO SERVICE: paid services open to all users
YPE & DESCRIPTION OF SERVICES PROVIDED: Provides library services. Has set up a
network linking 6 regional documentation centres.

55 - BOLIVIA-INSTITUTO NACIONAL DE ESTADÍSTICA

YNONYMOUS NAMES: INE;
Bolivia-National Institute of Statistics
ARENT ORGANIZATION: Ministerio de Planeamiento y Coordinación
DDRESS: Plaza Mario Guzmán Aspiazu No. 1,
Casilla Correo No. 6129,
La Paz,
BOLIVIA
TEL: 367443
REATED: 1936   *HEAD:* Mr. M. Mercado Lora, Executive Director
IZE OF STAFF: Professional: 1
YPE OF SERVICE: national; public
ORKING LANGUAGE(S): Spanish
UBJECT COVERAGE: statistics; social sciences; administrative sciences; demography;
economics; education; social welfare; sociology; transport; communication;
towns; housing; health; agriculture; industry; finance; energy
EOGRAPHICAL COVERAGE: Bolivia
ATA PROCESSING METHODS: manual
TORAGE MEDIA: fiches
YPE OF ACTIVITY: data collection; data analysis; distribution of information;
publication
ERIODICALS PUBLISHED:
- Boletin Bibliografico
- Censo Económico 1985
UBLICATIONS: - Catálogo de publicaciones
- Bolivia en CIFRA, 1985
- Censo nacional agropecuario
CCESS TO SERVICE: services open to all users against payment
YPE & DESCRIPTION OF SERVICES PROVIDED: Provides library services, bibliographic,
literature abstract and quantitative data searches of information, selective
dissemination of information, information on magnetic tapes or discs,
photcopies and translation of documents.

56 - FACULTAD LATINOAMERICANA DE CIENCIAS SOCIALES-PROGRAMA BOLIVIA, BIBLIOTECA

YNONYMOUS NAMES: FLACSO-Programa Bolivia, Library;
Latin American Faculty of Social Sciences, Bolivia, Library
ARENT ORGANIZATION: Facultad Latinoamericana de Ciencias Sociales
DDRESS: Av. Ecuador 2517,
Casilla 20803,
La Paz,
BOLIVIA
TEL: 37.27.32

CREATED: 1983   HEAD: Mr. E. García, Librarian
SIZE OF STAFF: Professional: 1
TYPE OF SERVICE: public; non-profit
WORKING LANGUAGE(S): Spanish
SUBJECT COVERAGE: social sciences; economics; political science; sociology
GEOGRAPHICAL COVERAGE: Bolivia; South America
DATA BEING PROCESSED AND SIZE: 500 books; 1,000 journals; 1,000 serials; 500 report
DATA PROCESSING METHODS: manual
TYPE OF ACTIVITY: data analysis; distribution of information; SSID scientific and
         methodological activities; publication
PERIODICALS PUBLISHED: - Estado y Sociedad
         - Cuadernos Populares
PUBLICATIONS: - Socioeconómicos relaciones internacionales
CLIENTELE: researchers
ACCESS TO SERVICE: open to all users free of charge
TYPE & DESCRIPTION OF SERVICES PROVIDED: Provides library services, bibliographic
         searches of information and selective dissemination of information.

**157 - UNIVERSITY OF BOTSWANA, NATIONAL INSTITUTE OF DEVELOPMENT RESEARCH AND
         DOCUMENTATION SERVICE**

SYNONYMOUS NAMES: NIR
ADDRESS: Private Bag 0022,
         Gaborone,
         BOTSWANA
         TEL: 356364/5 - TELEX: 2429 B
CREATED: 1975   HEAD: Mr. A. Datta, Director
TYPE OF SERVICE: international; public; non-profit
SYSTEMS & NETWORKS ATTACHED TO: Pan African Documentation and Information System
         (PADIS)
MATERIALS DESCRIBING THE SERVICE: - NIR brochure
WORKING LANGUAGE(S): English
SUBJECT COVERAGE: social sciences; economics; sociology; demography; education;
         information science; social anthropology; social welfare; health;
         development
GEOGRAPHICAL COVERAGE: Botswana; Southern Africa; Africa
DATA BEING PROCESSED AND SIZE: 7,000 documents including books, reports, articles,
         reports and on-going research
DATA PROCESSING METHODS: manual; partially computerized
HARDWARE USED: IBM PC AT
SOFTWARE USED: CDS/ISIS
STORAGE MEDIA: traditional shelving of publications
TYPE OF ACTIVITY: data collection; data analysis; distribution of information;
         publication
CLIENTELE: students, researchers, experts and general public
ACCESS TO SERVICE: open to all users free of charge (some paid services)
TYPE & DESCRIPTION OF SERVICES PROVIDED: Provides library services, bibliographic
         searches of information, selective dissemination of information, microform
         and photocopies.

Brazil / Brésil / Brasil

58 - CENTRO DE ESTUDOS AFRO-ASIÁTICOS, SERVIÇO DE DOCUMENTAÇÃO E INTERCAMBIO

SYNONYMOUS NAMES: Centre for African and Asian Studies. Documentation and Exchange
Service
PARENT ORGANIZATION: Conjunto Universitário Candido Mendes
ADDRESS: rua da Assembléia no. 10 sala 501,
Centro,
Rio de Janeiro, R.J.,
CEP 20011,
BRAZIL
TEL: (021) 221.3536
CREATED: 1973   *HEAD:* Mr. C. A. Hasenbalg,
SIZE OF STAFF: Professional: 3   Other: 2   Total: 5
TYPE OF SERVICE: national; private; non-profit
WORKING LANGUAGE(S): Portuguese
SUBJECT COVERAGE: social sciences; political science; sociology; history; economics
GEOGRAPHICAL COVERAGE: Africa; Asia; Caribbean area; Brazil (Afro-Brazilians)
DATA BEING PROCESSED AND SIZE: 6,000 books; 2,000 periodicals; reports; 45,000 press
cuttings
DATA PROCESSING METHODS: computerized
HARDWARE USED: microcomputer PC
SOFTWARE USED: DBASE III
STORAGE MEDIA: fiches; tapes; discs
TYPE OF ACTIVITY: data collection; data analysis; publication
PERIODICALS PUBLISHED: - Estudos Afro-Asiáticos
CLIENTELE: university students and researchers
ACCESS TO SERVICE: free of charge
TYPE & DESCRIPTION OF SERVICES PROVIDED: Provides library services, surveys,
bibliographic searches of information and photocopies.

59 - FUNDAÇÃO CASE DE RUI BARBOSA, CENTRO DE DOCUMENTAÇÃO

SYNONYMOUS NAMES: FCRB, Centro de Documentação
PARENT ORGANIZATION: Ministry of Culture
ADDRESS: rua São Clemente, 134,
22.260 Botafogo,
Rio de Janeiro RJ,
BRAZIL
TEL: 286-1297 - TELEX: 2137232
CREATED: 1966   *HEAD:* J. Conçalves de Araugo, Director
SIZE OF STAFF: Professional: 6   Other: 3   Total: 9
TYPE OF SERVICE: national; public; non-profit
MATERIALS DESCRIBING THE SERVICE: - Fundação Casa de Rui Barbosa, Centro de
Documentaçao. Canudos: subsídios para a sua reavalição histórica, Rio de
Janeiro, 1986. 548 p.
WORKING LANGUAGE(S): Portuguese
SUBJECT COVERAGE: history; law; linguistics; philology
GEOGRAPHICAL COVERAGE: Brazil; Portugal
DATA BEING PROCESSED AND SIZE: 60,000 books

DATA PROCESSING METHODS: manual
TYPE OF ACTIVITY: data collection; data analysis; distribution of information;
   publication
CLIENTELE: researchers, post-graduate students
TYPE & DESCRIPTION OF SERVICES PROVIDED: Provides library services, bibliographic &
   literature abstract searches of information, microforms and photocopies.

160 - FUNDAÇÃO SISTEMA ESTADUAL DE ANÁLISE DE DADOS, CENTRAL DE DADOS E REFERENCIAS

SYNONYMOUS NAMES: SEADE-CDR
ADDRESS: Av. Cásper Líbero, 464 - 3e And.,
   01033 São Paulo SP,
   BRAZIL
   TEL: 229.24.33 - TELEX: (011) 31390
CREATED: 1979   *HEAD:* Ms. M. Lopes Ginez de Lara, Head
TYPE OF SERVICE: public; non-profit
SYSTEMS & NETWORKS ATTACHED TO: DOCPAL (Sistema de Documentação sobre Población);
   INFOPLAN/BR (Sistema de Informações sobre o Planejamento/BR
WORKING LANGUAGE(S): Portuguese; Spanish; French
SUBJECT COVERAGE: social sciences; administrative sciences; demography; economics;
   education; political science; social welfare; sociology; statistics; socio
   economic indicators
GEOGRAPHICAL COVERAGE: São Paulo, Brazil
DATA BEING PROCESSED AND SIZE: books; journal articles; theses; seminar reports;
   project reports
DATA PROCESSING METHODS: partially computerized
HARDWARE USED: IBM 4341; IBM PC
SOFTWARE USED: ISIS V.4/MICRO-ISIS, DBASE III, LOTUS, WORDSTAR
TYPE OF ACTIVITY: data collection; data analysis; distribution of information;
   publication
PERIODICALS PUBLISHED: - São Paulo em Perspectiva, 4 p.a.
   - DOCPOP
   - Conjuntura Demográfica, 4 p.a.
   - São Paulo e Conjuntura, 12 p.a.
   - Indicadores Demográficos, 12 p.a.
PUBLICATIONS: - Análise demográfica regional
   - Anuário estatístico do Estado de São Paulo
   - Informe demográfico (series)
   - Um Retrato da Violência contra a mulher
   - São Paulo 80 (series)
CLIENTELE: public and private administrators (25,000 p.a.)
ACCESS TO SERVICE: services open to all users, both paid and free services
TYPE & DESCRIPTION OF SERVICES PROVIDED: Provides library services, bibliographic,
   literature and quantitative data searches of information, on-line services
   using own data bases: "SIM" (Sistema de Informações Municipais), "DOCPOP"
   (Sistema Documentação sobre População no Brasil), "DOCCDR" (Base de Dados
   de Informação Bibliográfica Sócio-econômica). Services also available
   include production of information on magnetic tapes or discs, provision of
   microforms and photocopies.

61 - INSTITUTO DE PLANEJAMENTO ECONOMICO E SOCIAL, CENTRO DE TREINAMENTO PARA O DESENVOLVIMENTO ECONOMICO, BIBLIOTECA

SYNONYMOUS NAMES: IPEA-CENDEC Biblioteca;
    Economic and Social Planning Institute, Processing Center for Economic
    Development
PARENT ORGANIZATION: Secretaria de Planejamento da Presidência da República
ADDRESS: SGAN - Quadra 908,
    Módulo E,
    Caixa Postal 040013,
    Brasilia, DF,
    CEP 70312,
    BRAZIL
    TEL: 2744105 - TELEX: (061) 1023
CREATED: 1966   *HEAD:* J. V. de Abreu Neto,
SIZE OF STAFF: Total: 2
TYPE OF SERVICE: international; public; non-profit
SUBJECT COVERAGE: economics; social sciences; administrative sciences; demography;
    education; political science; sociology
DATA BEING PROCESSED AND SIZE: books; reports; seminars; training courses;
    periodicals; official documents
DATA PROCESSING METHODS: manual
TYPE OF ACTIVITY: distribution of information
CLIENTELE: libraries
ACCESS TO SERVICE: open to all users, free of charge
TYPE & DESCRIPTION OF SERVICES PROVIDED: Provides library services, bibliographic
    searches, selective dissemination of information, information on magnetic
    tapes or discs and photocopies.

62 - INSTITUTO UNIVERSITARIO DE PESQUISAS DO RIO DE JANEIRO, SETOR DE COMUNICAÇÃO E DIVULGAÇÃO

SYNONYMOUS NAMES: IUPERJ
PARENT ORGANIZATION: Instituto Universitário de Pesquisas do Rio de Janeiro (IUPERJ)
ADDRESS: Rua da Matriz, 82,
    Botafogo, Rio de Janeiro,
    BRAZIL
    TEL: (021) 286-0996
HEAD: V. M. Monteiro,
SIZE OF STAFF: Professional: 2   Other: 2   Total: 4
TYPE OF SERVICE: national; public; non-profit
SUBJECT COVERAGE: sociology; political science; socio-economic indicators; urban
    planning
DATA BEING PROCESSED AND SIZE: books, periodicals, research reports, theses
DATA PROCESSING METHODS: manual; partially computerized
HARDWARE USED: IBM
SOFTWARE USED: various
STORAGE MEDIA: traditional shelving of publications; fiches; tapes; discs;
    microfiches
TYPE OF ACTIVITY: data collection; data analysis; publication
PUBLICATIONS: - O Ensino e a pesquisa no Instituto Universitário do Rio de Janeiro

- Brasilian bibliography in social sciences
- Social sciences index, 1979
- Catalogo de Teses
- Relatorios Anuais

CLIENTELE: students and researchers

ACCESS TO SERVICE: open to all users, free of charge or reimbursement of marginal
costs

TYPE & DESCRIPTION OF SERVICES PROVIDED: Provides library services, bibliographic,
literature abstracts and quantitative data searches as well as on-line
services using their own data bases SOCIAL INDICATORS, BRAZILIAN ELITES and
URBAN PLANNING.

163 - MINISTÉRIO DA FAZENDA, BIBLIOTECA

SYNONYMOUS NAMES: Ministry of Finance, Library

ADDRESS: Av. Presidente Antonio Carlos 375,
Sala 1238,
20020 Rio de Janeiro, RJ,
BRAZIL
TEL: 240-1120

CREATED: 1943   *HEAD:* Ms. L. Almeida Chaves, Head Librarian

SIZE OF STAFF: Professional: 14   Other: 10   Total: 24

TYPE OF SERVICE: public

MATERIALS DESCRIBING THE SERVICE: - Manual de serviço - Rotinas

SUBJECT COVERAGE: administrative sciences; economics; law; social sciences

DATA BEING PROCESSED AND SIZE: 76,900 books; 360 periodicals

DATA PROCESSING METHODS: manual

TYPE OF ACTIVITY: data collection; publication

CLIENTELE: lawyers, economists, students, public service (11,597 in all)

ACCESS TO SERVICE: services open to all users, free of charge (12,000 p.a.)

TYPE & DESCRIPTION OF SERVICES PROVIDED: Provides library services, bibliographic
searches of information, and photocopies.

164 - UNIVERSIDADE DE SÃO PAULO, CENTRO DE ESTUDOS DE DEMOGRAFIA HISTÓRICA DA AMÉRI
LATINA

SYNONYMOUS NAMES: CEDHAL

ADDRESS: C. P. 8105,
05508 São Paulo,
BRAZIL
TEL: (011) 210.2122

CREATED: 1985   *HEAD:* Prof. M. L. Marcilio, Director

SIZE OF STAFF: Professional: 2

TYPE OF SERVICE: international; public; non-profit

WORKING LANGUAGE(S): Portuguese; English; French; Spanish; Italian

SUBJECT COVERAGE: demography; history; historical demography; law; social
anthropology; cultural anthropology; sociology; geography; population;
children; youth; family

GEOGRAPHICAL COVERAGE: Latin America

DATA BEING PROCESSED AND SIZE: 10,000 documentation items
DATA PROCESSING METHODS: partially computerized
HARDWARE USED: IBM PC
SOFTWARE USED: DBASE III; Word Data; ISIS
STORAGE MEDIA: fiches; discs
TYPE OF ACTIVITY: data analysis; distribution of information; SSID scientific and
        methodological activities; SSID training
PERIODICALS PUBLISHED: - Estudos CEDHAL
PUBLICATIONS: - Marcílio, M. L., Caiçara. Terra e população, 1986
CLIENTELE: researchers, graduate students, undergraduates, faculty
ACCESS TO SERVICE: services open to specific categories of users, free of charge
TYPE & DESCRIPTION OF SERVICES PROVIDED: Provides bibliographic and quantitative data
        searches of information, on-line services using its own data bases on infant
        population in Brazilian history.

165 - UNIVERSIDADE FEDERAL DO ACRE, BIBLIOTECA CENTRAL RUY ALBERTO DA COSTA LINS

SYNONYMOUS NAMES: Federal University of Acre, Ruy Alberto da Costa Lins Central
        Library
ADDRESS: Campus Universitário BR,
        364 Km 4,
        CEP 69.900 Rio Brancho-Acre,
        BRAZIL
        TEL: (068) 224-2397 - TELEX: (069) 2532
HEAD: Mr. V. Augustinho, Director
SIZE OF STAFF: Professional: 3   Other: 23   Total: 26
TYPE OF SERVICE: national; public; non-profit
SYSTEMS & NETWORKS ATTACHED TO: National System of University Libraries
WORKING LANGUAGE(S): Portuguese
SUBJECT COVERAGE: social sciences; humanities; agriculture
GEOGRAPHICAL COVERAGE: north and northwest Brazil
DATA BEING PROCESSED AND SIZE: books; on-going research; seminars; articles; reports
DATA PROCESSING METHODS: manual
CLIENTELE: students, teachers, civil servants; (about 2,700 users)
ACCESS TO SERVICE: services open to all users, free of charge
TYPE & DESCRIPTION OF SERVICES PROVIDED: Provides library services, bibliographic,
        literature abstract and quantitative data searches, selective dissemination
        of information, microforms and photocopies.

166 - CENTAR ZA BIBLIOGRAFSKA INFORMACIJA

SYNONYMOUS NAMES: Centre of Bibliographic Information;
        CBI
PARENT ORGANIZATION: Cyril and Methodius National Library
ADDRESS: Boul. Tolbuhin 11,
        1504 Sofia,
        BULGARIA
        TEL: 88-28-11 ext. 230 - TELEX: 22432 Natlib

Bulgaria / Bulgarie / Bulgaria

CREATED: 1951   HEAD: Mrs. E. Laskova, Deputy Director
SIZE OF STAFF: Professional: 29   Other: 3   Total: 32
TYPE OF SERVICE: national; public; profit
SYSTEMS & NETWORKS ATTACHED TO: National System of Scientific and Technical
        Information
MATERIALS DESCRIBING THE SERVICE: - Cyril and Methodius National Library, 1878-1978.
        Sofia, Sofia Press, 1978, 50 p.
        - Parvanova, Y., Cuzdestranna bibliografska informacija v pomost na organit
        za socialno upravlenie in: Bibliotekar. 1978, no.9
SUBJECT COVERAGE: social sciences
GEOGRAPHICAL COVERAGE: global
DATA BEING PROCESSED AND SIZE: 15,700 books; 5,000 periodicals; 11,200 official
        publications; 750 archives of bibliographical references
DATA PROCESSING METHODS: manual
TYPE OF ACTIVITY: distribution of information
PERIODICALS PUBLISHED:
        - Bjuletin za Novonabaveni Knigi na Cuzdi Ezici. Mesecno Izdanie. Sofia,
        Narodna Biblioteka Kiril Metodij, 1954- Serija D. Obstestveni Nauki.
        Filologicni Nauki. Izkustvo
        - Novi zakoni v kapitalisticeskite strani. Informacionen bjuletin
        - Information bulletin of bibliographic references
CLIENTELE: researchers, civil servants
ACCESS TO SERVICE: open to all users, free of charge
TYPE & DESCRIPTION OF SERVICES PROVIDED: Provides library services, retrospective
        bibliographic searches, selective dissemination of information, photocopies
        and microforms.

**167 - CENTAR ZA NAUCNA INFORMACIJA PO PRIRODNI, MATEMATICESKI I OBSTESTVENI NAUKI PR
BALGARSKA AKADEMIJA NA NAUKITE**

SYNONYMOUS NAMES: CNI-BAN;
        Bulgarian Academy of Sciences Scientific Information Centre for Natural,
        Mathematical and Social Sciences
PARENT ORGANIZATION: Centralna Biblioteka pri Balgarska Akademia na Naukite
ADDRESS: 1, "7 Noembri" str.,
        Sofia 1040,
        BULGARIA
        TEL: 8.41.41./336
CREATED: 1959   HEAD: G. Svobodozarya, Director
SIZE OF STAFF: Professional: 35   Other: 70
TYPE OF SERVICE: national
SYSTEMS & NETWORKS ATTACHED TO: The National Scientific and Technical Information
        System (NSNTI) and Management Information Body of the Academic Information
        Network
SUBJECT COVERAGE: social sciences; statistics; science policy
DATA BEING PROCESSED AND SIZE: books; periodicals; microcopies; manuscripts
DATA PROCESSING METHODS: manual
HARDWARE USED: Hewlett-Packard 3000; BK 1302 (microcomputer)
SOFTWARE USED: POISK 4M
STORAGE MEDIA: fiches; tapes; discs; microfiches
TYPE OF ACTIVITY: data collection; data analysis; publication; SSID scientific and

methodological activities

PERIODICALS PUBLISHED:
- Bulletin of Scientific Achievements in the Field of Social Sciences at the Bulgarian Academy of Sciences
- Bulletin of Foreign and Bulgarian Methods Newly Introduced in the Practice
- Abstract Journals in the Field of Scientific Communism, Philosophy, Sociology, Science of Science and Scientific Information; Economics and Law; Linguistics and Literature; History, Archeology and Ethnography; Psychology and Pedagogics; Arts and Culture

ACCESS TO SERVICE: open to specific categories of users, some paid services

TYPE & DESCRIPTION OF SERVICES PROVIDED: The Centre uses the library holdings of the Central Library at the Bulgarian Academy of Sciences. It has its own data base "Sofia" and also has access to others such as COMPENDIX, INSPEC, BIOSIS, VINITI. Provides information retrieval services, selective dissemination of information, microfilms, photocopies and translation of documents.

168 - IKONOMICESKI INSTITUT PRI BALGARSKA, AKADEMIJA NA NAUKITE, NAPRAVLENIE ZA NAUCNA STATISTIKO-IKONOMICESKA INFORMACIJA I BIBLIOTEKA

SYNONYMOUS NAMES: Institute of Economics, Bulgarian Academy of Sciences, Department of Scientific and Statistical Economic Information and Library

ADDRESS: 3, Aksakov St.,
Sofia 1000,
BULGARIA
TEL: 8.41.21/812

CREATED: 1956   HEAD: T. Bantgheva, Senior Research Associate

TYPE OF SERVICE: public; private; non-profit

SYSTEMS & NETWORKS ATTACHED TO: The Information Network at the Bulgarian Academy of Sciences - Scientific Information Centre (CNI-BAN)

WORKING LANGUAGE(S): Russian

SUBJECT COVERAGE: economics; statistics; administrative sciences; demography; social welfare

DATA BEING PROCESSED AND SIZE: 26,400 books; 3,300 periodicals; 17 abstract journals; 88 microcopies

DATA PROCESSING METHODS: computerized

STORAGE MEDIA: traditional shelving of publications; fiches; microfilms

TYPE OF ACTIVITY: data collection; data analysis; distribution of information; publication

CLIENTELE: professors, junior and senior scientists, post-graduate students

ACCESS TO SERVICE: open to all users, free of charge

TYPE & DESCRIPTION OF SERVICES PROVIDED: Provides library services and bibliographic, literature and survey data searches, and translation of documents upon request. Has access to the International Social Sciences Information System (MISON), USSR.

169 - INSTITUT PO NAUKITE ZA DARZAVATA I PRAVOTO, SLUZBA ZA NAUCNA INFORMACIJA I DOKUMENTACIJA KAM

SYNONYMOUS NAMES: Institute of State and Legal Sciences, Office for Scientific
    Information and Documentation;
    Institut des Sciences de l'Etat et du Droit, Service d'Information
    Scientifique et de Documentation
PARENT ORGANIZATION: Balgarska Akademija na Naukite (Bulgarian Academy of Sciences)
ADDRESS: 3, Benkovski Str.,
    Sofia-1000,
    BULGARIA
    TEL: 87-56-84
CREATED: 1959   *HEAD:* A. K. Manov, Chief of the Office
SIZE OF STAFF: Professional: 15
TYPE OF SERVICE: national
SYSTEMS & NETWORKS ATTACHED TO: The Information Network at the Bulgarian Academy of
    Sciences (CNI-BAN)
WORKING LANGUAGE(S): Bulgarian; Russian; English; German; French; Hungarian; Czech;
    Polish; Rumanian; Italian; Spanish
SUBJECT COVERAGE: political science; law; social sciences; administrative sciences;
    philosophy; sociology
DATA BEING PROCESSED AND SIZE: 17,800 books; 9,485 periodicals; 1 abstract journal;
    94 microcopies
DATA PROCESSING METHODS: partially computerized
HARDWARE USED: APPLE
SOFTWARE USED: PFS
STORAGE MEDIA: traditional shelving of publications, fiches, discs, microfiches
TYPE OF ACTIVITY: data collection; data analysis; distribution of information;
    publication; SSID training
PERIODICALS PUBLISHED:
    - Bulletin for legal information
PUBLICATIONS: - Bibliography of legal literature
CLIENTELE: lawyers, scholars
ACCESS TO SERVICE: open to specific categories of users, free of charge
TYPE & DESCRIPTION OF SERVICES PROVIDED: Provides library services, bibliographic,
    literature and survey data searches, using its own database IIBC-KY,
    selective dissemination of information, production of information on
    magnetic tapes or discs, microfilms, photocopies and translation of
    documents. Has access to the International Social Sciences Information
    System (MISON), USSR.

170 - INSTITUT PO SOCIOLOGIJA, OTDEL ZA NAUCNA INFORMACIJA I DOKUMENTACIJA

SYNONYMOUS NAMES: Institute of Sociology, Department of Scientific Information and
    Documentation
PARENT ORGANIZATION: Balgarska Akademija na Naukite (Bulgarian Academy of Sciences)
ADDRESS: 13-A, Moskovska St.,
    1000 Sofia,
    BULGARIA
    TEL: 88-32-00
CREATED: 1968   *HEAD:* V. Nokov, Head of Department

SIZE OF STAFF: Professional: 9
TYPE OF SERVICE: national
SYSTEMS & NETWORKS ATTACHED TO: The Information Network at the Bulgarian Academy of
        Sciences (CNI-BAN)
SUBJECT COVERAGE: sociology
DATA BEING PROCESSED AND SIZE: 6,650 books; 2,600 periodicals; 130 abstract journals;
        360 manuscripts
DATA PROCESSING METHODS: manual
TYPE OF ACTIVITY: data collection
ACCESS TO SERVICE: open to specific categories of users, free of charge
TYPE & DESCRIPTION OF SERVICES PROVIDED: Provides library services, bibliographic
        data searches and selective dissemination of information. Has access to the
        International Social Sciences Information System (MISON), USSR. Also
        provides microforms, photocopies and translation of documents upon request.

**171 - INSTITUT ZA MEZDUNARODNI OTNOSENIJA I SOCIALISTICESKA INTEGRACIJA, NAUCEN
INFORMACIONEN CENTAR**

SYNONYMOUS NAMES: IMOSI-BAN;
        Institute for International Relations and Socialist Integration, Scientific
        Information Centre
PARENT ORGANIZATION: Balgarska Akademija na Naukite (Bulgarian Academy of Sciences)
ADDRESS: Boul. "P. Slavejkov" no. 15-a,
        Sofia,
        BULGARIA
        TEL: 52-30-75 - TELEX: 22310
CREATED: 1976   *HEAD:* V. Iskra, Director
SIZE OF STAFF: Professional: 26
SYSTEMS & NETWORKS ATTACHED TO: The Information Network at the Bulgarian Academy of
        Sciences (CNI-BAN)
SUBJECT COVERAGE: political science; economics; social sciences; international
        relations; international economic relations
DATA BEING PROCESSED AND SIZE: 19,000 books; 555 periodicals; 35 abstract journals;
        352 manuscripts
DATA PROCESSING METHODS: manual
STORAGE MEDIA: traditional shelving of publications
TYPE OF ACTIVITY: data collection; data analysis; publication
PERIODICALS PUBLISHED: - Mezdunarodni Otnosenija
ACCESS TO SERVICE: open to specific categories of users, free of charge
TYPE & DESCRIPTION OF SERVICES PROVIDED: Provides library services and information
        retrieval services. Has access to the International Information System for
        Social Sciences (MISON), USSR. Also provides photocopies and translation of
        documents.

172 - MEZDUNARODEN INFORMACIONEN CENTAR PO BALKANISTIKA

SYNONYMOUS NAMES: International Information Centre on Sources of Balkan and
        Mediterranean History;
        Centre international d'Information sur les Sources de l'Histoire Balkanique

et Méditerranéenne;
CIBAL

PARENT ORGANIZATION: Institute for Balkan Studies of the Bulgarian Academy of
Sciences

ADDRESS: 45, "Moskovska" St.,
Sofia 1000,
BULGARIA
TEL: 882283

CREATED: 1976   *HEAD:* J. Kabadaïev, Director of Secretariat

SIZE OF STAFF: Professional: 10   Other: 5   Total: 15

TYPE OF SERVICE: international; non-profit

MATERIALS DESCRIBING THE SERVICE: - CIBAL - Dix ans d'activités d'information
scientifique, 1986

WORKING LANGUAGE(S): Bulgarian; French

SUBJECT COVERAGE: history; literature; cultural anthropology; ethnography;
linguistics

GEOGRAPHICAL COVERAGE: the Balkans; Bulgaria; Yugoslavia; Albania; Greece; Turkey

DATA BEING PROCESSED AND SIZE: 9,468 books; 227 periodicals, 12 abstract journals;
500 microfilms

DATA PROCESSING METHODS: manual

STORAGE MEDIA: traditional shelving of publications; fiches, microfilms; microfiche
electrocopies

TYPE OF ACTIVITY: data collection; data analysis; distribution of information;
publication

PERIODICALS PUBLISHED: - Bibliographie d'Etudes Balkaniques, 1p.a.
- Bulletin d'Information CIBAL; 1 p.a.

PUBLICATIONS: - Stancev, K., Description et catalogue des manuscrits médievaux, 198
- Periodicals in the history, ethnography, literature, folklore and
linguistics of the Balkan peoples. Reference book, 1984
- Répertoire d'études balkaniques 1966-1975, 2 volumes, 1983/1984
- Linguistique balkanique. Bibliographie, 1983
- Les Etats balkaniques depuis la Deuxième guerre mondiale jusqu'à 1980,
développement politique, économique et culturel. Bibliographie, 1987

CLIENTELE: researchers, scientists (around 200 users)

ACCESS TO SERVICE: open to all users, free of charge

TYPE & DESCRIPTION OF SERVICES PROVIDED: Mainly concerned with history of the
Balkans. Provides library services, information retrieval from its
"Bibliographical Documents Archival" manual data base, selective
dissemination of information, microfilms and photocopies.

173 - VFSI "D. A. CENOV", SVISTOV, NAUCNA BIBLIOTEKA "AKADEMIK DR. NICOLAS MIHOV"

SYNONYMOUS NAMES: Higher Institute of Finance and Economics "D. A. Tsenov",
Svishtov, Academic Library "Dr. N. Mikhov";
Institut des Hautes Etudes Economiques et Financières, Svichtov,
Bibliothèque "Dr. Nicolas Mikhov"

PARENT ORGANIZATION: VFSI "D.A.-Cenov" Svistov

ADDRESS: 2, "EM. Tchakarov" St.,
Svishtov,
BULGARIA
TEL: 2-46-56, 2-27-21 (335)

CREATED: 1936   *HEAD:* Mr. S. Lalev, Director
SIZE OF STAFF: Professional: 5
TYPE OF SERVICE: national
SYSTEMS & NETWORKS ATTACHED TO: International Information System on Social Sciences
        in the Socialist Countries
SUBJECT COVERAGE: economics
DATA BEING PROCESSED AND SIZE: 181,052 books; 17,008 periodicals; 128 microcopies; 50
        manuscripts; 113 dissertations
DATA PROCESSING METHODS: manual
HARDWARE USED: ES - 10 - 20
SOFTWARE USED: IRMSS
STORAGE MEDIA: tapes
TYPE OF ACTIVITY: publication
ACCESS TO SERVICE: open to specific categories of users, paid services
TYPE & DESCRIPTION OF SERVICES PROVIDED: Provides library services and bibliographic,
        literature and survey data searches. Has its own data base "Social-Economic
        Knowledge".

174 - VISS INSTITUT PO IKONOMIKA "K. MARX", INFORMACIONEN CENTAR S BIBLIOTEKA

SYNONYMOUS NAMES: The "K. Marx" Higher Institute of Economics, Information Centre
        and Library
ADDRESS: Studentsky Grad "Christo Botev",
        Sofia 1100,
        BULGARIA
        TEL: 62-94-69 - TELEX: 22040
CREATED: 1980   *HEAD:* K. T. Banovski, Director
SIZE OF STAFF: Professional: 8
TYPE OF SERVICE: national
SYSTEMS & NETWORKS ATTACHED TO: The National Scientific and Technical Information
        System
SUBJECT COVERAGE: economics; administrative sciences; demography; education
DATA BEING PROCESSED AND SIZE: 73,561 books; 742 periodicals; 42 abstract journals
TYPE OF ACTIVITY: publication
PERIODICALS PUBLISHED:
        - Information Bulletin of Newly Registered Books, 6 p.a.
PUBLICATIONS: - The new economic approach and the new economic mechanism:
        bibliographical index, S., VII, "K. Marx", 1984
        - Bibliographical sources on the problems of economics in the library of VII
        "K. Marx". Annotated bibliographical index, S., VII "K. Marx", 1984
        - Karl Marx and the political economy: bibliographical index, S., VII "K.
        Marx", 1983, 63 p.
ACCESS TO SERVICE: open to specific categories of users, free of charge
TYPE & DESCRIPTION OF SERVICES PROVIDED: Provides library services, bibliographic and
        literature abstract searches, selective dissemination of information and
        translation of documents. Has access to the International Social Sciences
        Information System (MISON), USSR.

Burkina Faso

175 - CENTRE D'ETUDES ECONOMIQUES ET SOCIALES D'AFRIQUE OCCIDENTALE, BIBLIOTHÈQUE

SYNONYMOUS NAMES: CESAO Bibliothèque
ADDRESS: B.P. 305,
　　　Bobo-Dioulasso,
　　　BURKINA-FASO
　　　TEL: 98.27.78
CREATED: 1964　　*HEAD:* Mr. J. Ouandorah, Documentalist
SIZE OF STAFF: Professional: 2　　Total: 2
TYPE OF SERVICE: national; private; non-profit
WORKING LANGUAGE(S): French
SUBJECT COVERAGE: social sciences; sociology; economics; education; social
　　　anthropology; cultural anthropology
GEOGRAPHICAL COVERAGE: Western Africa
DATA BEING PROCESSED AND SIZE: 10,500 documentation items
STORAGE MEDIA: traditional shelving of publications
TYPE OF ACTIVITY: data collection
PERIODICALS PUBLISHED:
　　　- Liste d'Acquisition
CLIENTELE: students, teachers, researchers
ACCESS TO SERVICE: open to all users, free of charge
TYPE & DESCRIPTION OF SERVICES PROVIDED: Provides library reference services and
　　　selective bibliographies.

176 - CENTRE NATIONAL DE LA RECHERCHE SCIENTIFIQUE ET TECHNIQUE, DIRECTION DE L'INFORMATION SCIENTIFIQUE ET TECHNIQUE

SYNONYMOUS NAMES: CNRST, DIST
ADDRESS: B.P. 7047,
　　　Ouagadougou,
　　　BURKINA-FASO
　　　TEL: 33-23-94/95
CREATED: 1949　　*HEAD:* Ms. T. Hien, Director
SIZE OF STAFF: Professional: 7　　Other: 5　　Total: 12
TYPE OF SERVICE: national
SYSTEMS & NETWORKS ATTACHED TO: Réseau Sahélien d'Information et de Documentation
　　　Scientifiques et Techniques (RESADOC); Système d'Information sur les
　　　Recherches Agronomiques en Cours (CARIS)
MATERIALS DESCRIBING THE SERVICE: - Rapports d'activités du CNRST
WORKING LANGUAGE(S): French
SUBJECT COVERAGE: social sciences
GEOGRAPHICAL COVERAGE: Burkina-Faso; Africa; global
DATA BEING PROCESSED AND SIZE: books/reports (7,000 p.a.); articles (3,000 p.a.)
DATA PROCESSING METHODS: manual
STORAGE MEDIA: traditional shelving of publications; fiches; microfiches
TYPE OF ACTIVITY: scientific data collection; publication
PERIODICALS PUBLISHED:
　　　　- Liste Mensuelle d'Acquisitions
　　　　- Bulletin Bibliographique

PUBLICATIONS: - Répertoire des thèses et mémoires
          - Catalogue des périodiques
CLIENTELE: researchers, experts, teachers and students
ACCESS TO SERVICE: open to all users
TYPE & DESCRIPTION OF SERVICES PROVIDED: Provides library services, question-
          answering service and bibliographies.

**177 - COMITÉ PERMANENT INTER-ETATS DE LUTTE CONTRE LA SÉCHERESSE DANS LE SAHEL,
SERVICE D'INFORMATION ET DE DOCUMENTATION**

SYNONYMOUS NAMES: CILSS, Service d'Information et de Documentation;
          Permanent InterState Committee for Drought Control in the Sahel,
          Documentation and Information Service
ADDRESS: B. P. 7049,
          Ouagadougou,
          BURKINA-FASO
          TEL: 33.42.52 - TELEX: 5263 COMITER Ouaga
CREATED: 1973   HEAD: Mr. C. Elvalide Seye, Head
SIZE OF STAFF: Professional: 1
TYPE OF SERVICE: international; public
SYSTEMS & NETWORKS ATTACHED TO: Réseau Sahélien d'Information et de Documentation
          scientifiques et Techniques (RESADOC)
WORKING LANGUAGE(S): French; English
SUBJECT COVERAGE: demography; economics; geography; sociology
GEOGRAPHICAL COVERAGE: Sahel; Burkina-Faso; Cape Verde; Gambia; Guinea-Bissau; Mali;
          Mauritania; Niger; Senegal; Chad
DATA PROCESSING METHODS: manual
TYPE OF ACTIVITY: SSID scientific and methodological activities
PERIODICALS PUBLISHED: - Reflets Sahéliens
          - Liste d'Acquisitions
          - Bulletin Bibliographique
CLIENTELE: students, scientists, general public
ACCESS TO SERVICE: services open to all users, free of charge
TYPE & DESCRIPTION OF SERVICES PROVIDED: Provides searches of information, selective
          dissemination of information, microforms and photocopies.

**178 - AKADEMIA NAUK BELORUSSKOI SSR, OTDEL NAUCHNOI INFORMATSII PO OBSHCHESTVENNYM
NAUKAM**

SYNONYMOUS NAMES: ONION AN BSSR;
          Academy of Sciences of the Byelorussian Soviet Socialist Republic,
          Department of Scientific Information in Social Sciences
ADDRESS: ul. Akademicheskaya 25,
          BSSR Minsk, 220600,
          BYELORUSSIAN SSR
          TEL: 394543
CREATED: 1971   HEAD: L. F. Evmenov, Head
SIZE OF STAFF: Professional: 20   Other: 9   Total: 29

TYPE OF SERVICE: national
SYSTEMS & NETWORKS ATTACHED TO: State System of Scientific-Technological Informatic
(GSNTI)
MATERIALS DESCRIBING THE SERVICE: - Scientific digest (national literature)
WORKING LANGUAGE(S): Russian; Byelorussian
SUBJECT COVERAGE: economics; history; law; linguistics; literature; political
science; philosophy; arts
GEOGRAPHICAL COVERAGE: Byelorussian SSR; USSR
DATA BEING PROCESSED AND SIZE: 18,000 books
DATA PROCESSING METHODS: partially computerized
TYPE OF ACTIVITY: data analysis; publication
ACCESS TO SERVICE: services open to specific categories of users, free of charge
TYPE & DESCRIPTION OF SERVICES PROVIDED: Provides library services, bibliographic,
literature and survey data searches, selective dissemination of informatic
on-line services using INION's data bases, and translation of documents up
request.

**179 - INSTITUT DES SCIENCES HUMAINES, SERVICE DE LA BIBLIOTHÈQUE, DE LA DOCUMENTATI
ET DES PUBLICATIONS**

SYNONYMOUS NAMES: ISH/SBDP;
Institute of Human Sciences, Library, Documentation and Publications Servi
PARENT ORGANIZATION: Ministère de l'Enseignement Supérieur et de la Recherche
Scientifique (MESRES/ISH)
ADDRESS: B.P. 6170,
Yaoundé,
CAMEROON (UNITED REPUBLIC)
TEL: 22.16.74
CREATED: 1935   *HEAD:* Mr. M. Njikam, Head
SIZE OF STAFF: Professional: 2   Other: 16   Total: 21
TYPE OF SERVICE: national; public; non-profit
MATERIALS DESCRIBING THE SERVICE: - Répertoire de l'Institut des Sciences Humaines
WORKING LANGUAGE(S): English; French
SUBJECT COVERAGE: social sciences; rural development; rural sociology; migration;
regional Planning; archaeology; African languages
GEOGRAPHICAL COVERAGE: Cameroun; Central Africa; developing countries
DATA BEING PROCESSED AND SIZE: 20,000 books; 5,000 articles and reports; 100
periodicals
DATA PROCESSING METHODS: manual
STORAGE MEDIA: traditional shelving of publications; microfiches
TYPE OF ACTIVITY: data collection; data analysis; distribution of information;
publication
PERIODICALS PUBLISHED: - Revue Science et Technique. Série Sciences Humaines
- Quarterly Accessions List
PUBLICATIONS: - Travaux et documents de l'ISH
- Catalogue des acquisitions ISH
CLIENTELE: researchers, professors, students and visiting experts (1,000)
ACCESS TO SERVICE: services open to all users, free of charge
TYPE & DESCRIPTION OF SERVICES PROVIDED: Provides reference services and
bibliographies for researchers, selective dissemination of information,

microforms, photocopies, translation of documents upon request and distribution of own publications.

80 - INSTITUT PANAFRICAIN POUR LE DÉVELOPPMENT/AFRIQUE CENTRALE FRANCOPHONE, CENTRE DE DOCUMENTATION

YNONYMOUS NAMES: IPD/AC;
Panafrican Institute for Development, Documentation Centre
DDRESS: Boîte postale 4078,
Douala,
CAMEROON (UNITED REPUBLIC)
TEL: 42.37.70 - TELEX: 6048 KN
REATED: 1965   *HEAD:* Mr. E. Zocli, Chief
IZE OF STAFF: Professional: 2   Other: 2   Total: 4
YPE OF SERVICE: international; private; non-profit
YSTEMS & NETWORKS ATTACHED TO: Réseau Panafricain d'Information et de Documentation Rurales (REPIDOR)
ATERIALS DESCRIBING THE SERVICE: - Le Centre de Documentation de l'IPD-Afrique Centrale Francophone
ORKING LANGUAGE(S): French
UBJECT COVERAGE: social sciences; demography; economics; education; social welfare; sociology; agriculture
EOGRAPHICAL COVERAGE: French speaking Africa; Central Africa
ATA BEING PROCESSED AND SIZE: 10,000 books; 150 periodicals; 4,000 students' works; 2,100 brochures
ATA PROCESSING METHODS: manual
TORAGE MEDIA: traditional shelving of publications; fiches; microfiches
YPE OF ACTIVITY: data collection; data analysis; publication; SSID training, surveys
ERIODICALS PUBLISHED:
- Bulletin Analytique, 6 p.a.
- Bulletin Bibliographique, 4 p.a.
UBLICATIONS: - Bibliographies spécialisées
- Catalogue des publications de l'IPD/AC
- Annuaire des anciens étudiants de l'IPD/AC
- Catalogue des travaux d'étudiants de l'IPD/AC
- Catalogue des périodiques dépouillés
- Catalogue des travaux d'étudiants de l'IPD/AC
LIENTELE: teachers, researchers, students
CCESS TO SERVICE: services open to specific categories of users, free of charge
YPE & DESCRIPTION OF SERVICES PROVIDED: Provides bibliographic and literature searches, analytical bibliographies, country files and surveys, selective dissemination of information and photocopies.

81 - SOCIÉTÉ INTERNATIONALE DE LINGUISTIQUE CAMEROUN, SERVICE DE DOCUMENTATION

YNONYMOUS NAMES: SIL Cameroun
ARENT ORGANIZATION: Summer Institute of Linguistics International
DDRESS: B.P. 1299,
Yaoundé,

CAMEROON (UNITED REPUBLIC)
TEL: 22.39.48
CREATED: 1969   *HEAD:* Ms. Heiniger, Librarian
TYPE OF SERVICE: international; private; non-profit
MATERIALS DESCRIBING THE SERVICE: - Annual report 1986-1987
SUBJECT COVERAGE: linguistics; cultural anthropology; African languages
GEOGRAPHICAL COVERAGE: Cameroon (United Republic)
DATA BEING PROCESSED AND SIZE: 6,000 books; 52 periodicals; reports
DATA PROCESSING METHODS: computerized
TYPE OF ACTIVITY: data collection; data analysis; SSID scientific and methodological
        activities; SSID training; publication
PUBLICATIONS: - Bibliographies in two sections: "Scientific documents" and
        "Documents in national language"
ACCESS TO SERVICE: open to all users with paid services
TYPE & DESCRIPTION OF SERVICES PROVIDED: Provides library services, translation of
        documents and photocopies upon request.

182 - CANADIAN COUNCIL ON SOCIAL DEVELOPMENT, LIBRARY

SYNONYMOUS NAMES: CCSD Library;
        Conseil Canadien de Développement Social, Bibliothèque
ADDRESS: 55 Parkdale,
        P.O. Box 3505, Station C,
        Ottawa,
        Ontario K1Y 4G1,
        CANADA
        TEL: (613) 728-1865
CREATED: 1920   *HEAD:* Ms. O. Barrington, Library Officer
SIZE OF STAFF: Total: 1
TYPE OF SERVICE: national; private; non-profit
MATERIALS DESCRIBING THE SERVICE: - Printed notice
WORKING LANGUAGE(S): English; French
SUBJECT COVERAGE: criminology; social sciences; social welfare
GEOGRAPHICAL COVERAGE: Canada
DATA BEING PROCESSED AND SIZE: 21,000 printed documents including monographs; 45
        serial titles; bibliographies
DATA PROCESSING METHODS: manual
STORAGE MEDIA: traditional shelving of publications, fiches
TYPE OF ACTIVITY: publication
PERIODICALS PUBLISHED: - Perception
        - Vis-à-Vis - Overview - Self-help Newsletter
PUBLICATIONS: - List of publications of the CCSD
CLIENTELE: membership of council, organizations and governments
ACCESS TO SERVICE: open to all users
TYPE & DESCRIPTION OF SERVICES PROVIDED: Library services, limited reference servic

83 - CANADIAN INTERNATIONAL DEVELOPMENT AGENCY, DEVELOPMENT INFORMATION CENTRE

SYNONYMOUS NAMES: Agence Canadienne de Développement International, Centre
d'Information sur le Développement
ADDRESS: Place du Centre,
200 Promenade du Portage,
Hull,
Quebec, K1A 0G4,
CANADA
TEL: (819) 997-6212
CREATED: 1968   *HEAD:* Ms. N. Sansfaçon, Chief
SIZE OF STAFF: Professional: 5   Other: 4   Total: 9
TYPE OF SERVICE: private
WORKING LANGUAGE(S): English; French
SUBJECT COVERAGE: economics; history; political science; development
GEOGRAPHICAL COVERAGE: Asia; Caribbean area; Latin America; Africa; developing
countries
DATA BEING PROCESSED AND SIZE: 6,000 books; 1,600 periodicals titles; 30,000
unpublished reports
DATA PROCESSING METHODS: computerized
HARDWARE USED: IBM-PC
SOFTWARE USED: Ultracard, D-BASE III, Lotus 1-2-3, Wordperfect
STORAGE MEDIA: traditional shelving of publications, microfiches, hard discs
TYPE OF ACTIVITY: distribution of information
PERIODICALS PUBLISHED:
- Periodicals List
CLIENTELE: researchers
ACCESS TO SERVICE: services open to specific categories of users
TYPE & DESCRIPTION OF SERVICES PROVIDED: Provides library services, bibliographic,
literature and quantitative data searches of information, on-line services,
selective dissemination of information and photocopies. Has access to
external data bases through DIALOG, INFO GLOBE, IST-Informathèque, MEAD, QL
systems, CAN/OLE, MINISIS.

84 - CANADIAN SOCIO-ECONOMIC INFORMATION MANAGEMENT SYSTEM

SYNONYMOUS NAMES: CANSIM
PARENT ORGANIZATION: Statistics Canada
ADDRESS: Electronic Data Dissemination Division,
Statistics Canada,
Ottawa,
K1A 0T6 Ontario,
CANADA
CREATED: 1967   *HEAD:* E. Boyko,
SIZE OF STAFF: Total: 39
TYPE OF SERVICE: national; public; non-profit
MATERIALS DESCRIBING THE SERVICE: - CANSIM operation manual
- CANSIM user's manual
- CANSIM interactive system user's manual
WORKING LANGUAGE(S): English; French
SUBJECT COVERAGE: economics; socio-economic indicators

197

GEOGRAPHICAL COVERAGE: Canada; USA; Europe
DATA BEING PROCESSED AND SIZE: 400,000 economic time series
DATA PROCESSING METHODS: computerized
HARDWARE USED: IBM 3090
SOFTWARE USED: CANSIM
TYPE OF ACTIVITY: data collection; data analysis; distribution of information;
        publication
PUBLICATIONS: - CANSIM main base series directory
        - CANSIM minibase series directory
        - CANSIM university base series directory
CLIENTELE: experts, government officials, researchers
ACCESS TO SERVICE: paid services open to all users
TYPE & DESCRIPTION OF SERVICES PROVIDED: Provides library services, bibliographic
        quantitative data searches of information, on-line services using its own
        data bases, selective dissemination of information, information on magnetic
        tapes or discs, documents in French upon request.

185 - CARLETON UNIVERSITY, SOCIAL SCIENCE DATA ARCHIVE

SYNONYMOUS NAMES: SSDA
ADDRESS: A 715 LOEB Building,
        Colonel By Drive,
        Ottawa,
        Ontario K1S 5B6,
        CANADA
        TEL: (613) 564-7426- BITNET: SSDATA at CARLETON BITNET
CREATED: 1967   *HEAD:* Mr. H. Burshtyn, Director
SIZE OF STAFF: Professional: 1
TYPE OF SERVICE: international; public; non-profit
SYSTEMS & NETWORKS ATTACHED TO: IFDO, ICPSR, etc.
MATERIALS DESCRIBING THE SERVICE: - machine readable/searchable catalogue (in
        progress)
WORKING LANGUAGE(S): English
SUBJECT COVERAGE: social sciences; sociology; political science
GEOGRAPHICAL COVERAGE: Canada; USA; Australia; Europe
DATA BEING PROCESSED AND SIZE: data bases (censuses, statistical surveys, polls,
        social surveys, research studies): 600 machine readable data sets
DATA PROCESSING METHODS: computerized
HARDWARE USED: Honeywell Level 66, IBM Token Ring Network
SOFTWARE USED: SPSSX, OSIRIS, BMDP, SIR, ENABLE
STORAGE MEDIA: disks; magnetic tapes
TYPE OF ACTIVITY: data analysis
PUBLICATIONS: - Inventory of machine readable data on Canadian native people
        - Inventory of machine readable data on mental illness and allied phenomena
        in Canada, 1987
CLIENTELE: students, faculty members of Carleton University
ACCESS TO SERVICE: open to all users, against payment
TYPE & DESCRIPTION OF SERVICES PROVIDED: Provides quantitative data searches limited
        to inventories, data sets, and consultation regarding data acquisitions and
        analysis.

86 - CENTRE D'INFORMATION ET DOCUMENTATION SUR LE MOZAMBIQUE ET L'AFRIQUE AUSTRALE

SYNONYMOUS NAMES: CIDMAA
ADDRESS: 3738, St. Dominique,
       Montreal,
       Quebec H2X 2X9,
       CANADA
       TEL: (514) 499-0314
CREATED: 1982   HEAD: Ms. S. Garcia, Coordinator
SIZE OF STAFF: Professional: 5   Other: 1   Total: 6
TYPE OF SERVICE: non-profit
WORKING LANGUAGE(S): French; English; Portuguese
SUBJECT COVERAGE: social sciences
GEOGRAPHICAL COVERAGE: Southern Africa
DATA PROCESSING METHODS: partially computerized
HARDWARE USED: Macintosh
STORAGE MEDIA: traditional shelving of publications, fiches
TYPE OF ACTIVITY: distribution of information; SSID scientific and methodological
       activities; publication
PERIODICALS PUBLISHED: - Afrique, 4 p.a.
       - Africa Information Afrique, 52 p.a.
       - What's the Word, 12 p.a.
CLIENTELE: researchers, journalists, professors, students, trade unionists
ACCESS TO SERVICE: services free of charge
TYPE & DESCRIPTION OF SERVICES PROVIDED: Provides searches of information,
       information on magnetic tapes or discs, translation of documents, field
       survey research upon request.

87 - ECONOMIC COUNCIL OF CANADA, LIBRARY

SYNONYMOUS NAMES: Conseil Economique du Canada, Bibliothèque
PARENT ORGANIZATION: Government of Canada
ADDRESS: 333 Chemin River,
       Vanier,
       Ontario K1P 5V6,
       CANADA
       TEL: (613) 993-1253- TELKEFAX: (613) 991-4904
CREATED: 1963   HEAD: J. Fortin, Director, Information Division
TYPE OF SERVICE: national; public
WORKING LANGUAGE(S): English; French
SUBJECT COVERAGE: economics; finance; social sciences; statistics; employment; social
       policy
GEOGRAPHICAL COVERAGE: Canada
DATA BEING PROCESSED AND SIZE: 38,000 books and documents; reference works and
       periodicals
DATA PROCESSING METHODS: partially computerized
HARDWARE USED: IBM-PC, VAX 8250, MacIntosh Plus, other microcomputers
SOFTWARE USED: SAS, SPSS/PC, AREMOS, PASCAL, Dbase III, Lotus 1/2/3
STORAGE MEDIA: tapes, diskettes
TYPE OF ACTIVITY: data collection; data analysis; distribution of information;
       publication

PERIODICALS PUBLISHED: - Au Courant, 4 p.a.
CLIENTELE: government policy-makers, general public, media
ACCESS TO SERVICE: services open to all users, free of charge
TYPE & DESCRIPTION OF SERVICES PROVIDED: Provides current answering services and
          selective dissemination of information. The on-line reference service has
          access to CAN/OLE, INFOGLOBE AND DIALOG systems. It is also a depository
          library for certain federal government publications.

188 - EMPLOYMENT AND IMMIGRATION CANADA, LIBRARY

SYNONYMOUS NAMES: EIC, Library;
          Emploi et Immigration Canada, Bibliothèque;
          EIC, Bibliothèque
ADDRESS: Place du Portage, Phase IV,
          150 Promenade du Portage,
          Ottawa-Hull, K1A OJ9,
          CANADA
          TEL: 994-2603
CREATED: 1977   HEAD: P. E. Sunder-Raj,
SIZE OF STAFF: Professional: 7   Other: 10   Total: 17
TYPE OF SERVICE: public
MATERIALS DESCRIBING THE SERVICE: - The EIC Library (brochure)
WORKING LANGUAGE(S): English; French
SUBJECT COVERAGE: social sciences; administrative sciences; demography; economics;
          education; social welfare; sociology; labour force; employment; labour
          market; management; immigration; refugees
GEOGRAPHICAL COVERAGE: Canada
DATA BEING PROCESSED AND SIZE: 80,000 books and reports; 3,000 periodical titles
DATA PROCESSING METHODS: partially computerized
SOFTWARE USED: UTLAS system
STORAGE MEDIA: microfiches
TYPE OF ACTIVITY: distribution of information
PERIODICALS PUBLISHED:
          - List of Acquisitions. 2 p.a.
CLIENTELE: government employees; researchers (2,000 approx. p.a.)
ACCESS TO SERVICE: services open to specific categories of users
TYPE & DESCRIPTION OF SERVICES PROVIDED: Provides library services, question
          answering service, inter-library loans, bibliographic, literature,
          quantitative data searches of information and photocopying facilities. In
          addition to its own collection and outside resources, it has access to ov
          250 Canadian and American online databases. The Library maintains archiva
          collections of documents issued by Employment and Immigration.

189 - INSTITUT QUÉBÉCOIS DE RECHERCHE SUR LA CULTURE

SYNONYMOUS NAMES: IQRC
ADDRESS: 14, rue Haldimand,
          Quebec City,
          Quebec G1R 4N4,

CANADA
TEL: (418) 643-4695
EAD: Prof. F. Dumont, President
Mr. G. Lamy, Administrative Director
IZE OF STAFF: Professional: 36   Other: 15   Total: 51
YPE OF SERVICE: national; public; non-profit
ATERIALS DESCRIBING THE SERVICE: - Annual report
ORKING LANGUAGE(S): French
UBJECT COVERAGE: culture; regional history; philosophy; social anthropology;
cultural anthropology; social welfare; sociology; family
EOGRAPHICAL COVERAGE: Quebec, Canada
ATA BEING PROCESSED AND SIZE: 2,500 books; 250 periodicals; research reports
ATA PROCESSING METHODS: manual
YPE OF ACTIVITY: data collection; data analysis; distribution of information;
publication
UBLICATIONS: - Dumont, F., Une Société des jeunes? 1986
- Rudin, R., Histoire du Québec anglophone 1759-1980, 1986
- Helly, D., Les Chinois à Montréal 1877-1951, 1987
- Tessier, D. et al., Bibliographie de Lanaudière, 1987
- Desjardins, M., Bibliographie des Iles de la Madeline, 1987
- Aubin, P.; Côté, L.-M., Bibliographie de l'histoire du Québec et du
Canada, 1987
- Lemieux, D., Identités féminines: mémoire et créations, 1986
- Gauthier, M., Les Nouveaux visages de la pauvreté, 1987
- Blouin, J., Le Libre échange vraiment libre? 1986
- Dufresne, J., Le Procès du droit, 1987
- Laforce, H., Histoire de la sage-femme dans la région de Québec, 1985
CCESS TO SERVICE: services open to all users, against payment
YPE & DESCRIPTION OF SERVICES PROVIDED: Provides library services, bibliographic and
literature abstract searches of information and photocopies. On-line
searches available on its own data base "HISCABEC" (Bibliography on the
history of Quebec and Canada) including 70,000 references.

90 - INTERNATIONAL DEVELOPMENT RESEARCH CENTRE, LIBRARY

YNONYMOUS NAMES: IDRC Library;
Centre de Recherches pour le Développement International, Bibliothèque;
CRDI Bibliothèque
DDRESS: Information Sciences IDRC,
P.O. Box 8500,
Ottawa K1G KH9,
CANADA
TEL: (613) 236.6163 - TELEX: 053-3753
CABLE: RECENTRE
REATED: 1971
YPE OF SERVICE: international; public; non-profit
ATERIALS DESCRIBING THE SERVICE: - IDRIS (interagency Information System on
Development)
ORKING LANGUAGE(S): English; French; Spanish
UBJECT COVERAGE: social sciences; socio-economic development; development of rural
areas

Canada / Canada / Canadá

GEOGRAPHICAL COVERAGE: developing countries
DATA BEING PROCESSED AND SIZE: 47,000 books; 4,200 periodicals
DATA PROCESSING METHODS: computerized
HARDWARE USED: HP 3000 series 44
SOFTWARE USED: MINISIS
STORAGE MEDIA: microfiches
TYPE OF ACTIVITY: data collection; data analysis; SSID scientific and methodologic
        activities; publication
PERIODICALS PUBLISHED: - DEVINDEX: Index to Selected Literature on Economic and
        Social Development, 1 p.a.
PUBLICATIONS: - IDRC Library Thesaurus
CLIENTELE: researchers, educators
ACCESS TO SERVICE: open to all users, free of charge
TYPE & DESCRIPTION OF SERVICES PROVIDED: Provides library and information services
        third world development, selective dissemination of information,
        interlibrary loans and consultation.

191 - MCMASTER UNIVERSITY, LLYOD REEDS MAP LIBRARY, URBAN DOCUMENTATION CENTRE

ADDRESS: 1280 Main Street W.,
        Hamilton,
        Ontario L8S 4K1,
        CANADA
        TEL: (416) 525-9140
HEAD: Ms. C. Moulder, Curator
SIZE OF STAFF: Professional: 1   Other: 2   Total: 3
TYPE OF SERVICE: public; non-profit
MATERIALS DESCRIBING THE SERVICE: - Llyod Reeds Map Library / Urban Documentation
        Centre (Brochure)
WORKING LANGUAGE(S): English
SUBJECT COVERAGE: geography; history; urban planning
GEOGRAPHICAL COVERAGE: global
DATA BEING PROCESSED AND SIZE: 2,943 books; 90,910 maps; 20,134 documents
TYPE OF ACTIVITY: distribution of information; publication
PERIODICALS PUBLISHED:
        - Recent Acquisitions of the Urban Documentation Centre
PUBLICATIONS: - Periodicals index of the Urban Documentation Centre
        - Canadian urban affairs collection: a directory (1980)
ACCESS TO SERVICE: open to all users
TYPE & DESCRIPTION OF SERVICES PROVIDED: Provides library services. Municipal
        documents and university publications may be borrowed.

192 - PARLIAMENT OF CANADA, LIBRARY OF PARLIAMENT, INFORMATION AND REFERENCE BRANC

SYNONYMOUS NAMES: Parlement du Canada, Bibliothèque du Parlement, Service
        d'Information et de référence
ADDRESS: Parliament Bldgs.
        Ottawa,
        Ontario K1A 0A9,

CANADA
TEL: (613) 992-3122
REATED: 1871   *HEAD:* Mr. E. J. Spicer, Parliamentary Librarian
IZE OF STAFF: Professional: 167   Other: 71   Total: 238
YPE OF SERVICE: national; non-profit
ATERIALS DESCRIBING THE SERVICE: - Votre bibliothèque: services de la Bibliothèque
     du Parlement, 1985
ORKING LANGUAGE(S): English; French
UBJECT COVERAGE: political science; law; history; government; parliamentary systems;
     international relations; sociology; social welfare
EOGRAPHICAL COVERAGE: Canada; USA; United Kingdom; Commonwealth; France; global
ATA BEING PROCESSED AND SIZE: 7,600 books p.a.
ATA PROCESSING METHODS: partially computerized
OFTWARE USED: Dobis; D-Base; Lotus
YPE OF ACTIVITY: data collection; data analysis; distribution of information;
     publication
ERIODICALS PUBLISHED:
     - Selected Additions List
     - Selected Periodical Articles Index, 52 p.a.
     - Quorum
     - List of Press Clipping Books, 1 p.a.
UBLICATIONS: - Catalogue of bibliographies and reading lists
     - Catalogue of compilations
LIENTELE: senators, members of parliament, parliamentary gallery press members,
     members of the House of Commons, the Governor General; general public
CCESS TO SERVICE: open to the public for consultation, free of charge
YPE & DESCRIPTION OF SERVICES PROVIDED: Provides library services, bibliographic and
     quantitative data searches, on-line services using own data bases "DOBIS"
     and "COMPAS" as well as external databases including BADADUQ, BRS,
     CAN/OLE, Centrale des Bibliothèques, CSG Insight, DATASOLVE, DIALOG, DOW
     JONES, DUNSERVE, Info Globe, Informant on-line, lexis, Minisis, Orbit,
     Polis, QL, Questel, SOQUIS.

193 - PEACE RESEARCH INSTITUTE - DUNDAS

YNONYMOUS NAMES: PRI-D
DDRESS: 25 Dundana Avenue,
     Dundas,
     Ontario L9H 4E5,
     CANADA
     TEL: (416) 628-2356
REATED: 1964   *HEAD:* A. G. Newcombe, Director
                    Ms. H. Newcombe, Director
                    Ms. C. Peringer, Director
IZE OF STAFF: Professional: 3   Other: 5   Total: 8
YPE OF SERVICE: international; private; non-profit
ATERIALS DESCRIBING THE SERVICE: - A Guide to the use of peace research abstracts
     journal, 12 p.
     - Peace Research Institute - Dundas (leaflet)
     - Peace Research Abstracts coding manual
ORKING LANGUAGE(S): English

SUBJECT COVERAGE: social sciences
GEOGRAPHICAL COVERAGE: global
DATA BEING PROCESSED AND SIZE: 175,000 abstracts from articles and books
DATA PROCESSING METHODS: partially computerized
HARDWARE USED: IBM PC; Compaq
SOFTWARE USED: own
TYPE OF ACTIVITY: data collection; data analysis; distribution of information; publication
PERIODICALS PUBLISHED: - Peace Research Abstracts Journal
                   - Peace Research Review Journal
PUBLICATIONS: - Newcombe, H., Peace values for a better world, 1987
            - Newcombe, H. et al., Nations on record: United Nations General Assembl roll-call votes (1978-1983), 1986
            - Peringer, C., How we work for peace, 1987
            - Newcombe, H., Revamping the U.N. voting structure, 1987
            - Newcombe, H., Collective security, common security and alternative security: a conceptual comparison, 1986
            - Newcombe, H., A Prediction of war using the Tensiometer, 1988
CLIENTELE: 360 subscribers, mostly universities or colleges or research institute state libraries, foreign offices
ACCESS TO SERVICE: open to all subscribers
TYPE & DESCRIPTION OF SERVICES PROVIDED: Provides literature abstract searches, selective dissemination of information, on-line services using own data (175,000 citations).

194 - REGIONAL INDUSTRIAL EXPANSION, GOVERNMENT DOCUMENTATION CENTRE

SYNONYMOUS NAMES: Expansion Industrielle Régionale, Centre de Documentation Gouvernemental
PARENT ORGANIZATION: Government of Canada/Canadian Government
ADDRESS: 1800 Victoria Square, Suite 3800,
         P.O. Box 247,
         Montreal,
         Quebec H4Z 1E8,
         CANADA
         TEL: (514) 283-1274 - TELEX: 055-60768
HEAD: Ms. C. Laplante,
SIZE OF STAFF: Total: 2
TYPE OF SERVICE: international; public; private
SUBJECT COVERAGE: economics; political science; regional development
GEOGRAPHICAL COVERAGE: Quebec, Canada
DATA BEING PROCESSED AND SIZE: 8,000 books; 300 periodicals
DATA PROCESSING METHODS: partially computerized
TYPE OF ACTIVITY: distribution of information
PERIODICALS PUBLISHED:
         - Acquisitions Bulletin, 12 p.a.
ACCESS TO SERVICE: services open to all users, free of charge
TYPE & DESCRIPTION OF SERVICES PROVIDED: Provides library services, interlibrary loans, bibliographic searches, and on-line services on external data base CAN/OLE, QL Systems and QUESTEL accessed through DIALOG, ICIST and IST-Informatheque. Also provides selective dissemination of information and

photocopying facilities.

85 - STATISTICS CANADA, LIBRARY

NONYMOUS NAMES: Statistique Canada, Library
DDRESS: R. H. Coats Bldg.,
          Tunney's Pasture,
          Ottawa,
          Ontario K1A OT6,
          CANADA
          TEL: (613) 951-8219 - TELEX: 053-3585
REATED: 1918   *HEAD:* Ms. G. Ellis, Director
IZE OF STAFF: Professional: 9   Other: 18   Total: 27
YPE OF SERVICE: international; public; non-profit
YSTEMS & NETWORKS ATTACHED TO: Federal Library Network (DOBIS)
ATERIALS DESCRIBING THE SERVICE: - library services, brochure
ORKING LANGUAGE(S): English; French
UBJECT COVERAGE: statistics; statistical methodology; statistical analysis; social
          sciences; administrative sciences; demography; economics; education;
          geography; social welfare; sociology
ATA BEING PROCESSED AND SIZE: 150,000 books and documents; 1,800 periodicals and
          serials; microfiches; microfilms
ARDWARE USED: IBM-PC, DOBIS
OFTWARE USED: Wordperfect, Wordstar, Lotus 123, PC-talk, Findit
TORAGE MEDIA: traditional shelving of publications; fiches; microfiches
YPE OF ACTIVITY: distribution of information; publication
ERIODICALS PUBLISHED:
          - Accessions List, 6 p.a.
          - Current Contents List, 12 p.a.
UBLICATIONS: - Statistics Canada catalog
LIENTELE: libraries, researchers, consultants, students
CCESS TO SERVICE: services open to all users, free of charge
YPE & DESCRIPTION OF SERVICES PROVIDED: Provides library services, interlibrary
          loans, bibliographic, literature abstracts and quantitative data searches of
          information, on-line services using own data base STATCAN. Has access
          through DATAPAC to other data bases: DIALOG, CAN/OLE, QL systems, BRS,
          QUESTEL, Infoglobe, Infomart. Photocopying facilities are also available.

86 - UNIVERSITÉ DE MONTRÉAL, BIBLIOTHÈQUE DES LETTRES ET DES SCIENCES HUMAINES

YNONYMOUS NAMES: University of Montreal, Humanities and Social Sciences Library
DDRESS: 3100, rue Jean-Brillant,
          C.P. 6128 Succursale A,
          Montreal,
          Québec H3C 3J7,
          CANADA
          TEL: (514) 343-7430
REATED: 1968   *HEAD:* Mr. R. Greene, Director
IZE OF STAFF: Professional: 12   Other: 48   Total: 68

TYPE OF SERVICE: private; non-profit

MATERIALS DESCRIBING THE SERVICE: - Guide de l'usager, Bibliothèque des Lettres et des Sciences Humaines, Université de Montréal, 1987

WORKING LANGUAGE(S): French

SUBJECT COVERAGE: social sciences; demography; economics; history; linguistics; philosophy; political science; social anthropology; cultural anthropology; social welfare; sociology; criminology; labour relations; religion

GEOGRAPHICAL COVERAGE: Quebec, Canada

DATA BEING PROCESSED AND SIZE: 500,000 books; 3,700 periodicals

DATA PROCESSING METHODS: partially computerized

HARDWARE USED: DIGITAL

SOFTWARE USED: CLSI

STORAGE MEDIA: traditional shelving of publications; fiches; microforms

TYPE OF ACTIVITY: distribution of information

CLIENTELE: university teachers, researchers and students (20,000 p.a.)

ACCESS TO SERVICE: services open to specific categories of users, free of charge; some paid services

TYPE & DESCRIPTION OF SERVICES PROVIDED: Provides library services, bibliographic searches of information, microforms, photocopies, and on-line services using external data bases available through DIALOG and CAN/OLE.

197 - UNIVERSITÉ DU QUÉBEC, ECOLE NATIONALE D'ADMINISTRATION PUBLIQUE, CENTRE DE DOCUMENTATION

ADDRESS: 945 avenue Wolfe,
Sainte-Foy,
Québec G1V 3J9,
CANADA
TEL: (418) 657-2485

HEAD: Mr. J.-M. Alain, Director

SIZE OF STAFF: Total: 3

TYPE OF SERVICE: public

SYSTEMS & NETWORKS ATTACHED TO: SIGIRD of Quebec University

MATERIALS DESCRIBING THE SERVICE: - Gélinas, M., Guide d'orientation de l'usager, Québec, 1987

WORKING LANGUAGE(S): French

SUBJECT COVERAGE: administrative sciences; economics; political science; public administration

DATA BEING PROCESSED AND SIZE: 40,000 documentation items

DATA PROCESSING METHODS: computerized

HARDWARE USED: VAX 780

TYPE OF ACTIVITY: distribution of information

PERIODICALS PUBLISHED:
- Bulletin Signalétique des Acquisitions, 12 p.a.

PUBLICATIONS: - Alain, M.; Grasham, W. E., Administration publique canadienne, bibliographie, 1985
- Gelinas, M., Les Banques de données bibliographiques au service de l'administration publique, 1986
- Gelinas, M.; Chabot, J., Liste cumulative des publications et rapports de recherche du personnel de l'ENAP, 1986

CLIENTELE: post-graduate students, civil servants, researchers

CESS TO SERVICE: open to all users
PE & DESCRIPTION OF SERVICES PROVIDED: Provides library services, bibliographic
searches of information, selective dissemination of information with on-line
services using own data base "BADADUG". Has also access to external data
bases: Management Contents, Social Scisearch and Francis through DIALOG and
QUESTEL. Address in Montreal: 4835 Christophe Colomb, Montreal, PQ, H2J 3G8.

38 - UNIVERSITÉ LAVAL BIBLIOTHÈQUE GÉNÉRALE

DRESS: Cité Universitaire,
Sainte-Foy,
Québec G1K 7P4,
CANADA
TEL: (418) 656-5541
JBJECT COVERAGE: humanities; administrative sciences
ATA BEING PROCESSED AND SIZE: 1,000,000 books; 11,000 periodicals
TORAGE MEDIA: traditional shelving of publications; AV Library
YPE OF ACTIVITY: data collection; distribution of information; SSID training
CCESS TO SERVICE: open to the academic community
YPE & DESCRIPTION OF SERVICES PROVIDED: Provides library services, inter-library
loans, question-answering service and computerized bibliographic searches.

99 - UNIVERSITÉ LAVAL, CENTRE INTERNATIONAL DE RECHERCHES SUR LE BILINGUISME

YNONYMOUS NAMES: CIRB;
Laval University, International Centre for Research on Bilingualism;
ICRB
DDRESS: Pavillon Casault, 6th Fl.,
Ste Foy,
PQ, G1K 7P4,
CANADA
TEL: (418) 656-3232
REATED: 1967   *HEAD:* L. Laforge, Director
IZE OF STAFF: Professional: 3   Other: 8   Total: 11
YPE OF SERVICE: international; public; non-profit
ORKING LANGUAGE(S): French; English
UBJECT COVERAGE: linguistics; bilingualism; language didactics; bilingual education;
psycholinguistics; language surveys; sociolinguistics
EOGRAPHICAL COVERAGE: global; Canada
ATA BEING PROCESSED AND SIZE: 5,000 books; 250 publications (books, articles,
reports) produced by researchers of the Centre; 30,000 documents; 50
periodicals
ATA PROCESSING METHODS: partially computerized
OFTWARE USED: Word perfect; Acknowledgement
TORAGE MEDIA: traditional shelving of publications; fiches; tapes; discs;
microfiches
YPE OF ACTIVITY: data collection; data analysis; distribution of information;
publication
UBLICATIONS: - Serie "B": Documents, essays, theses, articles

- Serie "G": Research reports
- Serie "H": Brief studies on language contact throughout the world
- Serie "J": Bibliographie informatisée sur le bilinguisme et l'enseignement des langues officielles (BIBELO)
- Serie "K": Recherche en linguistique appliquée à l'informatique (RELAI)
- Serie "A": Basic studies, syntheses, proceedings
- Serie "E": Inventories
- Serie "F": Bibliographies

CLIENTELE: teachers, students, researchers, government officials, etc.
ACCESS TO SERVICE: services open to all users, free of charge
TYPE & DESCRIPTION OF SERVICES PROVIDED: Provides library services, bibliographic, literature and quantitative data searches of information, production of information on magnetic tapes or discs, provision of microforms and photocopies upon request.

200 - UNIVERSITÉ MCGILL, SERVICE D'ANALYSE DES CONVENTIONS COLLECTIVES SDA

SYNONYMOUS NAMES: McGill University, Labour Agreements Data Bank-SDA
ADDRESS: 1001 Sherbrooke Street West,
        Room 457,
        Montreal,
        P.Q. H3A 1G5,
        CANADA
        TEL: (514) 398-4004
CREATED: 1968   HEAD: Dr. C. Steinberg, Director
SIZE OF STAFF: Professional: 2   Other: 1   Total: 3
TYPE OF SERVICE: national; public; non-profit
SUBJECT COVERAGE: statistics; labour relations, collective bargaining
GEOGRAPHICAL COVERAGE: Canada
DATA BEING PROCESSED AND SIZE: 12,000 collective agreements
DATA PROCESSING METHODS: manual; computerized
HARDWARE USED: IBM 370/158
SOFTWARE USED: VM (Virtual Machine)
STORAGE MEDIA: traditional shelving of publications
TYPE OF ACTIVITY: data analysis; SSID scientific and methodological activities
PUBLICATIONS: - Reports made to user's specifications
        - Development of user collective agreement analysis systems
CLIENTELE: members of companies, unions, professors, students, labour lawyers, government agencies
ACCESS TO SERVICE: open to all users, against payment
TYPE & DESCRIPTION OF SERVICES PROVIDED: Provides library services; information on magnetic tapes, photocopies, consulting services on analysis of collective agreement and collective bargaining, and computerized analysis of collecti agreements. Also provides on-line services using own data base.

201 - UNIVERSITY OF ALBERTA, BOREAL INSTITUTE FOR NORTHERN STUDIES, LIBRARY

ADDRESS: Bio Sci Building,
        Edmonton,

Alberta T6G 2E9,
CANADA
TEL: (403) 432-4409 (Library) - TELEX: 037-2979 (U of A) Bins U of A -
TELEFAX: (403) 432-7219 Bins U of A
CABLE: BINS VALTAMTS (Electronic Mail)
REATED: 1960
YPE OF SERVICE: international; non-profit
ATERIALS DESCRIBING THE SERVICE: - Annual report of the Boreal Institute for
Northern Studies
ORKING LANGUAGE(S): English; French
UBJECT COVERAGE: social sciences; geography; social anthropology; cultural
anthropology
EOGRAPHICAL COVERAGE: Canada and northern circumpolar countries
ATA BEING PROCESSED AND SIZE: 110,000 documentation items
ATA PROCESSING METHODS: computerized
ARDWARE USED: University mainframe (access on Campus and nationally on CAN/OLE)
OFTWARE USED: SPIRES
TORAGE MEDIA: traditional shelving of publications; fiches; tapes; discs;
microfiches
YPE OF ACTIVITY: data collection; data analysis; distribution of information; SSID
scientific and methodological activities; SSID training; publication
ERIODICALS PUBLISHED: - Circumpolar Research Series
UBLICATIONS: - Annual Report of the Boreal Institute for Northern Studies, 1988
LIENTELE: undergraduate and graduate students, faculty members (approx. 250)
CCESS TO SERVICE: open to all users
YPE & DESCRIPTION OF SERVICES PROVIDED: Provides library services, inter-library
loans, photocopies, and bibliographic and literature abstract searches of
information. Also provides on-line services using own data base and external
data bases "ASTIS" and "SPRI" available through Arctic Institute for
Northern Research and Scott Polar Research Institute.

202 - UNIVERSITY OF ALBERTA, HUMANITIES AND SOCIAL SCIENCES LIBRARY

ADDRESS: Rutherford North,
Edmonton,
AB, T6G 2J8,
CANADA
TEL: (402) 432 57 91
HEAD: B. J. Busch, Area Coordinator
SIZE OF STAFF: Professional: 14   Other: 47   Total: 61
TYPE OF SERVICE: public; non-profit
MATERIALS DESCRIBING THE SERVICE: - University of Alberta Library guide
WORKING LANGUAGE(S): English
SUBJECT COVERAGE: social sciences; humanities
GEOGRAPHICAL COVERAGE: Alberta, Canada
DATA BEING PROCESSED AND SIZE: 1.3 million books; 130,000 bound periodicals; 7,500
journals and serials; 115 newspapers; 2.25 million microforms
DATA PROCESSING METHODS: partially computerized
HARDWARE USED: IBM
SOFTWARE USED: DOBIS
STORAGE MEDIA: traditional shelving of publications

Canada / Canada / Canadá

TYPE OF ACTIVITY: distribution of information; SSID training
PUBLICATIONS: - Bibliographies
CLIENTELE: students, teaching and non-teaching faculty, researchers, general public
ACCESS TO SERVICE: services open to specific categories of users, free of charge
TYPE & DESCRIPTION OF SERVICES PROVIDED: Provides library services, bibliographic,
        literature abstract and quantitative data searches, selective dissemination
        of information, microforms, photocopies as well as specialized instruction
        and conducted tours of facilities upon request by interested groups. Also
        provides on-line services using external data bases of all major vendors.

203 - UNIVERSITY OF BRITISH COLUMBIA, DATA LIBRARY

ADDRESS: Computing Centre,
        6356 Agricultural Road,
        Vancouver, B.C., V6T 1W5,
        CANADA
        TEL: (604) 228-5587
CREATED: 1972   HEAD: L. G. Ruus, Head
SIZE OF STAFF: Professional: 2   Other: 1   Total: 3
TYPE OF SERVICE: public; non-profit
SYSTEMS & NETWORKS ATTACHED TO: DATAPAC
MATERIALS DESCRIBING THE SERVICE: - Ruus, L. G., The University of British Columbia
        Data Library: an overview, 1982
WORKING LANGUAGE(S): English
SUBJECT COVERAGE: social sciences; sociology; demography; political science;
        economics; education; cultural anthropology; social anthropology;
        humanities; archaeology; social welfare; geography
GEOGRAPHICAL COVERAGE: global
DATA BEING PROCESSED AND SIZE: computer readable data files (4,700)
DATA PROCESSING METHODS: computerized
HARDWARE USED: Amdahl 470/V6
SOFTWARE USED: MTS Operating System
STORAGE MEDIA: computer readable magnetic tapes
TYPE OF ACTIVITY: distribution of information
PUBLICATIONS: - UBC Data Library catalogue "Comfiche"
CLIENTELE: faculty, students, researchers
ACCESS TO SERVICE: open to all users, free of charge
TYPE & DESCRIPTION OF SERVICES PROVIDED: The Library collects data files required to
        support the research and teaching activities of the university, and provide
        services appropriate to the collection, including on-line services using
        their data bases "DATALIB" AND "BIBLIO" and production of information on
        magnetic tapes. Also acts as a data archive for data files produced locally
        and elsewhere that may be of significance for future secondary analysis.

204 - UNIVERSITY OF BRITISH COLUMBIA LIBRARY, HUMANITIES AND SOCIAL SCIENCES DIVISION

ADDRESS: 1956 Main Hall,
        Vancouver,
        British Columbia V6T 1Y3,

CANADA
TEL: (604) 228-2725
CABLE: GREY POINT
REATED: 1984   *HEAD:* Ms. J. Foster, Head of Division
IZE OF STAFF: Professional: 11   Other: 6   Total: 17
YPE OF SERVICE: national; public; non-profit
ATERIALS DESCRIBING THE SERVICE: - UBC Library news. Special issue: Faculty library
        guide
ORKING LANGUAGE(S): English
UBJECT COVERAGE: social sciences; humanities
EOGRAPHICAL COVERAGE: British Columbia, Canada
ATA BEING PROCESSED AND SIZE: books; periodicals; reports
ATA PROCESSING METHODS: partially computerized
LIENTELE: students, teaching and non-teaching staff, researchers
CCESS TO SERVICE: open to all users, free of charge, except for some outside users
YPE & DESCRIPTION OF SERVICES PROVIDED: Provides library services, query answering
        service, current awareness services, selective dissemination of information,
        on-line bibliographic searches, and photocopies.

05 - UNIVERSITY OF MANITOBA, ELIZABETH DAFOE LIBRARY

ARENT ORGANIZATION: The University of Manitoba
DDRESS: Winnipeg,
        Manitoba R3T 2N2,
        CANADA
        TEL: (204) 474-9211 - TELEX: 07-587721 - TELEFAX: (204) 262-6629
REATED: 1885   *HEAD:* Mr. M. Angel, Head
IZE OF STAFF: Professional: 11   Other: 29   Total: 40
YPE OF SERVICE: non-profit
YSTEMS & NETWORKS ATTACHED TO: The University of Manitoba Libraries
ORKING LANGUAGE(S): English; French; German
UBJECT COVERAGE: social sciences; humanities
EOGRAPHICAL COVERAGE: global
ATA BEING PROCESSED AND SIZE: 733,000 books and bound periodicals volumes; 4,650
        periodical titles; 382,000 government publications; maps; microfiches;
        microfilms
ARDWARE USED: AMDAHL 470/V8
OFTWARE USED: Inhouse (BM/SP.31 operating system)
TORAGE MEDIA: traditional shelving of publications, microfiches, microfilms
YPE OF ACTIVITY: distribution of information
LIENTELE: students and faculty, government, business and private researchers
CCESS TO SERVICE: services open to all users, free of charge
YPE & DESCRIPTION OF SERVICES PROVIDED: Provides library services, interlibrary
        loans, bibliographic and literature abstract searches of information. Also
        provides on-line searches using own inhouse data base "UMSEARCH" and
        external data bases through INFOGLOBE, IDRC, CCINFO, DIALOG, BRS, CAN/OLE
        and CORN.

Canada / Canada / Canadá

206 - UNIVERSITY OF OTTAWA, MORISSET LIBRARY (HUMANITIES AND SOCIAL SCIENCES)

SYNONYMOUS NAMES: Université d'Ottawa, Bibliothèque Morisset (Sciences Sociales et
        Humaines)
ADDRESS: 65 Hastey Avenue,
        Ottawa,
        Ontario K1N 9A5,
        CANADA
        TEL: (613) 564-6880 - TELEX: 0533338
CREATED: 1972   *HEAD:* Mr. J.-J. Le Blanc,
SIZE OF STAFF: Professional: 30   Other: 107   Total: 137
TYPE OF SERVICE: international; public; non-profit
WORKING LANGUAGE(S): English; French
SUBJECT COVERAGE: social sciences; humanities
GEOGRAPHICAL COVERAGE: global
DATA BEING PROCESSED AND SIZE: 737,000 books; 9,500 periodicals; 622,000 microforms
        315,000 government documents; U.N. publications (depository)
DATA PROCESSING METHODS: computerized
HARDWARE USED: GEAC
SOFTWARE USED: GEAC
TYPE OF ACTIVITY: distribution of information; publication
PUBLICATIONS: - Reference guides
CLIENTELE: students, professors, researchers
ACCESS TO SERVICE: services open to all users, free of charge, some paid services
TYPE & DESCRIPTION OF SERVICES PROVIDED: Provides library services, interlibrary
        loans, photocopies, and on-line services using own data base "Library
        Catalogue" and other relevant external data bases available through BRS and
        Dialog.

207 - UNIVERSITY OF TORONTO, VICTORIA UNIVERSITY LIBRARY

ADDRESS: 71 Queen's Park Crescent, E.,
        Toronto,
        Ontario M5S 1K7,
        CANADA
        TEL: (416) 585-4472
HEAD: Dr. R. C. Brandeis, Chief Librarian
SIZE OF STAFF: Professional: 5   Other: 20   Total: 25
TYPE OF SERVICE: private; non-profit
SUBJECT COVERAGE: social sciences; economics; history; philosophy; political science
        humanities; religion
DATA BEING PROCESSED AND SIZE: 208,330 volumes; 830 periodicals
DATA PROCESSING METHODS: partially computerized
HARDWARE USED: ZENITH, OLIVETTI
STORAGE MEDIA: traditional shelving of publications
TYPE OF ACTIVITY: distribution of information
CLIENTELE: primarily academic users (6,000 p.a.)
ACCESS TO SERVICE: services open to specific categories of users
TYPE & DESCRIPTION OF SERVICES PROVIDED: Provides library services, bibliographic
        searches of information, inter-library loans and photocopies. Holds specia
        rare collections of books and manuscripts (Tennyson collection,

Woolf/Bloomsbury/Hogarth Press collection and others). Victoria University
Library houses its Arts College Collection in the E.J. Pratt Library.

208 - UNIVERSITY OF WATERLOO, DANA PORTER LIBRARY

ADDRESS: University Avenue,
Waterloo,
Ontario N2L 3G1,
CANADA
TEL: (519) 885-1211 - TELEX: 069-55259
CREATED: 1957   *HEAD:* Mr. M. C. Shepherd, Librarian
SIZE OF STAFF: Professional: 43   Other: 141   Total: 184
TYPE OF SERVICE: national; public; non-profit
WORKING LANGUAGE(S): English
SUBJECT COVERAGE: social sciences; humanities; special collections include rare
materials on the history of women
GEOGRAPHICAL COVERAGE: Canada
DATA BEING PROCESSED AND SIZE: 812,000 books and bound periodical volumes; 6,265
periodicals; 187,000 government documents, theses, newspapers; 470,000
microforms
DATA PROCESSING METHODS: computerized
HARDWARE USED: GEAC 8000 and 9000
SOFTWARE USED: own
STORAGE MEDIA: traditional shelving of publications; microfilms; microfiches
TYPE OF ACTIVITY: distribution of information; publication
PUBLICATIONS: - Bibliography series
- Technical papers series
- Functional requirements for an on-line bibliographic data access and
control system, 1982
CLIENTELE: graduates and under-graduates, faculty, local community borrowers and
alumnae (32,870 users p.a.)
ACCESS TO SERVICE: services open to specific categories of users, free of charge
TYPE & DESCRIPTION OF SERVICES PROVIDED: Provides library services, interlibrary
loans, bibliographic, literature abstract searches of information (on fee
basis) using its on-line catalogue. Has access to 750 external data bases
through DIALOG, BRS, CAN/OLE, QL, INFOGLOBE, MEDLINE, ORBIT, ETC. Microforms
and photocopies can be obtained upon request.

209 - UNIVERSITY OF WATERLOO, LEISURE STUDIES DATA BANK

SYNONYMOUS NAMES: LSDB;
Université de Waterloo, Banque de Données sur les Loisirs;
BDL
ADDRESS: Waterloo,
Ontario N2L 3G1,
CANADA
TEL: (519) 885-1211
CREATED: 1972   *HEAD:* Dr. R. Mannell, Director
Mrs. S. Wright, Coordinator

Canada / Canada / Canadá

SIZE OF STAFF: Total: 3
TYPE OF SERVICE: national; public; non-profit
SYSTEMS & NETWORKS ATTACHED TO: International Federation of Data Organizations
(IFDO); IASSIST
WORKING LANGUAGE(S): English; French
SUBJECT COVERAGE: sociology of tourism, leisure
GEOGRAPHICAL COVERAGE: Canada; USA; Europe
DATA BEING PROCESSED AND SIZE: machine readable numeric data; over 100 files
DATA PROCESSING METHODS: computerized
HARDWARE USED: IBM 4341; IBM XT-PC; DEC RAINBOW
SOFTWARE USED: VM/CMS; WYLBUR; SAS; BMD; SPSS; SCRIPT; IBM utilities etc.
STORAGE MEDIA: tapes; disks
TYPE OF ACTIVITY: data collection; data analysis; publication
PUBLICATIONS: - Avedon, E.M., Current holdings of the LSDB/BDL. Waterloo, Ontario
- General catalogue of holdings
CLIENTELE: academics, students, government officials, private and commercial
researchers
ACCESS TO SERVICE: open to specific categories of users, free of charge
TYPE & DESCRIPTION OF SERVICES PROVIDED: Provides consultation services on research
methods, machine readable data organization, machine readable data
processing and data analysis etc. Also provides data for secondary analysis
and training in the use of large-scale data files and computer techniques.

210 - UNIVERSITY OF WATERLOO, SPECIALIZED INFORMATION RETRIEVAL AND LIBRARY SERVICES

SYNONYMOUS NAMES: SIRLS
PARENT ORGANIZATION: University of Waterloo, Faculty of Human Kinetics and Leisure
Studies
ADDRESS: Waterloo,
Ontario N2L 3G1,
CANADA
TEL: (519) 885-1211, ext 2560 - TELEX: 069-55259
CREATED: 1971   *HEAD:* Ms. B. Millman, Database Manager & Consultant
SIZE OF STAFF: Professional: 1   Other: 2   Total: 3
TYPE OF SERVICE: national; public; non-profit
MATERIALS DESCRIBING THE SERVICE: - Brochure
WORKING LANGUAGE(S): English
SUBJECT COVERAGE: sociology; leisure; psychology; sport
GEOGRAPHICAL COVERAGE: global
DATA BEING PROCESSED AND SIZE: 2,672 books; 398 reports; 7,753 journal articles; 239
government documents; 2,409 proceedings; 921 theses; 1,612 unpublished
papers
DATA PROCESSING METHODS: computerized
HARDWARE USED: IBM 4341
SOFTWARE USED: SPIRES
TYPE OF ACTIVITY: data collection; distribution of information; publication
PERIODICALS PUBLISHED: - Sociology of Leisure and Sport Abstracts, 3 p.a.
PUBLICATIONS: - Bibliographies on various aspects of sport and leisure
CLIENTELE: students and faculty, external researchers, government agencies
ACCESS TO SERVICE: open to all users, paid services for external users
TYPE & DESCRIPTION OF SERVICES PROVIDED: Provides library services, on-line

accessibility to its own data base SIRLS, information on magnetic tapes and photocopies.

211 - UNIVERSITY OF WESTERN ONTARIO, SOCIAL SCIENCE COMPUTING LABORATORY

SYNONYMOUS NAMES: SSCL
ADDRESS: Faculty of Social Science,
London,
Ontario N6A 5C2,
CANADA
TEL: (519) 661-2152
CREATED: 1972   *HEAD:* Mr. D. G. Link, Director
SIZE OF STAFF: Professional: 10   Other: 6   Total: 16
SYSTEMS & NETWORKS ATTACHED TO: ICPSR (Inter-University Consortium for Political and
Social Research)
MATERIALS DESCRIBING THE SERVICE: - Introduction to the SSCL computing environment
SUBJECT COVERAGE: social sciences; demography; economics; political science;
psychology; sociology; statistics
DATA BEING PROCESSED AND SIZE: 230 machine readable files
HARDWARE USED: VAX11/785; VAX11/780; MicroVAX 11
TYPE OF ACTIVITY: data analysis; distribution of information; SSID scientific and
methodological activities; SSID training
CLIENTELE: students, researchers, faculty members
ACCESS TO SERVICE: paid services for outside users
TYPE & DESCRIPTION OF SERVICES PROVIDED: Provides statistical and computational
software, on-line biblographic and micro-data retrieval systems, custom
utilities and hardware resources. The Laboratory includes a Data Resources
Library which maintains the DRL Catalogue and the Canadian Register of
Research and Researchers in the Social Sciences (CANREG), a bilingual
computer-based information system containing biographical information on
over 8,000 social scientists, 5,000 research projects and 30,000
publications. It is available on-line through the Canadian Enquiry System
(CAN/OLE).

12 - YORK UNIVERSITY, INSTITUTE FOR SOCIAL RESEARCH, CANADIAN SOCIAL SCIENCE DATA ARCHIVE

ADDRESS: 4700 Keele Street,
North York,
Ontario M3J 1P3,
CANADA
TEL: (416) 736-5061 - TELEX: 065-24736
CREATED: 1967   *HEAD:* Ms. A. E. Oram, Data Archivist
SIZE OF STAFF: Professional: 4   Other: 3   Total: 7
TYPE OF SERVICE: national; public; non-profit
MATERIALS DESCRIBING THE SERVICE: - Canadian Social Science Data Archive, leaflet
SUBJECT COVERAGE: social sciences; sociology; immigration; education; political
science; elections; leisure; ethnic groups; housing; multiculturalism;
demography; surveys

GEOGRAPHICAL COVERAGE: Canada
DATA BEING PROCESSED AND SIZE: data bases: 300 numeric data files
DATA PROCESSING METHODS: computerized
HARDWARE USED: IBM 4341
SOFTWARE USED: SAS/SPSSX
STORAGE MEDIA: tapes, discs, diskettes
TYPE OF ACTIVITY: data analysis; publication
PUBLICATIONS: - Canadian Social Science Data Catalogue, 1985
CLIENTELE: students and researchers
ACCESS TO SERVICE: open to all users, against payment
TYPE & DESCRIPTION OF SERVICES PROVIDED: Its database includes 300 numeric data file
    providing information on magnetic tapes. Custom data analysis is also
    available.

213 - CENTER FOR STUDIES AND TRAINING IN DEVELOPMENT, DOCUMENTATION

SYNONYMOUS NAMES: CEFOD-Documentation
ADDRESS: B.P. 907,
    N'Djaména,
    CHAD
    TEL: 51.54.32
CREATED: 1983   *HEAD:* Ms. N. Vial, Head
SIZE OF STAFF: Professional: 1   Other: 4   Total: 5
TYPE OF SERVICE: national; public; non-profit
SYSTEMS & NETWORKS ATTACHED TO: IBISCUS, RESADOC
WORKING LANGUAGE(S): French; English
SUBJECT COVERAGE: economics; education; history; law; linguistics; social
    anthropology; cultural anthropology; sociology; statistics
GEOGRAPHICAL COVERAGE: Chad; Sahel
DATA PROCESSING METHODS: manual
PERIODICALS PUBLISHED:
    - Bulletin Bibliographique, 4 p.a.
PUBLICATIONS: - Bibliographie sur la ville de N'Djaména
CLIENTELE: approx. 500 users
ACCESS TO SERVICE: services open to all users, free of charge
TYPE & DESCRIPTION OF SERVICES PROVIDED: Provides question-answering services,
    photocopies, and microfiche reproduction on paper.

**214 - ACADEMIA DE HUMANISMO CRISTIANO, GRUPO DE INVESTIGACIONES AGRARIAS, BIBLIOTECA
    Y CENTRO DE DOCUMENTACIÓN**

PARENT ORGANIZATION: Grupo de Investigaciones Agrarias, Academia de Humanismo
    Cristiano
ADDRESS: Ricardo Matte Perez 0342,.
    Casilla 6122,
    Correo 22,
    Santiago,

CHILE
TEL: 223.06.45
CREATED: 1978   *HEAD:* Mrs. M. Giacaman, Head Librarian
SIZE OF STAFF: Total: 2
TYPE OF SERVICE: national; private; non-profit
SYSTEMS & NETWORKS ATTACHED TO: NGO's Libraries Network
WORKING LANGUAGE(S): Spanish
SUBJECT COVERAGE: social sciences; political science; social anthropology; sociology
GEOGRAPHICAL COVERAGE: Chile
DATA BEING PROCESSED AND SIZE: 6,000 books; 250 periodicals; 600 on-going research;
        2,000 seminars reports
DATA PROCESSING METHODS: computerized
HARDWARE USED: IBM AT
SOFTWARE USED: DBASE II
STORAGE MEDIA: fiches, discs
TYPE OF ACTIVITY: distribution of information; SSID training; publication
PUBLICATIONS: - Peasant bibliography
        - Chilean peasant bibliography
CLIENTELE: students, researchers (25 daily)
ACCESS TO SERVICE: services open to all users, free of charge or against payment
TYPE & DESCRIPTION OF SERVICES PROVIDED: Provides library services, bibliographic
        searches of information, selective dissemination of information and
        translation of documents upon request.

215 - CENTRO DE DOCUMENTACIÒN DE "VECTOR"

SYNONYMOUS NAMES: "Vector" Center of Economic and Social Studies, Documentation
        Centre
PARENT ORGANIZATION: "Vector" Center of Economic and Social Studies
ADDRESS: Pio Nono 81-3 Piso-A,
        Casilla 16831, Correo 9,
        Santiago,
        CHILE
        TEL: 775728
CREATED: 1984   *HEAD:* Mr. V. Càceres,
SIZE OF STAFF: Professional: 2   Other: 1   Total: 3
TYPE OF SERVICE: national; private; non-profit
MATERIALS DESCRIBING THE SERVICE: - Cambio
SUBJECT COVERAGE: economics; social sciences; trade unions
GEOGRAPHICAL COVERAGE: Latin America; North America; Europe
DATA BEING PROCESSED AND SIZE: books, serials, pamphlets, reports
DATA PROCESSING METHODS: manual
TYPE OF ACTIVITY: data collection; distribution of information
CLIENTELE: researchers, students, teachers
ACCESS TO SERVICE: services open to specific categories of users, free of charge
TYPE & DESCRIPTION OF SERVICES PROVIDED: Provides selective dissemination of
        information, current awareness services, retrospective searches and question
        answering service.

216 - CENTRO DE PERFECCIONAMIENTO EXPERIMENTACIÓN E INVESTIGACIONES PEDAGÓGICAS, SISTEMA NACIONAL DE INFORMACIÓN EDUCACIONAL, RED DOCUMENTAL

SYNONYMOUS NAMES: CPEIP, SINIE, RED Documental
ADDRESS: Casilla 16162, Correo 9,
Santiago,
CHILE
TEL: 471236
CREATED: 1984   *HEAD:* E. Martasoto, Director
M. A. Palavicino, Chef, Documentation and Data Bank Section
SIZE OF STAFF: Professional: 5   Other: 4   Total: 9
TYPE OF SERVICE: international; public; non-profit
SYSTEMS & NETWORKS ATTACHED TO: Services National Network of University Libraries
(RENIB); Red Académica Chilena (Programas Corporativos IBM); BITHET; REDUC
WORKING LANGUAGE(S): Spanish
SUBJECT COVERAGE: education; social sciences; administrative sciences; geography;
history; psychology; sociology; statistics; linguistics; philosophy; social
welfare
GEOGRAPHICAL COVERAGE: Chile
DATA BEING PROCESSED AND SIZE: books; articles; theses; reports; on-going research
DATA PROCESSING METHODS: computerized
HARDWARE USED: IBM 370 - Batch
SOFTWARE USED: STAIRS (on line) REDO-P-CARDIN A
STORAGE MEDIA: traditional shelving of publications; discs; microfiches; tapes
TYPE OF ACTIVITY: data collection; data analysis; distribution of information, SSID
scientific and methodological research, publication
PERIODICALS PUBLISHED: - INRED: Indice y Resúmenes en Educación, 2 p.a.
PUBLICATIONS: - Lykke Nielsen, M.; Sotomayor San Roman; Muñoz Gomez, A., Manual de
normas editoriales, 1984
- Munoz Gomez, A., Manual para la selección de documentos, 1985
- Sotomayor San Roman, G., Normas para la confección de resúmenes, 1985
CLIENTELE: administrators, researchers, university teachers, school teachers,
students, general public
ACCESS TO SERVICE: open to all users, free of charge
TYPE & DESCRIPTION OF SERVICES PROVIDED: Provides library services, literature and
quantitative data searches and on-line searches using data bases such as
RACH, REDUC, DIALOG and BITHET. Also provides microforms and photocopies.

217 - CONGRESO NACIONAL, BIBLIOTECA

SYNONYMOUS NAMES: Congress Library
ADDRESS: Hemeroteca,
Huerfanos 1117 - 2 piso,
Clasificador postal 1199,
Santiago de Chile,
CHILE
TEL: 6968062
CREATED: 1883   *HEAD:* Mr. N. Blanc Renard, Head Librarian
SIZE OF STAFF: Professional: 20   Other: 61   Total: 81
TYPE OF SERVICE: public; non-profit
SYSTEMS & NETWORKS ATTACHED TO: Northwestern On-Line Total Integrated System (NOTIS

WORKING LANGUAGE(S): Spanish

SUBJECT COVERAGE: law; administrative sciences; social sciences; education; geography; philosophy; political science; economics; history; cultural anthropology; social welfare; sociology

DATA BEING PROCESSED AND SIZE: 800,000 vols.; 4,500 periodicals; 60,000 leaflets; 2,300,000 Chilean press cuttings

DATA PROCESSING METHODS: manual; partially computerized

HARDWARE USED: IBM 4331, CICS/VS, OS/VS1, MVS

TYPE OF ACTIVITY: data collection; data analysis; distribution of information

PERIODICALS PUBLISHED:
- Boletín Bibliográfico, 4 p.a.
- Efímeros, irr.

PUBLICATIONS: - Bibliografías especializadas

ACCESS TO SERVICE: services open to all users, free of charge

TYPE & DESCRIPTION OF SERVICES PROVIDED: Provides library services, bibliographic searches of information, on-line services using own data bases, "RENIB , Banco de Datos Legales y Jurisprudenciales del Poder Legislativo", selective dissemination of information and photocopies upon request.

218 - FACULTAD LATINOAMERICANA DE CIENCIAS SOCIALES-PROGRAMA DE SANTIAGO, CHILE, CENTRO DE DOCUMENTACIÓN

SYNONYMOUS NAMES: CEDOC-FLACSO/Chile;
Latin American Faculty of Social Sciences, Chile, Documentation Centre

PARENT ORGANIZATION: Facultad Latinoamericana de Ciencias Sociales

ADDRESS: Leopoldo Urrutia 1950,
Casilla 3213 - C. Central,
Santiago,
CHILE
TEL: 2257 357 - TELEX: 341326 FLACSO CK

CREATED: 1982   HEAD: Mr. E. Hermosilla-Palma,

SIZE OF STAFF: Professional: 1   Other: 2   Total: 3

TYPE OF SERVICE: public; non-profit

SYSTEMS & NETWORKS ATTACHED TO: Integrated Library System, Santiago, Chile

WORKING LANGUAGE(S): English; French; Portuguese; Spanish

SUBJECT COVERAGE: social sciences; economics; political science; sociology; militarism; peace

GEOGRAPHICAL COVERAGE: Latin America

DATA BEING PROCESSED AND SIZE: 13,000 books, 520 periodicals

DATA PROCESSING METHODS: manual; computerized

SOFTWARE USED: MICRO ISIS, Unesco

TYPE OF ACTIVITY: distribution of information; SSID scientific and methodological activities; publication

PERIODICALS PUBLISHED: - Catálogo Bibliográfico, 2 p.a.
- Catálogo Publicaciones Periodicas, 1 p.a.

PUBLICATIONS: - Catálogo de publicaciones de Flacso-Programa Santiago 1958, 1986

CLIENTELE: students, politicians, academicians, researchers, reporters (1,200 persons p.a.)

ACCESS TO SERVICE: open to specific categories of users free of charge

TYPE & DESCRIPTION OF SERVICES PROVIDED: Provides library services, bibliographical searches of information and selective dissemination of information. Has also access to data bases through ECLA and CELADE.

219 - INSTITUTO DE ESTUDIOS INTERNACIONALES, BIBLIOTECA

SYNONYMOUS NAMES: Institute of International Studies, Library
ADDRESS: University of Chile,
        Avda. Condell 249,
        Casilla 14187, Sucursal 21,
        Santiago,
        CHILE
        TEL: 232-1797
CREATED: 1966   *HEAD:* M. L. Matte, Chief Librarian
SIZE OF STAFF: Professional: 2   Other: 1   Total: 3
TYPE OF SERVICE: national; public; non-profit
WORKING LANGUAGE(S): Spanish
SUBJECT COVERAGE: political science; law; international relations; international la
GEOGRAPHICAL COVERAGE: Chile
DATA BEING PROCESSED AND SIZE: 7,500 books; 450 periodicals
DATA PROCESSING METHODS: manual
TYPE OF ACTIVITY: data collection; publication
PERIODICALS PUBLISHED:
        - Accession List
CLIENTELE: researchers, professors, students, international officers
ACCESS TO SERVICE: open to all users
TYPE & DESCRIPTION OF SERVICES PROVIDED: Provides library services, question-
        answering services, interlibrary loans and reproduction of documents.

220 - OFICINA INTERNACIONAL DEL TRABAJO, PROGRAMA REGIONAL DEL EMPLEO PARA AMÉRICA LATINA Y EL CARIBE

SYNONYMOUS NAMES: OIT/PREALC;
        International Labour Office, Regional Employment Programme for Latin Amer
        and the Caribbean;
        ILO/PREALC
ADDRESS: Alonso de Córdova 4212,
        Casilla 618,
        Santiago,
        CHILE
        TEL: 486500-2289636 - TELEX: 340382 PREALC CK
        CABLE: PREALC
CREATED: 1968   *HEAD:* Ms. P. Etchevers, Chief Librarian
SIZE OF STAFF: Professional: 1   Other: 1   Total: 2
TYPE OF SERVICE: international
SYSTEMS & NETWORKS ATTACHED TO: SIB (Sistema Integrado de Bibliotecas)
WORKING LANGUAGE(S): Spanish; English
SUBJECT COVERAGE: social sciences; economics; sociology; employment
GEOGRAPHICAL COVERAGE: Latin America; Caribbean area
DATA BEING PROCESSED AND SIZE: 15,000 documentation items
DATA PROCESSING METHODS: partially computerized

HARDWARE USED: EPSON EQUITY 1
SOFTWARE USED: MicroISIS
TYPE OF ACTIVITY: data collection; data analysis; publication
PERIODICALS PUBLISHED:
        - Catálogo Mensual
CLIENTELE: researchers, professors, alumnae, university students, trade unions
ACCESS TO SERVICE: services open to all users, free of charge
TYPE & DESCRIPTION OF SERVICES PROVIDED: Provides library services, bibliographic
        searches of information, photocopies and distribution of documents.

21 - PRESIDENCIA DE LA REPUBLICA, OFICINA DE PLANIFICACIÓN NACIONAL, BIBLIOTECA

SYNONYMOUS NAMES: ODEPLAN, Biblioteca;
        Office of the President of the Republic, National Planning Office, Library
ADDRESS: Ahumada 48,Piso 4,
        Casilla 9140,
        Santiago,
        CHILE
        TEL: 6980104 - TELEX: 341400 ODEPLACK
CREATED: 1966   *HEAD:* Ms. C. Sánchez, Head Librarian
SIZE OF STAFF: Professional: 3   Other: 1   Total: 4
TYPE OF SERVICE: national; public; non-profit
SUBJECT COVERAGE: demography; economics; law; social welfare; economic planning;
        social planning
DATA BEING PROCESSED AND SIZE: 10,300 books
DATA PROCESSING METHODS: manual
SOFTWARE USED: MICRO ISIS
STORAGE MEDIA: traditional shelving of publications
TYPE OF ACTIVITY: data collection; data analysis; distribution of information;
        publication
PUBLICATIONS: - Yearbooks
        - Indexes
CLIENTELE: consultants (3,500), university students, teachers, economists
ACCESS TO SERVICE: services open to all users, free of charge
TYPE & DESCRIPTION OF SERVICES PROVIDED: Provides library services, bibliographic
        searches of information and photocopies (against payment).

22 - PROGRAMA INTERDISCIPLINARIO DE INVESTIGACIONES EN EDUCACIÓN, BIBLIOTECA

SYNONYMOUS NAMES: PIIE, Biblioteca;
        Interdisciplinary Research Program on Education, Library
PARENT ORGANIZATION: Academia de Humanismo Cristiano (Academy of Catholic Christian
        Humanism)
ADDRESS: Eliodoro Yáñez 890,
        Santiago,
        CHILE
        TEL: 746656 - TELEX: CK 340412
CREATED: 1977   *HEAD:* Mrs. M. I. Ortega, Head
SIZE OF STAFF: Professional: 1   Other: 1   Total: 2

TYPE OF SERVICE: national; private; non-profit
SYSTEMS & NETWORKS ATTACHED TO: SIB (Integrated Libraries System)
WORKING LANGUAGE(S): Spanish; English; French
SUBJECT COVERAGE: social sciences; education; political science; psychology; social
      anthropology; sociology; statistics; adult education; educational planning
      educational development; rural development
GEOGRAPHICAL COVERAGE: Latin America; global
DATA BEING PROCESSED AND SIZE: 5,000 documentation items; 35 periodicals
DATA PROCESSING METHODS: computerized
HARDWARE USED: Microcomputer IBM PC (hard disc)
SOFTWARE USED: CDS/Micro ISIS
STORAGE MEDIA: fiches; discs
TYPE OF ACTIVITY: data collection; data analysis; distribution of information;
      publication
PERIODICALS PUBLISHED:
     - Accession List
CLIENTELE: researchers, students, teachers
ACCESS TO SERVICE: open to all users
TYPE & DESCRIPTION OF SERVICES PROVIDED: Provides library services, bibliographic
      searches, information on magnetic tapes and photocopies. Has its own data
      base: DOCS and has access to REDUC through RAE (analytical abstracts on
      education).

223 - UNIVERSIDAD DE CHILE, CENTRO DE ESTUDIOS DE CULTURA JUDÁICA

SYNONYMOUS NAMES: University of Chile, Center for the Study of Jewish Culture
ADDRESS: Miguel Claro 182,
      P.O. Box 13583, Correo 21,
      Santiago,
      CHILE
      TEL: 497720
CREATED: 1967   *HEAD:* Prof. Dr. G. Böhm,
SIZE OF STAFF: Professional: 1   Other: 4   Total: 5
TYPE OF SERVICE: international; public; non-profit
WORKING LANGUAGE(S): Spanish; English; Hebrew; German
SUBJECT COVERAGE: history; Jewish minorities; religion; language; culture; art
GEOGRAPHICAL COVERAGE: South America; Caribbean area
DATA PROCESSING METHODS: manual
STORAGE MEDIA: fiches
TYPE OF ACTIVITY: data collection; publication
PERIODICALS PUBLISHED: - Cuadernos Judáicos
     - Judáica Iberoamericana
PUBLICATIONS: - History of the Jews in South America and the Caribbean islands
     - Jewish art
CLIENTELE: university students and teachers, general public
ACCESS TO SERVICE: services open to all users, free of charge
TYPE & DESCRIPTION OF SERVICES PROVIDED: Provides library services and bibliographic
      searches.

24 - UNIVERSIDAD DE CHILE, INSTITUTO DE CIENCIA POLÍTICA, BIBLIOTECA

SYNONYMOUS NAMES: University of Chile, Political Science Institute, Library
ADDRESS: Maria Guerrero, 940,
　　　　Providencia,
　　　　P.O. Box 258-V,
　　　　Correo 21,
　　　　Santiago de Chile,
　　　　CHILE
　　　　TEL: 49.22.47 - TELEX: 340436 PBVTR CIPOLUCH
CREATED: 1982　　*HEAD:* Ms. M. Tagle, Library Chief
SIZE OF STAFF: Professional: 6
TYPE OF SERVICE: international; public
SYSTEMS & NETWORKS ATTACHED TO: BITNET Network
WORKING LANGUAGE(S): Spanish
SUBJECT COVERAGE: political science; administrative sciences; sociology; geopolitics;
　　　　political history; political geography
DATA PROCESSING METHODS: partially computerized
TYPE OF ACTIVITY: data collection; data analysis; distribution of information; SSID
　　　　scientific and methodological activities
CLIENTELE: academic researchers, specialists, students
ACCESS TO SERVICE: services open to all users, free of charge
TYPE & DESCRIPTION OF SERVICES PROVIDED: Provides library services, bibliographic and
　　　　literature abstract searches of information. Photocopies and translation of
　　　　documents upon request.

25 - WEN XIAN QING BAO ZHONG XIN

SYNONYMOUS NAMES: Chinese Academy of Sciences, Center for Documentation and
　　　　Information
PARENT ORGANIZATION: Chinese Academy of Social Sciences
ADDRESS: 5 Jianguomennei Dajie,
　　　　Beijing,
　　　　CHINA (PEOPLE'S REPUBLIC)
　　　　TEL: 5007744-2707
　　　　CABLE: CASS
CREATED: 1985　　*HEAD:* Ru Xin, Director
SIZE OF STAFF: Professional: 150　　Other: 20　　Total: 170
TYPE OF SERVICE: national; public; non-profit
SYSTEMS & NETWORKS ATTACHED TO: APINESS (Asia-Pacific Information Network in the
　　　　Social Sciences)
WORKING LANGUAGE(S): Chinese
SUBJECT COVERAGE: social sciences
DATA BEING PROCESSED AND SIZE: 300,000 books, periodicals and reports
DATA PROCESSING METHODS: manual
STORAGE MEDIA: traditional shelving of publications, microfiches
TYPE OF ACTIVITY: data collection; distribution of information; SSID scientific and
　　　　methodological activities; publication
PERIODICALS PUBLISHED: - Social Sciences Abroad, 12 p.a.
　　　　- New Trends in Social Sciences Abroad, 12 p.a.

- Diogenes (Chinese edition)
- Abstracts of Social Science Articles in Recent Foreign Periodicals, 12 p.a.

PUBLICATIONS: - Index of social science papers in foreign countries
- Index of economic literature in foreign countries
- Social science academic abstracts and summaries of theses
- Collection of titles of social science literature in China

CLIENTELE: social science researchers and students, policy-makers

ACCESS TO SERVICE: services open to specific categories of users, partly free of charge

TYPE & DESCRIPTION OF SERVICES PROVIDED: Information service linked to the 32 research institutes of the Chinese Academy of Social Sciences and providing bibliographic and literature searches of information and library services. Has incorporated in 1985 the Institute for Social Science Information (Qing Bao Yan Jiu Suo).

226 - ASOCIACIÓN NACIONAL DE INDUSTRIALES, BIBLIOTECA, CENTRO DE DOCUMENTACIÓN E INFORMACIÓN INDUSTRIAL

SYNONYMOUS NAMES: ANDI, Library and Industrial Documentation and Information Centre

ADDRESS: Centro Coltejer,
Calle 52, No. 47-48, pisos 8 y 9,
Apartado Aéreo 997,
Medellín,
COLOMBIA
TEL: 251.44.44 - TELEX: 66631
CABLE: ANDI

CREATED: 1977   *HEAD:* Ms. L. M. Upegui Gaviria,

SIZE OF STAFF: Professional: 1   Other: 2   Total: 3

TYPE OF SERVICE: national; private; non-profit

SYSTEMS & NETWORKS ATTACHED TO: RECIDE, GUIE

MATERIALS DESCRIBING THE SERVICE: - Restrepo, A.; Upegui, L.M., A design for a documentation and industrial information service at Andi. Medellín, 1977, 6 p.
- Processing manual. Medellín, Andi, 1977 (short comments on the official publications of Andi)

WORKING LANGUAGE(S): Spanish

SUBJECT COVERAGE: administrative sciences; economics; social sciences

GEOGRAPHICAL COVERAGE: Colombia

DATA BEING PROCESSED AND SIZE: 19,200 books, articles, seminar reports

DATA PROCESSING METHODS: computerized

TYPE OF ACTIVITY: data collection; data analysis; publication

PERIODICALS PUBLISHED:
- New Publications Received, daily report

PUBLICATIONS: - List of periodicals currently received by the Andi Library
- List of sources of information received by the Andi Library
- Bibliographies in: Noticiero: Noticias técnicas

CLIENTELE: students, researchers

ACCESS TO SERVICE: open to specific categories of users, free of charge

TYPE & DESCRIPTION OF SERVICES PROVIDED: Library services, query answering service,

provision of photocopies, retrospective bibliographic searches, selective
dissemination of information. Internal network for service of the main
office and 7 branches located in Bogota, Barranquilla, Bucaramanga, Cali,
Cartagena, Manizales and Pereira.

27 - CENTRO NACIONAL DE DOCUMENTACIÓN SOBRE DESARROLLO URBANO Y VIVIENDA

ANONYMOUS NAMES: CENDUVI
ADDRESS: Ciudad Universitaria,
         Calle 45-Carrera 30,
         Apartado Aereo 34219,
         Bogota, DE,
         COLOMBIA
         TEL: (2) 680818
CREATED: 1974   *HEAD:* Mr. O. F. Gomez Villa, Executive Director
SIZE OF STAFF: Professional: 7   Other: 18   Total: 25
TYPE OF SERVICE: international; public; private; non-profit
WORKING LANGUAGE(S): Spanish
SUBJECT COVERAGE: social sciences; economics; urban development; urban planning;
         architecture
GEOGRAPHICAL COVERAGE: Colombia
DATA PROCESSING METHODS: manual; computerized
HARDWARE USED: PC EPSON EQUITY II; PC TEXAS INSTRUMENTS
SOFTWARE USED: LOTUS, SIMPHONY, DBASE III+, BASIC, COBOL, WORD
STORAGE MEDIA: discs; fiches; microfiches
TYPE OF ACTIVITY: data collection; data analysis; distribution of information; SSID
         scientific and methodological activities; publication
ACCESS TO SERVICE: services open to all users free of charge, some paid services
TYPE & DESCRIPTION OF SERVICES PROVIDED: Provides library services and bibliographic
         searches of information.

28 - COLEGIO MAYOR DE NUESTRA SEÑORA DEL ROSARIO, BIBLIOTECA

ADDRESS: Calle 14, no. 6-25,
         Bogota,
         COLOMBIA
         TEL: 82.00.88
CREATED: 1953   *HEAD:* Ms. M. Molina Passega, Head Librarian
SIZE OF STAFF: Professional: 1   Other: 10   Total: 11
TYPE OF SERVICE: private; non-profit
WORKING LANGUAGE(S): Spanish
SUBJECT COVERAGE: law; administrative sciences; economics; history; linguistics;
         philosophy; political science
DATA BEING PROCESSED AND SIZE: books; seminars; periodicals
DATA PROCESSING METHODS: partially computerized
TYPE OF ACTIVITY: data collection; data analysis; distribution of information; SSID
         scientific and methodological activities; SSID training
CLIENTELE: students, professors, civil servants
ACCESS TO SERVICE: services open to specific categories of users, free of charge

TYPE & DESCRIPTION OF SERVICES PROVIDED: Provides library services, bibliographic and literature abstract searches, selective dissemination of information, photocopies, and on-line services using own data base.

229 - FONDO COLOMBIANO DE INVESTIGACIONES CIENTÍFICAS Y PROYECTOS ESPECIALES "FRANCISCO JOSE DE CALDAS", BIBLIOTECA Y DIVISIÓN DE LA DOCUMENTACIÓN

SYNONYMOUS NAMES: COLCIENCIAS
ADDRESS: Transversal 9A. no. 133-28,
Apartado Aéreo 051580,
Bogotá,
COLOMBIA
TEL: 274.0004 - TELEX: 44305
CREATED: 1969   HEAD: Ms. I. Forero de Moreno, Head
SIZE OF STAFF: Professional: 4   Other: 3   Total: 7
TYPE OF SERVICE: national; public
SYSTEMS & NETWORKS ATTACHED TO: SNI (Systema Nacional de Información)
SUBJECT COVERAGE: political science; social sciences
GEOGRAPHICAL COVERAGE: global
DATA BEING PROCESSED AND SIZE: 7,500 documentation items
DATA PROCESSING METHODS: computerized
HARDWARE USED: IBM PC
SOFTWARE USED: MicroISIS; Lotus-Scimate
STORAGE MEDIA: traditional shelving of publications; diskettes; fiches
TYPE OF ACTIVITY: data collection; distribution of information
PERIODICALS PUBLISHED:
    - Carta de COLCIENCIAS
PUBLICATIONS: - Directorio de unidades de información
    - Colombia: ciencia y tecnología
CLIENTELE: researchers
ACCESS TO SERVICE: services open to specific categories of users, free of charge or against payment
TYPE & DESCRIPTION OF SERVICES PROVIDED: Provides library services, on-line searches using its own data bases: Memoria Institucional, Política Científica y Tecnológia, Información e Informática. Has also access to BRS and DIALOG data bases. Also provides selective dissemination of information and photocopies.

230 - INSTITUTO COLOMBIANO DE BIENESTAR FAMILIAR, BIBLIOTECA

SYNONYMOUS NAMES: ICBF, Biblioteca;
    Colombian Institute of Family Welfare, Library
ADDRESS: Avenida 68 por calle 64,
Apartado Aereo 18116,
Bogota,
COLOMBIA
TEL: (2) 314-556
CREATED: 1972   HEAD: Ms. S. Sánchez García, Head
SIZE OF STAFF: Professional: 2   Other: 5   Total: 7

YPE OF SERVICE: public; non-profit
YSTEMS & NETWORKS ATTACHED TO: SNI (Sistema Nacional de Información); SNICS
(Subsistema Nacional de Información en Ciencias de la Salud)
ORKING LANGUAGE(S): Spanish
UBJECT COVERAGE: social welfare; education; law; psychology; sociology; nutrition;
women; family life; child psychology
EOGRAPHICAL COVERAGE: Colombia
ATA BEING PROCESSED AND SIZE: 14,000 documentation items
ATA PROCESSING METHODS: manual
TORAGE MEDIA: traditional shelving of publications; fiches
YPE OF ACTIVITY: distribution of information
ERIODICALS PUBLISHED:
- Listas Mensuales de Adquisiciones
LIENTELE: 80 users per day
CCESS TO SERVICE: services open to all users, free of charge
YPE & DESCRIPTION OF SERVICES PROVIDED: Provides library services, inter-library
loans, bibliographic searches, selective dissemination of information, and
photocopies.

31 - UNIVERSIDAD AUTÓNOMA DE BUCARAMANGA, FACULTAD DE COMUNICACIÓN SOCIAL, CENTRO DE DOCUMENTACIÓN PARA LAS COMUNICACIONES

YNONYMOUS NAMES: UNAB/CDC
DDRESS: Calle 48 no. 39-234,
Apartado Aéreo No. 1642,
Bucaramanga,
COLOMBIA
TEL: 75111
REATED: 1983   *HEAD:* Mrs. G. M. Rojas de Hernandez, Director
IZE OF STAFF: Professional: 1   Other: 3   Total: 4
YPE OF SERVICE: public
YSTEMS & NETWORKS ATTACHED TO: Sistema Colombiano de Información Bibliográfica
(SCIB)
ORKING LANGUAGE(S): Spanish
UBJECT COVERAGE: social sciences; social communication; mass media; public opinion
EOGRAPHICAL COVERAGE: Latin America
ATA BEING PROCESSED AND SIZE: 4,000 books; 10,000 documents; 400 serials; 15
periodicals
ATA PROCESSING METHODS: partially computerized
OFTWARE USED: SCIB
TORAGE MEDIA: traditional shelving of publications, disquettes and microfiches
YPE OF ACTIVITY: data collection; data analysis; distribution of information;
publication
UBLICATIONS: - Catálogo del Centro de Documentación y Bibliografía
LIENTELE: professors, researchers, students
CCESS TO SERVICE: services open to all users, against payment
YPE & DESCRIPTION OF SERVICES PROVIDED: Provides library services, bibliographic
search of information and photocopies.

232 - UNIVERSIDAD DE LA AMAZONIA, BIBLIOTECA CENTRAL

SYNONYMOUS NAMES: Amazonia University, Central Library
ADDRESS: Av. Circunvalación,
  Apartado Aéreo 192,
  Florencia,
  Caquetá,
  COLOMBIA
  TEL: 2904
CREATED: 1971   *HEAD:* Mr. C. A. Moreno Mendoza, Director
SIZE OF STAFF: Total: 5
TYPE OF SERVICE: public
SYSTEMS & NETWORKS ATTACHED TO: SouthWestern Organization of the Provinces (Tolima,
  Quindio, Huila and Caquetá)
SUBJECT COVERAGE: administrative sciences; education; geography; history;
  linguistics; psychology
GEOGRAPHICAL COVERAGE: Colombia
DATA BEING PROCESSED AND SIZE: 9,000 books; 400 documents; 350 publications
DATA PROCESSING METHODS: partially computerized
SOFTWARE USED: Micro Columbia 15001-3/11
STORAGE MEDIA: traditional shelving of publications, fiches
TYPE OF ACTIVITY: data collection; data analysis; distribution of information
PERIODICALS PUBLISHED: - Matemáticas Review, 4 p.a.
  - University de la Amazonia, 1 p.a.
CLIENTELE: students, general public
ACCESS TO SERVICE: services open to all users, free of charge
TYPE & DESCRIPTION OF SERVICES PROVIDED: Provides library services, selective
  dissemination and searches of information through the Centro de
  Documentación de la Amazonia Colombiana and the Centro de Información del
  Instituto de Investigaciones amazonicas (IAMI). Photocopying facilities are
  available.

233 - UNIVERSIDAD DE LOS ANDES, FACULTAD DE ECONOMÍA, CENTRO DE ESTUDIOS DEL DESARROLLO ECONÓMICO, BIBLIOTECA

SYNONYMOUS NAMES: CEDE-UNIANDES, Biblioteca
ADDRESS: Apartado Aéreo 4976,
  Carrera 1aE No. 18A-10,
  Bogotá,
  COLOMBIA
  TEL: 282.40.66/189
CREATED: 1958   *HEAD:* Ms. C. Morales, Director
SIZE OF STAFF: Professional: 1   Other: 5   Total: 6
TYPE OF SERVICE: national; private; non-profit
MATERIALS DESCRIBING THE SERVICE: - Activities report
WORKING LANGUAGE(S): Spanish; English
SUBJECT COVERAGE: economics; social sciences; sociology; economic development
GEOGRAPHICAL COVERAGE: Colombia; Latin America; USA
DATA BEING PROCESSED AND SIZE: 26,370 books; 380 periodicals; 320 theses; 520 CEDE
  publications; 3,000 papers
DATA PROCESSING METHODS: manual

TORAGE MEDIA: traditional shelving of publications: fiches; tapes; discs
YPE OF ACTIVITY: data collection; distribution of information; publication
ERIODICALS PUBLISHED:
   - Accession List
UBLICATIONS: - Printed catalogues of periodical publications
   - Printed catalogues of CEDE publications
   - Printed catalogues of degree theses
LIENTELE: students, teachers, researchers
CCESS TO SERVICE: services open to specific categories of users
YPE & DESCRIPTION OF SERVICES PROVIDED: Provides library services.

34 - UNIVERSIDAD DE SAN BUENAVENTURA, BIBLIOTECA

YNONYMOUS NAMES: San Buenaventura University, Library
DDRESS: La Umbria,
   Apartado Aéreo 7154,
   Cali,
   COLOMBIA
   TEL: 391079
REATED: 1971   *HEAD:* Ms. A. Henao Jaramillo, Director
IZE OF STAFF: Professional: 9
YPE OF SERVICE: private
UBJECT COVERAGE: social sciences; administrative sciences; economics; law;
   education; political science
ATA BEING PROCESSED AND SIZE: 20,000 books
ATA PROCESSING METHODS: manual
TORAGE MEDIA: traditional shelving of publications
YPE OF ACTIVITY: data analysis
ERIODICALS PUBLISHED:
   - Boletin Bibliografico de Nuevas Adquisiciones
LIENTELE: students, teachers, researchers (3,000)
CCESS TO SERVICE: services open to specific categories of users
YPE & DESCRIPTION OF SERVICES PROVIDED: Provides library services, bibliographic
   information searches, selective dissemination of information, and
   photocopies.

**35 - UNIVERSIDAD PONTIFICIA BOLIVARIANA, CENTRO DE INVESTIGACIONES PARA EL
   DESARROLLO INTEGRAL, CENTRO DE DOCUMENTACIÓN "RAFAEL M. SALAS"**

DDRESS: Apartado Aereo 1178,
   Medellin,
   COLOMBIA
   TEL: 248-6892
   CABLE: 65047 UPB
REATED: 1969   *HEAD:* L. M. Franco, Chief
IZE OF STAFF: Professional: 1   Other: 5   Total: 6
YPE OF SERVICE: national; private; non-profit
ORKING LANGUAGE(S): Spanish
UBJECT COVERAGE: social sciences; demography; philosophy; sociology

Costa Rica

GEOGRAPHICAL COVERAGE: Colombia
DATA BEING PROCESSED AND SIZE: 1,500 books; 4,000 documents and 250 microfiches
DATA PROCESSING METHODS: partially computerized
HARDWARE USED: NEC APC IV
SOFTWARE USED: CDS/ISIS
STORAGE MEDIA: traditional shelving of publications; microfiches; discs
TYPE OF ACTIVITY: data collection; distribution of information
PERIODICALS PUBLISHED: - Contaminación Ambiental
      - Cuadernos del CIDI
      - Boletín Técnico
CLIENTELE: students and teachers
ACCESS TO SERVICE: open to all users
TYPE & DESCRIPTION OF SERVICES PROVIDED: Provides library services, selective
dissemination of information, bibliographic, literature and quantitative
data searches, and photocopies. The Center has access to DIALOG (on-line
services).

Costa Rica

236 - INSTITUTO GEOGRÁFICO NACIONAL, BIBLIOTECA

SYNONYMOUS NAMES: National Geographic Institute, Library
ADDRESS: C.9, av. 20 y 22,
      Apartado Postal 2272,
      San Jose,
      COSTA RICA
      TEL: 27.21.88
CREATED: 1975   *HEAD:* Mr. F. M. Rudin Rodríguez,
TYPE OF SERVICE: national; public; non-profit
WORKING LANGUAGE(S): Spanish; English
SUBJECT COVERAGE: geography; social sciences
GEOGRAPHICAL COVERAGE: Costa Rica; Central America
DATA PROCESSING METHODS: manual
TYPE OF ACTIVITY: data collection; distribution of information; SSID scientific and
methodological activities; publication
PERIODICALS PUBLISHED: - Informe Semestral
CLIENTELE: technical and professional users, university students and school teacher
ACCESS TO SERVICE: services open to specific categories of users
TYPE & DESCRIPTION OF SERVICES PROVIDED: Provides bibliographic information searche
and photocopies.

237 - UNIVERSIDAD DE COSTA RICA, BIBLIOTECA EUGENIO FONSECA TORTOS

SYNONYMOUS NAMES: University of Costa Rica, Eugenio Fonseca Tortos Library
ADDRESS: Facultad de Ciencias Sociales,
      Apdo. 41, Ciudad Universitaria "Rodrigo Facio",
      San José,
      COSTA RICA
      TEL: 25.55.55
CREATED: 1980   *HEAD:* Ms. A. L. S. Echavarría, Director

SIZE OF STAFF: Professional: 2   Other: 2   Total: 4
TYPE OF SERVICE: public; non-profit
SYSTEMS & NETWORKS ATTACHED TO: National Network of Planning (REDNAPLAN); Red Mujer
        (Women Network)
WORKING LANGUAGE(S): Spanish; English; French
SUBJECT COVERAGE: social sciences
GEOGRAPHICAL COVERAGE: global
DATA BEING PROCESSED AND SIZE: 25,000 books and periodicals; 200 maps; 700 theses; 50
        reports on on-going research
DATA PROCESSING METHODS: computerized
TYPE OF ACTIVITY: data collection; data analysis
CLIENTELE: 3,000 teachers and students
ACCESS TO SERVICE: services open to specific categories of users, free of charge
TYPE & DESCRIPTION OF SERVICES PROVIDED: Provides retrospective bibliographies,
        reference services, dissemination of information and analysis of documents
        for REDNAPLAN.

**238 - UNIVERSIDAD DE COSTA RICA, INSTITUTO DE INVESTIGACIONES SOCIALES, UNIDAD DE
INVESTIGACIÓN DOCUMENTAL E INFORMACIÓN**

SYNONYMOUS NAMES: UNIDI, IIS;
        UNIDI, Institute of Social Research
ADDRESS: Ciudad Universitaria "Rodrigo Facio",
        Código 2060,
        San Jose,
        COSTA RICA
        TEL: 24.67.81
        CABLE: UNICORI (I.I.S.)
CREATED: 1975   HEAD: Mrs. M. A. Mora Ledezma,
SIZE OF STAFF: Professional: 5   Other: 3   Total: 8
TYPE OF SERVICE: national; public; non-profit
SYSTEMS & NETWORKS ATTACHED TO: CLADES; CEDESC-CSUCA; REDNAPLAN-INFOPLAN
MATERIALS DESCRIBING THE SERVICE: - Centro de Documentación, 1979 (leaflet)
WORKING LANGUAGE(S): Spanish
SUBJECT COVERAGE: social sciences
GEOGRAPHICAL COVERAGE: Central America; Costa Rica
DATA BEING PROCESSED AND SIZE: 5,000 printed documents, periodicals, reports on on-
        going research
HARDWARE USED: Burroughs B 6920
SOFTWARE USED: DMS II
STORAGE MEDIA: magnetic tapes
TYPE OF ACTIVITY: data collection; data analysis; publication
PERIODICALS PUBLISHED:
        - Información Documental, since 1978
PUBLICATIONS: - Avances de investigación (series)
        - Investigaciones (series)
CLIENTELE: researchers, students, professionals
ACCESS TO SERVICE: open to specific categories of users, free of charge
TYPE & DESCRIPTION OF SERVICES PROVIDED: Provides library services and bibliographic
        data searches of information.

Côte d'Ivoire

239 - CENTRE IVOIRIEN DE RECHERCHES ECONOMIQUES ET SOCIALES, BIBLIOTHÈQUE

SYNONYMOUS NAMES: CIRES Bibliothèque
PARENT ORGANIZATION: Université Nationale
ADDRESS: B.P. 1295,
    Abidjan 08,
    COTE D'IVOIRE
    TEL: 44-09-53 - TELEX: 26138 RECTU
CREATED: 1971   *HEAD:* Mr. A. Kouapa, Documentalist
SIZE OF STAFF: Professional: 1   Other: 3   Total: 4
TYPE OF SERVICE: national; public
SYSTEMS & NETWORKS ATTACHED TO: REDACI: Réseau National de Documentation Agricole e
    Côte d'Ivoire
WORKING LANGUAGE(S): French; English
SUBJECT COVERAGE: demography; economics; sociology
GEOGRAPHICAL COVERAGE: Cote d'Ivoire; Western Africa
DATA BEING PROCESSED AND SIZE: 8,000 books; 200 periodicals
DATA PROCESSING METHODS: computerized
HARDWARE USED: IBM PC XT
SOFTWARE USED: CDS/ISIS
TYPE OF ACTIVITY: publication
PERIODICALS PUBLISHED: - Cahiers du CIRES, 4 p.a.
    - Bulletin de Sommaires des Revues
CLIENTELE: researchers, professors, postgraduate students
ACCESS TO SERVICE: open to specific categories of users
TYPE & DESCRIPTION OF SERVICES PROVIDED: Provides library services, searches of
    information and photocopies.

240 - INSTITUT AFRICAIN POUR LE DÉVELOPPEMENT ECONOMIQUE ET SOCIAL, CENTRE DE DOCUMENTATION

SYNONYMOUS NAMES: INADES Documentation;
    African Institute for Economic and Social Development, Documentation Centr
ADDRESS: 08/B.P. 8,
    Abidjan 08,
    COTE D'IVOIRE
    TEL: 44-15-94
CREATED: 1962   *HEAD:* Mr. Y. Morel,
SIZE OF STAFF: Professional: 5   Other: 5   Total: 10
TYPE OF SERVICE: national; private; non-profit
SYSTEMS & NETWORKS ATTACHED TO: Association IBISCUS
MATERIALS DESCRIBING THE SERVICE: - Annual report
WORKING LANGUAGE(S): French
SUBJECT COVERAGE: social sciences; rural development
GEOGRAPHICAL COVERAGE: French speaking Africa
DATA BEING PROCESSED AND SIZE: 42,000 books; 300 periodicals; micro-fiches;
    audiovisual documents
DATA PROCESSING METHODS: partially computerized
HARDWARE USED: GOUPIL G4

SOFTWARE USED: TEXTO LOGOTEL
STORAGE MEDIA: fiches; discs; microfiches
TYPE OF ACTIVITY: data collection; data analysis; SSID training
PERIODICALS PUBLISHED: - Bibliographies Commentées, 4 p.a.
         - Livres Enregistrés à la Bibliothèque, 3 p.a.
         - Fichier Afrique, fiches miméo, 2 p.a.
CLIENTELE: students, researchers
TYPE & DESCRIPTION OF SERVICES PROVIDED: Provides libary services, query answering
      service, bibliographic and literature searches of information, selective
      dissemination of information, information on magnetic tapes or discs,
      microforms and photocopies.

241 - MINISTÈRE DE L'ECONOMIE ET DES FINANCES, SERVICE AUTONOME DE LA DOCUMENTATION, DES ARCHIVES ET DES PUBLICATIONS

SYNONYMOUS NAMES: SADAP
ADDRESS: B.P.V. 125,
        Abidjan,
        COTE D'IVOIRE
        TEL: 32-05-66
CREATED: 1975   *HEAD:* Mr. A. M. Kadio,
SIZE OF STAFF: Professional: 4   Other: 6   Total: 10
TYPE OF SERVICE: international; public; non-profit
WORKING LANGUAGE(S): French
SUBJECT COVERAGE: economics; statistics; social sciences; law; political science;
      social welfare; agriculture
GEOGRAPHICAL COVERAGE: Western Africa
DATA BEING PROCESSED AND SIZE: 8,000 books; 250 periodicals; 2,000 files
DATA PROCESSING METHODS: manual
TYPE OF ACTIVITY: data analysis; publication
PERIODICALS PUBLISHED: - Revue Economique et Financière de la Côte d'Ivoire
PUBLICATIONS: - Catalogue des publications du Ministère de l'Economie et des Finances
        - Etudes économiques et financières
        - Etudes et conjonctures
CLIENTELE: general public, students, teachers, advisors, ambassadors
ACCESS TO SERVICE: open to specific categories of users, free of charge
TYPE & DESCRIPTION OF SERVICES PROVIDED: Provides library services, bibliographic and
      literature abstract searches, selective dissemination of information and
      translation of documents upon request.

242 - CENTRO DE ESTUDIOS SOBRE AMERÍCA, UNIDAD DE INFORMACIÓN

SYNONYMOUS NAMES: CEA, Unidad de Información;
      Center of Studies on America, Information Unit
ADDRESS: Ave. 3A No. 1805 entre 18 y 20 Miramar,
      Playa,
      Havana,
      CUBA

TEL: 296745
CREATED: 1978   *HEAD:* Mr. L. S. Salazar,
SIZE OF STAFF: Total: 3
TYPE OF SERVICE: non-profit
WORKING LANGUAGE(S): English; Spanish; French; Russian
SUBJECT COVERAGE: social sciences; demography; economics; history; law; philosophy;
        political science; social anthropology; social welfare; sociology;
        international relations; foreign policy
GEOGRAPHICAL COVERAGE: America
DATA BEING PROCESSED AND SIZE: 6,000 books; 500 periodicals
DATA PROCESSING METHODS: partially computerized
HARDWARE USED: NEC-PC 9801 M
SOFTWARE USED: DBase III
STORAGE MEDIA: 700 fiches; 15 floppy disks
TYPE OF ACTIVITY: data collection; distribution of information; publication
PERIODICALS PUBLISHED:
        - Accessions List
        - Signal Information Bulletin
CLIENTELE: researchers (around 40)
ACCESS TO SERVICE: services open to specific categories of users
TYPE & DESCRIPTION OF SERVICES PROVIDED: Provides library services, bibliographic and
        quantitative data searches of information, selective dissemination of
        information and photocopies. Also provides on-line services using its own
        data base "CEALIB".

**243 - CESKOSLOVENSKA AKADEMIE VED, USTAV PRO FILOZOFII A SOCIOLOGII, STREDISKO
VEDECKÝCH INFORMACÍ**

SYNONYMOUS NAMES: Czechoslovak Academy of Sciences, Institute for Philosophy and
        Sociology, Centre for Scientific Information;
        UFS CVAV SVI
ADDRESS: Jilska 1,
        CS-110 00 Prague 1,
        CZECHOSLOVAKIA
        TEL: 26.01.75
CREATED: 1956   *HEAD:* F. Pospisil, Head
SIZE OF STAFF: Total: 14
TYPE OF SERVICE: public; non-profit
SYSTEMS & NETWORKS ATTACHED TO: Scientific Information System of the Czechoslovak
        Academy of Sciences
SUBJECT COVERAGE: philosophy; sociology; science philosophy
GEOGRAPHICAL COVERAGE: global
DATA BEING PROCESSED AND SIZE: 64,000 vols.; 379 periodicals; 25 abstract journals;
        40 microcopies
DATA PROCESSING METHODS: manual
STORAGE MEDIA: traditional shelving of publications; microfiches
TYPE OF ACTIVITY: data collection; publication
ACCESS TO SERVICE: services open to specific categories of users, free of charge
TYPE & DESCRIPTION OF SERVICES PROVIDED: Provides library services, bibliographic,
        literature abstract and survey data searches, and selective dissemination of

information.

44 - CESKOSLOVENSKO-SOVETSKÝ INSTITUT, KNIHOVNA

YNONYMOUS NAMES: CSI, Knihovna;
    Czechoslovak-Soviet Institute, Library
ARENT ORGANIZATION: Ceskoslovenská Akademie Ved (CSAV)/Czechoslovak Academy of
    Sciences
DDRESS: Thunovská 22,
    CS-118 28 Prague 1,
    CZECHOSLOVAKIA
    TEL: 530-127
REATED: 1964   *HEAD:* A. Cerný, Library
IZE OF STAFF: Professional: 14   Other: 1   Total: 15
YPE OF SERVICE: public; non-profit
YSTEMS & NETWORKS ATTACHED TO: Ceskoslovenská Akademie Ved, Základní Knihovna -
    Utredí Vedeckýeh Informaci
ORKING LANGUAGE(S): Czech
UBJECT COVERAGE: history; social sciences
EOGRAPHICAL COVERAGE: Eastern Europe
ATA BEING PROCESSED AND SIZE: 59,280 books; 400 periodicals
ATA PROCESSING METHODS: manual
YPE OF ACTIVITY: data collection; publication
UBLICATIONS: - Bibliografické prirucky (Series)
       - Knizni prirustky Knihovny CSI CSAV
LIENTELE: researchers
CCESS TO SERVICE: services free of charge, open to specific categories of users
YPE & DESCRIPTION OF SERVICES PROVIDED: Services provided are: library services,
    bibliographic searches of information and translation of documents upon
    request.

45 - EKONOMICKÝ ÚSTAV CSAV, ÚTVAR VEDECKÝCH INFORMACI

YNONYMOUS NAMES: ÚVI EÚ CSAV;
    Institute of Economics, Scientific Information Section;
    CAS
ARENT ORGANIZATION: Ceskoslovenská Akademie Ved/Czechoslovak Academy of Sciences
DDRESS: Trída Politických veznú 7,
    CS-111 73 Prague 1,
    CZECHOSLOVAKIA
    TEL: 26.87.41
REATED: 1953   *HEAD:* F. Bezan, Head
IZE OF STAFF: Professional: 25   Other: 8   Total: 33
YPE OF SERVICE: international; public; non-profit
YSTEMS & NETWORKS ATTACHED TO: MISON
UBJECT COVERAGE: economics
ATA BEING PROCESSED AND SIZE: 55,000 books; 480 periodicals; 30 abstract journals;
    6,000 microcopies
ATA PROCESSING METHODS: manual

TYPE OF ACTIVITY: data collection; distribution of information; publication
CLIENTELE: researchers, students
ACCESS TO SERVICE: services open to all users, free of charge
TYPE & DESCRIPTION OF SERVICES PROVIDED: Provides library services, bibliographic,
     literature abstract and survey data searches, selective dissemination of
     information and photocopies.

246 - ORIENTÁLNÍ ÚSTAV CSAV, STREDISKO VEDECKÝCH INFORMACÍ

SYNONYMOUS NAMES: Oú Csav, Svi;
     Oriental Institute, Czechoslovak Academy of Sciences, Centre of Scientific
     Information
PARENT ORGANIZATION: Ceskoslovenská Akademie Ved, Základní Knihovna/Czechoslovak
     Academy of Sciences, Fundamental Library
ADDRESS: Lázenská 4,
     CS-118 37 Prague 1 - Malá Strana,
     CZECHOSLOVAKIA
     TEL: 533051-53
     CABLE: ORIENTINSTITUTE Praha 011
CREATED: 1922   HEAD: Dr. J. Prosecký, Head
SIZE OF STAFF: Professional: 17   Other: 4   Total: 21
TYPE OF SERVICE: national; public; non-profit
WORKING LANGUAGE(S): Czech
SUBJECT COVERAGE: history; economics; linguistics; literature; political science;
     philosophy; sociology
DATA BEING PROCESSED AND SIZE: 120,000 books; 1,500 periodicals, 3,000 microcopies,
     1,000 manuscripts
DATA PROCESSING METHODS: manual
STORAGE MEDIA: traditional shelving of publications; microfiches; microfilms
TYPE OF ACTIVITY: publication; distribution of information
PERIODICALS PUBLISHED:
     - Ceskoslovenská akademie Ved Orientální Ústav Vseobecná Knihovna Výber z
     Nových Knih (Accessions List), 4 p.a.
CLIENTELE: researchers
ACCESS TO SERVICE: services open to specific categories of users, free of charge
TYPE & DESCRIPTION OF SERVICES PROVIDED: Provides library services, bibliographic a
     literature abstracts, searches of information, on-line services,
     photocopies, microfilms, microforms and translation of documents upon
     request. Has also access to data base AIS MISON through Ceskoslovenská
     Akademie Ved, Základní knihovna.

247 - PSYCHOLOGICKÝ ÚSTAV CSAV, STREDISKO VEDECKÝCH INFORMACÍ

SYNONYMOUS NAMES: Psychological Institute of Czechoslovak Academy of Sciences,
     Information Centre
PARENT ORGANIZATION: Základní Knihovňa - ÚVI CSAV/Fundamental Library of Czechoslov
     Academy of Sciences
ADDRESS: Husova 4,
     CS-110 00 Prague 1,

CZECHOSLOVAKIA
TEL: 24.93.91
CREATED: 1969   *HEAD:* M. Svecová,
SIZE OF STAFF: Professional: 2   Other: 1   Total: 3
WORKING LANGUAGE(S): Czech; Russian; English
SUBJECT COVERAGE: psychology
DATA BEING PROCESSED AND SIZE: 10,050 books; 101 periodicals; 4 abstract journals; 31
    microcopies
DATA PROCESSING METHODS: manual
TYPE OF ACTIVITY: publication
ACCESS TO SERVICE: services open to specific categories of users
TYPE & DESCRIPTION OF SERVICES PROVIDED: Provides library services and
    bibliographies.

248 - SLEZSKÝ ÚSTAV CSAV, STREDISKO VEDECKÝCH INFOMACI

SYNONYMOUS NAMES: Sleský Ústav;
    The Czechoslovak Academy of Sciences, Silesian Institute Opava, Sciences
    Information Centre
ADDRESS: Nádrazni Okruh 31,
    CS-74655 Opava,
    CZECHOSLOVAKIA
    TEL: 214764
CREATED: 1972   *HEAD:* Dr. D. Kupcová,
SIZE OF STAFF: Professional: 4   Other: 3   Total: 7
TYPE OF SERVICE: national; non-profit
WORKING LANGUAGE(S): Czech
SUBJECT COVERAGE: demography; economics; history; philosophy; political science;
    sociology
GEOGRAPHICAL COVERAGE: Europe
DATA BEING PROCESSED AND SIZE: 150,000 books, articles, reports, on-going research
DATA PROCESSING METHODS: manual
STORAGE MEDIA: traditional shelving of publications
TYPE OF ACTIVITY: data collection; distribution of information
PERIODICALS PUBLISHED:
    - Průmyslové Oblasti. Vseobecné Dejiny 18.-20. století.
    - Výberová Bibliografie
CLIENTELE: researchers, professionals
ACCESS TO SERVICE: services open to specific categories of users, free of charge
TYPE & DESCRIPTION OF SERVICES PROVIDED: Provides library services, bibliographic
    searches, selective dissemination of information and photocopies.

249 - SLOVENSKEJ AKAÉMIE VIED, ÚSTREDNÁ KNIZNICA INFORMACNÉ CENTRUM

SYNONYMOUS NAMES: UK SAV;
    The Slovak Academy of Sciences, Central Library Information Centre
PARENT ORGANIZATION: Presidium Slovenskej Akadémie Vied/Presidium of the Slovak
    Academy of Sciences
ADDRESS: Klemensova 19,

CS-814 67 Bratislava,
CZECHOSLOVAKIA
TEL: 517 33 - TELEX: 934 64 UK SAV C
CREATED: 1953   *HEAD:* Dr. F. Kyselica, Director
SIZE OF STAFF: Professional: 27   Other: 19   Total: 46
SYSTEMS & NETWORKS ATTACHED TO: System of Scientific and Technical Information (VTE
       Unit System of Libraries (JSK)
SUBJECT COVERAGE: social sciences
DATA BEING PROCESSED AND SIZE: 486,040 books; 1,525 periodicals; 52,378 manuscript
       books
DATA PROCESSING METHODS: manual; partially computerized
STORAGE MEDIA: traditional shelving of publications; fiches
TYPE OF ACTIVITY: data collection; data analysis; publication; SSID scientific and
       methodological activities; SSID training
PERIODICALS PUBLISHED:
       - PZK, Prírastky Zahranicných Kníh. Série D. Matematickofyzikálne a
       Geologické Vedy/New foreign books in the Slovak Academy of Sciences.
       Mathematics, Physics, Geology, 10 p.a.
       - Informacné Bulletin ÚK SAV/Information Bulletin, 2 p.a.
CLIENTELE: 5,900 users approximately
ACCESS TO SERVICE: services open to all users, free of charge
TYPE & DESCRIPTION OF SERVICES PROVIDED: Provides library services, on-line service
       bibliographic, literature and survey data searches using data base
       consisting of 2,378 items on research reports and dissertation theses. Has
       access to data bases produced by other suppliers, i.e.: MISON (Internation
       Information System on Social Sciences), Slovak National Bibliography,
       Management Contents, Psycinfo, IEAB, FNL through Central Technical Base -
       Prague, and Czechoslovak National Centre for Automated Access. Also provid
       selective dissemination of information, microfilms and photocopies.

250 - ÚSTAV CESKOSLOVENSKÝCH A SVETOVÝCH DEJIN CSAV, ODDELENÍ VEDECKÝCH INFORMACÍ

SYNONYMOUS NAMES: Institute of Czechoslovak and World History, Department of
       Scientific Information
PARENT ORGANIZATION: Ceskoslovenská Akademie Ved/Czechoslovak Academy of Sciences
ADDRESS: Vysehradská 49,
       CS-128 26 Prague 2,
       CZECHOSLOVAKIA
       TEL: 29.64.51
CREATED: 1952   *HEAD:* Dr. M. Kudelásek, Head
SIZE OF STAFF: Professional: 10   Other: 6   Total: 16
TYPE OF SERVICE: national; public; non-profit
SUBJECT COVERAGE: history
GEOGRAPHICAL COVERAGE: Czechoslovakia
DATA BEING PROCESSED AND SIZE: 154,050 books; 408 periodicals; 1,030 microcopies; 1
       serials
DATA PROCESSING METHODS: manual
TYPE OF ACTIVITY: data collection; data analysis; publication
PUBLICATIONS: - Bibliografie dejin Ceskoslovenska/Bibliography of the history of
       Czechoslovakia
ACCESS TO SERVICE: services free of charge and open to specific categories of users

YPE & DESCRIPTION OF SERVICES PROVIDED: Provides library services, bibliographic
   searches of information, microforms, microfilms and photocopies. Also has
   access to DIALOG, USA and MISON, USSR.

251 - ÚSTAV PRO JAZYK ČESKÝ CSAV, ÚTVAR VEDECKÝCH INFORMACÍ

SYNONYMOUS NAMES: ÚJC - ÚVI;
   The Institute for Czech Language, Department of Scientific Information
PARENT ORGANIZATION: Ceskoslovenská Akademie ved (CSAV)/Czechoslovak Academy of
   Sciences
ADDRESS: U Sorových mlýnů 2,
   CS-11800 Prague 1,
   CZECHOSLOVAKIA
   TEL: 53.33.15
CREATED: 1966   *HEAD:* J. Sommerová, Head
SIZE OF STAFF: Professional: 3   Other: 4.5   Total: 7.5
TYPE OF SERVICE: international; public; non-profit
SYSTEMS & NETWORKS ATTACHED TO: Základní Knihovna - Ústredí Vedeckých Informaci CSAV
   (ZK-ÚVI CSAV)/Fundamental Library of the Czechoslovak Academy of Sciences
SUBJECT COVERAGE: linguistics
GEOGRAPHICAL COVERAGE: USSR; some European countries
DATA BEING PROCESSED AND SIZE: 44,000 books; 27 abstract journals; 239 periodicals
DATA PROCESSING METHODS: manual
STORAGE MEDIA: fiches
TYPE OF ACTIVITY: data collection; data analysis; publication
PERIODICALS PUBLISHED:
   - Bibliography of Czech Linguistic, 1 p.a.
ACCESS TO SERVICE: services free of charge and open to specific categories of users
TYPE & DESCRIPTION OF SERVICES PROVIDED: Provides library services, bibliographic,
   literature and survey data searches using its own data base (including
   25,000 bibliographical files).

252 - USTAV STÁTU A PRÁVA CSAV, ÚTVAR VEDECKÝCH INFORMACÍ

SYNONYMOUS NAMES: Institute of Law, Czechoslovak Academy of Sciences, Documentation
   and Information Service;
   Institut des Sciences Juridiques de l'Académie Tchécoslovaque des Sciences,
   Service de Documentation et d'Information
PARENT ORGANIZATION: Ceskoslovenská Akademie Ved, Zakladni Knihovna-Ústredí Vedeckých
   Informaci-Metodické Centrum/Czechoslovak Academy of Sciences, Central
   Library Information Service Centre-Methodological Centre
ADDRESS: Národni trida 18,
   CS-116 91 Prague 1,
   CZECHOSLOVAKIA
   TEL: 20.38.63
CREATED: 1954   *HEAD:* Dr E. Dloutý,
SIZE OF STAFF: Professional: 7   Other: 2   Total: 9
TYPE OF SERVICE: national; public; non-profit
WORKING LANGUAGE(S): Czech; Russian; English; German

Czechoslovakia / Tchécoslovaquie / Checoslovaquia

SUBJECT COVERAGE: law; political science; criminology
GEOGRAPHICAL COVERAGE: Czechoslovakia
DATA BEING PROCESSED AND SIZE: 36,000 books; 415 periodicals; 10 abstract journals; microcopies
DATA PROCESSING METHODS: manual
STORAGE MEDIA: traditional shelving of publications
TYPE OF ACTIVITY: data collection; distribution of information; publication
CLIENTELE: scientific research workers
ACCESS TO SERVICE: services open to specific categories of users, free of charge
TYPE & DESCRIPTION OF SERVICES PROVIDED: The documentation centre provides library services, bibliographic literature and survey data searches, selective dissemination of information, photocopies and translation of documents upon request.

253 - USTREDI VEDECKÝCH INFORMACÍ CESKOSLOVENSKÉ AKADEMIE VED, ZÁKLASNI KNIHOVNA

SYNONYMOUS NAMES: ZK-UVI CSAV;
   Scientific Information Centre of Czechoslovak Academy of Sciences, Main Library
ADDRESS: Národni Tr. 3,
   115 22 Prague 1,
   CZECHOSLOVAKIA
   TEL: 235 80 65 - TELEX: 121040 AKAD C
CREATED: 1952   HEAD: J. Zahradil, Director
SIZE OF STAFF: Professional: 92   Other: 29   Total: 121
TYPE OF SERVICE: national; public; non-profit
SYSTEMS & NETWORKS ATTACHED TO: CSAV
MATERIALS DESCRIBING THE SERVICE: - Vedecké informace ZK-ÚVI CSAV (Users Manuals)
SUBJECT COVERAGE: social sciences
GEOGRAPHICAL COVERAGE: global
DATA BEING PROCESSED AND SIZE: 902,000 documentation items
DATA PROCESSING METHODS: partially computerized
HARDWARE USED: IBM 370; IBM 4331-2; EC 1040; EC 1045
SOFTWARE USED: USS (Unified Software System)
STORAGE MEDIA: traditional shelving of publications; magnetic tapes
TYPE OF ACTIVITY: data collection; data analysis; distribution of information; publication; SSID training
CLIENTELE: researchers (21,300 p.a.)
ACCESS TO SERVICE: open to specific categories of users, free of charge
TYPE & DESCRIPTION OF SERVICES PROVIDED: Provides library services, retrospective bibliographic data searches, microforms, photocopies, selective dissemination of information. Has its own data bases "Union catalogue of periodicals of the CSAV", and ASEP (Bibliographic data base). Has also access to 100 data bases covering scientific literature through NCADE/Úvte ÚTZ (Czechoslovak National Centre).

54 - ÚSTREDNÁ EKONOMICKÁ KNIZNICA

ANONYMOUS NAMES: ÚEK;
Central Economic Library, Bratislava
PARENT ORGANIZATION: Vysoká Skola Ekonomická v Bratislave (Bratislava School of
Economics)
ADDRESS: Palisády 22,
814 80 Bratislava,
CZECHOSLOVAKIA
TEL: 316.023
CREATED: 1959   *HEAD:* Dr. V. Rak, Director
SIZE OF STAFF: Professional: 27   Other: 22   Total: 49
TYPE OF SERVICE: national; public; non-profit
SYSTEMS & NETWORKS ATTACHED TO: Czechoslovak Scientific Library Network
SUBJECT COVERAGE: economics; social sciences; administrative sciences; education;
social welfare
GEOGRAPHICAL COVERAGE: Czechoslovakia
DATA BEING PROCESSED AND SIZE: 387,500 books, articles, reports and special
literature
DATA PROCESSING METHODS: partially computerized
STORAGE MEDIA: traditional shelving of publications; tapes; discs; microfiches
TYPE OF ACTIVITY: data collection; data analysis; distribution of information; SSID
scientific and methodological activities; publication
PERIODICALS PUBLISHED:
- EKO Index
- Acqusitions of Foreign Books. Series B: Economics
CLIENTELE: students, teachers, economists (2,500)
ACCESS TO SERVICE: services open to all users, free of charge
TYPE & DESCRIPTION OF SERVICES PROVIDED: Provides library services, bibliographic,
literature and quantitative data searches using its own data base EKO-Index
and other data bases such as MISON, INSPEC and COMPENDEX accessed
respectively through the Central Library of the Slovak Academy of Sciences
and the Institute of Applied Cybernetics. Also provides selective
dissemination of information, information on magnetic tapes, photocopies,
translation of documents upon request and consultation services.

55 - ÚSTREDNÍ EKONOMICKÁ KNIHOVNA

ANONYMOUS NAMES: Central Library of Economic Sciences
PARENT ORGANIZATION: Státní Knihovna CSR (State Library of the Czech Socialist
Republic)
ADDRESS: ÚEK, nám, A Západockého 4,
CS-130 00 Prague 3,
CZECHOSLOVAKIA
TEL: 22.63.71
CREATED: 1959   *HEAD:* Mr. M. Ponavic, Head
SIZE OF STAFF: Professional: 17   Other: 21   Total: 38
SUBJECT COVERAGE: economics; administrative sciences; social sciences
DATA BEING PROCESSED AND SIZE: 255,900 books; 3,230 periodicals; 60 microcopies;
10,000 manuscripts
DATA PROCESSING METHODS: manual

STORAGE MEDIA: traditional shelving of publications; microfiches
TYPE OF ACTIVITY: data collection; data analysis; publication; SSID scientific and
         methodological activities
ACCESS TO SERVICE: services open to specific categories of users; payment is
         conditioned by the kind of service
TYPE & DESCRIPTION OF SERVICES PROVIDED: Provides library services, bibliographic
         searches of information, selective dissemination of information and
         photocopies. Also has access to MISON (International Information System of
         Social Sciences, Moscow).

256 - DANMARKS STATISTIK

SYNONYMOUS NAMES: The Danish National Bureau of Statistics
PARENT ORGANIZATION: Økonomiministeriet/Ministry of Economic Affairs
ADDRESS: Sejrøgade 11,
         P.O. Box 2550,
         DK-2100 Copenhagen Ø,
         DENMARK
         TEL: (01) 29.82.22 - TELEX: 1 62 36 - TELEFAX: 01 18 48 01
CREATED: 1849   *HEAD:* N. V. Skak-Nielsen, National Statistician
SIZE OF STAFF: Total: 662
MATERIALS DESCRIBING THE SERVICE: - Act on Danmarks Statistik
         - Annual report and work programme (in Danish)
WORKING LANGUAGE(S): Danish; English
SUBJECT COVERAGE: demography; statistics; economics
DATA BEING PROCESSED AND SIZE: 151,000 documentation items
DATA PROCESSING METHODS: computerized
HARDWARE USED: NAS A$/9000
STORAGE MEDIA: tapes; discs
TYPE OF ACTIVITY: data collection; data analysis; distribution of information;
         publication
PERIODICALS PUBLISHED: - Monthly Review of Statistics, 12 p.a. (in Danish)
         - Statistical Yearbook, 1 p.a. (in Danish)
         - Guide to Official Statistics, every 3 years (in Danish)
         - News from Denmarks Statistiks, 260 p.a. (in Danish)
PUBLICATIONS: - Statistical ten-year review (in Danish)
ACCESS TO SERVICE: open to all users, condition of payment is by the kind of servic
TYPE & DESCRIPTION OF SERVICES PROVIDED: Provides library services and on-line
         services using its own data banks DSTB and KSDB.

257 - FOLKETINGETS BIBLIOTEK OG OPLYSNINGSTJENESTE

SYNONYMOUS NAMES: The Danish Parliament, Library and Information Service
ADDRESS: Christiansborg,
         DK-1240 Copenhagen K,
         DENMARK
         TEL: (01) 11.66.00 - TELEX: (01) 328536
CREATED: 1849   *HEAD:* K. Hvidt, Head

ZE OF STAFF: Professional: 9   Other: 5   Total: 14
PE OF SERVICE: national; public; non-profit
RKING LANGUAGE(S): Danish; English
BJECT COVERAGE: social sciences; administrative sciences; economics; history; law;
        political science
OGRAPHICAL COVERAGE: Europe; USA
TA BEING PROCESSED AND SIZE: 185,000 books; 600 periodicals
TA PROCESSING METHODS: partially computerized
ORAGE MEDIA: traditional shelving of publications, microfiches
PE OF ACTIVITY: data collection; publication
RIODICALS PUBLISHED:
        - List of New Acquisitions, 8 p.a.
        - Tamanumme
BLICATIONS: - Bibliography of Danish Commission reports 1850-1975, 2 vol.
        - Various bibliographical volumes issued in collaboration with the
        parliamentary libraries of the Nordic countries
        - Bibliography of Danish Commission reports 1850-1985, 4 vol.
IENTELE: members and staff of the Parliament, civil servants of the government
        departments, graduate students
CESS TO SERVICE: open to all users, free of charge
PE & DESCRIPTION OF SERVICES PROVIDED: Provides library services, selective
        dissemination of information and photocopies. Also provides bibliographic,
        literature, survey and quantitative data searches using its own data base
        Folketingets Information System or external bases CELEX, RETSINFORMATION,
        DCTIME, SAMKAT, MINIBIB, SCAD, SCANP, SCIMP, POLTXT or BASIS.

8 - HANDELEHØJSKOLENS AARHUS, BIBLIOTEKET

NONYMOUS NAMES: Aarhus Graduate School of Management and Modern Languages, Library
RENT ORGANIZATION: Handelshøjskolen i Aarhus
DRESS: 4 Fuglesangsallé,
        DK-8210 Aarhus V,
        DENMARK
        TEL: 45615.5588 - TELEFAX: 06-150188
EATED: 1941   *HEAD:* Mr. A. Mølgaard Frandsen, Chief Librarian
ZE OF STAFF: Professional: 11   Other: 14   Total: 25
PE OF SERVICE: national; public; non-profit
STEMS & NETWORKS ATTACHED TO: EBSLG (European Business School Librarians Group)
RKING LANGUAGE(S): Danish; English; German; French; Spanish
BJECT COVERAGE: administrative sciences; economics; urban planning; regional
        planning; statistics; linguistics
TA BEING PROCESSED AND SIZE: 130,000 books; 3,000 periodicals; 15 abstract journals
TA PROCESSING METHODS: manual
ORAGE MEDIA: traditional shelving of publications
PE OF ACTIVITY: data collection; distribution of information
RIODICALS PUBLISHED: - Tilvaekstfortegnelse, Økonomi, 4 p.a.
        - Tilvaekstfortegnelse, Sporog, 4 p.a.
        - Tidsskriftkatalog, 1 p.a.
IENTELE: students, researchers, experts
CESS TO SERVICE: services open to all users, free of charge
PE & DESCRIPTION OF SERVICES PROVIDED: Provides library services, bibliographic,

literature, survey and quantitative on-line data searches using Dialog,
Datastar, Fintel, Euronet, Helicon. Also provides photocopies.

259 - HANDELSHØJSKOLENS BIBLIOTEK, KOBENHAVN

SYNONYMOUS NAMES: Copenhagen School of Economics and Business Administration, Libra
ADDRESS: 31, Rosenørns alle,
      DK-1970 Frederiksberg C,
      DENMARK
      TEL: 01.39.66.77
CREATED: 1922   *HEAD:* Mr. M. Cotta Schoenberg, Chief Librarian
SIZE OF STAFF: Professional: 32   Other: 8   Total: 40
TYPE OF SERVICE: national; public; non-profit
SYSTEMS & NETWORKS ATTACHED TO: SAMKAT
SUBJECT COVERAGE: economics; administrative sciences; law; statistics; linguistics
GEOGRAPHICAL COVERAGE: Denmark
DATA BEING PROCESSED AND SIZE: 200,000 books (7,000 p.a.)
DATA PROCESSING METHODS: partially computerized
HARDWARE USED: PRIME 550
SOFTWARE USED: own
STORAGE MEDIA: traditional shelving of publications
TYPE OF ACTIVITY: data collection; distribution of information
PUBLICATIONS: - Alfabetisk katalog 1965-82
       - Alfabetisk katalog 1983-
       - Systematisk katalog 1965-82
       - Systematisk katalog 1983-
       - Aktuelle tidsskriftartiklen
CLIENTELE: teachers, researchers, students
ACCESS TO SERVICE: services open to all users, free of charge, some services agains
      payment
TYPE & DESCRIPTION OF SERVICES PROVIDED: Provides library services, bibliographic,
      literature abstracts and quantitative data searches of information. Also
      provides photocopies upon request.

260 - DET KONGELIGE BIBLIOTEK

SYNONYMOUS NAMES: The Royal Library
ADDRESS: P.O. Box 2149,
      DK-1016 Copenhagen K,
      DENMARK
      TEL: (01) 93.01.11 - TELEX: 15009
CREATED: 1954   *HEAD:* E. K. Nielsen, Director General
SIZE OF STAFF: Professional: 131   Other: 178   Total: 309
TYPE OF SERVICE: national; public; non-profit
MATERIALS DESCRIBING THE SERVICE: - The Royal Library guide, 1986
WORKING LANGUAGE(S): Danish; English
SUBJECT COVERAGE: social sciences; humanities; criminology; demography; economics;
      geography; history; law; linguistics; political science; psychology; socia
      anthropology; cultural anthropology; sociology

TA BEING PROCESSED AND SIZE: 3,000,000 documentation items; 8,985 Danish journals; 12,540 foreign journals

TA PROCESSING METHODS: computerized

RDWARE USED: RC8000 minicomputer

ORAGE MEDIA: traditional shelving of publications

PE OF ACTIVITY: data analysis; distribution of information; publication

RIODICALS PUBLISHED: - Psykologisk Litteratur i Danske Forskningsbiblioteker
- Sociologisk Litteratur i Danske Forskningsbiblioteker
- Fund og Forskning i Det kgl. Biblioteks Samlinger
- Magasin fra Det kgl. Bibliotek og Universitetsbiblioteket
- Subject Bibliographies
- Nyhedsbrev (Newsletter)

IENTELE: 8,000 mainly from the University of Copenhagen

CESS TO SERVICE: services open to all users, free of charge except for on-line information retrieval

PE & DESCRIPTION OF SERVICES PROVIDED: Provides on-line catalog of own documents; information retrieval in public databases in the social sciences; manual reference services; research in social science, humanities and information science; printed bibliographies; circulation of documents; user education programs.

1 - NORDISK DOKUMENTATIONSCENTRAL FOR MASSEKOMMUNIKATIONS-FORSKNING

NONYMOUS NAMES: NORDICOM;
Nordic Documentation Center for Mass Communication Research

DRESS: Statsbiblioteket,
Universitetsparken,
DK-8000 Aarhus C,
DENMARK

EATED: 1973   *HEAD:* Dr. L. Weibull, Chairman
C. K. Hansen, Secretary

ZE OF STAFF: Professional: 6   Other: 1   Total: 7

PE OF SERVICE: international; public; non-profit

STEMS & NETWORKS ATTACHED TO: International Network of Documentation Centres on Communication Research and Policies (COMNET)

RKING LANGUAGE(S): Danish; Swedish; Norwegian; Finnish; English

BJECT COVERAGE: mass communication

OGRAPHICAL COVERAGE: Northern Europe; Denmark; Finland; Norway; Sweden

TA BEING PROCESSED AND SIZE: 11,500 books, articles, reports and gray material

TA PROCESSING METHODS: computerized

RDWARE USED: IBM

FTWARE USED: BRS/CCL

ORAGE MEDIA: discs

RIODICALS PUBLISHED: - NORDICOM Review of Nordic Mass Communication Research, 2 p.a.
- NORDICOM-INFORMATION om Massekommunikations-Forskning i Norden (Newsletter), 4 p.a.

CESS TO SERVICE: services open to all users, free of charge except bibliographies and on-line database searches

PE & DESCRIPTION OF SERVICES PROVIDED: Provides bibliographies and on-line searches using its own database "NCOM".

245

Denmark / Danemark / Dinamarca

262 - ODENSE UNIVERSITET, DANSK DATA ARKIV

SYNONYMOUS NAMES: DDA;
        Odense University, Danish Data Archives
ADDRESS: Niels Bohrs Allé 25,
        DK-5230 Odense M,
        DENMARK
        TEL: (09) 157920
        CABLE: DENARCHIVES
CREATED: 1973   *HEAD:* P. Nielsen, Archive Director
SIZE OF STAFF: Professional: 4   Other: 6   Total: 10
TYPE OF SERVICE: national; public; non-profit
SYSTEMS & NETWORKS ATTACHED TO: IFDO (International Federation of Data Organization
MATERIALS DESCRIBING THE SERVICE: - Danish data guide, 1986
WORKING LANGUAGE(S): Danish; English
SUBJECT COVERAGE: social sciences; political science; social welfare; history;
        sociology
GEOGRAPHICAL COVERAGE: Denmark
DATA BEING PROCESSED AND SIZE: 6,000 books; .300 periodicals; approx. 1,500 datasets
DATA PROCESSING METHODS: computerized
HARDWARE USED: AMDAHL-MVS/TSO; IBM=VM/CMS; Micros
SOFTWARE USED: OSIRIS, SAS, SPSS, In-house produced software
STORAGE MEDIA: tapes, microfiches
TYPE OF ACTIVITY: data collection; data analysis; publication; SSID scientific and
        methodological activities; SSID training
PERIODICALS PUBLISHED:
        - DDA-NYT, Quarterly Newsletter, since 1976
CLIENTELE: researchers, graduate students, employees in the public and quasi-publi
        sectors and other members of the social science community
ACCESS TO SERVICE: open to all users, free of charge
TYPE & DESCRIPTION OF SERVICES PROVIDED: Provides library reference services only,
        selective dissemination of information, information on magnetic tapes.
        Provides quantitative data searches using its own data base DDAGUIDE (an
        line catalogue of holdings).

263 - ROSKILDE UNIVERSITETSBIBLIOTEK

SYNONYMOUS NAMES: RUB;
        Roskilde University Library;
        Roskilde University Centre;
        RUC
PARENT ORGANIZATION: Roskilde Universitetscenter
ADDRESS: P. O. Box 258,
        DK-4000 Roskilde,
        DENMARK
        TEL: 2-757711 - TELEX: 43158
CREATED: 1972   *HEAD:* Mr. N. S. Clausen, Director
SIZE OF STAFF: Professional: 14   Other: 48   Total: 62
TYPE OF SERVICE: public
SYSTEMS & NETWORKS ATTACHED TO: ALBA / SAMKAT
WORKING LANGUAGE(S): Danish

BJECT COVERAGE: social sciences; humanities
TA BEING PROCESSED AND SIZE: 380,000 books, periodicals and reports
TA PROCESSING METHODS: partially computerized
RDWARE USED: UNISYS (as a Hostmachine)
FTWARE USED: Forskningsbibliotekernes Bibliografiske EDB-System
ORAGE MEDIA: traditional shelving of publications
PE OF ACTIVITY: distribution of information; SSID scientific and methodological
    activities; publication
RIODICALS PUBLISHED:
    - Skriftserie fra Roskilde Universitetsbibliotek
IENTELE: university staff and students, the general public
CESS TO SERVICE: services open to all users, free of charge
PE & DESCRIPTION OF SERVICES PROVIDED: Provides library services, microforms,
    photocopies and on-line searches.

4 - STATSBIBLIOTEKET ÅRHUS

NONYMOUS NAMES: State and University Library of Arhus
DRESS: Universitetsparken,
    DK-8000 Arhus C,
    DENMARK
    TEL: (45) 612.20.22 - TELEX: 64515 - TELEFAX: (45) 613.72.07
REATED: 1902   *HEAD:* Mr. N. Mark, Acting Director
ZE OF STAFF: Professional: 97 Other: 104 Total: 201
PE OF SERVICE: international; public; non-profit
RKING LANGUAGE(S): Danish; English
BJECT COVERAGE: social sciences
EOGRAPHICAL COVERAGE: global
TA BEING PROCESSED AND SIZE: 1,837,300 vols. including books, periodicals and
    reports
ATA PROCESSING METHODS: computerized
RDWARE USED: RC 8000
FTWARE USED: RCLIB
ORAGE MEDIA: traditional shelving of periodicals; Danish newspapers microfilmed
PE OF ACTIVITY: distribution of information; publication
BLICATIONS: - Danish politics after the year 1920
    - Social sciences, current bibliographies
CESS TO SERVICE: services open to all users, free of charge
PE & DESCRIPTION OF SERVICES PROVIDED: Provides library services, on-line services
    using own data base "SOL" (catalogue on-line), microforms and photocopies.

5 - CENTRO DE DOCUMENTACIÓN E INFORMACIÓN DE LOS MOVIMIENTOS SOCIALES DEL ECUADOR

NONYMOUS NAMES: CEDIME;
    Documentation and Information Center on Ecuador's Social Movements
DRESS: Juan Larrea 657 y Rio de Janeiro,
    Casilla 18-C,
    Quito,

ECUADOR
TEL: 552-382
CREATED: 1981   *HEAD:* Dr. R. Moya, General Coordinator
SIZE OF STAFF: Professional: 1
TYPE OF SERVICE: national; private; non-profit
SYSTEMS & NETWORKS ATTACHED TO: CEAAL (Consejo de Educación de Adultos de América Latina)
WORKING LANGUAGE(S): Spanish; Quichua
SUBJECT COVERAGE: social sciences; economics; education; geography; history; linguistics; political science; social anthropology; cultural anthropolog social welfare; sociology; Quichua culture; ethnology; oral history; urba poverty; political system; bilingual teaching methodology; social movemen trade unions; collective bargaining; ecology; religious sects
GEOGRAPHICAL COVERAGE: Highlands, Amazonic jungle region of Ecuador
DATA BEING PROCESSED AND SIZE: books; manuals; pamphlets; articles; reports; photographs; slides
DATA PROCESSING METHODS: manual; partially computerized
SOFTWARE USED: Apple Mackintosh
STORAGE MEDIA: traditional shelving of publications; discs; fiches; tapes
TYPE OF ACTIVITY: data collection; data analysis; distribution of information; SSI scientific and methodological activities; SSID training; publication
CLIENTELE: trade unions, native people's federations, confederations, communes and cooperatives, students, urban community organizations
ACCESS TO SERVICE: services open to specific categories of users, free of charge
TYPE & DESCRIPTION OF SERVICES PROVIDED: Provides library services, selective dissemination of information and photocopies.

266 - CENTRO INTERNACIONAL DE ESTUDIOS SUPERIORES DE COMUNICACIÓN PARA AMERICA LATINA, CENTRO DE DOCUMENTACIÓN

SYNONYMOUS NAMES: CIESPAL;
International Centre of Higher Studies on Communication in Latin America, Documentation Centre
ADDRESS: Avenida Amazonas 1615,
Apartado 584,
Quito,
ECUADOR
TEL: 236-144
CABLE: CIESPAL
CREATED: 1960   *HEAD:* L. Eladio Proaño,
SIZE OF STAFF: Professional: 5   Other: 3   Total: 8
TYPE OF SERVICE: international; public; non-profit
SYSTEMS & NETWORKS ATTACHED TO: Red Internacional de Centros de Información para 1 Investigación de la Comunicación Colectiva (COMNET)
WORKING LANGUAGE(S): Spanish; English; French
SUBJECT COVERAGE: mass communication; social sciences; political science; social anthropology; cultural anthropology; education
GEOGRAPHICAL COVERAGE: Latin America; Spain; Portugal; Europe; Canada; USA
DATA BEING PROCESSED AND SIZE: 10,000 books, periodicals, grey literature; manuscripts; printed documents
DATA PROCESSING METHODS: manual; computerized

BLICATIONS: - Favor, asunto bibliográfico de la bibliografía preliminar
- Hancock, A., Planificación de la comunicación para el desarrollo, 1981
IENTELE: researchers, students, civil servants
CESS TO SERVICE: open to all users, free of charge
PE & DESCRIPTION OF SERVICES PROVIDED: Provides photocopies upon request.

7 - PROGRAMA DE LAS NACIONES UNIDAS PARA EL DESARROLLO, BIBLIOTECA

NONYMOUS NAMES: PNUD Biblioteca;
            PNUD Library
DRESS: Av. 10 de Agosto 5470 y Villalengua,
        Apartado 4731,
        Quito,
        ECUADOR
        TEL: 458 666 - TELEX: 2177
        CABLE: UNDEVPRO QUITO
AD: Ms. S. Endara,
ZE OF STAFF: Professional: 1   Other: 1   Total: 2
PE OF SERVICE: private; non-profit
RKING LANGUAGE(S): Spanish; English
BJECT COVERAGE: economics; education; demography; social sciences
TA PROCESSING METHODS: manual
PE OF ACTIVITY: data collection; distribution of information; publication
IENTELE: high school and university students
CESS TO SERVICE: services open to specific categories of users, free of charge
PE & DESCRIPTION OF SERVICES PROVIDED: Provides library services, bibliographic
        searches of information, selective dissemination of information, photocopies
        and translation of documents upon request.

8 - AIN-SHAMS UNIVERSITY, CENTER OF CHILDHOOD STUDIES

DRESS: Abassia,
        Cairo,
        EGYPT
REATED: 1977   *HEAD:* Prof. Dr. A. S. A. Ghaffar,
PE OF SERVICE: national; public; non-profit
RKING LANGUAGE(S): Arabic
BJECT COVERAGE: social sciences; education; psychology; social welfare; children
EOGRAPHICAL COVERAGE: Egypt
TA BEING PROCESSED AND SIZE: reports; on-going research; seminars; training courses
TA PROCESSING METHODS: partially computerized
ORAGE MEDIA: traditional shelving of publications
PE OF ACTIVITY: distribution of information; SSID scientific and methodological
        activities; publication
BLICATIONS: - Bibliographies of childhood books, and of graduate theses
CESS TO SERVICE: open to all users, free of charge
PE & DESCRIPTION OF SERVICES PROVIDED: Provides library services, bibliographic and
        quantitative data searches of information, selective dissemination of

information and photocopies.

269 - AMERICAN UNIVERSITY IN CAIRO, SOCIAL RESEARCH CENTER, REGIONAL INFORMATION NETWORK ON ARAB WOMEN

SYNONYMOUS NAMES: SRC/RINAW
ADDRESS: 113 Sharia Kasr El-Aini Street,
P.O. Box 2511,
Cairo,
EGYPT
TEL: 21916 - TELEX: 92224 AUCAI UN
CABLE: Victorious, Cairo
CREATED: 1987   *HEAD:* Dr. S. Abdel Kader, Interim Coordinator
SIZE OF STAFF: Professional: 3   Other: 2   Total: 5
TYPE OF SERVICE: international; private; non-profit
MATERIALS DESCRIBING THE SERVICE: - Proceedings, recommendations and summary of presentations, preparatory meeting: the creation of a Regional Informatio Network on Arab Women, Social Research Center, American University in Cai 1987
WORKING LANGUAGE(S): English; French; Arabic
SUBJECT COVERAGE: social sciences; women
GEOGRAPHICAL COVERAGE: Arab countries
DATA PROCESSING METHODS: computerized
HARDWARE USED: Micronet PC
TYPE OF ACTIVITY: data collection; distribution of information; SSID scientific an methodological activities; publication
ACCESS TO SERVICE: services open to specific categories of users
TYPE & DESCRIPTION OF SERVICES PROVIDED: Provides bibliographic, literature abstra and quantitative data searches of information, on-line services using its own data bases and selective dissemination of information.

270 - CENTER FOR SOCIAL SCIENCE RESEARCH AND DOCUMENTATION FOR THE ARAB REGION

SYNONYMOUS NAMES: ARCSS;
Centre Régional Arabe pour la Recherche et la Documentation en Sciences Sociales
ADDRESS: Zamalek P.O.,
Cairo,
EGYPT
TEL: 3470019
CABLE: NASOCRI Cairo
CREATED: 1978   *HEAD:* Dr. A. M. Khalifa, Director General
TYPE OF SERVICE: international; non-profit
SYSTEMS & NETWORKS ATTACHED TO: Arab Network for Communication Research and Polici (COMNET)
MATERIALS DESCRIBING THE SERVICE: - Brochure
WORKING LANGUAGE(S): Arabic; English
SUBJECT COVERAGE: social sciences; psychology; social anthropology; cultural anthropology; social welfare; sociology

OGRAPHICAL COVERAGE: Arab countries
TA BEING PROCESSED AND SIZE: books, periodicals, reports
TA PROCESSING METHODS: manual; partially computerized
ORAGE MEDIA: traditional shelving of publications, fiches, microfiches
PE OF ACTIVITY: distribution of information; SSID scientific and methodological
        activities; SSID training; publication
RIODICALS PUBLISHED:
       - Newsletter, 3 p.a.
BLICATIONS: - Social and culture patterns in Arab society
       - Information system in the social sciences
       - Arab index of social sciences
       - Directory of social sciences research and documentation
IENTELE: researchers, information specialists
CESS TO SERVICE: services open to specific categories of users free of charge
PE & DESCRIPTION OF SERVICES PROVIDED: Provides library services, bibliographic
        searches of information, microforms, photocopies and translation of
        documents upon request.

1 - CENTRE D'ETUDES ET DE DOCUMENTATION JURIDIQUE, ECONOMIQUE ET SOCIALE

NONYMOUS NAMES: CEDEJ
RENT ORGANIZATION: Ministry of Foreign Affairs, Centre National de la Recherche
        Scientique
DRESS: 22, Sharia Al Fawakeh,
        Mohandessin-Dokki,
        Cairo,
        EGYPT
        TEL: 717728 - TELEX: 93088 CEFEC UN
EATED: 1968   *HEAD:* Mr. J. C. Vatin, Director
ZE OF STAFF: Professional: 27
PE OF SERVICE: national; public; non-profit
BJECT COVERAGE: social sciences; law; economics; sociology; history; political
        science; cultural anthropology; social life; participation
OGRAPHICAL COVERAGE: Middle East; Egypt; Europe; France
TA BEING PROCESSED AND SIZE: 8,000 books and serials; 80 periodicals
TA PROCESSING METHODS: manual
ORAGE MEDIA: traditional shelving of publications; microfiches
PE OF ACTIVITY: data collection; publication
RIODICALS PUBLISHED: - Dossier du CEDEJ, 4 p.a.
       - Cahiers du CEDEJ, 2 p.a.
       - Bulletin du CEDEJ, 4 p.a.
       - Revue de la Presse Egyptienne, 4 p.a.
BLICATIONS: - Collection "Recherche"
IENTELE: librarians, documentalists, students, researchers, academics
CESS TO SERVICE: open to specific categories of users, free of charge
PE & DESCRIPTION OF SERVICES PROVIDED: Provides library services and retrospective
        bibliographic searches. Also provides photocopies and translation of
        documents upon request.

272 - INSTITUTE OF ARAB RESEARCH AND STUDIES, LIBRARY

SYNONYMOUS NAMES: IARS, Information Library
PARENT ORGANIZATION: Arab Educational Cultural and Scientific Organization-League
        Arab States
ADDRESS: 1, El Tolombat Street,
        Garden City,
        Cairo,
        EGYPT
        TEL: 3540651 - TELEX: 92642 Alesco UN
        CABLE: IREALEA-Cairo
CREATED: 1953
TYPE OF SERVICE: international; public; non-profit
SYSTEMS & NETWORKS ATTACHED TO: ALECSO
WORKING LANGUAGE(S): Arabic; English
SUBJECT COVERAGE: social sciences
GEOGRAPHICAL COVERAGE: Arab countries
DATA BEING PROCESSED AND SIZE: 68,070 books; 870 periodicals
DATA PROCESSING METHODS: manual
TYPE OF ACTIVITY: data collection; SSID scientific and methodological activities;
        SSID training; publication
ACCESS TO SERVICE: open to all users
TYPE & DESCRIPTION OF SERVICES PROVIDED: Provides library services, searches of
        information and photocopies.

273 - NATIONAL POPULATION COUNCIL, LIBRARY

SYNONYMOUS NAMES: NPC Library
ADDRESS: P.O. Box 1036,
        Cairo,
        EGYPT
        TEL: 350-2207 - TELEX: 94086 USRAH CAIRO
CREATED: 1985 · *HEAD:* Prof. M. Mahran, Secretary General
SIZE OF STAFF: Professional: 97   Other: 96   Total: 193
TYPE OF SERVICE: national; public; non-profit
WORKING LANGUAGE(S): Arabic; English
SUBJECT COVERAGE: social sciences; demography; family planning
GEOGRAPHICAL COVERAGE: Egypt
DATA BEING PROCESSED AND SIZE: 100 books p.a.; 60 periodicals p.a.; research report
DATA PROCESSING METHODS: partially computerized
TYPE OF ACTIVITY: data analysis; distribution of information; SSID scientific and
        methodological activities; publication
PERIODICALS PUBLISHED: - Population Studies Journal, 4 p.a.
ACCESS TO SERVICE: open to all users, free of charge
TYPE & DESCRIPTION OF SERVICES PROVIDED: Provides library services, bibliographic
        quantitative searches of information, photocopies, and translation of
        documents upon request.

El Salvador

4 - BANCO CENTRAL DE RESERVA DE EL SALVADOR, BIBLIOTECA "LUIS ALFARO DURAN"

DRESS: Calle Poniente y 9a av. Norte,
Apartado postal (06) 106,
San Salvador,
EL SALVADOR
TEL: 22-5802
CABLE: BACEN
EATED: 1954   *HEAD:* Ms B. Soto, Head
ZE OF STAFF: Professional: 6   Other: 6   Total: 12
PE OF SERVICE: international; public
RKING LANGUAGE(S): Spanish
BJECT COVERAGE: economics; administrative sciences; law; psychology; social
sciences
TA BEING PROCESSED AND SIZE: 22,320 books; 436 periodicals; documents
TA PROCESSING METHODS: manual; partially computerized
RDWARE USED: Hewlett Packard 3000
ORAGE MEDIA: discs
PE OF ACTIVITY: distribution of information; SSID scientific and methodological
activities; publication
RIODICALS PUBLISHED:
- Boletin Bimensual, 6 p.a.
IENTELE: students, researchers
CCESS TO SERVICE: open to specific categories of users, free of charge
PE & DESCRIPTION OF SERVICES PROVIDED: Provides bibliographic information searches,
interlibrary loans, selective dissemination of information and photocopies.

5 - UNIVERSIDAD CENTROAMERICANA "JOSÉ SIMEÓN CAÑAS", BIBLIOTECA

NONYMOUS NAMES: Central American University "José Simeón Cañas", Library
ARENT ORGANIZATION: CIDAI: Centro de Información, Documentación y Apoyo a la
Investigación de la UCA. CIDAI is a centre which is independent of the
Library
DDRESS: Col. Jardines de Guadalupe,
Apartado Postal (0i) 168,
San Salvador,
EL SALVADOR
TEL: 24-0011
REATED: 1965   *HEAD:* Ms. M. Arteaga, Head Librarian
IZE OF STAFF: Professional: 5   Other: 10   Total: 15
PE OF SERVICE: national; private; non-profit
ORKING LANGUAGE(S): Spanish
UBJECT COVERAGE: economics; administrative sciences; law; human rights; philosophy;
psychology; sociology; literature
EOGRAPHICAL COVERAGE: El Salvador; Central America
ATA BEING PROCESSED AND SIZE: 42,000 books; 10,000 collections; 17,652 periodicals;
5,700 theses; 113 maps
ATA PROCESSING METHODS: manual
TORAGE MEDIA: traditional shelving of publications; microfilms

TYPE OF ACTIVITY: publication
PERIODICALS PUBLISHED:
- Boletín de Nuevas Investigaciones, 12 p.a.
- Boletín DSI: Difusión Selectiva de Información, 6 p.a.
- Accession List
CLIENTELE: university teachers and students (7,000 p.a.)
ACCESS TO SERVICE: services open to all users, free of charge
TYPE & DESCRIPTION OF SERVICES PROVIDED: Provides library services, searches of
information, especially on human rights, selective dissemination of
information, and photocopies.

276 - ADDIS ABABA UNIVERSITY, INSTITUTE OF ETHIOPIAN STUDIES, INFORMATION SERVICE

ADDRESS: P.O. Box 1176,
Addis Ababa,
ETHIOPIA
TEL: 119469 - TELEX: 21205
CABLE: A.A. UNIV
CREATED: 1963   *HEAD:* T. Taddese Beyene, Director
TYPE OF SERVICE: national; public; non-profit
SUBJECT COVERAGE: cultural anthropology; social anthropology; humanities; history;
social sciences; linguistics; sociology; cultural heritage; oral tradition
literature
GEOGRAPHICAL COVERAGE: Ethiopia and the Horn of Africa
DATA PROCESSING METHODS: manual
STORAGE MEDIA: traditional shelving of publications; fiches; tapes; discs; microfil
TYPE OF ACTIVITY: data collection; data analysis; SSID scientific and methodologica
activities; publication
PERIODICALS PUBLISHED: - Journal of Ethiopian Studies, 2 p.a.
PUBLICATIONS: - List of current periodical publications
- Dictionary of Ethiopian biography
CLIENTELE: students and researchers
ACCESS TO SERVICE: services open to specific categories of users, free of charge
TYPE & DESCRIPTION OF SERVICES PROVIDED: Provides library services, bibliographic a
literature abstracts searches of information, photocopies and translation
upon request.

277 - ASMARA UNIVERSITY, INSTITUTE OF AFRICAN STUDIES, LIBRARY

SYNONYMOUS NAMES: IAS, Library
ADDRESS: P.O. Box 1220,
Asmara,
ETHIOPIA
TEL: (04) 113600 - TELEX: 42091
CABLE: ASMUNIV
CREATED: 1982   *HEAD:* Mr. A. Negash, Principal Library Assistant
SIZE OF STAFF: Professional: 1   Other: 1   Total: 2
TYPE OF SERVICE: national

BJECT COVERAGE: social sciences; economics; education; geography; history; law;
        linguistics; social anthropology; cultural anthropology
TA PROCESSING METHODS: manual
ORAGE MEDIA: traditional shelving of publications
CESS TO SERVICE: open to all users
PE & DESCRIPTION OF SERVICES PROVIDED: Provides library services, searches of
        information, photocopies and translation of documents upon request.

Fiji / Fidji / Fiji

8 - UNIVERSITY OF THE SOUTH PACIFIC, PACIFIC INFORMATION CENTRE

DRESS: University of the South Pacific Library,
        P.O. Box 1168,
        Suva,
        FIJI
        TEL: 313900 - TELEX: 2276 USP FJ
REATED: 1983   HEAD: Ms. E. Williams, University Librarian
ZE OF STAFF: Professional: 2   Other: 2   Total: 4
PE OF SERVICE: national; public; non-profit
TERIALS DESCRIBING THE SERVICE: - Annual report
ORKING LANGUAGE(S): English
BJECT COVERAGE: social sciences; agriculture; health; education; environment; rural
        development; technology; culture
EOGRAPHICAL COVERAGE: South Pacific area; Polynesia and Micronesia; Melanesia
ATA BEING PROCESSED AND SIZE: 10,000 documentation items
ATA PROCESSING METHODS: manual
PE OF ACTIVITY: publication
RIODICALS PUBLISHED: - South Pacific Bibliography, 1 p.a.
        - South Pacific Union List of Periodicals, 1 p.a.
        - South Pacific Periodicals Index, 1 p.a.
        - United Nations Documents Relating to the South Pacific, 1 p.a.
        - South Pacific Research Register, 1 p.a.
        - Quarterly Newsletter, 4 p.a.
JBLICATIONS: - Bibliography of plant protection in the area of the South Pacific
        Commission, 1982
        - Bibliography of soils information from the South Pacific, 1982
        - Bibliography on population education
        - Environmental issues in the South Pacific, 1983
        - Women in the South Pacific, 1982
LIENTELE: academic staff and students, researchers
CCESS TO SERVICE: open to all users

Finland / Finlande / Finlandia

79 - EDUSKUNNAN KIRJASTO/RIKSDAGSBIBLIOTEKET

YNONYMOUS NAMES: Library of Parliament
ARENT ORGANIZATION: Suomen Eduskunta/Finlands Riksdag - The Parliament of Finland
DDRESS: Aurorankatu 6,
        SF-00102 Helsinki 10,

FINLAND
TEL: 0-4321 - TELEX: 121464 ekirj sf
CREATED: 1872   *HEAD:* E.-M. Tammekann, Chief Librarian
SIZE OF STAFF: Professional: 20   Other: 21   Total: 41
TYPE OF SERVICE: national; public; non-profit
SYSTEMS & NETWORKS ATTACHED TO: Finnish System of Legal Information (FINLEX), Finni
        Bibliographical Data Base (KATI)
MATERIALS DESCRIBING THE SERVICE: - Eduskunnan kirjaston kertomus/Annual report (in
        Finnish). Hki 1983, 14 p.
        - Riksdagsbibliotekets berättelse/Annual report (in Swedish). Hki 1983, 14
        p.
WORKING LANGUAGE(S): Finnish; Swedish; English
SUBJECT COVERAGE: political science; law; administrative sciences; criminology;
        history; social welfare; parliamentary systems; international organization
DATA BEING PROCESSED AND SIZE: 508,500 books, periodicals, abstract journals; 125,0
        microcopies; manuscripts
DATA PROCESSING METHODS: partially computerized
HARDWARE USED: Nokia Mikko 3/18 (processing); Mikromikko 2 (retrieval)
SOFTWARE USED: several softwares ex. Minttu
STORAGE MEDIA: traditional shelving of publications; microfilms; microfiches
TYPE OF ACTIVITY: distribution of information; publication
PERIODICALS PUBLISHED:
        - Accessions List
PUBLICATIONS: - Valtion virallisjulkaisut, statens officiella publikationer,
        Riksdagbiblioteket, 1983
        - Suomen lainopillinen kirjallisuuus, Finlands juridiska litteratur,.
        bibliographia juridica fennica
ACCESS TO SERVICE: open to all users, free of charge, some paid services. Some
        special services in the field of information retrieval are open only to MP
        and the staff of the parliament
TYPE & DESCRIPTION OF SERVICES PROVIDED: Library services are provided, and also
        bibliographic searches of information in its own data bases, FINLEX and
        Bibliographia Juridica Fennica, as well as other Finnish, Scandinavian and
        American data bases. Other services such as provision of microfilms and
        photocopies are also available.

280 - HELSINGIN KAUPPAKORKEAKOULUN KIRJASTO

SYNONYMOUS NAMES: Helsinki School of Economics Library
ADDRESS: Runeberginkatu 22-24,
        00100 Helsinki 10,
        FINLAND
        TEL: 0-4313422 - TELEX: 122220 ekon sf - TELEFAX: 358 0 4313 539 HSE FINLA
CREATED: 1911   *HEAD:* H. Broms, Chief Librarian
SIZE OF STAFF: Professional: 15   Other: 25   Total: 40
TYPE OF SERVICE: national; public; non-profit
SYSTEMS & NETWORKS ATTACHED TO: DATAPAK, DIANE, TYMNET
SUBJECT COVERAGE: economics; management; administrative sciences; social sciences;
        sociology; mass communication; demography; law; statistics
GEOGRAPHICAL COVERAGE: global
DATA BEING PROCESSED AND SIZE: 220,000 books; 1,300 periodicals; 100 abstract

journals; 45,000 microforms

DATA PROCESSING METHODS: computerized

HARDWARE USED: Hewlett-Packard HP 3000/42

SOFTWARE USED: IMAGE

STORAGE MEDIA: traditional shelving of publications; fiches; magnetic tapes; microfiches

TYPE OF ACTIVITY: data collection; distribution of information; publication; SSID training

PERIODICALS PUBLISHED:
  - Accession List
  - List of Journals

PUBLICATIONS: - Series of annual bibliographies on special subjects
  - BILD/FINP/THES thesaurus
  - Selective list of publications 1960-1987
  - Directory of economic and business libraries in Scandinavia, 1987
  - Search program for Helicon data bases, 1987

ACCESS TO SERVICE: a public service open to anyone interested in the field of economics and business administration (free of charge or against payment)

TYPE & DESCRIPTION OF SERVICES PROVIDED: Provides library services, selective dissemination of information, information on magnetic tapes, photocopies, and on-line bibliographic, literature and survey data searches. Acts as a host to "HELECON" data base family which includes several databases in the fields of economics and management: SCIMP contains articles from 160 periodicals in various languages; SCANP contains articles, research reports from 450 Scandinavian sources; BILD covers books; FINP covers articles from 600 periodicals in Finnish; THES covers theses in economics and management in Finland; and IBS the international bibliography of the social sciences. Has also access to other data bases such as LOCKHEED, SDC, BLAISE and QUESTEL.

281 - HELSINGIN YLIOPISTON KEHITYSMAAINSTITUTTIN KIRJASTO

SYNONYMOUS NAMES: University of Helsinki, Institute of Development Studies, Library

PARENT ORGANIZATION: Helsingin Yliopisto

ADDRESS: Annankatu 42 D,
    SF-00100 Helsinki 10,
    FINLAND
    TEL: (358-0) 4027410 - TELEX: 124690 UNIH SF - TELEFAX: 656591

CREATED: 1978   *HEAD:* Ms. R. Saar, Librarian

SIZE OF STAFF: Professional: 1

TYPE OF SERVICE: national; public; non-profit

WORKING LANGUAGE(S): Finnish

SUBJECT COVERAGE: social sciences; development

GEOGRAPHICAL COVERAGE: East Africa; India

DATA BEING PROCESSED AND SIZE: 4,000 books; 200 periodicals

DATA PROCESSING METHODS: manual

TYPE OF ACTIVITY: distribution of information

CLIENTELE: researchers, students, general public (2,000 p.a.)

ACCESS TO SERVICE: services open to all users, free of charge

TYPE & DESCRIPTION OF SERVICES PROVIDED: Provides library services.

282 - HELSINGIN YLIOPISTON VALTIOTIETEELLISSEN TIEDEKUNNAN KIRJASTO

SYNONYMOUS NAMES: University of Helsinki, Social Science Library
ADDRESS: Aleksanterinkatu 7,
        SF-00100 Helsinki,
        FINLAND
        TELEX: 90-1912547
CREATED: 1950   *HEAD:* Ms. M.-L. Harju-Khadr, Librarian
SIZE OF STAFF: Professional: 5   Other: 6   Total: 11
TYPE OF SERVICE: national; public; non-profit
WORKING LANGUAGE(S): Finnish; Swedish; English
SUBJECT COVERAGE: social sciences
GEOGRAPHICAL COVERAGE: global
DATA BEING PROCESSED AND SIZE: 80,000 books; periodicals; theses
DATA PROCESSING METHODS: partially computerized
STORAGE MEDIA: traditional shelving of publications; microfiches
TYPE OF ACTIVITY: data collection; data analysis; publication
PERIODICALS PUBLISHED: - Opinnäytetïvistelmäluettelo, (Annual list of thesis
        abstracts)
        - Uutuusluettelo, (Accession catalogue)
        - Lehtiluettelo, (Periodicals catalogue)
PUBLICATIONS: - Accession catalogue
        - Periodical catalogue
        - Annual list of thesis abstracts
CLIENTELE: university teachers and students
ACCESS TO SERVICE: services open to specific categories of users, free of charge
TYPE & DESCRIPTION OF SERVICES PROVIDED: Provides library services, bibliographic
        searches, selective dissemination of information, microforms, and
        photocopies. Also provides on-line services using own data base "SOSIO"
        (secondary data base of KATI) and external data bases available through
        KDOK/Minttu, HELECON, DIALOG and NSI.

283 - OULUN YLIOPISTON KIRJASTO

SYNONYMOUS NAMES: Oulu University Library
ADDRESS: Box 186,
        SF-90101 Oulu,
        FINLAND
        TEL: 981-353505
CREATED: 1959   *HEAD:* Mr. V. Kaufto, Director
                    Ms. I. Kujala, Head of the Information Service Department
SIZE OF STAFF: Professional: 31   Other: 41   Total: 72
TYPE OF SERVICE: public; non-profit
WORKING LANGUAGE(S): Finnish; Swedish; English; German
SUBJECT COVERAGE: social sciences; economics; education; history
GEOGRAPHICAL COVERAGE: Northern Finland
DATA BEING PROCESSED AND SIZE: 350,000 books; 250,000 periodicals
DATA PROCESSING METHODS: partially computerized
HARDWARE USED: Ericsson PC, Mikromikko 2
TYPE OF ACTIVITY: distribution of information; publication
PUBLICATIONS: - Oulun yliopiston kirjaston julkaisuja (publications of Oulu

University Library)‑

LIENTELE: students, researchers and teachers of Oulu University (8,300)

CCESS TO SERVICE: services open to all users, some paid services

YPE & DESCRIPTION OF SERVICES PROVIDED: Provides library services, bibliographic searches of information, on-line services from Finnish data bases: KATI, KOTI, KAUKO, IBS, FINP, BILD, SCIMP, SCANP, THES, LEO; foreign data banks: Dialog, STN, Data-Star, ESA, Byggdok, Pergamon/Infoline and SDC. Also provides photocopies.

84 - TILASTOKESKUS/TILASTOKIRJASTO

YNONYMOUS NAMES: Central Statistical Office, Library on Statistics

DDRESS: Annankatu 44,
P.O. Box 504,
SF-00101 Helsinki,
FINLAND
TEL: 0-1734225 - TELEX: 10002111 TILASTO SF

REATED: 1867   *HEAD:* Mrs. H. Myllys, Acting Chief Librarian

IZE OF STAFF: Professional: 9   Other: 5   Total: 14

YSTEMS & NETWORKS ATTACHED TO: National Network of Central Research Libraries (10 libraries in different fields of science)

ATERIALS DESCRIBING THE SERVICE: - Brochure

ORKING LANGUAGE(S): Finnish; English

UBJECT COVERAGE: statistics; economics; demography; sociology; social sciences; information science

EOGRAPHICAL COVERAGE: Finland

ATA BEING PROCESSED AND SIZE: 225,000 library holdings of which 4,700 are periodicals; 10,000 manuscripts

ATA PROCESSING METHODS: partially computerized

ARDWARE USED: microcomputer 'Mikro Mikko 2' (Oy Nokia Ab); IBM PC XT(2)

OFTWARE USED: Info Star

TORAGE MEDIA: traditional shelving of publications; microfiches; tapes, discs

YPE OF ACTIVITY: publication; distribution of information; SSID training

ERIODICALS PUBLISHED: - Government Statistics, 12 p.a.
- Government Statistics, 1 p.a.
- Accessions List, 12 p.a.

UBLICATIONS: - Tilastokeskuksen julkaisuja. Tilastotiedotukset 1968-1980 ja Tilastokatsausten artikkelit 1924-1978. CSO, Helsinki 1984

LIENTELE: private enterprises, government officials, researchers, teachers

CCESS TO SERVICE: services free of charge, paid services for information retrieval requiring more than one hour work

YPE & DESCRIPTION OF SERVICES PROVIDED: The library produces bibliographic information to the national and foreign literature data bases of the Finnish Research Libraries in the field of statistics. Services offered are: library services, selective dissemination of information, provision of photocopies and bibliographic, literature and survey data searches using its own data base, LISTSTAT (a joint database containing the holdings of official statistical publications from the whole world at the statistical libraries in Norway, Finland and Denmark). Has also access to other data bases: I.P. SHARP, CISI, DATA-CENTRALEN, DIALOG, HELECON through DATAPAK.

France / France / Francia

285 - ULKOPOLIITTINEN INSTITUUTTI, BIBLIOTEKET

SYNONYMOUS NAMES: The Finnish Institute of International Affairs, Library;
    FIIA, Library
ADDRESS: Pursimiehenkatu 8,
    Helsinki SF-00150,
    FINLAND
    TEL: 90-170 434
    CABLE: 98 97-3
CREATED: 1961   *HEAD:* Ms. K. Slakala, Librarian
TYPE OF SERVICE: private; non-profit
WORKING LANGUAGE(S): Finnish; Swedish; English
SUBJECT COVERAGE: political science; economics; international affairs
GEOGRAPHICAL COVERAGE: Northern Europe; USSR; Europe
DATA BEING PROCESSED AND SIZE: 10,000 books; 350 periodicals; 5 abstract journals
DATA PROCESSING METHODS: manual
TYPE OF ACTIVITY: publication
PERIODICALS PUBLISHED: - Yearbook of Finnish Foreign Policy
        - Ulkopolitikka/Foreign Policy
PUBLICATIONS: - Suomen turvalisuuspolitikan bibliografia, 1983
CLIENTELE: scholars, students
ACCESS TO SERVICE: services open to specific categories of users
TYPE & DESCRIPTION OF SERVICES PROVIDED: Provides library services, bibliographic
        searches of information and photocopies.

France / France / Francia

286 - ASSEMBLÉE PERMANENTE DES CHAMBRES DE COMMERCE ET D'INDUSTRIE, SERVICE DE DOCUMENTATION

SYNONYMOUS NAMES: APCCI, Service de Documentation
ADDRESS: 45, avenue d'Iéna,
    75116 Paris,
    FRANCE
    TEL: (1) 47.23.01.11 - TELEX: 610396 APCCI
CREATED: 1964   *HEAD:* Mr. M. Filleul, Information & Communication Director
SIZE OF STAFF: Total: 12
TYPE OF SERVICE: national; public; non-profit
SYSTEMS & NETWORKS ATTACHED TO: CCI (161 local and 21 regional chambers)
MATERIALS DESCRIBING THE SERVICE: - Les Chambres de commerce et d'industrie, 1985
        (brochure)
WORKING LANGUAGE(S): French
SUBJECT COVERAGE: economics; education; trade; tourism; transport
GEOGRAPHICAL COVERAGE: France
DATA BEING PROCESSED AND SIZE: monographs; periodicals
HARDWARE USED: IN 8000 (Intertechnique)
SOFTWARE USED: IN 2 (specific programs)
STORAGE MEDIA: traditional shelving of publications; microfiches
TYPE OF ACTIVITY: distribution of information; SSID training; publication
PERIODICALS PUBLISHED: - L'Interconsulaire: France Régions
CLIENTELE: chambers of commerce and industry, miscellaneous organizations
ACCESS TO SERVICE: services open to all users free of charge, some services against

payment

YPE & DESCRIPTION OF SERVICES PROVIDED: Provides library services, searches of
information, information on magnetic tapes and photocopies. Also provides
on-line services using own data bases "DELPHES", "TELEFIRM",
"TELEXPORT", "DOCPRATIC", "VECTRA" and "LINGUATEL", as well as
external data bases in conjunction with consular services.

87 - ASSOCIATION IBISCUS, SYSTÈME D'INFORMATION SUR LES PAYS EN DÉVELOPPEMENT

YNONYMOUS NAMES: IBISCUS Association, Information System on Developing Countries
DDRESS: 1 bis, avenue de Villars,
75007 Paris,
FRANCE
TEL: (1) 45.51.93.12
REATED: 1983   *HEAD:* Mr. M. Guignard, Délégué général
IZE OF STAFF: Professional: 5   Other: 5   Total: 10
YPE OF SERVICE: international; non-profit
ATERIALS DESCRIBING THE SERVICE: - "IBISCUS", Système d'Information sur les Pays
en Développement, leaflet
ORKING LANGUAGE(S): French
UBJECT COVERAGE: economics; development; rural development; industrial development;
trade; economic structure
EOGRAPHICAL COVERAGE: developing countries
ATA BEING PROCESSED AND SIZE: books (25%); articles (50%); grey literature (15%);
miscellaneous (10%)
ATA PROCESSING METHODS: computerized
ARDWARE USED: HONEYWELL BULL (Mini 6); MSDOS (micros)
OFTWARE USED: TEXTO-LOGOTEL
TORAGE MEDIA: traditional shelving of publications
YPE OF ACTIVITY: data collection; data analysis; distribution of information; SSID
scientific and methodological activities; SSID training in developing
countries; publication
UBLICATIONS: - Thesaurus thématique: 3 vol., 1984-1987
- Lexique régional, 1986
- Lexique d'organismes: 2 vol., 1988
- Manuel d'indexation, 1986
- Catalogue des périodiques, 1987
- Femmes et développement, 1985
- Epargne et développement, 1987
LIENTELE: members of IBISCUS network as well as researchers, students, development
specialists, public and private enterprises, NGOs
CCESS TO SERVICE: services open to all users, against payment for non members
YPE & DESCRIPTION OF SERVICES PROVIDED: Provides on-line services on their own data
base "IBISCUS" accessible through G. CAM and including 40,000
bibliographical references and 600 institutions. Also offers selective
dissemination of information, information on magnetic tapes or discs,
microforms and photocopies.

France / France / Francia

288 - BIBLIOTHÈQUE DE DOCUMENTATION INTERNATIONALE CONTEMPORAINE ET MUSÉE DES DEUX GUERRES MONDIALES

SYNONYMOUS NAMES: BDIC
PARENT ORGANIZATION: Ministère de l'Education Nationale, Universités de Paris
ADDRESS: 6, allée de l'Université,
      92001 Nanterre Cedex,
      FRANCE
      TEL: (1) 47.21.40.22
CREATED: 1914   *HEAD:* Mr. J. Uhue, Director
SIZE OF STAFF: Professional: 32   Other: 5   Total: 37
TYPE OF SERVICE: national; public; non-profit
SYSTEMS & NETWORKS ATTACHED TO: CCN (Catalogue Collectif National des Publications e
      Série)
MATERIALS DESCRIBING THE SERVICE: - leaflet
WORKING LANGUAGE(S): French
SUBJECT COVERAGE: history; international relations; world wars; international
      treaties
GEOGRAPHICAL COVERAGE: global; especially Europe for the two World Wars
DATA BEING PROCESSED AND SIZE: 500,000 books; 50,000 periodicals; 2,000 files; 800
      microfilms; 25,000 posters; 300,000 slides
DATA PROCESSING METHODS: manual
STORAGE MEDIA: card files
PUBLICATIONS: - Liste des périodiques en cours reçus par la bibliothèque. Nanterre,
      BDIC, 1978
      - Bibliographie de la deuxième guerre dans "Revue d'histoire de la deuxième
      guerre et des conflits contemporains"
CLIENTELE: 22,000 researchers, professors, journalists, writers (French and foreign)
ACCESS TO SERVICE: open to all users, free of charge
TYPE & DESCRIPTION OF SERVICES PROVIDED: Provides library services, photocopies and
      microforms.

289 - CENTRE D'ETHNOLOGIE FRANÇAISE/MUSÉE DES ARTS ET TRADITIONS POPULAIRES

PARENT ORGANIZATION: CNRS; Direction des Musées Nationaux
ADDRESS: 6, avenue du Mahatma Gandhi,
      75116 Paris,
      FRANCE
      TEL: (1) 47.47.69.80
CREATED: 1937   *HEAD:* J. Cuisenier, Conservateur en Chef
SIZE OF STAFF: Professional: 10   Total: 150
TYPE OF SERVICE: national; public; non-profit
SYSTEMS & NETWORKS ATTACHED TO: Documentary network of the Ministry of Culture
MATERIALS DESCRIBING THE SERVICE: - Informatique et sciences humaines, no. 37-38
WORKING LANGUAGE(S): French
SUBJECT COVERAGE: social sciences; history; social anthropology; cultural
      anthropology; sociology
GEOGRAPHICAL COVERAGE: France
DATA BEING PROCESSED AND SIZE: 70,000 books; 500 periodicals; 7,218 manuscripts;
      200,000 slides; 64,708 phonogrammes
DATA PROCESSING METHODS: partially computerized

HARDWARE USED: IRIS 80, IBM 158
SOFTWARE USED: MISTRAL
TYPE OF ACTIVITY: data collection; data analysis; publication
PUBLICATIONS: - Système descriptif des objets domestiques
   - Richard, P., Documentation des collections ethnographiques dans: Hier pour
   demain: arts, traditions et patrimoine
CLIENTELE: specialists, professors, students
ACCESS TO SERVICE: open to all users, free of charge
TYPE & DESCRIPTION OF SERVICES PROVIDED: Provides library services, bibliographies
   and information on on-going research.

290 - CENTRE D'ETUDE ET DE DOCUMENTATION SUR L'AFRIQUE NOIRE ET MADAGASCAR

SYNONYMOUS NAMES: CEDAM
PARENT ORGANIZATION: Direction de la Documentation Française au Secrétariat Général
   du Gouvernement
ADDRESS: 29-31, quai Voltaire,
   75340 Paris Cedex 07,
   FRANCE
   TEL: (1) 40.15.71.61 - TELEX: 204826 DOCFRAM PARIS
CREATED: 1962 *HEAD:* Ms. L. Porgès, Chief
SIZE OF STAFF: Professional: 6 Other: 3 Total: 9
TYPE OF SERVICE: national; public; non-profit
MATERIALS DESCRIBING THE SERVICE: - Le CEDAM, 4 p., leaflet
WORKING LANGUAGE(S): French
SUBJECT COVERAGE: history; social sciences; administrative sciences; demography;
   economics; education; geography; law; linguistics; political science;
   sociology
GEOGRAPHICAL COVERAGE: Africa South of the Sahara; Madagascar; Mauritius; Comoros
   Islands; Seychelles
DATA BEING PROCESSED AND SIZE: 60,000 books; 400 current periodicals; reports;
   seminars; newspaper cuttings; 70,000 photos
DATA PROCESSING METHODS: manual
STORAGE MEDIA: traditional shelving of publications
TYPE OF ACTIVITY: data collection; data analysis; publication
PERIODICALS PUBLISHED: - Afrique Contemporaine, 4 p.a.
   - Liste Mensuelle d'Acquisitions d'Ouvrages
CLIENTELE: professors, students, research workers, civil servants
ACCESS TO SERVICE: open to all, free of charge
TYPE & DESCRIPTION OF SERVICES PROVIDED: The Centre is organized in two distinct
   units: the "Service de Documentation" which holds press files on Africa
   South of the Sahara and islands of the Indian Ocean and the "Photothèque
   Afrique" which includes photographic documents mostly on French speaking
   Africa.

291 - CENTRE D'ETUDE ET DE DOCUMENTATION SUR L'URSS, LA CHINE ET L'EUROPE DE L'EST

SYNONYMOUS NAMES: CEDUCEE
PARENT ORGANIZATION: La Documentation Française - Secrétariat Général du Gouvernement

France / France / Francia

ADDRESS: 31, quai Voltaire,
        75340 Paris Cedex 07,
        FRANCE
        TEL: (1) 40.15.71.47 - TELEX: 204826 DOCFRAN Paris
CREATED: 1967   HEAD: Mme F. Barry, Head
SIZE OF STAFF: Professional: 15   Other: 4   Total: 19
TYPE OF SERVICE: public; non-profit
MATERIALS DESCRIBING THE SERVICE: - CEDUCEE, leaflet
WORKING LANGUAGE(S): French
SUBJECT COVERAGE: economics; geography; statistics; demography; economic development
        economic relations
GEOGRAPHICAL COVERAGE: Eastern Europe; USSR; China (People's Republic); Viet-nam
        (Socialist Republic); Korea (Democratic People's Republic); Albania;
        Mongolia; Cuba
DATA BEING PROCESSED AND SIZE: 22,000 Russian books; 7,000 West European books; 320
        yearbooks; 360 East European periodicals; 150 West European periodicals;
        3,000 dossiers of press cuttings
DATA PROCESSING METHODS: manual
TYPE OF ACTIVITY: data collection; data analysis; SSID training; publication
PERIODICALS PUBLISHED:
        - Le Courrier des Pays de l'Est, 11 p.a.
        - Liste d'Acquisitions Soviétiques
        - Liste des Périodiques Reçus et Exploités par le CEDUCEE
        - L'URSS et l'Europe de l'Est en..., 1 p.a.
CLIENTELE: public organizations, scholars, students, industrialists and the media
ACCESS TO SERVICE: services open to specific categories of users by appointment, free
        of charge
TYPE & DESCRIPTION OF SERVICES PROVIDED: Provides library services, exchange of
        publications, bibliographic information and surveys.

292 - CENTRE D'ETUDES AFRICAINES, LABORATOIRE DE SOCIOLOGIE ET GÉOGRAPHIE AFRICAINES
       BIBLIOTHÈQUE

PARENT ORGANIZATION: Ecole des Hautes Etudes en Sciences Sociales (EHESS)/Centre
        National de la Recherche Scientifique
ADDRESS: 54, boulevard Raspail,
        75270 Paris,
        FRANCE
        TEL: (1) 45.44.39.79
CREATED: 1958   HEAD: Mme O. Darkowska-Nidzgorski, Responsable de la Bibliothèque
SIZE OF STAFF: Professional: 1   Other: 1   Total: 2
TYPE OF SERVICE: national; public; non-profit
WORKING LANGUAGE(S): French
SUBJECT COVERAGE: social anthropology; cultural anthropology; history; sociology;
        geography; social sciences
GEOGRAPHICAL COVERAGE: Africa South of the Sahara; Western Indian Ocean
DATA BEING PROCESSED AND SIZE: 11,500 books; 410 periodicals; 500 theses
DATA PROCESSING METHODS: manual
STORAGE MEDIA: traditional shelving of publications
TYPE OF ACTIVITY: data collection; publication
CLIENTELE: 200 p.m.

ACCESS TO SERVICE: open to specific categories of users, e.g., researchers, students,
          free of charge
TYPE & DESCRIPTION OF SERVICES PROVIDED: Library services.

293 - CENTRE D'ETUDES, DE DOCUMENTATION, D'INFORMATION ET D'ACTION SOCIALES, BIBLIOTHÈQUE

SYNONYMOUS NAMES: CEDIAS-Musée Social
ADDRESS: 5, rue Las-Cases,
          75007 Paris,
          FRANCE
          TEL: (1) 45.51.66.10
CREATED: 1895
SIZE OF STAFF: Professional: 5   Other: 8   Total: 13
TYPE OF SERVICE: international; private; non-profit
WORKING LANGUAGE(S): French
SUBJECT COVERAGE: social welfare; social history; social movements
GEOGRAPHICAL COVERAGE: France
DATA BEING PROCESSED AND SIZE: 90,000 books; 50,000 index cards
DATA PROCESSING METHODS: manual; computerized
HARDWARE USED: IBM (3 AT 2)
SOFTWARE USED: GESBIB III
STORAGE MEDIA: traditional shelving of publications; fiches; tapes; discs;
          microfiches
TYPE OF ACTIVITY: data analysis; distribution of information; publication
PERIODICALS PUBLISHED: - Vie Sociale, 12 p.a.
PUBLICATIONS: - Initiation à la documentation sociale
          - Problèmes de documentation dans les centres de formation des travailleurs
          sociaux
          - Manual de placement
CLIENTELE: researchers, social workers and general public
ACCESS TO SERVICE: open to all users, free of charge
TYPE & DESCRIPTION OF SERVICES PROVIDED: Provides library services, bibliographic and
          literature abstract searches of information and selective dissemination of
          information.

294 - CENTRE D'ETUDES DE GÉOGRAPHIE TROPICALE, CENTRE DE DOCUMENTATION

SYNONYMOUS NAMES: CEGET, Centre de Documentation
PARENT ORGANIZATION: Centre National de la Recherche Scientifique
ADDRESS: Domaine Universitaire de Bordeaux,
          33405 Talence Cedex,
          FRANCE
          TEL: 56.80.60.00
CREATED: 1968
SIZE OF STAFF: Professional: 7   Other: 4
TYPE OF SERVICE: national; public; non-profit
SYSTEMS & NETWORKS ATTACHED TO: GRECO, Amérique Latine; IBISCUS
MATERIALS DESCRIBING THE SERVICE: - Annual report

France / France / Francia

WORKING LANGUAGE(S): French
SUBJECT COVERAGE: geography; social sciences
GEOGRAPHICAL COVERAGE: tropical countries; developing countries
DATA BEING PROCESSED AND SIZE: 19,000 books; 900 periodicals; 900 theses; 2,700
        microfiches; 14,000 cards; 16,000 photographs; 9,000 slides
DATA PROCESSING METHODS: computerized
HARDWARE USED: IRIS 80
SOFTWARE USED: SPLEEN
STORAGE MEDIA: traditional shelving of publications; tapes; discs; microfiches
TYPE OF ACTIVITY: data collection; data analysis; publication
PUBLICATIONS: - Travaux et documents de géographie tropicale (series)
        - Mémoires du Centre d'Etudes de Géographie Tropicale (series)
CLIENTELE: graduate students, researchers
ACCESS TO SERVICE: open to all users, free of charge
TYPE & DESCRIPTION OF SERVICES PROVIDED: Provides photocopies and microforms of
        documents, question answering service, selective dissemination of
        information, standard profiles and searches of information using own
        database CEGET (25,000 references) available through CDSH (Francis).

295 - CENTRE D'ETUDES ET DE RECHERCHES SUR LES SOCIÉTÉS DE L'OCÉAN INDIEN

SYNONYMOUS NAMES: CERSOI
PARENT ORGANIZATION: Université d'Aix-Marseille 3
ADDRESS: 3, avenue R. Schuman,
        13628 Aix-en-Provence Cedex,
        FRANCE
        TEL: 42.59.40.76
CREATED: 1974   *HEAD:* Mr. H. Gerbeau, Director
SIZE OF STAFF: Professional: 2
TYPE OF SERVICE: public; non-profit
SYSTEMS & NETWORKS ATTACHED TO: Réseau Documentaire Océan Indien (REDOCOI), GRECO
        Océan Indien, CNRS
WORKING LANGUAGE(S): French; English; Malgasian
SUBJECT COVERAGE: social sciences; social anthropology; cultural anthropology;
        political science; history; economics; law; administrative sciences
GEOGRAPHICAL COVERAGE: Western Indian Ocean; South Asia; Eastern Africa
DATA BEING PROCESSED AND SIZE: 700 documents per year
DATA PROCESSING METHODS: partially computerized
HARDWARE USED: TRANSPAC
SOFTWARE USED: Mistral V4 (Questel Télésystèmes)
STORAGE MEDIA: discs
TYPE OF ACTIVITY: data collection; data analysis; publication; conference-
        organization
PERIODICALS PUBLISHED: - Annuaire des Pays de l'Océan Indien
        - Etudes Créoles
CLIENTELE: researchers, experts
ACCESS TO SERVICE: open to specific categories of users
TYPE & DESCRIPTION OF SERVICES PROVIDED: Provides library services, bibliographies,
        and research in the social sciences.

296 - CENTRE D'ETUDES PROSPECTIVES ET D'INFORMATIONS INTERNATIONALES

SYNONYMOUS NAMES: CEPII;
        Center for International Prospective Studies
ADDRESS: 9, rue Georges Pitard,
        75015 Paris,
        FRANCE
        TEL: (1) 48.42.64.64
        CABLE: CEPIREM 206 735 F
CREATED: 1978   *HEAD:* Mr. J.-M. Charpin, Director
                        Ms. C. Duparc, Head of the Documentation Service
SIZE OF STAFF: Professional: 3   Other: 2   Total: 5
TYPE OF SERVICE: national; public; non-profit
SYSTEMS & NETWORKS ATTACHED TO: ECODOC
MATERIALS DESCRIBING THE SERVICE: - CEPIREM brochure (in vol. 19 no. 3)
        - Centre d'Etudes Prospectives et d'Informations Internationales (leaflet)
WORKING LANGUAGE(S): French
SUBJECT COVERAGE: economics; world economy; international trade; economic
        forecasting; models
GEOGRAPHICAL COVERAGE: global; Western Europe; Eastern Europe; USA; Japan; Asia;
        Latin America; Middle East; Northern Africa
DATA BEING PROCESSED AND SIZE: 15,000 books; 3,500 periodicals
DATA PROCESSING METHODS: computerized
HARDWARE USED: HP 3000XE
SOFTWARE USED: MINISIS
STORAGE MEDIA: traditional shelving of publications; fiches; discs
TYPE OF ACTIVITY: distribution of information; publication
PERIODICALS PUBLISHED: - Economie Prospective Internationale, 4 p.a.
        - La Lettre du CEPII
        - Bulletin de Documentation du CEPII
PUBLICATIONS: - Economie mondiale 1980-1990: la fracture, 1984
        - La Drôle de crise, de Kaboul à Genève, 1979-1985, 1986
        - L'Après dollar, 1986
        - Le Pétrole, 1986
CLIENTELE: government officials, professional and trade union associations
ACCESS TO SERVICE: services open to specific categories of users, free of charge
TYPE & DESCRIPTION OF SERVICES PROVIDED: Provides bibliographic and quantitative data
        searches of information, on-line services using own data base "CHELEM"
        (Harmonized Trade and World Economy Accounts) also available through GSI-
        ECO, 45, rue de la Procession, 75015 Paris. Also provides selective
        dissemination of information.

297 - CENTRE DE DOCUMENTATION JUIVE CONTEMPORAINE

SYNONYMOUS NAMES: CDJC;
        Center for Jewish Contemporary Documentation
ADDRESS: 17, rue Geoffroy l'Asnier,
        75004 Paris,
        FRANCE
        TEL: (1) 42.77.44.72
CREATED: 1943   *HEAD:* Ms. C. Cohen-Naar, Director

SIZE OF STAFF: Professional: 3   Other: 1   Total: 4
TYPE OF SERVICE: national; private; non-profit
WORKING LANGUAGE(S): French; English; German; Hebrew; Yiddish; Polish
SUBJECT COVERAGE: history; political science; Second World war; racial
          discrimination; antisemitism
GEOGRAPHICAL COVERAGE: global
DATA BEING PROCESSED AND SIZE: 30,000 books; periodicals; photographs
DATA PROCESSING METHODS: manual
TYPE OF ACTIVITY: publication
PERIODICALS PUBLISHED:
          - Le Monde Juif, 4 p.a. since 1975
ACCESS TO SERVICE: open to all users, free of charge
TYPE & DESCRIPTION OF SERVICES PROVIDED: Provides library services, query answering
          service and reproduction of documents.

298 - CENTRE DE DOCUMENTATION - MIGRANTS

PARENT ORGANIZATION: Centre National de Documentation Pédagogique, Ministère de
          l'Education Nationale
ADDRESS: 91, rue Gabriel Péri,
          92120 Montrouge,
          FRANCE
          TEL: (1) 46.57.11.67
CREATED: 1973   *HEAD:* Mr. J.-P. Tauvel, Head
SIZE OF STAFF: Professional: 1   Other: 5   Total: 6
TYPE OF SERVICE: national; public; non-profit
SYSTEMS & NETWORKS ATTACHED TO: Groupement de Recherches Coordonnées (GRECO 13);
          Mémoire de l'Education (CNDP)
WORKING LANGUAGE(S): French
SUBJECT COVERAGE: sociology; migrations; migrant labour; minority groups; children ⌐
          migrants; migrant education
GEOGRAPHICAL COVERAGE: France
DATA BEING PROCESSED AND SIZE: 4,000 books; 190 periodicals
DATA PROCESSING METHODS: manual
STORAGE MEDIA: traditional shelving of publications
TYPE OF ACTIVITY: data collection; publication
PERIODICALS PUBLISHED:
          - Migrants-Formation
          - Migrants Nouvelles
PUBLICATIONS: - Dossier d'information sur les migrants en France
          - Répertoire de travaux universitaires sur l'immigration, 1986
          - Liste de matériel pédagogique pour adultes migrants
CLIENTELE: teachers, adult trainers, social workers, students and researchers
ACCESS TO SERVICE: open to all users, free of charge
TYPE & DESCRIPTION OF SERVICES PROVIDED: Provides library services and bibliographic
          searches on the data base: Mémoire de l'Education produced by the Centre
          National de Documentation Pédagogique.

99 - CENTRE DE DOCUMENTATION TIERS-MONDE

SYNONYMOUS NAMES: CDTM
ADDRESS: 20, rue Rochechouart,
      F-75009 Paris,
      FRANCE
      TEL: (1) 42.82.07.51
CREATED: 1980   *HEAD:* Ms. B. de Boischevalier, Documentalist
SIZE OF STAFF: Professional: 2   Total: 2
TYPE OF SERVICE: private; non-profit
SYSTEMS & NETWORKS ATTACHED TO: Réseau d'Information Tiers-Monde des Centres de
      Documentation pour le Développement (RITIMO)
WORKING LANGUAGE(S): French
SUBJECT COVERAGE: demography; economics; education; geography; history; law;
      political science; social anthropology; cultural anthropology; sociology
GEOGRAPHICAL COVERAGE: Africa; Asia; Latin America; developing countries
DATA BEING PROCESSED AND SIZE: 700 books; 200 periodicals; brochures
DATA PROCESSING METHODS: partially computerized
HARDWARE USED: compatible PC AT
SOFTWARE USED: TEXTO
STORAGE MEDIA: fiches
TYPE OF ACTIVITY: data collection; distribution of information
CLIENTELE: students, teachers, researchers, journalists (800 p.a.)
ACCESS TO SERVICE: services open to all users, against payment
TYPE & DESCRIPTION OF SERVICES PROVIDED: Provides bibliographic and literature
      abstract searches of information, selective dissemination of information, ·
      photocopies and press reviews.

100 - CENTRE DE DOCUMENTATION, VILLES EN DÉVELOPPEMENT

PARENT ORGANIZATION: Institut des Sciences et des Techniques de l'Equipememt et de
      l'Environnement pour le Développement (ISTED)
ADDRESS: 64, rue de la Fédération,
      75015 Paris,
      FRANCE
      TEL: (1) 45.67.97.39 - TELEX: 200789 F ISTED
CREATED: 1962   *HEAD:* Mrs. F. Reynaud, Head
SIZE OF STAFF: Professional: 3   Other: 1   Total: 4
TYPE OF SERVICE: non-profit
MATERIALS DESCRIBING THE SERVICE: - Urbamet brochure
WORKING LANGUAGE(S): French
SUBJECT COVERAGE: urban development; regional planning; human settlements
GEOGRAPHICAL COVERAGE: developing countries
DATA BEING PROCESSED AND SIZE: 8,000 books and reports; 7,000 articles
HARDWARE USED: computerized
SOFTWARE USED: Mistral
STORAGE MEDIA: traditional shelving of publications; fiches; microfiches
TYPE OF ACTIVITY: data collection; data analysis; distribution of information; SSID
      scientific and methodological activities; SSID training
PERIODICALS PUBLISHED: - Cahiers de Documentation
CLIENTELE: planners, experts, researchers, teachers, students

ACCESS TO SERVICE: open to all users, free of charge
TYPE & DESCRIPTION OF SERVICES PROVIDED: Provides library services, bibliographic and literature abstract searches of information using own data base "URBAMET" available through Télésytèmes-Questel and Minitel. Also provides selective dissemination of information. microforms and photocopies.

301 - CENTRE DE HAUTES ETUDES SUR L'AFRIQUE ET L'ASIE MODERNES, BIBLIOTHÈQUE

SYNONYMOUS NAMES: CHEAM, Bibliothèque
ADDRESS: 13, rue du Four,
    75006 Paris,
    FRANCE
    TEL: (1) 43.26.96.90
CREATED: 1936   *HEAD:* Ms. A. Malecot, Conservateur
SIZE OF STAFF: Professional: 1   Other: 1   Total: 2
TYPE OF SERVICE: public
SYSTEMS & NETWORKS ATTACHED TO: CCN (Catalogue Collectif National): CCOE
SUBJECT COVERAGE: social sciences; political science; Islam
GEOGRAPHICAL COVERAGE: Africa; Asia; Arab countries; Caribbean area; Pacific area; Indian Ocean
DATA BEING PROCESSED AND SIZE: 15,000 books, reports and leaflets; 350 periodicals
DATA PROCESSING METHODS: manual
STORAGE MEDIA: traditional shelving of publications
TYPE OF ACTIVITY: data collection; distribution of information; publication
PERIODICALS PUBLISHED: - l'Afrique et L'Asie Modernes, 4 p.a.
        - Lettre d'Information
CLIENTELE: researchers and experts (2,500 p.a.)
ACCESS TO SERVICE: services open to specific categories of users, free of charge
TYPE & DESCRIPTION OF SERVICES PROVIDED: Provides library services, bibliographic searches of information, photocopies and advice to researchers.

302 - CENTRE DE RECHERCHES ET D'ETUDES SUR LES SOCIÉTÉS MÉDITERRANÉENNES, SERVICE DE DOCUMENTATION

PARENT ORGANIZATION: Centre National de la Recherche Scientifique, Université de Provence, Université d'Aix-Marseille III
ADDRESS: Maison de la Mediterranée,
    3-5, avenue Pasteur,
    13100 Aix-en-Provence,
    FRANCE
    TEL: 42.96.27.81
CREATED: 1962   *HEAD:* Mr. M. Flory,
SIZE OF STAFF: Professional: 14
TYPE OF SERVICE: national; public; non-profit
MATERIALS DESCRIBING THE SERVICE: - Le CRESM 1962-1976. 2eme ed., 1977, 50 p.
WORKING LANGUAGE(S): French; Arabic; English; Italian; Spanish; German
SUBJECT COVERAGE: social sciences
GEOGRAPHICAL COVERAGE: Maghreb; Algeria; Morocco; Tunisia; Libyan Arab Jamahiriya
DATA BEING PROCESSED AND SIZE: 10,200 books, 210 periodicals, reports; 3,300

documents in arabic; films
DATA PROCESSING METHODS: computerized
HARDWARE USED: IBM 33-30
SOFTWARE USED: TEXTO
STORAGE MEDIA: traditional shelving of publications
TYPE OF ACTIVITY: data analysis; publication
PERIODICALS PUBLISHED:
      - Listes d'Acquisitions, 4 p.a. since 1965
      - Bibliographies in: Annuaire d'Afrique du Nord, 1 p.a. since 1962
CLIENTELE: researchers, teachers, students
ACCESS TO SERVICE: restricted to specific categories of users, free of charge
TYPE & DESCRIPTION OF SERVICES PROVIDED: Services include library services,
communication of documentary dossiers, query answering service, provision of
bibliographies. Maintains a database on the social sciences in the Maghreb.

803 - CENTRE DE RECHERCHES ET DE DOCUMENTATION SUR LA CHINE CONTEMPORAINE

SYNONYMOUS NAMES: CRDCC
PARENT ORGANIZATION: Ecole des Hautes Etudes en Sciences Sociales (EHESS)
ADDRESS: 54, boulevard Raspail,
      75270 Paris Cedex 06,
      FRANCE
      TEL: (1) 45.44.38.49
      CABLE: CENTRE CHINE 54 bd Raspail
CREATED: 1958   *HEAD:* Mr. P.-E. Will,
                    Mr. Y. Chevrier,
SIZE OF STAFF: Professional: 4   Other: 5   Total: 9
TYPE OF SERVICE: national; public; non-profit
MATERIALS DESCRIBING THE SERVICE: - EASL newsletter
WORKING LANGUAGE(S): French; English; Chinese
SUBJECT COVERAGE: social sciences
GEOGRAPHICAL COVERAGE: China (People's Republic); Taiwan
DATA BEING PROCESSED AND SIZE: 15,000 books and monographs; 1,350 periodicals; 1,000
      microforms
DATA PROCESSING METHODS: manual
STORAGE MEDIA: traditional shelving of publications; fiches; microfiches
TYPE OF ACTIVITY: data collection; distribution of information; publication
PERIODICALS PUBLISHED: - Cahiers du Centre Chine, (5 titles published) irr.
      - Documents et Inventaires, (2 titles published)
      - Bulletin de Liaison pour les Etudes Chinoises en Europe, 1 p.a. from 1968
      to 1973
CLIENTELE: students, research staff
ACCESS TO SERVICE: restricted to researchers, free of charge
TYPE & DESCRIPTION OF SERVICES PROVIDED: Provides library services.

804 - CENTRE DES HAUTES ETUDES TOURISTIQUES

PARENT ORGANIZATION: Université de Droit, d'Economie et des Sciences d'Aix-Marseille
ADDRESS: Fondation Vasarely,

1, avenue Marcel Pagnol,
13090 Aix-en-Provence,
FRANCE
TEL: 42.20.09.73

CREATED: 1975   *HEAD:* Mr. R. Baretje, Director
SIZE OF STAFF: Professional: 2   Total: 2
TYPE OF SERVICE: national; public; non-profit
MATERIALS DESCRIBING THE SERVICE: - Centre des Hautes Etudes Touristiques, Rapport
        d'activités
WORKING LANGUAGE(S): French; English
SUBJECT COVERAGE: .tourism; leisure; social sciences
GEOGRAPHICAL COVERAGE: global
DATA BEING PROCESSED AND SIZE: 33,500 books; 50 periodicals
DATA PROCESSING METHODS: manual; computerized
HARDWARE USED: IBM
STORAGE MEDIA: traditional shelving of publications; fiches, tapes
TYPE OF ACTIVITY: data collection; data analysis; distribution of information; SSID
        scientific and methodological activities; SSID training; publication
PERIODICALS PUBLISHED: - Etudes et Mémoires
        - Cahiers du Tourisme
        - Essais
        - Documentation Touristique: Bibliographie Analytique Internationale, 4 p.a
        - Touristic Analysis Review, 4 p.a.
CLIENTELE: researchers, experts, teachers
ACCESS TO SERVICE: services open to specific categories of users, free of charge
TYPE & DESCRIPTION OF SERVICES PROVIDED: Provides library services, bibliographic,
        literature abstract and quantitative data searches and on-line services
        using its own data bases. Also provides selective dissemination of
        information and photocopies.

305 - CENTRE NATIONAL DE LA RECHERCHE SCIENTIFIQUE, RÉSEAU DOCUMENTAIRE AMÉRIQUE LATINE

SYNONYMOUS NAMES: Greco 26 - CNRS
ADDRESS: Université de Toulouse-le Mirail,
        5, allées A. Machado,
        31058 Toulouse Cedex,
        FRANCE
        TEL: 61.41.11.05
CREATED: 1980   *HEAD:* Ms. H. Rivière d'Arc, Director
                Ms. N. Percot,
SIZE OF STAFF: Total: 13
TYPE OF SERVICE: national; public; non-profit
WORKING LANGUAGE(S): French
SUBJECT COVERAGE: social sciences; economics; education; geography; history;
        political science; social anthropology; sociology
GEOGRAPHICAL COVERAGE: Latin America
DATA BEING PROCESSED AND SIZE: 5,000 documentation items
DATA PROCESSING METHODS: computerized
SOFTWARE USED: SPLEEN (CDSH-CNRS)
STORAGE MEDIA: traditional shelving of publications, discs, microfiches

TYPE OF ACTIVITY: data analysis; publication; distribution of information
PERIODICALS PUBLISHED:
- Bulletin Bibliographique Amérique Latine
PUBLICATIONS: - Catalogue collectif de périodiques sur l'Amérique latine disponibles
en France, 1985
- Répertoire des centrès de recherche et des chercheurs américanistes en
France
- Thèses sur l'Amérique latine soutenues en France. Répertoire
bibliographique
CLIENTELE: those interested in Latin America, principally researchers and students
ACCESS TO SERVICE: paid services open to all users
TYPE & DESCRIPTION OF SERVICES PROVIDED: Provides library services, bibliographic and
literature searches, on-line services using data base "Amérique Latine -
Francia". Also provides selective dissemination of information and
provision of microforms and photocopies.

306 - CHAMBRE DE COMMERCE ET D'INDUSTRIE DE PARIS, CENTRE D'OBSERVATION ECONOMIQUE

SYNONYMOUS NAMES: COE
ADDRESS: 27, avenue Friedland,
75382 Paris Cedex 08,
FRANCE
TEL: (1) 42.89.70.77
CREATED: 1956   *HEAD:* Mr. E. Devaud, Secretary General
SIZE OF STAFF: Professional: 22
TYPE OF SERVICE: international; public; non-profit
WORKING LANGUAGE(S): French
SUBJECT COVERAGE: economics; statistics; economic situation; statistical analysis
GEOGRAPHICAL COVERAGE: France; global
DATA BEING PROCESSED AND SIZE: statistical investigations
DATA PROCESSING METHODS: computerized
HARDWARE USED: VAX DIGITAL
STORAGE MEDIA: discs and magnetic tapes
TYPE OF ACTIVITY: distribution of information; publication
PERIODICALS PUBLISHED: - Indicateurs du COE, 11 p.a.
- Lettre Mensuelle de Conjoncture, 11 p.a.
ACCESS TO SERVICE: open to all users

307 - CHAMBRE DE COMMERCE ET D'INDUSTRIE DE PARIS, CENTRE DE DOCUMENTATION ECONOMIQUE

SYNONYMOUS NAMES: Paris Chamber of Trade and Industry, Documentation Centre
ADDRESS: 16, rue Chateaubriand,
75382 Paris Cedex 08,
FRANCE
TEL: (1) 45.89.70.00 - TELEX: 650 100 CCI PARIS F
CREATED: 1803   *HEAD:* Ms. M. F. Marminia, Head
SIZE OF STAFF: Professional: 19   Other: 16   Total: 35
TYPE OF SERVICE: national; public; non-profit
SYSTEMS & NETWORKS ATTACHED TO: National Network: Comité Technique des Centres de

Documentation des Chambres de Commerce
MATERIALS DESCRIBING THE SERVICE: - Centre de Documentation Economique (leaflet)
- ISIS, Banque de Données d'Informatique Economique, présentation générale (booklet)
- Guide d'utilisation ISIS
WORKING LANGUAGE(S): French
SUBJECT COVERAGE: economics; law; management
GEOGRAPHICAL COVERAGE: France and the French regions, 150 foreign countries
DATA BEING PROCESSED AND SIZE: 300,000 books; 1,500 collections of yearbooks; 8,000 collections of periodicals, French and foreign; 1,500 cards and atlas (25,000 per year)
DATA PROCESSING METHODS: partially computerized
SOFTWARE USED: STAIRS/BRS
STORAGE MEDIA: traditional shelving of publications
TYPE OF ACTIVITY: data collection; publication
PERIODICALS PUBLISHED: - ISIS-Afrique, Marches à Terme et Options
PUBLICATIONS: - Répertoire alphabétique des périodiques reçus, 1985
- Thésaurus: système DES, 5th ed., 1988
- Thésaurus géographique, 1988
- Répertoire des annuaires français, 1986
CLIENTELE: 32,000 per year: business executives, experts, documentalists, researchers, students
ACCESS TO SERVICE: open to specific categories of users
TYPE & DESCRIPTION OF SERVICES PROVIDED: Provides library services and on-line servicesusing own database ISIS.

308 - COMITÉ FRANÇAIS FISE/UNICEF, CENTRE DE DOCUMENTATION

SYNONYMOUS NAMES: FISE/UNICEF
PARENT ORGANIZATION: UNICEF
ADDRESS: 35, rue Félicien-David,
75016 Paris,
FRANCE
TEL: (1) 45.24.60.00 - TELEX: 610638
HEAD: Ms. C Hentgen, Responsable de l'Information et de l'Education au Développement
TYPE OF SERVICE: national; non-profit
WORKING LANGUAGE(S): French; English
SUBJECT COVERAGE: children; women; health; nutrition; education; social welfare
GEOGRAPHICAL COVERAGE: developing countries
DATA BEING PROCESSED AND SIZE: books, brochures and periodicals; films; photos; slides; video cassettes
DATA PROCESSING METHODS: manual; computerized
SOFTWARE USED: ORIADOC
STORAGE MEDIA: traditional shelving of publications; fiches
TYPE OF ACTIVITY: data collection; data analysis; publication
PERIODICALS PUBLISHED: - Dossiers de Presse
- Revue de Presse, 6 p.a.
- Info-Doc, 6 p.a.
- Les Enfants du Monde, 5 p.a.
- Liste d'Acquisitions
- Revue des Sommaires, 12 p.a.

France / France / Francia

LIENTELE: students, teachers, researchers, trainees, documentalists, animators, international organizations
CCESS TO SERVICE: services open to all users, free of charge
YPE & DESCRIPTION OF SERVICES PROVIDED: Provides library services, bibliographic and literature searches, selective dissemination of information, photocopies and on-line services using own data base UNICEF, and outside data base IPS accessible through TELENET. Participates in a national network ORIADOC (Réseau National d'Orientation et d'Accès aux Sources d'Information et de Documentation).

09 - CONSEIL ECONOMIQUE ET SOCIAL, BIBLIOTHÈQUE ET DOCUMENTATION

YNONYMOUS NAMES: Economic and Social Council, Library and Documentation
ARENT ORGANIZATION: Conseil Economique et Social
DDRESS: Palais d'Iéna,
1, avenue d'Iéna,
75775 Paris Cedex 16,
FRANCE
TEL: (1) 47.23.72.34
REATED: 1947   *HEAD:* Mrs. Lasne, Librarian
Mrs. Mamert, Head Documentation Service
IZE OF STAFF: Professional: 2   Other: 6   Total: 8
YPE OF SERVICE: national; public; non-profit
YSTEMS & NETWORKS ATTACHED TO: Répertoire des Bibliothèques du Catalogue Collectif National (RBCCN)
ORKING LANGUAGE(S): French
UBJECT COVERAGE: social sciences; economics; political science; education; history; law; statistics; finance; planning; international relations
EOGRAPHICAL COVERAGE: France; global
ATA BEING PROCESSED AND SIZE: 30,000 books; 310 periodicals; official gazettes; statistical yearbooks; reports and studies on special funding; extensive analytical reports on sessions of the Social and Economic Council
ATA PROCESSING METHODS: manual; computerized
ARDWARE USED: teletype terminal
TORAGE MEDIA: traditional shelving of publications; fiches; dossiers
YPE OF ACTIVITY: data analysis; data collection; distribution of information
ERIODICALS PUBLISHED:
- Liste Sélective des Livres Entrés à la Bibliothèque
- Compte Rendu de la Presse Hebdomadaire de Grande Diffusion
- Compte Rendu des Publications Périodiques
LIENTELE: researchers and students upon request to the Secretary-General
CCESS TO SERVICE: services open to specific categories of users, free of charge
YPE & DESCRIPTION OF SERVICES PROVIDED: Provides library services, bibliographic, literature abstract, survey and quantitative data searches, photocopies and selective dissemination of information. Also provides on-line searches using external data bases: G.CAM, Serveur télésystème, Questel, Juridial, SCAD, Celex, etc..

France / France / Francia

310 - DEUTSCHES HISTORISCHES INSTITUT PARIS

SYNONYMOUS NAMES: DHIP;
      Institut Historique Allemand de Paris;
      IHAP;
      German Historical Institute Paris
PARENT ORGANIZATION: Bundesministerium für Forschung und Technologie (Ministère
      Fédéral de la Recherche et de la Technologie)
ADDRESS: 9, rue Maspéro,
      75116 Paris,
      FRANCE
      TEL: (1) 45.20.25.55
CREATED: 1964   *HEAD:* Prof. Dr. K. F. Werner,
SIZE OF STAFF: Professional: 10   Other: 9   Total: 19
TYPE OF SERVICE: national; public; non-profit
MATERIALS DESCRIBING THE SERVICE: - Deutsches Historisches Institut Paris/Institut
      Historique Allemand Paris 1958-1983, brochure
WORKING LANGUAGE(S): German; French
SUBJECT COVERAGE: history; political science
GEOGRAPHICAL COVERAGE: Western Europe (especially France, Germany (Federal Republic)
      Belgium, Luxembourg and the Netherlands)
DATA BEING PROCESSED AND SIZE: 50,000 books and reviews (2,000 p.a.)
DATA PROCESSING METHODS: manual
STORAGE MEDIA: traditional shelving of publications, microfiches and microfilms
TYPE OF ACTIVITY: data collection; publication
PERIODICALS PUBLISHED: - Francia, 1 p.a.
PUBLICATIONS: - Beihefte der Francia
      - Dokumentation Westeuropa
      - Documentations et recherches
      - Pariser historische Studien
CLIENTELE: scholars, students, journalists, editors, documentalists, researchers
ACCESS TO SERVICE: paid services open to all users
TYPE & DESCRIPTION OF SERVICES PROVIDED: Provides library services, advice to
      readers, bibliographic research and interlibrary loans. Also offers
      scholarships to historians and financial aid for publications.

311 - DIRECTION DE LA DOCUMENTATION FRANÇAISE, BIBLIOTHÈQUE

PARENT ORGANIZATION: Secrétariat Général du Gouvernement, Direction de la
      Documentation Française
ADDRESS: 29-31 quai Voltaire,
      75340 Paris CEDEX 07,
      FRANCE
      TEL: (1) 40.15.70.00 - TELEX: 204 826 DOCFRAN, Paris
CREATED: 1945   *HEAD:* Mrs. C. Dumaine, Head
SIZE OF STAFF: Professional: 13   Other: 12   Total: 25
TYPE OF SERVICE: national; public; non-profit
SYSTEMS & NETWORKS ATTACHED TO: CCNP (Catalogue Collectif National des Périodiques)
MATERIALS DESCRIBING THE SERVICE: - Readers' guide, leaflet
WORKING LANGUAGE(S): French; English
SUBJECT COVERAGE: political science; administrative sciences; economics; history of

colonialism
GEOGRAPHICAL COVERAGE: France; Africa; global; Southeast Asia
DATA BEING PROCESSED AND SIZE: 195,000 books and reports; articles; official reports
    and studies; underground literature
DATA PROCESSING METHODS: manual
STORAGE MEDIA: traditional shelving of publications; fiches; microfiches
TYPE OF ACTIVITY: data collection; publication
PERIODICALS PUBLISHED: - Catalogue des Publications de la Documentation Française, 1
    p.a. since 1971
PUBLICATIONS: - Indexes, accession lists, current contents of periodicals
CLIENTELE: 200 readers per day (40% students)
ACCESS TO SERVICE: open to all users, free of charge
TYPE & DESCRIPTION OF SERVICES PROVIDED: Provides bibliographic information and
    library services.

812 - LA DOCUMENTATION FRANÇAISE, BANQUE D'INFORMATION POLITIQUE ET D'ACTUALITÉ

SYNONYMOUS NAMES: BIPA
PARENT ORGANIZATION: Secrétariat Général du Governement, Direction de la
    Documentation Française
ADDRESS: 8, avenue de l'Opéra,
    75001 Paris,
    FRANCE
    TEL: (1) 42.96.14.22
CREATED: 1979   HEAD: Mrs M. C. Marquet, Head
SIZE OF STAFF: Professional: 18   Other: 6
TYPE OF SERVICE: national; public; non-profit
MATERIALS DESCRIBING THE SERVICE: - La BIPA, Paris 1982, 32 p. (brochure)
WORKING LANGUAGE(S): French
SUBJECT COVERAGE: political science; administrative sciences; economics; social
    welfare
GEOGRAPHICAL COVERAGE: France
DATA BEING PROCESSED AND SIZE: 250,000 documents (books; articles; speeches; press
    cuttings on LOGOS database); 60,000 documents (speeches, communications on
    SAGA database)
DATA PROCESSING METHODS: computerized
HARDWARE USED: BULL DP7/IBM
SOFTWARE USED: Questel (Télésystèmes); BRS (G-CAM serveur)
STORAGE MEDIA: microfiches; discs
TYPE OF ACTIVITY: data analysis; distribution of information; SSID training
PERIODICALS PUBLISHED:
    - Bulletin Signalétique d'Information Administrative/BIBLIOS, 10 p.a.
    - Lettre d'Information
PUBLICATIONS: - Thesaurus de la BIPA
    - Manuel d'utilisation de la banque de données LOGOS
CLIENTELE: government officers, teachers, researchers, students, journalists,
    managers
ACCESS TO SERVICE: open to all users, against payment
TYPE & DESCRIPTION OF SERVICES PROVIDED: Provides query answering services, on-line
    bibliographic searches using its own data base "LOGOS" (including 230,000
    bibliographic references and full text documents) accessed through QUESTEL

France / France / Francia

and "SAGA" accessed through G-CAM. Provides selective dissemination of
information and photocopies.

313 - DOCUMENTATION FRANÇAISE, CENTRE D'INFORMATION ET DE DOCUMENTATION
INTERNATIONALE CONTEMPORAINE

SYNONYMOUS NAMES: CIDIC
PARENT ORGANIZATION: Documentation Française
ADDRESS: 31, quai Voltaire,
      75007 Paris,
      FRANCE
      TEL: (1) 40.15.72.18
CREATED: 1945   *HEAD:* Ms. D. Lhuillier, Head
SIZE OF STAFF: Professional: 10   Other: 3   Total: 13
TYPE OF SERVICE: public
MATERIALS DESCRIBING THE SERVICE: - CIDIC, leaflet
SUBJECT COVERAGE: political science; administrative sciences; demography; economics
    education; social welfare
GEOGRAPHICAL COVERAGE: Western Europe; Asia; Northern Africa; North America; Latin
    America
DATA BEING PROCESSED AND SIZE: documents, brochures
DATA PROCESSING METHODS: manual
STORAGE MEDIA: traditional shelving of publications; microfiches
TYPE OF ACTIVITY: data collection; distribution of information
CLIENTELE: 3,200 users p.a.
ACCESS TO SERVICE: services open to all users, free of charge
TYPE & DESCRIPTION OF SERVICES PROVIDED: Provides library services from its themati
    files, searches of information and photocopies.

314 - FONDATION NATIONALE DE GÉRONTOLOGIE, CENTRE DE DOCUMENTATION VIEILLISSEMENT
VIEILLESSE

SYNONYMOUS NAMES: National Foundation of Gerontology, Documentation Centre
ADDRESS: 49, rue Mirabeau,
      75016 Paris,
      FRANCE
      TEL: (1) 45.25.92.80
CREATED: 1977   *HEAD:* Mrs. A. Boullet, Head
SIZE OF STAFF: Professional: 2   Other: 1   Total: 3
TYPE OF SERVICE: national; semi-public; non-profit
SYSTEMS & NETWORKS ATTACHED TO: RESHUS (Réseau des Sciences Humaines de la
    Santé/CNRS) and RAMIS (Réseau pour l'Amélioration de l'Information en Sant
    Publique)
MATERIALS DESCRIBING THE SERVICE: - Centre de documentation vieillissement et
    vieillesse (leaflet)
WORKING LANGUAGE(S): French
SUBJECT COVERAGE: demography; medical sciences; psychology; social welfare;
    sociology; gerontology; old age
GEOGRAPHICAL COVERAGE: France; global

DATA BEING PROCESSED AND SIZE: 4,000 books; 210 periodicals; 300 press cuttings; reports· theses
DATA PROCESSING METHODS: manual
STORAGE MEDIA: traditional shelving of publications, fiches
TYPE OF ACTIVITY: data collection; data analysis; SSID training; publication
PERIODICALS PUBLISHED: - Gérontologie et Société, 4 p.a.
    - Liste d'Acquisitions, 6 p.a.
PUBLICATIONS: - Les Bénéficiaires de l'allocation compensatrice, 1987
    - Maladie d'Alzheimer, autre démence senile, 1984
    - Démence du sujet âgé et environnement, 1985
    - Thérapeutique de la démence, 1986
    - Vieillissement cérébral, moral et pathologique, 1988
    - Les Grands parents, la vieillesse et la mort dans la littérature enfantine, 1985
    - Education et personnes âgées, 1986
    - Soins de longue durée en institutions, 1987
CLIENTELE: researchers, students, medical doctors, architects, social workers, journalists, education professionals
ACCESS TO SERVICE: open to all users, free of charge
TYPE & DESCRIPTION OF SERVICES PROVIDED: Provision of bibliographies.

315 - FONDATION NATIONALE DES SCIENCES POLITIQUES, SERVICES DE DOCUMENTATION

ADDRESS: 27, rue Saint Guillaume,
    75341 Paris Cedex 07,
    FRANCE
    TEL: (1) 45.49.50.50 - TELEX: F. 201002 SCIPOL
CREATED: 1945   *HEAD:* Mr. J. Meyriat, Director
SIZE OF STAFF: Professional: 47   Other: 55   Total: 102
TYPE OF SERVICE: national; private; non-profit
SYSTEMS & NETWORKS ATTACHED TO: SPES (Sciences Politiques, Economiques et Sociales)
MATERIALS DESCRIBING THE SERVICE: - Les Services de documentation, 1987
WORKING LANGUAGE(S): Frencb
SUBJECT COVERAGE: social sciences
GEOGRAPHICAL COVERAGE: global
DATA BEING PROCESSED AND SIZE: 565,000 books; 6,500 serials (current titles); 26,000 articles p.a.; 100,000 press cuttings p.a.
DATA PROCESSING METHODS: partially computerized
HARDWARE USED: IBM 9375
SOFTWARE USED: Dobis-Libis
STORAGE MEDIA: traditional shelving of publications; fiches; tapes; discs
TYPE OF ACTIVITY: data collection; data analysis; distribution of information; SSID scientific and methodological activities; SSID training; publication
PERIODICALS PUBLISHED:
    - Liste Mensuelle des Ouvrages Entrés à la Bibliothèque, 12 p.a. since 1951
    - Bulletin Analytique de Documentation Politique, Economique et Sociale Contemporaine, 12 p.a. since 1946
    - Bibliographie Courante sur Fiches d'Articles de Périodiques, 100 p.a. since 1955
PUBLICATIONS: - Catalogue général des périodiques reçus par la Fondation Nationale des Sciences Politiques, Paris, Colin, 1968 - Supplément, 1971

- Bibliographie courante d'articles de périodiques postérieurs à 1944 sur les problèmes politiques, économiques et sociaux. 17 vol. Supplément 12 vol
- Bibliographies françaises de sciences sociales (non-periodical collection since 1960)
- Guide du Lecteur (1 p.a. since 1975)

CLIENTELE: research workers, teachers, students (9,500 users p.a.)
ACCESS TO SERVICE: services open to specific categories of users, free of charge
TYPE & DESCRIPTION OF SERVICES PROVIDED: Provides library services, bibliographic an literature searches, on-line services, selective dissemination of information, files of bibliographical references and press cuttings, microforms and photocopies. Has access to external data bases through LOCKHEED DIALOG, QUESTEL and DATA STAR.

316 - INSTITUT D'ETUDES CRÉOLES ET FRANCOPHONES

SYNONYMOUS NAMES: IECF
ADDRESS: Université de Provence,
   29, avenue R. Schuman,
   13621 Aix-en-Provence,
   FRANCE
   TEL: 42.64.39.90
CREATED: 1983   *HEAD:* Prof. R. Chaudenson, Director
TYPE OF SERVICE: non-profit
WORKING LANGUAGE(S): French
SUBJECT COVERAGE: linguistics; sociolinguistics
GEOGRAPHICAL COVERAGE: Africa; Caribbean area; Québec (Canada)
DATA PROCESSING METHODS: computerized
HARDWARE USED: IBM PC/XT
SOFTWARE USED: SUPERDOC
TYPE OF ACTIVITY: data collection; data analysis; distribution of information; publication
PERIODICALS PUBLISHED:
   - Langues et développement, 4 p.a.
TYPE & DESCRIPTION OF SERVICES PROVIDED: Provides library services, bibliographies from own data base: "Aménagement Linguistique et Développement" and reproduction of documents. Has set up a documentation network on African an French specialists on linguistics.

317 - INSTITUT D'HISTOIRE DU TEMPS PRÉSENT, BIBLIOTHÈQUE

SYNONYMOUS NAMES: IHTP Bibliothèque
PARENT ORGANIZATION: Centre National de la Recherche Scientifique (CNRS)
ADDRESS: 44, rue de l'Amiral Mouchez,
   75014 Paris,
   FRANCE
   TEL: (1) 45.80.90.46
CREATED: 1978   *HEAD:* Mr. D. Peschanski, Head of Documentation/Archives Section
SIZE OF STAFF: Professional: 2
TYPE OF SERVICE: national; public; non-profit

WORKING LANGUAGE(S): French
SUBJECT COVERAGE: history; social sciences; sociology; political science; Second
    World War
GEOGRAPHICAL COVERAGE: France; Europe; North America
DATA BEING PROCESSED AND SIZE: 15,000 books; periodicals; newspapers; microfilms;
    press cuttings
DATA PROCESSING METHODS: manual
STORAGE MEDIA: traditional shelving of publications
TYPE OF ACTIVITY: data collection; data analysis; publication
PERIODICALS PUBLISHED:
    - Bulletin de l'IHTP, 4 p.a. with supplements
    - Les Cahiers de l'IHTP, 3/4 p.a.
PUBLICATIONS: - Le Développement des sciences sociales en France au tourant des
    années soixante, 1983
    - Pierre Mendès France et le mendésisme, 1985
    - Le Parti communiste français des années sombres, 1986
    - De Monnet à Massé: enjeux politiques et objectifs économiques dans le
    cadre des quatre premiers Plans (1946-1965), 1986
    - Le Mémoire des Français: quarante ans de commémorations de la Seconde
    guerre mondiale, 1986
    - Les Chemins de la décolonisation de l'Empire français (1936-1956), 1986
CLIENTELE: researchers
ACCESS TO SERVICE: open to specific categories of users

318 - INSTITUT DE L'INFORMATION SCIENTIFIQUE ET TECHNIQUE-SCIENCES HUMAINES ET SOCIALES

SYNONYMOUS NAMES: INIST
PARENT ORGANIZATION: Centre National de la Recherche Scientifique (CNRS)
ADDRESS: 54, boulevard Raspail,
    B.P. 140,
    75270 Paris Cedex 06,
    FRANCE
    TEL: (1) 45.44.38.49 - TELEX: 203104 MSH F
CREATED: 1970   HEAD: Ms. F. Gourd, Head
SIZE OF STAFF: Professional: 30   Other: 50   Total: 80
TYPE OF SERVICE: national; public; non-profit
MATERIALS DESCRIBING THE SERVICE: - FRANCIS, l'information en sciences humaines,
    sociales et économiques au Centre de Documentation Sciences Humaines
WORKING LANGUAGE(S): French
SUBJECT COVERAGE: social sciences; education; humanities; economics; administrative
    sciences; law; linguistics; philosophy; social anthropology; cultural
    anthropology; social welfare; sociology; ethnology; religion; arts;
    archaeology; literature; health; economy; energy
GEOGRAPHICAL COVERAGE: global
DATA BEING PROCESSED AND SIZE: 1,130,000 bibliographic references (85% periodical
    articles)
DATA PROCESSING METHODS: computerized
HARDWARE USED: NAS 9180, IBM 3090/200, Siemens VP200, Bull DPS8/62M
SOFTWARE USED: SPLEEN II, PSILOG
TYPE OF ACTIVITY: data analysis; SSID scientific and methodological activities; SSID

training; publication
PERIODICALS PUBLISHED: - Reshus
- Economie de l'Energie, 6 p.a., since 1971
- Informatique et Sciences Juridiques, 1 p.a., since 1971
- Emploi et Formation
- DOGE
- ECODOC
- BRISES (Bulletin de Recherches sur l'Information en Sciences Economiques, Humaines et Sociales), 2 p.a.
- Bibliographie Géographique Internationale, 4 p.a. since 1977
- Bibliographie Annuelle de l'Histoire de France, 1 p.a. since 1953
- 11 specialized sections of the Bulletin Signalétique du Centre National de la Recherche Scientifique, devoted to various social or human sciences, 4 p.a., published (under different titles) since 1947
CLIENTELE: researchers, all interested persons
ACCESS TO SERVICE: open to all users, against payment depending on the services
TYPE & DESCRIPTION OF SERVICES PROVIDED: Provides limited library services, bibliographic references, on-line bibliographical searches on FRANCIS data bases accessible through Questel and SINORG-G.CAM. Also provides current awareness service, selective dissemination of information, reproduction of documents, information on magnetic tapes or discs, photocopies and information about on-going research (CNRSLAB). Formerly known as: Centre de Documentation Sciences Humaines.

319 - INSTITUT DE RECHERCHE SUR LES SOCIÉTÉS CONTEMPORAINES, SERVICE DE DOCUMENTATION ET D'INFORMATION

SYNONYMOUS NAMES: IRESCO, Service de Documentation et d'Information
PARENT ORGANIZATION: Centre National de la Recherche Scientifique
ADDRESS: 59-61, rue Pouchet,
75849 Paris Cedex 17,
FRANCE
TEL: (1) 40.25.11.90
CREATED: 1986
SIZE OF STAFF: Total: 3
TYPE OF SERVICE: national; public; non-profit
WORKING LANGUAGE(S): French
SUBJECT COVERAGE: social sciences; sociology
GEOGRAPHICAL COVERAGE: global
DATA BEING PROCESSED AND SIZE: yearbooks; directories; periodicals; conference reports
DATA PROCESSING METHODS: manual; computerized
HARDWARE USED: Zenith
SOFTWARE USED: Wordstar; DBase III
STORAGE MEDIA: traditional shelving of publications; fiches; discs
TYPE OF ACTIVITY: data collection; distribution of information; publication
PUBLICATIONS: - Institut de Recherche sur les Sociétés Contemporaines, 1987 (27 fiches)
- Annuaire des sociologues
CLIENTELE: students, researchers, professors, journalists, social workers
ACCESS TO SERVICE: services open to all users, free of charge

YPE & DESCRIPTION OF SERVICES PROVIDED: Provides library services, searches of
    information, assistance to researchers, selective dissemination of
    information and production of information on magnetic tapes or discs.
    Information can also be obtained from Minitel by dialing 40.25.12.77.

320 - INSTITUT DE RECHERCHES JURIDIQUES COMPARATIVES, BIBLIOTHÈQUE

SYNONYMOUS NAMES: IRJC
PARENT ORGANIZATION: Centre National de la Recherche Scientifique
ADDRESS: 27, rue Paul Bert,
    94204 Ivry Cedex,
    FRANCE
    TEL: (1) 46.70.11.52
CREATED: 1952   HEAD: Mr. M. Burda, Director
                    Mrs. L. Khaïat, Director
SIZE OF STAFF: Total: 3
TYPE OF SERVICE: international; public; non-profit
WORKING LANGUAGE(S): French
SUBJECT COVERAGE: law; political science; administrative sciences; comparative law;
    state; political institutions; communism; family law; sociology of law
GEOGRAPHICAL COVERAGE: USSR; Eastern Europe; China (People's Republic); Western
    Europe; USA; Italy; Germany (Federal Republic); United Kingdom; France
DATA BEING PROCESSED AND SIZE: 7,000 books; 300 periodicals
DATA PROCESSING METHODS: manual
TYPE OF ACTIVITY: data collection; data analysis; publication
CLIENTELE: researchers, professors
ACCESS TO SERVICE: open to professors and postgraduates by appointment, free of
    charge
TYPE & DESCRIPTION OF SERVICES PROVIDED: Two separate sections provide library and
    reference services dealing with the USSR and Communist countries on one hand
    and Western Europe and the USA on the other.

321 - INSTITUT DES HAUTES ETUDES DE L'AMÉRIQUE LATINE, BIBLIOTHÈQUE ET CENTRE DE DOCUMENTATION

SYNONYMOUS NAMES: Institute of Advanced Latin American Studies, Library and
    Documentation Centre
PARENT ORGANIZATION: Université de Paris
ADDRESS: 28, rue Saint-Guillaume,
    75007 Paris,
    FRANCE
    TEL: (1) 42.22.35.93
CREATED: 1955   HEAD: Ms. A. Lefort, Librarian
                    Cl. Duport, Librarian
                    Ms. M. N. Pellegrin, Documentalist
SIZE OF STAFF: Professional: 6   Other: 3
TYPE OF SERVICE: national; public; non-profit
SYSTEMS & NETWORKS ATTACHED TO: Groupement de Recherches Coordonnées (GRECO 26
    Amérique latine), CNRS

WORKING LANGUAGE(S): French; English; Spanish; Portuguese; German; Italian
SUBJECT COVERAGE: social sciences
GEOGRAPHICAL COVERAGE: Latin America; Caribbean area
DATA BEING PROCESSED AND SIZE: 70,000 books (3,000 p.a.); 2,400 periodicals (150,00 articles indexed); 7,000 reports; 5,200 maps; 1,500 serial photographs; 1,200 theses (60 p.a.); 170 microforms
DATA PROCESSING METHODS: manual; partially computerized
SOFTWARE USED: SPLEEN
STORAGE MEDIA: traditional shelving of publications; fiches; microfiches
TYPE OF ACTIVITY: data collection; publication
PERIODICALS PUBLISHED: - Bibliographie Latinoaméricaine d'Articles/Latin American Bibliography of Periodical Literature, 2 p.a.
            - Bulletin d'Acquisitions Récentes, 2 p.a.
PUBLICATIONS: - Catalogue collectif des périodiques sur l'Amérique Latine disponibl en France
CLIENTELE: students, scientific and private researchers (about 1,600 monthly)
ACCESS TO SERVICE: open to all users, free of charge
TYPE & DESCRIPTION OF SERVICES PROVIDED: Provides library services, bibliographic, literature and quantitative data searches, question-answering service and inter-library loans.

322 - INSTITUT NATIONAL DE LA RECHERCHE AGRONOMIQUE - STATION D'ECONOMIE ET DE SOCIOLOGIE RURALES, SERVICE DE DOCUMENTATION

SYNONYMOUS NAMES: INRA ESA
PARENT ORGANIZATION: Ministère de l'Agriculture, Unité de Formation et de Recherche en Sciences Sociales
ADDRESS: 9, place Viala,
            34060 Montpellier Cedex,
            FRANCE
            TEL: 67.61.25.51 - TELEX: INRAMON 490 818 F
CREATED: 1962   HEAD: Mr. D. Boulet,
SIZE OF STAFF: Professional: 4   Other: 1   Total: 5
TYPE OF SERVICE: public; non-profit
SYSTEMS & NETWORKS ATTACHED TO: Agropolis, RESAGRI
MATERIALS DESCRIBING THE SERVICE: - Economie et sociologie rurale et agroalimentair leaflet
WORKING LANGUAGE(S): French; English; Spanish; German; Russian
SUBJECT COVERAGE: economics; geography; history; political science; sociology; agricultural economics; rural sociology; rural development
GEOGRAPHICAL COVERAGE: France; Africa; South America; Eastern Europe; developing countries
DATA BEING PROCESSED AND SIZE: 15,000 books; 400 periodicals
DATA PROCESSING METHODS: computerized
HARDWARE USED: IM 5000; Système Pye
SOFTWARE USED: OPSYS
STORAGE MEDIA: discs
TYPE OF ACTIVITY: data collection; distribution of information; training of students in documentation
CLIENTELE: teachers and researchers, students, agricultural professionals
ACCESS TO SERVICE: open to all users

YPE & DESCRIPTION OF SERVICES PROVIDED: Provides library services, bibliographic and literature searches, on-line interrogation of the INRA-ESA data base, and production of information on magnetic discs.

823 - INSTITUT NATIONAL DE LA STATISTIQUE ET DES ETUDES ECONOMIQUES, DIVISION "DOCUMENTATION"

SYNONYMOUS NAMES: INSEE, Division "Documentation";
National Institute for Statistics and Economic Studies, Documentation Division
ADDRESS: 18, boulevard Adolphe Pinard,
75675 Paris Cedex 14,
FRANCE
TEL: (1) 45.40.12.12
CREATED: 1946   *HEAD:* Mr. B. Chevalier, Chief of the Division
SIZE OF STAFF: Professional: 10   Other: 33   Total: 43
TYPE OF SERVICE: national; public; non-profit
WORKING LANGUAGE(S): French
SUBJECT COVERAGE: statistics; economics; demography
GEOGRAPHICAL COVERAGE: France; global
DATA BEING PROCESSED AND SIZE: 200,000 books (5,000 p.a.); 12,000 periodicals (5,000 articles p.a.)
DATA PROCESSING METHODS: computerized
HARDWARE USED: IBM
SOFTWARE USED: DOBIS, LIBIS AND STAIRS
STORAGE MEDIA: microfiches; tapes; discs
TYPE OF ACTIVITY: data collection; data analysis; distribution of information; publication
PERIODICALS PUBLISHED:
- Scribeco, 6 p.a.
- Bulletin Bibliographique, 3 p.a.
CLIENTELE: civil servants, researchers
ACCESS TO SERVICE: open to all users with some restrictions, free of charge. Interrogation of database provided against payment
TYPE & DESCRIPTION OF SERVICES PROVIDED: Provides library services, bibliographic searches, selective dissemination of information, photocopies and microforms of documents, on-line searches using its own data bases: "SPHINX" (including 43,000 bibliographical references) and "BdM" (macroeconomic information including 200,000 time series) and "SIC" (including statistical data related to the French economic situation) and external databases. INSEE databases are available through G.CAM.

324 - LABORATOIRE D'INFORMATION ET DE DOCUMENTATION EN GÉOGRAPHIE

SYNONYMOUS NAMES: INTERGEO
PARENT ORGANIZATION: Centre National de la Recherche Scientifique
ADDRESS: 191, rue Saint Jacques,
75005 Paris,
FRANCE

TEL: (1) 46.33.74.31
CREATED: 1976   *HEAD:* Dr. P. Pirazzoli, Director
SIZE OF STAFF: Professional: 13   Other: 6   Total: 19
TYPE OF SERVICE: national; public; non-profit
SYSTEMS & NETWORKS ATTACHED TO: Network of the "Centre de Documentation des Science
    Humaines" of the C.N.R.S., international network of correspondents for
    "Bibliographie géographique internationale", Intergéo national network
MATERIALS DESCRIBING THE SERVICE: - In: Images de la recherche en géographie, CNRS,
    1984
WORKING LANGUAGE(S): French; Russian; English; European languages
SUBJECT COVERAGE: geography; environment; regional planning
GEOGRAPHICAL COVERAGE: global
DATA BEING PROCESSED AND SIZE: articles, books, maps, atlases, pictures, slides, on
    going research
DATA PROCESSING METHODS: partially computerized
HARDWARE USED: IBM
SOFTWARE USED: PASCAL III and SPLEEN
STORAGE MEDIA: traditional shelving of publications; fiches; tapes; discs
TYPE OF ACTIVITY: data collection; data analysis; distribution of information; SSID
    scientific and methodological activities; publication
PERIODICALS PUBLISHED: - Bibliographie Géographique Internationale, 4 p.a. since 19
    - Intergéo-Bulletin, 4 p.a. since 1966
    - Lettre d'Intergéo, 8 p.a. since 1978
PUBLICATIONS: - Répertoire des géographes français. 4th ed., 1984
    - Répertoire des formations françaises en géographie. 1st ed., 1982
    - Thesaurus: géographie physique, géographie humaine, noms de lieux
CLIENTELE: researchers, teachers and geographers
ACCESS TO SERVICE: open to researchers, free of charge (except for SDI)
TYPE & DESCRIPTION OF SERVICES PROVIDED: Provides library services including maps a
    photos, retrospective bibliographic searches using its own database:
    "Bibliographie Géographique Internationale" (including 70,000
    bibliographic references). Also provides selective dissemination of
    information on on-going research and surveys and translations upon request

325 - LIAISONS SOCIALES

ADDRESS: 5, avenue de la République,
    75541 Paris CEDEX 11,
    FRANCE
    TEL: (1) 48.05.91.05
CREATED: 1945   *HEAD:* Mr. Galan, General Delegate
SIZE OF STAFF: Total: 80
TYPE OF SERVICE: national; private; profit
WORKING LANGUAGE(S): French
SUBJECT COVERAGE: social welfare; economics; social law; labour relations; statisti
GEOGRAPHICAL COVERAGE: France; French speaking countries
DATA BEING PROCESSED AND SIZE: books; articles; reports
DATA PROCESSING METHODS: manual
STORAGE MEDIA: traditional shelving of publications; microfiches
TYPE OF ACTIVITY: data collection; publication
PERIODICALS PUBLISHED:

- Liaisons sociales, daily
- Mémo social, 1 p.a.
- Barème Social Périodique, 4 p.a.
- Social Pratique, 24 p.a.
- La Lettre Sociale, 52 p.a.

ACCESS TO SERVICE: open to all users; paid services

326 - MERLIN GERIN - SERVICE DOCUMENTATION

SYNONYMOUS NAMES: Merlin Gerin - Information Department
ADDRESS: 38050 Grenoble Cedex,
          FRANCE
          TEL: 76.57.94.60 - TELEX: 320842
HEAD: R. Arnaud, Head
SIZE OF STAFF: Professional: 5   Other: 4   Total: 9
TYPE OF SERVICE: international; private; non-profit
SUBJECT COVERAGE: economics; administrative sciences; management; marketing
GEOGRAPHICAL COVERAGE: global
DATA BEING PROCESSED AND SIZE: 200 books p.a.; 2,000 articles p.a.
DATA PROCESSING METHODS: computerized
HARDWARE USED: PRIME 550
SOFTWARE USED: own
STORAGE MEDIA: traditional shelving of publications; discs
TYPE OF ACTIVITY: data analysis; distribution of information; publication
PERIODICALS PUBLISHED:
          - Analyses des Revues Françaises et Etrangères sur l'Economie et la Gestion
CLIENTELE: 500 internal users and 200 external organizations
ACCESS TO SERVICE: paid services open to all users
TYPE & DESCRIPTION OF SERVICES PROVIDED: Provides on-line searches using own data
          base "MERL-ECO" containing about 30,000 citations with abstracts.

327 - MINISTÈRE DE L'EQUIPEMENT, DU LOGEMENT, DE L'AMÉNAGEMENT DU TERRITOIRE ET DES TRANSPORTS, SERVICE TECHNIQUE DE L'URBANISME, CENTRE DE DOCUMENTATION

ADDRESS: 64, rue de la Fédération,
          75015 Paris,
          FRANCE
          TEL: (1) 45.67.35.36 - TELEX: 260090
CREATED: 1967   *HEAD:* Mr. M. Griffon, Director
SIZE OF STAFF: Professional: 13   Other: 2   Total: 15
TYPE OF SERVICE: national; public; non-profit
MATERIALS DESCRIBING THE SERVICE: - printed notice
WORKING LANGUAGE(S): French
SUBJECT COVERAGE: regional planning; urban planning; urbanization; housing;
          environment; transport
GEOGRAPHICAL COVERAGE: global, especially France
DATA BEING PROCESSED AND SIZE: 20,000 books and reports; 300 periodicals
DATA PROCESSING METHODS: partially computerized
HARDWARE USED: BULL-DPS 7-70

SOFTWARE USED: MISTRAL
STORAGE MEDIA: traditional shelving of publications; fiches; discs; microfiches
TYPE OF ACTIVITY: data analysis; distribution of information; publication
PERIODICALS PUBLISHED:
      - Fiches Analytiques de la Recherche Urbaine, 1 p.a. since 1974
PUBLICATIONS: - Catalogue des publications
CLIENTELE: students, researchers, ministries, professionals, local authorities
ACCESS TO SERVICE: services open to all users; payment for on-line searches
TYPE & DESCRIPTION OF SERVICES PROVIDED: Provides library services, bibliographic a█
      factual information searches, selective dissemination of information,
      microforms and videodiscs; and on-line search of coproduced data bases
      URBAMET (Réseau d'Information sur l'Urbanisme, l'Aménagement,
      l'Environnement et les Transports) and URBATEL.

328 - MINISTÈRE DE LA COOPÉRATION, CENTRE DE DOCUMENTATION

ADDRESS: 1 bis, avenue de Villars,
      75007 Paris,
      FRANCE
      TEL: (1) 45.55.95.44
CREATED: 1961   *HEAD:* Ms A. Rageau, Head
SIZE OF STAFF: Professional: 2   Other: 4   Total: 6
TYPE OF SERVICE: national; public
SYSTEMS & NETWORKS ATTACHED TO: IBISCUS (Système d'Information sur les Pays en
      Développement)
MATERIALS DESCRIBING THE SERVICE: - leaflet
WORKING LANGUAGE(S): French
SUBJECT COVERAGE: social sciences
GEOGRAPHICAL COVERAGE: French speaking Africa; Indian Ocean; Antilles
DATA BEING PROCESSED AND SIZE: 22,000 books, reports, proceedings and documents; 55█
      periodicals; 1,500 press cutting files; 1,200 maps
DATA PROCESSING METHODS: partially computerized
HARDWARE USED: Micro AT (40 Mega)
SOFTWARE USED: Texto
STORAGE MEDIA: traditional shelving of publications
TYPE OF ACTIVITY: data collection; data analysis; distribution of information; SSID
      training; publication
PERIODICALS PUBLISHED:
      - Accessions List
CLIENTELE: civil servants, technical advisers, general public
ACCESS TO SERVICE: services open to all users by appointment
TYPE & DESCRIPTION OF SERVICES PROVIDED: Provides library services, query answering
      service, selective dissemination of information, abstract searches of
      information using IBISCUS and other national and international data bases.

329 - MUSÉE DE L'HOMME, BIBLIOTHÈQUE

PARENT ORGANIZATION: Direction des Bibliothèques, des Musées et de l'Information
      Scientifique et Technique du Ministère de l'Education Nationale

DDRESS: Palais de Chaillot,
place du Trocadéro,
75116 Paris,
FRANCE
TEL: (1) 45.53.70.60
REATED: 1928   *HEAD:* Mrs. J. Dubois, Director
IZE OF STAFF: Professional: 9   Other: 7   Total: 16
YPE OF SERVICE: national; public; non-profit
UBJECT COVERAGE: social anthropology; cultural anthropology; prehistory; ethnology
EOGRAPHICAL COVERAGE: global
ATA BEING PROCESSED AND SIZE: 200,000 books; 4,500 periodicals
ATA PROCESSING METHODS: manual
TORAGE MEDIA: traditional shelving of publications; fiches; microfiches
YPE OF ACTIVITY: distribution of information; publication
ERIODICALS PUBLISHED: - Objets et Mondes, 4 p.a.
      - Liste d'Acquisitions
LIENTELE: 4,000 users p.a.
CCESS TO SERVICE: open to all users, free of charge
YPE & DESCRIPTION OF SERVICES PROVIDED: Provides library services, national and
      international loans and photocopies, on-line services. Has access to FRANCIS
      and QUESTEL data bases.

**30 - OBSERVATOIRE ECONOMIQUE DE PARIS, INSTITUT NATIONAL DE LA STATISTIQUE ET DES
ETUDES ECONOMIQUES**

ARENT ORGANIZATION: Ministère de l'Economie et des Finances
DDRESS: 195, rue de Bercy,
      Tour Gamma A,
      75582 Paris Cedex 12,
      FRANCE
      TEL: (1) 43.45.73.74 - TELEX: 230541F INSEE OEP
REATED: 1974   *HEAD:* Mr. J.-F. Royer, Director
IZE OF STAFF: Professional: 55   Other: 40   Total: 95
YPE OF SERVICE: national; public; non-profit
ATERIALS DESCRIBING THE SERVICE: - Padieu, R., Les Observatoires économiques
      régionaux et leurs utilisateurs. Economie et statistique no. 56, mai 1974:
      57-64
      - Royer, J. F.j, L'Observatoire économique de Paris: mode d'emploi. Courrier
      des statistiques, no. 35, juillet 1985, 6 p.
ORKING LANGUAGE(S): French
UBJECT COVERAGE: statistics; demography; economics
EOGRAPHICAL COVERAGE: France
ATA BEING PROCESSED AND SIZE: BDM-SIC File: (statistical series on French social and
      economic conjuncture); SIRF File: (statistical data and indicators on French
      departments and regions); BDL File: (data on French communes); Population
      censuses, National economic accounts, industrial and commercial enterprises
ATA PROCESSING METHODS: computerized
ARDWARE USED: IBM, TELEX terminals
OFTWARE USED: SPHINX (derived from STAIRS); special software for each main file
TORAGE MEDIA: traditional shelving of publications; fiches; tapes; discs;
      microfiches

France / France / Francia

TYPE OF ACTIVITY: data collection; data analysis; publication
PERIODICALS PUBLISHED:
- Bloc Note de l'Observatoire Economique de Paris, 12 p.a. since 1978
- Note d'Information, Irr.
CLIENTELE: mainly small and medium size enterprises, local communities, researchers
ACCESS TO SERVICE: open to all users and post-graduate students
TYPE & DESCRIPTION OF SERVICES PROVIDED: National network of 22 regional economic
observatories, giving more or less similar services to customers in the
various French regions, on the basis of the same files. Devoted to the
preparation of statistical publications, production of statistical tables
and maps, statistical calculations, provision and dissemination of social
and economic data. Provides library services, bibliographic, literature and
quantitative data services, on-line services of own data bases, BDL, BDM,
SIRF, and also Minitel 3615-INSEE, selective dissemination of information,
production of information on magnetic tapes, microforms and photocopies.

331 - RÉSEAU DE DOCUMENTATION EN ECONOMIE AGRICOLE

SYNONYMOUS NAMES: RESAGRI
PARENT ORGANIZATION: Ministère de l'Agriculture
ADDRESS: 78, rue de Varenne,
         75700 Paris,
         FRANCE
         TEL: (1) 45.55.95.50
CREATED: 1973   HEAD: Mrs. S. Julien, Secretary General
SIZE OF STAFF: Professional: 3   Other: 1   Total: 4 (Network: 140 indexers)
TYPE OF SERVICE: national; non-profit
MATERIALS DESCRIBING THE SERVICE: - Résagri, Brochure
         - Manuel d'interrogation
WORKING LANGUAGE(S): French
SUBJECT COVERAGE: agriculture; agricultural policy; agricultural economics;
         agricultural development; rural planning; rural life; rural population;
         rural sociology; labour law; social policy
GEOGRAPHICAL COVERAGE: France
DATA BEING PROCESSED AND SIZE: 70% periodicals; 30% books, reports, on-going
         research, theses, seminars
DATA PROCESSING METHODS: computerized
HARDWARE USED: DP S7 BULL
SOFTWARE USED: MISTRAL V5
STORAGE MEDIA: traditional shelving of publications, microfiches
TYPE OF ACTIVITY: data collection; data analysis; distribution of information; SSID
         training
PERIODICALS PUBLISHED:
         - Manual users
         - List of reviews
PUBLICATIONS: - RESAGRI thesaurus (for RESADEC and RESAPHO data bases)
         - Geographical thesaurus
         - AGROVOC thesaurus (for TECAGRI data base)
         - Liste des périodiques dépouillés
CLIENTELE: 400 users
ACCESS TO SERVICE: services open to all users, free of charge

PE & DESCRIPTION OF SERVICES PROVIDED: Provides question-answering service,
        selective dissemination of information, on-line services from own data bases
        RESADEC (agricultural economy), TECAGRI (agricultural technology) and
        RESAPHO (audio visual documents), including a total of 225,000 references.

32 - SÉNAT, SERVICE DES IMPRESSIONS DE LA DOCUMENTATION PARLEMENTAIRE ET DE L'INFORMATIQUE

NONYMOUS NAMES: French Senate, Parliamentary Documentation and Information Printing
        Service
ARENT ORGANIZATION: Sénat
DDRESS: 5, rue de Vaugirard,
        75291 Paris Cedex 6,
        FRANCE
        TEL: (1) 42.34.20.14 - TELEX: 260.430 SENAT PARIS
EAD: Mr. M. Vilain, Director
IZE OF STAFF: Total: 8
PE OF SERVICE: national; public; non-profit
RKING LANGUAGE(S): French
BJECT COVERAGE: law; political science
ATA BEING PROCESSED AND SIZE: machine readable data
ATA PROCESSING METHODS: computerized
ARDWARE USED: Hewlett Packard
FTWARE USED: MINISIS
ORAGE MEDIA: tapes, magnetic discs
PE OF ACTIVITY: distribution of information
IENTELE: senators, Senat civil servants, political officials
CCESS TO SERVICE: open to all users
PE & DESCRIPTION OF SERVICES PROVIDED: Provides on-line services using own data
        bases "QSO1", "SINT", "SENA" and "PARL" available through the
        central server G-CAM.

33 - SOCIÉTÉ D'ETUDES ET D'INFORMATION SUR LA RECHERCHE

NONYMOUS NAMES: SEIREC
DDRESS: 61, rue Meslay,
        75003 Paris,
        FRANCE
        TEL: (1) 42.29.79.60
REATED: 1985   HEAD: Mr. G. Tchibozo, Secretary-General
IZE OF STAFF: Professional: 1   Other: 2   Total: 3
PE OF SERVICE: international; private; profit
RKING LANGUAGE(S): French; English
BJECT COVERAGE: social sciences; law; economics; political science; history;
        humanities; international relations; development
EOGRAPHICAL COVERAGE: global
ATA BEING PROCESSED AND SIZE: 150 theses; 1,000 books; 50 on-going research
ATA PROCESSING METHODS: manual
PE OF ACTIVITY: data collection; publication

PERIODICALS PUBLISHED:
- Le Bulletin des Thèses
CLIENTELE: professors, students, researchers, lawyers (2,000 p.a.)
ACCESS TO SERVICE: paid services open to all users
TYPE & DESCRIPTION OF SERVICES PROVIDED: Provides bibliographic and literature
    abstract searches and selective dissemination of information on university
    research.

**334 - UNIVERSITÉ DE MONTPELLIER, INSTITUT DE RECHERCHES ET D'ETUDES POUR LE
TRAITEMENT DE L'INFORMATION JURIDIQUE**

SYNONYMOUS NAMES: IRETIJ
ADDRESS: 39, rue de l'Université,
    34060 Montpellier Cedex,
    FRANCE
    TEL: 67 604555
CREATED: 1971   HEAD: Prof. C. Mouly,
TYPE OF SERVICE: international; public; profit
WORKING LANGUAGE(S): French
SUBJECT COVERAGE: law; legal information systems; legal sociology; computer assisted
    legal education; linguistics; artificial intelligence
DATA BEING PROCESSED AND SIZE: 200,000 documents and articles
DATA PROCESSING METHODS: computerized
HARDWARE USED: IBM
SOFTWARE USED: own
TYPE OF ACTIVITY: data collection; distribution of information; SSID scientific and
    methodological activities; SSID training
PERIODICALS PUBLISHED:
- Rapport Annuel
PUBLICATIONS: - Bibliographie de l'IRETIJ
CLIENTELE: jurists, lawyers, judges, professors, students, researchers
ACCESS TO SERVICE: services open to specific categories of users, against payment
TYPE & DESCRIPTION OF SERVICES PROVIDED: Provides library services, bibliographic,
    literature abstract and quantitative data searches using own data bases
    "JURIDOC", "JURILIC" and "JURINPI".

**335 - UNIVERSITÉ DE PARIS VII, LABORATOIRE DE PSYCHOLOGIE SOCIALE, SERVICE DE
DOCUMENTATION**

SYNONYMOUS NAMES: SERDOC/LPS
PARENT ORGANIZATION: CNRS
ADDRESS: 18 bis, rue de la Sorbonne,
    75230 Paris Cedex,
    FRANCE
CREATED: 1954   HEAD: Mr. B. Matalon, Director of LPS
TYPE OF SERVICE: national; public; non-profit
WORKING LANGUAGE(S): French
SUBJECT COVERAGE: psychology; social psychology
DATA BEING PROCESSED AND SIZE: 17,000 books; reports; 127 periodicals

PERIODICALS PUBLISHED:
- Publications des Membres du Laboratoire, 2 p.a.
TYPE & DESCRIPTION OF SERVICES PROVIDED: Provides library services, bibliographic
searches, query-answering service.

86 - UNIVERSITÉ DE PARIS-NANTERRE, GROUPE D'ANALYSE MACROÉCONOMIQUE APPLIQUÉE

SYNONYMOUS NAMES: GAMA
ADDRESS: 2, rue de Rouen,
92001 Nanterre,
FRANCE
TEL: (1) 47.25.92.34 - TELEX: 638898 UPX NANT
CREATED: 1987   HEAD: Prof. R. Courbis, Director
SIZE OF STAFF: Professional: 7   Other: 7   Total: 14
TYPE OF SERVICE: national; non-profit
WORKING LANGUAGE(S): French
SUBJECT COVERAGE: economics; econometrics; economic forecasting; econometric
modelling; world economy
GEOGRAPHICAL COVERAGE: France; Western Europe
DATA BEING PROCESSED AND SIZE: statistical data
DATA PROCESSING METHODS: manual; partially computerized; computerized
TYPE OF ACTIVITY: data collection; data analysis; publication
PERIODICALS PUBLISHED: - Etudes Prévisionnelles du GAMA, 12 p.a.
- Prévision et Analyse Economique, 3 p.a.
CLIENTELE: government and business enterprises
ACCESS TO SERVICE: services open to all users against payment
TYPE & DESCRIPTION OF SERVICES PROVIDED: Provides computerized economic forecasts and
simulation models. Also provides on-line searches using own data bases
"Prévisions Economiques (Macroéconomiques et Sectorielles)".

**87 - UNIVERSITÉ DES SCIENCES SOCIALES DE GRENOBLE, FACULTÉ DE DROIT, CENTRE DES
DROITS DE L'HOMME, SERVICES D'INFORMATION**

ADDRESS: Domaine Universitaire de Saint-Martin d'Hères,
B.P. 47 X,
38040 Grenoble Cedex,
FRANCE
TEL: 76.54.81.78
CREATED: 1986   HEAD: Mr. P. Arsac, Director
TYPE OF SERVICE: national; public; non-profit
WORKING LANGUAGE(S): French
SUBJECT COVERAGE: law; history; education; social welfare; human rights
GEOGRAPHICAL COVERAGE: France
DATA PROCESSING METHODS: computerized
STORAGE MEDIA: traditional shelving of publications; fiches
TYPE OF ACTIVITY: distribution of information; SSID scientific and methodological
activities
ACCESS TO SERVICE: services open to all users, free of charge
TYPE & DESCRIPTION OF SERVICES PROVIDED: Provides library services. Has set up a data

base.

338 - UNIVERSITÉ TOULOUSE LE MIRAIL, CENTRE DE DOCUMENTATION SUR L'AMÉRIQUE LATINE

SYNONYMOUS NAMES: CEDOCAL
ADDRESS: 5 Allées Antonio Machado,
31058 Toulouse Cedex,
FRANCE
TEL: 61.41.11.05
CREATED: 1979   *HEAD:* Mr. M. Poinard,
SIZE OF STAFF: Professional: 1   Other: 1   Total: 2
TYPE OF SERVICE: international; public
SYSTEMS & NETWORKS ATTACHED TO: Réseau Documentaire Amérique Latine (GRECO 26 du CNRS)
SUBJECT COVERAGE: social sciences; demography; geography; history; linguistics; social anthropology; cultural anthropology; sociology
GEOGRAPHICAL COVERAGE: Latin America
DATA PROCESSING METHODS: partially computerized
HARDWARE USED: CNRS database: CDSH
SOFTWARE USED: ISIS
STORAGE MEDIA: traditional shelving of publications; microfiches
TYPE OF ACTIVITY: data analysis; distribution of information; publication
PERIODICALS PUBLISHED:
- Bulletin de Sommaire de Revues sur l'Amérique Latine
- Bulletin Bibliographique Amérique Latine
PUBLICATIONS: - Répertoire des recherches latinoaméricainistes en France
ACCESS TO SERVICE: services open to all users, some paid services
TYPE & DESCRIPTION OF SERVICES PROVIDED: Provides library services, bibliographic a literature abstract searches, selective dissemination of information, microforms and photocopies. Also provides on-line services using own data base "Amérique Latine".

339 - CENTRE INTERNATIONAL DES CIVILISATIONS BANTU

SYNONYMOUS NAMES: CICIBA;
International Center of Bantu Civilizations
PARENT ORGANIZATION: Bantu Information Service
ADDRESS: B.P. 770,
Libreville,
GABON
TEL: 72.33.14 - TELEX: 5689 GO
CREATED: 1983   *HEAD:* J. Kwenzi-Mikala, Data Bank Director
SIZE OF STAFF: Professional: 11   Other: 1   Total: 12
TYPE OF SERVICE: international
WORKING LANGUAGE(S): French; English
SUBJECT COVERAGE: social anthropology; cultural anthropology; history; sociology; linguistics; geography; education; law; archaeology; music; traditional medicine

EOGRAPHICAL COVERAGE: Bantu; Africa
ATA BEING PROCESSED AND SIZE: 1,150 books; 1,500 articles; 50 theses; 50 discs; 10
     films
ATA PROCESSING METHODS: computerized
ARDWARE USED: IBM/ATE + local NETWORK
OFTWARE USED: TEXTO and TELECOM NETWORK
TORAGE MEDIA: traditional shelving of publications, fiches, microfiches, discs
YPE OF ACTIVITY: data collection; data analysis; distribution of information; SSID
     training; publication
ERIODICALS PUBLISHED:
     - Bulletin Bibliographique des Nouvelles Acquisitions
LIENTELE: university students; general public
CCESS TO SERVICE: open to all users
YPE & DESCRIPTION OF SERVICES PROVIDED: Provides bibliographies, on-line searches,
     microfiches and microfilms.

**40 - AKADEMIE DER WISSENSCHAFTEN DER DDR, ZENTRUM FÜR GESELLSCHAFTSWISSENSCHAFTLICHE
INFORMATION**

YNONYMOUS NAMES: Academy of Sciences of the German Democratic Republic, Centre for
     Social Science Information
DDRESS: Leipzigerstrasse 3/4,
     1086 Berlin,
     GERMAN DEMOCRATIC REPUBLIC
     TEL: 2236220
REATED: 1985   *HEAD:* Prof. Dr. M. Krausse, Director
YPE OF SERVICE: national; public; non-profit
YSTEMS & NETWORKS ATTACHED TO: International Social Science Information System,
     (MISON)
ORKING LANGUAGE(S): German
UBJECT COVERAGE: social sciences; political science; peace research; social aspects
     of the implementation of scientific progress and technical progress; global
     problems of world development; computer-aided methods in social sciences;
     statistical analysis
EOGRAPHICAL COVERAGE: global
ATA BEING PROCESSED AND SIZE: books, articles, reports, on-going research, seminars,
     training courses
ATA PROCESSING METHODS: partially computerized
TORAGE MEDIA: traditional shelving of publications, tapes, discs
YPE OF ACTIVITY: data collection; data analysis; distribution of information; SSID
     scientific and methodological activities; SSID training; publication
ERIODICALS PUBLISHED: - Mathematics and Computer-aided Methods in Social Sciences
UBLICATIONS: - Social science research (information and studies)
LIENTELE: researchers, teachers in higher education institutions, research
     management
CCESS TO SERVICE: services open to all users, free of charge, some paid services
YPE & DESCRIPTION OF SERVICES PROVIDED: Provides bibliographic, literature abstract,
     quantitative data searches and on-line services using external data bases.

341 - ARBEITSKREIS FÜR INTERNATIONALE WISSENSCHAFTSKOMMUNIKATION

SYNONYMOUS NAMES: AIW;
  Association for International Scientific Communication;
  AISC
ADDRESS: c/o Institut für Völkerkunde,
  Theaterplatz 15,
  D-3400 Göttingen,
  GERMANY (FEDERAL REPUBLIC)
  TEL: 0551/39-7892
CREATED: 1980   HEAD: R. Husmann,
SIZE OF STAFF: Professional: 12   Other: 3   Total: 15
TYPE OF SERVICE: international; non-profit
MATERIALS DESCRIBING THE SERVICE: - AISC program
WORKING LANGUAGE(S): English; German
SUBJECT COVERAGE: social anthropology; cultural anthropology; geography; archaeolog
  sociology; folklore; human settlements; urbanization; ethnography
GEOGRAPHICAL COVERAGE: developing countries
DATA BEING PROCESSED AND SIZE: 500 documents (books, articles) p.a.
DATA PROCESSING METHODS: manual
TYPE OF ACTIVITY: data collection; publication
PERIODICALS PUBLISHED: - Abstracts in German Anthropology
  - Research
TYPE & DESCRIPTION OF SERVICES PROVIDED: Aims to promote contacts and exchange of
  information among anthropologists.

342 - ARBEITSSTELLE FRIEDENSFORSCHUNG BONN

SYNONYMOUS NAMES: AFB;
  Peace Research Information Unit Bonn;
  Centre d'Information des Recherches sur la Paix Bonn
PARENT ORGANIZATION: Hessische Stiftung Friedens- und Konfliktforschung Frankfurt a
  Main (HSFK) and the Peace Research Institute, Frankfurt (PRIF)
ADDRESS: Beethovenallee 4,
  5300 Bonn 2 Bad Godesberg,
  GERMANY (FEDERAL REPUBLIC)
  TEL: (0228) 35.60.32
CREATED: 1984   HEAD: Mr. K. H. Koppe, Director
SIZE OF STAFF: Professional: 3   Other: 1   Total: 4
TYPE OF SERVICE: national; public; non-profit
WORKING LANGUAGE(S): German; English
SUBJECT COVERAGE: political science; social sciences; peace; education for peace;
  international conflict
GEOGRAPHICAL COVERAGE: global
DATA BEING PROCESSED AND SIZE: 4,890 books; 60 periodicals
DATA PROCESSING METHODS: computerized
HARDWARE USED: PC
SOFTWARE USED: DMS, Wordstar
STORAGE MEDIA: traditional shelving of publications

ERIODICALS PUBLISHED:
- AFB-Info. Mitteilungen der Arbeitsstelle Friedensforschung Bonn
- AFB-Texte

LIENTELE: researchers, educators, students, practitioners

CCESS TO SERVICE: services open to all users, free of charge

YPE & DESCRIPTION OF SERVICES PROVIDED: Provides information on East/West and North/South relations.

43 - BIBLIOTHEK FÜR ZEITGESCHICHTE

YNONYMOUS NAMES: BfZ;
Library for Contemporary History

DDRESS: Postfach 769,
Konrad-Adenauer-Str. 8,
D-7000 Stuttgart 1,
GERMANY (FEDERAL REPUBLIC)
TEL: 0711/244 117

REATED: 1915   *HEAD:* Prof. Dr. J. Rohwer, Director

IZE OF STAFF: Professional: 8   Other: 4   Total: 12

YPE OF SERVICE: national; public; non-profit

YSTEMS & NETWORKS ATTACHED TO: Württembergische Landesbibliothek (WLB)

ATERIALS DESCRIBING THE SERVICE: - Festchrift zum 50. Jährigen Bestehen der Bibliothek für Zeitgeschichte-Weltkriegs-bücherei Stuttgart, München, Bernand und Graefe, 1966

ORKING LANGUAGE(S): German; correspondence English and French

UBJECT COVERAGE: history; political science; international relations; foreign affairs; military affairs

EOGRAPHICAL COVERAGE: global

ATA BEING PROCESSED AND SIZE: 220,000 books and monographs; 790 periodicals; 300 abstract journals; 1,000 microcopies; 400 manuscripts

ATA PROCESSING METHODS: manual

TORAGE MEDIA: traditional shelving of publications

YPE OF ACTIVITY: data collection; publication

ERIODICALS PUBLISHED: - Jahresbibliographie der Bibliothek für Zeitgeschichte, 1 p.a. since 1924
- Schriften der Bibliothek für Zeitgeschichte, irr. since 1962
- Dokumentation der Bibliothek für Zeitgeschichte, irregular, since 1968

UBLICATIONS: - Katalog der Bibliothek für Zeitgeschichte-Weltkriegsbücherei, 31 vols. 1968

LIENTELE: general public

CCESS TO SERVICE: open to all users, free of charge

YPE & DESCRIPTION OF SERVICES PROVIDED: Provides library services, selective dissemination of information, photocopies and microforms. Also provides bibliographic, literature, survey and quantitative data searches.

44 - BUNDESKRIMIMALAMT, COMPUTERGESTUETZES DOKUMENTATIONSSYSTEM FÜR LITERATUR

YNONYMOUS NAMES: COD-Literatur

DDRESS: Postfach 1820,

6200 Wiesbaden 1,
GERMANY (FEDERAL REPUBLIC)
CREATED: 1974   *HEAD:* Dr. P. Poerting,
SIZE OF STAFF: Professional: 5   Other: 3   Total: 8
TYPE OF SERVICE: national; public; non-profit
SYSTEMS & NETWORKS ATTACHED TO: INPOL (Informationssystem der Polizen)
MATERIALS DESCRIBING THE SERVICE: - Poerting, P.; Störzer, H. U., Das "COD-
     Literatur". Weniger Arbeit für allee!!, in Kripo-Campus, Heft 9, 1985
     - Göbel, R.; Störzer, H. U., Das "Computer-gestützte Dokumentationssystem
     für Literatur", in Rechtsinformationssystem, Heft 22, 1987
SUBJECT COVERAGE: law; psychology; sociology; criminology; penal law
GEOGRAPHICAL COVERAGE: Germany (Federal Republic); Austria; Switzerland; German
     Democratic Republic
DATA BEING PROCESSED AND SIZE: 23,000 periodical articles
DATA PROCESSING METHODS: computerized
HARDWARE USED: Siemens 7760
SOFTWARE USED: Golem
TYPE OF ACTIVITY: data collection; distribution of information; publication
PERIODICALS PUBLISHED: - COD-Literatur-Reihe
CLIENTELE: police agencies and officers, researchers
ACCESS TO SERVICE: services open to specific categories of users, free of charge
TYPE & DESCRIPTION OF SERVICES PROVIDED: Provides library services, bibliographic
     literature abstract searches, selective dissemination of information and
     photocopies.

345 - BUNDESMINISTERIUM DER JUSTIZ, JURISTISCHES INFORMATIONSSYSTEM FÜR DIE BUNDESREPUBLIK DEUTSCHLAND

SYNONYMOUS NAMES: JURIS;
     Federal Ministry of Justice, Legal Information System for the Federal
     Republic of Germany
PARENT ORGANIZATION: Bundesministerium der Justiz / Federal Ministry of Justice
ADDRESS: Gutenbergstrasse 23,
     D-6600 Saarbrücken,
     GERMANY (FEDERAL REPUBLIC)
     TEL: (0681) 58660
CREATED: 1973   *HEAD:* Mr. W. Stewen,
                          Mr. G. Käfer,
SIZE OF STAFF: Total: 40
TYPE OF SERVICE: public
MATERIALS DESCRIBING THE SERVICE: - JURIS: das juristische Informationssystem in de
     praktischen Erprobung
SUBJECT COVERAGE: law
GEOGRAPHICAL COVERAGE: Germany (Federal Republic)
DATA BEING PROCESSED AND SIZE: 600,000 documents including books, articles,
     bibliographic references, legal statutes, court decisions, legal literatur
     administrative provisions
DATA PROCESSING METHODS: computerized
HARDWARE USED: Siemens
SOFTWARE USED: Golem/Passat
STORAGE MEDIA: discs

Germany, Federal Rep. / Allemagne, Rép féd / Alemania, Rep Fed

YPE OF ACTIVITY: data analysis; publication
LIENTELE: lawyers (1,200 p.a.)
CCESS TO SERVICE: open to all users
YPE & DESCRIPTION OF SERVICES PROVIDED: Computerized legal information system
providing bibliographic, literature abstract and survey data searches on its
own data base, JURIS.

46 - DEUTSCHE STIFTUNG FÜR INTERNATIONALE ENTWICKLUNG, ZENTRALE DOKUMENTATION

YNONYMOUS NAMES: DSE/ZD;
German Foundation for International Development, Documentation Centre
DDRESS: Postfach 300380,
Hans-Böckler-Str. 5,
D-5300 Bonn 3,
GERMANY (FEDERAL REPUBLIC)
TEL: 0228/4001-0 - TELEX: 886710
CABLE: DEUTSCHSTIFTUNG-BONN
REATED: 1961   *HEAD:* D. L. Steinert, Head
IZE OF STAFF: Professional: 20   Other: 7   Total: 27
YPE OF SERVICE: national; public; non-profit
ATERIALS DESCRIBING THE SERVICE: - Zentrale Dokumentation der deutschen Stiftung für
internationale Entwicklung, 1988, (brochure)
ORKING LANGUAGE(S): German; English; French
UBJECT COVERAGE: social sciences; education; geography; political science;
sociology; economics; development; international cooperation; development
policy; strategies; project evaluation; cultural change
EOGRAPHICAL COVERAGE: developing countries
ATA BEING PROCESSED AND SIZE: 80,000 books, articles, reports; 350,000 newspaper
clippings
ATA PROCESSING METHODS: computerized; manual
ARDWARE USED: IBM
OFTWARE USED: STAIRS (retrieval); SFP/PANVALET (input)
TORAGE MEDIA: traditional shelving of publications; magnetic discs; file cards
YPE OF ACTIVITY: data collection; publication
ERIODICALS PUBLISHED: - Development and Cooperation, 6 p.a.
- Neuerwerbungen der Bibliothek, 2 p.a.
- Zeitschriftenliste, every two years
- Seminare, Kurse und Konferenzen auf dem Gebiet der Entwicklungshilfe im
In- und Ausland, 4 p.a.
- Entwicklungsländer-Studien: Bibliographie der Entwicklungsländer-
Forschung, 1 p.a. since 1964
- Themendienst der Zentralen Dokumentation
UBLICATIONS: - Bibliographies, guides, reports, directories of German development
institutions
- Thesaurus für Wirtschaftliche und Soziale Entwicklung, 1987
LIENTELE: researchers, administrators, politicians, students, experts, teaching
staff (17,000 p.a.)
CCESS TO SERVICE: open to all users, free of charge (some services are subject to
charges)
YPE & DESCRIPTION OF SERVICES PROVIDED: Provides library services, selective
dissemination of information, bibliographic, literature and survey data

searches using its own data base "Literatur" consisting of 50,000 data
files. Also provides referral services and photocopies upon request.

347 - DEUTSCHES BUCHARCHIV MÜNCHEN

SYNONYMOUS NAMES: German Archives of Books in Munich
PARENT ORGANIZATION: Institut für Buchwissenschaften - Gemeinnützige Stiftung
      Privaten Rechts
ADDRESS: Erhardtstrasse 8,
      D-8000 Munich 5,
      GERMANY (FEDERAL REPUBLIC)
      TEL: 089/2021328 - TELEX: 529813 debig d
CREATED: 1948   *HEAD:* L. Delp,
SIZE OF STAFF: Professional: 1   Other: 3   Total: 4
TYPE OF SERVICE: national; public; non-profit
MATERIALS DESCRIBING THE SERVICE: - Das Deutsche Bucharchiv München UND seine IUD-
      Arbeit für das Medium Bach, 1982
SUBJECT COVERAGE: computer science; social sciences; economics; education; history
      law; political science; mass media
GEOGRAPHICAL COVERAGE: Germany (Federal Republic)
DATA BEING PROCESSED AND SIZE: 20,000 books; 240 periodicals; 4,200 reports; films
      microforms; magnetic tapes and newspaper cuttings
DATA PROCESSING METHODS: manual
TYPE OF ACTIVITY: publication
PUBLICATIONS: - Scientific articles, information, bibliographies on the laws of the
      press, book trade, radio and T.V.
      - Buchwissenschaftliche Beiträge aus den Deutschen Bucharchiv München
      (contribution of scientific books from the DBM)
ACCESS TO SERVICE: open to all users, free of charge
TYPE & DESCRIPTION OF SERVICES PROVIDED: Provides library services, bibliographic
      literature searches of information, selective dissemination of information
      photocopies and microforms.

348 - DEUTSCHES JUGENDINSTITUT, ABTEILUNG DOKUMENTATION UND INFORMATION

SYNONYMOUS NAMES: German Youth Institute, Department of Documentation and Informat
PARENT ORGANIZATION: German Youth Institute
ADDRESS: Freibadstr. 30,
      8000 Munich 90,
      GERMANY (FEDERAL REPUBLIC)
      TEL: (089) 62306-131
CREATED: 1963   *HEAD:* Dr. R. Mayer, Head
SIZE OF STAFF: Professional: 10   Other: 10   Total: 20
TYPE OF SERVICE: public; non-profit
SYSTEMS & NETWORKS ATTACHED TO: Dokumentationsring Pädagogik (DOPAED)
WORKING LANGUAGE(S): German
SUBJECT COVERAGE: youth; family
GEOGRAPHICAL COVERAGE: Germany (Federal Republic); Austria
DATA BEING PROCESSED AND SIZE: 80,000 books, articles of journals and grey literatu

ATA PROCESSING METHODS: manual; partially computerized
ARDWARE USED: CTM
YPE OF ACTIVITY: data collection; data analysis; publication
ERIODICALS PUBLISHED: - Dokumentation Sozialisation und Sozialpädagogik, 4 p.a.
CCESS TO SERVICE: open to all users
YPE & DESCRIPTION OF SERVICES PROVIDED: Provides library services and on-line
    interrogation of own database Bibliographie "Sozialisation und
    Sozialpädagogik".

49 - DEUTSCHES ÜBERSEE-INSTITUT, ÜBERSEE-DOKUMENTATION

YNONYMOUS NAMES: German Overseas Institute, Overseas Documentation
DDRESS: Neuer Jungfernstieg 21,
         D-2000 Hamburg 36,
         GERMANY (FEDERAL REPUBLIC)
         TEL: (040) 3562589
REATED: 1966   *HEAD:* Dr. U. Gehrke, Head of Department
IZE OF STAFF: Professional: 12   Other: 4   Total: 16
YPE OF SERVICE: national; public; non-profit
YSTEMS & NETWORKS ATTACHED TO: IB + LK, Internationale Beziehungen und Länderkunde
    (International Relations and Area Studies)
ATERIALS DESCRIBING THE SERVICE: - Deutsches Übersee-Institut, Übersee-
    Dokumentation, 1987, 15 p.
ORKING LANGUAGE(S): German
UBJECT COVERAGE: social sciences; economics; political science; sociology;
    demography; administrative sciences; education; geography; social
    anthropology; social welfare; law; history
EOGRAPHICAL COVERAGE: Africa; Asia; Pacific area; Latin America; Middle East
ATA BEING PROCESSED AND SIZE: 280,000 books, articles, journals and serials
ATA PROCESSING METHODS: manual; computerized
ARDWARE USED: Philips Minicomputer P859
OFTWARE USED: Domestic
TORAGE MEDIA: card catalogues; magnetic discs
YPE OF ACTIVITY: data collection; distribution of information; publication
ERIODICALS PUBLISHED: - Ausgewählte Neuere Literatur, 4 p.a.
UBLICATIONS: - Spezialbibliographien (series)
    - Länderkatalog Afrika der Übersee-Dokumentation Hamburg (1979-1984), 1986
    - Fritsche, K., Non-Alignment and the Non-Aligned Movement. A bibliography,
    1984
LIENTELE: researchers, students, administrators, economists, journalists, interested
    public (2,500 p.a.)
CCESS TO SERVICE: paid services (nominal charges) open to all users
YPE & DESCRIPTION OF SERVICES PROVIDED: Provides retrospective bibliographic and
    literature searches. Comprises four sections: Afrika (AFDOC), Asien und
    Südpazific (ASDOK), Lateinamerika (LADOK) and Vorderer Orient (ORDOK).

Germany, Federal Rep. / Allemagne, Rép féd / Alemania, Rep Fed

350 - FORSCHUNGSINSTITUT FÜR FRIEDENSPOLITIK, INFORMATIONSBÜRO

SYNONYMOUS NAMES: FF/IBF;
Research Institute for Peace Policy, Information Office
ADDRESS: Postfach 1308,
D-8130 Starnberg,
GERMANY (FEDERAL REPUBLIC)
TEL: 0 81 51/41 15 - TELEX 5 270 220 ibff d
CREATED: 1982   *HEAD:* Mr. B. J. Huck, Head
SIZE OF STAFF: Professional: 2   Other: 2   Total: 4
TYPE OF SERVICE: non-profit
MATERIALS DESCRIBING THE SERVICE: - Prospectus
WORKING LANGUAGE(S): German
SUBJECT COVERAGE: political science; peace research; conflict
GEOGRAPHICAL COVERAGE: Germany (Federal Republic); German Democratic Republic
DATA BEING PROCESSED AND SIZE: 4,000 books and reports; 120 periodicals; newspapers
factual records
DATA PROCESSING METHODS: partially computerized
HARDWARE USED: IBM PC/AT
SOFTWARE USED: CICADE; WORD; F & A; EASY
STORAGE MEDIA: traditional shelving of publications
TYPE OF ACTIVITY: data collection; data analysis; distribution of information;
publication
PERIODICALS PUBLISHED:
- fpk (Friedenspolitischer Kurier)
- FriedensBrief, (English language newsletter)
PUBLICATIONS: - Directories
CLIENTELE: researchers of parent organizations; affiliates of the West German Peace
Movement
ACCESS TO SERVICE: services open to specific categories of users, free of charge
TYPE & DESCRIPTION OF SERVICES PROVIDED: The IBF acts as a communication network an
information center for the whole peace movement, and also as a mail order
sales service and publishing house for peace-related literature. Has its o
data base: "Waffen-, Standort- und Rüstungsfirmenarchiv" (WSRA).
Translating and photocopying facilities are available.

351 - FORSCHUNGSINSTITUT FÜR INTERNATIONALE POLITIK UND SICHERHEIT, STIFTUNG WISSENSCHAFT UND POLITIK. BIBLIOTHEK UND DOKUMENTATION

SYNONYMOUS NAMES: Research Institute for International Politics and Security, Scien
and Politics Foundation. Library and Documentation Service
ADDRESS: Haus Eggenberg,
D-8026 Ebenhausen/Isar,
GERMANY (FEDERAL REPUBLIC)
TEL: (08178) 70-1 - TELEFAX: (08178) 70312
CREATED: 1964   *HEAD:* D. Seydel,
SIZE OF STAFF: Professional: 20   Other: 12   Total: 32
TYPE OF SERVICE: national; public; non-profit
SYSTEMS & NETWORKS ATTACHED TO: Fachinformationsverbund internationale Beziehungen
und Länderkunde
WORKING LANGUAGE(S): German

UBJECT COVERAGE: economics; political science; social anthropology; cultural
        anthropology; international security; international economics
EOGRAPHICAL COVERAGE: global
ATA BEING PROCESSED AND SIZE: 34,000 books; reports; 110,000 articles; periodicals;
        yearbooks; 25,000 documents
ATA PROCESSING METHODS: computerized
ARDWARE USED: Philips P857, Philips P859
OFTWARE USED: DOMESTIC
TORAGE MEDIA: discs
YPE OF ACTIVITY: data collection; data analysis; publication
LIENTELE: public administration, researchers
CCESS TO SERVICE: open to specific categories of users
YPE & DESCRIPTION OF SERVICES PROVIDED: Provides bibliographies, literature
        searches, magnetic tape service and on-line access.

52 - FRAUNHOFER-GESELLSCHAFT, INFORMATIONSZENTRUM RAUM UND BAU

YNONYMOUS NAMES: FhG IRB;
        Fraunhofer Society, Information Centre for Regional Planning and Building
        Construction
DDRESS: Nobelstrasse 12,
        D-7000 Stuttgart 80,
        GERMANY (FEDERAL REPUBLIC)
        TEL: (711) 68.68.600 - TELEX: 7255167 IRB D - TELEFAX: (711) 6868-399
EAD: Dr. Ing. W Wissmann,
IZE OF STAFF: Total: 100
YPE OF SERVICE: international; profit
YSTEMS & NETWORKS ATTACHED TO: CIB-International Council for Building Research,
        Studies and Documentation; IVDB-Internationaler Verein für Dokumentation im
        Bauwesen
ATERIALS DESCRIBING THE SERVICE: - Brochure
ORKING LANGUAGE(S): German; English
UBJECT COVERAGE: regional planning; urban planning; housing; architecture
EOGRAPHICAL COVERAGE: Germany (Federal Republic); global
ATA BEING PROCESSED AND SIZE: 223,000 citations in RSWB; 1,000 periodicals; 145,000
        citations in ICONDA
ATA PROCESSING METHODS: computerized
OFTWARE USED: ICONDA, RSWB, BODO, BAUFO, FORS, PASCALBAT, PICA, VWAB
TORAGE MEDIA: card files and catalogues
YPE OF ACTIVITY: data collection; data analysis; distribution of information;
        publication
ERIODICALS PUBLISHED:
        - Kurzberichte aus der Bauforschung, 12 p.a.
        - Bulldok Bauschöden, 4 p.a.
        - Bulldok Betonbau, 4 p.a.
        - Bulldok Holzbau, 4 p.a.
        - Bulldok Bauphysik (Wärme), 4 p.a.
UBLICATIONS: - Mikrofors
        - Findex
        - Katalog der IRB-Literaturauslesen
        - Forschungsdokumentation Raumordrung Städtebau Wohnungswesen, 2 vol.

ACCESS TO SERVICE: paid services open to all users
TYPE & DESCRIPTION OF SERVICES PROVIDED: Provides library services, on-line service
    information services on personal request, periodical services on personal
    request, standardized periodical services (journals), publications and
    microfiche services and consultation in formation. Its data bases include:
    RSWB (building construction literature); BODO (facts concerning planning of
    buildings); BAUFO (research in building construction); FORS (research in
    urban planning); PASCALBAT (building construction literature in French);
    PICA (building construction literature in English); VWAB (hydraulic
    engineering literature). Operates also ICONDA (international construction
    database).

353 - GESELLSCHAFT FÜR BETRIEBSWIRTSCHAFTLICHE INFORMATION MBH

SYNONYMOUS NAMES: GBI
ADDRESS: Pafiser Strasse 42,
    Postfach 80 07 23,
    D-8000 Munich 40,
    GERMANY (FEDERAL REPUBLIC)
    TEL: (089) 448.28.04
CREATED: 1978   HEAD: Dr. P. Müller-Bader.
SIZE OF STAFF: Professional: 4   Other: 2   Total: 6
TYPE OF SERVICE: international; public; profit
WORKING LANGUAGE(S): German
SUBJECT COVERAGE: administrative sciences; economics
GEOGRAPHICAL COVERAGE: Germany (Federal Republic); Switzerland; Austria
DATA BEING PROCESSED AND SIZE: articles; reports
DATA PROCESSING METHODS: computerized
HARDWARE USED: Data General
SOFTWARE USED: Sudok
STORAGE MEDIA: discs
TYPE OF ACTIVITY: data collection; data analysis; distribution of information;
    publication
PUBLICATIONS: - BZD (Betriebswirtschaftliche Zeitschriftendokumentation)
        - Betriebswirtschaftliche Forschungsbeiträge
        - Betriebswirtschaftliche Studientexte
        - Volkswirtschaftliche Fortschungsbeiträge
        - Produktforschung und Industriedesign
CLIENTELE: information professionals, universities, companies (2,000 p.a.)
ACCESS TO SERVICE: paid services open to all users
TYPE & DESCRIPTION OF SERVICES PROVIDED: Provides bibliographic, literature abstract
    and quantitative data searches, selective dissemination of information,
    information on magnetic tapes or discs and photocopies. Also provides on-
    line services from own data bases: FINF (Firmeninformationssystem); BLISS
    (Betriebswirtschaftliches Literature-Suchsystem); MANEX (Management Experte
    Nachweis); BONMOT; HADOSS (online-ordering von HWWA Dossiers); PROGNO
    (Prognosen, Trends, Entwicklungen).

354 - HWWA-INSTITUT FÜR WIRTSCHAFTSFORSCHUNG - HAMBURG, INFORMATIONSZENTRUM

SYNONYMOUS NAMES: HWWA-Institute of Economic Research - Hamburg, Information Centre
ADDRESS: Neuer Jungfernstieg 21,
            2000 Hamburg 36,
            GERMANY (FEDERAL REPUBLIC)
            TEL: (040) 3562-1 - TELEX: 211 458 hwwa d - TELEFAX: (040) 351900
CREATED: 1908   *HEAD:* H. G. Striefler,
SIZE OF STAFF: Professional: 75   Other: 34   Total: 109
TYPE OF SERVICE: public; non-profit
MATERIALS DESCRIBING THE SERVICE: - HWWA Institut für Wirtschaftsforschung - Hamburg
WORKING LANGUAGE(S): European languages
SUBJECT COVERAGE: economics; political science; international economics
GEOGRAPHICAL COVERAGE: global
DATA BEING PROCESSED AND SIZE: 850,000 books; 14,8 million press cuttings; 3,500
            magazines; 80 daily newspapers; 9,000 yearbooks; 3,600 reports
DATA PROCESSING METHODS: manual
TYPE OF ACTIVITY: data collection; distribution of information; SSID training;
            publication
PERIODICALS PUBLISHED: - Bibliographie der Wirtschaftspresse, 12 p.a.
            - Neuerwerbungen der Bibliothek des HWWA-Institüt für Wirtschaftsforschung
            Hamburg, 12 p.a.
CLIENTELE: visitors: 68,400 p.a.; services: 3,100 p.a.
ACCESS TO SERVICE: services open to all users; some services are subject to charges
TYPE & DESCRIPTION OF SERVICES PROVIDED: Provides library services, bibliographic and
            quantitative data searches and selective dissemination of information on all
            fields of national and international economics and related disciplines. Also
            provides photocopies. As a depository library of the UN, FAO, GATT, OECD and
            the EC, it contains nearly all publications of these organizations.

355 - IFO-INSTITUT FÜR WIRTSCHAFTSFORSCHUNG, IFO-DATENBANK UND BIBLIOTEK

SYNONYMOUS NAMES: Ifo Institute for Economic Research, Ifo-Data Bank and Library
ADDRESS: Poschingerstrasse 5,
            Postfach 86.04.60,
            8 Munich 86,
            GERMANY (FEDERAL REPUBLIC)
            TEL: 089-9224-0 - TELEX: 5-22269
CREATED: 1949   *HEAD:* G. Goldrian, Head
SIZE OF STAFF: Professional: 5
TYPE OF SERVICE: national; private; non-profit
MATERIALS DESCRIBING THE SERVICE: - Ifo Institute for Economic Research, booklet
SUBJECT COVERAGE: economics; statistics; economic forecasting; models
GEOGRAPHICAL COVERAGE: Germany (Federal Republic)
DATA BEING PROCESSED AND SIZE: 50,000 economic time series, 85,000 books; 1,000
            periodicals
DATA PROCESSING METHODS: computerized
HARDWARE USED: Siemens 7.865-2
SOFTWARE USED: own software
STORAGE MEDIA: discs
TYPE OF ACTIVITY: distribution of information

PUBLICATIONS: - Ifo Datenbanksystem Verzeichnis der Reihen aus der amtlichen
        Statistik
        - Ifo Datenbanksystem Verzeichnis der Reihen aus dem Ifo-Konjunkturtest
CLIENTELE: firms, public administrations
ACCESS TO SERVICE: services open to all users, against payment
TYPE & DESCRIPTION OF SERVICES PROVIDED: Provides library services, selective
        dissemination of information, information on magnetic tapes or discs, and
        quantitative searches of information on its own data bank (IFO-Data Bank).

356 - INFORMATIONSZENTRUM SOZIALWISSENSCHAFTEN

SYNONYMOUS NAMES: I Z
PARENT ORGANIZATION: Arbeitsgemeinschaft Sozialwissenschaftlicher Institute
ADDRESS: Lennéstrasse 30,
        D-5300 Bonn 1,
        GERMANY (FEDERAL REPUBLIC)
        TEL: (0228) 22 81-0
CREATED: 1969   HEAD: Mr. K. A. Stroetmann, Director
SIZE OF STAFF: Professional: 16   Other: 4
TYPE OF SERVICE: National; private; non-profit
MATERIALS DESCRIBING THE SERVICE: - Organisation - Aufgaben - Entwicklung, printed
        notice, Sept. 1977
SUBJECT COVERAGE: social sciences; sociology; political science; economics;
        education; psychology; communication
GEOGRAPHICAL COVERAGE: Germany (Federal Republic); Austria; Switzerland
DATA PROCESSING METHODS: computerized
HARDWARE USED: SIEMENS 4004/151
SOFTWARE USED: GOLEM 2
TYPE OF ACTIVITY: data collection; data analysis; SSID training; publication
PERIODICALS PUBLISHED:
        - Tätig-Keitsbericht, 1 p.a.
PUBLICATIONS: - Herfurth, M.; Stroetmann, K. A., Information strategy and informatic
        policy in the social sciences: recent developments in Germany (FRG), 1986
CLIENTELE: scientists, administrators
ACCESS TO SERVICE: open to all users, against payment
TYPE & DESCRIPTION OF SERVICES PROVIDED: Advice to interested people, elaboration of
        statistics, provision of data for secondary analysis, selective
        dissemination of information: standard profiles, retrospective
        bibliographies searches. Data bases FORIS (42,000 references) and SOLIS
        (73,500 references) on social science projects and literature on the German
        speaking area provide on-line service on primary information.

357 - INSTITUT FÜR ARBEITSMARKT-UND BERUFSFORSCHUNG DER BUNDESANSTALT FÜR ARBEIT, INFORMATIONSDIENSTE

SYNONYMOUS NAMES: IAB, Informationsdienste;
        Institute of Labour Market and Occupational Research of the Federal
        Employment Agency, Information Service
PARENT ORGANIZATION: Bundesanstalt für Arbeit

ADDRESS: Regensburger Strasse 104,
8500 Nürnberg,
GERMANY (FEDERAL REPUBLIC)
TEL: 0911/17-1
CREATED: 1967   *HEAD:* G. Peters,
SIZE OF STAFF: Professional: 8   Other: 10   Total: 18
TYPE OF SERVICE: national; public; non-profit
WORKING LANGUAGE(S): German
SUBJECT COVERAGE: economics; social sciences; sociology; demography; social welfare;
labour market; labour relations
GEOGRAPHICAL COVERAGE: Germany (Federal Republic); Western Europe; EEC; USA; Japan
DATA BEING PROCESSED AND SIZE: 35,000 books; 500 periodicals
DATA PROCESSING METHODS: computerized
HARDWARE USED: Siemens
STORAGE MEDIA: traditional shelving of publications; tapes; discs; microfiches
TYPE OF ACTIVITY: data collection; distribution of information; publication
PUBLICATIONS: - Literatur Dokumentation für Arbeitsmarkt und Berufsforschung
- Forschungsdokumentation für Arbeitsmarkt und Berufsforschung
- Mitteilungen aus der Arbeitsmarkt-und Berufsforschung
CLIENTELE: students, professors, administrators
ACCESS TO SERVICE: open to all users, paid services
TYPE & DESCRIPTION OF SERVICES PROVIDED: Provides library reference services,
selective dissemination of information and bibliographic data searches in
the fields of labour market and occupational research using its own data
base LITDOK and FODOK comprising 40,000 bibliographical items (including
literature and research documentation).

358 - INSTITUT FÜR AUSLANDSBEZIEHUNGEN, BIBLIOTHEK

SYNONYMOUS NAMES: Institute for Foreign Cultural Relations Library
ADDRESS: Charlottenplatz 17,
D-7000 Stuttgart 1,
GERMANY (FEDERAL REPUBLIC) ·
TEL: (0711) 2225-147 - TELEX: 07-23772 - TELEFAX: 49.711 - 224346
CREATED: 1917   *HEAD:* Mr. G Kuhn, Director
SIZE OF STAFF: Professional: 11   Other: 4   Total: 15
TYPE OF SERVICE: international; public; non-profit
MATERIALS DESCRIBING THE SERVICE: - Kuhn, G.; Pflüger, E., Auswärtige
Kulturbeziehungen und die Dokumentations- und Informationstätigkeit im
Institut für Auslandsbeziehungen in Zeitschrift für Kulturaustausch, 1978
WORKING LANGUAGE(S): German
SUBJECT COVERAGE: cultural anthropology; social sciences; sociology; cultural policy;
ethnic groups; minorities
GEOGRAPHICAL COVERAGE: global
DATA BEING PROCESSED AND SIZE: 320,000 books; 4,800 periodicals and newspapers; 5,600
microfilms, 11,000 maps
DATA PROCESSING METHODS: manual
TYPE OF ACTIVITY: data collection; data analysis
PUBLICATIONS: - Kuhn, G., Verzeichnis deutsch-auslandischer Gesellschaften und
ausländischer Gesellschaften in der Bundesrepublik Deutschland und Berlin
(West), 1986

CLIENTELE: 15,000 users p.a.
ACCESS TO SERVICE: open to all users, free of charge
TYPE & DESCRIPTION OF SERVICES PROVIDED: Provides library services, prepares materia
    for scientific papers, bibliographies and photocopies.

359 - INSTITUT FÜR WISSENSCHAFTLICHE ZUSAMMENARBEIT MIT ENTWICKLUNGSLÄNDERN

SYNONYMOUS NAMES: Institute for Scientific Cooperation
ADDRESS: Landhausstrasse 18,
    D-7400 Tübingen 1,
    GERMANY (FEDERAL REPUBLIC)
    TEL: (07071) 21871
CREATED: 1966   *HEAD:* Prof. Dr. J. Hohnholz, Director
SIZE OF STAFF: Professional: 7   Other: 18   Total: 25
TYPE OF SERVICE: non-profit
SUBJECT COVERAGE: sociology; political science; economics; law; education;
    humanities; international law, international history; languages philosophy
GEOGRAPHICAL COVERAGE: America; Africa; Asia
DATA PROCESSING METHODS: manual
TYPE OF ACTIVITY: data collection; publication
PERIODICALS PUBLISHED: - German studies
      - Economics
      - Universitas, Zeitschrift für Wissenschaft, Kunstund Literatur
PUBLICATIONS: - Recent German research in international economics, 1984
      - Indien-Probleme eines Schwellenlandes, 1983
      - Lateinamerika: ein Kontinent im Umbruch, 2000 Jahre nach Simon Boliva,
    1983
CLIENTELE: 35,000 users
ACCESS TO SERVICE: some paid services
TYPE & DESCRIPTION OF SERVICES PROVIDED: Its aim is to make recent research in the
    Federal Republic of Germany available to specialists and institutions in
    countries outside Europe. Provides bibliographic and literature searches.

360 - MAX-PLANCK-INSTITUT FÜR AUSLÄNDISCHES ÖFFENTLICHES RECHT UND VÖLKERRECHT, BIBLIOTHEK

SYNONYMOUS NAMES: Max Planck Institute for Comparative Public Law and International
    Law, Library
PARENT ORGANIZATION: Max-Planck-Gesellschaft zur Förderung der Wissenschaften e.V.
ADDRESS: Berliner Strasse 48,
    D-6900 Heidelberg 1,
    GERMANY (FEDERAL REPUBLIC)
    TEL: (06221) 482-1
CREATED: 1924   *HEAD:* Mr. J. Schwietzke, Head of Service
SIZE OF STAFF: Professional: 10   Other: 10   Total: 20
TYPE OF SERVICE: public; non-profit
MATERIALS DESCRIBING THE SERVICE: - Folders in English and French
WORKING LANGUAGE(S): English; French; German
SUBJECT COVERAGE: administrative sciences; political science; law; public

international law; treaties
GEOGRAPHICAL COVERAGE: global
DATA BEING PROCESSED AND SIZE: 315,793 books; 4,176 periodicals (including court
        reports)
DATA PROCESSING METHODS: manual; partially computerized
HARDWARE USED: RC-Partner 750 Personal-Computer
SOFTWARE USED: Genesys IuD-Software System; DBASE II; Word Star
STORAGE MEDIA: traditional shelving of publications; microcards; microfiches;
        microfilms
TYPE OF ACTIVITY: data collection; data analysis; publication
PERIODICALS PUBLISHED: - Fontes Iuris Gentium, series a, b and c
        - ZAÖRV: Journal of Comparative Public Law and International Law
        - Public International Law
        - Accessions List
PUBLICATIONS: - Beiträge zum ausländischen öffentlichen Recht und Völkerrecht
        (Contributions on comparative public law and international law)
        - Encyclopedia of Public International Law
CLIENTELE: researchers, postgraduate students, officials of national and
        international organizations and law courts
ACCESS TO SERVICE: services open to all users (documents of organizations for which
        the library is a depository library, for instance the UN and specialized
        agencies), free of charge
TYPE & DESCRIPTION OF SERVICES PROVIDED: Provides bibliographies from its index of
        articles (300,710 references), and index of treaties (57,700 references) and
        photocopies. Also provides on-line services using external data bases,
        BELINDIS, CED, CELEX, DBI, DEINJUNINET, DFN, DIALOG, ECHO, JNKA, JURIS,
        LEXIS, QUESTEL.

361 - MAX-PLANCK-INSTITUT FÜR AUSLÄNDISCHES UND INTERNATIONALES PATENT-, URHEBER- UND
        WETTBEWERBSRECHT, BIBLIOTHEK

SYNONYMOUS NAMES: Max-Planck-Institute for Foreign and International Patent,
        Copyright and Competition Law, Library
PARENT ORGANIZATION: Max-Planck-Gesellschaft zur Förderung der Wissenschaften e.v.
ADDRESS: Siebertstrasse 3,
        D-8000 Munich 80,
        GERMANY (FEDERAL REPUBLIC)
        EL: (089) 9246-1 - TELEX: (05) 23965 mapat
CREATED: 1966   HEAD: F.-K. Beier, Managing Director
                        G. Schricker, Director
SIZE OF STAFF: Professional: 4
TYPE OF SERVICE: national; private; non-profit
WORKING LANGUAGE(S): German
SUBJECT COVERAGE: law; international law
GEOGRAPHICAL COVERAGE: global
DATA BEING PROCESSED AND SIZE: 70,000 books
DATA PROCESSING METHODS: manual
TYPE OF ACTIVITY: data collection; data analysis; publication
PUBLICATIONS: - Bibliograhies on European patent law
        - Bibliographies on biotechnology and patent law
CLIENTELE: researchers

ACCESS TO SERVICE: open to specific categories of users, free of charge
TYPE & DESCRIPTION OF SERVICES PROVIDED: Provides library services.

362 - PHILIPPS-UNIVERSITÄT, MARBURG, INFORMATIONSZENTRUM FÜR FREMDSPRACHENFORSCHUNG

SYNONYMOUS NAMES: IFS;
    Philipps University, Foreign Language Research Information Center
ADDRESS: Hans-Meerwein-Strasse,
    Lahnberge,
    D-3550 Marburg,
    GERMANY (FEDERAL REPUBLIC)
    TEL: (06421) 282-141 - TELEX: 482372 UMRD
CREATED: 1967   *HEAD:* Dr. R. Freudenstein, Director
SIZE OF STAFF: Professional: 5   Other: 2   Total: 7
TYPE OF SERVICE: international; public; non-profit
SYSTEMS & NETWORKS ATTACHED TO: Dokumentationsring Päedagogik (DOPAED)
MATERIALS DESCRIBING THE SERVICE: - Freudenstein, R., IFS - Informationen für
    Sprachlehrer (also in English), 1983
WORKING LANGUAGE(S): German
SUBJECT COVERAGE: education; linguistics; modern foreign language teaching and
    research
GEOGRAPHICAL COVERAGE: Austria; Canada; France; German Democratic Republic; Germany
    (Federal Republic); United Kingdom; Italy; Latin America; USSR; Spain;
    Switzerland; USA
DATA BEING PROCESSED AND SIZE: books; periodicals; working papers; project reports;
    informal tests; commercial and non-commercial teaching materials;
    microfiches
DATA PROCESSING METHODS: computerized
HARDWARE USED: IBM PC
SOFTWARE USED: LIDOS
STORAGE MEDIA: fiches; discs; hard-disc
TYPE OF ACTIVITY: data analysis; data collection; distribution of information;
    publication
PERIODICALS PUBLISHED: - Bibliographie Moderner Fremdsprachenunterricht, 4 p.a.
    - Dokumentation Neusprachlicher Unterricht
CLIENTELE: student teachers and teachers of foreign languages, in-service training
    seminars, universities, documentation centers
ACCESS TO SERVICE: open to all users, free of charge
TYPE & DESCRIPTION OF SERVICES PROVIDED: Provides bibliographic, literature abstract
    and survey searches, selective dissemination of information and photocopies

363 - PRESS UND INFORMATIONSAMT DER BUNDESREGIERUNG

SYNONYMOUS NAMES: BPA;
    Federal Press and Information Office
PARENT ORGANIZATION: Zentrales Dokumentationssystem
ADDRESS: Welckerstrasse 11,
    5300 Bonn,
    GERMANY (FEDERAL REPUBLIC)

TEL: 02221/ 2082455 - TELEX: 0886741/743
CREATED: 1967
SIZE OF STAFF: Professional: 16   Other: 11   Total: 27
TYPE OF SERVICE: national; public; non-profit
MATERIALS DESCRIBING THE SERVICE: - Fachinformation/Programme der Bundesregierung,
         1985-1988
         - Das Presse- und Informationsamt der Bundesregierung
WORKING LANGUAGE(S): German
SUBJECT COVERAGE: political science; politics
GEOGRAPHICAL COVERAGE: Germany (Federal Republic)
DATA BEING PROCESSED AND SIZE: periodicals, reports; 1,250.000 press clippings, news
         from news agencies, evaluation reports on TV and radio programmes
DATA PROCESSING METHODS: computerized
HARDWARE USED: SIEMENS 7550 D
SOFTWARE USED: GOLEM, PASSAT, FIDAS, EDOR
TYPE OF ACTIVITY: distribution of information
CLIENTELE: members of the federal ministries and agencies, parliament and political
         parties, universities, publishing houses, radio and television stations,
         general public concerned with politics
ACCESS TO SERVICE: open to specific categories of users, free of charge
TYPE & DESCRIPTION OF SERVICES PROVIDED: Provides bibliographic and literature
         searches of information using its own data base BPA-DOK, selective
         dissemination of information, photocopies and microforms upon request.

364 - STATISTISCHES BUNDESAMT, ABT. BIBLIOTHEK-DOCUMENTATION-ARCHIV

SYNONYMOUS NAMES: Federal Statistical Office, Library-Documentation-Archives Services
ADDRESS: Gustav-Stresemann-Ring 11,
         Postach 5528,
         D-6200 Wiesbaden 1,
         GERMANY (FEDERAL REPUBLIC)
CREATED: 1948   *HEAD:* Steiger, Head
SIZE OF STAFF: Professional: 9   Other: 18   Total: 27
TYPE OF SERVICE: national; public; non-profit
WORKING LANGUAGE(S): German; English; French
SUBJECT COVERAGE: statistics; economics; demography
GEOGRAPHICAL COVERAGE: global
DATA BEING PROCESSED AND SIZE: books; articles
DATA PROCESSING METHODS: partially computerized
HARDWARE USED: Siemens
SOFTWARE USED: own
STORAGE MEDIA: traditional shelving of publications; microfiches
TYPE OF ACTIVITY: distribution of information; publication
PERIODICALS PUBLISHED: - Neues aus Zeitschriften, (Current contents of statistical
         periodicals)
         - Neue Bücher und Aufsätze, (Accession list including articles)
         - Zeitschriftenverzeichnis, (list of periodicals)
PUBLICATIONS: - Profildienst = Selective Dissemination of Information
CLIENTELE: scientists and students
ACCESS TO SERVICE: services open to specific categories of users, free of charge
TYPE & DESCRIPTION OF SERVICES PROVIDED: Provides library services, literature

abstract and survey searches, selective dissemination of information and photocopies. Also provides on-line searches using own data base "STALIS Statistical Literature Information System".

365 - UNIVERSITÄT DÜSSELDORF, FORSCHUNGSABTEILUNG FÜR PHILOSOPHISCHEN INFORMATION UN DOKUMENTATION

SYNONYMOUS NAMES: University of Düsseldorf, Research Division for Philosophy
        Information and Documentation, Philosophy Information Service
ADDRESS: Philosophisches Institut Geb. 2321,
        Universitätsstr. 1,
        D-4000 Düsseldorf 1,
        GERMANY (FEDERAL REPUBLIC)
        TEL: (49-211) 311-2913 - TELEX: 8547-348 UNI D
CREATED: 1967   *HEAD:* Prof. Dr. N. Henrichs, Head
SIZE OF STAFF: Professional: 2   Other: 2   Total: 4
TYPE OF SERVICE: international; public; non-profit
SYSTEMS & NETWORKS ATTACHED TO: DFN (German Research Network)
WORKING LANGUAGE(S): German; English; French
SUBJECT COVERAGE: philosophy; science philosophy; logic; culture; sociology; ethics;
        metaphysics; cultural anthropology
GEOGRAPHICAL COVERAGE: global
DATA BEING PROCESSED AND SIZE: 50,000 articles, including biographical data, letters
        of philosophers (1750-1850)
HARDWARE USED: SIEMENS 7.580-S (BS 2000)
SOFTWARE USED: GOLEM
STORAGE MEDIA: discs; microfiches
TYPE OF ACTIVITY: data analysis; distribution of information; SSID training;
        publication
PUBLICATIONS: - Indexes
CLIENTELE: academics, students, general public (approx. 700 p.a.)
ACCESS TO SERVICE: services open to all users, free of charge
TYPE & DESCRIPTION OF SERVICES PROVIDED: Provides bibliographic, literature abstract
        and quantitative data searches, selective dissemination of information,
        magnetic tapes and microforms. Also provides on-line services using own dat
        bases "PHILIS" and "EPISTOLOGRAPHIE".

366 - UNIVERSITÄT KIEL, INSTITUT FÜR WELTWIRTSCHAFT, BIBLIOTHEK

SYNONYMOUS NAMES: University of Kiel, Institute of World Economics, Library;
        Zentralbibliothek der Wirtschaftswissenschaften in der Bundesrepublik
        Deutschland;
        National Library of Economics in the Federal Republic of Germany
ADDRESS: Düsternbrooker Weg 120-122,
        Postfach 4309,
        D-2300 Kiel 1,
        GERMANY (FEDERAL REPUBLIC)
        TEL: (0431) 884-1 - TELEX: 02 92 479
CREATED: 1914   *HEAD:* Dr. E. Heidemann, Director

SIZE OF STAFF: Professional: 16   Other: 120   Total: 136
TYPE OF SERVICE: national; public; non-profit
MATERIALS DESCRIBING THE SERVICE: - Seusing, E., the Information activities of the
        National Library of Economics in the Federal Republic of Germany.
        "INSPEL.IFLA-Division of Special Libraries", Den Haag, 1986
WORKING LANGUAGE(S): German; English and other important languages
SUBJECT COVERAGE: economics; macroeconomics
GEOGRAPHICAL COVERAGE: global
DATA BEING PROCESSED AND SIZE: 740,345 books and reprints; 17,800 periodicals
DATA PROCESSING METHODS: partially computerized
HARDWARE USED: Siemens 7.570
SOFTWARE USED: BIS (Fa, Dabis, Hamburg)
STORAGE MEDIA: traditional shelving of publications
TYPE OF ACTIVITY: distribution of information
PERIODICALS PUBLISHED: - Bibliographie der Wirtschaftswissenschaften, 2 p.a.
        - Kieler Schrifttumskunden zu Wirtschaft und Gesellschaft, irr. since 1960
PUBLICATIONS: - Zeitschriftenverzeichnisse
CLIENTELE: faculty students, scholars, all interested persons
ACCESS TO SERVICE: open to all users, free of charge, some paid services
TYPE & DESCRIPTION OF SERVICES PROVIDED: Provides library services, selective
        dissemination of information and bibliographic, literature and survey
        searches using its 8,518,989 items card catalogue and ECONIS (Economics
        Information System) database. Also provides microforms and photocopies.

**367 - UNIVERSITÄT TRIER, ZENTRALSTELLE FÜR PSYCHOLOGISCHE INFORMATION UND
        DOKUMENTATION**

SYNONYMOUS NAMES: ZPID;
        Trier University, Center for Psychological Information and Documentation
ADDRESS: Tarforst,
        Postfach 3825,
        D-5500 Trier,
        GERMANY (FEDERAL REPUBLIC)
        TEL: (0651) 2012877
CREATED: 1972   *HEAD:* Prof. Dr. L. Montada,
SIZE OF STAFF: Professional: 8   Other: 8   Total: 16
TYPE OF SERVICE: national; public
SYSTEMS & NETWORKS ATTACHED TO: Fachinformationssystem 1 (FIS 1) Gesundheitswesen,
        Medizin, Biologie, Sport
MATERIALS DESCRIBING THE SERVICE: - Informationsmaterial
WORKING LANGUAGE(S): English; German
SUBJECT COVERAGE: psychology
GEOGRAPHICAL COVERAGE: German language literature from Germany (Federal Republic),
        German Democratic Republic, Austria and Switzerland
DATA BEING PROCESSED AND SIZE: 5,000 books; 26,000 articles; 6,000 reports and
        dissertations
DATA PROCESSING METHODS: computerized
HARDWARE USED: SIEMENS
SOFTWARE USED: GRIPS
STORAGE MEDIA: traditional shelving of publications; discs; tapes
TYPE OF ACTIVITY: data collection; data analysis; distribution of information; SSID

scientific and methodological activities; SSID training; publication
PERIODICALS PUBLISHED: - Psychologischer Index. Referatedienst über die
psychologische Literatur aus den deutschsprachigen Ländern, 4 p.a.
- Psyndexinfo
PUBLICATIONS: - Bibliographie deutschsprachiger psychologischer Dissertationen
- Bibliographien zur Psychologie
ACCESS TO SERVICE: open to the general public, paid services
TYPE & DESCRIPTION OF SERVICES PROVIDED: Provides bibliographic and literature
searches using its own data base PSYNDEX, as well as other data bases such
as PsycINFO, MEDLARS, EMBASE, Social SCIsearch through DIMDI.

368 - UNIVERSITÄT ZU KÖLN, ZENTRALARCHIV FÜR EMPIRISCHE SOZIALFORSCHUNG

SYNONYMOUS NAMES: University of Cologne, Central Archive for Empirical Social
Research
ADDRESS: Bachemer Strasse 40,
D-5000 Cologne 41,
GERMANY (FEDERAL REPUBLIC)
TEL: (0221) 44.40.88
CREATED: 1960   *HEAD:* Mr. E. Mochmann, Director
SIZE OF STAFF: Professional: 1   Other: 39   Total: 40
TYPE OF SERVICE: national; public; non-profit
SYSTEMS & NETWORKS ATTACHED TO: International Federation of Data Organizations for
the Social Sciences
MATERIALS DESCRIBING THE SERVICE: - ZA - data service
WORKING LANGUAGE(S): German; English
SUBJECT COVERAGE: social sciences; sociology; social welfare; political science;
education; mass communication; statistics
GEOGRAPHICAL COVERAGE: global; Germany (Federal Republic); Austria; Switzerland
DATA BEING PROCESSED AND SIZE: 1100 data sets; 8000 books; 1500 research reports
DATA PROCESSING METHODS: computerized
HARDWARE USED: IBM 4331, IBM 370/MDS 2400 (for data manipulation), CDC 72/76 (local
clientele), SIEMENS 4004 (tape conversion)
SOFTWARE USED: ZAR-System. For data preparation: in house programs: ZADCL, OSIRIS,
CROSS TABS, UTILITY CODER; For analysis: SPSS, OSIRIS
STORAGE MEDIA: tapes, disks
TYPE OF ACTIVITY: data collection; data analysis; consulting
PERIODICALS PUBLISHED:
- ZA Information, 2 p.a. since 1977
- Empirical Social Research, 1 p.a.
PUBLICATIONS: - ZA list of holdings
- Norporth, H., Wählerverhalten in der Bundesrepublik, 1980
- Mochmann, E., Computerstrategien für die Kommunikationsanalyse, 1980
CLIENTELE: researchers
ACCESS TO SERVICE: open to specific categories of users, reimbursement of marginal
costs
TYPE & DESCRIPTION OF SERVICES PROVIDED: Compiles information on empirical social
research. Includes library services, provision of surveys, data sets and
code books for secondary analysis or for immediate analysis.

69 - ZENTRALE DOKUMENTATIONSSTELLE DER FREIEN WOHLFAHRTSPFLEGE FÜR FLÜCHTLINGE

SYNONYMOUS NAMES: ZDWF;
        Refugee Documentation Center
ADDRESS: Hans Boeckler Str. 3,
        Postfach 301069,
        5300 Bonn 3,
        GERMANY (FEDERAL REPUBLIC)
        TEL: (0228) 462047
CREATED: 1980   *HEAD:* Mr. B. Martens-Parrée,
SIZE OF STAFF: Professional: 5   Other: 5   Total: 10
TYPE OF SERVICE: international; public; private; non-profit
SYSTEMS & NETWORKS ATTACHED TO: HURIDOCS (Human Rights Documentation System)
MATERIALS DESCRIBING THE SERVICE: - ZDWF/Refugee Documentation Center (leaflet)
SUBJECT COVERAGE: law; social welfare; refugees problems
GEOGRAPHICAL COVERAGE: all countries concerned with refugees problems
DATA BEING PROCESSED AND SIZE: 4,500 books; 2,000 press clippings; 1,000 reports;
        1,000 articles; 5,000 legal decisions; unpublished literature
DATA PROCESSING METHODS: computerized
SOFTWARE USED: GRIPS
STORAGE MEDIA: traditional shelving of publications, tapes, discs
TYPE OF ACTIVITY: data collection; distribution of information; publication
PUBLICATIONS: - Reference works
CLIENTELE: parliamentary members, public administrations, research institutes, law-
        courts, lawyers, social counsellors, social workers, general public
ACCESS TO SERVICE: services open to all users, free of charge
TYPE & DESCRIPTION OF SERVICES PROVIDED: Provides library services, bibliographic and
        literature abstract searches of information, selective dissemination of
        information regarding new tendencies and new material in the field of
        jurisdiction, provision of situation reports on crisis areas and countries
        of origin, provision of compilations on legal and administrative practices
        of German federal states. Access to this information is available through
        ASYLDOC data base containing 19,000 entries.

70 - ZENTRUM FÜR HISTORISCHE SOZIALFORSCHUNG

SYNONYMOUS NAMES: ZHSF;
        Center for Historical Social Research
PARENT ORGANIZATION: Zentralarchiv für Empirische Sozialforschung, Universität zu
        Köln
ADDRESS: Bachemerstr. 40,
        D-5000 Cologne 41,
        GERMANY (FEDERAL REPUBLIC)
        TEL: (0221) 4470-3157
CREATED: 1977   *HEAD:* Dr. W. H. Schröder, Director
SIZE OF STAFF: Total: 7
TYPE OF SERVICE: non-profit
SYSTEMS & NETWORKS ATTACHED TO: International Federation of Data Organizations (IFDO)
MATERIALS DESCRIBING THE SERVICE: - Printed reports
SUBJECT COVERAGE: sociology; history; political science
GEOGRAPHICAL COVERAGE: Germany (Federal Republic); Austria; Switzerland

Germany, Federal Rep. / Allemagne, Rép féd / Alemania, Rep Fed

DATA PROCESSING METHODS: computerized
TYPE OF ACTIVITY: data collection; data analysis
PERIODICALS PUBLISHED: - Historical Social Research/Historische Sozialforschung, 4
      p.a.
PUBLICATIONS: - Historisch-sozialwissenschaftliche Forschungen, vols. 1-22, 1988
CLIENTELE: university researchers
ACCESS TO SERVICE: open to all users, free of charge
TYPE & DESCRIPTION OF SERVICES PROVIDED: Archives and disseminates machine-readable
      historical data for comparative and for secondary analyses.

371 - DEUTSCHES INSTITUT FÜR URBANISTIK, ARBEITSBEREICH INFORMATION UND DOKUMENTATIC

SYNONYMOUS NAMES: German Institute of Urban Affairs, Information and Documentation
      Division
ADDRESS: Str. des 17. Juni 110,
      Postfach 12 62 24,
      D-1000 Berlin 12,
      BERLIN (WEST)
      TEL: 030-39001 - TELEX: 8882617 DST
HEAD: Prof. Dr. D. Sanberzweig,
TYPE OF SERVICE: national; non-profit
SYSTEMS & NETWORKS ATTACHED TO: ORLIS (Literaturdatenbank zur Orts-Regional-und
      Landes Planung); DBI (Deutsches Bibliotheksinstitut); INKA
      (Informationssystem Karlsruhe)
MATERIALS DESCRIBING THE SERVICE: - Orlis Benutzerinformation
SUBJECT COVERAGE: administrative sciences; urban development
GEOGRAPHICAL COVERAGE: Germany (Federal Republic)
DATA BEING PROCESSED AND SIZE: books; journals articles; surveys; on-going research,
      planning reports; grey literature
HARDWARE USED: GOLEM Siemens BS 2000
SOFTWARE USED: GOLEM; own software
STORAGE MEDIA: traditional shelving of publications
TYPE OF ACTIVITY: data collection; data analysis; distribution of information; SSID
      scientific and methodological activities; publication
PERIODICALS PUBLISHED:
      - Kommunalwissenschaftliche Dissertationen
CLIENTELE: municipal administrators, executors
ACCESS TO SERVICE: services open to specific categories of users
TYPE & DESCRIPTION OF SERVICES PROVIDED: Provides bibliographic, literature abstrac
      and quantitative data searches of information, on-line services using its
      own data base "ORLIS", and production of information on magnetic tapes or
      discs.

372 - FREIE UNIVERSITÄT BERLIN, INFORMATIONSZENTRUM POLITIK UND MASSENKOMMUNIKATION

SYNONYMOUS NAMES: IPM;
      Free University of Berlin, Information Centre for Politics and Mass
      Communication
ADDRESS: Paulinenstrasse 22,

        *The interests of Berlin (West) are represented in the United Nations
        by the Federal Republic of Germany

D-1000 Berlin 45,
BERLIN (WEST)
TEL: (030) 8337027
CREATED: 1983   *HEAD:* Prof. Dr. W. Krumholz, Director
SIZE OF STAFF: Professional: 11   Other: 6   Total: 17
TYPE OF SERVICE: national; public; non-profit
MATERIALS DESCRIBING THE SERVICE: - Forschungsmarkt Berlin, Kooperationsangebote der
    öffentlich geförderten Forschungseinrichtungen in Berlin in die Praxis,
    Hrsg: Der Senator für Wissenschaft und Forschung. Der Senator für
    Wissenschaft und Verkehr, Berlin 1983, 15-16 p.
SUBJECT COVERAGE: political science; mass communication
DATA BEING PROCESSED AND SIZE: 5,000 books; 8,600 newspapers; 5,000 research reports
DATA PROCESSING METHODS: partially computerized
HARDWARE USED: Siemens
SOFTWARE USED: GOLEM; FIDAS
STORAGE MEDIA: discs
TYPE OF ACTIVITY: data collection; distribution of information; publication; SSID
    training
PERIODICALS PUBLISHED:
    - Politische Dokumentation, POLDOK. Referatedienst Deutschsrachije
    Zeitschriften
CLIENTELE: professors, students, practitioners in politics and mass communication
ACCESS TO SERVICE: open to all users; payment is conditioned by the kind of service
TYPE & DESCRIPTION OF SERVICES PROVIDED: Provides bibliographic, literature and
    survey searches and expertises. Its data bases are: POLDOK-Lit with 33,000
    items in politics; POLDOK-FODOK with 6,000 items in politics, PUBLDOK-Lit
    with 20,000 items in mass communication, and PUBL DOK-INST with 3,000
    factual items in mass communication, via GENIOS, Düsseldorf.

**73 - GHANA INSTITUTE OF MANAGEMENT AND PUBLIC ADMINISTRATION, LIBRARY AND
    DOCUMENTATION CENTRE**

SYNONYMOUS NAMES: GIMPA Library and Documentation Centre
ADDRESS: P.O. Box 50,
    Greenhill,
    GHANA
    TEL: 77625
    CABLE: GIMPA, ACHIMOTA
CREATED: 1961   *HEAD:* E. Cabutey-Adodoadji, Librarian
SIZE OF STAFF: Professional: 3   Other: 12   Total: 15
TYPE OF SERVICE: international; public; non-profit
SYSTEMS & NETWORKS ATTACHED TO: The African Network of Administration Information
    (ANAI)
MATERIALS DESCRIBING THE SERVICE: - Ghana Institute of Management & Public
    Administration: Calendar, 1977-78, pp. 41-43
    - Ghana 1977: an official handbook. Accra, Information Services Department,
    1977. pp. 382-383
SUBJECT COVERAGE: administrative sciences; economics; history; law; political
    science; psychology; social anthropology; cultural anthropology; social
    sciences; sociology; statistics; management; public finance; economic

The interests of Berlin (West) are represented in the United Nations
by the Federal Republic of Germany

planning; development planning; demography
GEOGRAPHICAL COVERAGE: Ghana; Africa
DATA BEING PROCESSED AND SIZE: official government documents dating back to 1895,
30,000 books; 200 serials; reports, etc.
DATA PROCESSING METHODS: Manual
STORAGE MEDIA: media resource equipment, e.g. video
PERIODICALS PUBLISHED: - Greenhill Administration Sources, 4 p.a.
- GIMPA Library Bulletin, 6 p.a.
- Theses and Research Projects
CLIENTELE: course participants, faculty members, researchers and administrative sta
(over 200 users)
ACCESS TO SERVICE: for internal users, open to researchers free of charge
TYPE & DESCRIPTION OF SERVICES PROVIDED: Provides subject bibliographies, reading
lists, selective dissemination of information, inter-library loans,
photocopies and film shows.

374 - RESEARCH LIBRARY ON AFRICAN AFFAIRS

PARENT ORGANIZATION: Ghana Library Board
ADDRESS: P.O. Box 2970,
Accra,
GHANA
TEL: 28402
CREATED: 1961   HEAD: Ms. C. D. T. Kwei,
SIZE OF STAFF: Professional: 3
TYPE OF SERVICE: national; public; non-profit
MATERIALS DESCRIBING THE SERVICE: - Guide to the services of the Research Library o
African Affairs, 1986, 5 p.
WORKING LANGUAGE(S): English
SUBJECT COVERAGE: social sciences; economics; education; geography; history;
linguistics; social anthropology; cultural anthropology
GEOGRAPHICAL COVERAGE: Ghana; Africa
DATA BEING PROCESSED AND SIZE: 32,000 books; 4,000 pamphlets; 2,500 periodicals; 50
microfilms, microfiches
DATA PROCESSING METHODS: manual
PERIODICALS PUBLISHED: - Ghana national bibliography, 1 p.a.
- Ghana: a current bibliography, 6 p.a.
- Special subject bibliographies, irr. since 1962
PUBLICATIONS: - Union list of Africana periodicals in Balme Library, Institute of
African Studies Library and the Research Library on African Affairs
CLIENTELE: researchers, civil servants, diplomats, general public
ACCESS TO SERVICE: open to all users, free of charge
TYPE & DESCRIPTION OF SERVICES PROVIDED: Provides library services, query answering
service, retrospective bibliographic searches, and photocopies.

Greece / Grèce / Grecia

375 - ETHNIKON KENTRON KINONIKON EREVNON

SYNONYMOUS NAMES: National Centre of Social Research
PARENT ORGANIZATION: Secretariat of Research and Technology
ADDRESS: 1, Sophocleous Street,
105 59 Athens,
GREECE
TEL: 32.12.611
CREATED: 1961   *HEAD:* Prof. K. Tsoukalas, Research Director
SIZE OF STAFF: Total: 3
SUBJECT COVERAGE: social sciences
GEOGRAPHICAL COVERAGE: Greece
DATA BEING PROCESSED AND SIZE: 30,000 vols.
DATA PROCESSING METHODS: manual
PERIODICALS PUBLISHED: - Epitheoresi Koinonikon Evevnon, 4 p.a.
PUBLICATIONS: - Reference books, Athens, 1975
- Current foreign language periodicals: subject catalogue, Athens, 1975
- Migration: a listing of items on migration in the library, Athens, 1976
CLIENTELE: researchers, professionals and students
ACCESS TO SERVICE: open to all users, free of charge
TYPE & DESCRIPTION OF SERVICES PROVIDED: Provides library services, bibliographic and
photocopies upon request.

Grenada / Grenade / Granada

376 - MINISTRY OF PLANNING, DEVELOPMENT AND TRAINING, NATIONAL DOCUMENTATION CENTRE

ADDRESS: St. George's,
GRENADA
TEL: 440-2731 - TELEX: 3481
CREATED: 1981   *HEAD:* Ms. C. Robinson, Documentalist
SIZE OF STAFF: Professional: 1   Other: 1   Total: 3
TYPE OF SERVICE: national; public; non-profit
SYSTEMS & NETWORKS ATTACHED TO: OECSS INFONET (Organization of Eastern Caribbean
States Information Network); CARISPLAN (Caribbean Information System for
Social and Economic Planning)
WORKING LANGUAGE(S): English
SUBJECT COVERAGE: social sciences
GEOGRAPHICAL COVERAGE: Grenada; global
DATA BEING PROCESSED AND SIZE: books, articles, reports, seminars, courses
DATA PROCESSING METHODS: partially computerized
HARDWARE USED: IBM/PC
SOFTWARE USED: CDS micro ISIS
STORAGE MEDIA: traditional shelving of publications
TYPE OF ACTIVITY: data collection; distribution of information; publication
CLIENTELE: government officers, students, researchers
ACCESS TO SERVICE: services open to specific categories of users, free of charge
TYPE & DESCRIPTION OF SERVICES PROVIDED: Provides library services, bibliographic and
literature abstract searches of information and selective dissemination of
information.

Guatemala

377 - SECRETARÍA PERMANENTE DEL TRATADO GENERAL DE INTEGRACIÓN ECONÓMICA CENTROAMERICANA, CENTRO DE DOCUMENTACIÓN E INFORMACIÓN

SYNONYMOUS NAMES: SIECA/CDI;
      Permanent Secretariat of the General Treaty for the Economic Integration of Central America, Information and Documentation Centre
ADDRESS: 4a. av. 10-25, Zona 14,
      Apartado Postal 1237,
      01914 Guatemala,
      GUATEMALA
      TEL: 682151 - TELEX: 5676 ANSTEL-GU-SIECA
      CABLE: Integración Sieca
CREATED: 1968   *HEAD:* Ms. I. de González, Head
SIZE OF STAFF: Professional: 3   Other: 3   Total: 6
TYPE OF SERVICE: international; public; non-profit
WORKING LANGUAGE(S): Spanish
SUBJECT COVERAGE: social sciences; demography; economics; law; social welfare
GEOGRAPHICAL COVERAGE: Guatemala; El Salvador; Honduras; Nicaragua; Costa Rica
DATA BEING PROCESSED AND SIZE: 400 books; 10,000 documents
DATA PROCESSING METHODS: manual
TYPE OF ACTIVITY: publication
PERIODICALS PUBLISHED:
      - Boletines de Nuevas Adquisiciones
CLIENTELE: students, researchers, government officials
ACCESS TO SERVICE: services open to all users
TYPE & DESCRIPTION OF SERVICES PROVIDED: Provides bibliographies, information searches and selective dissemination of information.

378 - UNIVERSIDAD DE SAN CARLOS DE GUATEMALA, BIBLIOTECA CENTRAL

SYNONYMOUS NAMES: San Carlos University of Guatemala, Central Library
ADDRESS: Ciudad Universitaria, zona 12,
      Ciudad de Guatemala 01012,
      GUATEMALA
      TEL: 760790-4
CREATED: 1967   *HEAD:* Mr. V. Castillo Lopez, Director
SIZE OF STAFF: Professional: 15   Other: 35   Total: 54
TYPE OF SERVICE: international; public; non-profit
SUBJECT COVERAGE: social sciences; economics; education; history; law; linguistics; philosophy
GEOGRAPHICAL COVERAGE: Central America
DATA BEING PROCESSED AND SIZE: 200,000 books
DATA PROCESSING METHODS: manual
STORAGE MEDIA: fiches
TYPE OF ACTIVITY: publication
PERIODICALS PUBLISHED:
      - Boletin de Nuevas Adquisiciones
      - Boletin de Libros Clasificados
CLIENTELE: faculty members, teachers, researchers and students (50,000 p.a.)

CCESS TO SERVICE: paid services open to all users
YPE & DESCRIPTION OF SERVICES PROVIDED: Provides library services, bibliographic and
 literature abstract searches, selective dissemination of information, and
 photocopies.

Guyana

*79 - STATE PLANNING SECRETARIAT

SYNONYMOUS NAMES: SPS
ADDRESS: 229 South Road,
 Lacytown,
 Georgetown,
 GUYANA
SIZE OF STAFF: Professional: 50   Other: 35   Total: 85
TYPE OF SERVICE: national; non-profit
SYSTEMS & NETWORKS ATTACHED TO: Ministry of Planning and Development
MATERIALS DESCRIBING THE SERVICE: - State Planning Commission Act (a legal document
 outlining the scope of the Commission's activities)
WORKING LANGUAGE(S): English
SUBJECT COVERAGE: economics; education
GEOGRAPHICAL COVERAGE: Guyana
DATA BEING PROCESSED AND SIZE: 10,000 books; 3,000 articles; 4,000 papers; 200
 training courses; reports including research and seminars
DATA PROCESSING METHODS: partially computerized for loans only
HARDWARE USED: IBM PC XT
SOFTWARE USED: Dbase III PLUS
STORAGE MEDIA: traditional shelving of publications
TYPE OF ACTIVITY: data collection; data analysis; distribution of information
CLIENTELE: planners, research assistants, secondary-school and university students
ACCESS TO SERVICE: services open to specific categories of users, free of charge
TYPE & DESCRIPTION OF SERVICES PROVIDED: Provides library services, bibliographic and
 quantitative data searches, selective dissemination of information, and
 photocopies. Also provides on-line services using external data bases.

Haiti / Haïti / Haiti

880 - INSTITUT HAÏTIEN DE STATISTIQUES ET D'INFORMATIQUE

SYNONYMOUS NAMES: IHSI
PARENT ORGANIZATION: Ministère des Finances
ADDRESS: Blvd. Harry Truman,
 Cité Exposition,
 Port-au-Prince,
 HAITI
 TEL: 2-1011
CREATED: 1951   *HEAD:* Mr. L. Smith, Director General
SIZE OF STAFF: Professional: 3
TYPE OF SERVICE: national; public; non-profit
MATERIALS DESCRIBING THE SERVICE: - L'Institut Haïtien de Statistiques, son
 organisation, ses réalisations, 1980

- Rapport d'évaluation et programme de travail de l'IHSI, 1983
SUBJECT COVERAGE: economics; statistics; demography
GEOGRAPHICAL COVERAGE: Haiti
DATA BEING PROCESSED AND SIZE: Data bases (censuses, statistical surveys); economic
    activities; administrative processes, research
DATA PROCESSING METHODS: computerized
HARDWARE USED: Wang 2200; Wang VS 80; IBMXT; AT
SOFTWARE USED: own programmes with BASIC, COBOL and FORTRAN
STORAGE MEDIA: tapes, discs, disquettes
TYPE OF ACTIVITY: data collection; data analysis; distribution of information;
    publication
PERIODICALS PUBLISHED:
    - Bulletin Trimestriel de Statistique, 4. p.a.
    - Bulletin de Statistique, Supplément Annuel, 1 p.a.
    - Enquête Trimestrielle de Conjoncture, 4 p.a.
CLIENTELE: general public
ACCESS TO SERVICE: open to all users, free of charge
TYPE & DESCRIPTION OF SERVICES PROVIDED: Provision of data for secondary analysis.

Honduras

381 - CENTRO DE DOCUMENTACIÓN DE HONDURAS

SYNONYMOUS NAMES: CEDOH
ADDRESS: Apartado Postal 1882,
        Tegucigalpa, D.C.,
        HONDURAS
CREATED: 1980   *HEAD:* Mr. V. Meza, Director
SIZE OF STAFF: Total: 5
TYPE OF SERVICE: national; private; non-profit
SUBJECT COVERAGE: economics; political science
GEOGRAPHICAL COVERAGE: Honduras; Central America
DATA PROCESSING METHODS: manual
TYPE OF ACTIVITY: data collection; publication
PERIODICALS PUBLISHED:
    - Boletín Informativo del Centro de Documentación de Honduras
ACCESS TO SERVICE: services open to all users, free of charge
TYPE & DESCRIPTION OF SERVICES PROVIDED: Provides library services, information
        searches, selective dissemination of information and photocopies.

Hungary / Hongrie / Hungría

382 - FOVÁROSI SZABÓ ERVIN KÖNYVTÁR SZOCIOLÓGIAI DOKUMENTÁCIÓS OSZTÁLY

SYNONYMOUS NAMES: Metropolitan Ervin Szabo Library, Budapest, Sociology Department
ADDRESS: Szabó Ervin tér 1,
        H-1371 Budapest,
        HUNGARY
        TEL: 34.15.76
        CABLE: 1371 Budapest 5 Pf. 487
CREATED: 1968   *HEAD:* Mr. J. Báthory, Head

IZE OF STAFF: Professional: 7   Other: 2   Total: 9
YPE OF SERVICE: national; public; non-profit
ORKING LANGUAGE(S): Hungarian; English
UBJECT COVERAGE: sociology; social sciences; social welfare
ATA BEING PROCESSED AND SIZE: 100,000 books and 20,000 volumes of bound periodicals,
     integrated with the holdings of the Metropolitan Ervin Szabó Library
ATA PROCESSING METHODS: partially computerized
ARDWARE USED: IBM PC AT
OFTWARE USED: Microisis
TORAGE MEDIA: traditional shelving of publications; card catalogues; discs
YPE OF ACTIVITY: data collection; data analysis; publication; SSID scientific and
     methodological activities
ERIODICALS PUBLISHED:
     - Sociological Information; Selected Bibliography of Hungarian Sociological
     Literature, 4 p.a.
UBLICATIONS: - Thematic sociological bibliographies
LIENTELE: 1,400 readers per year
CCESS TO SERVICE: services open to all users, some paid services, some free of
     charge
YPE & DESCRIPTION OF SERVICES PROVIDED: Provides library services, bibliographic,
     literature and survey searches, selective dissemination of information and
     photocopies. The data bases are "Sociological Information", containing
     30,000 bibliographical items covering the Hungarian sociological literature,
     and "SDI-Sociology" containing 500 bibliographical items covering
     abstracts of articles from current foreign journals.

83 - KOPINT-DATORG KONJUNKTURA- PIACKUTATÓ ÉS INFORMATIKAI INTÉZET

YNONYMOUS NAMES: KOPINT-DATORG Institute for Economics, Market Research and
     Informatics
DDRESS: Dorottya u.6,
     H-1051 Budapest,
     HUNGARY
     TEL: 184-055 - TELEX: 225646
     KONJUNKTURA BUDAPEST
REATED: 1964   *HEAD:* Mr. J. Deák, General Director
YPE OF SERVICE: international; public; private; profit; non-profit
ORKING LANGUAGE(S): Hungarian; English
UBJECT COVERAGE: economics; foreign trade
EOGRAPHICAL COVERAGE: global
ATA BEING PROCESSED AND SIZE: books; journals; periodicals; unpublished studies;
     statistics
ATA PROCESSING METHODS: partially computerized
ARDWARE USED: Siemens; IBM PC's
OFTWARE USED: own
TORAGE MEDIA: traditional shelving of publications; tapes; discs; microfiches
YPE OF ACTIVITY: data analysis; data collection; distribution of information
ERIODICALS PUBLISHED: - Directory of Hungarian Foreign Trade Companies, 1 p.a.
     - Business Partner Hungary, in Hungarian and German
LIENTELE: economic researchers, management and marketing consultants (50-500 in the
     case of multi-client services)

Hungary / Hongrie / Hungría

ACCESS TO SERVICE: paid services open to all users
TYPE & DESCRIPTION OF SERVICES PROVIDED: Provides library services, bibliographic,
    literature abstract, survey and quantitative data searches, selective
    dissemination of information, magnetic tapes, microforms, photocopies and
    translation upon request. Also provides on-line services using own data
    base: Macrostatistics on Hungary's Foreign Trade.

384 - KÖZPONTI STATISZTIKAI HIVATAL KÖNYVTÁR ÉS DOKUMENTÁCIÓS SZOLGÁLAT

SYNONYMOUS NAMES: Central Statistical Office, Library and Documentation Service
ADDRESS: Keleti Károly utca 5,
        H-1525 Budapest, Pf. 10,
        HUNGARY
        TEL: 350-734 - TELEX: 22 4308
CREATED: 1867   *HEAD:* Dr. I. Csahók, Director
SIZE OF STAFF: Professional: 54   Other: 45   Total: 99
TYPE OF SERVICE: national; public; non-profit
MATERIALS DESCRIBING THE SERVICE: - Brochure
WORKING LANGUAGE(S): Hungary
SUBJECT COVERAGE: statistics; economics; demography; geography; sociology;
        statistical methodology; social statistics
GEOGRAPHICAL COVERAGE: global
DATA BEING PROCESSED AND SIZE: 455,000 books; 85,000 periodicals; 60 microcopies;
        4,800 manuscripts; 10,000 maps
DATA PROCESSING METHODS: partially computerized
HARDWARE USED: IBM 370/155, IBM PC/XT
SOFTWARE USED: TEXT-PAC / IBM programme package, CDS/ISIS, Micro CDS/ISIS
STORAGE MEDIA: traditional shelving of publications; fiches; tapes; microfiches;
        discs
TYPE OF ACTIVITY: data collection; distribution of information; publication
CLIENTELE: researchers
ACCESS TO SERVICE: services open to all users, some paid and some free of charge
TYPE & DESCRIPTION OF SERVICES PROVIDED: Provides library services, bibliographic a
        literature searches, on-line searches using its own data base STATINFORM,
        selective dissemination of information and photocopies.

385 - MAGYAR TUDOMÁNYOS AKADÉMIA KÖNYVTÁRA

SYNONYMOUS NAMES: Hungarian Academy of Sciences, Library
ADDRESS: V. Akadémia u.2,
        P.O.B. 7,
        H-1361 Budapest,
        HUNGARY
        TEL: 382-344 - TELEX: 224132
CREATED: 1826   *HEAD:* Dr. G. Rózsa, General Director
SIZE OF STAFF: Professional: 95   Other: 63   Total: 158
TYPE OF SERVICE: national; public; non-profit
SYSTEMS & NETWORKS ATTACHED TO: ECSSID; MISON/International Social Science
        Information System of Socialist Countries

MATERIALS DESCRIBING THE SERVICE: - The services of the Library of the Hungarian
        Academy of Sciences, 1984, leaflet (in Hungarian)
        - The catalogues and the information sources of the Library of the Hungarian
        Academy of Sciences, 1984, leaflet
        - Rozsa, G., The love for sciences and arts. Writings on the Library of the
        Hungarian Academy of Sciences, Budapest, 1987, 166 p. (in Hungarian)
SUBJECT COVERAGE: social sciences; history; linguistics; literature; philosophy;
        information science
GEOGRAPHICAL COVERAGE: global
DATA BEING PROCESSED AND SIZE: 948,000 books, 15,000 periodicals; 21,000 microcopies;
        542,000 manuscripts
DATA PROCESSING METHODS: manual; computerized
HARDWARE USED: IBM 370
SOFTWARE USED: IDMS
TYPE OF ACTIVITY: data collection; data analysis; publication; SSID scientific and
        methodological activities
PERIODICALS PUBLISHED:
        - Analecta Linguistica
        - Scientometrics
        - Kutatás-Fejlesztés. Tudományszervezési Tájékoztató/Research-Development.
        Bulletin of Science Organization
PUBLICATIONS: - Catalogi collectionis manuscriptorum Bibliothecae Academiae
        Scientiarum Hungaricae
        - Keleti tanulmányok/Oriental studies
        - Informatika és tudományelemzés/Informatics and scientometrics
ACCESS TO SERVICE: open to specific categories of users, free of charge
TYPE & DESCRIPTION OF SERVICES PROVIDED: Provides library services, selective
        dissemination of information, bibliographic, literature and survey data
        searches using its own data base "Publication Data Bank of the Hungarian
        Academy of Sciences" comprising 12,000 bibliographic items, microfilms and
        photocopies.

886 - MAGYAR TUDOMÁNYOS AKADÉMIA KÖZGAZDASÁGI INFORMÁCIÓS SZOLGÁLAT

SYNONYMOUS NAMES: Hungarian Academy of Sciences, Economic Information Unit
ADDRESS: Budaörsi ut 45,
        H-1112 Budapest,
        HUNGARY
        TEL: 850-878 - TELEX: Ecnat 227030
CREATED: 1973   *HEAD:* Mr. T. Földi, Head
SIZE OF STAFF: Professional: 6   Other: 6   Total: 12
TYPE OF SERVICE: national; public; non-profit
SYSTEMS & NETWORKS ATTACHED TO: International Institute of Economic Problems of the
        Socialist System, Moscow
MATERIALS DESCRIBING THE SERVICE: - ECHO user's guide, 1986
SUBJECT COVERAGE: economics; international economic relations; economic policy;
        statistics
GEOGRAPHICAL COVERAGE: global; Western Europe; Eastern Europe
DATA BEING PROCESSED AND SIZE: 500 books; 70 periodicals; reports
DATA PROCESSING METHODS: manual
STORAGE MEDIA: traditional shelving of publications; fiches

TYPE OF ACTIVITY: data collection; data analysis; distribution of information; SSID
     scientific and methodological activities
PUBLICATIONS: - Földi, T., Economic information and decision-making in Hungary, 198
CLIENTELE: economic and scientific policy makers
ACCESS TO SERVICE: paid services open to all users
TYPE & DESCRIPTION OF SERVICES PROVIDED: Provides bibliographic, literature abstrac
     and quantitative data searches and translations upon request.

387 - MAGYAR TUDOMÁNYOS AKADÉMIA VILÁGGAZDASÁGI KUTATÓ INTÉZET

SYNONYMOUS NAMES: Institute for World Economics of the Hungarian Academy of Science
ADDRESS: Kálló Esperes utca 15,
     P.O. Box 36,
     H-1531 Budapest XII,
     HUNGARY
     TEL: 260-661 - TELEX: 227713 MTAVG H
     CABLE: BUWORLDINST BUDAPEST
CREATED: 1970   HEAD: Dr. T. Felvinczi, Head
SIZE OF STAFF: Professional: 15   Other: 4   Total: 19
TYPE OF SERVICE: national; public; non-profit
WORKING LANGUAGE(S): Hungarian; English
SUBJECT COVERAGE: economics
DATA BEING PROCESSED AND SIZE: 48,000 books; 810 periodicals; 15,300 manuscripts
DATA PROCESSING METHODS: manual'
STORAGE MEDIA: traditional shelving of publications
TYPE OF ACTIVITY: data collection; data analysis; publication
ACCESS TO SERVICE: services open to all users, free of charge
TYPE & DESCRIPTION OF SERVICES PROVIDED: Provides library services, bibliographic,
     literature and survey data searches and photocopies.

388 - MARX KÁROLY KÖZGAZDASÁGTUDOMÁNYI EGYETEM KÖZPONTI KÖNYVTÁRA

SYNONYMOUS NAMES: Karl Marx University of Economic Sciences, Central Library;
     ⁻ ECONIMFORM
PARENT ORGANIZATION: Marx Károly Közgazdaságtudományi Egyetem
ADDRESS: Zsil u.2.,
     H-1093 Budapest,
     HUNGARY
     TEL: 175-827 - TELEX: 224186 mkke, 1828. BP. 5. PF. 489
CREATED: 1850   HEAD: Dr. H. Huszár, Director General
SIZE OF STAFF: Professional: 37   Other: 82   Total: 119
TYPE OF SERVICE: public; national; non-profit
MATERIALS DESCRIBING THE SERVICE: - Walleshausen, G., Olvasószolgálat: szabadpolc
     modell a Marx Károly Közgazdaságtudományi Egyetem Könyvtárában = Könyvtári
     Figyelo, 1984. 1 sz. 34-43 p.
     - Huszár, E., A A közgazdasági szakirodalmi információ jelentosége =
     Marketing - Piackutatás, 1983. 4. sz. 249-251 p.
WORKING LANGUAGE(S): Hungarian
SUBJECT COVERAGE: economics; administrative sciences; sociology; economic history;

finance; political economy; business economics
GEOGRAPHICAL COVERAGE: global; Hungary
DATA BEING PROCESSED AND SIZE: 465,000 books; 1,270 periodicals; 23 abstract
          journals; 32,000 manuscripts
DATA PROCESSING METHODS: partially computerized
HARDWARE USED: MØ8X PC, OK XTPC, MAXON PC
SOFTWARE USED: STAIRS, MICRO-ISIS
STORAGE MEDIA: traditional shelving of publications; fiches; tapes; microfiches
TYPE OF ACTIVITY: publication; SSID Scientific and methodological activities;
          distribution of information; SSID training
PUBLICATIONS: - Hungarian economic literature
          - The Literary activity of the teaching staff of the Karl Marx University of
          Economic Sciences
          - Doctoral theses at the Karl Marx University of Economic Sciences
          - Information on the foreign economic literature
CLIENTELE: 129,000 visitors p.a., 7,500 registered users p.a. (students, faculties,
          others)
ACCESS TO SERVICE: services open to all users, free of charge, some paid services
TYPE & DESCRIPTION OF SERVICES PROVIDED: Provides library services, bibliographic,
          literature and survey data searches using its own data base containing
          30,000 items, selective dissemination of information, photocopies and
          microfilms. Also has access to ABBIINFORM, ELI, SOLSCISEARCH (economic and
          business related data bases) through DIALOG and DATASTAR.

389 - MTA KÖZGAZDASÁGTUDOMÁNYI INTÉZETE, KÖNYVTÁR ÉS DOKUMENTÁCIÓ

SYNONYMOUS NAMES: Institute of Economics at the Hungarian Academy of Sciences,
          Library and Documentation
PARENT ORGANIZATION: Magyar Tudományos Akadémia/Hungarian Academy of Sciences
ADDRESS: Budaörsi ut 45,
          1112 Budapest XI,
          HUNGARY
          TEL: 850-777 - TELEX: 22 70 30
CREATED: 1955   *HEAD:* Dr. S. Szalay, Director
SIZE OF STAFF: Professional: 4   Other: 11   Total: 15
TYPE OF SERVICE: public; non-profit
WORKING LANGUAGE(S): English; French; German; Hungarian; Russian
SUBJECT COVERAGE: economics; social welfare; economic growth; standard of living;
          economic integration; foreign trade; agricultural economics
DATA BEING PROCESSED AND SIZE: 27,000 books; 18,000 periodicals; 500 abstract
          journals; 5,000 manuscripts
DATA PROCESSING METHODS: manual
TYPE OF ACTIVITY: data collection; publication
PERIODICALS PUBLISHED:
          - Accession List
PUBLICATIONS: - Selected list of Hungarian economic books and articles
ACCESS TO SERVICE: services open to specific categories of users, free of charge
TYPE & DESCRIPTION OF SERVICES PROVIDED: Provides library services, bibliographical,
          literature and survey data searches, selective dissemination of information,
          and translation of documents upon request.

390 - NÉPRAJZI MUZEUM KÖNYVTÁRA

SYNONYMOUS NAMES: Ethnographical Museum, Library
ADDRESS: Kossuth Lajos tér 12,
   H-1055 Budapest,
   HUNGARY
   TEL: 128.250
CREATED: 1872 HEAD: Mrs. A. Lay, Chief Librarian
SIZE OF STAFF: Professional: 6 Other: 1 Total: 7
TYPE OF SERVICE: public
WORKING LANGUAGE(S): German; English; French
SUBJECT COVERAGE: cultural anthropology; social anthropology; demography; history;
   sociology; ethnology; ethnography; folklore; arts
DATA BEING PROCESSED AND SIZE: 58,300 books. 73,640 periodicals; 1,230 manuscripts
DATA PROCESSING METHODS: manual
STORAGE MEDIA: traditional shelving of publications
PUBLICATIONS: - Néprajzi értesito ethnographia
   - Néprajzi közlemények
   - Néprajzi hirek
CLIENTELE: researchers, students (around 2,000 p.a.)
ACCESS TO SERVICE: services open to specific categories of users, free of charge
TYPE & DESCRIPTION OF SERVICES PROVIDED: Library services consist of international
   book exchange, interlibrary loans (national and international). Also
   provides bibliographic searches of information and photocopies.

391 - ORSZÁGGYÜLÉSI KÖNYVTÁR

SYNONYMOUS NAMES: Library of the Hungarian Parliament
ADDRESS: Kossuth Lajos tér 1-3,
   H-1357 Budapest,
   HUNGARY
   TEL: 120-600 - TELEX: 227463 OK H
CREATED: 1849 HEAD: Dr. K. Balázs-Veredy, Director-General
SIZE OF STAFF: Professional: 69 Other: 46 Total: 115
TYPE OF SERVICE: public
MATERIALS DESCRIBING THE SERVICE: - Valyi, G., The history and function of the
   Library of the Hungarian Parliament in Parliament und Bibliothek.
   Internationale Festeschrift für Wolfgang Dietz zum 65, 1986
SUBJECT COVERAGE: law; international relations; political science; administrative
   sciences; history
DATA BEING PROCESSED AND SIZE: 600,000 books; 500,000 articles; UN documents;
   parliamentary papers; 10,000 microfiches
DATA PROCESSING METHODS: computerized
HARDWARE USED: VT 16
SOFTWARE USED: INFDO87
STORAGE MEDIA: traditional shelving of publications
TYPE OF ACTIVITY: data analysis; distribution of information; publication
PERIODICALS PUBLISHED: - Világpolitikai Információk Permutált Indexe, 2 p.a.
   - Külföldi Jogi Dokumentáció Permutált Indexe, 2 p.a.
   - Külföldi Jogszabályok Permutált Indexe, 1 p.a.
   - A Magyar állam- és Jogtudományi Irodalom Bibliográfiája, 2 p.a.

PUBLICATIONS: - Állam- és jogtudományi Bibliográfia. Bibliográfia iuridica Hungarica, every 2-3 years

CLIENTELE: researchers, teachers and students of higher-education institutions, government officers, etc. (58,000 p.a.)

ACCESS TO SERVICE: services open to specific categories of users, free of charge and some paid services

TYPE & DESCRIPTION OF SERVICES PROVIDED: The data base consists of 50,000 items concerning international relations and law. Provides library services, bibliographic, literature and survey data searches, photocopies and translation of documents upon request.

392 - ORSZÁGOS MŰSZAKI INFORMÁCIÓS KÖZPOINTÉS KÖNYVTAR

SYNONYMOUS NAMES: OMIKK;
National Technical Information Centre and Library

PARENT ORGANIZATION: Országos Műszaki Fejlesztési Bizottság "OMFB"/State Office of Technical Development

ADDRESS: P.O.B. 12,
Muzeum U.17,
H-1428 Budapest,
HUNGARY
TEL: 336-300 - TELEX: 22-4944 OMIKK H

CREATED: 1883   *HEAD:* M. Agoston, Director General

SIZE OF STAFF: Professional: 301   Other: 199   Total: 500

TYPE OF SERVICE: national

SYSTEMS & NETWORKS ATTACHED TO: member of the International Scientific and Technical Information System of the CMEA countries; focal point of UNESCO/PGI, INTIB/UNESCO and INIS/IAEA

MATERIALS DESCRIBING THE SERVICE: - Brochure

WORKING LANGUAGE(S): English; Russian; Hungarian

SUBJECT COVERAGE: administrative sciences; economics; information science; statistics; urban planning; regional planning

DATA BEING PROCESSED AND SIZE: 500,000 books; 320,000 periodicals; 5,000 current titles; 300 abstract journals; 135,000 microcopies; 625,000 translations

DATA PROCESSING METHODS: partially computerized

STORAGE MEDIA: traditional shelving of publications; microfiches etc.

TYPE OF ACTIVITY: data analysis; distribution of information; SSID scientific and methodological activities; publication

PERIODICALS PUBLISHED: - Hungarian Research and Development Abstracts Science and Technology, 4 p.a.
- Szakirodalmi Tájékoztatók, 12 p.a.
- Tudományos es Műszaki Tájékoztatás, 12 p.a. (Journal of Scientific and Technical Information)
- Műszaki Gazdasági Tájékoztacó, monthly review and digest

ACCESS TO SERVICE: services open to all users, free of charge and some paid services

TYPE & DESCRIPTION OF SERVICES PROVIDED: Provides library services, bibliographic, literature and survey data searches. Also provides on-line services, selective dissemination of information, photocopies, visual materials and translation of documents upon request. The data base is the "Central Catalog of Periodicals in the Technical Libraries" comprising 7,500 bibliographical items covering 450 technical libraries.

393 - ORSZÁGOS VEZETÓKÉPZÓ KÖZPONT, TUDOMÁNYOS TÁJÉKOZTATÓ SZOLGÁLAT

SYNONYMOUS NAMES: OVK TTSZ;
       National Management Development Centre, Service for Scientific Information
PARENT ORGANIZATION: Ministry of Culture
ADDRESS: H-1476 Budapest VIII,
       Könyves Kálmán krt. 48-52,
       HUNGARY
       TEL: 344-500, 342-355 - TELEX: 22-4221
CREATED: 1967   *HEAD:* Dr. L. Gober,
SIZE OF STAFF: Professional: 12   Other: 2   Total: 14
TYPE OF SERVICE: national; public; non-profit
MATERIALS DESCRIBING THE SERVICE: - Activities, results and tasks of the National
       Management Development Centre, 1987
SUBJECT COVERAGE: social sciences; administrative sciences; management; sociology
GEOGRAPHICAL COVERAGE: Hungary
DATA BEING PROCESSED AND SIZE: 28,000 books, 600 travel reports, 400 periodicals,
       4,500 pamphlets, 750 dissertations, 12,000 translations; 18,000 items
DATA PROCESSING METHODS: computerized
TYPE OF ACTIVITY: distribution of information
PERIODICALS PUBLISHED: - Hungarian language (summary in English)
       - Documentary Review, 4 p.a.
       - Gyorstájekoztató a Szakkönyvtár Legujabb Gyarapodásáról/New acquisitions
       of the Library, 12 p.a. since 1968
PUBLICATIONS: - Vezetéstudomány dokumentácios szemle, 1976 (Management science)
CLIENTELE: teachers and researchers of Hungarian management development institutions
ACCESS TO SERVICE: open to specific categories of users, free of charge
TYPE & DESCRIPTION OF SERVICES PROVIDED: Provides current and retrospective
       bibliographic searches of information, selective dissemination of
       information, syntheses, loan of documents and reproduction of articles.

394 - A. N. SINHA INSTITUTE OF SOCIAL STUDIES, LIBRARY

ADDRESS: Patna 800001,
       Bihar,
       INDIA
       TEL: 26226
       CABLE: ANSISS
CREATED: 1958   *HEAD:* Dr. S. F. Rab, Head
SIZE OF STAFF: Professional: 5   Other: 5   Total: 10
TYPE OF SERVICE: international; public; non-profit
SYSTEMS & NETWORKS ATTACHED TO: ICSSR, New Delhi
WORKING LANGUAGE(S): English; Hindi
SUBJECT COVERAGE: social sciences; administrative sciences; demography; economics;
       political science; psychology; social anthropology; cultural anthropology;
       social welfare; sociology
GEOGRAPHICAL COVERAGE: India
DATA BEING PROCESSED AND SIZE: 20,000 books; 200 periodicals; reports
DATA PROCESSING METHODS: partially computerized
STORAGE MEDIA: traditional shelving of publications; microfiches

YPE OF ACTIVITY: data collection; data analysis; distribution of information; SSID
        scientific and methodological activities; publication
LIENTELE: research scholars (30-35 per day)
CCESS TO SERVICE: paid services open to specific categories of users
YPE & DESCRIPTION OF SERVICES PROVIDED: Provides library services, bibliographic
        searches, selective dissemination of information and photocopies.

95 - AMERICAN STUDIES RESEARCH CENTRE

SYNONYMOUS NAMES: ASRC
ADDRESS: Osamania University Campus,
        Hyderabad 500007,
        Andhra Pradesh,
        INDIA
        TEL: 71608
        CABLE: AMCENTRE
CREATED: 1964   HEAD: Dr. J. W. Bjorkman, Director
SIZE OF STAFF: Professional: 17   Other: 25   Total: 42
TYPE OF SERVICE: international; non-profit
WORKING LANGUAGE(S): English
SUBJECT COVERAGE: social sciences; economics; education; history; law; philosophy;
        political science; sociology
GEOGRAPHICAL COVERAGE: USA; South Asia
DATA BEING PROCESSED AND SIZE: 96,000 books; 15,000 periodicals, brochures and other
        documents
DATA PROCESSING METHODS: manual
STORAGE MEDIA: microfilms; microfiches; tapes; discs; cassettes
TYPE OF ACTIVITY: data analysis; distribution of information; publication
PERIODICALS PUBLISHED: - Indian Journal of American Studies, 2 p.a.
        - ASRC Newsletter, 2 p.a.
        - Acquisition List
        - The Month at ASRC, 12 p.a.
        - American Studies Index to Indian Periodicals, irr.
PUBLICATIONS: - Catalogue of serials
        - Indian essays in American literature
        - American history by Indian historians
        - Themes and perspectives in American history: essays on historiography
        - Indian contributions in American studies
        - Union catalog of American studies and periodicals in India, Ceylon and
        Nepal, 1972
        - Indian research in American studies
        - Crunden, R.M. et al., New perspectives on American and South Asia, 1984
        - Crunden, R. M., Traffic of ideas between India and America, 1984
        - Kar, P. C. : Ramakrishna, D., American classics revisted: recent studies
        of American literature, 1986
        - Krishnamoorthy, P. S., A Scholar's guide to modern American science
        fiction, 1983
CLIENTELE: researchers (3,000 members)
ACCESS TO SERVICE: services open to specific categories of users
TYPE & DESCRIPTION OF SERVICES PROVIDED: The Centre's main activities are to provide
        reference service, prepare specialized checklist and assist scholars,

universities and other institutions of higher learning with bibliographical problems. Also provides library services, bibliographic searches, literatu* abstracts, selective dissemination of information and photocopies. Conduct short-term courses, seminars, etc. Also arranges lectures and shows VTR's and films.

396 - ANTHROPOLOGICAL SURVEY OF INDIA

PARENT ORGANIZATION: Ministry of Human Resources Development
ADDRESS: 27, Jawaharlal Nehru Road,
   Indian Museum,
   Calcutta 700016,
   INDIA
   TEL: 29-8733
   CABLE: ANTHROPOS
CREATED: 1945 *HEAD:* Dr. K. S. Singh, Director General
TYPE OF SERVICE: international; public; non-profit
WORKING LANGUAGE(S): Hindi; English
SUBJECT COVERAGE: anthropology; linguistics; demography; geography; psychology;
   social anthropology; cultural anthropology
GEOGRAPHICAL COVERAGE: India
DATA BEING PROCESSED AND SIZE: 10,000 documentation items
DATA PROCESSING METHODS: manual
TYPE OF ACTIVITY: data collection; data analysis; publication
PERIODICALS PUBLISHED: - Human Science, 4 p.a.
CLIENTELE: research scholars and university students
ACCESS TO SERVICE: services open to specific categories, free of charge
TYPE & DESCRIPTION OF SERVICES PROVIDED: Provides library services, bibliographies
   and exchange of information on research with research organizations in
   anthropology and allied disciplines.

397 - ASSOCIATION OF INDIAN UNIVERSITIES, LIBRARY AND DOCUMENTATION CENTRE

SYNONYMOUS NAMES: AIU Library and Documentation Centre
ADDRESS: AIU House,
   16 Kotla Marg,
   New Delhi 110002,
   INDIA
   TEL: 3310059 - TELEX: 31 5578 AIU IN
   CABLE: ASINDU
CREATED: 1925 *HEAD:* Shri S. Singh,
SIZE OF STAFF: Professional: 6 Other: 3 Total: 9
TYPE OF SERVICE: national; public; non-profit
WORKING LANGUAGE(S): English
SUBJECT COVERAGE: education; social sciences; psychology; sociology; economics;
   political science; law; history; geography
GEOGRAPHICAL COVERAGE: India
DATA BEING PROCESSED AND SIZE: books, periodicals, reports, on-going research,
   newspaper clippings

DATA PROCESSING METHODS: manual
STORAGE MEDIA: traditional shelving of publications
TYPE OF ACTIVITY: data collection; distribution of information; publication
PERIODICALS PUBLISHED: - Bibliography of Doctoral Dissertations, 1 p.a. in two
        volumes 1) Natural Sciences and 2) Social Sciences and Humanities
PUBLICATIONS: - Education and economic development
CLIENTELE: researchers
ACCESS TO SERVICE: services open to specific categories of users
TYPE & DESCRIPTION OF SERVICES PROVIDED: Provides library services, bibliographies,
        photocopies and information concerning university courses.

398 - BANARAS HINDU UNIVERSITY, CENTRE FOR THE STUDY OF NEPAL, LIBRARY WITH DOCUMENTATION SERVICES

ADDRESS: Faculty of Social Sciences,
        Varanasi 221005,
        INDIA
CREATED: 1976
SIZE OF STAFF: Total: 3
TYPE OF SERVICE: international; public; non-profit
WORKING LANGUAGE(S): English; Hindi; Nepali
SUBJECT COVERAGE: social sciences
GEOGRAPHICAL COVERAGE: Nepal
DATA BEING PROCESSED AND SIZE: 2,066 books; 31 periodicals
DATA PROCESSING METHODS: manual
STORAGE MEDIA: traditional shelving of publications, tapes, microfiches
TYPE OF ACTIVITY: data collection; data analysis; distribution of information;
        publication
PUBLICATIONS: - Jha, S. N., Bibliography on the political development in Nepal
        - Jha, S. N., Bibliography on economic development and planning in Nepal
CLIENTELE: students, research scholars
ACCESS TO SERVICE: services open to all users, free of charge
TYPE & DESCRIPTION OF SERVICES PROVIDED: Provides library services, bibliographic and
        literature abstract searches, production of information on magnetic tapes,
        microforms and photocopies.

399 - BHANDARKAR ORIENTAL RESEARCH INSTITUTE, LIBRARY

ADDRESS: Deccan Gymkhana,
        Pune 411 004,
        INDIA
        TEL: 56936
        CABLE: BORI
CREATED: 1917   *HEAD:* Prof. R. N. Dandekar, Honorary Secretary
SIZE OF STAFF: Total: 5
TYPE OF SERVICE: international; public; non-profit
SYSTEMS & NETWORKS ATTACHED TO: University of Poona
WORKING LANGUAGE(S): English; Sanskrit
SUBJECT COVERAGE: history; philosophy; linguistics; sociology; psychology; oriental

and Indological studies
GEOGRAPHICAL COVERAGE: global
DATA BEING PROCESSED AND SIZE: books, periodicals, 20,000 manuscripts
DATA PROCESSING METHODS: manual
STORAGE MEDIA: traditional shelving of publications
TYPE OF ACTIVITY: data collection; distribution of information; SSID scientific and
methodological activities; SSID training; publication
PERIODICALS PUBLISHED: - Annals of the Bhandarkar Oriental Research Institute
PUBLICATIONS: - Bombay Sanskrti and Prakrit series
- Government Oriental series
- Bhandarkar Oriental series
- Descriptive catalogues of government manuscripts
CLIENTELE: scholars, researchers
ACCESS TO SERVICE: services open to all users, some paid services
TYPE & DESCRIPTION OF SERVICES PROVIDED: Provides library services, bibliographic and
literature abstract searches of information and photocopies.

400 - CENTRE FOR DEVELOPMENT STUDIES LIBRARY

ADDRESS: Aakulam Road,
Ulloor,
Trivandrum 695011,
Kerala,
INDIA
TEL: 8881-84 - TELEX: 435-227-CDS
CABLE: CENTPED
CREATED: 1971   *HEAD:* G. Ravindran Nair, Librarian
SIZE OF STAFF: Professional: 12   Other: 6   Total: 18
TYPE OF SERVICE: national; non-profit
MATERIALS DESCRIBING THE SERVICE: - Brochure
WORKING LANGUAGE(S): English
SUBJECT COVERAGE: social sciences; demography; economics; education; history;
sociology; development
GEOGRAPHICAL COVERAGE: Kerala, India
DATA BEING PROCESSED AND SIZE: 83,000 books; 440 periodicals; 6,500 working papers;
900 microforms
DATA PROCESSING METHODS: manual
TYPE OF ACTIVITY: distribution of information; publication

401 - CENTRE FOR POLICY RESEARCH, LIBRARY

SYNONYMOUS NAMES: CPR Library
ADDRESS: Dharma Marg,
Chakayapuri,
New Delhi 110021,
INDIA
TEL: 3015273
CABLE: CENPOLRES
CREATED: 1973   *HEAD:* K. Jit Kumar, Librarian

SIZE OF STAFF: Professional: 2   Other: 1   Total: 3
TYPE OF SERVICE: national; non-profit
MATERIALS DESCRIBING THE SERVICE: - CPR (brochure)
WORKING LANGUAGE(S): English
SUBJECT COVERAGE: political science; demography; economics; public policy; foreign
        policy; international affairs
GEOGRAPHICAL COVERAGE: global
DATA BEING PROCESSED AND SIZE: 7,200 documentation items (750 p.a.)
DATA PROCESSING METHODS: computerized
HARDWARE USED: IBM/PC
SOFTWARE USED: DBase III
STORAGE MEDIA: traditional shelving of publications
TYPE OF ACTIVITY: data collection; data analysis; distribution of information;
        publication
PERIODICALS PUBLISHED:
        - CPR Report
        - CPR Annual Report
CLIENTELE: faculty members; research scholars
ACCESS TO SERVICE: services open to specific categories of users, free of charge
TYPE & DESCRIPTION OF SERVICES PROVIDED: Provides library services, bibliographic and
        literature abstract searches, selective dissemination of information and
        microforms.

402 - CENTRE FOR RESEARCH AND DEVELOPMENT

ADDRESS: 175 Dr. Dadabhai Nauroji Road,
        Bombay 400 001,
        Maharashtra,
        INDIA
        TEL: 260308
        CABLE: DEVSUPPORT, BOMBAY
CREATED: 1972
SIZE OF STAFF: Professional: 1
TYPE OF SERVICE: national; private; non-profit
SYSTEMS & NETWORKS ATTACHED TO: Indian Council of Social Science Research; ADIPA/ADPC
        Development Information Clearinghouse & Referral Service
MATERIALS DESCRIBING THE SERVICE: - Annual report
WORKING LANGUAGE(S): English
SUBJECT COVERAGE: social sciences; administrative sciences; economics; social
        anthropology; cultural anthropology; social welfare; sociology; social
        defence; rehabilitation; Leprosy
GEOGRAPHICAL COVERAGE: India
DATA BEING PROCESSED AND SIZE: books; articles; reports; on-going research; seminars;
        training courses
DATA PROCESSING METHODS: manual
STORAGE MEDIA: traditional shelving of publications
TYPE OF ACTIVITY: data collection; data analysis; distribution of information;
        publication
CLIENTELE: government and international agencies
ACCESS TO SERVICE: services open to all users against payment
TYPE & DESCRIPTION OF SERVICES PROVIDED: Provides library services, search of

information, selective dissemination of information and translation of documents upon request.

403 - CENTRE FOR STUDIES IN SOCIAL SCIENCES, CALCUTTA, LIBRARY

ADDRESS: 10, Lake Terrace,
Calcutta 700029,
INDIA
TEL: 46-7958
CABLE: SOCRECENT
CREATED: 1973   *HEAD:* A. K. Ghosh, Librarian
SIZE OF STAFF: Professional: 4   Other: 2   Total: 6
TYPE OF SERVICE: national; public; non-profit
WORKING LANGUAGE(S): English; Bengali
SUBJECT COVERAGE: social sciences; demography; economics; geography; history; political science; social anthropology; sociology; socio-economic development; urban sociology; rural sociology; technology transfer; regiona planning; economic history
GEOGRAPHICAL COVERAGE: India; developing countries
DATA BEING PROCESSED AND SIZE: 12,000 books; government reports; journals; maps; atlases
DATA PROCESSING METHODS: manual
STORAGE MEDIA: traditional shelving of publications; microfilms; microfiches
TYPE OF ACTIVITY: data collection; distribution of information
CLIENTELE: research scholars (25 per day)
ACCESS TO SERVICE: services open to specific categories of users, free of charge
TYPE & DESCRIPTION OF SERVICES PROVIDED: Provides library services, bibliographic an literature abstract searches, selective dissemination of information, inter library loans, photocopies, newspaper clippings and translation of documents.

404 - CENTRE FOR THE STUDY OF DEVELOPING SOCIETIES, DATA UNIT

SYNONYMOUS NAMES: CSDS, Data Unit
ADDRESS: 29 Rajpur Road,
Delhi 110054,
INDIA
TEL: 231190, 2517131
CABLE: POLITY
CREATED: 1963   *HEAD:* Prof. D. L. Sheth, Director
SIZE OF STAFF: Professional: 2   Other: 3   Total: 5
TYPE OF SERVICE: national; public; non-profit
MATERIALS DESCRIBING THE SERVICE: - printed notice
WORKING LANGUAGE(S): English
SUBJECT COVERAGE: political science; philosophy; social anthropology; sociology
GEOGRAPHICAL COVERAGE: India; global
DATA BEING PROCESSED AND SIZE: 200 reports, by-products of research studies; data bases: 600 censuses, 9000 surveys, polls
DATA PROCESSING METHODS: computerized

336

HARDWARE USED: computer IBM 360/44 (Delhi University)
SOFTWARE USED: SPSSG, OSIRIS
TYPE OF ACTIVITY: data collection; data analysis; SSID training; publication
PERIODICALS PUBLISHED: - Alternatives, 4 p.a.
        - China Report, 4 p.a.
CLIENTELE: research scholars
ACCESS TO SERVICE: restricted to specific categories of users, against payment
TYPE & DESCRIPTION OF SERVICES PROVIDED: Provides library services, bibliographic and
        quantitative data searches, selective dissemination of information and
        photocopies.

05 - GANDHI PEACE FOUNDATION

ADDRESS: 221/223 Deen Dayal Upadhyaya,
        New Delhi 110002,
        INDIA
        TEL: 3317491
        CABLE: SATYARGAHA, New Delhi
CREATED: 1961   *HEAD:* K. S. Radhakrishna, Secretary
TYPE OF SERVICE: national; private; non-profit
WORKING LANGUAGE(S): Hindi; English
SUBJECT COVERAGE: peace; nonviolence; social sciences; education; sociology
GEOGRAPHICAL COVERAGE: India
DATA BEING PROCESSED AND SIZE: books; periodicals
DATA PROCESSING METHODS: manual
TYPE OF ACTIVITY: data collection; distribution of information
PERIODICALS PUBLISHED: - Gandhi Marg, 12 p.a.
ACCESS TO SERVICE: services open to specific categories of users, free of charge
TYPE & DESCRIPTION OF SERVICES PROVIDED: Provides training courses on Gandhi, library
        services, information searches, selective dissemination of information,
        information on magnetic tapes and information about constructive work
        organizations and peace organizations.

06 - GOKHALE INSTITUTE OF POLITICS AND ECONOMICS, LIBRARY

ADDRESS: Deccan Gymkhana,
        Pune 411004 (Maharashtra),
        INDIA
        TEL: 54287
        CABLE: GOKHALINST
CREATED: 1930   *HEAD:* Prof. V. S. Chitre, Director
SIZE OF STAFF: Professional: 2   Other: 19   Total: 21
TYPE OF SERVICE: national; non-profit
WORKING LANGUAGE(S): English
SUBJECT COVERAGE: demography; economics; sociology
GEOGRAPHICAL COVERAGE: India
DATA PROCESSING METHODS: partially computerized
HARDWARE USED: Kelikom 8; IBM/PC; IBM/XT
SOFTWARE USED: Wordstar; Lotus; Supercale DBASE II & III; MSDOS; CP/M

STORAGE MEDIA: traditional shelving of publications; discs; microfiches
TYPE OF ACTIVITY: data collection; data analysis; distribution of information; publication
PERIODICALS PUBLISHED: - Artha Vijnana
CLIENTELE: research scholars (40 per day)
ACCESS TO SERVICE: services open to specific categories of users
TYPE & DESCRIPTION OF SERVICES PROVIDED: Provides library services and bibliographic searches.

407 - GOKHALE INSTITUTE OF PUBLIC AFFAIRS, LIBRARY

SYNONYMOUS NAMES: GIPA, Library
ADDRESS: Bull Temple Road,
N.R. Colony,
Bangalore-560019,
INDIA
TEL: 602436.
CREATED: 1945
SIZE OF STAFF: Total: 2
TYPE OF SERVICE: national; public; non-profit
WORKING LANGUAGE(S): English; Kannada
SUBJECT COVERAGE: social welfare; administrative sciences; economics; education; history; philosophy
DATA BEING PROCESSED AND SIZE: 60,000 books
DATA PROCESSING METHODS: manual
TYPE OF ACTIVITY: data collection
PERIODICALS PUBLISHED: - Public Affairs, 12 p.a.
CLIENTELE: researchers
TYPE & DESCRIPTION OF SERVICES PROVIDED: Provides library services.

408 - GUJARAT VIDYAPITH GRANTHALAYA, BIBLIOGRAPHICAL AND DOCUMENTATION SERVICE

ADDRESS: Ashram Road,
Ahmedabad 380014,
INDIA
TEL: 446148
CREATED: 1920   *HEAD:* K. L. Shah, Librarian
SIZE OF STAFF: Total: 9
TYPE OF SERVICE: international; public; non-profit
MATERIALS DESCRIBING THE SERVICE: - Brochure
WORKING LANGUAGE(S): Gujarati; Hindi; English
SUBJECT COVERAGE: social sciences; humanities
GEOGRAPHICAL COVERAGE: India; global
DATA BEING PROCESSED AND SIZE: 357,000 books; 740 periodicals; reports
DATA PROCESSING METHODS: partially computerized
HARDWARE USED: Nelco Force 20; MC-68020 (UNIX based OS)
SOFTWARE USED: UNIFY relational data base
STORAGE MEDIA: traditional shelving of publications; discs
TYPE OF ACTIVITY: data collection; data analysis; distribution of information; SSID

training; publication
UBLICATIONS: - Bibliography of books and articles on community education, 1982
  - Catalogue of copyright books published before 1900 (1867-1900)
  - Bibliography of epigraphical studies
  - Social anthropology: a bibliography of books on tribal peoples
LIENTELE: students; general public
CCESS TO SERVICE: services open to all users, free of charge
YPE & DESCRIPTION OF SERVICES PROVIDED: Provides library services, bibliographic and
  literature abstract searches, on-line searches of external data base of the
  Unify Corporation, selective dissemination of information, production of
  information on magnetic tapes, photocopies and translation of documents.

09 - INDIAN COUNCIL FOR RESEARCH ON INTERNATIONAL ECONOMIC RELATIONS, DOCUMENTATION
    CENTRE

YNONYMOUS NAMES: ICRIER, Documentation Centre
DDRESS: 40 Lodi Estate,
        New Delhi 110003,
        INDIA
        TEL: 616329
        CABLE: ECOINST
REATED: 1981   HEAD: S. R. Gupta, Chief
IZE OF STAFF: Professional: 2   Other: 1   Total: 3
YPE OF SERVICE: non-profit
ATERIALS DESCRIBING THE SERVICE: - Current contents
ORKING LANGUAGE(S): English
UBJECT COVERAGE: economics; international economic relations
EOGRAPHICAL COVERAGE: Asia; Africa; Europe; Americas
ATA BEING PROCESSED AND SIZE: books; periodicals; press clippings; reports
ATA PROCESSING METHODS: manual; computerized
ARDWARE USED: Neptune PC/AT
OFTWARE USED: DBase III
TORAGE MEDIA: discs
YPE OF ACTIVITY: data collection; data analysis; distribution of information;
        publication
LIENTELE: researchers and visiting scholars
CCESS TO SERVICE: services open to specific categories of users, free of charge
YPE & DESCRIPTION OF SERVICES PROVIDED: Provides library services, bibliographic
        searches, selective dissemination of information, photocopies and
        information on magnetic tapes.

10 - INDIAN INSTITUTE OF ISLAMIC STUDIES, NEW DELHI, LIBRARY

ARENT ORGANIZATION: Hamdard National Foundation
DDRESS: Tughlaqabad Institutional Area,
        Hamdard Nagar,
        New Delhi 110062,
        INDIA
        TEL: 643.9625

CREATED: 1963   HEAD: Mr. A. S. Khan, Librarian
SIZE OF STAFF: Professional: 7   Other: 11   Total: 18
TYPE OF SERVICE: international; public; non-profit
WORKING LANGUAGE(S): English
SUBJECT COVERAGE: history; cultural anthropology; sociology; Islamic studies
GEOGRAPHICAL COVERAGE: global
DATA BEING PROCESSED AND SIZE: books; periodicals; seminars
DATA PROCESSING METHODS: manual
STORAGE MEDIA: traditional shelving of publications; microfilms
TYPE OF ACTIVITY: data collection; distribution of information
CLIENTELE: research scholars
ACCESS TO SERVICE: services open to specific categories of users, free of charge
TYPE & DESCRIPTION OF SERVICES PROVIDED: Provides library services, microforms,
        photocopies and translation of documents upon request.

411 - INDIAN INSTITUTE OF MANAGEMENT, BANGALORE, MANAGEMENT LIBRARY

SYNONYMOUS NAMES: IIM-B Library
ADDRESS: Bilekahalli,
        Bannerghatta Road,
        Bangalore 560076,
        INDIA
        TEL: 642511 - TELEX: 0845-472
        CABLE: MANAGEMENT
CREATED: 1973   HEAD: Mr. Chikkamallaiah, Librarian
SIZE OF STAFF: Professional: 6   Other: 28   Total: 34
TYPE OF SERVICE: national; public; non-profit
SUBJECT COVERAGE: administrative sciences; economics; management; social sciences
GEOGRAPHICAL COVERAGE: India; global
DATA BEING PROCESSED AND SIZE: 85,000 documentation items
DATA PROCESSING METHODS: manual
TYPE OF ACTIVITY: distribution of information; publication
PERIODICALS PUBLISHED:
            - Recent Additions (Books/Government Reports), 12 p.a.
            - Current Press Clippings, 12 p.a.
            - Current Contents: IIMB, 24 p.a.
PUBLICATIONS: - Review of sectoral research, 1982
            - PGP profile 1974-84
            - Periodical holdings (1973-1986)
CLIENTELE: faculty, researchers, students, programme participants
ACCESS TO SERVICE: services open to all users, free of charge
TYPE & DESCRIPTION OF SERVICES PROVIDED: Provides library services, query-answering
        service, bibliographic, literature abstract and quantitative data searches
        microforms, photocopies and translation of documents upon request.

412 - INDIAN INSTITUTE OF MANAGEMENT, CALCUTTA, BIDHAN CHANDRA ROY MEMORIAL LIBRARY

PARENT ORGANIZATION: Indian Institute of Management Calcutta
ADDRESS: P.O. Joka,

Dist. 24 Parganas,
West Bengal 743512,
INDIA
TEL: 77-2329 - TELEX: 021-2501
CABLE: INMANAC
REATED: 1961   *HEAD:* R. Mukherji, Librarian
ZE OF STAFF: Professional: 18   Other: 19   Total: 37
PE OF SERVICE: international; public; non-profit
RKING LANGUAGE(S): English
BJECT COVERAGE: administrative sciences; management; systems analysis
OGRAPHICAL COVERAGE: India; global
TA BEING PROCESSED AND SIZE: 74,000 books; 900 periodicals; 17,940 bound volumes;
         800 annual reports
TA PROCESSING METHODS: manual
RDWARE USED: IBM 447; Micro-200 of Hindustan Computers
PE OF ACTIVITY: data collection; distribution of information; publication
RIODICALS PUBLISHED:
         - Library Bulletin
IENTELE: scholars, students, researchers
CESS TO SERVICE: services open to specific categories of users, free of charge
PE & DESCRIPTION OF SERVICES PROVIDED: Provides library services, bibliographic and
         quantitative data searches, selective dissemination of information,
         microforms and photocopies.

3 - INDIAN INSTITUTE OF MASS COMMUNICATION, LIBRARY AND DOCUMENTATION UNIT

NONYMOUS NAMES: IIMC, Library
DRESS: Saheed Jit Singh Marg,
         Jawaharlal Nehru University Complex no. 13,
         New Delhi 110067,
         INDIA
         TEL: 6-57492
         CABLE: MASS MEDIA
EATED: 1965   *HEAD:* B. K. Prasad, Senior Librarian
ZE OF STAFF: Professional: 8   Other: 4   Total: 12
PE OF SERVICE: international; public; non-profit
TERIALS DESCRIBING THE SERVICE: - IIMC Library
RKING LANGUAGE(S): English; Hindi
BJECT COVERAGE: mass communication
OGRAPHICAL COVERAGE: global
TA BEING PROCESSED AND SIZE: 18,000 books and reports; periodicals; on-going
         research
TA PROCESSING METHODS: manual
ORAGE MEDIA: traditional shelving of publications
PE OF ACTIVITY: distribution of information; publication
RIODICALS PUBLISHED: - Communication, 4 p.a.
         - Current Awareness Service, 12 p.a.
BLICATIONS: - Mass communication in India: an annotated bibliography
IENTELE: students, teachers, researchers, government officers (5,000 p.a.)
CESS TO SERVICE: services open to all users, free of charge
PE & DESCRIPTION OF SERVICES PROVIDED: Provides library services, bibliographic and

literature abstract searches, selective dissemination of information and photocopies.

414 - INDIAN INSTITUTE OF PUBLIC ADMINISTRATION, DOCUMENTATION AND REFERENCE SERVIC

ADDRESS: Indraprastha Estate,
Ring Road East,
New Delhi 110 002,
INDIA
TEL: 3317561
CABLE: ADMNIST, New Delhi
CREATED: 1954   *HEAD:* M. C. Ragavan, Librarian
SIZE OF STAFF: Professional: 12   Other: 15   Total: 27
TYPE OF SERVICE: national; non-profit
WORKING LANGUAGE(S): English
SUBJECT COVERAGE: administrative sciences; social sciences
GEOGRAPHICAL COVERAGE: global
DATA BEING PROCESSED AND SIZE: 140,000 documentation items (yearly: 2,000 books,
1,500 public documents, 2,500 articles, 6,000 press clippings, research reports)
DATA PROCESSING METHODS: manual
STORAGE MEDIA: traditional shelving of publications
TYPE OF ACTIVITY: distribution of information; SSID scientific and methodological activities; SSID training; publication
PERIODICALS PUBLISHED: - Indian Journal of Public Administration
- Documentation in Public Administration
- Weekly Documentation List
- Recent additions to Library, 12 p.a.
PUBLICATIONS: - Municipal government, a bibliography
- Civil service & personnel administration
CLIENTELE: teachers and scholars (3,500 p.a.)
ACCESS TO SERVICE: services open to specific categories of users, free of charge
TYPE & DESCRIPTION OF SERVICES PROVIDED: Provides library services, bibliographic, literature and quantitative data searches, selective dissemination of information and photocopies.

415 - INDIAN INTERNATIONAL CENTRE, LIBRARY

ADDRESS: 40-Max Mueller Marg,
New Delhi 110003,
INDIA
TEL: 619431
CABLE: INTERCIND
CREATED: 1962   *HEAD:* Mr. H. K. Kaul, Librarian
SIZE OF STAFF: Professional: 3   Other: 4   Total: 7
TYPE OF SERVICE: international; private; non-profit
WORKING LANGUAGE(S): English
SUBJECT COVERAGE: social sciences
GEOGRAPHICAL COVERAGE: South Asia with special reference to India

ATA BEING PROCESSED AND SIZE: 24,410 books; 300 periodicals
ATA PROCESSING METHODS: manual
TORAGE MEDIA: traditional shelving of publications
YPE OF ACTIVITY: data collection; distribution of information; publication
LIENTELE: scientists, philosophers, historians, lawyers
CCESS TO SERVICE: open to all users, free of charge
YPE & DESCRIPTION OF SERVICES PROVIDED: Provides library services, bibliographic
        searches of information, selective dissemination of information, microforms
        and photocopies.

16 - INDIAN LAW INSTITUTE, LIBRARY

DDRESS: Bhagwandas Road,
        New Delhi 110001,
        INDIA
        TEL: 387526
        CABLE: INSTITUTE
REATED: 1956   *HEAD:* Mr. R. S. Palhak, President
IZE OF STAFF: Professional: 15
YPE OF SERVICE: national; public
ORKING LANGUAGE(S): English
UBJECT COVERAGE: law; administrative law; constitutional law; criminal law; labour
        law; family law; comparative law
ATA BEING PROCESSED AND SIZE: 50,000 books and periodicals
ATA PROCESSING METHODS: manual
YPE OF ACTIVITY: data collection; SSID scientific and methodological activities;
        SSID training
ERIODICALS PUBLISHED: - Journal of the Indian Law Institute, 4 p.a.
        - Annual Survey of Indian Law
        - Index to Indian Legal Periodicals, 2 p.a.
        - Annual Report
LIENTELE: law teachers, students, advocates, researchers
CCESS TO SERVICE: services open to specific categories of users
YPE & DESCRIPTION OF SERVICES PROVIDED: Provides library services, bibliographic
        searches and photocopies.

17 - INDIAN SOCIAL INSTITUTE, DOCUMENTATION CENTRE

YNONYMOUS NAMES: ISI-DC
DDRESS: 10, Institutional Area,
        Lodi Road,
        New Delhi 110003,
        INDIA
        TEL: 622379
        CABLE: INSOCIN
REATED: 1961   *HEAD:* Dr. W. Fernandes, Director
IZE OF STAFF: Professional: 8
YPE OF SERVICE: national; public; non-profit
YSTEMS & NETWORKS ATTACHED TO: FNDP, Namur, Belgium; UFSIA, Antwerp, Belgium

WORKING LANGUAGE(S): English; Hindi
SUBJECT COVERAGE: social sciences; law; psychology; sociology
GEOGRAPHICAL COVERAGE: India
DATA BEING PROCESSED AND SIZE: books; periodicals; reports; on-going research; seminars
DATA PROCESSING METHODS: partially computerized
HARDWARE USED: Microcomputer (PC/AT compatible); 2 printers; tape drive
SOFTWARE USED: own
STORAGE MEDIA: traditional shelving of publications; fiches; tapes; discs
TYPE OF ACTIVITY: data collection; data analysis; distribution of information; publication
CLIENTELE: experts, teachers (600 p.a.)
ACCESS TO SERVICE: services open to all users, free of charge
TYPE & DESCRIPTION OF SERVICES PROVIDED: Provides library services, bibliographic searches, literature abstract and quantitative data searches, selective dissemination of information and photocopies.

418 - INDIAN SOCIETY OF AGRICULTURAL ECONOMICS

ADDRESS: 46-48, Esplanade Mansions,
    Mahatma Gandhi Road, Fort,
    Bombay 400001,
    INDIA
    TEL: 24.25.42
    CABLE: INDAGRECON
CREATED: 1939
SIZE OF STAFF: Professional: 2   Other: 5   Total: 7
TYPE OF SERVICE: private; non-profit
WORKING LANGUAGE(S): English
SUBJECT COVERAGE: agricultural economics; rural development
GEOGRAPHICAL COVERAGE: global
DATA BEING PROCESSED AND SIZE: 16,200 books; 130 periodicals; seminars
DATA PROCESSING METHODS: computerized
STORAGE MEDIA: tapes
TYPE OF ACTIVITY: data collection; distribution of information; publication
PERIODICALS PUBLISHED: - Indian Journal of Agricultural Economics
ACCESS TO SERVICE: paid services open to all users
TYPE & DESCRIPTION OF SERVICES PROVIDED: Provides library services, bibliographic searches of information and photocopies.

419 - INSTITUTE FOR DEFENCE STUDIES AND ANALYSES, LIBRARY, DOCUMENTATION AND INFORMATION SERVICE

SYNONYMOUS NAMES: IDSA Library, Documentation and Information Service
PARENT ORGANIZATION: Institute for Defence Studies and Analyses
ADDRESS: Sapru House,
    Barakhamba Road,
    New Delhi 110001,
    INDIA

TEL: 331 19 55
REATED: 1965   HEAD: Mr. J. Singh, Director
IZE OF STAFF: Professional: 5   Other: 9   Total: 14
YPE OF SERVICE: national; public; non-profit
ORKING LANGUAGE(S): English
UBJECT COVERAGE: political science; international relations; stratégies; war; peace;
        defence; weapons; system; disarmament
EOGRAPHICAL COVERAGE: global
ATA BEING PROCESSED AND SIZE: 21,000 books; 4,000 periodicals
ATA PROCESSING METHODS: manual
YPE OF ACTIVITY: data collection; data analysis; SSID training; publication
ERIODICALS PUBLISHED:
        - Accession List, 12 p.a.
        - Index to Current Literature, 12 p.a.
LIENTELE: researchers and army personnel (2,700 regular members, 6,000 occasional
        users p.a.)
CCESS TO SERVICE: open to all users, free of charge
YPE & DESCRIPTION OF SERVICES PROVIDED: Provides library services, bibliographic,
        literature and quantitative data searches of information and photocopies. A
        4-month Applied Librarianship training can be given to students holding a
        post-MA B.Lib.Sc..

20 - INSTITUTE FOR SOCIAL AND ECONOMIC CHANGE, LIBRARY

YNONYMOUS NAMES: ISECL, Library
DDRESS: Nagarbhavi P.O.,
        Bangalore 560072,
        INDIA
        TEL: 606224
        CABLE: ECOSOCI
REATED: 1972   HEAD: N. Samba Murthy, Librarian
IZE OF STAFF: Professional: 5   Other: 9   Total: 14
YPE OF SERVICE: national
ATERIALS DESCRIBING THE SERVICE: - Annual report of the institute
ORKING LANGUAGE(S): English
UBJECT COVERAGE: social sciences
EOGRAPHICAL COVERAGE: India
ATA BEING PROCESSED AND SIZE: 25,530 books; 26,000 reports and documents (back
        volumes of periodicals); 8,260 pamphlets; 224 maps, 400 periodicals
        (current)
ATA PROCESSING METHODS: manual
TORAGE MEDIA: traditional shelving of publications
ERIODICALS PUBLISHED: - Index to Current Articles on Social and Economic Change, 4
        p.a., since 1978
        - Agriculture and Rural Development Abstracts, 1984-1986
LIENTELE: doctoral students, faculty members, researchers
CCESS TO SERVICE: services open to all users free of charge
YPE & DESCRIPTION OF SERVICES PROVIDED: Provides library services, retrospective
        bibliographic searches, selective dissemination of information, current
        awareness service, photocopies and microforms.

India / Inde / India

421 - INSTITUTE OF CONSTITUTIONAL AND PARLIAMENTARY STUDIES, LIBRARY

ADDRESS: 18-21 Vithalbhai Patel House,
Rafi Marg,
New Delhi 110001,
INDIA
TEL: 383177
CABLE: CONPARLIST
CREATED: 1985   *HEAD:* S. Rangswami,
SIZE OF STAFF: Professional: 1   Total: 1
TYPE OF SERVICE: national; private; non-profit
SUBJECT COVERAGE: political science; law; parliamentary systems
GEOGRAPHICAL COVERAGE: India
DATA BEING PROCESSED AND SIZE: 9,000 books; 8,000 periodicals and reports
DATA PROCESSING METHODS: manual
TYPE OF ACTIVITY: distribution of information
CLIENTELE: research scholars (1,200)
ACCESS TO SERVICE: services open to specific categories of users
TYPE & DESCRIPTION OF SERVICES PROVIDED: Provides library services and information
searches of information.

422 - INSTITUTE OF ECONOMIC GROWTH LIBRARY

ADDRESS: University Enclave,
Delhi 110007,
INDIA
TEL: 2522524
CABLE: GROWTH DELHI
CREATED: 1958   *HEAD:* Mr. S. C. Bhatia, Librarian
SIZE OF STAFF: Professional: 6   Other: 11   Total: 17
TYPE OF SERVICE: international; public; non-profit
WORKING LANGUAGE(S): English
SUBJECT COVERAGE: economics; economic growth; economic history; economic development
GEOGRAPHICAL COVERAGE: global; Asia
DATA PROCESSING METHODS: computerized
STORAGE MEDIA: traditional shelving of publications; microfiches
TYPE OF ACTIVITY: distribution of information
PERIODICALS PUBLISHED:
- Asian Social Science Bibliography, 1 p.a.
- Selected List of Books and Periodicals Added to the Library, 12 p.a.
PUBLICATIONS: - Statistical annuals: list of IEG holdings, 1984
- Investment planning and project evaluation: bibliography
- Holding list of bound periodicals, 1985
- Environmental economics, a bibliography, 1986
CLIENTELE: research faculty and scholars; students
TYPE & DESCRIPTION OF SERVICES PROVIDED: Provides library services, bibliographic
search, on-line searches on external data bases, selective dissemination of
information and photocopies.

346

23 - INSTITUTE OF PUBLIC ENTERPRISE, LIBRARY

SYNONYMOUS NAMES: IPE, Library
ADDRESS: Osmania University Campus,
Hyderabad 500 007,
INDIA
HEAD: Mr. N. K. Gopalakrishnan, Chief, Library & Documentation
TYPE OF SERVICE: national
WORKING LANGUAGE(S): English
SUBJECT COVERAGE: economics; administrative sciences; management sciences; public
enterprise
GEOGRAPHICAL COVERAGE: India
DATA BEING PROCESSED AND SIZE: 10,000 books and 150 journals; parliamentary
publications; reports
DATA PROCESSING METHODS: manual; computerized
TYPE OF ACTIVITY: data collection; SSID training; publication
PERIODICALS PUBLISHED:
- COMPUT Newsletter, 4 p.a.
CLIENTELE: faculty and researchers of the Institute, students, university
researchers, enterprise managers
ACCESS TO SERVICE: open to all users
TYPE & DESCRIPTION OF SERVICES PROVIDED: The Library has established institutional
linkage for exchange of information and data with enterprises and public
systems in the country and their administrative department. Has also an
exchange arrangement with economic research institutions in India and with
an International Centre for Public Enterprises in Developing Countries at
Ljubljana, Commonwealth Secretariat at London, etc..

24 - INTERNATIONAL INSTITUTE FOR POPULATION SCIENCES, LIBRARY

SYNONYMOUS NAMES: IIPS
ADDRESS: Govandi Station Road,
Deonar,
Bombay 40088,
INDIA
TEL: 5511.13.47
CABLE: DEMOGRAPHY, CHEMBUR, BOMBAY
CREATED: 1956
SIZE OF STAFF: Professional: 5   Other: 10   Total: 15
TYPE OF SERVICE: international; public; non-profit
WORKING LANGUAGE(S): English
SUBJECT COVERAGE: demography; population
GEOGRAPHICAL COVERAGE: global
DATA BEING PROCESSED AND SIZE: 46,000 books; 250 journals
DATA PROCESSING METHODS: partially computerized
HARDWARE USED: Vax 11/780
STORAGE MEDIA: tapes; discs; microfiches
TYPE OF ACTIVITY: distribution of information; SSID scientific and methodological
activities; SSID training
CLIENTELE: researchers, government officials, international organizations (1,500
p.a.)

ACCESS TO SERVICE: services open to specific categories of users
TYPE & DESCRIPTION OF SERVICES PROVIDED: Provides bibliographic and library service

425 - JAWAHARLAL NEHRU UNIVERSITY, NEW DELHI, LIBRARY

ADDRESS: New Mehrauli Road,
         New Delhi 110067,
         INDIA
         TEL: 667676 - TELEX: 031-4967
         CABLE: JAYENU
HEAD: V. B. Nanda, University Librarian
SIZE OF STAFF: Professional: 42   Other: 96   Total: 138
TYPE OF SERVICE: national; public; non-profit
SYSTEMS & NETWORKS ATTACHED TO: DEVINSA (Development Information Network on South
         Asia)
WORKING LANGUAGE(S): English
SUBJECT COVERAGE: social sciences; humanities
GEOGRAPHICAL COVERAGE: global
DATA BEING PROCESSED AND SIZE: 332,000 books, periodicals and reports (10,000 p.a.)
DATA PROCESSING METHODS: manual
STORAGE MEDIA: traditional shelving of publications; microfiches; microfilms
TYPE OF ACTIVITY: data collection; distribution of information; publication
PERIODICALS PUBLISHED:
         - Suchika: Monthly Index to Periodical Literature on Social Sciences and
         Area Studies, 12 p.a.
         - Monthly List of Additions
CLIENTELE: faculty, research scholars, students (3,500)
ACCESS TO SERVICE: services open to all users, free of charge (except for
         photocopies)
TYPE & DESCRIPTION OF SERVICES PROVIDED: Provides bibliographic searches, selective
         dissemination of information and photocopies.

426 - KARVE INSTITUTE OF SOCIAL SERVICE

ADDRESS: Karvenagar,
         Pune 411052,
         INDIA
         TEL: 34203
CREATED: 1963
SIZE OF STAFF: Professional: 11
TYPE OF SERVICE: national; public; non-profit
SYSTEMS & NETWORKS ATTACHED TO: Association of Schools of Social Work in India; As
         Pacific Association for Social Work Education (APASWE); International
         Association of School of Social Work
WORKING LANGUAGE(S): English
SUBJECT COVERAGE: social welfare; social work; education; psychology; sociology
GEOGRAPHICAL COVERAGE: Maharashtra State and other states of India
DATA BEING PROCESSED AND SIZE: 9,360 books, reports and periodicals
DATA PROCESSING METHODS: manual

TORAGE MEDIA: traditional shelving of publications
YPE OF ACTIVITY: data collection; data analysis; distribution of information; SSID
        scientific and methodological activities; SSID training
ERIODICALS PUBLISHED:
        - Annual Report
        - Souvenir
CCESS TO SERVICE: services open to all users, some paid services
YPE & DESCRIPTION OF SERVICES PROVIDED: Provides library services, bibliographic and
        literature abstract searches and selective dissemination of information.

27 - MADRAS INSTITUTE OF DEVELOPMENT STUDIES

YNONYMOUS NAMES: MIDS
ARENT ORGANIZATION: Indian Council of Social Science Research
DDRESS: 79, Second Main Road,
        Gandhi Nagar,
        Adyar,
        Madras 600020,
        INDIA
        TEL: 412589
        CABLE: INSDEV
REATED: 1971   HEAD: Dr. C. T. Kurien, Director
IZE OF STAFF: Professional: 21   Other: 36   Total: 57
YPE OF SERVICE: national; private; non-profit
ORKING LANGUAGE(S): English
UBJECT COVERAGE: social sciences; development
ATA BEING PROCESSED AND SIZE: books; periodicals; reports; on-going research;
        seminars
ATA PROCESSING METHODS: partially computerized
YPE OF ACTIVITY: data collection; data analysis; distribution of information; SSID
        scientific and methodological activities; SSID training; publication
ERIODICALS PUBLISHED:
        - Bulletin
LIENTELE: research scholars; institutions
CCESS TO SERVICE: services open to specific categories of users
YPE & DESCRIPTION OF SERVICES PROVIDED: Provides library services, bibliographic and
        literature abstract searches, selective dissemination of information,
        information on magnetic tape and photocopies.

28 - MAHARASHTRA INSTITUTE OF LABOUR STUDIES

ARENT ORGANIZATION: Government of Maharashtra, Department of Labour
DDRESS: Dadabhai Chamarbaugwala Road,
        Parel,
        Bombay 400 012,
        INDIA
        TEL: 413.53.32 - TELEX: MILS, Parel, Bombay
REATED: 1947   HEAD: Dr. V. G. Mhetras, Director
IZE OF STAFF: Professional: 17

TYPE OF SERVICE: national; public; non-profit
MATERIALS DESCRIBING THE SERVICE: - Maharashtra Institute of Labour Studies, brochu
WORKING LANGUAGE(S): English; Marathi
SUBJECT COVERAGE: social sciences; administrative sciences; economics; education;
      law; psychology; social welfare; sociology; labour
GEOGRAPHICAL COVERAGE: Maharastra State, India
DATA PROCESSING METHODS: manual
TYPE OF ACTIVITY: data collection; data analysis; distribution of information; SSID
      scientific and methodological activities; SSID training; publication
PUBLICATIONS: - Personnel administration, 1986
         - Industrial relations, 1986
         - Industrial development and environment, 1986
         - Mhetras, V. G., Status of women workers, 1985
         - Mhetras, V. G., Women leaders of rural workers, 1985
         - Mhetras, V. G., Status of part-time women workers, 1985
ACCESS TO SERVICE: services open to specific categories of users, free of charge
TYPE & DESCRIPTION OF SERVICES PROVIDED: Provides library services, information
      searches, selective dissemination of information and translation of
      documents upon request.

429 - MANAGEMENT DEVELOPMENT INSTITUTE, LIBRARY

SYNONYMOUS NAMES: MDI Library
ADDRESS: Post Box No.60,
      Mehrahli Road,
      Gurgaon 122001,
      Haryana,
      INDIA
      TEL: 22117 - TELEX: 0342-212
      CABLE: MANDEVIN
CREATED: 1973   *HEAD:* M. M. Goyal, Librarian
SIZE OF STAFF: Professional: 6   Other: 4   Total: 10
TYPE OF SERVICE: national; public; non-profit
WORKING LANGUAGE(S): English
SUBJECT COVERAGE: management; administrative sciences; economics
GEOGRAPHICAL COVERAGE: India
DATA BEING PROCESSED AND SIZE: 30,000 books and repints; 2,400 journals; 190
      periodicals; 13 newspapers
DATA PROCESSING METHODS: manual
TYPE OF ACTIVITY: data collection; distribution of information; publication
PERIODICALS PUBLISHED: - Management Development Abstracts, 4 p.a.
         - MDI Management Journal
         - MDI Quarterly, 4 p.a.
ACCESS TO SERVICE: services open to specific categories of users, free of charge
TYPE & DESCRIPTION OF SERVICES PROVIDED: Provides library services, bibliographic a
      literature abstract searches, selective dissemination of information and
      photocopies.

30 - MINISTRY OF HUMAN RESOURCE DEVELOPMENT, DEPARTMENT OF CULTURE, CENTRAL SECRETARIAT LIBRARY

ADDRESS: 'G' Wing,
Shastgri Bhavan,
New Delhi 110001,
INDIA
TEL: 389383
CREATED: 1891   *HEAD:* Mr. S. C. Biswas, Director
SIZE OF STAFF: Professional: 52   Other: 74   Total: 126
TYPE OF SERVICE: national; public; non-profit
WORKING LANGUAGE(S): English; Hindi
SUBJECT COVERAGE: social sciences; education; history; government publications
GEOGRAPHICAL COVERAGE: Delhi and New Delhi, India
DATA BEING PROCESSED AND SIZE: 700,000 documents; 900 periodicals
DATA PROCESSING METHODS: partially computerized
HARDWARE USED: HP 3000
SOFTWARE USED: Minisis
STORAGE MEDIA: traditional shelving of publications; microfiches
TYPE OF ACTIVITY: data collection; distribution of information
CLIENTELE: government officials, research scholars, students and general public (500 per day)
ACCESS TO SERVICE: services open to all users, free of charge
TYPE & DESCRIPTION OF SERVICES PROVIDED: Provides library services, bibliographic searches of information, selective dissemination of information, microforms and photocopies.

31 - NATIONAL COUNCIL OF APPLIED ECONOMIC RESEARCH, DOCUMENTATION SERVICE

SYNONYMOUS NAMES: NCAER Documentation Service
ADDRESS: Parisila Bhawan,
11, Indraprastha Estate,
New Delhi 110 002,
INDIA
TEL: 331-7861-68 - TELEX: 3165880 NCAR IN
CABLE: ARTHSANDAN
CREATED: 1956
SIZE OF STAFF: Professional: 4   Other: 4   Total: 8
TYPE OF SERVICE: national; private; non-profit
WORKING LANGUAGE(S): English
SUBJECT COVERAGE: economics; social sciences
GEOGRAPHICAL COVERAGE: India
DATA BEING PROCESSED AND SIZE: 52,000 books and reports
DATA PROCESSING METHODS: partially computerized
HARDWARE USED: HP 3000
SOFTWARE USED: MINISIS
STORAGE MEDIA: traditional shelving of publications; microfiches
TYPE OF ACTIVITY: data collection; distribution of information; publication
PERIODICALS PUBLISHED: - Margin, 4 p.a.
- ArthaSuchi: Quarterly Index to Indian Economic Literature
CLIENTELE: researchers (150 p.a.)

ACCESS TO SERVICE: open to all users
TYPE & DESCRIPTION OF SERVICES PROVIDED: Provides library services, selective
dissemination of information, photocopies and microforms. Also provides on-
line services using own data base "ArthaSuchi" containing more than 8,500
entries.

432 - NATIONAL DOCUMENTATION CENTRE FOR HEALTH AND FAMILY WELFARE

PARENT ORGANIZATION: National Institute of Health and Family Welfare
ADDRESS: Munirka,
New Delhi-110067,
INDIA
TEL: 666059
CABLE: SWASTHPARIVAR
CREATED: 1976   *HEAD:* M. S. Gowtham, Senior Documentation Officer
SIZE OF STAFF: Professional: 11   Other: 9   Total: 20
TYPE OF SERVICE: national; public; non-profit
SYSTEMS & NETWORKS ATTACHED TO: Population Information Network of ESCAP (POPIN)
MATERIALS DESCRIBING THE SERVICE: - National Institute of Health and Family Welfare,
introduction. NIHFW, New Delhi, n.d. 16 p.
SUBJECT COVERAGE: population; family; welfare; demography; social sciences;
sociology; social welfare; statistics; psychology; economics; education;
law; social anthropology; cultural anthropology; health care
GEOGRAPHICAL COVERAGE: global
DATA BEING PROCESSED AND SIZE: monographs, books, reports, conference proceedings,
theses, and serial articles
DATA PROCESSING METHODS: manual; computerized
HARDWARE USED: HP 3000
SOFTWARE USED: Local
STORAGE MEDIA: traditional shelving of publications; floppy discs
TYPE OF ACTIVITY: distribution of information; SSID training; publication
PERIODICALS PUBLISHED:
- Health and Family Welfare Documentation Bulletin
- NIHFW Accession List
PUBLICATIONS: - Bibliographical series
- Health and family welfare critiques
CLIENTELE: researchers, trainers, program planners, trainees
ACCESS TO SERVICE: open to all users free of charge
TYPE & DESCRIPTION OF SERVICES PROVIDED: Provides selective dissemination of
information, current awareness service, query answering service,
retrospective bibliographic and literature searches, provision of microform
and photocopies. Orientation training is given to health, family welfare and
population librarians. Acts as clearing house for information on on-going
research in health care delivery system.

433 - NATIONAL INSTITUTE OF PUBLIC FINANCE AND POLICY, LIBRARY

ADDRESS: 18/2 Satsang Vihar Marg,
Special Institutional Area,

New Delhi 110067,
INDIA
TEL: 669303
CABLE: NIPUBFIN
REATED: 1976   *HEAD:* R. Kumar Sharma, Librarian
IZE OF STAFF: Professional: 3   Other: 5   Total: 8
YPE OF SERVICE: national; public; non-profit
ORKING LANGUAGE(S): English
UBJECT COVERAGE: economics; public finance; public policy
EOGRAPHICAL COVERAGE: India
ATA BEING PROCESSED AND SIZE: books; periodicals; reports; on-going research;
         seminars; training courses (4,000 p.a.)
ATA PROCESSING METHODS: partially computerized
ARDWARE USED: Wipro PC/AT
TORAGE MEDIA: traditional shelving of publications; fiches
YPE OF ACTIVITY: distribution of information
UBLICATIONS: - Aspects of the black economy in India (Black Money report), 1986
         - Inflation accounting and corporate taxation, 1987
         - Sales tax system in Manipur, 1987
         - Stamp duties and registration fees in West Bengal, 1986
         - An Appraisal of Provident Fund and allied schemes: opinion survey of
         subscribers, 1986
         - A Study on terminal tax in New Delhi, 1986
LIENTELE: faculty members, researchers
CCESS TO SERVICE: services open to specific categories of users
YPE & DESCRIPTION OF SERVICES PROVIDED: Provides library services, information
         searches and photocopies.

34 - NATIONAL INSTITUTE OF RURAL DEVELOPMENT, LIBRARY

YNONYMOUS NAMES: NIRD, Library;
         Centre on Rural Documentation
DDRESS: Rajendranagar,
         Hyderabad 500 030,
         INDIA
REATED: 1958   *HEAD:* Mr. A. Ahmad Khan,
IZE OF STAFF: Professional: 6   Other: 9   Total: 15
YPE OF SERVICE: national; public; non-profit
ORKING LANGUAGE(S): English
UBJECT COVERAGE: social sciences; administrative sciences; demography; economics;
         education; political science; psychology; social anthropology; cultural
         anthropology; social welfare; sociology; rural development
EOGRAPHICAL COVERAGE: India; developing countries
ATA BEING PROCESSED AND SIZE: 60,000 books; 70,000 periodical articles indexed
ATA PROCESSING METHODS: manual
YPE OF ACTIVITY: data collection; publication
ERIODICALS PUBLISHED: - CORD Index, 12 p.a.
         - CORD Abstracts, 6 p.a.
         - CORD Accessions, 4 p.a.
UBLICATIONS: - Rural development. A register of research in India, 1983-84
LIENTELE: researchers and trainees

ACCESS TO SERVICE: open to all users, services free of charge (reimbursement of
marginal costs)
TYPE & DESCRIPTION OF SERVICES PROVIDED: Provides library services, bibliographies
and photocopies upon request.

435 - NATIONAL SOCIAL SCIENCE DOCUMENTATION CENTRE

SYNONYMOUS NAMES: NASSDOC
PARENT ORGANIZATION: Indian Council of Social Science Research
ADDRESS: 35, Ferozeshah Road,
        New Delhi 110 001,
        INDIA
        TEL: 384353 - TELEX: 3161083-ISSR-IN
        CABLE: ICSORES
CREATED: 1970   *HEAD:* Mr. S. P. Agrawal, Director
SIZE OF STAFF: Professional: 25   Other: 30   Total: 55
TYPE OF SERVICE: national; public; non-profit
SYSTEMS & NETWORKS ATTACHED TO: National Information System in Social Sciences
        (NISSS); Asia Pacific Information Network in the Social Sciences (APINESS)
MATERIALS DESCRIBING THE SERVICE: - NASSDOC: How it works, 1987
        - NASSDOC Dockets
WORKING LANGUAGE(S): English
SUBJECT COVERAGE: social sciences
GEOGRAPHICAL COVERAGE: global
DATA BEING PROCESSED AND SIZE: 20,000 books, research reports and theses; 100,000
        periodicals
DATA PROCESSING METHODS: partially computerized
TYPE OF ACTIVITY: data collection; data analysis; publication; SSID scientific and
        methodological activities
PERIODICALS PUBLISHED:
        - Conference Alert, a quarterly calendar
        - Acquisition Update
        - Paging Review of Periodical Contents
        - Social Science News: Index to Select Newspapers in English
PUBLICATIONS: - Union catalogue of social science serials
        - Indian economic bibliography
        - Mahatma Gandhi bibliography, 1984
        - Research project reports in SSDC: an annotated bibliography, 1984
        - Social sciences research methodology: a bibliography, 1983
        - Bibliography of bibliographies in SSDC, 1983
        - Reference sources in SSDC: a bibliography, 1984
        - Inventory of social science institutions and organisations in India, 1985
        - Library and information science literature: SSDC resources, 1985
        - Periodicals in SSDC: Current list 1985
        - Social Sciences in the present day world since 1970: a bibliography, 1986
        - Social science information and documentation: search for relevance India,
        1986
        - Union catalogue of Library science and informatics publications: Delhi
        Librairies, 1986
        - Indian social science periodicals: a survey, 1986
        - Goa, Daman and Diu: a preliminary list, 1986

- Thesauri, glossaries, terminologies and dictionaries in NASSDOC: a resource list, 1987

CLIENTELE: researchers, students (8,000 p.a.)

ACCESS TO SERVICE: open to specific categories of users, free of charge and some paid services

TYPE & DESCRIPTION OF SERVICES PROVIDED: Provides library services, query answering service, retrospective bibliographic searchers, inter-library loans, financial assistance for collection of material for research, provision of data for secondary analysis and photocopies.

436 - NETAJI INSTITUTE FOR ASIAN STUDIES

SYNONYMOUS NAMES: NIAS
PARENT ORGANIZATION: Government of West Bangal, Higher Education Department
ADDRESS: 1, Woodburn Park,
Calcutta 700020,
INDIA
TEL: 44-3145
CREATED: 1980   *HEAD:* Dr. R. Chakrabarti, Director
TYPE OF SERVICE: international; non-profit
WORKING LANGUAGE(S): English
SUBJECT COVERAGE: social sciences
GEOGRAPHICAL COVERAGE: South Asia; Southeast Asia
DATA BEING PROCESSED AND SIZE: 1,000 books and reports; 45 periodicals; 20 seminars
DATA PROCESSING METHODS: manual
STORAGE MEDIA: traditional shelving of publications
TYPE OF ACTIVITY: data collection; data analysis; distribution of information; SSID scientific and methodological activities; publication
PERIODICALS PUBLISHED: - Asian Studies, 4 p.a.
PUBLICATIONS: - Dhar, S., Transformation and trend of Buddhism in the 20th Century
- Ramachandra, G. P., Kampuchea: an artificial problem in international relations
- Majumdar, A. K., Indian foreign policy and Marxist opposition parties in Parliament
CLIENTELE: scholars
ACCESS TO SERVICE: services open to specific categories of users, free of charge
TYPE & DESCRIPTION OF SERVICES PROVIDED: Provides library services, bibliographic searches, selective dissemination of information and photocopies.

437 - OSMANIA UNIVERSITY, REGIONAL CENTRE FOR URBAN AND ENVIRONMENTAL STUDIES

ADDRESS: Hyderabad 500007,
Andhra Pradesh,
INDIA
TEL: 703394
HEAD: Prof. D. Ravindra Prasad, Director
TYPE OF SERVICE: national; public; non-profit
WORKING LANGUAGE(S): English
SUBJECT COVERAGE: administrative sciences; social sciences; urban planning;

environmental planning
GEOGRAPHICAL COVERAGE: Southern States of India
DATA BEING PROCESSED AND SIZE: books; periodicals; reports; on-going research;
       seminars; training courses
DATA PROCESSING METHODS: manual
STORAGE MEDIA: traditional shelving of publications
TYPE OF ACTIVITY: data collection; data analysis; distribution of information; SSID
       scientific and methodological activities; publication
PUBLICATIONS: - Property tax administration
        - Urban government and administration
        - Reforms in municipal government
        - Public housing
        - Municipal tax on mineral rights
        - Urban conservation
CLIENTELE: academics, administrators, practitioners and other urban government
       officers
ACCESS TO SERVICE: paid services open to specific categories of users
TYPE & DESCRIPTION OF SERVICES PROVIDED: Provides library services.

438 - PARLIAMENT LIBRARY AND REFERENCE, RESEARCH, DOCUMENTATION AND INFORMATION SERVICE

SYNONYMOUS NAMES: LARRDIS
PARENT ORGANIZATION: Lok Sabha Secretariat
ADDRESS: Lok Sabha Secretariat,
       Parliament House,
       New Delhi-110001,
       INDIA
       TEL: 695752 - TELEX: 31.66156 LSS IN
       CABLE: LOKSABHA, NEW DELHI
CREATED: 1921   HEAD: Mr. S. R. C. Bhardwaj, Director
SIZE OF STAFF: Total: 186
TYPE OF SERVICE: national; public; non-profit
MATERIALS DESCRIBING THE SERVICE: - LARRDIS no. 63 (PPR)
        - A Guide to Parliament Library
        - Parliament Library rules
WORKING LANGUAGE(S): English; Hindi
SUBJECT COVERAGE: political science; law; public administration; constitutional law;
       social sciences; parliamentary systems
GEOGRAPHICAL COVERAGE: global
DATA BEING PROCESSED AND SIZE: 650,000 printed documents (15,000 p.a.)
DATA PROCESSING METHODS: manual
STORAGE MEDIA: traditional shelving of publications
TYPE OF ACTIVITY: data collection; publication
PERIODICALS PUBLISHED: - Abstracts of Books, Reports and Articles, 4 p.a.
        - Journal of Parliamentary Information, 4 p.a.
        - Sansadiya Patrika (Hindi), 4 p.a.
        - Digest of Central Acts, 4 p.a.
        - Digest of Legislative and Constitutional Cases, 4 p.a.
        - Diary of Political Events, 12 p.a.
        - Digest of News and Views on Public Undertakings, 12 p.a.

- Masik Samachar Saar (Hindi)
- Sarkari Upakrama Samachar aur Abhimat Saar (Hindi)
- Documentation, 24 p.a.
- Parliament Library Bulletin

CLIENTELE: members of Parliament, government officials, research scholars
TYPE & DESCRIPTION OF SERVICES PROVIDED: Provides library and reference services,
documentation and press clippings, research assistance and press and public
relations services.

439 - PEACE RESEARCH CENTRE

PARENT ORGANIZATION: Gujarat Vidyapith
ADDRESS: Ashram Road,
Ahmadabad 380014,
INDIA
CREATED: 1970   *HEAD:* Prof. R. Parikh, Director
SIZE OF STAFF: Professional: 1   Other: 1   Total: 2
TYPE OF SERVICE: international; public; non-profit
SYSTEMS & NETWORKS ATTACHED TO: International Peace Research Association, Finland
SUBJECT COVERAGE: peace research; nonviolence; conflict resolution
DATA PROCESSING METHODS: partially computerized
STORAGE MEDIA: traditional shelving of publications; tapes; microfiches
TYPE OF ACTIVITY: data collection; data analysis; distribution of information; SSID
scientific and methodological activities; SSID training; publication
PERIODICALS PUBLISHED:
- SETU: a bulletin of documentation on peace research
CLIENTELE: mainly social science researchers
ACCESS TO SERVICE: open to speicific categories of users, free of charge
TYPE & DESCRIPTION OF SERVICES PROVIDED: Provides library services, bibliographic,
literature abstract and quantitative data searches, on-line searches of own
data base on conflict situation in Guyana State, selective dissemination of
information and photocopies.

440 - RESEARCH AND INFORMATION SYSTEM FOR THE NON-ALIGNED AND OTHER DEVELOPING COUNTRIES, DOCUMENTATION CENTRE AND DATA ARCHIVES

ADDRESS: 40-B, Lodhi Estate,
New Delhi-110 003,
INDIA
TEL: 617136
CABLE: RISNODEC, NEW DELHI-110 003
CREATED: 1984   *HEAD:* Dr. V. R. Panchamukhi, Director
SIZE OF STAFF: Professional: 4   Other: 24   Total: 28
TYPE OF SERVICE: international; public; non-profit
SYSTEMS & NETWORKS ATTACHED TO: MSIN (Multi-Sectorial Information Network)
MATERIALS DESCRIBING THE SERVICE: - Brochure
WORKING LANGUAGE(S): English
SUBJECT COVERAGE: social sciences; economics; international economics; self-reliance
GEOGRAPHICAL COVERAGE: developing countries

DATA BEING PROCESSED AND SIZE: 2,100 books; 2,700 working papers; 2,500 pamphlets;
          130 periodicals
DATA PROCESSING METHODS: manual; computerized
HARDWARE USED: IBM PC/Compatibles
SOFTWARE USED: DBASE; Word Star; Supper Cala, Basic, Cobol, Fortran
STORAGE MEDIA: disks; diskettes (5 1/2" and 8"); tapes
TYPE OF ACTIVITY: data collection; data analysis; distribution of information; SSID
          scientific and methodological activities; publication
PERIODICALS PUBLISHED:
          - RIS Digest, 4 p.a.
          - Acquisitions List
PUBLICATIONS: - RIS bibliographical services
          - The World economy in the mid-eighties
          - V. R. Panchamukhi et al; , The Third World and the world economic system,
          1986
          - V. R. Panchamukhi, Capital formation and output in the Third World, 1986
          - South-South economic cooperation, 1987
          - Low income Developing Countries : problems and prospects, 1987
CLIENTELE: research institutions in India and other countries, research scholars
ACCESS TO SERVICE: open to specific categories of users, free of charge
TYPE & DESCRIPTION OF SERVICES PROVIDED: Provides library and inter-library loan
          services, selective dissemination of information, bibliographic, literature
          and quantitative data searches using its own data base as well as those of
          UN, UNCTAD and the World Bank. Also provides computer print-outs,
          information on magnetic tapes and photocopies. Specializes in research on
          issues related to economic and technological cooperation among non-aligned
          and other developing countries.

441 - SHRI RAM CENTRE FOR INDUSTRIAL RELATIONS AND HUMAN RESOURCES

ADDRESS: 4E/16, Jhandewalan Extension,
          New Delhi 110055,
          INDIA
          TEL: 519064
          CABLE: SRICIR
CREATED: 1963   *HEAD:* A. Joshi, Executive Director
SIZE OF STAFF: Total: 38
TYPE OF SERVICE: national; private; non-profit
MATERIALS DESCRIBING THE SERVICE: - Brochure
WORKING LANGUAGE(S): English
SUBJECT COVERAGE: economics; psychology; sociology; labour relations; surveys
GEOGRAPHICAL COVERAGE: India
DATA BEING PROCESSED AND SIZE: 30,000 books
DATA PROCESSING METHODS: manual
TYPE OF ACTIVITY: data collection; data analysis; publication
PERIODICALS PUBLISHED: - Indian Journal of Industrial Relations, 4 p.a.
ACCESS TO SERVICE: open to all users free of charge
TYPE & DESCRIPTION OF SERVICES PROVIDED: Provides library services, bibliographies,
          literature searches and surveys. Specializes in labour relations.

442 - SNDT WOMEN'S UNIVERSITY, RESEARCH CENTRE FOR WOMEN'S STUDIES, REFERENCE SERVICE AND DOCUMENTATION CENTRE

ADDRESS: Vithaldas Vidyavihar,
Santacruz,
Bombay 400049,
INDIA
CREATED: 1974   *HEAD:* Ms. S. Deokattey, Documentalist
SIZE OF STAFF: Professional: 4   Other: 3   Total: 7
TYPE OF SERVICE: international; public; non-profit
WORKING LANGUAGE(S): English
SUBJECT COVERAGE: women; womens studies
GEOGRAPHICAL COVERAGE: India
DATA BEING PROCESSED AND SIZE: books; periodicals; reports; on-going resarch;
seminars; training courses (200-300 books p.a.; 500-600 non-book material)
DATA PROCESSING METHODS: manual
STORAGE MEDIA: traditional shelving of publications
TYPE OF ACTIVITY: data collection; distribution of information; publication
PUBLICATIONS: - Directory of organizations for women
- Women's studies: an index to Indian periodical literature
- Women' studies index, 1986
- Women and Marathi press: a list of 19th century periodicals on women's issues
CLIENTELE: researchers, activists, journalists, students (15-20 per day)
ACCESS TO SERVICE: services open to all users, free of charge
TYPE & DESCRIPTION OF SERVICES PROVIDED: Provides library searches, bibliographic searches, selective dissemination of information, current awareness services, photocopies and translation of documents upon request.

443 - SRI VENKATESWARA UNIVERSITY, POPULATION STUDIES CENTRE

ADDRESS: Tirupati 517502,
INDIA
TEL: 2781
CREATED: 1973   *HEAD:* Dr. P. Jayarami Reddy, Head
SIZE OF STAFF: Professional: 11   Other: 7   Total: 18
TYPE OF SERVICE: international; public; non-profit
MATERIALS DESCRIBING THE SERVICE: - Brochure
WORKING LANGUAGE(S): English
SUBJECT COVERAGE: demography; economics; geography; psychology; sociology; fertility; mortality; population education; rural development; social change; migration; population growth; family planning
GEOGRAPHICAL COVERAGE: global
DATA BEING PROCESSED AND SIZE: 4,000 documentation items
DATA PROCESSING METHODS: computerized
STORAGE MEDIA: traditional shelving of publications; discs
TYPE OF ACTIVITY: SSID scientific and methodological activities; SSID training; publication
PUBLICATIONS: - Sociology of fertility
- Decision-making and diffusion in family planning
- Strategies for population control

- Infant and childhood mortality in India
- Fertility and mortality

CLIENTELE: students, faculty members

ACCESS TO SERVICE: services open to all users

TYPE & DESCRIPTION OF SERVICES PROVIDED: Provides library services, literature abstract searches, on-line services using external data bases and selective dissemination of information.

444 - TATA ECONOMIC CONSULTANCY SERVICES

SYNONYMOUS NAMES: TECS

PARENT ORGANIZATION: TECS

ADDRESS: Orient House,
Mangalore Street,
Ballard Estate,
Bombay 400038,
INDIA
TEL: 267621 - TELEX: 011-2618
CABLE: TECSTATA

CREATED: 1970   *HEAD:* Mr. D. N. Poonegar, Executive Director

SIZE OF STAFF: Professional: 85   Other: 35   Total: 120

TYPE OF SERVICE: international; private; profit

MATERIALS DESCRIBING THE SERVICE: - An Introduction to Tata Economic Consultancy Services

WORKING LANGUAGE(S): English

SUBJECT COVERAGE: economics; social sciences; social welfare; psychology; demography market research; feasibility reports; economic studies

GEOGRAPHICAL COVERAGE: India; global

DATA BEING PROCESSED AND SIZE: 1,530 reports, on-going research, seminars (90-100 p.a.)

DATA PROCESSING METHODS: partially computerized

STORAGE MEDIA: traditional shelving of publications

TYPE OF ACTIVITY: data collection; data analysis; distribution of information; SSID scientific and methodological activities; publication

CLIENTELE: 1,500 clients

ACCESS TO SERVICE: paid services open to all users

TYPE & DESCRIPTION OF SERVICES PROVIDED: Provides library services, quantitative dat searches and selective dissemination of information.

445 - UNIVERSITY OF DELHI, DEPARTMENT OF SOCIAL WORK, DOCUMENTATION CENTRE

ADDRESS: 3 University Road,
Delhi 110007,
INDIA
TEL: 2523981
CABLE: SOCIWORK

MATERIALS DESCRIBING THE SERVICE: - UN Asian Development Institute, Directory of Development Documentation and Information Facilities in Asia and the Pacific, 1976

WORKING LANGUAGE(S): English
SUBJECT COVERAGE: social welfare; social work
GEOGRAPHICAL COVERAGE: India; Asia
DATA BEING PROCESSED AND SIZE: books; periodicals; reports
TYPE OF ACTIVITY: data collection; data analysis; distribution of information;
        publication
PERIODICALS PUBLISHED:
        - Accession List
CLIENTELE: social scientists, research scholars, students
ACCESS TO SERVICE: paid services open to specific categories of users
TYPE & DESCRIPTION OF SERVICES PROVIDED: Provides library services, bibliographic and
        literature abstract searches of information and photocopies.

446 - XAVIER LABOUR RELATIONS INSTITUTE, LIBRARY

SYNONYMOUS NAMES: XLRI, Library
ADDRESS: Post Box 222,
        Circuit House Area (East),
        Jamshedpur 831001,
        INDIA
        TEL: 25231 - TELEX: 626240 XLRI IN
        CABLE: EXCEL
CREATED: 1949
SIZE OF STAFF: Total: 10
TYPE OF SERVICE: national; public; non-profit
WORKING LANGUAGE(S): English
SUBJECT COVERAGE: administrative sciences; social sciences; labour relations
GEOGRAPHICAL COVERAGE: India
DATA BEING PROCESSED AND SIZE: books
DATA PROCESSING METHODS: partially computerized
HARDWARE USED: WIPRO Series 6820; Neptune PC/XT
SOFTWARE USED: SPSS
STORAGE MEDIA: disks, tapes
TYPE OF ACTIVITY: data collection; data analysis; distribution of information
PERIODICALS PUBLISHED: - Management and Labour Studies Journal
CLIENTELE: postgraduates, industry and commerce experts
ACCESS TO SERVICE: services free of charge, some paid services
TYPE & DESCRIPTION OF SERVICES PROVIDED: Provides bibliographic searches of
        information.

447 - CENTRE FOR STRATEGIC AND INTERNATIONAL STUDIES, LIBRARY

SYNONYMOUS NAMES: CSIS Library
PARENT ORGANIZATION: CSIS Library
ADDRESS: Jalan Tanah Abang III/27,
        Jakarta 10160,
        INDONESIA
        TEL: 356532 - TELEX: 45164 CSIS IA

CABLE: CSIS Jakarta
CREATED: 1971   *HEAD:* T. Murdani, Chief
SIZE OF STAFF: Professional: 3   Other: 16   Total: 19
TYPE OF SERVICE: national; public; non-profit
WORKING LANGUAGE(S): English; Indonesia
SUBJECT COVERAGE: political science; demography; economics; education; history; law
GEOGRAPHICAL COVERAGE: Jakarta, Indonesia
DATA BEING PROCESSED AND SIZE: 20,000 books; 350 periodicals
DATA PROCESSING METHODS: manual
STORAGE MEDIA: traditional shelving of publications
TYPE OF ACTIVITY: distribution of information
CLIENTELE: students, researchers (40 per day)
ACCESS TO SERVICE: services open to all users, free of charge
TYPE & DESCRIPTION OF SERVICES PROVIDED: Provides library services, newspaper
        clippings, selective dissemination of information and photocopies.

448 - LEMBAGA PENELITIAN PENDIDIKAN DAN PENERANGAN EKONOMI DAN SOSIAL, PERPUSTAKAAN

SYNONYMOUS NAMES: LEPPES;
        Institute for Economic and Social Research, Education and Information
        Library
ADDRESS: Jalan S. Parman no. 81, Slipi,
        P.O. Box 493,
        Jakarta 10002,
        INDONESIA
        TEL: 591528
        CABLE: LEPPES, Jakarta
CREATED: 1971
SIZE OF STAFF: Professional: 2   Other: 3   Total: 5
TYPE OF SERVICE: national; private; non-profit
SYSTEMS & NETWORKS ATTACHED TO: Jaringan Dokumentasi ilmu-ilmu sosial (Social Scienc
        Documentation Network System)
SUBJECT COVERAGE: economics; social sciences; small scale industry; rural
        development; urban development
GEOGRAPHICAL COVERAGE: Indonesia
DATA BEING PROCESSED AND SIZE: 4,000 written documents; 225 bibliographical
        references; on-going research; statistical series
DATA PROCESSING METHODS: manual
PERIODICALS PUBLISHED:
        - Accessions List
        - Information Bulletin
PUBLICATIONS: - Clipping index
        - Current content service
ACCESS TO SERVICE: services open to specific categories of users
TYPE & DESCRIPTION OF SERVICES PROVIDED: Provides retrospective bibliographic
        searches of information and question answering service.

449 - LEMBAZA STUDI PEMBANGUNAN

SYNONYMOUS NAMES: Institute for Development Studies
PARENT ORGANIZATION: Lembaga Studi Pembangunan
ADDRESS: P.O. Box 1 KBY SB/JAKSEL,
      Jakarta,
      INDONESIA
      TEL: 512-608; 512-672 - TELEX: 62399 CARE IA, Indonesia
CREATED: 1976   *HEAD:* A. Sasono, Director
TYPE OF SERVICE: national; private; non-profit
SYSTEMS & NETWORKS ATTACHED TO: Third World Network (TWN); South-East Asian Forum for
      Development Alternatives (SEAFDA)
MATERIALS DESCRIBING THE SERVICE: - Brochure
WORKING LANGUAGE(S): Indonesian; English
SUBJECT COVERAGE: economics; development
GEOGRAPHICAL COVERAGE: Indonesia
DATA PROCESSING METHODS: partially computerized
HARDWARE USED: IBM PC
SOFTWARE USED: Dbase III, Spreadsheet, Lotus, Framework, WS-2000, Multiplan
STORAGE MEDIA: traditional shelving of publications
TYPE OF ACTIVITY: data collection; data analysis; distribution of information;
      publication
PERIODICALS PUBLISHED:
      - Grassroots
CLIENTELE: scholars, students, institutes
ACCESS TO SERVICE: services open to specific categories of users, free of charge
TYPE & DESCRIPTION OF SERVICES PROVIDED: Provides library services, bibliographic,
      literature abstract and quantitative data searches, on-line searches on own
      data base INSAN, selective dissemination of information, production of
      information on magnetic tapes and translation of documents.

450 - PUSAT PELAYANAN KEADILAN DAN PENGABDIAN HUKUM

SYNONYMOUS NAMES: PPK-PH;
      University of Indonesia, Center for Justice and the Rule of Law
ADDRESS: Jalan Salemba Raya, 4,
      Jakarta,
      INDONESIA
      TEL: 330292
CREATED: 1948   *HEAD:* Mr. M. Reksodiputro, Head
TYPE OF SERVICE: national; private; non-profit
WORKING LANGUAGE(S): Indonesian
SUBJECT COVERAGE: law; criminology; criminal law
GEOGRAPHICAL COVERAGE: Jakarta, Indonesia
DATA BEING PROCESSED AND SIZE: 5,500 books and reports
DATA PROCESSING METHODS: manual
STORAGE MEDIA: fiches
TYPE OF ACTIVITY: SSID scientific and methodological activities; publication
PERIODICALS PUBLISHED:
      - Banaha, 4 p.a.
CLIENTELE: students, lecturers

Indonesia / Indonésie / Indonesia

ACCESS TO·SERVICE: services open to specific categories of users, free of charge
TYPE & DESCRIPTION OF SERVICES PROVIDED: Provides library services, bibliographic
     searches and photocopies.

451 - PUSAT PENELITIAN DAN PENGEMBANGAN PERKOTAAN DAN LINGKUNGAN, BAGIAN DOKUMENTASI
     DAN INFORMASI

SYNONYMOUS NAMES: Centre for Urban and Environmental Research and Development,
     Documentation and Information Section for Urban and Environmental Problems
     PPPPL-DKI Jakarta, DOCINFO
ADDRESS: Jalan Rsuna Said Kuningan,
     Jakarta Selatan,
     INDONESIA
     TEL: 516174
CREATED: 1972
SIZE OF STAFF: Professional: 2   Other: 1   Total: 3
TYPE OF SERVICE: international; private; profit
WORKING LANGUAGE(S): Indonesian
SUBJECT COVERAGE: urban development; environment
GEOGRAPHICAL COVERAGE: Jakarta, Indonesia
DATA PROCESSING METHODS: manual
TYPE OF ACTIVITY: data collection; distribution of information; SSID scientific and
     methodological activities; SSID training; publication
PUBLICATIONS: - Annotated bibliography for urban and environment development (in
     Indonesian)
ACCESS TO SERVICE: services open to specific categories of users
TYPE & DESCRIPTION OF SERVICES PROVIDED: Provides library services, bibliographic
     searches and selective dissemination of information.

452 - PUSAT PENELITIAN UNIKA ATMA JAYA, PERPUSTAKAAN

SYNONYMOUS NAMES: Atma Jaya Research Centre, Library
PARENT ORGANIZATION: Atma Jaya Foundation
ADDRESS: Jalan Jenderal Sudirman 49A,
     P.O.Box 2639,
     Jakarta 10001,
     INDONESIA
     TEL: 586491
     CABLE: UNIKATOLIK Jakarta
CREATED: 1972   *HEAD:* K. J. Veeger,
SIZE OF STAFF: Professional: 35   Other: 13   Total: 48
TYPE OF SERVICE: international; private; non-profit
WORKING LANGUAGE(S): Indonesian; English
SUBJECT COVERAGE: social sciences; demography; economics; education; psychology;
     social anthropology; cultural anthropology; social welfare; sociology
GEOGRAPHICAL COVERAGE: Indonesia; Asia; USA; Europe; Australia
DATA BEING PROCESSED AND SIZE: 46,000 books and reports; 660 periodicals
DATA PROCESSING METHODS: partially computerized
TYPE OF ACTIVITY: data collection; data analysis; distribution of information; SSID

scientific and methodological activities; SSID training; publication
PERIODICALS PUBLISHED:
- Atma Jaya Research Centre Library Bulletin
ACCESS TO SERVICE: services open to all users, free of charge
TYPE & DESCRIPTION OF SERVICES PROVIDED: Provides library services, bibliographic,
literature abstract and quantitative data searches, on-line service using
own data bases and external data bases, selective dissemination of
information, microforms, photocopies and translation of documents.

53 - UNIVERSITY OF INDONESIA, FACULTY OF ECONOMICS, THE DEMOGRAPHIC INSTITUTE, LIBRARY

ADDRESS: Jalan Salemba Raya no. 4,
P.O. Box 427,
Jakarta 10002,
INDONESIA
TEL: 336434
CABLE: FEKODEM
CREATED: 1971   *HEAD:* S. Sri Suyatni, Head
SIZE OF STAFF: Professional: 2   Other: 3   Total: 5
TYPE OF SERVICE: national; public; non-profit
SYSTEMS & NETWORKS ATTACHED TO: Population and Family Planning Information Network
(Indonesia) and ASEAN POPINS
WORKING LANGUAGE(S): Indonesian; English
SUBJECT COVERAGE: demography; economics; social welfare; sociology
GEOGRAPHICAL COVERAGE: Indonesia; Asia; Pacific area
DATA BEING PROCESSED AND SIZE: 9,100 books; 410 journals; newspaper clippings; 600
other documentation items
DATA PROCESSING METHODS: manual
TYPE OF ACTIVITY: data collection; publication
PERIODICALS PUBLISHED:
- Indeks Artikel, (Articles index)
- Warta Demografi, (Demographic newsletter)
PUBLICATIONS: - Bibliographies
- Index of newspaper articles
CLIENTELE: students, researchers, teaching staff, general public
ACCESS TO SERVICE: open to all users
TYPE & DESCRIPTION OF SERVICES PROVIDED: Provides library services, bibliographic
searches of information, selective dissemination of information,
photocopies.

54 - YAYASAN IDAYU, PERPUSTAKAAN

SYNONYMOUS NAMES: Idayu Foundation, Library
ADDRESS: Gedung Kebangkitan Nasional,
Jalan Dr. Abdulrahman Saleh 26,
Jakarta Pusat,
INDONESIA
TEL: 361261 - TELEX: 011.44359

CABLE: Yayasanidayu Jakarta
CREATED: 1966   HEAD: D. Asif, Acting Executive Chairman/Librarian
SIZE OF STAFF: Professional: 16   Other: 26   Total: 42
TYPE OF SERVICE: national; public; non-profit
SYSTEMS & NETWORKS ATTACHED TO: Social Sciences Documentation Center of the Indones
         Council of Sciences (PDIS)
SUBJECT COVERAGE: social sciences; economics; geography; history; law; mass
         communication; political science; statistics; administrative sciences;
         psychology; social welfare; sociology
GEOGRAPHICAL COVERAGE: Indonesia
DATA BEING PROCESSED AND SIZE: 173,664 books; 2,223 periodicals; 325,000 newspaper
         clippings; photos and films
DATA PROCESSING METHODS: manual
TYPE OF ACTIVITY: data collection; distribution of information; publication
PERIODICALS PUBLISHED:
         - Berita Idayu Bibliografi, book-news. 12 p.a.
         - Indeks Pers, bulletin, 12 p.a.
CLIENTELE: 300 students per day
ACCESS TO SERVICE: open to specific categories of users, paid services
TYPE & DESCRIPTION OF SERVICES PROVIDED: Provides library services, bibliographies
         and photocopies.

455 - IRANIAN DOCUMENTATION CENTRE

SYNONYMOUS NAMES: IRANDOC
PARENT ORGANIZATION: Ministry of Culture and Higher Education
ADDRESS: P.O. Box 13185/1371,
         1188 Engelab Ave.,
         Tehran,
         IRAN (ISLAMIC REPUBLIC)
         TEL: 662223
         CABLE: ASNAD IRAN
CREATED: 1968   HEAD: M. N. Mahdavi, Director
SIZE OF STAFF: Total: 60
TYPE OF SERVICE: national; public; non-profit
SYSTEMS & NETWORKS ATTACHED TO: UNISIST
MATERIALS DESCRIBING THE SERVICE: - IRANDOC, 1984, Leaflet
WORKING LANGUAGE(S): Farsi; English
SUBJECT COVERAGE: science; social sciences
DATA BEING PROCESSED AND SIZE: 32,500 books and technical reports; 4,000 periodical
         and serials with current subscription to 125 titles; 8,000 theses and
         dissertations
DATA PROCESSING METHODS: manual
STORAGE MEDIA: traditional shelving of publications
TYPE OF ACTIVITY: data collection; data analysis; publication; SSID scientific and
         methodological activities; SSID Training
PUBLICATIONS: - Contents pages: science and social science journals 1969-1973 (in
         Persian)
         - Index to Iranian government publications available in IRANDOC, 1983 (In
         Persian)

- Iranian national union list of serials, 1983
- Directory of documentation centres, special libraries and universtiy libraries of Iran, 1983 (in Persian)
- Index of the non-book materials in Iranian Documentation Centre, 1983 (in Persian)
- Bibliography of management

LIENTELE: researchers

CCESS TO SERVICE: services open to specific categories of users

YPE & DESCRIPTION OF SERVICES PROVIDED: Provides selective dissemination of information, lending and reference services to scientists and specialists, publication of bibliographic references. Engages in planning and coordinating the project of national scientific and technical information network and serves as a link in the world scientific information network (UNISIST).

Ireland / Irlande / Irlanda

56 - UNIVERSITY COLLEGE DUBLIN, DEVELOPMENT STUDIES INFORMATION CENTRE AND LIBRARY

DDRESS: Belfield,
          Dublin 4,
          IRELAND
          TEL: 69.32.44 - TELEX: 24114

REATED: 1986   *HEAD:* Ms. M. Riordan, Librarian

IZE OF STAFF: Total: 2

YPE OF SERVICE: public; non-profit

ORKING LANGUAGE(S): English

UBJECT COVERAGE: social sciences; economics; political science; social anthropology; cultural anthropology; sociology; development; agriculture; food policy

EOGRAPHICAL COVERAGE: developing countries

ATA BEING PROCESSED AND SIZE: 1,000 books; 100 periodicals

ATA PROCESSING METHODS: computerized

ARDWARE USED: ERICSSON P.C.

OFTWARE USED: INMAGIC

YPE OF ACTIVITY: distribution of information; publication

ERIODICALS PUBLISHED:
          - Accessions List
          - List of Periodicals

LIENTELE: students, researchers, aid agencies, Department of Foreign Affairs, other libraries, general public

CCESS TO SERVICE: services open to all users, free of charge

YPE & DESCRIPTION OF SERVICES PROVIDED: Provides library services, bibliographic, literature abstracts and quantitative data searches of information, and on-line services. Has access to DIALOG, ESA, Development Index data base through ODA. Also provides selective dissemination of information and photocopies.

457 - AL-HAQ/LAW IN THE SERVICE OF MAN, LIBRARY

ADDRESS: P.O. Box 1413,
          Ramallah,
          West Bank,
          ISRAEL
          TEL: 02/952421
SIZE OF STAFF: Professional: 5
TYPE OF SERVICE: international; private; non-profit
SYSTEMS & NETWORKS ATTACHED TO: International Commission of Jurists
MATERIALS DESCRIBING THE SERVICE: - 1986 Programme Report
WORKING LANGUAGE(S): Arabic; English
SUBJECT COVERAGE: law; international law; human rights
GEOGRAPHICAL COVERAGE: Middle East; West Bank, occupied Palestine
DATA BEING PROCESSED AND SIZE: 1,500 books and journals; reports; on-going research;
          seminars; training courses; affidavits; photographs
DATA PROCESSING METHODS: computerized
STORAGE MEDIA: traditional shelving of publications; microfiches
TYPE OF ACTIVITY: data collection; data analysis; distribution of information;
          publication
PERIODICALS PUBLISHED:
          - Newsletter, 6 p.a.
PUBLICATIONS: - Playfair, E., Administrative detention in the occupied West Bank,
          1985
          - Israel's deportation policy in the occupied West Bank and Gaza, 1986
          - Rishmawi, M., Palestinian women: their historical experience and legal
          situation, 1986
          - Rishmawi, M., Planning in whose interest? Land use planning as a strategy
          for Judaization, 1986
          - The Rights of workers in the West Bank, 1986
          - Hiltermann, J., Response to the Chapter on Israel and the occupied
          territories in the U.S. State Department's 1985 "country reports on Human
          rights practices for 1984", 1986
          - Fallon, V., Excessive secrecy, lack of guidelines: a report on military
          censorship in the West Bank, 1984
          - Hillier, T., The Reply of law in the service of man to the 1983 U.S.
          Report on Human Rights Practices in the territories occupied by Israel, 198
CLIENTELE: lawyers; researchers; university and school students; general public
ACCESS TO SERVICE: services open to all users, free of charge
TYPE & DESCRIPTION OF SERVICES PROVIDED: Provides library services, on-line services
          using its own data base, and selective dissemination of information.

**458 - HEBREW UNIVERSITY OF JERUSALEM, HARRY S. TRUMAN RESEARCH INSTITUTE FOR THE
ADVANCEMENT OF PEACE, LIBRARY AND DOCUMENTATION CENTER**

ADDRESS: Mount Scopus,
          Jerusalem 91905,
          ISRAEL
          TEL: (02) 882300 - TELEX: 26458

CABLE: SCOPUS
REATED: 1966   *HEAD:* Mr. C. Panzer, Senior Librarian
IZE OF STAFF: Total: 12
YPE OF SERVICE: private; non-profit
YSTEMS & NETWORKS ATTACHED TO: ALEPH (Automated Library Network on University
          Libraries in Israel)
ORKING LANGUAGE(S): English; French; German; Spanish; Portuguese; Italian; Hebrew;
          Arabic; Chinese; Japanese
UBJECT COVERAGE: sociology; political science; history
EOGRAPHICAL COVERAGE: Asia; Africa; Latin America; Middle East; developing countries
ATA BEING PROCESSED AND SIZE: 2,000 periodicals; 80 newspapers; documents
ATA PROCESSING METHODS: computerized
TORAGE MEDIA: traditional shelving of publications; microfiches
YPE OF ACTIVITY: data collection; publication
UBLICATIONS: - Avimor, S. (ed.), Guide to selected documentation on relations
          between Israel and Asian and African states, no.2, Israel-Cambodia, 1986
LIENTELE: students, faculty members, government officers, media
YPE & DESCRIPTION OF SERVICES PROVIDED: Also compiles the bibliographical Index
          database "Dictionary of Prominent Palestinian Arabs".

59 - THE HEBREW UNIVERSITY OF JERUSALEM, SOCIAL SCIENCES DATA ARCHIVE

YNONYMOUS NAMES: SSDA
ARENT ORGANIZATION: The Hebrew University of Jerusalem
DDRESS: Mount Scopus,
          Jerusalem 91905,
          ISRAEL
          TEL: 02-883007 - TELEX: 26485
REATED: 1975   *HEAD:* Ms. M. Peleg, Director
IZE OF STAFF: Professional: 5   Other: 1   Total: 6
YPE OF SERVICE: national; public; non-profit
YSTEMS & NETWORKS ATTACHED TO: IFDO (International Federation of Data Organizations)
ORKING LANGUAGE(S): Hebrew; English
UBJECT COVERAGE: social sciences; demography; economics; statistics; geography;
          sociology; political science; social welfare; psychology; psychology; mass
          communication; social anthropology; cultural anthropology; education
EOGRAPHICAL COVERAGE: Israel
ATA BEING PROCESSED AND SIZE: national surveys micro-data; census micro-data; census
          SAS aggregate data; attitudes studies; election studies; longitudinal
          studies; cohort studies; national economy time series; world time-series;
          foreign economic and demographic data-sets (total 200 data sets and
          5,500,000 records)
ATA PROCESSING METHODS: computerized
ARDWARE USED: CDC Cyber 170-855; PRIME 750; IBM 4381 and IBM PC-AT
OFTWARE USED: Database: DBMS, SIR, SPSS
TORAGE MEDIA: tapes, discs
YPE OF ACTIVITY: data collection; data analysis; distribution of information
ERIODICALS PUBLISHED: - SSDA Newsletter, 1 p.a.
UBLICATIONS: - Computerized on-line catalog system
LIENTELE: university students, researchers, experts
CCESS TO SERVICE: services open to all users, payment conditioned by the kind of

service provided
TYPE & DESCRIPTION OF SERVICES PROVIDED: The SSDA provides data-sets and sub-files
from its holdings. It has data processing capabilities and provides this
service for users who have no access to data processing and data analysis.
The SSDA has built several on-line data bases for holding national as well
as international time series files. It provides its users with friendly
access to these data bases as well as information on magnetic tapes and
discs.

460 - THE HENRIETTA SZOLD INSTITUTE, INFORMATION RETRIEVAL FOR THE SOCIAL SCIENCES

ADDRESS: 9, Colombia Street,
Kiryat Menachem,
Jerusalem 96583,
ISRAEL
TEL: 02-419191
CREATED: 1971   *HEAD:* Mrs. S. Langerman, Head
SIZE OF STAFF: Professional: 7   Other: 3   Total: 11
TYPE OF SERVICE: international; public; non-profit
MATERIALS DESCRIBING THE SERVICE: - The Information Retrieval Center, leaflet
- Langerman, S., Israel's Information Retrieval Center for the Social
Sciences: data base products and services, in Behavioural and Social
Sciences Librarian, 1986
WORKING LANGUAGE(S): Hebrew; English
SUBJECT COVERAGE: social sciences; education; sociology; psychology; social welfare;
economics; political science; administrative sciences; criminology
GEOGRAPHICAL COVERAGE: Israel
DATA BEING PROCESSED AND SIZE: 10,000 books, articles, reports on on-going research
(1,200 p.a.)
DATA PROCESSING METHODS: computerized
HARDWARE USED: Mini-computer PDP 11/44
SOFTWARE USED: QDMS
STORAGE MEDIA: hard discs
TYPE OF ACTIVITY: data collection; distribution of information; publication
PERIODICALS PUBLISHED: - Current Research in the Social Sciences, 4 p.a.
PUBLICATIONS: - Union catalog of research tools
- The Ethiopian Jews and their absorption in Israel. Bibliography, 1985
CLIENTELE: researchers, students, teachers, social workers (100 per month)
ACCESS TO SERVICE: services open to all users, free of charge but paid computer
services
TYPE & DESCRIPTION OF SERVICES PROVIDED: Provides bibliographic searches on its 4
data bases: Current research in the social sciences in Israel (13,000
records); Union catalogue for research tools (3,500 records); Innovative ar
special programs; Computers in education. Also provides on-line searches
using other data bases such as ERIC, Psychological Abstracts, Sociological
Abstracts, library services, selective dissemination of information and
photocopies.

Italy / Italie / Italia

61 - ARCHIVIO DATI E PROGRAMMI PER LE SCIENZE SOCIALI

SYNONYMOUS NAMES: ADPSS;
        Social Science Data and Programs Archive
PARENT ORGANIZATION: Istituto Superiore di Sociologia
ADDRESS: Via Giovanni Cantoni 4,
        20144 Milan,
        ITALY
        TEL: 02/49.86.187
CREATED: 1973   *HEAD:* Prof. S. Draghi, Director
SIZE OF STAFF: Professional: 5   Other: 1   Total: 6
TYPE OF SERVICE: international; public; non-profit
SYSTEMS & NETWORKS ATTACHED TO: IFDO (International Federation of Data Organizations)
SUBJECT COVERAGE: social sciences; social welfare; political science; sociology
GEOGRAPHICAL COVERAGE: Italy
DATA BEING PROCESSED AND SIZE: since 1983, 85 machine-readable data files
DATA PROCESSING METHODS: computerized
HARDWARE USED: DEC VAX-11/750
SOFTWARE USED: VMS SPSSx
TYPE OF ACTIVITY: data analysis; distribution of information; SSID training
CLIENTELE: public administration officers, research workers, academics
ACCESS TO SERVICE: open to all users, free of charge
TYPE & DESCRIPTION OF SERVICES PROVIDED: Provides quantitative data searches,
        selective dissemination of information and production of information on
        magnetic tapes.

62 - ARCHIVIO DISARMO, CENTRO DI DOCUMENTAZIONE SULLA PACE SUL DISARMO

ADDRESS: Via di Torre Argentina 18,
        00186 Rome,
        ITALY
        TEL: (06) 687-5447
CREATED: 1982   *HEAD:* Mr. F. Battistelli, Secretary-General
SIZE OF STAFF: Professional: 5   Other: 2   Total: 7
TYPE OF SERVICE: national; private; non-profit
MATERIALS DESCRIBING THE SERVICE: - Archivio disarmo, leaflet
WORKING LANGUAGE(S): Italian; English; French
SUBJECT COVERAGE: law; political science; armaments; disarmament; peace; arms
        control; defence; Italian military industry
DATA BEING PROCESSED AND SIZE: 3,000 books; 80 periodicals; 80,000 reports and
        materials
DATA PROCESSING METHODS: manual
HARDWARE USED: Olivetti M 24
TYPE OF ACTIVITY: data collection; data analysis; distribution of information; SSID
        scientific and methodological activities; SSID training; publication
PERIODICALS PUBLISHED: - Armamenti ed Economica, 1 p.a.
        - Arms Race and Arms Control (abridged edition in Italian)
CLIENTELE: students, researchers, peace movements, trade unions
ACCESS TO SERVICE: services open to all users, free of charge

Italy / Italie / Italia

TYPE & DESCRIPTION OF SERVICES PROVIDED: Provides library services, bibliographic and
quantitative data searches of information, selective dissemination of
information and photocopies.

463 - CENTRO DI DOCUMENTAZIONE BIBLIOGRAFICA IN MATERIA DI DIRITTO E PROCEDURA PENALE

SYNONYMOUS NAMES: Centre of Bibliographic Documentation on Criminal Law and Procedure
PARENT ORGANIZATION: Istituto per la Documentazione Giuridica del Consiglio Nazionale
delle Ricerche
ADDRESS: Presso l'Instituto per la Documentazione Giuridica del Consiglio Nazionale
delle Ricerche,
Via Panciatichi, 56/16,
50127 Florence,
ITALY
TEL: (055) 431.722
CREATED: 1974   *HEAD:* M. Fameli, Director
SIZE OF STAFF: Professional: 4   Other: 6   Total: 10
TYPE OF SERVICE: public; non-profit
SYSTEMS & NETWORKS ATTACHED TO: Network of the Computer Centre of the Italian Corte
di Cassazione
MATERIALS DESCRIBING THE SERVICE: - Fameli, M., Il Materiale Bibliografico di Diritto
e Procedura Penale Nell'Archivio
- Fameli, M., The Criminal Law Bibliographical Data Base of the Instituto
per la Documentazione Giuridica (IDG) of the Italian National Research
Council, 1987
SUBJECT COVERAGE: law; social anthropology; cultural anthropology; social welfare;
sociology; criminal law; criminology
GEOGRAPHICAL COVERAGE: Italy
DATA BEING PROCESSED AND SIZE: reports, seminars, articles
DATA PROCESSING METHODS: computerized
HARDWARE USED: Olivetti OC 5320
SOFTWARE USED: STAIRS
STORAGE MEDIA: tapes, discs
TYPE OF ACTIVITY: data collection; data analysis; distribution of information;
publication
PERIODICALS PUBLISHED: - Bibliografia IDG. Rassegna Automatica di Dottrina Giuridica
Sezione C, Diritto e Procedura Penale, 1 p.a.
PUBLICATIONS: - Rivista delle Riviste, Rassegna di Dottrina Giuridica Penalistica de
1984
CLIENTELE: legal operators
ACCESS TO SERVICE: services open to specific categories of users, against payment
TYPE & DESCRIPTION OF SERVICES PROVIDED: Provides bibliographic and literature
searches of information, on-line services using its own data bases DOTTR an
DOCT. Also produces information on magnetic tapes or discs.

464 - CENTRO DI RECERCA E DOCUMENTAZIONE FEBBRAIO '74

SYNONYMOUS NAMES: CERFE
ADDRESS: Via Flaminia, 160,

00196 Rome,
ITALY
TEL: 06/63.77.940; 36.00.851
REATED: 1980   *HEAD:* G. Quinti,
IZE OF STAFF: Professional: 25   Other: 22   Total: 47
YPE OF SERVICE: international; private; profit
UBJECT COVERAGE: social sciences; development; international cooperation; studies;
        civil defence; education
EOGRAPHICAL COVERAGE: America; Africa; Europe; Asia
ATA BEING PROCESSED AND SIZE: reports; evaluation documents; projects of
        international cooperation; proceedings
ATA PROCESSING METHODS: computerized
ARDWARE USED: McIntosh, Apple, IBM PC
OFTWARE USED: Visicalc, DBase III, Lotus, Excell, Word Star
YPE OF ACTIVITY: data collection; data analysis; SSID scientific and methodological
        activities
ERIODICALS PUBLISHED: - Laboratorio di Scienze dell'Uomo
        - F74 Informazioni
UBLICATIONS: - Quaranta, G. C., Governabilità e democrazia diretta, 1981
        - Quaranta, G. C., L'Associazione invisible, 1981
        - Quaranta, G. C., L'Era dello sviluppo, 1986
        - Technology, culture and development, 1984
        - Le Rapport entre ville et campagne en Afrique Occidentale et le transfert
        de technologie, 1986
CCESS TO SERVICE: services open to specific categories of users, free of charge

65 - CENTRO INTERNAZIONALE DI STUDI E DOCUMENTAZIONE SULLE COMUNITÀ EUROPEE

YNONYMOUS NAMES: CISDCE;
        International Centre of Studies and Documentation on the European Community
DDRESS: Palazzo delle Stelline,
        Corso Magenta, 61,
        20123 Milan,
        ITALY
        TEL: (02) 865-547
REATED: 1958   *HEAD:* Mr. F. Capelli, Prof.
IZE OF STAFF: Professional: 7   Other: 7   Total: 14
YPE OF SERVICE: international; public; non-profit
ATERIALS DESCRIBING THE SERVICE: - Statuto, C.I.S.D.C.E., 1972, 7p. (internal
        publication)
        - Centro Internazionale di Studi e Documentazione sulle Comunità Europee,
        1958-1968; pp. 69-70
        - Centro Internazionale di Studie et Documentazione sulle Comunità Europee:
        3 aggiornamento dell'attivita del luglio 1971 al dicembre 1974
ORKING LANGUAGE(S): Italian
UBJECT COVERAGE: social sciences; political science; economics; history; social
        welfare; law and economy of the E.E.C.
EOGRAPHICAL COVERAGE: Europe
ATA BEING PROCESSED AND SIZE: printed documents: 26,000 books, monographs and
        reports, 150 periodicals
ATA PROCESSING METHODS: manual; partially computerized

TYPE OF ACTIVITY: distribution of information
PERIODICALS PUBLISHED: - Euroinformazioni, 48 p.a.
- Relazione Annuale sull'Attività del CISDCE dal 1977 ad oggi
PUBLICATIONS: - Reports on specialized studies and conference records
CLIENTELE: students, teachers, officials, bankers, lawyers, insurance companies
ACCESS TO SERVICE: services open to all users, paid services (free of charge for students)
TYPE & DESCRIPTION OF SERVICES PROVIDED: Provides library services, query-answering service, searches of information, preparation of documentary dossiers, photocopies and microforms.

466 - ISTITUTO CENTRALE DI STATISTICA, BANCHE DATI

SYNONYMOUS NAMES: Central Institute of Statistics, Data Base
ADDRESS: Via Cesare Balbo, 16,
00184 Rome,
ITALY
TEL: 06/4673 - TELEX: 610338 - 626282
CREATED: 1929   *HEAD:* Prof. V. Siesto, Director
TYPE OF SERVICE: national; public; non-profit
MATERIALS DESCRIBING THE SERVICE: - Statistiche: Sanitarie; Protezione Sociale; Giustizia; Istruzione; Culturali; Lavoro
SUBJECT COVERAGE: social welfare; agriculture
GEOGRAPHICAL COVERAGE: Italy
DATA PROCESSING METHODS: partially computerized
HARDWARE USED: IBM 3090/180; Olivetti 6480/190
TYPE OF ACTIVITY: data collection; data analysis; distribution of information; SSID scientific and methodological activities; publication
PERIODICALS PUBLISHED:
- Bolletino Mensile di Statistica, 12 p.a.
- Indicacatori Mensili, 12 p.a.
- Statistiche del Commercio con l'Estero, 4 p.a.
- Conti Economica Trimenstrali, 4 p.a.
ACCESS TO SERVICE: Services open to all users, free of charge, some paid services
TYPE & DESCRIPTION OF SERVICES PROVIDED: Provides on-line services on its own data base ISTAT (Sistema Informativo Statistico), selective dissemination of information and information on magnetic tapes or discs.

467 - ISTITUTO PER LA SCIENZA DELL'AMMINISTRAZIONE PUBBLICA I CENTRO DI BIBLIOGRAFI AMMINISTRATIVA INTERNAZIONALE, BIBLIOTECA

SYNONYMOUS NAMES: Institute of Public Administration and International Administrati Bibliography Center, Library
ADDRESS: Piazza Castelo 3,
20121 Milan,
ITALY
TEL: 873241, 873270, 873316
CREATED: 1959   *HEAD:* Prof. G. Rotelli, President
Prof. E. Rotelli, Director-General

SIZE OF STAFF: Professional: 2   Other: 2
TYPE OF SERVICE: national; public; non-profit
MATERIALS DESCRIBING THE SERVICE: - Printed notice in: ISAP notizie
WORKING LANGUAGE(S): Italian
SUBJECT COVERAGE: administrative sciences
GEOGRAPHICAL COVERAGE: global
DATA BEING PROCESSED AND SIZE: 15,000 books; 245 periodicals
DATA PROCESSING METHODS: manual
PERIODICALS PUBLISHED: - Amministrare, 4 p.a.
        - Rivista Trimestrale di Diritto Pubblico, 4 p.a.
CLIENTELE: scholars, students, civil servants
ACCESS TO SERVICE: open to all users, free of charge
TYPE & DESCRIPTION OF SERVICES PROVIDED: Provides library services, photocopies and
        microforms of documents, query answering service and selective dissemination
        of information (standard profiles).

**468 - ISTITUTO PER LE RELAZIONI TRA L'ITALIA E I PAESI DELL'AFRICA, AMERICA LATINA E
        MEDIO ORIENTE, BIBLIOTECA**

SYNONYMOUS NAMES: IPALMO Biblioteca
ADDRESS: Via de Tritone 62-B,
        I-00187 Rome,
        ITALY
        TEL: 6792734 - TELEX: 621594
CREATED: 1971   HEAD: Ms. C. Luciani, Librarian
SIZE OF STAFF: Professional: 2   Total: 2
TYPE OF SERVICE: national; private; non-profit
WORKING LANGUAGE(S): Italian; English; French; Spanish
SUBJECT COVERAGE: social sciences; economics; political science; demography;
        geography; history; administrative sciences; law; sociology
GEOGRAPHICAL COVERAGE: developing countries
DATA BEING PROCESSED AND SIZE: 10,000 books, reports and documents; 500 periodicals
DATA PROCESSING METHODS: manual
TYPE OF ACTIVITY: distribution of information; publication
PERIODICALS PUBLISHED: - Politica Internazionale
        - Elenco dei Periodici Preolarmente Ricevuti, 1 p.a.
        - Biblioteca IPALMO, Nuovo Acquisizioni, 4 p.a.
CLIENTELE: students, researchers
ACCESS TO SERVICE: services open to all users, free of charge
TYPE & DESCRIPTION OF SERVICES PROVIDED: Provides library services, bibliographic,
        literature abstract and quantiative data searches of information, selective
        dissemination of information and photocopies.

**469 - UFFICIO RICERCHE, DOCUMENTAZIONE E MONITORAGGIO, DIREZIONE GENERALE DEGLI
        AFFARI PENALI**

SYNONYMOUS NAMES: Bureau for Research, Documentation and Monitoring of the
        Directorate of Criminal Affairs
PARENT ORGANIZATION: Ministero di Grazia e Giustizia

Italy / Italie / Italia

ADDRESS: Via Arenula, 70,
       00186 Rome,
       ITALY
       TEL: 65102503
CREATED: 1981   *HEAD:* Mr. C. Sarzana, Director
SIZE OF STAFF: Professional: 5   Other: 7   Total: 12
TYPE OF SERVICE: international; public; non-profit
WORKING LANGUAGE(S): Italian
SUBJECT COVERAGE: law; sociology; criminology
GEOGRAPHICAL COVERAGE: Italy
DATA PROCESSING METHODS: manual
TYPE OF ACTIVITY: data collection; data analysis
PUBLICATIONS: - Sarzana C.; Tinebra, G., Il Monitoraggio sull'amministrazione della
      giustizia penale: finalità e prospettive, 1986
ACCESS TO SERVICE: services open to specific categories of users, free of charge
TYPE & DESCRIPTION OF SERVICES PROVIDED: Provides library services, bibliographic,
      literature and quantitative data searches of information, selective
      dissemination of information and photocopies.

470 - UNIVERSITÀ DI BOLOGNA, DIPARTIMENTO DI SOCIOLOGIA, CENTRO INTERNAZIONALE DI DOCUMENTAZIONE E STUDI SOCIOLOGICI SUI PROBLEMI DEL LAVORO

SYNONYMOUS NAMES: Cidospel-Università di Bologna;
      University of Bologna, Sociology Department, International Documentation
      Centre for Sociological Studies on Labour Problems
ADDRESS: Casella Postale 413,
      Via delle Belle Arti 42,
      40126 Bologna,
      ITALY
      TEL: 051-233380 - TELEX: 511650 UNIVBOI
CREATED: 1971   *HEAD:* Prof. M. La Rosa, Director
SIZE OF STAFF: Other: 1
TYPE OF SERVICE: international; public; non-profit
MATERIALS DESCRIBING THE SERVICE: - Siutesi dell'attività 1970-1985 (allegato)
WORKING LANGUAGE(S): Italian
SUBJECT COVERAGE: sociology; sociology of work; labour relations; industrial
      sociology; social sciences; social welfare
GEOGRAPHICAL COVERAGE: Italy
TYPE OF ACTIVITY: SSID scientific and methodological activities; SSID training;
      publication
PERIODICALS PUBLISHED: - Sociologia del Lavoro, 3 p.a.
CLIENTELE: students, university teachers and graduate students
ACCESS TO SERVICE: services open to specific categories of users
TYPE & DESCRIPTION OF SERVICES PROVIDED: Provides library services, bibliographic,
      literature abstract and survey data searches.

Jamaica / Jamaïque / Jamaica

471 - JAMAICA INFORMATION SERVICE, LIBRARY

SYNONYMOUS NAMES: JIS
PARENT ORGANIZATION: Office of the Prime Minister
ADDRESS: 58A Half Way Tree Road,
       P.O. Box 2222,
       Kingston 10,
       JAMAICA
       TEL: 92-63740 - TELEX: 2393
CREATED: 1974   *HEAD:* Ms. A. Barrett, Chief Librarian
SIZE OF STAFF: Professional: 3   Other: 14   Total: 17
TYPE OF SERVICE: national; public; non-profit
SYSTEMS & NETWORKS ATTACHED TO: National Information System (NATIS)/Socio-Economic
      Network (SECIN)
WORKING LANGUAGE(S): English
SUBJECT COVERAGE: geography; history; social sciences
GEOGRAPHICAL COVERAGE: Jamaica
DATA BEING PROCESSED AND SIZE: newspaper articles; new releases; journals; books;
     films/video; photographs; tapes
DATA PROCESSING METHODS: manual
STORAGE MEDIA: traditional shelving of publications
TYPE OF ACTIVITY: data collection; distribution of information
PUBLICATIONS: - Directory of information units in Jamaica: libraries, archives and
     documentation services
CLIENTELE: 15 researchers (tertiary level) daily, 50-75 users from public in general
ACCESS TO SERVICE: services open to all users, free of charge
TYPE & DESCRIPTION OF SERVICES PROVIDED: Provides references and question answering
     services, pamphlets, government documents and photocopies.

472 - NATIONAL PLANNING AGENCY, DOCUMENTATION CENTRE

SYNONYMOUS NAMES: NPA Documentation Centre
ADDRESS: 39-41 Barbados Avenue,
     Kingston 5,
     JAMAICA
     TEL: 92-61480
CREATED: 1962   *HEAD:* Ms. A. Ononaiwu, Acting Chief Librarian
SIZE OF STAFF: Professional: 2   Other: 7   Total: 9
TYPE OF SERVICE: private; non-profit
SYSTEMS & NETWORKS ATTACHED TO: Socio-economic Information Network SECIN (focal
     point) and Caribbean Information System
MATERIALS DESCRIBING THE SERVICE: - Introducing the NPA Library/Documentation Centre,
     1983 (brochure)
WORKING LANGUAGE(S): English
SUBJECT COVERAGE: social sciences; socio-economic development; planning; agriculture;
     industrial development; housing; human resources; development; manpower;
     social development; public services
DATA BEING PROCESSED AND SIZE: books, serials, reports, feasibility studies,
     articles, newspaper clippings (2,500 p.a.); audio visual material:

microfiche, microfilm (20 p.a.)
DATA PROCESSING METHODS: manual
TYPE OF ACTIVITY: publication
PERIODICALS PUBLISHED: - Journal of the Socio-Economic Information Network
            - SECIN newsletter
            - SECIN abstracts
CLIENTELE: researchers, students from high schools and tertiary institutions
ACCESS TO SERVICE: services open to specific categories of users, free of charge
TYPE & DESCRIPTION OF SERVICES PROVIDED: Provides library services, bibliographic
            searches of information and photocopies.

473 - UNIVERSITY OF THE WEST INDIES, INSTITUTE OF SOCIAL AND ECONOMIC RESEARCH, DOCUMENTATION AND DATA CENTRE

ADDRESS: Mona Campus,
        Kingston 7,
        JAMAICA
        TEL: 927-6661
        CABLE: UNIVERS
CREATED: 1982   HEAD: R. Robb, Documentalist
SIZE OF STAFF: Professional: 3   Other: 4   Total: 7
TYPE OF SERVICE: national; public; non-profit
SYSTEMS & NETWORKS ATTACHED TO: Socio-Economic Information Network (SECIN), The
            National Planning Agency, Government of Jamaica
WORKING LANGUAGE(S): English; Spanish
SUBJECT COVERAGE: social sciences
GEOGRAPHICAL COVERAGE: global, with emphasis on the Caribbean area
DATA BEING PROCESSED AND SIZE: 253 serials; 22,000 reports, papers, policy documents
            monographs, journal articles; 17,000 colonial office Commonwealth Caribbean
            documents; oral history tapes
DATA PROCESSING METHODS: partially computerized
HARDWARE USED: IBM 370/138-1 Megabyte
SOFTWARE USED: VM/CMS, DOS/VS, POWER/VS, MUSIC, CICS
STORAGE MEDIA: traditional shelving of publications; tapes; films; microforms
TYPE OF ACTIVITY: data collection; data analysis; SSID training; publication
PUBLICATIONS: - Index to social and economic studies, vol. 1-26, 1953-1977, Kingston
            U.W.I., 1980
CLIENTELE: teachers, post-graduate students, researchers and practitioners
ACCESS TO SERVICE: services open to specific categories of users, free of charge
TYPE & DESCRIPTION OF SERVICES PROVIDED: Reference service providing specific data as
            well as documents and/or bibliographical references, selective dissemination
            of information, production of biblio-critical studies, compilation of
            research registers and directories, retrospective bibliographic searches and
            reproduction of documents.

474 - AICHIKEN KINRO KAIKAN RODO TOSYO SIRYOSHITU

SYNONYMOUS NAMES: Aichi Prefectural Labour Centre, Labour Reference Library
ADDRESS: 1-2-32 Tsurumai,
        Showaku,
        Nagoya 466,
        JAPAN
        TEL: 052-733-1141
CREATED: 1970   *HEAD:* S. Kobayashi, Chief Librarian
SIZE OF STAFF: Professional: 5   Other: 1   Total: 6
TYPE OF SERVICE: public; non-profit
MATERIALS DESCRIBING THE SERVICE: - Annual report of Aichi Prefectural Labour Centre
WORKING LANGUAGE(S): Japanese
SUBJECT COVERAGE: social sciences; labour; employment; personnel management; working
        conditions; workers' life; labour management relations; labour movement;
        labour laws; labour culture; labour problems
GEOGRAPHICAL COVERAGE: Japan
DATA BEING PROCESSED AND SIZE: 40,315 books; 10,579 pamphlets; 334 serial
        publications
DATA PROCESSING METHODS: manual
STORAGE MEDIA: traditional shelving of publications; fiches of newspapers related to
        labour
TYPE OF ACTIVITY: distribution of information; publication
PERIODICALS PUBLISHED: - Labour Documents, 1 p.a.
PUBLICATIONS: - Catalogue of labour material
        - Indexes of periodicals related to labour
CLIENTELE: office staff, junior executives, union officials, unionists and others
        interested in labour problems and university studies
ACCESS TO SERVICE: open to all users, free of charge
TYPE & DESCRIPTION OF SERVICES PROVIDED: Provides library services, bibliographic
        search of information, question-answering service, lending and photocopying
        services.

475 - HITOTSUBASHI DAIGAKU, KEIZAI KENKYUSHO SHIRYOSHITSU

SYNONYMOUS NAMES: Hitotsubashi University, the Institute of Economic Research,
        Library
ADDRESS: Kunitachi-shi,
        Tokyo 186,
        JAPAN
        TEL: 0425-72-1101 - TELEX: 2842107 HITOTSJ - TELEFAX: 0425-75-4856
        CABLE: IECONRHU KUNITACHI TOKYO
CREATED: 1940   *HEAD:* T. Saegusa, Chief Librarian
SIZE OF STAFF: Professional: 9   Other: 1   Total: 10
TYPE OF SERVICE: national; non-profit
MATERIALS DESCRIBING THE SERVICE: - Information bulletin of the Institute of Economic
        Research (description of the institute including the library)
WORKING LANGUAGE(S): Japanese
SUBJECT COVERAGE: economics; social sciences

Japan / Japon / Japón

GEOGRAPHICAL COVERAGE: global
DATA BEING PROCESSED AND SIZE: 255,000 books (7,112 p.a.); 6,000 microfilm reels (10
     p.a.); 86,000 microfiche sheets (7,977 p.a.)
DATA PROCESSING METHODS: manual
PERIODICALS PUBLISHED:
    - Recent Acquisitions List
CLIENTELE: faculty members and graduate students (3,000 p.a.)
ACCESS TO SERVICE: open to researchers
TYPE & DESCRIPTION OF SERVICES PROVIDED: Provides library services.

476 - HITOTSUBASHI DAIGAKU SHAKAIKAGAKU KOTENSHIRYO SENTA

SYNONYMOUS NAMES: Hitotsubashi University, Center for Historical Social Science
    Literature
ADDRESS: 2-1 Naka,
    Kunitachi-shi,
    Tokyo-to,
    JAPAN
    TEL: 0425-72-1101
CREATED: 1978   *HEAD:* T. Morita, Director
SIZE OF STAFF: Professional: 4   Total: 4
TYPE OF SERVICE: national; public; non-profit
MATERIALS DESCRIBING THE SERVICE: - Hitotsubashi Daigaku Shakaikagaku Kotenshiryo
    Senta, 1986
    - A Brief guide to the Center for Historical Social Science Literature, 198
WORKING LANGUAGE(S): Japanese
SUBJECT COVERAGE: history; law; political science; social sciences; statistics;
    literature
GEOGRAPHICAL COVERAGE: Japan
DATA BEING PROCESSED AND SIZE: 63,000 books and periodicals; training courses
DATA PROCESSING METHODS: manual
STORAGE MEDIA: traditional shelving of publications
TYPE OF ACTIVITY: data collection; distribution of information; publication
PERIODICALS PUBLISHED:
    - Hitotsubashi Daigaku Shakaikagaku Koten Shiryo Senta Nenpo (Bulletin of
    the Center for Historical Social Science Literature)
PUBLICATIONS: - Catalogue of old and rare foreign books mainly from the general
    collections, 1976
    - Center for Historical Social Science Literature (study series)
CLIENTELE: researchers (around 300 p.a.)
ACCESS TO SERVICE: services open to specific categories of users, free of charge
TYPE & DESCRIPTION OF SERVICES PROVIDED: Provides library services, searches of
       information, selective dissemination of information, microforms and
       photocopies. Specializes in the historical literature of social science in
       Western languages (mainly before 1851).

477 - HITOTSUBASHIDAIGAKU, KEIZAKENKYUJO NIPPON KEIZAI TOKEI BUNKEN SENTA

SYNONYMOUS NAMES: Hitotsubashi University, the Documentation Centre for Japanese
      Economic Statistics
PARENT ORGANIZATION: Institute of Economic Research (Hitotsubashi University)
ADDRESS: 2-1 Naka,
      Kunitachi,
      Tokyo 186,
      JAPAN
      TEL: 0425-72-1101 - TELEX: 2842107 HITOTS J - TELEFAX: 0425-75-4856
      CABLE: IECONRHU
CREATED: 1963   *HEAD:* Prof. E. Hidekazu, Director
SIZE OF STAFF: Professional: 4   Other: 7   Total: 11
TYPE OF SERVICE: national; public; non-profit
MATERIALS DESCRIBING THE SERVICE: - Coki Keizai Tokei (LTES) Deita Beisu no Kenkyu
      (Summary report of the compiling of the LTES data base, in Japanese with
      English summary)
      - Information bulletin of Institute of Economic Research
      - Bunken Senta no riyo annai (guide for the users of documentation centre)
WORKING LANGUAGE(S): Japanese
SUBJECT COVERAGE: economics; statistics; demography; education; history; political
      science; social welfare; sociology; econometrics
GEOGRAPHICAL COVERAGE: Japan and the former colonies of the Japanese empire
DATA BEING PROCESSED AND SIZE: 91,000 books; 400 periodicals; statistical dates
DATA PROCESSING METHODS: manual; partially computerized
HARDWARE USED: HITAC M-240 D
SOFTWARE USED: Fortran, PL/1; RDB1; SAS; housemade DBMS
STORAGE MEDIA: traditional shelving of publications; magnetic tapes; microforms
TYPE OF ACTIVITY: data collection; data analysis; distribution of information; SSID
      scientific and methodological activities; publication
PUBLICATIONS: - Nihon Keizai Tokei Bunken Senta Shojo
      - Annotated bibliography of the Japanese economic statistics of the Meiji
      period, 4 vols (in Japanese)
      - Summary report of the compiling LTES data base (in Japanese with English
      summary)
      - Catalogue of the microfilms processed by the Centre (in Japanese)
      - Summary report of the compiling LTES data base, long term economic
      statistics (in Japanese)
      - Catalogue of the archival documents of the iron and steel industry of
      Japan and Manchuria during war period; documents and manuscripts possessed
      by the late Toshio Suitsu in 2 vols. (in Japanese)
      - Analytical bibliography of the provincial summary statistical materials in
      Meiji-era (in Japanese)
      - Catalogue of Gunze-Chosonze; rural reconstruction surveys (in Japanese)
      - Annotated bibliography of the prefectural statistical materials published
      in Meiji-era (in Japanese)
      - Detailed report of survey of social scientists' demand for Japan's socio-
      economic statistics
      - Matsuda, Y., Social scientists' demand for Japan's socio-economic
      statistics, 1986
CLIENTELE: researchers, scholars, students, administrative workers, producers or
      handlers of statistics (around 550 users p.a.)
ACCESS TO SERVICE: open to specific categories of users

TYPE & DESCRIPTION OF SERVICES PROVIDED: Provides library service, bibliographic and quantitative data searches of information, on-line services, information on magnetic tapes or discs, microforms and photocopies.

478 - HOKKAIDO DAIGAKU, SURABU KENKYU SENTA

SYNONYMOUS NAMES: SRC;
        Hokkaido University, Slavic Research Center
ADDRESS: Kita-9,
        Nishi-7,
        Sapporo 060,
        JAPAN
        TEL: 011-716-2111
CREATED: 1953   *HEAD:* T. Ito, Director
SIZE OF STAFF: Professional: 10   Other: 1   Total: 11
TYPE OF SERVICE: national; non-profit
SYSTEMS & NETWORKS ATTACHED TO: International Committee for Soviet and East European Studies (ICSEES)
WORKING LANGUAGE(S): Japanese; English; Slavic languagues
SUBJECT COVERAGE: social sciences; administrative sciences; economics; geography; history; political science
GEOGRAPHICAL COVERAGE: USSR; Eastern Europe
DATA BEING PROCESSED AND SIZE: 47,000 books; 180 periodicals
DATA PROCESSING METHODS: computerized
SOFTWARE USED: NEC ACOS610/10 system
STORAGE MEDIA: fiches; microfiches
TYPE OF ACTIVITY: data collection; distribution of information; publication
PERIODICALS PUBLISHED: - Bibliography of Slavic and East European Studies in Japan, p.a.
        - Acta Slavica Iaponica, 1 p.a.
        - Slavic Studies/Surabu Kenkyu, 1 p.a.
CLIENTELE: researchers
ACCESS TO SERVICE: services open to researchers only
TYPE & DESCRIPTION OF SERVICES PROVIDED: Provides library services, bibliographic searches, on-line searches using own data base and selective dissemination of information.

479 - HOSEI UNIVERSITY, OHARA SHAKAIMONDAI KENKYUSHO

SYNONYMOUS NAMES: Hosei University, Ohara Institute for Social Research
ADDRESS: 4342 Aihara-machi,
        Machida-shi,
        Tokyo 194-02,
        JAPAN
        TEL: (0427) 83-2306
CREATED: 1919   *HEAD:* Mr. Y. Koreeda, Librarian
SIZE OF STAFF: Professional: 2   Other: 5   Total: 7
TYPE OF SERVICE: national; public; non-profit
SYSTEMS & NETWORKS ATTACHED TO: Association for Documentation in Economics (Keizai

Shiryo Kyogikai)

MATERIALS DESCRIBING THE SERVICE: - Rodo kankei bunken shiryo geturoku (in Chingin to shakaihosho), 12 p.a., 10 p.

- Ohara Institute for Social Research, brochure, 1987

WORKING LANGUAGE(S): Japanese

SUBJECT COVERAGE: history; economics; social sciences; trade unions movement, labour problems

GEOGRAPHICAL COVERAGE: Japan

DATA BEING PROCESSED AND SIZE: 76,800 books; 1,038 periodicals

DATA PROCESSING METHODS: partially computerized

HARDWARE USED: NEC PC 9801VX

SOFTWARE USED: Data Box

STORAGE MEDIA: traditional shelving of publications

TYPE OF ACTIVITY: data collection; SSID scientific and methodological activities; publication

PERIODICALS PUBLISHED: - Nihon Rodo Nenkan (the Labour Yearbook of Japan), 1 p.a.
- Nihon Shakai Undo Shiryo
- Ohara Shakai Mondai Kenkyusho Zasshi (Ohara Institute for Social Research Journal)

PUBLICATIONS: - Chronological tables of social and labour movement (in Japanese), 1987
- Ohara shakai mondai kenkyusho kenkyu sosho (Institute publications series)

CLIENTELE: professors, students, researchers (1,100 p.a.)

ACCESS TO SERVICE: open to all users, free of charge

TYPE & DESCRIPTION OF SERVICES PROVIDED: Provides library services and bibliographic searches of information.

480 - INSTITUTE OF DEVELOPING ECONOMIES, LIBRARY AND STATISTICAL RESEARCH DEPARTMENT

ADDRESS: 42 Ichigaya-Hommura-cho,
Shinjuku-ku,
Tokyo 162,
JAPAN
TEL: (03) 353-4231 - TELEX: AJIKEN J32473
CABLE: AJIKEN TOKYO

CREATED: 1958   *HEAD:* N. Suzuki, Director, Statistical Research Department
K. Nonaka, Director, Library

SIZE OF STAFF: Professional: 57

TYPE OF SERVICE: national; public; non-profit

SYSTEMS & NETWORKS ATTACHED TO: University of Toronto Library Automation System (UTLAS)

MATERIALS DESCRIBING THE SERVICE: - Annual report

WORKING LANGUAGE(S): Japanese

SUBJECT COVERAGE: economics; social sciences; political science; demography; education; history; law; sociology

GEOGRAPHICAL COVERAGE: developing countries; Asia; Middle East; Latin America; Africa

DATA BEING PROCESSED AND SIZE: 240,500 books; 170 newspapers; 2,000 journals; 26,560 maps; 47,790 reels of microfilm

DATA PROCESSING METHODS: computerized

HARDWARE USED: IBM 4381-M 12

SOFTWARE USED: OS/VS 1; CMS

Japan / Japon / Japón

STORAGE MEDIA: traditional shelving of publications, microfilms (newspaper, serials)
TYPE OF ACTIVITY: data collection; data analysis; distribution of information;
 publication
PERIODICALS PUBLISHED:
 - Library Bulletin, 12 p.a.
PUBLICATIONS: - Annotated bibliography of modern Chinese studies in mainland China
 1978-1983, 1985
 - Regional cooperation in ASEAN: an annotated bibliography, with ASEAN
 chronicles, 1984
 - Developing countries in Japanese writings: an annual bibliography, 1986
 - Union catalogue of Chinese periodicals and newspapers in Japan, 1986
 - Union catalogue of Korean periodicals and newspapers in Japan, 1987
CLIENTELE: librarians, researchers
ACCESS TO SERVICE: services open to specific categories of users, free of charge
TYPE & DESCRIPTION OF SERVICES PROVIDED: Provides library services, selective
 dissemination of information, bibliographic searches of information using
 on-line services, i.e. AID/XT, YART, JART. Has also access to UTLAS by
 telephone. Microforms and photocopies are also provided.

481 - KEIDANREN TOSHOKAN

SYNONYMOUS NAMES: Keidanren Library
PARENT ORGANIZATION: Keizai Dantai Rengokai (Federation of Economic Organizations)
ADDRESS: 1-9-4 Ohtemachi,
 Chiyoda-ku,
 Tokyo 100,
 JAPAN
 TEL: 03-279-1411 - TELEX: 02223188 KDR TOK J
 KEIDANREN TOKYO
CREATED: 1946 *HEAD:* N. Hanamura, Chief
TYPE OF SERVICE: national; private; non-profit
WORKING LANGUAGE(S): Japanese
SUBJECT COVERAGE: economics
GEOGRAPHICAL COVERAGE: Japan
DATA BEING PROCESSED AND SIZE: 24,000 Japanese books; 3,200 foreign books; 1,137
 Japanese serials; 579 foreign serials; newspapers; pamphlets; films
DATA PROCESSING METHODS: partially computerized
STORAGE MEDIA: traditional shelving of publications
TYPE OF ACTIVITY: distribution of information; SSID scientific and methodological
 activities; publication
PERIODICALS PUBLISHED: - Keidenren Review, 4 p.a., in English
 - Economic Picture of Japan, 1 p.a. in English and French
 - Accession List
ACCESS TO SERVICE: services open to specific categories of users
TYPE & DESCRIPTION OF SERVICES PROVIDED: Provides library services.

482 - KEIO GIJUKU DAIGAKU MITA JOHO SENTA

SYNONYMOUS NAMES: Keio University Mita Library and Information Center
PARENT ORGANIZATION: Keio Gijuku Daigaku
ADDRESS: 2-15-45 Mita,
          Minato-ku,
          Tokyo 108,
          JAPAN
          TEL: 03-453-4511
CREATED: 1970   *HEAD:* R. Shimizu, Director
SIZE OF STAFF: Professional: 40   Other: 39   Total: 79
TYPE OF SERVICE: national; private; non-profit
SYSTEMS & NETWORKS ATTACHED TO: National Center for Science Information System
MATERIALS DESCRIBING THE SERVICE: - Toshokan riyo annai shirizu (Series of guide to
          the Keio University library), no. 1-18
          - Guide to the Keio University Library, no. 5 of the series, in English
WORKING LANGUAGE(S): Japanese; English
SUBJECT COVERAGE: social sciences; humanities
GEOGRAPHICAL COVERAGE: Japan
DATA BEING PROCESSED AND SIZE: 1,200,000 books and 290,000 volumes of bound journals
          (16,000 titles)
DATA PROCESSING METHODS: partially computerized
HARDWARE USED: FACOM M360, FACOM K280
SOFTWARE USED: own
STORAGE MEDIA: traditional shelving of publications
TYPE OF ACTIVITY: data collection; publication
PUBLICATIONS: - PICC (Union List of Periodicals in Keio University)
          - Bunken Shirizu (Bibliographical Series)
CLIENTELE: faculty members, undergraduates and graduate students
ACCESS TO SERVICE: open to researchers, free of charge
TYPE & DESCRIPTION OF SERVICES PROVIDED: Provides library services, retrospective
          bibliographic searches, query-answering service, reference service and
          reproduction of documents.

483 - KOBE DIAGAKU KEIZAI KEIEI KENKYUSHO TOSHOSHITSU

SYNONYMOUS NAMES: Kobe University, Research Institute for Economics and Business
          Administration, Library
ADDRESS: Rokkodai-cho,
          Nada-ku,
          Kobe 657,
          JAPAN
          TEL: 078-881-1212
CREATED: 1919   *HEAD:* Mr. T. Maeda, Chief Librarian
SIZE OF STAFF: Professional: 3   Other: 3   Total: 6
TYPE OF SERVICE: national; public; non-profit
WORKING LANGUAGE(S): Japanese
SUBJECT COVERAGE: economics; business administration
GEOGRAPHICAL COVERAGE: global
DATA BEING PROCESSED AND SIZE: 184,000 books; 2,500 periodicals; 320,000 microfiches
DATA PROCESSING METHODS: manual

STORAGE MEDIA: traditional shelving of publications; microfiches
TYPE OF ACTIVITY: data collection; distribution of information
CLIENTELE: researchers
TYPE & DESCRIPTION OF SERVICES PROVIDED: Provides library services, bibliographic
  searches, microforms and photocopies.

484 - KOKURITSU FUJIN KYOIKU KAIKAN

SYNONYMOUS NAMES: National Women's Education Centre
PARENT ORGANIZATION: Monbu-sho (Ministry of Education, Science and Culture)
ADDRESS: 728 Sugaya Ranzan-machi,
  Hiki-gun,
  Saitama 355-02,
  JAPAN
  TEL: 0493-62-6711
  CABLE: NWEC HIGASHIMATSUYAMA
CREATED: 1977   *HEAD:* Ms. M. Maeda, Director-General
SIZE OF STAFF: Professional: 11   Other: 30   Total: 41
TYPE OF SERVICE: national; public; non-profit
WORKING LANGUAGE(S): Japanese
SUBJECT COVERAGE: education; women; family
GEOGRAPHICAL COVERAGE: Japan
DATA BEING PROCESSED AND SIZE: 45,000 books and reports; 750 periodicals (in
  Japanese); 250 periodicals (non-Japanese); 130 video tapes; 100 cassette
  tapes
DATA PROCESSING METHODS: partially computerized
HARDWARE USED: HITAC L70/28; HITAC L30
STORAGE MEDIA: traditional shelving of publications; discs; optical discs
TYPE OF ACTIVITY: data collection; data analysis; distribution of information;
  publication
PERIODICALS PUBLISHED: - Fujin Kyoiku Joho (The Japanese Journal of Education for
  Women), 2 p.a.
  - NWEC Newsletter, 2 p.a.
  - Kokuritsu Fujin Kyoiku Kaikan News (National Women's Education Centre
  News), 4 p.a.
CLIENTELE: 12,000 p.a.
ACCESS TO SERVICE: services open to all users, free of charge
TYPE & DESCRIPTION OF SERVICES PROVIDED: Provides library services, bibliographic,
  literature abstract and quantitative data searches, on-line service using
  own data base and external data bases, and photocopies.

485 - KOKURITSU KOKKAI TOSHOKAN, CHIKUJI KANKOBUTSU-BU, SAKUIN-KA

SYNONYMOUS NAMES: National Diet Library, Indexing Division, Serials Department
ADDRESS: 1-10-1 Nagata-cho,
  Chiyoda-ku,
  Tokyo 100,
  JAPAN
  TEL: 03-581-2331

```
        CABLE: NADLIB N004
REATED: 1948      HEAD: Mr. Y. Iibuchi,
IZE OF STAFF: Professional: 9    Other: 4    Total: 13
YPE OF SERVICE: national; public; non-profit
UBJECT COVERAGE: social sciences
EOGRAPHICAL COVERAGE: Japan
ATA BEING PROCESSED AND SIZE: 76,000 articles p.a.
ATA PROCESSING METHODS: computerized
ARDWARE USED: HITAC M-280H
OFTWARE USED: Japanese periodicals index's system (user program)
TORAGE MEDIA: traditional shelving of publications, magnetic tapes
YPE OF ACTIVITY: distribution of information; publication
ERIODICALS PUBLISHED:
       - Japanese periodicals index; humanities and social sciences, 4 p.a.
LIENTELE: public libraries, university libraries and the general public
CCESS TO SERVICE: open to all users, free of charge
YPE & DESCRIPTION OF SERVICES PROVIDED: Provides library services, searches of
       information, on-line services as well as information on magnetic tapes or
       discs. Has its own data base: Japanese Periodicals Index.
```

86 - KYOTO DAIGAKU JINBUNKAGAKU KENKYUJYO FUZOKU, TOYOGAKU BUNKEN SENTA

```
NONYMOUS NAMES: Kyoto University, the Documentation Center for Oriental Studies
ARENT ORGANIZATION: Research Institute for Humanistic Studies
DDRESS: 47 Higashiogura-cho,
        Kitashirakawa,
        Sakyo-ku,
        Kyoto,
        JAPAN
        TEL: 075-781-3405
REATED: 1965     HEAD: Y. Ozaki, Director
IZE OF STAFF: Professional: 2    Other: 6    Total: 8
YPE OF SERVICE: public; non-profit
UBJECT COVERAGE: humanities; history; linguistics; sinology
EOGRAPHICAL COVERAGE: global; Asia; China (People's Republic)
ATA PROCESSING METHODS: manual
TORAGE MEDIA: microfilms
ERIODICALS PUBLISHED: - Annual Bibliography of Oriental Studies
UBLICATIONS: - Catalogue of the Chinese classical books, 2 vols., 1965
LIENTELE: scholars, researchers and students
CCESS TO SERVICE: open to researchers against payment
YPE & DESCRIPTION OF SERVICES PROVIDED: Provides microfilms and photocopies.
```

87 - KYOTO DAIGAKU, TONAN AZIA KENKYU SENTA

```
NONYMOUS NAMES: Kyoto University, Center for Southeast Asian Studies;
        CSEAS
DDRESS: 46 Shimoadachi-cho, Yoshida,
        Sakyo-ku,
```

Kyoto 606,
JAPAN
TEL: (075) 771-0431
CABLE: KYODAI ASIA KYOTO
CREATED: 1965   *HEAD:* Y. Ishii, Director
TYPE OF SERVICE: international; public; non-profit
WORKING LANGUAGE(S): Japanese; English
SUBJECT COVERAGE: social sciences; economics
GEOGRAPHICAL COVERAGE: Southeast Asia
DATA BEING PROCESSED AND SIZE: 45,000 books
DATA PROCESSING METHODS: manual
TYPE OF ACTIVITY: data collection; distribution of information; SSID scientific and methodological activities; publication
PERIODICALS PUBLISHED: - Southeast Asian Studies, 4 p.a.
ACCESS TO SERVICE: services open to specific categories of users
TYPE & DESCRIPTION OF SERVICES PROVIDED: Provides library services and bibliographic searches of information.

488 - NIHON RODOKYOKAI, RODO TOSHOKAN

SYNONYMOUS NAMES: The Japan Institute of Labour, Labour Reference Library
ADDRESS: Chutaikin Bldg.,
7-6 Shibakoen, 1-chome,
Minato-ku,
Tokyo 105,
JAPAN
TEL: 03-436-0151
CREATED: 1958   *HEAD:* M. Nanzan, Director
SIZE OF STAFF: Total: 4
TYPE OF SERVICE: national; public; non-profit
SYSTEMS & NETWORKS ATTACHED TO: Japan Special Library Association
WORKING LANGUAGE(S): Japanese; English
SUBJECT COVERAGE: economics; labour
GEOGRAPHICAL COVERAGE: Japan
DATA BEING PROCESSED AND SIZE: 59,000 books; 900 periodicals
DATA PROCESSING METHODS: manual; partially computerized
SOFTWARE USED: Oasis Mate (Fujitsu)
STORAGE MEDIA: traditional shelving of publications; microfilms
TYPE OF ACTIVITY: distribution of information; publication
CLIENTELE: researchers from institutes, labour unions, management and governmental bodies, mass media etc. about 1,600 p.a.
ACCESS TO SERVICE: open to all users, free of charge
TYPE & DESCRIPTION OF SERVICES PROVIDED: Provides library services, query-answering services and photocopies.

489 - NIKKEI ECONOMIC ELECTRONIC DATABANK SYSTEM

SYNONYMOUS NAMES: NEEDS;
Nikkei Telecom Japan News and Retrieval

PARENT ORGANIZATION: Nihon Keizai Shimbun, Inc.
ADDRESS: 1-9-5, Ohtemachi,
       Chiyoda-ku,
       Tokyo, 100,
       JAPAN
       TEL: (03) 270-0251 - TELEX: J22308 NIKKEI
       CABLE: NIHONKEIZAI
CREATED: 1970   HEAD: T. Suzuki, Director
SIZE OF STAFF: Professional: 120   Other: 40   Total: 160
TYPE OF SERVICE: international; private; profit
SYSTEMS & NETWORKS ATTACHED TO: Regarding NEEDS data in general, some of the data
       bases are transferred to Data Resources, Inc. (U.S.)'s DRINET, and Control
       Data Corp's SBC network
MATERIALS DESCRIBING THE SERVICE: - NEEDS
         - NEEDS-ASIA
         - NEEDS-TS
         - NEEDS-Bulk
         - Nikkei Telecom Japan News and Retrieval
WORKING LANGUAGE(S): Japanese; English
SUBJECT COVERAGE: demography; economics
GEOGRAPHICAL COVERAGE: Japan; North America; Western Europe; Middle East; Southeast
       Asia; Australia
DATA BEING PROCESSED AND SIZE: 2,000,000 time series
DATA PROCESSING METHODS: computerized
HARDWARE USED: Burroughs A-15
SOFTWARE USED: Burroughs CANDE, Needs application softwares CAMP, MARS, MERLIN
STORAGE MEDIA: magnetic tapes, on-line disk
TYPE OF ACTIVITY: data collection; data analysis; publication
PERIODICALS PUBLISHED: - NEEDS Macro Forecast, 4 p.a.
       - NEEDS Energy Forecast, 4 p.a.
       - NEEDS Money Forecast, 4 p.a.
       - NEEDS Report, 6 p.a.
       - NEEDS Review, irr.
PUBLICATIONS: - Retrieval code books
       - Software manuals
CLIENTELE: 3,282 passwords issued to users
ACCESS TO SERVICE: open to all users, paid services
TYPE & DESCRIPTION OF SERVICES PROVIDED: Provides a wide range of information from
       numeric, economic data to bibliographic information. Provides on-line
       services using its own data bases Needs-Company, Nikkei Financial File,
       Nikkei Stock and Bond Price File, Needs-Economy, Needs-Money, Needs-
       World/Macro Forecast, Needs-IO, Needs-IFS, Needs-Energy. Also provides
       magnetic tapes as well as hardcopies.

O - NOMURA RESEARCH INSTITUTE, JAPAN ECONOMIC AND BUSINESS DATA BASE

SYNONYMOUS NAMES: NRI/E, Japan Economic and Business Data Bank
ADDRESS: 1-11-1, Nihonbashi,
       Chuo-ku,
       Tokyo 103,
       JAPAN

TEL: (03) 276-4762 - TELEX: NRITKJ J27586 - TELEFAX: (03) 276-4787
CABLE: NRITKY J
CREATED: 1965   *HEAD:* Mr. A. Kuwamori, Director of Information Service and
Development Dept.
SIZE OF STAFF: Professional: 5   Other: 10   Total: 15
TYPE OF SERVICE: international; public; profit
SYSTEMS & NETWORKS ATTACHED TO: Mark III/GE (General Electric Company); IDC
(Interactive Data Corporation)
MATERIALS DESCRIBING THE SERVICE: - NRI/E Japan Economic and Business Data Base
(manual)
- NRI/E Japan Economic and Business Data Base (brochure)
WORKING LANGUAGE(S): English
SUBJECT COVERAGE: economics; technology; economy; industry; economic forecasting;
model; simulation
GEOGRAPHICAL COVERAGE: Japan; global
DATA BEING PROCESSED AND SIZE: mainly government publications
DATA PROCESSING METHODS: computerized
SOFTWARE USED: XSIM
STORAGE MEDIA: discs
TYPE OF ACTIVITY: data analysis
CLIENTELE: personnel in corporate planning
ACCESS TO SERVICE: paid services, open to all users
TYPE & DESCRIPTION OF SERVICES PROVIDED: NRI/E is a machine-readable file containing
annual time series relating to Japan's economy and industry, including
macroeconomic data, financial data and forecasts. It is available through
the time sharing network "MARK III" of General Electric Information
Services.

491 - OSAKA KEIZAI DAIGAKU TOSMOKAN

SYNONYMOUS NAMES: Osaka University of Economics, Library
ADDRESS: 2-chome, Osumi,
Higashiyodogawa-ku,
Osaka 533,
JAPAN
TEL: 06-328-2431
CREATED: 1935   *HEAD:* T. Nabesima, Director
SIZE OF STAFF: Professional: 20   Other: 5   Total: 25
TYPE OF SERVICE: national; public; non-profit
WORKING LANGUAGE(S): English; Japanese
SUBJECT COVERAGE: economics; administrative sciences; social sciences
GEOGRAPHICAL COVERAGE: mainly Japan
DATA BEING PROCESSED AND SIZE: 432,000 books; 3,990 periodicals; 6,000 manuscripts
DATA PROCESSING METHODS: manual
PERIODICALS PUBLISHED: - Toshokan Newsletter, 4 p.a.
PUBLICATIONS: - Bunken-siryo no sagasikata, user's guide for material research
CLIENTELE: faculty members (100 p.a.); students (6,100 p.a.)
ACCESS TO SERVICE: services open to specific categories of users
TYPE & DESCRIPTION OF SERVICES PROVIDED: Provides library services and bibliograph'
searches of information.

492 - OSAKA SHOKO KAIGISHO SHOKO-TOSHOKAN

SYNONYMOUS NAMES: Osaka Chamber of Commerce and Industry Library
PARENT ORGANIZATION: Osaka Shoko Kaigisho
ADDRESS: 58-7 Uchihon-machi,
        Hashizume-cho,
        Higashi-ku,
        Osaka 540,
        JAPAN
        TEL: (06) 944-6317
        CABLE: OSAKACHAMBER OSAKA
CREATED: 1922   *HEAD:* T. Mori, Director
SIZE OF STAFF: Professional: 5   Other: 7   Total: 12
TYPE OF SERVICE: national; private; non-profit
MATERIALS DESCRIBING THE SERVICE: - Profile of Osaka Chamber of Commerce and Industry
        Library (in Japanese)
WORKING LANGUAGE(S): Japanese
SUBJECT COVERAGE: economics; social sciences; statistics
GEOGRAPHICAL COVERAGE: Osaka City in Japan
DATA BEING PROCESSED AND SIZE: 4,775 books p.a.; 1,117 periodicals; 1,060 microfilm
        reels; 786 microfiches
DATA PROCESSING METHODS: partially computerized
STORAGE MEDIA: traditional shelving of publications, discs, microfiches
CLIENTELE: mainly businessmen
ACCESS TO SERVICE: open to all users, paid services
TYPE & DESCRIPTION OF SERVICES PROVIDED: Provides library services, reference
        service, photocopies and microfilm copying, commercial database information
        retrieval.

**493 - SOPHIA UNIVERSITY INSTITUTE OF COMPARATIVE CULTURE, INTERNATIONAL MANAGEMENT
DEVELOPMENT SEMINARS**

SYNONYMOUS NAMES: SUICC/IMDS
ADDRESS: 4 Yonbancho,
        Chiyoda-ku,
        Tokyo 102,
        JAPAN
        TEL: (03) 238-4080 - TELEFAX: (03) 238-4088
        CABLE: SOPHIAUNIV
CREATED: 1964   *HEAD:* Prof. R. J. Ballon,
SIZE OF STAFF: Professional: 6   Other: 3   Total: 9
TYPE OF SERVICE: international; private
WORKING LANGUAGE(S): English
SUBJECT COVERAGE: economics; law; sociology; business management
GEOGRAPHICAL COVERAGE: Japan; East Asia
DATA PROCESSING METHODS: manual
TYPE OF ACTIVITY: data collection; data analysis; distribution of information;
        publication
PUBLICATIONS: - Abegglen, J. C., Kaisha, the Japanese corporation, 1985 (also in
        Japanese and German)
        - Gregory, G., Japanese electronics technology: enterprise and innovation,

1985
CLIENTELE: business executives (600 p.a.)
ACCESS TO SERVICE: paid services
TYPE & DESCRIPTION OF SERVICES PROVIDED: Provides quantitative data searches,
          selective dissemination of information, translation of documents and
          training and development for multinational corporations.

494 - TENRI UNIVERSITY, TENRI CENTRAL LIBRARY

ADDRESS: 1050 Somanouchi-cho,
          Tenri,
          Nara 632,
          JAPAN
          TEL: 07436-3-1511
CREATED: 1930   *HEAD:* Rev. H. Ueda, Chief Librarian
SIZE OF STAFF: Professional: 48   Other: 19   Total: 67
TYPE OF SERVICE: international; public; non-profit
MATERIALS DESCRIBING THE SERVICE: - Steele, C., Major libraries of the world: a
          selective guide, Bowker, London, 1976
WORKING LANGUAGE(S): English
SUBJECT COVERAGE: philosophy; religion; linguistics; history; geography; social
          anthropology; cultural anthropology
GEOGRAPHICAL COVERAGE: global
DATA BEING PROCESSED AND SIZE: 1,350,000 books
DATA PROCESSING METHODS: manual
STORAGE MEDIA: data collection; distribution of information; publication
TYPE OF ACTIVITY: data collection; distribution of information; publication
PERIODICALS PUBLISHED:
          - Biblia: Bulletin of the Tenri Central Library
PUBLICATIONS: - Tenri Central Library series
ACCESS TO SERVICE: services open to all users, free of charge
TYPE & DESCRIPTION OF SERVICES PROVIDED: Provides library services, bibliographic
          searches, microforms and photocopies.

495 - TOKYO DAIGAKU SHAKAI KAGAKU KENKYUSHO

SYNONYMOUS NAMES: University of Tokyo, Institute of Social Science
ADDRESS: 3-1, 7-chome, Hongo,
          Bunkyo-ku,
          Tokyo 113,
          JAPAN
          TEL: (03) 812-2111
CREATED: 1946   *HEAD:* Prof. Y. Okudaira, Director
TYPE OF SERVICE: international
WORKING LANGUAGE(S): Japanese
SUBJECT COVERAGE: economics; law; political science
GEOGRAPHICAL COVERAGE: Japan; Americas; Western Europe; USSR; Eastern Europe
DATA BEING PROCESSED AND SIZE: 220,000 books; 16,000 periodicals/serials
DATA PROCESSING METHODS: partially computerized

TORAGE MEDIA: traditional shelving of publications; microfilms; microfiches
YPE OF ACTIVITY: data collection; data analysis; publication
ERIODICALS PUBLISHED: - Tokyo Daigaku Shakai Kagaku Kenkyusho Yoran, every 2 years
        - Annals of the Institute of Social Science, 1 p.a. from 1987
        - Shakai Kagaku Kenkyu, 6 p.a.
LIENTELE: researchers
CCESS TO SERVICE: services open to specific categories of users
YPE & DESCRIPTION OF SERVICES PROVIDED: Provides library services and selective
        dissemination of information.

96 - TOKYO DAIGAKU TOYOBUNKA KENKYUJO

YNONYMOUS NAMES: University of Tokyo, Institute of Oriental Culture
DDRESS: 7-3-1 Hongo,
        Bunkyo-ku,
        Tokyo 113,
        JAPAN
        TEL: (03) 812-2111
        CABLE: TODAITOYO Tokyo
REATED: 1941   *HEAD:* Prof. T. Yamazaki, Director
YPE OF SERVICE: national
ATERIALS DESCRIBING THE SERVICE: - Institute of Oriental Culture, University of
        Tokyo, 1984
ORKING LANGUAGE(S): Japanese; English
UBJECT COVERAGE: social sciences; culture
EOGRAPHICAL COVERAGE: Asia
ATA BEING PROCESSED AND SIZE: books; periodicals; on-going research; seminars
ATA PROCESSING METHODS: manual
TORAGE MEDIA: traditional shelving of publications; microfiches; microfilms
YPE OF ACTIVITY: data collection; data analysis; distribution of information; SSID
        scientific and methodological activities; publication
ERIODICALS PUBLISHED: - The Memoirs of the Institute of Oriental Culture
        - Oriental Culture
LIENTELE: researchers
CCESS TO SERVICE: services open to specific categories of users, free of charge
YPE & DESCRIPTION OF SERVICES PROVIDED: Provides library services and photocopies.

97 - TOKYO KEIZAIDAIGAKU TOSHOKAN

YNONYMOUS NAMES: Tokyo Keizai University Library
DDRESS: 1-7 Minamicho,
        Kokubunji,
        Tokyo 185,
        JAPAN
        TEL: 0423-21-1941
REATED: 1900   *HEAD:* T. Fukuo, Librarian
IZE OF STAFF: Professional: 19   Other: 4   Total: 23
YPE OF SERVICE: national; private; non-profit
ORKING LANGUAGE(S): Japanese

SUBJECT COVERAGE: social sciences; administrative sciences; economics; law; politica science; social welfare; sociology
GEOGRAPHICAL COVERAGE: global
DATA BEING PROCESSED AND SIZE: 350,000 books; 3,000 periodicals
DATA PROCESSING METHODS: manual
STORAGE MEDIA: traditional shelving of publications
TYPE OF ACTIVITY: data collection; data analysis; distribution of information
CLIENTELE: undergraduate students, postgraduate students, faculties
ACCESS TO SERVICE: open to researchers, free of charge
TYPE & DESCRIPTION OF SERVICES PROVIDED: Provides library services, bibliographic
        searches, photocopies and on-line services using external data bases
        accessed through DIALOG and NACCIS.

498 - TOKYO SHISEI CHOSAKAI, SHISEI SEMMON TOSHOKAN

SYNONYMOUS NAMES: The Tokyo Institute for Municipal Research, Municipal Reference
        Library
ADDRESS: c/o Shisei Kaikan 1-3,
        Hibiya-koen,
        Chiyoda-ku,
        Tokyo 100,
        JAPAN
        TEL: 03-591-1201
CREATED: 1922
SIZE OF STAFF: Professional: 5
TYPE OF SERVICE: private; non-profit
MATERIALS DESCRIBING THE SERVICE: - The Tokyo Institute for Municipal Research and
        its work (in English)
WORKING LANGUAGE(S): Japanese; English; French; German
SUBJECT COVERAGE: social sciences; local government; urban areas
GEOGRAPHICAL COVERAGE: global
DATA BEING PROCESSED AND SIZE: 118,000 books; articles; reports; 275 periodicals (2
        Japanese, 65 foreign)
DATA PROCESSING METHODS: manual
STORAGE MEDIA: traditional shelving of publications
TYPE OF ACTIVITY: data collection; publication
CLIENTELE: students, teaching staff, researchers, experts (1,200 p.a.)
ACCESS TO SERVICE: services open to professors, researchers, public employees and
        students, free of charge
TYPE & DESCRIPTION OF SERVICES PROVIDED: Provides library services, bibliographic a
        literature searches.

499 - TOKYO SHOKO KAIGISHO SHOKO TOSHOKAN

SYNONYMOUS NAMES: The Tokyo Chamber of Commerce and Industry, Commercial and
        Industrial Library
ADDRESS: 3-2-2 Marunouchi,
        Chiyoda-ku,
        Tokyo 100,

JAPAN
TEL: 03-283-7690
REATED: 1926   *HEAD:* S. Oshima, Chief Librarian
IZE OF STAFF: Professional: 4   Other: 2   Total: 6
YPE OF SERVICE: national; public; non-profit
MATERIALS DESCRIBING THE SERVICE: - Toshokan Annai, leaflet (Japanese edition only)
WORKING LANGUAGE(S): Japanese; English
SUBJECT COVERAGE: economics; administrative sciences; law; political science
GEOGRAPHICAL COVERAGE: Japan mainly around Tokyo area
DATA BEING PROCESSED AND SIZE: 139,000 books (115,000 Japanese, 24,000 English);
         1,600 periodicals (1,500 Japanese, 100 English)
DATA PROCESSING METHODS: partially computerized
HARDWARE USED: FUJITSU K-10
STORAGE MEDIA: traditional shelving of publications; microfilms
YPE OF ACTIVITY: distribution of information
CLIENTELE: 16,000 persons p.a. mostly from service industries
ACCESS TO SERVICE: open to all users, free of charge
YPE & DESCRIPTION OF SERVICES PROVIDED: Provides bibliographic, literature abstract
         and quantitative data searches, query-answering services, on-line searches
         using external data bases, and photocopies.

500 - UNIVERSIDAD SOFÍA, INSTITUTO IBEROAMERICANO

SYNONYMOUS NAMES: Sophia University, Iberoamerican Institute
ADDRESS: 7-1 Kioicno,
         Chiyoda-ku,
         Tokyo 102,
         JAPAN
         TEL: 03-238-3530 - TELEFAX: 03-238-3885
CREATED: 1964   *HEAD:* G. Andrade Lleras, Director
IZE OF STAFF: Professional: 14   Other: 4   Total: 18
YPE OF SERVICE: national; private; non-profit
WORKING LANGUAGE(S): Japanese; Spanish; Portuguese; English
SUBJECT COVERAGE: social sciences; history; geography; philosophy
GEOGRAPHICAL COVERAGE: Latin America
DATA BEING PROCESSED AND SIZE: 23,000 books; 420 periodicals; on-going research;
         courses
DATA PROCESSING METHODS: manual
STORAGE MEDIA: traditional shelving of publications; fiches; tapes; discs;
         microfiches
YPE OF ACTIVITY: data collection; distribution of information; SSID scientific and
         methodological activities; SSID training; publication
PERIODICALS PUBLISHED: - Revista Iberoamericana, 2 p.a.
         - Serie de Investigaciones Latinoamericanas
         - Bibliografia de publicaciones Japonesas sobre América Latina, 1 p.a.
         - Boletin Informativo
         - Accessions List
PUBLICATIONS: - Latin American monograph series
CLIENTELE: students, researchers, general public (3,000 p.a.)
ACCESS TO SERVICE: services open to all users, some paid services
YPE & DESCRIPTION OF SERVICES PROVIDED: Provides library services, bibliographic,

literature abstract and quantitative data searches, microforms and
photocopies.

501 - CENTRE FOR RESEARCH, DOCUMENTATION AND UNIVERSITY EXCHANGE

SYNONYMOUS NAMES: CREDU;
   Centre de Recherches, d'Echanges et de Documentation Universitaire
ADDRESS: Maendeleo House,
   P.O. Box 58480,
   Nairobi,
   KENYA
   TEL: 21911
CREATED: 1980 *HEAD:* Dr. J. Copans, Director
SIZE OF STAFF: Professional: 3 Other: 2 Total: 5
TYPE OF SERVICE: international; public; non-profit
WORKING LANGUAGE(S): English; French
SUBJECT COVERAGE: social sciences
GEOGRAPHICAL COVERAGE: Eastern Africa and Southern Africa
DATA BEING PROCESSED AND SIZE: books, periodicals, reports on on-going research,
   seminars
DATA PROCESSING METHODS: manual
STORAGE MEDIA: traditional shelving of publications
TYPE OF ACTIVITY: data collection; data analysis; distribution of information
PERIODICALS PUBLISHED:
   - CREDU Newsletter/Lettre d'Information du CREDU
   - Working papers/Travaux et Documents
ACCESS TO SERVICE: services open to all users
TYPE & DESCRIPTION OF SERVICES PROVIDED: Provides bibliographic and literature
   abstracts searches, selective dissemination of information, photocopies and
   translation of documents upon request.

502 - HIGH COURT OF KENYA, LIBRARY

ADDRESS: Law Courts,
   POB 30041,
   Nairobi,
   KENYA
   TEL: 21221
CREATED: 1935 *HEAD:* Mr. L. Kimathi Rukaria, Librarian
SIZE OF STAFF: Professional: 1 Other: 8 Total: 9
TYPE OF SERVICE: national
WORKING LANGUAGE(S): English; Kiswalhi
SUBJECT COVERAGE: law
TYPE OF ACTIVITY: distribution of information
CLIENTELE: special libraries
ACCESS TO SERVICE: services open to specific categories of users
TYPE & DESCRIPTION OF SERVICES PROVIDED: Provides information searches.

503 - KENYA INSTITUTE OF ADMINISTRATION, LIBRARY

SYNONYMOUS NAMES: KIA, Library
ADDRESS: PO Lower Kabete,
KENYA
TEL: 582311
HEAD: Mr. J. F. Lilech,
SIZE OF STAFF: Professional: 5
TYPE OF SERVICE: national; public; non-profit
MATERIALS DESCRIBING THE SERVICE: - Brochure
SUBJECT COVERAGE: administrative sciences
DATA BEING PROCESSED AND SIZE: 40,000 books; 200 periodicals
TYPE OF ACTIVITY: data collection
ACCESS TO SERVICE: services open to specific categories of users
TYPE & DESCRIPTION OF SERVICES PROVIDED: Provides library services and includes an
audio-visual centre and language laboratory.

504 - KOREA INSTITUTE FOR POPULATION AND HEALTH, LIBRARY-DATA MANAGEMENT UNIT

ADDRESS: San 42-14, Bulgwang-dong,
Seoul 122,
KOREA (REPUBLIC)
TEL: 388-8003-7
CABLE: INSPOHELTH SEOUL
CREATED: 1981   *HEAD:* Mr. Soo Young Lee, Director
SIZE OF STAFF: Professional: 2
TYPE OF SERVICE: national; public; non-profit
MATERIALS DESCRIBING THE SERVICE: - KIPH brochure, 1986, 18p.
WORKING LANGUAGE(S): Korean; English
SUBJECT COVERAGE: population; public health; social welfare; family planning; social
sciences
GEOGRAPHICAL COVERAGE: Korea (Republic)
DATA BEING PROCESSED AND SIZE: 17,000 books; 3,500 articles; 300 journals
DATA PROCESSING METHODS: manual; partially computerized
HARDWARE USED: Perkin Elner 3210
SOFTWARE USED: Reliance Data Base System, 44 tapes; discs
TYPE OF ACTIVITY: data collection; publication; data analysis; distribution of
information
PERIODICALS PUBLISHED: - Journal of Population and Health Studies, 2 p.a.
- KIPH Bulletin
PUBLICATIONS: - Bibliography on population and health in Korea
CLIENTELE: researchers and experts, professors, students (300 p.month)
ACCESS TO SERVICE: open to all users, free of charge
TYPE & DESCRIPTION OF SERVICES PROVIDED: Provides library services, bibliographic
searches of information, on-line services using own data base KIPHLINE, and
photocopies.

Korea, Republic of / Rép. de Corée / Rep. de Corea

505 - THE KOREA SOCIAL SCIENCE RESEARCH LIBRARY

PARENT ORGANIZATION: The Lee In Pyo Foundation
ADDRESS: C.P.O. Box 6607,
      Seoul,
      KOREA (REPUBLIC)
      TEL: 738-5015 - TELEX: K26289 ESQUIRE
      CABLE: ESQUIRE
CREATED: 1983   *HEAD:* Mrs. L. Pongsoon, Director
SIZE OF STAFF: Professional: 6   Other: 9   Total: 15
TYPE OF SERVICE: national; private; non-profit
WORKING LANGUAGE(S): Korean; English
SUBJECT COVERAGE: political science; administrative sciences; economics; law;
      psychology; sociology; anthropology
GEOGRAPHICAL COVERAGE: Korea (Republic)
DATA BEING PROCESSED AND SIZE: 18,000 books; 600 periodicals; microfilms; microfiche
DATA PROCESSING METHODS: manual
STORAGE MEDIA: microfiches, films, video tapes
TYPE OF ACTIVITY: data collection; publication
PERIODICALS PUBLISHED:
      - Accession List
      - Periodicals List
CLIENTELE: undergraduate and graduate school students, professors, researchers (150-
      160 daily)
ACCESS TO SERVICE: services open to specific categories of users, free of charge
TYPE & DESCRIPTION OF SERVICES PROVIDED: Provides library services, reference
      service, bibliographies, selective dissemination of information, indexes and
      abstracts and photocopies upon request. The Library is the deposit center of
      the Royal Asiatic Society, Korea Branch Publications. It acts as the
      distribution center for the 8th US Army Excess Library Books.

506 - KOREAN SOCIAL SCIENCE RESEARCH COUNCIL

SYNONYMOUS NAMES: KOSSREC
ADDRESS: 304-28, Sachick-Dong,
      Chongro-ku,
      Seoul,
      KOREA (REPUBLIC)
CREATED: 1976   *HEAD:* Ki-seon Chung, Executive Secretary
TYPE OF SERVICE: international; public; non-profit
SYSTEMS & NETWORKS ATTACHED TO: Association of Asian Social Science Research Council
      (AASSREC); International Federation of Social Science Organizations (IFSSO)
WORKING LANGUAGE(S): English; Korean
SUBJECT COVERAGE: social sciences
GEOGRAPHICAL COVERAGE: Korea
DATA BEING PROCESSED AND SIZE: books; peridoicals; reports; on-going research report
      and seminar reports
DATA PROCESSING METHODS: manual
STORAGE MEDIA: traditional shelving of publications; tapes
TYPE OF ACTIVITY: data collection; distribution of information; publication
PERIODICALS PUBLISHED: - Social Science Review, 1 p.a. since 1983 (in Korean)

- Korea Social Science Journal
- Newsletter, 2 p.a.

CLIENTELE: graduate students
ACCESS TO SERVICE: services open to all users, free of charge
TYPE & DESCRIPTION OF SERVICES PROVIDED: Provides library services and selective dissemination of information.

Lesotho

507 - NATIONAL UNIVERSITY OF LESOTHO, INSTITUTE OF SOUTHERN AFRICAN STUDIES DOCUMENTATION CENTRE

SYNONYMOUS NAMES: ISAS Documentation Centre
ADDRESS: P.O.B.,
180 Roma,
LESOTHO
TEL: (050) 64247 - TELEX: 4303 LO
CABLE: Uniter Roma
SIZE OF STAFF: Professional: 2   Other: 3   Total: 5
TYPE OF SERVICE: national; non-profit
MATERIALS DESCRIBING THE SERVICE: - ISAS annual report
WORKING LANGUAGE(S): English; Sesotho
SUBJECT COVERAGE: social sciences; human rights; socio-political change
GEOGRAPHICAL COVERAGE: Southern Africa
DATA BEING PROCESSED AND SIZE: 3,000 documentation items
DATA PROCESSING METHODS: partially computerized
HARDWARE USED: MITAC, IBM compatible
SOFTWARE USED: Mini micro CDS/ISIS
STORAGE MEDIA: traditional shelving of publications
TYPE OF ACTIVITY: data collection; data analysis; distribution of information; SSID scientific and methodological activities
CLIENTELE: researchers, university students, etc. (60 per week)
ACCESS TO SERVICE: services open to specific categories of users
TYPE & DESCRIPTION OF SERVICES PROVIDED: Provides library services, bibliographic and literature abstract searches of information, selective dissemination of information and photocopies. In the process of computerization, ISAS plans to join with sister Centres in Botswana and Swaziland through SASSI (Southern African Social Science Index) Project.

Madagascar

508 - CENTRE NATIONAL DE LA RECHERCHE APPLIQUÉE AU DÉVELOPPEMENT RURAL, CENTRE DE DOCUMENTATION POUR LA RECHERCHE AGRICOLE

SYNONYMOUS NAMES: CENRADERU;
National Centre of Applied Research to Research Development, Documentation Centre for Agricultural Research
ADDRESS: Route circulaire-Bel Air,
B.P.1690,
Antananarivo 101,
MADAGASCAR

Madagascar

TEL: 303-96
CREATED: 1976   *HEAD:* Mr. J. Rakotonirina, Head
SIZE OF STAFF: Professional: 2   Other: 12   Total: 14
TYPE OF SERVICE: public; national; non-profit
SYSTEMS & NETWORKS ATTACHED TO: AGRIS-CARIS
WORKING LANGUAGE(S): French
SUBJECT COVERAGE: agriculture; rural development; agricultural development
GEOGRAPHICAL COVERAGE: Madagascar
DATA BEING PROCESSED AND SIZE: 2,000 books, articles, reports, on-going research
DATA PROCESSING METHODS: manual
STORAGE MEDIA: traditional shelving of publications; fiches; microfiches
TYPE OF ACTIVITY: data collection; publication
PERIODICALS PUBLISHED:
        - Aquisitions List
PUBLICATIONS: - Archives du FOFIFA
CLIENTELE: researchers, students
ACCESS TO SERVICE: services open to specific categories of users, free of charge
TYPE & DESCRIPTION OF SERVICES PROVIDED: Provides library services, bibliographic
        searches of information, selective dissemination of information, microforms
        and photocopies.

**509 - MINISTÈRE DE LA RECHERCHE SCIENTIFIQUE ET TECHNOLOGIQUE POUR LE DÉVELOPPEMENT,
CENTRE D'INFORMATION ET DE DOCUMENTATION SCIENTIFIQUE ET TECHNIQUE**

SYNONYMOUS NAMES: MRSTD, CIDST;
        Ministry of Scientific and Technological Research for Development,
        Scientific and Technical Information and Documentation Centre
ADDRESS: B.P. 6224,
        rue Fernand Kasanga, Tsimbazaza,
        Antananarivo (101),
        MADAGASCAR
        TEL: 217-18 - TELEX: 22539 MRSTD MG
CREATED: 1987   *HEAD:* Ms. J. Ratsimandrava, Director
SIZE OF STAFF: Professional: 20   Other: 56   Total: 76
TYPE OF SERVICE: national; public; non-profit
MATERIALS DESCRIBING THE SERVICE: - Journal officiel de la République Démocratique de
        Madagascar no. 1821, 1987
WORKING LANGUAGE(S): French
SUBJECT COVERAGE: social sciences; science; technology; development
GEOGRAPHICAL COVERAGE: Madagascar
DATA BEING PROCESSED AND SIZE: 3,900 encyclopedias, dictionaries, directories,
        general information, books, reports, theses and memoirs, bibliographic
        series, catalogues
DATA PROCESSING METHODS: manual
STORAGE MEDIA: traditional shelving of publications; fiches
TYPE OF ACTIVITY: data analysis; distribution of information; publication
PERIODICALS PUBLISHED:
        - Information Interne
        - Au Fil des Jours
        - Recherche pour le Développement, Série Sciences de l'Homme et de la
        Société

PUBLICATIONS: - Population de Madagascar: situation actuelle et perspectives d'avenir
CLIENTELE: researchers, students, decision-makers
ACCESS TO SERVICE: open to all users
TYPE & DESCRIPTION OF SERVICES PROVIDED: Provides library services, bibliographic and
        literature searches and photocopies; translation of documents upon request.

510 - PRÉSIDENCE DE LA RÉPUBLIQUE, DIRECTION GÉNÉRALE DE LA BANQUE DE DONNÉES

PARENT ORGANIZATION: Ministry of Finance and Economy
ADDRESS: B.P. 485,
        Antananarivo 101,
        MADAGASCAR
        TEL: 20081
CREATED: 1985   *HEAD:* Mr. A. R. Randrianarivony, Director General
TYPE OF SERVICE: national; public; non-profit
WORKING LANGUAGE(S): French
SUBJECT COVERAGE: demography; economics; statistics
DATA PROCESSING METHODS: computerized
HARDWARE USED: IBM 370/138
SOFTWARE USED: Cobol, Fortran
STORAGE MEDIA: tapes, discs
TYPE OF ACTIVITY: data collection; data analysis; distribution of information
PERIODICALS PUBLISHED: - Recensement Industriel, 1 p.a.
        - Annuaire Statistique, every 5 years
        - Bulletin Mensuel de Statistique
PUBLICATIONS: - Commerce extérieur
        - Situation économique
        - Résultats des enquêtes statistiques
CLIENTELE: public services; international institutions; economists
ACCESS TO SERVICE: services open to all users, free of charge
TYPE & DESCRIPTION OF SERVICES PROVIDED: Provides library services, literature and
        quantitative data searches, selective dissemination of information,
        statistical tables ordered through the mail or consultancies on the
        premises.

Malaysia / Malaisie / Malasia

511 - UNIT PENYELIDEKAN SOSIOEKONOMI

SYNONYMOUS NAMES: UPSE;
        Socio-Economic Research Unit;
        SERU
PARENT ORGANIZATION: Prime Minister's Department
ADDRESS: Prime Minister's Department,
        Ground Floor, Wisma Mirama,
        Jalan Wisma Putra,
        Kuala Lumpur 50529,
        MALAYSIA
        TEL: 03-2485155
CREATED: 1980   *HEAD:* Mr. A. Rahim bin Mohd. Zain, Director General

SIZE OF STAFF: Professional: 19
TYPE OF SERVICE: national; public; non-profit
WORKING LANGUAGE(S): Bahasa; Malay; English
SUBJECT COVERAGE: social sciences; development
GEOGRAPHICAL COVERAGE: Malaysia
DATA BEING PROCESSED AND SIZE: 2,400 (120 p.a.) documentation items
DATA PROCESSING METHODS: partially computerized
HARDWARE USED: IBM
SOFTWARE USED: SAS/SPSS Packages
STORAGE MEDIA: traditional shelving of publications
TYPE OF ACTIVITY: data collection; data analysis; publication
PERIODICALS PUBLISHED: - Forum Pembangunan, 2 p.a.
          - Development Forum, 2 p.a.
          - Perspectif, 4 p.a.
PUBLICATIONS: - Directory of on-going research in Malaysia
          - Directory of social science researchers and research organizations
          - Bibliography of research reports prepared by researchers registered with
          SERU
CLIENTELE: government officials, academic staff of local universities and foreign
          researchers
ACCESS TO SERVICE: services open to specific categories of users, free of charge
TYPE & DESCRIPTION OF SERVICES PROVIDED: Mainly concerned with the impact evaluation
          of the development projects of the Malaysian government. Services provided
          include the use of library facilities and searches of information.

512 - INSTITUT DU SAHEL, PROGRAMME DE RÉSEAU SAHÉLIEN DE DOCUMENTATION ET D'INFORMATION SCIENTIFIQUES ET TECHNIQUES

SYNONYMOUS NAMES: RESADOC
ADDRESS: B.P. 1530,
          Bamako,
          MALI
          TEL: 22.21.78 - TELEX: INSAH 432
CREATED: 1978   *HEAD:* Mr. Z. Bamba, Coordinator p.i.
TYPE OF SERVICE: international; non-profit
SYSTEMS & NETWORKS ATTACHED TO: POPIN-AFRICA (Réseau International d'Information en
          Matière de Population); PADIS (Système Panafricain de Documentation et
          d'Information)
WORKING LANGUAGE(S): French; English; Portuguese
SUBJECT COVERAGE: demography; education; economics; social anthropology; cultural
          anthropology; social welfare; sociology
GEOGRAPHICAL COVERAGE: Sahel; Burkina-Faso; Cape Verde; Guinea-Bissau; Gambia; Mali;
          Mauritania; Niger; Senegal; Chad
DATA BEING PROCESSED AND SIZE: 11,215 reference items
DATA PROCESSING METHODS: computerized
HARDWARE USED: HP 3000, serial 37
SOFTWARE USED: MINISIS
TYPE OF ACTIVITY: distribution of information; SSID scientific and methodological
          activities; SSID training; publication
PERIODICALS PUBLISHED:

- Lettre d'Information RESADOC
- POP-Sahel: Bulletin d'Information sur la Population et le Développement

UBLICATIONS: - Selected bibliographies
- Répertoire des Unités d'information au Sahel
- RESINDEX: Bibliographie sur le Sahel

LIENTELE: approximately 340 users p.a.

CCESS TO SERVICE: open to all users free of charge

YPE & DESCRIPTION OF SERVICES PROVIDED: Provides library services, bibliographic and literature abstract searches of information, selective dissemination of information, microforms and photocopies.

Mexico / Mexique / México

13 - BIBLIOTECA BENJAMIN FRANKLIN

YNONYMOUS NAMES: Benjamin Franklin Library

ARENT ORGANIZATION: United States Information Agency

DDRESS: Londres 16,
Col. Juarez,
06600 Mexico, D.F.,
MEXICO
TEL: 211.00.42, Ext. 3443

REATED: 1942   *HEAD:* Ms. I. de Perez Monroy,

IZE OF STAFF: Total: 20

YPE OF SERVICE: public

UBJECT COVERAGE: social sciences; economics; history; political science

EOGRAPHICAL COVERAGE: Mexico

ATA BEING PROCESSED AND SIZE: 30,000 books; 5,000 pamphlets; audio visual materials

ATA PROCESSING METHODS: partially computerized

ARDWARE USED: IBM

OFTWARE USED: LOGICAT, LOGIPRES, WORDSTAR

TORAGE MEDIA: traditional shelving of publications; microfiches

YPE OF ACTIVITY: data collection; distribution of information; SSID training

ERIODICALS PUBLISHED:
- Selección de Adquisiciones Recientes

LIENTELE: general public, university students, academics, professionals, and government officials

CCESS TO SERVICE: services open to all users, free of charge

YPE & DESCRIPTION OF SERVICES PROVIDED: Provides library services, bibliographic searches, selective dissemination of information, microforms, photocopies, and on-line services using external data bases.

14 - BIBLIOTECA NACIONAL DE ANTROPOLOGÍA E HISTORIA

YNONYMOUS NAMES: National Library of Anthropology and History

ARENT ORGANIZATION: Instituto Nacional de Antropologia e Historia, Secretaria de Educación Publica

DDRESS: Paseo de la Reforma y Calzada Gandhi,
11560 México, D. F.,
MEXICO

TEL: 553.62.42
CREATED: 1880   *HEAD:* Ms Y. Mercader Martínez, Director
SIZE OF STAFF: Professional: 20   Other: 35
TYPE OF SERVICE: public
SUBJECT COVERAGE: history; linguistics; social anthropology; cultural anthropology;
       ethnography
GEOGRAPHICAL COVERAGE: Latin America; global
DATA BEING PROCESSED AND SIZE: 500,000 books; 11,000 periodicals
DATA PROCESSING METHODS: manual
PERIODICALS PUBLISHED:
       - Información al Día en Antropología y Ciencias Sociales, 6 p.a.
PUBLICATIONS: - Serie archivo histórico
       - Serie bibliografía
       - Serie códices
       - Serie investigación
CLIENTELE: students, professors
ACCESS TO SERVICE: open to all users
TYPE & DESCRIPTION OF SERVICES PROVIDED: Provides bibliographies, selective
       dissemination of information and reproduction of documents and microfilms.

515 - CENTRO DE ESTUDIOS DEMOGRÁFICOS Y DE DESARROLLO URBANO

SYNONYMOUS NAMES: CEDDU;
       Center for Demographic and Urban Development Studies
PARENT ORGANIZATION: El Colegio de México
ADDRESS: El Colegio de México,
       Camino al Ajusco 20,
       Apdo. Postal 20-671,
       01000 Mexico 20, D.F.,
       MEXICO
       TEL: 568.60.33 - TELEX: 1777585 COLME
       CABLE: COLMEX
CREATED: 1964   *HEAD:* Dr. G. Garza, Director
TYPE OF SERVICE: public
WORKING LANGUAGE(S): Spanish
SUBJECT COVERAGE: demography; economics; political science; social anthropology;
       social welfare; sociology
GEOGRAPHICAL COVERAGE: Mexico
DATA PROCESSING METHODS: partially computerized
HARDWARE USED: Printaform
SOFTWARE USED: SPSS, Stata, MCPD, PANDEM
TYPE OF ACTIVITY: data collection; data analysis; distribution of information; SSID
       scientific and methodological activities
ACCESS TO SERVICE: services open to specific categories of users, free of charge
TYPE & DESCRIPTION OF SERVICES PROVIDED: Provides production of information on
       magnetic tapes or discs. Has own data bases: "Datos Municipales" and
       "Encuestas Nacionales". Photocopying facilities are also available.

16 - EL COLEGIO DE LA FRONTERA NORTE, BIBLIOTECA

SYNONYMOUS NAMES: COLEF, Biblioteca;
College of the Northern Border, Library
ADDRESS: José Ma. Velasco 28,
Zona del Río,
Tijuana,
Baja California 22320,
MEXICO
TEL: (66) 84-29-36
HEAD: Mr. R. Quintanilla-Cardenas, Director
SIZE OF STAFF: Total: 6
TYPE OF SERVICE: international; national; public; profit; non-profit
WORKING LANGUAGE(S): Spanish; English
SUBJECT COVERAGE: social sciences; administrative sciences; demography; economics;
geography; history; political science; social welfare; sociology; migration;
environmental sciences; culture; public administration; ethnic groups;
urbanization; labour; tourism
GEOGRAPHICAL COVERAGE: USA; Mexico border
DATA BEING PROCESSED AND SIZE: books; articles; reports; on-going research; seminars;
training courses; microfiches; periodicals; special collections; photocopies
materials
DATA PROCESSING METHODS: manual; partially computerized
HARDWARE USED: PC IBM compatible
STORAGE MEDIA: traditional shelving of publications and discs
TYPE OF ACTIVITY: data analysis; distribution of information; SSID scientific and
methodological activities; SSID training
CLIENTELE: researchers, students, professors, executives
ACCESS TO SERVICE: open to all users, free of charge and some paid services
TYPE & DESCRIPTION OF SERVICES PROVIDED: Provides library services, bibliographic and
literature abstract searches of information, on-line services using its own
data bases, Current Awareness Information Services and a weekly bilingual
(English/Spanish) automated index. Also provides selective dissemination of
information, production of information on magnetic tapes and discs and
photocopies. Has access to SIE Economic Information System via satellite and
BANXICO Banco de Mexico.

**17 - CONSEJO NACIONAL DE POBLACIÓN, CENTRO DE DOCUMENTACIÓN "ANTONIO CARRILLO
FLORES"**

SYNONYMOUS NAMES: National Population Council, Documentation Center "Antonio
Carrillo Flores"
ADDRESS: Angel Urraza 1137,
Col. del Valle,
C.P. 03100 México, D.F.,
MEXICO
TEL: 559-61-10
CREATED: 1983   *HEAD:* Mr. A. Filio Moreno, Head
SIZE OF STAFF: Professional: 8   Other: 3   Total: 11
TYPE OF SERVICE: national; public; non-profit
WORKING LANGUAGE(S): Spanish

SUBJECT COVERAGE: demography; social sciences; economics; population; development; women
GEOGRAPHICAL COVERAGE: Mexico
DATA BEING PROCESSED AND SIZE: books; articles; reports; seminars; on-going research
DATA PROCESSING METHODS: manual; computerized
HARDWARE USED: IBM Mod. 60 (PS2) 70 MB
SOFTWARE USED: CDS/MICROISIS
STORAGE MEDIA: discs; microfiches
TYPE OF ACTIVITY: data analysis; distribution of information; publication
PERIODICALS PUBLISHED: - Revista de Resúmenes sobre Población
CLIENTELE: researchers (60%); students (30%); general public (10%)
ACCESS TO SERVICE: services open to all users, free of charge
TYPE & DESCRIPTION OF SERVICES PROVIDED: Provides library services, bibliographic and
literature abstract information searches, selective dissemination of
information, on-line services using own data base DOCPAL/CONAPO-MEXICO
(Sistema de Documentación sobre Población de México). Has also access to
DOCPAL/CELADE (Sistema de Documentación sobre Población en América Latina)
Photocopying facilities are available.

518 - EL COLEGIO DE MÉXICO, BIBLIOTECA "DANIEL COSÍO VILLEGAS", SECCIÓN DE INFORMACIÓN Y SELECCIÓN

ADDRESS: Camino al Ajusco 20,
Apartado Postal 20-671,
01000 Mexico, D.F.,
MEXICO
TEL: 568-60-33 - TELEX: 1777585 COLME
CABLE: COLMEX
CREATED: 1940   HEAD: Ms. S. Ainsworth,
SIZE OF STAFF: Professional: 17
TYPE OF SERVICE: private
MATERIALS DESCRIBING THE SERVICE: - La Biblioteca Daniel Cosio Villegas, booklet
- Manual del Rector
WORKING LANGUAGE(S): Spanish; English; oriental languages
SUBJECT COVERAGE: social sciences; demography; economics; history; linguistics; political science; sociology
GEOGRAPHICAL COVERAGE: Latin America; Asia; Africa; USA; Europe
DATA BEING PROCESSED AND SIZE: 400,000 books; 3,600 journals; maps
DATA PROCESSING METHODS: partially computerized
HARDWARE USED: ALTOS 586
SOFTWARE USED: in-house
STORAGE MEDIA: traditional shelving of publications; microfiches; tapes
TYPE OF ACTIVITY: distribution of information; publication
PERIODICALS PUBLISHED: - Lista de Obras Catalogadas, 12 p.a.
CLIENTELE: researchers and university students
ACCESS TO SERVICE: services open to specific categories of users, free of charge
TYPE & DESCRIPTION OF SERVICES PROVIDED: Provides library services, bibliographic
searches of information, and photocopies. Also provides on-line services
using external data bases avalaible through DIALOG, BRS, QUESTEL, BLAISE,
ESA-IRS, MEXICAN DATA BANKS.

19 - EL COLEGIO DE MICHOACÁN, BIBLIOTECA

SYNONYMOUS NAMES: College of Michoacan, Library
ADDRESS: Martínez de Navarrete No. 505,
      Esq. con Avenida del Arbol,
      Fracc. Las Fuentes,
      59690 Zamora, Michoacán,
      MEXICO
      TEL: 29997
CREATED: 1979   *HEAD:* Ms. E. Vega Méndez, Head Librarian
SIZE OF STAFF: Professional: 5   Other: 4   Total: 9
TYPE OF SERVICE: international; public; non-profit
SUBJECT COVERAGE: social sciences
GEOGRAPHICAL COVERAGE: Mexico
DATA BEING PROCESSED AND SIZE: 90,000 books and documents
DATA PROCESSING METHODS: manual
TYPE OF ACTIVITY: distribution of information; SSID scientific and methodological
      activities; publication
CLIENTELE: faculty, researchers and graduate students
ACCESS TO SERVICE: services open to specific categories of users, free of charge
TYPE & DESCRIPTION OF SERVICES PROVIDED: Provides library services, bibliographic
      searches, on-line services, selective dissemination of information,
      microforms and photocopies.

20 - FACULTAD LATINOAMERICANA DE CIENCIAS SOCIALES-SEDE ACADEMIA MÉXICO, BIBLIOTECA

SYNONYMOUS NAMES: FLACSO-Sede Academia México, Biblioteca;
      Latin American Faculty of Social Sciences, Library
PARENT ORGANIZATION: Facultad Latinoamericana de Ciencias Sociales
ADDRESS: Apartado Postal 20-021,
      Delegación Alvaro Obregon,
      01000 Mexico, D. F.,
      MEXICO
      TEL: 568.66.99 - TELEX: 1772150 FLACME
CREATED: 1975   *HEAD:* Ms. S. Hernández Acosta, Director
SIZE OF STAFF: Professional: 7
TYPE OF SERVICE: public; non-profit
WORKING LANGUAGE(S): Spanish
SUBJECT COVERAGE: social sciences
GEOGRAPHICAL COVERAGE: Latin America
DATA BEING PROCESSED AND SIZE: 20,000 books; 300 periodicals, 4,200 reports
DATA PROCESSING METHODS: partially computerized
HARDWARE USED: Printaform PC5512
SOFTWARE USED: Logicat version 3.0
STORAGE MEDIA: traditional shelving of publications, fiches
TYPE OF ACTIVITY: distribution of information; SSID scientific and methodological
      activities; SSID training; publication
PERIODICALS PUBLISHED:
      - Boletín BIbliográfico, 3 p.a.
CLIENTELE: 4,200 p.a.
ACCESS TO SERVICE: open to all users free of charge

TYPE & DESCRIPTION OF SERVICES PROVIDED: The Centre provides library services,
bibliographic and literature abstract searches. Also provides selective
dissemination of information and photocopies upon request.

521 - FUNDACIÓN JAVIER BARROS SIERRA, BIBLIOTECA

SYNONYMOUS NAMES: FJBAC Biblioteca
ADDRESS: Sierra, A.C.,
Apdo. Postal 20-061,
01000 Mexico, D.F.,
MEXICO
TEL: 568-96-39
HEAD: Mr. J. A. Luna Gonzalez,
SIZE OF STAFF: Total: 3
TYPE OF SERVICE: national; public; private
SUBJECT COVERAGE: futurology; social sciences; demography; economics; education;
history; political science; psychology; social welfare; sociology;
statistics; tourism; communication; transport; health
DATA BEING PROCESSED AND SIZE: 10,000 volumes; 750 periodicals
TYPE OF ACTIVITY: publication
CLIENTELE: researchers and professors
ACCESS TO SERVICE: services open to all users, free of charge
TYPE & DESCRIPTION OF SERVICES PROVIDED: Provides library services, bibliographic and
quantitative data searches of information, selective dissemination of
information, photocopies and translation of documents upon requests.

522 - INSTITUTO DE INVESTIGACIONES ANTROPOLÓGICAS, BIBLIOTECA

PARENT ORGANIZATION: Universidad Nacional Autonoma de Mexico
ADDRESS: Ciudad Universitaria,
Delegación Coyoacán,
04510 Mexico D. F.,
MEXICO
TEL: 550.53.11
CREATED: 1973   *HEAD:* I. Garcia Ortiz, Librarian
SIZE OF STAFF: Total: 11
TYPE OF SERVICE: national; public
MATERIALS DESCRIBING THE SERVICE: - Manual de uso de la biblioteca, 1978
- Cómo consultar los listados en la biblioteca, 1981
WORKING LANGUAGE(S): English; Spanish
SUBJECT COVERAGE: anthropology
GEOGRAPHICAL COVERAGE: Mexico; global
DATA BEING PROCESSED AND SIZE: 50,000 books; 1,450 periodicals; 7,000 theses
DATA PROCESSING METHODS: computerized
HARDWARE USED: Burroughs 7800
SOFTWARE USED: ALGOL (ONIONS)
TYPE OF ACTIVITY: data collection; data analysis; publication
PERIODICALS PUBLISHED:
- Boletin Nuevas Adquisiciones

CLIENTELE: 3,000 p.a.
ACCESS TO SERVICE: open to students and researchers free of charge
TYPE & DESCRIPTION OF SERVICES PROVIDED: Provides library services and computerized
        bibliographical research.

523 - INSTITUTO LATINOAMERICANO DE LA COMUNICACIÓN EDUCATIVA, CENTRO DE DOCUMENTACIÓN
        PARA AMÉRICA LATINA Y EL CARIBE

SYNONYMOUS NAMES: ILCE/CEDAL;
        ILCE, Documentation Centre for Latin America and the Caribbean
ADDRESS: Juan Luis Vives 200, 1,
        Col. Chapultepec Morales,
        Apartado Postal 11570,
        Mexico, D.F.,
        MEXICO
        TEL: 395-0600
CREATED: 1956   HEAD: Mr. R. Delgado Hurtado de Mendoza, Head
SIZE OF STAFF: Total: 5
TYPE OF SERVICE: international; public
WORKING LANGUAGE(S): Spanish; English
SUBJECT COVERAGE: education; communication
GEOGRAPHICAL COVERAGE: Latin America
DATA BEING PROCESSED AND SIZE: 10,000 books
DATA PROCESSING METHODS: manual
TYPE OF ACTIVITY: distribution of information; publication
PERIODICALS PUBLISHED: - Tecnologia y Comunicación Educativas, 4 p.a.
CLIENTELE: researchers, students
ACCESS TO SERVICE: services open to specific categories of users
TYPE & DESCRIPTION OF SERVICES PROVIDED: Provides library services, bibliographic and
        literature abstract searches of information, microforms, photocopies and
        translation of documents upon request.

524 - INSTITUTO TECNOLÓGICO AUTÓNOMO DE MEXICO, BIBLIOTECA

ADDRESS: Rio Hondo No. 1,
        Col. Progreso Tizapán,
        Del. A. Obregón,
        01000 México, D. F.,
        MEXICO
        TEL: 550-9300
CREATED: 1947   HEAD: Mr. J. Orozco-Tenorio, Director
SIZE OF STAFF: Professional: 3
TYPE OF SERVICE: private; non-profit
WORKING LANGUAGE(S): Spanish
SUBJECT COVERAGE: social sciences; administrative sciences; economics; sociology
DATA BEING PROCESSED AND SIZE: 72,600 documentation items
DATA PROCESSING METHODS: manual
STORAGE MEDIA: traditional shelving of publications
TYPE OF ACTIVITY: data collection; distribution of information

CLIENTELE: university students (3,500 p.a.)
ACCESS TO SERVICE: paid services open to specific categories
TYPE & DESCRIPTION OF SERVICES PROVIDED: Provides library services, bibliographic
        searches, selective dissemination of information, microforms and
        photocopies. Also provides on-line services using external data bases,
        DIALOG, ORBIT and SIE-BANXICO.

525 - INSTITUTO TECNOLÓGICO Y ESTUDIOS SUPERIORES MONTERREY, BIBLIOTECA

SYNONYMOUS NAMES: ITESM, Biblioteca
ADDRESS: Av. Eugenio Garza Sada 2501,
        Sucursal de Correos J.,
        64849 Monterrey, N.L.,
        MEXICO
        TEL: 58-20-00 - TELEX: 446222 - TELEFAX: (52-83) 58.89.31
CREATED: 1944   HEAD: Mr. S. Martínez, Director
SIZE OF STAFF: Professional: 7
TYPE OF SERVICE: private
SYSTEMS & NETWORKS ATTACHED TO: Acuerdo Regional
MATERIALS DESCRIBING THE SERVICE: - Guia del usuario. Biblioteca ITESM.
SUBJECT COVERAGE: social sciences; administrative sciences; demography; economics;
        geography; history; linguistics; psychology; labour relations; business
        management; mass media
DATA BEING PROCESSED AND SIZE: 70,000 books; 2,500 periodicals; 5,000 articles and
        reports
DATA PROCESSING METHODS: partially computerized
HARDWARE USED: Altos 2086; IBM PC XT; IBM 4381; Macintosh
SOFTWARE USED: in-house
STORAGE MEDIA: traditional shelving of publications; magnetic tapes and discs
TYPE OF ACTIVITY: distribution of information; SSID training; publication
PERIODICALS PUBLISHED:
        - Bibliotec
        - Catálogo de Software
        - Boletin de Adquisiciones Recientes
CLIENTELE: university students, professors and researchers (10,000 p.a.)
ACCESS TO SERVICE: paid services open to specific category of users
TYPE & DESCRIPTION OF SERVICES PROVIDED: Provides library services, bibliographic
        searches, selective dissemination of information, magnetic tapes, CD ROM
        discs, and photocopies. Also provides on-line services, using own data bas
        "TABCO" and external data bases available through BRS and DIALOG, and
        including loans of softwares.

526 - SECRETARÍA DE RELACIONES EXTERIORES, BIBLIOTECA "JOSÉ MA. LAFRAGUA"

SYNONYMOUS NAMES: Ministry of Foreign Affairs, Library "José Ma. Lafragua"
ADDRESS: R. Flores Magón 1,
        06995 México D.F.,
        MEXICO
        TEL: 782.43.20

REATED: 1976 *HEAD:* Ms M. E. Ibañez, Director
IZE OF STAFF: Total: 13
YPE OF SERVICE: public; non-profit
ORKING LANGUAGE(S): Spanish; English; French
UBJECT COVERAGE: history; economics; geography; law; political science; sociology;
social sciences; public international law; private international law
ATA BEING PROCESSED AND SIZE: 40,000 books
CCESS TO SERVICE: services open to all users, free of charge
YPE & DESCRIPTION OF SERVICES PROVIDED: Provides library services and bibliographic
searches of information.

27 - UNIVERSIDAD AUTÓNOMA DE YUCATÁN, CENTRO DE INVESTIGACIONES REGIONALES "DR. HIDEYO NOGUCHI", UNIDAD DE APOYO A LA INVESTIGACIÓN CIENTÍFICA

DDRESS: Apdo. Post. 2-1213,
C.P. 97240,
Mérida, Yucatán,
MEXICO
TEL: 23-97-71
REATED: 1979 *HEAD:* Mr. F. Anda Vela, Coordinator
IZE OF STAFF: Professional: 5 Other: 3 Total: 8
YPE OF SERVICE: international
YSTEMS & NETWORKS ATTACHED TO: Bancos Nacionales CONACYT
ATERIALS DESCRIBING THE SERVICE: - Información a los usuarios de la Unidad de Apoyo
(brochure)
ORKING LANGUAGE(S): Spanish
UBJECT COVERAGE: social sciences; economics; economic history; political history;
social history; economic problems
EOGRAPHICAL COVERAGE: Yucatán Peninsular; Caribbean area
ATA BEING PROCESSED AND SIZE: 5,000 books, 150 publications
ATA PROCESSING METHODS: partially computerized
ARDWARE USED: Elektra
TORAGE MEDIA: discs, fiches, microfilms, microfiches
YPE OF ACTIVITY: data collection; data analysis; distribution of information; SSID
scientific and methodological activities; SSID training; publication
ERIODICALS PUBLISHED: - Yucatán: Historia y Economia
- Boletin de Adquisiciones del Banco de Información, 6 p.a.
UBLICATIONS: - Lara Y Lara, H.; Aguilar, P. C., Catálogo bibliográfico microfilmado
en la Biblioteca Particular del Prof. A. B. Vásquez
CCESS TO SERVICE: services open to all users
YPE & DESCRIPTION OF SERVICES PROVIDED: Provides library services, bibliographic,
literature abstracts and quantitative data searches of information, on-line
services using QUESTEL, DIALOG, MEDLARS, ORBIT, BRS data bases. Also
provides selective dissemination of information, information on magnetic
tapes or discs, provision of microforms and photocopies.

528 - UNIVERSIDAD NACIONAL AUTÓNOMA DE MÉXICO, CENTRO DE INFORMACIÓN CIENTÍFICA Y HUMANÍSTICA

SYNONYMOUS NAMES: CICH
ADDRESS: Ciudad Universitaria,
Apartado Postal 70-392,
04510 México, D.F.,
MEXICO
TEL: 548-08-58; 550-59-05 - TELEX: 01774523 UNAMME
CREATED: 1971   *HEAD:* Ms. M. Almada de Ascencio, Director
SIZE OF STAFF: Professional: 52   Other: 40   Total: 92
TYPE OF SERVICE: public; non-profit
SYSTEMS & NETWORKS ATTACHED TO: Aquatic Sciences and Fisheries Information System
(ASFIS); Population Information Network (POPIN)
MATERIALS DESCRIBING THE SERVICE: - Centro de Información Científica y Humanística
(folleto descriptivo)
WORKING LANGUAGE(S): Spanish; Portuguese; English
SUBJECT COVERAGE: social sciences
GEOGRAPHICAL COVERAGE: Latin America
DATA BEING PROCESSED AND SIZE: 4,000 journals; 45,000 articles; 3,000 reports
DATA PROCESSING METHODS: computerized
HARDWARE USED: HP 3000/XE: PC compatible
SOFTWARE USED: MINISIS, CDS/ISIS, MICRO BRS
STORAGE MEDIA: traditional shelving of publications; magnetic tapes; microfiches;
discs; compact discs
TYPE OF ACTIVITY: data collection; data analysis; distribution of information;
publication
PERIODICALS PUBLISHED: - CLASE (Citas latinoamericanas en sociologia, economía y
humanidades), 4 p.a. since 1976
- PERIODICA (Indice de revistas mexicanas en ciencias), since 1978
- PORTAL (Accession list in library and information science), since 1981
- Bibliografía Médica Mexicana
PUBLICATIONS: - Bibliografía latinoamericana I, papers published by Latin-Americans
in foreign reviews, 1980
- Bibliografía latinoamericana II, papers on Latin-America published in
foreign reviews, 1980
CLIENTELE: researchers, academic staff, graduate students (3,000-5,000 p.a.)
ACCESS TO SERVICE: services open to all users, free of charge
TYPE & DESCRIPTION OF SERVICES PROVIDED: Provides library services, bibliographic
searches, on-line services using own data base CLASE and BIBLAT, selective
dissemination of information, information on magnetic tapes and photocopie

**529 - UNIVERSIDAD NACIONAL AUTÓNOMA DE MEXICO, CENTRO DE INVESTIGACIONES
INTERDISCIPLINARIAS EN HUMANIDADES, DEPARTAMENTO DE INFORMACIÓN Y
DOCUMENTACIÓN**

ADDRESS: Torre 2 de Humanidades, 4 piso,
Ciudad Universitaria,
04510 Mexico D.F.,
MEXICO
TEL: 550-59-43

REATED: 1986   *HEAD:* Lic. E. Koppen, Chief
IZE OF STAFF: Professional: 3   Other: 1   Total: 4
YPE OF SERVICE: national; public; non-profit
ORKING LANGUAGE(S): Spanish
UBJECT COVERAGE: social sciences
EOGRAPHICAL COVERAGE: Mexico; Latin America
ATA BEING PROCESSED AND SIZE: 1,000 books; periodicals; papers; bibliographies
ATA PROCESSING METHODS: partially computerized
ARDWARE USED: IBM PC
OFTWARE USED: Dbase III
TORAGE MEDIA: fiches; discs
YPE OF ACTIVITY: data collection; distribution of information
ERIODICALS PUBLISHED: - Cuadernos del CIIH: Serie Fuentes
          - Accession List
LIENTELE: researchers
CCESS TO SERVICE: services open to specific categories of users
YPE & DESCRIPTION OF SERVICES PROVIDED: Provides library services and bibliographic
          searches of information.

**30 - UNIVERSIDAD NACIONAL AUTONOMA DE MEXICO, ESCUELA NACIONAL DE ESTUDIOS
     PROFESIONALES ACATLÁN, CENTRO DE INFORMACIÓN Y DOCUMENTACIÓN**

YNONYMOUS NAMES: UNAM, ENEP, Acatlán, Centro de Información y Documentación;
          UNAM, ENEP, Acatlan, Center of Documentaion and Information
DDRESS: Alcanfores y San Juan Totoltepec,
          53150 Santa Cruz Acatlan,
          Edo. de Mexico,
          MEXICO
          TEL: 560-75-81
REATED: 1975   *HEAD:* Mr. A. Estevez Guzman, Coordinator
IZE OF STAFF: Professional: 24   Other: 23   Total: 47
YPE OF SERVICE: national; public
YSTEMS & NETWORKS ATTACHED TO: Catalogo Colectivo del Sistema Bibliotecario de la
          UNAM (LIBRUNAM)
ATERIALS DESCRIBING THE SERVICE: - Manual de orientación a usuarios
UBJECT COVERAGE: social sciences; humanities
EOGRAPHICAL COVERAGE: Mexico
ATA PROCESSING METHODS: manual; partially computerized
YPE OF ACTIVITY: data collection; data analysis
ERIODICALS PUBLISHED:
          - Boletin Bibliografico
LIENTELE: university students, professors, researchers (19,000 users p.a.)
CCESS TO SERVICE: services open to all users, free of charge
YPE & DESCRIPTION OF SERVICES PROVIDED: Provides library services, bibliographic,
          literature abstract and quantitative data searches of information, on-line
          services, selective dissemination of information and photocopies.

Mexico / Mexique / México

531 - UNIVERSIDAD NACIONAL AUTÓNOMA DE MÉXICO, FACULTAD DE CIENCIAS POLÍTICAS Y SOCIALES, CENTRO DE DOCUMENTACIÓN

ADDRESS: Ciudad Universitaria,
Apdo. Postal 70-266,
Coy. 04510,
Mexico 20, D. F.,
MEXICO
TEL: 550.52.15
CREATED: 1971　　*HEAD:* Ms M.G. Ferrer Andrade, Coordinator
TYPE OF SERVICE: public
SUBJECT COVERAGE: sociology; political science; public administration; international relations
GEOGRAPHICAL COVERAGE: Mexico; Latin America; developing countries
DATA PROCESSING METHODS: manual
TYPE OF ACTIVITY: data collection; data analysis; distribution of information; publication
PERIODICALS PUBLISHED:
- México-Artículos Clasificados, 12 p.a.
PUBLICATIONS: - Lista de revistas
ACCESS TO SERVICE: open to all users
TYPE & DESCRIPTION OF SERVICES PROVIDED: Provides library services relating to social sciences periodicals analyzed and indexed in the Centre.

532 - UNIVERSIDAD NACIONAL AUTONÓMA DE MÉXICO, INSTITUTO DE INVESTIGACIONES SOCIALES BIBLIOTECA

SYNONYMOUS NAMES: IISUNAM Biblioteca;
IISUNAM Library
ADDRESS: Torre II de Humanidades,
6o Piso,
Ciudad Universitaria,
C.P. 04510,
México D.F.,
MEXICO
TEL: 550-52-15
CREATED: 1939　　*HEAD:* Mr. L. Villanueva,
SIZE OF STAFF: Professional: 1　　Other: 6　　Total: 7
TYPE OF SERVICE: public
SYSTEMS & NETWORKS ATTACHED TO: Librunam, University Library Network, UNAM
SUBJECT COVERAGE: social sciences; political science; government; sociology; social demography
DATA BEING PROCESSED AND SIZE: 25,000 books; 300 periodicals; 300 theses
DATA PROCESSING METHODS: partially computerized
HARDWARE USED: PC I Hard Disk 25 MG
SOFTWARE USED: DBase III Plus; MicroISIS
STORAGE MEDIA: catalogue fiches
TYPE OF ACTIVITY: distribution of information; publication
PERIODICALS PUBLISHED:
- Boletín de Adquisiciones Bibliográficas
- Información Sociológica: Boletín de Publicaciones Periódicas

414

IENTELE: 15-20 readers per day
CCESS TO SERVICE: open to all users
PE & DESCRIPTION OF SERVICES PROVIDED: Provides library services, bibliographic
        searches, on-line services using own data base LIBRUNAM, selective
        dissemination of information and interlibrary loans.

33 – UNIVERSIDAD NATIONAL AUTÓNOMA DE MEXICO, COORDINACIÓN DE SERVICIOS
        BIBLIOTECARIOS

YNONYMOUS NAMES: Biblioteca Isidro Fabela;
        COSEBI
ARENT ORGANIZATION: Universidad Nacional Autónoma de México, Facultad de Ciencias
        Políticas y Sociales
DDRESS: Facultad de Ciencias Políticas y Sociales, UNAM,
        Apartado Postal 70-266,
        C.P. 04510,
        México, D.F.,
        MEXICO
        TEL: 550-52015
REATED: 1951   *HEAD:* Mr. M. Barragan Rojas, Coordinator
IZE OF STAFF: Professional: 10   Other: 49   Total: 59
YPE OF SERVICE: national; public; non-profit
YSTEMS & NETWORKS ATTACHED TO: Catalogue Librunam on Microcard (LIBRUNAM)
ATERIALS DESCRIBING THE SERVICE: – Información general y reglamento (Facultad de
        Ciencias Políticas y Sociales, Coordinación de servicios bibliotecarios
        – Triptico de servicios (Facultad de Ciencias Políticas y Sociales,
        Coordinación de servicios bibliotecarios)
ORKING LANGUAGE(S): Spanish
UBJECT COVERAGE: social sciences; sociology; political science; administrative
        sciences; history; economics; law; philosophy
EOGRAPHICAL COVERAGE: Mexico
ATA BEING PROCESSED AND SIZE: 100,148 books; 2,135 periodicals
ATA PROCESSING METHODS: manual
TORAGE MEDIA: microfiches
YPE OF ACTIVITY: data collection; distribution of information; publication
ERIODICALS PUBLISHED:
        – Cienpoliticas, Boletin Bibliografico, 6 p.a.
UBLICATIONS: – Amoxmachiotl, catálogo de publicaciones periódicas
LIENTELE: university students
CCESS TO SERVICE: services open to all users
YPE & DESCRIPTION OF SERVICES PROVIDED: Provides library services, bibliographic and
        literature abstract searches, selective dissemination of information,
        microforms and photocopies.

34 – CENTRE NATIONAL DE DOCUMENTATION

YNONYMOUS NAMES: CND;
        National Documentation Centre

PARENT ORGANIZATION: Ministère·du Plan
ADDRESS: Charii maa Al Ainain,
   P.O. Box 826,
   Haut-Agdal,
   Rabat,
   MOROCCO
   TEL: 749-44 - TELEX: CND 310-52 M
CREATED: 1968 *HEAD:* Mr. A. Fassi-Fihri,
SIZE OF STAFF: Professional: 34 Other: 71 Total: 105
TYPE OF SERVICE: national; public; non-profit
SYSTEMS & NETWORKS ATTACHED TO: SDS/RECON of European Spatial Agency; Projet ARISNE
   (Arab Information Network); ANAI; PADIS; AGRIS; CARIS; INFOTERRA
MATERIALS DESCRIBING THE SERVICE: - Meskine, A., Eight years of services for users,
   Rabat, 1976, 8 p.
   - The National Documentation Centre Rabat, 1982
   - Evaluation report of the NDC achievements. Rabat, 1969-1980: evaluation
   seminar/NDC, Rabat, March 27, 1981, 24p.
   - Activity report of the NDC, Rabat, 1982
WORKING LANGUAGE(S): Arabic; French; English
SUBJECT COVERAGE: social sciences; agriculture; economics; science; culture
GEOGRAPHICAL COVERAGE: Morocco
DATA BEING PROCESSED AND SIZE: more than 104,000 books, articles, reports on on-going
   research, theses, memoires, studies, seminars etc.
DATA PROCESSING METHODS: computerized
HARDWARE USED: Minicomputer MP 3000
SOFTWARE USED: MINISIS
STORAGE MEDIA: microfiches, magnetic tapes
TYPE OF ACTIVITY: distribution of information; SSID scientific and methodological
   activities; publication
PERIODICALS PUBLISHED:
   - Bulletin de Coordination
PUBLICATIONS: - Index démographie Maroc
   - MAKNAZ thesaurus, 1980
   - Index économie
   - Index patrimoine culturel
   - Répertoire des bibliothèques et centres de documentation du Maroc, 1986
   - Répertoire national de la recherche agronomique en cours, 1985
CLIENTELE: 3,500 students, teachers, officials, researchers
ACCESS TO SERVICE: services open to all users, free of charge
TYPE & DESCRIPTION OF SERVICES PROVIDED: Query answering service, on-line
   bibliographic, literature and quantitative data searches using both its own
   data base and external data bases. Provides selective dissemination of
   information, photocopies and microforms.

535 - UNIVERSIDADE EDUARDO MONDLANE, ARQUIVO HISTÓRICO DE MOÇAMBIQUE

ADDRESS: CP 2033,
   Maputo,
   MOZAMBIQUE
   TEL: 21177

EATED: 1934   *HEAD:* Mrs. M. I. Gonçalves, Director
                 Mrs. I. Nogueira da Costa, Director
'ZE OF STAFF: Professional: 15   Other: 18   Total: 33
'PE OF SERVICE: national; public; non-profit
'TERIALS DESCRIBING THE SERVICE: - Nogueira da Costa, I., Apontamento sobre o
        Arquivo Histórico dé Moçambique, 1987
'RKING LANGUAGE(S): Portuguese
'BJECT COVERAGE: history
'OGRAPHICAL COVERAGE: Mozambique
'TA BEING PROCESSED AND SIZE: 17,000 books; 1,000 periodicals
'TA PROCESSING METHODS: manual
'ORAGE MEDIA: traditional shelving of publications; microfiches
'PE OF ACTIVITY: SSID scientific and methodological activities; publication
'RIODICALS PUBLISHED:
        - ARQUIVO: Boletim Semestral do Arquivo Histórico de Moçambique, since 1987
'BLICATIONS: - Collection "documents"
        - Collection "études"
        - Collection "instruments de recherche"
'IENTELE: university students, researchers, journalists (2,650 p.a.)
'CESS TO SERVICE: services open to specific categories of users, free of charge
'PE & DESCRIPTION OF SERVICES PROVIDED: Provides library services, microforms and
        photocopies.

Netherlands Antilles / Antilles néerlandaises / Antillas Neerlandesas

36 - DEPARTEMENT VAN ONDERWIJS CURAÇAO, BIBLIOTHEEK

'NONYMOUS NAMES: Curaçao Department of Education, Library
'DRESS: Afd. Bibliotheek,
        Sta Rosa 48,
        Curaçao,
        NETHERLANDS ANTILLES
        TEL: 674466
EATED: 1981   *HEAD:* Miss B. Peters, Librarian
'ZE OF STAFF: Professional: 1   Other: 1   Total: 2
'PE OF SERVICE: national; public; non-profit
'RKING LANGUAGE(S): Dutch
'BJECT COVERAGE: education; information science; linguistics; mass communication;
        psychology; sociology; statistics
'OGRAPHICAL COVERAGE: Netherlands Antilles; Caribbean area; Netherlands
'TA BEING PROCESSED AND SIZE: written documents (books, serials, journals, reports),
        bibliographical references, grey literature, research and administrative
        records
'TA PROCESSING METHODS: manual
'ORAGE MEDIA: traditional shelving of publications, files
'PE OF ACTIVITY: publication
'RIODICALS PUBLISHED: - Annual Report of the Library
        - Annual List of Periodicals
        - Monthly Acquisition List
'IENTELE: educators, experts, students, library and documentation services,
        academics
'CESS TO SERVICE: open to all users against annual payment

417

TYPE & DESCRIPTION OF SERVICES PROVIDED: Provides bibliographic and literature
searches on request, library and reference services, exchange of
publications and photocopies.

537 - AFRIKA-STUDIECENTRUM, AFDELING BIBLIOTHEEK EN DOCUMENTATIE

SYNONYMOUS NAMES: African Studies Centre, Library and Documentation Department
ADDRESS: Stationsplein 10-12,
2312 AK Leiden,
NETHERLANDS
TEL: 071-273354
CABLE: AFRICEN
CREATED: 1947   *HEAD:* J. van der Meulen, Librarian
SIZE OF STAFF: Professional: 9   Other: 2   Total: 11
TYPE OF SERVICE: national; public; non-profit
WORKING LANGUAGE(S): Dutch; English
SUBJECT COVERAGE: social sciences; culture; statistics; education; history; law;
political science; social anthropology; cultural anthropology; economics;
religion
GEOGRAPHICAL COVERAGE: Africa
DATA BEING PROCESSED AND SIZE: 60,000 documentation items; 1,200 periodicals; 14
abstract journals; 1,200 microfiches
DATA PROCESSING METHODS: partially computerized
HARDWARE USED: Macintosh
STORAGE MEDIA: traditional shelving of publications
TYPE OF ACTIVITY: data analysis; publication
PERIODICALS PUBLISHED:
- Documentatieblad: the Abstract Journal of the African Studies Centre
Leiden, 4 p.a.
- Accession List, 2 p.a.
CLIENTELE: students, social scientists, general public (4,600 p.a.)
ACCESS TO SERVICE: open to all users, free of charge
TYPE & DESCRIPTION OF SERVICES PROVIDED: Provides library services, bibliographic,
literature and survey data searches and photocopies.

538 - BIBLIOTHEEK VAN HET VREDESPALEIS

SYNONYMOUS NAMES: Peace Palace Library
PARENT ORGANIZATION: Carnegie Stichting (Carnegie Foundation)
ADDRESS: Carnegieplein 2,
2517 KJ The Hague,
NETHERLANDS
TEL: (0)70-469680
CREATED: 1913   *HEAD:* J. C. Schalekamp, Director
SIZE OF STAFF: Total: 17
TYPE OF SERVICE: international; public; non-profit
SYSTEMS & NETWORKS ATTACHED TO: PICA
MATERIALS DESCRIBING THE SERVICE: - The Peace Palace: residence for justice, domici

of learning, 1988
RKING LANGUAGE(S): Dutch; English; French
BJECT COVERAGE: law; public law; private law; comparative law; jurisprudence;
political history; peace movements; grotiana
OGRAPHICAL COVERAGE: global
TA BEING PROCESSED AND SIZE: 600,000 volumes
TA PROCESSING METHODS: partially computerized
ORAGE MEDIA: traditional shelving of publications, microfiches
PE OF ACTIVITY: data collection; publication
RIODICALS PUBLISHED:
- Peace Palace Library Acquisitions
- Selective Bibliography for the Center for Studies and Research of the
Hague Academy of International Law
BLICATIONS: - Publication of the Association of Dutch Law Libraries (GJB)
- Bibliography of the International Court of Justice
IENTELE: lawyers, scientists and students especially from the International Court
of Justice and the Hague Academy of International Law
CESS TO SERVICE: services open to all users free of charge
PE & DESCRIPTION OF SERVICES PROVIDED: Provides library services, bibliographic
searches and photocopies.

89 - DOCUMENTATIECENTRUM JEUGDVOORZIENINGEN

NONYMOUS NAMES: Documentation Centre Child Care
DDRESS: Catharijnesingel 47,
Postbus 19272,
3501 DG Utrecht,
NETHERLANDS
TEL: 030-316510
REATED: 1947   *HEAD:* W. H. Coenen, Director
ZE OF STAFF: Professional: 4   Other: 1   Total: 5
STEMS & NETWORKS ATTACHED TO: SAGEMA-Pool
BJECT COVERAGE: social welfare; psychology; children; child care and protection
TA BEING PROCESSED AND SIZE: 31,000 books; 250 periodicals
PE OF ACTIVITY: distribution of information; publication
CESS TO SERVICE: open to all users
PE & DESCRIPTION OF SERVICES PROVIDED: Provides library services, interlibrary
loans and bibliographic and literature abstract data searches using own
catalogues. Photocopies can also be obtained.

40 - ERASMUS UNIVERSITEIT ROTTERDAM, SRM-DOCUMENTATION CENTRE

NONYMOUS NAMES: Erasmus University Rotterdam, Social Research Methodology
Documentation Centre
DDRESS: Burgemeester oudlaan 50,
P.O. Box 1738,
3000 DR Rotterdam,
NETHERLANDS
TEL: 010-4525511 - TELEX: 24421

CREATED: 1970   HEAD: Mrs. G. W. Kantebeen, Executive Manager
SIZE OF STAFF: Total: 7
TYPE OF SERVICE: national; public; non-profit
MATERIALS DESCRIBING THE SERVICE: - brochure
WORKING LANGUAGE(S): English
SUBJECT COVERAGE: social sciences; demography; education; history; mass
        communication; political science; psychology; social anthropology; cultural
        anthropology; sociology; statistics; research methodology
GEOGRAPHICAL COVERAGE: global
DATA BEING PROCESSED AND SIZE: articles from 100 periodicals
DATA PROCESSING METHODS: manual
STORAGE MEDIA: fiches
TYPE OF ACTIVITY: data collection; publication
PERIODICALS PUBLISHED: - Social Research Methodology Abstracts
        - Social Research Methodology Bibliography
PUBLICATIONS: - Van de Merwe, C., Thesaurus of sociological research terminology,
        1976
TYPE & DESCRIPTION OF SERVICES PROVIDED: Its main activity is the indexing and
        preparation of abstracts. Provides specialized information in research
        methodology and techniques using its own data base "SRM-Data Base"
        including 24,000 items. Also provides selective dissemination of
        information.

541 - GEOGRAFISCH INSTITUUT, BIBLIOTHEEK

SYNONYMOUS NAMES: Geographical Institute, Library
PARENT ORGANIZATION: Universiteitsbibliotheek/University Library
ADDRESS: Post Order Box 800,
        9700 AV Groningen,
        NETHERLANDS
        TEL: 050-633918
CREATED: 1951   HEAD: Dr. H. J. C. vanGeel, Librarian
SIZE OF STAFF: Professional: 1
WORKING LANGUAGE(S): Dutch; English; German
SUBJECT COVERAGE: geography; social sciences; demography
DATA BEING PROCESSED AND SIZE: 35,000 books; 500 periodicals; 45 abstract journals;
        35 microcopies; 2,200 manuscripts; 6,000 brochures
STORAGE MEDIA: traditional shelving of publications
TYPE OF ACTIVITY: distribution of information
CLIENTELE: students, scientific staff
ACCESS TO SERVICE: services open to specific categories of users, free of charge
TYPE & DESCRIPTION OF SERVICES PROVIDED: Provides library services, bibliographic,
        literature and survey data searches, selective dissemination of information
        and photocopies. Has its own terminal connected with the Central University
        Library, Groningen.

42 - INSTITUTE OF SOCIAL STUDIES, LIBRARY AND DOCUMENTATION DEPARTMENT

SYNONYMOUS NAMES: ISS, Library and Documentation Department
ADDRESS: Badhuisweg 251,
(Postbox 90733),
2509 LS The Hague,
NETHERLANDS
TEL: (0)70-510100 - TELEX: 31491 ISS NL
CABLE: SOCINST
CREATED: 1952   *HEAD:* J. Lamein, Head
SIZE OF STAFF: Professional: 6   Other: 8   Total: 14
TYPE OF SERVICE: international; public; non-profit
MATERIALS DESCRIBING THE SERVICE: - Guide to the ISS Library, 1987 (leaflet)
WORKING LANGUAGE(S): English
SUBJECT COVERAGE: social sciences; agricultural development; rural development;
labour; regional development; regional economic planning; women and
development; international relations
GEOGRAPHICAL COVERAGE: developing countries
DATA BEING PROCESSED AND SIZE: 60,000 books and documents; 500 periodicals
DATA PROCESSING METHODS: manual; partially computerized
HARDWARE USED: Tulip PC
SOFTWARE USED: DBase III; REFLEX; WORDMARC
STORAGE MEDIA: traditional shelving of publications; microfiches
TYPE OF ACTIVITY: distribution of information; SSID training; publication
PERIODICALS PUBLISHED:
- Accessions List
CLIENTELE: researchers, academics, students
ACCESS TO SERVICE: services open to specific categories of users, free of charge
TYPE & DESCRIPTION OF SERVICES PROVIDED: Provides library services, bibliographic and
literature abstract searches of information, on-line services using external
data bases (ESA, Dialog), and photocopies.

43 - INSTITUUT VOOR INTERNATIONALE STUDIEN

SYNONYMOUS NAMES: IIS;
Institute for International Studies
PARENT ORGANIZATION: Rijksuniversiteit Leiden
ADDRESS: P.O. Box 9515,
NL-22300 RA Leiden,
NETHERLANDS
TEL: 71-272228
CREATED: 1970   *HEAD:* Dr. P. P. Everts, Director
SIZE OF STAFF: Professional: 6   Other: 2   Total: 8
TYPE OF SERVICE: national; public; non-profit
WORKING LANGUAGE(S): Dutch; English
SUBJECT COVERAGE: political science; history; social sciences; international
relations; peace research; development problems; public opinion; foreign
policy; defence
GEOGRAPHICAL COVERAGE: Netherlands; Europe
DATA BEING PROCESSED AND SIZE: 2,000 items from public opinion polls; 15,000
newspaper articles

DATA PROCESSING METHODS: manual; partially computerized
HARDWARE USED: Commodore PC10 and PC20
SOFTWARE USED: DBase III, Displaywrite 3
STORAGE MEDIA: traditional shelving of publications; fiches
TYPE OF ACTIVITY: data collection; data analysis; publication
PUBLICATIONS: - Everts, Ph. P.; Vaneker, Ch.; H. D. Vaneker (eds), Buitenlandse
        politiek in de Nederlandse publieke opinie, 1975-1984, 1985
CLIENTELE: scientists and students
ACCESS TO SERVICE: services open to all users free of charge

544 - INTERNATIONAAL INFORMATIECENTRUM EN ARCHIEF VOOR DE VROUWENBEWEGING

SYNONYMOUS NAMES: IIAV;
        International Information Centre and Archives for the Women's Movement
ADDRESS: Keizersgracht 10,
        1015 CN Amsterdam,
        NETHERLANDS
        TEL: 020-244268
CREATED: 1988   *HEAD:* Ms. C. Posthumus, Librarian
SIZE OF STAFF: Professional: 8   Other: 7   Total: 15
TYPE OF SERVICE: international; public; non-profit
WORKING LANGUAGE(S): Dutch
SUBJECT COVERAGE: status of women; womens liberation movement; emancipation, femin
GEOGRAPHICAL COVERAGE: global
DATA BEING PROCESSED AND SIZE: 30,000 books; 18,000 grey literature; 750 periodical
        25,000 article descriptions; leaflets, press cuttings, posters (50,000)
DATA PROCESSING METHODS: manual; partially computerized
HARDWARE USED: UNISYS PC Network
SOFTWARE USED: PC Pals
STORAGE MEDIA: traditional shelving of publications; fiches
TYPE OF ACTIVITY: data collection; data analysis; distribution of information;
        publication
PERIODICALS PUBLISHED: - Lover, 4 p.a.
        - Knipselkrant, 8 p.a.
        - Overzicht, 4 p.a.
        - Signaleringsbulletin, 6 p.a.
        - Weet ik Veel, 1 p.a.
PUBLICATIONS: - Hall, G. K., Catalogue of the International Information Centre and
        Archives for the Women's Movement, 1980
        - Weet ik veel. Inventarisatie vrouwenstudies, 1986
CLIENTELE: from 7,500 to 10,000 visitors p.a.
ACCESS TO SERVICE: services open to all users, free of charge
TYPE & DESCRIPTION OF SERVICES PROVIDED: Provides library services, bibliographic
        searches of information, information on women's demonstration and
        photocopies.

45 - INTERNATIONAAL INSTITUUT VOOR SOCIALE GESCHIEDENIS

YNONYMOUS NAMES: IISG;
           International Institute of Social History
ARENT ORGANIZATION: Koninklijke Nederlandse Akademie van Wetenschappen/Royal
           Netherlands Academy of Sciences (KNAW)
DDRESS: Kabelweg 51,
           1014 BA Amsterdam,
           NETHERLANDS
           TEL: 020-843695
REATED: 1935   *HEAD:* Dr. E. J. Fischer, Director
IZE OF STAFF: Professional: 40   Other: 55   Total: 95
YPE OF SERVICE: international; public; non-profit
ATERIALS DESCRIBING THE SERVICE: - Annual report, 1988
           - History and activities
ORKING LANGUAGE(S): Dutch; German; English; French; Russian; Spanish
UBJECT COVERAGE: history; sociology; social history; trade unions; international
           organizations; anarchism
EOGRAPHICAL COVERAGE: global
ATA BEING PROCESSED AND SIZE: 800,000 books; 65,000 periodicals; audiovisual
           materials
ATA PROCESSING METHODS: computerized
ARDWARE USED: GEAC
OFTWARE USED: GEAC
TORAGE MEDIA: traditional shelving of publications; microfilms and fiches
YPE OF ACTIVITY: data collection; data analysis; distribution of information;
           publication
ERIODICALS PUBLISHED: - International Review of Social History, 3 p.a. (some special
           issues)
           - Accession List
UBLICATIONS: - Moore, B., Refugees from Nazi Germany in the Netherlands 1933-1940,
           1986
           - Devreese, D. E. (ed.), Documents relatifs aux militants belges de
           l'Association Internationale des Travailleurs en Belgique: correspondance
           1865-1872, 1986
           - Sapir, B., Russian series on social history (vol. III and IV), 1986
           - Mervand, M., Socialisme et liberté: la pensée et l'action de
           MicolasOlgarev (1813-1877), 1984
           - Holzer, J., "Solidarität", Dieeschichte einer freien Gewerkschaft in
           Polen ("Solidarité", Histoire de l'indépendance d'un syndicat en Pologne)
           1985
LIENTELE: 9,000 visitors per year
CCESS TO SERVICE: open to all users
YPE & DESCRIPTION OF SERVICES PROVIDED: Provides library services, on-line services,
           inventories, bibliographies, microforms, microfilms and photocopies.

46 - INTERNATIONAL STATISTICAL RESEARCH CENTRE

ARENT ORGANIZATION: International Statistical Institute
DDRESS: 428 Prinses Beatrixlaan,
           P. O. Box 950,

2270 AZ Voorburg,
NETHERLANDS
TEL: (070) 69 43 41 - TELEX 32260 isi nl
CABLE: STATIST
HEAD: Dr. D. J. Finney,
SIZE OF STAFF: Total: 8
TYPE OF SERVICE: non-profit
WORKING LANGUAGE(S): English; French
SUBJECT COVERAGE: social sciences; demography; economics; statistics
GEOGRAPHICAL COVERAGE: global
HARDWARE USED: Hewlett Packard
SOFTWARE USED: own
TYPE OF ACTIVITY: data collection; data analysis; distribution of information;
publication
CLIENTELE: private individuals, research centers, national governments, internation
agencies
ACCESS TO SERVICE: services open to all users, free of charge
TYPE & DESCRIPTION OF SERVICES PROVIDED: Provides on-line services using own data
bases and external data bases and information on magnetic tapes or discs.

547 - KATHOLIEKE UNIVERSITEIT NIJMEGEN, DERDE WERELD CENTRUM

SYNONYMOUS NAMES: Catholic University of Nijmegen, Third World Center
ADDRESS: Thomas van Aquinostraat 1,
Postbus 9108,
6500 HK Nijmegen,
NETHERLANDS
TEL: 080-513058
CREATED: 1973   *HEAD:* Prof. Dr. G. Huizer,
SIZE OF STAFF: Professional: 2   Total: 2
TYPE OF SERVICE: national; non-profit
WORKING LANGUAGE(S): Dutch; English; Spanish
SUBJECT COVERAGE: social sciences; economics
GEOGRAPHICAL COVERAGE: developing countries
DATA BEING PROCESSED AND SIZE: reports; seminars; articles; press-clippings; review
DATA PROCESSING METHODS: partially computerized
TYPE OF ACTIVITY: data collection
PUBLICATIONS: - Landervorming in Portugal 1975-1986: een bibliografie, 1987
CLIENTELE: about 50 users a week
ACCESS TO SERVICE: open to all users
TYPE & DESCRIPTION OF SERVICES PROVIDED: Provides library services, searches of
information and photocopies.

548 - KONINKLIJK INSTITUUT VOOR DE TROPEN, INFORMATIE EN DOKUMENTATIE AFDELING

SYNONYMOUS NAMES: KIT/ID;
Royal Tropical Institute, Department of Information and Documentation
ADDRESS: 63 Mauritskade,
1092 AD Amsterdam,

424

NETHERLANDS
TEL: (020) 5688290 - TELEX: 15080 KITNL - FAX (0)20-568.84.84
CABLE: INTROPEN AMSTERDAM
REATED: 1916   *HEAD:* Dr. J. H. W. van Hartevelt, Head
IZE OF STAFF: Professional: 11   Other: 9   Total: 20
YPE OF SERVICE: international; public; non-profit
ATERIALS DESCRIBING THE SERVICE: - Royal Tropical Institute, 1987, brochure
ORKING LANGUAGE(S): English
UBJECT COVERAGE: agriculture; rural development; demography; economics; education;
          social anthropology; social welfare; sociology; labour; nutrition; women
EOGRAPHICAL COVERAGE: Africa; Asia; Latin America; developing countries; tropical
          and subtropical regions
ATA BEING PROCESSED AND SIZE: 160,000 books; 6,000 periodicals; reports; theses;
          conference proceedings; 600,000 abstracts
ATA PROCESSING METHODS: computerized
ARDWARE USED: Mini: HP (Library), 5 micro's IBM and Philips (ID)
OFTWARE USED: Query V4.1, Freebase (ID); Minisis (library)
TORAGE MEDIA: discs; tapes; microfiches
YPE OF ACTIVITY: data collection; distribution of information; SSID scientific and
          methodological activities; data analysis; SSID training; publication
ERIODICALS PUBLISHED: - Abstracts on Rural Development in the Tropics, 4 p.a.
          - Abstracts on Tropical Agriculture, 12 p.a.
LIENTELE: businessmen, extension workers, researchers, development workers,
          students, other information services
CCESS TO SERVICE: open to all users, paid computer searches
YPE & DESCRIPTION OF SERVICES PROVIDED: Provides library services, computerized
          literature abstract searches using its own data base "TROPAG" available
          through ORBIT, as well as external data bases accessed through DIALOG, DIMDI
          and ESA. Also provides selective dissemination of information, question-
          answering and consultancy services, and information on magnetic tapes and
          photocopies.

49 - KONINKLIJK INSTITUUT VOOR TAAL-, LAND- EN VOLKENKUNDE

YNONYMOUS NAMES: KITLV;
          Royal Institute of Linguistics and Anthropology;
          RILA;
          Real Instituto de Antropologia y Linguistica
DDRESS: P.O. Box 9515,
          Reuvensplaats 2,
          2300 RA Leiden,
          NETHERLANDS
          TEL: 071-272295 - TELEX: 39427 BORUL NL
REATED: 1851   *HEAD:* Dr. J. Noorduyn, General Secretary
IZE OF STAFF: Professional: 18   Other: 18   Total: 36
ATERIALS DESCRIBING THE SERVICE: - Royal Institute of Linguistics and Anthropology,
          Leiden, the Netherlands, brochure, 1987
UBJECT COVERAGE: linguistics; social anthropology; cultural anthropology; geography;
          history; law; social sciences
EOGRAPHICAL COVERAGE: Caribbean area; Indonesia; Southeast Asia; Oceania
ATA BEING PROCESSED AND SIZE: 120,000 books; 1,000 periodicals; 21,000 microcopies;

1,600 manuscripts; 10,000 maps; 100,000 photographs and drawings
DATA PROCESSING METHODS: manual; partially computerized
STORAGE MEDIA: traditional shelving of publications; fiches; tapes; discs;
    microfiches
TYPE OF ACTIVITY: data collection; publication; SSID scientific and methodological
    activities
PERIODICALS PUBLISHED: - Bijdragen Tot de Toal-, Land- en Volkenkunde, 4 p.a.
    - Excerpta Indonesia, 2 p.a.
    - Boletín de Estudios Latinoamericanos y del Caribe, 2 p.a.
PUBLICATIONS: - Union catalogue of Caribbean publications
    - Lamur, C., The American takeover. Industrial emergence and Alcoa's
    expansion in Guyana and Suriname, 1985
    - Cohen Stuart, W., Women in the Caribbean: a bibliography, 1985
    - van Andel, J. D., Caribbean traditional architecture. The traditional
    architecture of Philipsburg, St. Martin, 1985
    - Central catalogue Caraïbiana
    - Dubelaar, C. N., South American and Caribbean petroglyphs, 1986
    - Koulen, I.; Oostindie, G., The Netherlands Antilles: social scientific
    research, 1967-1985 and beyond, 1986
    - Carrington, S. H., The British West Indies during the American revolutio
    a study in colonial economy and politics 1770-1787, 1987
    - Koelewijn, C.; Riviere, P., The Oral literature of the trio Indians of
    Suriname, 1987
    - Whitehead, N. L., The Conquest of the Caribs of the Orinoco Basin 1498-
    1771, 1987
    - Bibliotheca Indonesica (text editions of manuscripts in Indonesian
    languages, together with an English translation), 26 vols.
    - Caribbean series (monographs on the Caribbean), 6 vols.
    - Indonesian reprints (reprints of older publications in English and Dutch
    7 vols.
    - Directory of West European Indonesianists (EURISIS), 1987
ACCESS TO SERVICE: open to users by letter of introduction, some paid services
TYPE & DESCRIPTION OF SERVICES PROVIDED: Provides library reference service and
    bibliographic, literature and survey data searches, microfilms, microforms
    photocopies and translation of documents.

550 - MINISTERIE VAN SOCIALE ZAKEN, BIBLIOTHEEK EN DOCUMENTATIE

SYNONYMOUS NAMES: BIDOC-SOZA;
    Ministry of Social Affairs, Library and Documentation Service
ADDRESS: P.O. Box 20801,
    2500 EV The Hague.
    NETHERLANDS
    TEL: 070-715911 - TELEX: 32226
CREATED: 1933   *HEAD:* W. Mazure, Director
SIZE OF STAFF: Professional: 25   Other: 7   Total: 32
TYPE OF SERVICE: national; public; non-profit
WORKING LANGUAGE(S): Dutch
SUBJECT COVERAGE: social welfare; economics; law; sociology; social sciences;
    employment; labour; health; income policy; social security; women's
    emancipation; working conditions; wages

DATA BEING PROCESSED AND SIZE: 108,000 books; 1,400 periodicals; 28 abstract journals
HARDWARE USED: Philips P 7000
SOFTWARE USED: STAIRS (RCC data base)
STORAGE MEDIA: traditional shelving of publications
TYPE OF ACTIVITY: distribution of information; publication
PERIODICALS PUBLISHED: - Uitgelezen (abstracts journal)
CLIENTELE: policy makers (1,000 p.a.)
ACCESS TO SERVICE: services open to all users, some paid services
TYPE & DESCRIPTION OF SERVICES PROVIDED: Library services include lending and
    interlibrary loans within the country. Provides selective dissemination of
    information and photocopies against payment, and bibliographic, literature
    and survey data searches through on-line services. Has also access to KSZW
    data base through RCC Apeldoorn.

**551 - NEDERLANDS CENTRUM GEESTELIJKE VOLKSGEZONDHEID, BIBLIOTHEEK EN DOCUMENTATIE-
    DIENST**

SYNONYMOUS NAMES: NcGv, Bibliotheek en Documentaie-Dienst;
    Netherlands Institute for Mental Health, Library and Documentation Service
ADDRESS: Da Costakade 45,
    Postbus 5103,
    3502 JC Utrecht,
    NETHERLANDS
    TEL: (030) 935141
CREATED: 1972   *HEAD:* Mr. A. J. Heerma van Voss,
SIZE OF STAFF: Total: 5
TYPE OF SERVICE: national; public; non-profit
SYSTEMS & NETWORKS ATTACHED TO: Sagema-pool: Ministry of Welfare, Health and Cultural
    Affairs
MATERIALS DESCRIBING THE SERVICE: - Jaarverslag 1986. Utrecht, 1987
    - Werkprogramma 1988. Utrecht, 1987
WORKING LANGUAGE(S): Dutch
SUBJECT COVERAGE: social sciences; medical sciences; psychology; social welfare;
    sociology; mental health
DATA BEING PROCESSED AND SIZE: 25,000 books; 350 periodicals; 5 abstract journals
DATA PROCESSING METHODS: manual
STORAGE MEDIA: fiches
TYPE OF ACTIVITY: publication
PERIODICALS PUBLISHED:
    - Literatuurbulletin Geestelijke Volksgezondheid
    - Accession List
PUBLICATIONS: - Gids geestelijke gezondheidszorg, 1986-87, 1986
CLIENTELE: mental health workers, students, professional workers (psychologists,
    psychiatrists, etc.)
ACCESS TO SERVICE: services open to all users, free of charge
TYPE & DESCRIPTION OF SERVICES PROVIDED: Provides library services and bibliographic,
    literature and survey data searches.

Netherlands / Pays-Bas / Países Bajos

552 - NEDERLANDS CENTRUM VOOR RECHTSHISTORISCHE DOCUMENTATIE EN RECHTSICONOGRAFIE

SYNONYMOUS NAMES: Dutch Centre for Documentation of Legal History and Lexiconography
        Library
PARENT ORGANIZATION: Koninklijke Bibliotheek
ADDRESS: O. Z. Achterburgwal 217,
        1012-DL Amsterdam,
        NETHERLANDS
        TEL: (020) 525-3410
CREATED: 1967   *HEAD:* Mr. M. A. Becker-Moelands, Director
SIZE OF STAFF: Professional: 4   Other: 1   Total: 5
TYPE OF SERVICE: national; public; non-profit
SYSTEMS & NETWORKS ATTACHED TO: PICA, Centrum voor Bibliotheekautomatisering
WORKING LANGUAGE(S): Dutch
SUBJECT COVERAGE: history; legal history; law
GEOGRAPHICAL COVERAGE: Belgium; Netherlands; Luxembourg
DATA BEING PROCESSED AND SIZE: 700 books; reports; articles
DATA PROCESSING METHODS: partially computerized
HARDWARE USED: Olivetti M24
SOFTWARE USED: Micro OPC; PICA term
STORAGE MEDIA: traditional shelving of publications; 14,000 partially computerized
        fiches; microfiches
TYPE OF ACTIVITY: distribution of information
PUBLICATIONS: - Bibliografie van de Nederlandse rechtsgeschiedenis
CLIENTELE: lawyers, historians, art historians, students, economists, sociologists,
        those interested in women's studies
ACCESS TO SERVICE: services open to all users, free of charge
TYPE & DESCRIPTION OF SERVICES PROVIDED: Provides bibliographic and quantitative dat
        searches and on-line services using own data base: NCRD.

**553 - NEDERLANDS INSTITUUT VOOR RUIMTELIJKE ORDENING EN VOLKSHUISVESTING EN DE
        RIJKSPLANOLOGISCHE DIENST, BIBLIOTHEEK VAN BEIDE INSTELLINGEN**

SYNONYMOUS NAMES: RPD/NIROV
ADDRESS: Willem Witsenplein 6,
        Postbus 90618,
        2596 LP The Hague,
        NETHERLANDS
        TEL: (070) 264201
CREATED: 1941   *HEAD:* Ms. J. Kroes, Head
SIZE OF STAFF: Total: 13
TYPE OF SERVICE: national; public; non-profit
WORKING LANGUAGE(S): Dutch
SUBJECT COVERAGE: demography; geography; sociology
GEOGRAPHICAL COVERAGE: Netherlands; Western Europe/North America; to a lesser extent
        Eastern Europe and the Third World
DATA BEING PROCESSED AND SIZE: RPD: 85,000 books; NIROV: 20,000 books
DATA PROCESSING METHODS: manual
TYPE OF ACTIVITY: data collection; data analysis; data collection; distribution of
        information
CLIENTELE: regional planners, geographers (about 1,000)

ACCESS TO SERVICE: services open to all users, free of charge
TYPE & DESCRIPTION OF SERVICES PROVIDED: Provides library services, bibliographic and
literature abstract searches and photocopies. Also provides on-line services
using external data bases VROMDOC and GOVERNMENTAL.

554 - NEDERLANDS INSTITUUT VOOR SOCIAAL SEXUOLOGISCH ONDERZOEK, AFDELING BIBLIOTHEEK & DOCUMENTATIE

SYNONYMOUS NAMES: NISSO, Afdeling Bibliotheek and Documentatie;
Netherlands Institute for Social Sexological Research, Library &
Documentation Section;
NISSO, Library and Documentation Section
ADDRESS: Da Costakade 45,
3521 VS Utrecht,
NETHERLANDS
TEL: 030-946246
CREATED: 1966   *HEAD:* Ms. E. Evenhuis, Librarian
Ms. M. van Berckel, Research, Information, Documentation
Officer
SIZE OF STAFF: Professional: 3   Other: 1   Total: 4
TYPE OF SERVICE: national; public; private; non-profit
SYSTEMS & NETWORKS ATTACHED TO: Samenwerking literatuurdocumentatie geestelijke
gezondheidszorg en maatschappelijk welzijn (SAGEMA)
MATERIALS DESCRIBING THE SERVICE: - Nisso jaarverslag
WORKING LANGUAGE(S): Dutch; English
SUBJECT COVERAGE: psychology; sociology; sexual behaviour; marriage; family;
interpersonal relations
GEOGRAPHICAL COVERAGE: Western Europe; North America
DATA BEING PROCESSED AND SIZE: 4,050 books; 80 periodicals; 2 abstract journals;
7,800 reprints; photocopies; brochures; leaflets
DATA PROCESSING METHODS: manual
TYPE OF ACTIVITY: data collection; publication
PERIODICALS PUBLISHED:
- Acquisitions List
- Annotated Bibliography for the Literature Bulletin "Tydschrifte voor
Seksuologie" (Journal for Sexology)
CLIENTELE: scientists, press and other media, physicians, therapists, students,
individuals
ACCESS TO SERVICE: open to all users, free of charge
TYPE & DESCRIPTION OF SERVICES PROVIDED: Provides library services and bibliographic,
literature, survey and quantitative data searches, and photocopies.

555 - RIJKSUNIVERSITEIT LEIDEN, DOCUMENTATIEBUREAU VOOR OOSTEUROPEES RECHT

SYNONYMOUS NAMES: DBOER;
University of Leiden, Documentation Office for East European Law
ADDRESS: P.O. Box 9521,
NL-2300 RA Leiden,
NETHERLANDS

TEL: (071) 277 814
CREATED: 1953   *HEAD:* F. J. M. Feldbrugge,
SIZE OF STAFF: Professional: 5   Other: 3   Total: 8
TYPE OF SERVICE: national; public; non-profit
SUBJECT COVERAGE: law
GEOGRAPHICAL COVERAGE: Eastern Europe
DATA BEING PROCESSED AND SIZE: 21,000 books, abstract journals and periodicals; 8,50
        microcopies
DATA PROCESSING METHODS: manual
PERIODICALS PUBLISHED: - Law in Eastern Europe, 4 p.a.
        - Review of Socialist Law, 4 p.a.
        - List of Acquisitions
PUBLICATIONS: - Feldbrugge, F. J. M. (ed.), Law in Eastern Europe (series already
        consisting of 15 vol.)
CLIENTELE: university staff, students, lawyers, political scientists
ACCESS TO SERVICE: open to all users, free of charge for larger research
TYPE & DESCRIPTION OF SERVICES PROVIDED: Provides retrospective bibliographic
        searches, photocopies and translation upon request.

**556 - RIJKSUNIVERSITEIT LEIDEN, ONDERZOEK EN DOKUMENTATIE CENTRUM VROUWEN EN
        AUTONOMIE**

SYNONYMOUS NAMES: University of Leiden, Research and Documentation Centre Women and
        Autonomy
ADDRESS: Stationsplein 10,
        2312 AK Leiden,
        NETHERLANDS
        TEL: 071-273484
CREATED: 1925   *HEAD:* Prof. Dr. E. Postel-Coste,
SIZE OF STAFF: Professional: 18   Other: 3   Total: 21
TYPE OF SERVICE: international; public; non-profit
MATERIALS DESCRIBING THE SERVICE: - Documentation Centre Women and Autonomy, leaflet
WORKING LANGUAGE(S): Dutch; English
SUBJECT COVERAGE: social anthropology; cultural anthropology; sociology; womens
        studies; women and development
GEOGRAPHICAL COVERAGE: developing countries
DATA BEING PROCESSED AND SIZE: 4,000 books, articles, reports and seminars
DATA PROCESSING METHODS: partially computerized
STORAGE MEDIA: traditional shelving of publications
TYPE OF ACTIVITY: data collection; distribution of information; publication
PUBLICATIONS: - Boesveld, M., Bibliography: women in the third world, 1986
        - Boesveld, M. et al, Towards autonomy for women. Research and action to
        support a development process, 1986
        - Schrijvers, J., Mothers for live. Motherhood and marginalization in the
        north central province of Sri Lanka, 1986
        - Catalogue of the Documentation Centre Women and Autonomy, 1988
ACCESS TO SERVICE: services open to all users
TYPE & DESCRIPTION OF SERVICES PROVIDED: Provides library services, bibliographic ar
        literature abstract searches of information.

557 - SOCIAAL-WETENSCHAPPELIJK INFORMATIE-EN DOCUMENTATIECENTRUM

SYNONYMOUS NAMES: SWIDOC;
   Social Science Information and Documentation Centre
PARENT ORGANIZATION: Koninklijke Nederlandse Akademie van Wetenschappen (KNAW)/Royal
   Netherlands Academy of Arts and Sciences
ADDRESS: Herengracht 410-412,
   1017 BX Amsterdam,
   NETHERLANDS
   TEL: (020) 22.50.61
CREATED: 1963   *HEAD:* Dr. A. F. Marks, Director
SIZE OF STAFF: Total: 20
TYPE OF SERVICE: national; public; non-profit
SYSTEMS & NETWORKS ATTACHED TO: Coordinatiegroep Informatiesystemen Lopend Onderzoek
       - CILO (Coordination Information Current Research); Samenwerking
       Literatuurdocumentatie Geestelijke Gezondheidszorg en Maatschappelijk
       Welzijn - SAGEMA (Cooperation Literature on Mental Health Care and Social
       Welfare); PICA (Project Integrated Catalogue Automation); ECSSID; ICPSR;
       ECPR; IFDO; IASSIST
MATERIALS DESCRIBING THE SERVICE: - SWIDOC, leaflet
WORKING LANGUAGE(S): English; Dutch
SUBJECT COVERAGE: social sciences; social anthropology; cultural anthropology;
       psychology; education; political science; administrative sciences; mass
       communication; social gerontology; demography; regional planning; sociology
       of law; criminology; social economics; social history
GEOGRAPHICAL COVERAGE: Netherlands
DATA BEING PROCESSED AND SIZE: 35,000 books; 200 periodicals; 3,700 doctoral theses;
       1,500 on-going research projects p.a.; 200 research data sets for secondary
       analysis
DATA PROCESSING METHODS: partially computerized
HARDWARE USED: Cyber 73-28; Data-point 2200 mini-computer; minicomputers TAB-Bullet,
       Schneider/Amstrad, Olivetti May
SOFTWARE USED: RIQS (Remote Information Query System), SPSS, DBASE III, Superfile
STORAGE MEDIA: traditional shelving of publications; fiches; tapes; discs;
       microfiches; on-line catalogues
TYPE OF ACTIVITY: data collection; data analysis; distribution of information; SSID
       scientific and methodological activities; publication
PERIODICALS PUBLISHED:
       - Titels van Sociaal-Wetenschappelijk Onderzoek, 12 p.a.
PUBLICATIONS: - Periodieken parade
       - Steinmetzarchief: catalogue and guide
       - Wegwijzer maatschappijwetenschappen, bibliotheken en documentatie
       instellingen
       - Overzicht van provinciale, regionale en lokale historische verengingen in
       Nederland
       - Informatie lopend onderzoek
       - Onderzoek onderzocht (gerontology)
       - Bibliotheken met belangrijke collecties maatschappijwetenschappen
       - Dissertaties maatschappijwetenschappen
       - Doctoraalscripties geschiedenis
       - Dux femina facti
       - Some problems of networks: the case of CILO, 1983
       - Political terrorism

- Ontwikkelingsgericht underrock
- Onderzoek etnische groepen

CLIENTELE: students, professors, research workers, provincial and municipal services
foundations, private institutes, industrial enterprises

ACCESS TO SERVICE: open to all users, free of charge (paid services for computer
time)

TYPE & DESCRiPTION OF SERVICES PROVIDED: Integrated documentation centre specialized
in the collection of grey literature in the social sciences and on-going
research projects. Provides library services, search of information,
selective dissemination of information, information on magnetic tapes and
on-line literature retrieval using its own data base "Steinmetz Archives"
as well as other such as Dialog, Euronet/DIANE, SDC, Questel, Star-data.

558 - STEINMETZARCHIEF

SYNONYMOUS NAMES: Steinmetz Archive
PARENT ORGANIZATION: Social Science Information and Documentation Centre of the Roya
Netherlands Academy of Arts and Sciences (SWIDOC)
ADDRESS: Herengracht 410-412,
1017 BX Amsterdam,
NETHERLANDS
TEL: (020) 225061
CREATED: 1964   *HEAD:* P. F. A. de Guchteneire, Director
SIZE OF STAFF: Total: 8
TYPE OF SERVICE: national; public; non-profit
SYSTEMS & NETWORKS ATTACHED TO: CESSDA (Committee of European Social Data Archives);
IFDO (International Federation of Data Organizations)
MATERIALS DESCRIBING THE SERVICE: - Steinmetz Archive data catalogue and guide, 1986
500 p.
SUBJECT COVERAGE: social sciences
GEOGRAPHICAL COVERAGE: Netherlands
DATA BEING PROCESSED AND SIZE: 1,900 machine-readable data files; 900 public opinion
polls; some census-data and statistics
DATA PROCESSING METHODS: computerized
HARDWARE USED: CDC-CYBER of the Stichting Academisch Rekencentrum Amsterdam (SARA)
and micro-computer network
SOFTWARE USED: SPSS, SAS
STORAGE MEDIA: tapes
TYPE OF ACTIVITY: data collection; distribution of information
PERIODICALS PUBLISHED:
- Data Nieuws
CLIENTELE: social scientists
ACCESS TO SERVICE: open to all users (some data files are restricted)
TYPE & DESCRIPTION OF SERVICES PROVIDED: Central organization for documentation and
secondary analysis of machine readable research material in social sciences
Provides information on magnetic tape or discs.

559 - STUDIE- EN INFORMATIECENTRUM MENSENRECHTEN

SYNONYMOUS NAMES: SIM;
            Netherlands Institute of Human Rights
PARENT ORGANIZATION: Rijksuniversiteit te Utrecht
ADDRESS: Boothstraat 8,
            3512 BW Utrecht,
            NETHERLANDS
            TEL: (030) 39.40.33 - TELEX: 70779 SIM NL
            CABLE: SIMCABLE
CREATED: 1982   *HEAD:* Mr. J. G. H. Thoolen, Director
SIZE OF STAFF: Professional: 5   Other: 3   Total: 8
TYPE OF SERVICE: national; non-profit
SYSTEMS & NETWORKS ATTACHED TO: Human Rights Information and Documentation System
            (HURIDOCS)
WORKING LANGUAGE(S): English
SUBJECT COVERAGE: law; human rights
GEOGRAPHICAL COVERAGE: global
DATA BEING PROCESSED AND SIZE: 4,200 documentation references in its own data bases
DATA PROCESSING METHODS: computerized
SOFTWARE USED: SAT
PERIODICALS PUBLISHED:
            - SIM Newsletter
            - SIM Specials
PUBLICATIONS: - Declaration of the basic duties of ASEAM peoples and governments,
            1983
            - Alston, P.; Tomasevski, K. (eds.), The Right to food, 1984
            - Ethnic violence, development and human rights, 1985
            - Thoolen, H.; Verstappen, B.-bHuman rights missions: a study of the fact-
            finding practice of non-governmental organizations, 1986
CLIENTELE: students, experts, non-governmental organizations
ACCESS TO SERVICE: open to all users free of charge
TYPE & DESCRIPTION OF SERVICES PROVIDED: Maintains 3 data bases: SIMDOC (3,000
            references on general human rights documents), MERLIN (1,000 references on
            human rights documents in the Dutch language) and DIGEST (200 references on
            human rights case law).

560 - TMC ASSER INSTITUUT VOOR INTERNATIONAAL EN EUROPEES RECHT

SYNONYMOUS NAMES: Institute for International Law
ADDRESS: Alexanderstraat 20-22,
            P.O. Box 30461,
            2500 GL The Hague,
            NETHERLANDS
            TEL: 970) 630900 - TELEX: 34273 Asser nl. - TELEXFAX: (70) 638171
CREATED: 1965   *HEAD:* Dr. C. C. A. Voskuil, Director
SIZE OF STAFF: Professional: 21   Other: 21   Total: 42
MATERIALS DESCRIBING THE SERVICE: - de Jongh, J. S., Interuniversitair Instituut voor
            Internationaal Recht, 1985 (Brochure)
SUBJECT COVERAGE: international law; private international law; public international
            law; European Community Law

GEOGRAPHICAL COVERAGE: Netherlands; European Community
DATA BEING PROCESSED AND SIZE: 4,000 books; 400 periodicals; 15 abstract journals;
        25,000 manuscripts
DATA PROCESSING METHODS: manual; partially computerized
STORAGE MEDIA: traditional shelving of publications; fiches; discs; microfiches etc.
TYPE OF ACTIVITY: data collection; data analysis; distribution of information;
        publication; SSID scientific and methodological activities; SSID training
PERIODICALS PUBLISHED: - Netherlands International Law Review - International Law,
        Conflict of Laws, Comparative Law, 3 p.a.
        - Netherlands Yearbook of International Law, 1 p.a.
PUBLICATIONS: - Repertorium op de Nederlandse Volkenrechtelijke Rechtspraak 1840-
        1983, 1986
        - Bos, A.; Siblesz, H. (eds.), Realism in law-making; essays on
        international law in honour of W. Riphagen, 1986
        - Wellens, K. C., Peace and security: justice and development: report of a
        congress held on the occasion of 40 years United Nations, 1986
CLIENTELE: academic, legal practice and public administration institutions
ACCESS TO SERVICE: open to specific categories of users free of charge, some paid
        services
TYPE & DESCRIPTION OF SERVICES PROVIDED: Library services include reference use only
        Also provides bibliographic, literature and survey data searches,
        information on magnetic tapes or discs, microforms, on-line services using
        external data bases accessible through DATANET 1; photocopies and
        translation of documents upon request.

561 - UNIVERSITEIT NIJMEGEN, STUDIECENTRUM VOOR VREDESVRAAGSTUKKEN

SYNONYMOUS NAMES: University of Nijmegen, Peace Research Centre
ADDRESS: Thomas van Aquinostraat 1,
        P.O. Box 9108,
        6500 HK Nijmegen,
        NETHERLANDS
        TEL: (080) 515687
CREATED: 1965   HEAD: Drs. L. Wecke, Director
SIZE OF STAFF: Professional: 10   Other: 5   Total: 15
TYPE OF SERVICE: non-profit
WORKING LANGUAGE(S): Dutch
SUBJECT COVERAGE: political science; history; peace; defence
GEOGRAPHICAL COVERAGE: global
DATA BEING PROCESSED AND SIZE: 15,000 documentation items
DATA PROCESSING METHODS: manual; computerized
HARDWARE USED: Olivetti PC M24; Apple III
SOFTWARE USED: DBASE III
STORAGE MEDIA: traditional shelving of publications, fiches, discs
TYPE OF ACTIVITY: data collection; distribution of information; publication
PERIODICALS PUBLISHED:
        - Cahiers DOS-Schriften
CLIENTELE: students and professors
ACCESS TO SERVICE: open to all users, some paid services
TYPE & DESCRIPTION OF SERVICES PROVIDED: Provides library services and photocopies.

562 - UNIVERSITEIT VAN AMSTERDAM, EUROPA INSTITUUT, BIBLIOTHEEK

SYNONYMOUS NAMES: University of Amsterdam, Europa Institute, Library
ADDRESS: BG gebouw 1,
Grimburgwal 10,
NL-1012 GA Amsterdam,
NETHERLANDS
TEL: (020) 525.2161
CREATED: 1960   HEAD: Mrs. P. Sprengers, Librarian
SIZE OF STAFF: Professional: 1   Other: 2   Total: 3
TYPE OF SERVICE: public; non-profit
WORKING LANGUAGE(S): Dutch; English
SUBJECT COVERAGE: law; economics; political science; European integration
GEOGRAPHICAL COVERAGE: Europe
DATA PROCESSING METHODS: manual
STORAGE MEDIA: traditional shelving of publications
TYPE OF ACTIVITY: data collection; publication
PERIODICALS PUBLISHED: - Legal Issues of European Integration, 2 p.a.
PUBLICATIONS: - Europese monografieën (in Dutch)
CLIENTELE: university students; lawyers; researchers (40 per day)
ACCESS TO SERVICE: open to all users
TYPE & DESCRIPTION OF SERVICES PROVIDED: Provides library services including
        interlibrary loans. The library has the official status of European
        Documentation Centre of the European Communities.

563 - NEW ZEALAND DEPARTMENT OF STATISTICS, INFORMATION SCIENCES DIVISION

SYNONYMOUS NAMES: NZSTATS Information Sciences Division
ADDRESS: P.O. Box 2922,
Wellington,
NEW ZEALAND
TEL: (04) 729-119 - TELEX: 31313 - TELEFAX: (04) 729-135
CREATED: 1925   HEAD: Mr. K. Eddy, Director
SIZE OF STAFF: Professional: 27   Other: 22   Total: 49
TYPE OF SERVICE: national; public; non-profit
SYSTEMS & NETWORKS ATTACHED TO: New Zealand Bibliographic Network (NZBN)
MATERIALS DESCRIBING THE SERVICE: - Directory of Official Information
WORKING LANGUAGE(S): English
SUBJECT COVERAGE: statistics; social sciences; demography; economics
GEOGRAPHICAL COVERAGE: New Zealand
DATA PROCESSING METHODS: computerized
HARDWARE USED: IBM
SOFTWARE USED: own
STORAGE MEDIA: tapes; discs
TYPE OF ACTIVITY: data collection; data analysis; distribution of information;
        publication
PERIODICALS PUBLISHED: - New Zealand Official Yearbook
        - New Zealand Pocket Digest of Statistics
CLIENTELE: government, public and private enterprises, international organizations,
        academics, researchers, schools, private individuals

ACCESS TO SERVICE: paid services open to all users
TYPE & DESCRIPTION OF SERVICES PROVIDED: Provides library services, quantitative dat
    searches of information, on-line searches using own data base "INFOS"
    (Information Network for Official Statistics), selective dissemination of
    information, information on magnetic tapes or discs, microforms, photocopie
    and CD-ROM.

564 - NEW ZEALAND INSTITUTE OF ECONOMIC RESEARCH, LIBRARY

ADDRESS: P.O. Box 3479,
    Wellington,
    NEW ZEALAND
    TEL: 721880
CREATED: 1959   *HEAD:* Mrs. M. Malan, Librarian
SIZE OF STAFF: Professional: 1   Other: 1   Total: 2
TYPE OF SERVICE: national; private; non-profit
SUBJECT COVERAGE: economics
DATA BEING PROCESSED AND SIZE: 2,000 books; 150 journals
DATA PROCESSING METHODS: manual
STORAGE MEDIA: traditional shelving of publications; microfiches
TYPE OF ACTIVITY: distribution of information
CLIENTELE: researchers
ACCESS TO SERVICE: services open to all users, some paid services
TYPE & DESCRIPTION OF SERVICES PROVIDED: Provides library services, bibliographic ar
    literature abstract searches, selective dissemination of information and
    photocopies. External data bases are searched through NZBN and DIALOG at t
    New Zealand National Library.

565 - SOCIAL SCIENCES RESEARCH FUND COMMITTEE

SYNONYMOUS NAMES: SSRFC
ADDRESS: P.O. Box 27-042,
    Wellington 1,
    NEW ZEALAND
    TEL: (064) 4-846209
CREATED: 1979   *HEAD:* Dr. T. M. Loomis, Director
SIZE OF STAFF: Professional: 2   Other: 2   Total: 4
TYPE OF SERVICE: national; public; non-profit
WORKING LANGUAGE(S): English
SUBJECT COVERAGE: social sciences
GEOGRAPHICAL COVERAGE: New Zealand
DATA BEING PROCESSED AND SIZE: discussion papers; reports; seminars; periodicals
DATA PROCESSING METHODS: computerized
HARDWARE USED: IBM PC compatible
SOFTWARE USED: DBase III; Wordstar 2000; Lotus 1-2-3
STORAGE MEDIA: traditional shelving of publications; discs
TYPE OF ACTIVITY: data collection; distribution of information; SSID scientific and
    methodological activities; publication
PERIODICALS PUBLISHED:

- Newsletter
CLIENTELE: researchers
ACCESS TO SERVICE: open to all users
TYPE & DESCRIPTION OF SERVICES PROVIDED: Provides information from "SOCNET" (Social
    Science Research Network) and "SOCWIP" (Social Science Research - Work in
    Progress). Also provides bibliographic searches, selective dissemination of
    information, production of information on magnetic tapes and photocopies.

566 - UNIVERSITY OF CANTERBURY, CENTRE FOR RESOURCE MANAGEMENT

SYNONYMOUS NAMES: University of Canterbury, CRM
ADDRESS: Lincoln College,
        P.O. Box 56,
        Canterbury,
        NEW ZEALAND
        TEL: (03) 252-811 - TELEX: (64)(3) 252944
CREATED: 1982   *HEAD:* Dr. J. Hayward, Director
SIZE OF STAFF: Professional: 19   Other: 4   Total: 23
TYPE OF SERVICE: national; public; non-profit
WORKING LANGUAGE(S): English
SUBJECT COVERAGE: social sciences; economics; sociology; ecology; resource policy and
        planning; natural resource management
GEOGRAPHICAL COVERAGE: New Zealand
DATA PROCESSING METHODS: partially computerized
HARDWARE USED: Apricot; Exzel (IBM compatible), Brother; Dot-Matrix
SOFTWARE USED: Volkswriter; Superwriter; Wordperfect
STORAGE MEDIA: discs
TYPE OF ACTIVITY: data analysis; distribution of information; SSID scientific and
        methodological activities; publication
PUBLICATIONS: - Jowett, W.; Stephenson I.; Coates, F., Mountain Beech forest: an
        educational resource, 1986
        - Howell, J. (ed.), Environment and ethics: a New Zealand perspective, 1986
        - Taylor, C. N.; Blake-Kelly, A.; Leathers, K. L., A Social economic study
        of land development for farm settlement at Butlers, 1985
        - Taylor, C. N.;1 Abrahamson, M.; Williams, T., Rural change: issues for
        social research, social assessment and integrated rural policy, 1987
        - Kerr, G. N., Introduction to non-market valuation: theory and methods,
        1986
        - Kerr, G. N.; Sharp, B. M. H., Valuing the environment: economic theory and
        applications, 1987
CLIENTELE: decision-makers (bureaucrats and politicians); resource management
        professionals; students
ACCESS TO SERVICE: services open to all users, free of charge
TYPE & DESCRIPTION OF SERVICES PROVIDED: Provides library services and selective
        dissemination of information.

Nicaragua

567 - MINISTERIO DE EDUCACIÓN, CENTRO DE DOCUMENTACIÓN Y BIBLIOTECA

SYNONYMOUS NAMES: Ministry of Education, Library and Documentation Centre
ADDRESS: Apartado 108,
        Complejo Cívico "Modulo K",
        Managua,
        NICARAGUA
        TEL: 50195
CREATED: 1979   *HEAD:* Ms. G. M. Morales Arévalo,
SIZE OF STAFF: Professional: 2   Other: 5   Total: 7
TYPE OF SERVICE: national; non-profit
SYSTEMS & NETWORKS ATTACHED TO: Sistema Nacional de Información Documental
WORKING LANGUAGE(S): Spanish
SUBJECT COVERAGE: education; social sciences; linguistics; philosophy; psychology;
        sociology
GEOGRAPHICAL COVERAGE: Nicaragua
DATA PROCESSING METHODS: manual
TYPE OF ACTIVITY: publication
PERIODICALS PUBLISHED:
        - Boletín de Resúmenes Analíticos de Educación
        - Boletín de Últimas Adquisiciones
        - Alertas
ACCESS TO SERVICE: services open to specific categories of users, free of charge
TYPE & DESCRIPTION OF SERVICES PROVIDED: Provides selective dissemination of
        information.

Nigeria / Nigéria / Nigeria

568 - CENTRE FOR MANAGEMENT DEVELOPMENT, LIBRARY FOR MANAGEMENT STUDIES

SYNONYMOUS NAMES: LMS
ADDRESS: Management Village,
        Shangisha,
        P.M.B. 21578,
        Ikeja,
        Lagos,
        NIGERIA
        TEL: 901120-29
CREATED: 1976   *HEAD:* Ms. J. O. Akinsete, Assistant Chief Librarian
SIZE OF STAFF: Professional: 8   Other: 16   Total: 24
TYPE OF SERVICE: national; public; non-profit; private
WORKING LANGUAGE(S): English; Hausa, Igbo, Yoruba
SUBJECT COVERAGE: administrative sciences; economics; management; public enterprise
        development, consultancy, training, research
GEOGRAPHICAL COVERAGE: Nigeria
DATA BEING PROCESSED AND SIZE: 20,000 books, articles and reports
DATA PROCESSING METHODS: manual
STORAGE MEDIA: traditional shelving of publications
TYPE OF ACTIVITY: data collection; distribution of information; publication
CLIENTELE: management educators, students, practitioners

ACCESS TO SERVICE: services open to specific categories of users, free of charge
TYPE & DESCRIPTION OF SERVICES PROVIDED: Provides library services including
bibliographic and literature searches of information, photocopying services
and translation of documents upon request.

569 - NIGERIAN INSTITUTE OF INTERNATIONAL AFFAIRS, LIBRARY AND DOCUMENTATION SERVICES

ADDRESS: Kofo Abayomi Road,
Victoria Island,
P.O. Box 1727,
Lagos,
NIGERIA
TEL: 615606 - TELEX: 22638 NG
CABLE: INTERNATIONS, LAGOS
CREATED: 1961   *HEAD:* A. O. Banjo, Director
SIZE OF STAFF: Professional: 8
TYPE OF SERVICE: national; public; non-profit
MATERIALS DESCRIBING THE SERVICE: - Akinola, C. I., The Organization and utilization
of resources in the Nigerian Institute of International Affairs Library,
1984
WORKING LANGUAGE(S): English
SUBJECT COVERAGE: political science; economics; history; law; international relations
GEOGRAPHICAL COVERAGE: global
DATA PROCESSING METHODS: manual
TYPE OF ACTIVITY: data collection; data analysis; distribution of information;
publication
PUBLICATIONS: - Banjo, A. O., Problems in the storage and dissemination of newspaper
information: a Nigerian example, 1985
CLIENTELE: university staff, students, civil servants, military
ACCESS TO SERVICE: services open to specific categories of users, free of charge
TYPE & DESCRIPTION OF SERVICES PROVIDED: Provides library services, current awareness
service, bibliographic searches of information, photocopies, and translation
of documents upon request.

570 - NIGERIAN INSTITUTE OF SOCIAL AND ECONOMIC RESEARCH, LIBRARY

SYNONYMOUS NAMES: NISER Library
ADDRESS: P.M.B. No. 5,
U.I.P.O.,
Ibadan,
NIGERIA
CABLE: NISER IBADAN
CREATED: 1960   *HEAD:* J. A. Akisanya, Institute Librarian
SIZE OF STAFF: Professional: 5   Other: 19   Total: 24
TYPE OF SERVICE: public; non-profit
WORKING LANGUAGE(S): English
SUBJECT COVERAGE: economics; sociology; political science; demography; social
sciences; criminology; education; geography; psychology; social anthropology
GEOGRAPHICAL COVERAGE: Nigeria

DATA BEING PROCESSED AND SIZE: monographs, government publications
DATA PROCESSING METHODS: manual
HARDWARE USED: Data General MV4000 & IBM 370
SOFTWARE USED: SPSS
STORAGE MEDIA: tapes
TYPE OF ACTIVITY: data analysis
PERIODICALS PUBLISHED:
- Accession List, 4 p.a.
- List of Books, Articles and Government Publications, 1 p.a.
PUBLICATIONS: - Communication: index of periodical articles in NISER Library
CLIENTELE: researchers, university academic staff and post-graduate students
ACCESS TO SERVICE: open to specific categories of users
TYPE & DESCRIPTION OF SERVICES PROVIDED: Provides library services, bibliographic
searches of information, selective dissemination of information and
photocopies.

571 - CHR. MICHELSENS INSTITUTT, AVDELING FOR SAMFUNNSVITENSKAP OG UTVIKLING, BIBLIOTEKET

SYNONYMOUS NAMES: CMI/ASU, Library;
Chr. Michelsen Institute, Department of Social Science and Development,
Library
ADDRESS: Fantoftvegen 38,
5036 Fantoft,
NORWAY
TEL: 47.5.28.44.10 - TELEX: 40 006 CMI - TELEFAX: 47 5 28 56 13
CABLE: DERAP
CREATED: 1930   *HEAD:* K. Hagen Andersen, Head of Library
SIZE OF STAFF: Professional: 2   Other: 1   Total: 3
TYPE OF SERVICE: private; non-profit
MATERIALS DESCRIBING THE SERVICE: - Chr. Michelsen Institute. Department of Social
Science and Development, Annual report
- Chr. Michelsen Institute of Science and Intellectual Freedom, 1987
(brochure)
WORKING LANGUAGE(S): Norwegian; English
SUBJECT COVERAGE: social sciences; demography; economics; geography; political
science; social anthropology; cultural anthropology; women; human rights;
development aid
GEOGRAPHICAL COVERAGE: developing countries; Norway; Eastern Africa; Southeast Asia
DATA BEING PROCESSED AND SIZE: 25,000 books; 450 periodicals
DATA PROCESSING METHODS: computerized
HARDWARE USED: Olivetti Personal Computer M24
SOFTWARE USED: Revelation
TYPE OF ACTIVITY: distribution of information; publication
PERIODICALS PUBLISHED:
- List of Periodicals
- Library Acquisition List
PUBLICATIONS: - Norwegian development research catalogue, 1987
CLIENTELE: researchers, students, other libraries and institutions
ACCESS TO SERVICE: services open to all users, free of charge

TYPE & DESCRIPTION OF SERVICES PROVIDED: Provides library services, on-line services using own data base and external data bases accessed through DIALOG, SAMKAT (Norway) DEIN (United Nations). Also provides photocopies.

672 - INSTITUTT FOR FREDSFORSKNING, BIBLIOTEKET

SYNONYMOUS NAMES: PRIO, Library;
International Peace Research Institute, Oslo, Library
ADDRESS: Fuglehauggata 11,
N-0260 Oslo 2,
NORWAY
TEL: (02) 55.71.50
CABLE: PEACERESEARCH, Oslo
HEAD: A. Helseth, Librarian
SYSTEMS & NETWORKS ATTACHED TO: Norwegian Library Service
MATERIALS DESCRIBING THE SERVICE: - PRIO, 1988, brochure
SUBJECT COVERAGE: political science; peace
DATA BEING PROCESSED AND SIZE: 13,000 books; 400 journals
ACCESS TO SERVICE: open to the public
TYPE & DESCRIPTION OF SERVICES PROVIDED: Provides library services for reference only, bibliographic data searches on own data bases as well as international data bases. Copying facilities are also available.

673 - NAVFS EDB-SENTER FOR HUMANISTISK FORSKNING

SYNONYMOUS NAMES: Norwegian Computing Centre for the Humanities
PARENT ORGANIZATION: Norwegian Research Council for Science and the Humanities
ADDRESS: Universitetet Boøks 53,
N-5014 Bergen,
NORWAY
TEL: (475) 212954
CREATED: 1972
SIZE OF STAFF: Professional: 8   Other: 8   Total: 16
TYPE OF SERVICE: national; public; non-profit
SYSTEMS & NETWORKS ATTACHED TO: Operating agency of the International Computer Archive of Modern English (ICAME)
MATERIALS DESCRIBING THE SERVICE: - The Norwegian Computing Centre for the Humanities, 1986, brochure
WORKING LANGUAGE(S): Norwegian; English
SUBJECT COVERAGE: humanities; computer science; demography; history; linguistics; philosophy; ethnology; religion; architecture; archaeology
GEOGRAPHICAL COVERAGE: Norway; Scandinavia
DATA PROCESSING METHODS: computerized
HARDWARE USED: UNIVAC 1100/82; Mino computer MacIntosh
STORAGE MEDIA: traditional shelving of publications; tapes; discs; micro-fiches; CD-ROM; digital optical WORM (Write Once Read Many) disks
TYPE OF ACTIVITY: data collection; data analysis; distribution of information; SSID scientific and methodological activities; publication
PERIODICALS PUBLISHED: - Humanistiske Data, 3 p.a.

- Annual Report
PUBLICATIONS: - Report series
CLIENTELE: researchers from universities, colleges, academic archives, museums,
cultural organizations
ACCESS TO SERVICE: services open to all users free of charge, some paid services
TYPE & DESCRIPTION OF SERVICES PROVIDED: Provides library services, quantitative data
searches, selective dissemination of information, information on magnetic
tapes or discs, microforms, photocopies, computing services and teaching.
Has access to EARN, JANET and Arpanet international networks.

574 - NAVFS INFORMASJONSTJENESTE FOR SAMFUNNSVITENSKAPELIGE FORSKNINGSPROSJEKTER

SYNONYMOUS NAMES: Norwegian Research Council for Science and the Humanities,
Information and Documentation Service for On-Going Research in the Social
Sciences and the Humanities
PARENT ORGANIZATION: Norges Allenvitenskapelige Forskningsråd and Norsk
Samfunnsvitenskapelig Datatjeneste
ADDRESS: c/o Norwegian Social Science Data Services,
Hans Holmboesgate 22,
N-5007 Bergen,
NORWAY
TEL: (05) 21.21.17
CREATED: 1984   HEAD: Mr. B. Henrichsen, Director
SIZE OF STAFF: Professional: 1   Other: 1   Total: 2
TYPE OF SERVICE: national; public; non-profit
WORKING LANGUAGE(S): Norwegian
SUBJECT COVERAGE: social sciences
GEOGRAPHICAL COVERAGE: Norway
DATA BEING PROCESSED AND SIZE: 2,000 projects; 4,000 publications
DATA PROCESSING METHODS: partially computerized
HARDWARE USED: Univac 1100/82
TYPE OF ACTIVITY: data collection; data analysis; publication
PUBLICATIONS: - Samfunnsvitenskapelig Forskning i Norge. Projeticatalog 1985-1986
ACCESS TO SERVICE: open to all users; payment is conditioned by the kind of service
TYPE & DESCRIPTION OF SERVICES PROVIDED: Its purpose is to collect information on
on-going research in the social sciences in Norway and distribute this
information to researchers, authorities and the public. Provides
bibliographic searches of information using data-bases through the host
computer at the University of Bergen.

575 - NORSK INSTITUTT FOR BY- OG REGIONFORSKNING, BIBLIOTEKET

SYNONYMOUS NAMES: NIBR Biblioteket;
Norwegian Institute for Urban and Regional Research, Library
ADDRESS: P.O. Box 15 Grefsen,
0409 Oslo 4,
NORWAY
TEL: (02) 15.53.10
CREATED: 1970   HEAD: Ms. I. H. Andresen, Head Librarian

IZE OF STAFF: Professional: 1
YPE OF SERVICE: national; public; non-profit
ORKING LANGUAGE(S): Norwegian; English
UBJECT COVERAGE: urban planning; regional planning; social planning; sociology;
    social welfare; demography; economics; geography; political science
ATA BEING PROCESSED AND SIZE: 20,000 books; 200 periodicals; 12 abstract journals
ATA PROCESSING METHODS: partially computerized
ARDWARE USED: NORD 100 computer
OFTWARE USED: POLYDOC
TORAGE MEDIA: traditional shelving of publications
YPE OF ACTIVITY: data collection; distribution of information; publication
CCESS TO SERVICE: open to all users
YPE & DESCRIPTION OF SERVICES PROVIDED: Provides library services, bibliographic
    searches of information using own data base covering most fields within
    social planning. Has also access to ALIS, DIALOG, POLYDOC, (BYGGDOK), SCANP,
    UBO:BOK through SCANNET, TELENET, TYMNET.

76 - NORSK SAMFUNNSVITENSKAPELIG DATAJENESTE

YNONYMOUS NAMES: NSD;
    Norwegian Social Science Data Services
ARENT ORGANIZATION: Norges Allmenvitenskapelige Forskningsråd/Norwegian Research
    Council for Science and the Humanities (NAVF)
DDRESS: Hans Holmboesgate 22,
    N-5007 Bergen,
    NORWAY
    TEL: (05) 21.21.17
REATED: 1971   *HEAD:* Mr. B. Henrichsen, Executive Director
IZE OF STAFF: Professional: 16   Other: 4   Total: 20
YPE OF SERVICE: national; public; non-profit
YSTEMS & NETWORKS ATTACHED TO: CESSDA (The Committee of European Social Science Data
    Archives); IFDO (International Federation of Data Organizations for the
    Social Sciences)
ATERIALS DESCRIBING THE SERVICE: - Norsk Samfunnvitenskapelig Datajeneste:
    datakatalog, Bergen, 1986
ORKING LANGUAGE(S): Norwegian
UBJECT COVERAGE: social sciences
EOGRAPHICAL COVERAGE: Norway
ATA BEING PROCESSED AND SIZE: censuses, statistical surveys, by-products of economic
    activities, administrative processes, research studies
ATA PROCESSING METHODS: computerized
ARDWARE USED: UNIVAC 110/82
OFTWARE USED: SPSS, SIR, own software, CALFORM
TORAGE MEDIA: tapes, discs
YPE OF ACTIVITY: data collection
ERIODICALS PUBLISHED:
    - NSD Brukermelding, newsletter
    - European Political Data Newsletter
LIENTELE: students of the Norwegian universities and regional colleges
CCESS TO SERVICE: open to all users, free of charge
YPE & DESCRIPTION OF SERVICES PROVIDED: Provision of quantitative data for secondary

analysis. Its basic data systems are: Data bank on Norwegian Communes 1969 1987, Ecological Archive for Inter-War period, Archive on Members of Parliament and Cabinet Ministers, Archive on Norwegian Government Official Archive of Criminal Statistics, Archive of Nordic Regional Statistical Dat Survey Data, Archive of Norwegian Voluntary Association.

577 - NORSK UTENRIKSPOLITISK INSTITUTT, BIBLIOTEKET

SYNONYMOUS NAMES: NUPI, Library;
  Norwegian Institute of International Affairs, Library
ADDRESS: Bydøy Allé 3,
  P.B. 8159, Dep.,
  0033 Oslo 1,
  NORWAY
  TEL: (02) 44.58.20
  CABLE: NORWINTAFF
CREATED: 1960   *HEAD:* D. Hermansen, Librarian
SIZE OF STAFF: Professional: 15   Other: 19   Total: 34
WORKING LANGUAGE(S): Norwegian; English
SUBJECT COVERAGE: political science; international relations; economics; history; social anthropology
DATA BEING PROCESSED AND SIZE: 11,000 books; 350 periodicals; 4 abstract journals; 1,200 microcopies
HARDWARE USED: Olivetti PC
SOFTWARE USED: Révélation
STORAGE MEDIA: traditional shelving of publications; tapes; microfiches
TYPE OF ACTIVITY: data collection; SSID scientific and methodological activities
ACCESS TO SERVICE: open to specific categories of users, paid services
TYPE & DESCRIPTION OF SERVICES PROVIDED: Provides library reference services, bibliographic, literature and survey data searches.

578 - THE ROYAL NORWEGIAN MINISTRY OF DEVELOPMENT COOPERATION, LIBRARY

SYNONYMOUS NAMES: DUH/NORAD, Library
ADDRESS: P.O. Box 8142 Dep.,
  0033 Oslo 1,
  NORWAY
  TEL: 47-2-314055 - TELEX: 76548 NORAD-N
HEAD: K. Brekke, Head
SIZE OF STAFF: Professional: 3   Other: 2   Total: 5
TYPE OF SERVICE: international; public
SUBJECT COVERAGE: social sciences; economics; geography; political science; sociolo
GEOGRAPHICAL COVERAGE: developing countries
DATA BEING PROCESSED AND SIZE: 20,000 books; 350 periodicals; reports
DATA PROCESSING METHODS: partially computerized
HARDWARE USED: Olivetti Micro-computers
SOFTWARE USED: Revelation-"Bibelation"
STORAGE MEDIA: traditional shelving of publications
TYPE OF ACTIVITY: distribution of information

LIENTELE: students, researchers, aid agencies, libraries, general public
CCESS TO SERVICE: services open to all users, free of charge
YPE & DESCRIPTION OF SERVICES PROVIDED: Provides library services, bibliographic,
    literature and quantitative data searches of information, on-line services,
    selective dissemination of information, photocopies.

79 - STATISTISK SENTRALBYRÅS BIBLIOTEK

YNONYMOUS NAMES: Central Bureau of Statistics, the Library
DDRESS: Skippergt. 15,
    P.O. Box 8131,
    N-0033 Oslo 1 Dep,
    NORWAY
    TEL: (472) 41.38.20
    CABLE: STATISTIKK
REATED: 1850   HEAD: Mrs. H. Rødland, Chief Librarian
IZE OF STAFF: Professional: 7   Other: 4   Total: 11
YPE OF SERVICE: public
UBJECT COVERAGE: statistics; economics; demography
ATA BEING PROCESSED AND SIZE: 160,000 books; 680 periodicals; 4,200 serials; 8
    abstract journals; 30 microcopies
ATA PROCESSING METHODS: computerized
ARDWARE USED: IBM
YPE OF ACTIVITY: data collection; publication
ERIODICALS PUBLISHED: - Løpende Tidsskrifter, 1 p.a.
       - Biblioteksnytt, Accession List, 12 p.a.
CCESS TO SERVICE: open to all users, free of charge
YPE & DESCRIPTION OF SERVICES PROVIDED: Provides library services, bibliographic and
    quantitative data searches using its own database DOBIS-LIBIS. Has also
    access to DIALOG, DOP and UBO:BOK data bases through DATAPAK and USE.

80 - UNITED NATIONS ASSOCIATION OF NORWAY, DATA AND INFORMATION SERVICES

YNONYMOUS NAMES: UNA of Norway, Data and Information Services
ARENT ORGANIZATION: FN-Sambandet i Norge
DDRESS: Langes gate 4,
    0165 Oslo 1,
    NORWAY
    TEL: (02) 20.91.70 - TELEFAX: (02) 20.81.42
    CABLE: NORWUNA
REATED: 1946   HEAD: Ms. M. Clifford, Head of Library
IZE OF STAFF: Professional: 1   Other: 1   Total: 2
YPE OF SERVICE: public; non-profit
ATERIALS DESCRIBING THE SERVICE: - Annual report (in Norwegian)
       - UNA of Norway (pamphlet)
ORKING LANGUAGE(S): Norwegian
UBJECT COVERAGE: social sciences; demography; economics; education; political
    science; social anthropology; cultural anthropology
ATA BEING PROCESSED AND SIZE: 4,000 books; 250 periodicals

DATA PROCESSING METHODS: computerized
HARDWARE USED: OLIVETTI M 240
SOFTWARE USED: Revelation
STORAGE MEDIA: traditional shelving of publications
TYPE OF ACTIVITY: distribution of information; publication
PERIODICALS PUBLISHED:
          - List of Periodicals
          - Acquisitions List
CLIENTELE: students, teachers, journalists
ACCESS TO SERVICE: services open to all users, free of charge
TYPE & DESCRIPTION OF SERVICES PROVIDED: Provides library services and on-line
          services, using own data base. Has also access to DEIN data base through th
          UN. Provision of photocopies upon request.

581 - PAKISTAN INSTITUTE OF DEVELOPMENT ECONOMICS, LIBRARY AND DOCUMENTATION CENTRE

SYNONYMOUS NAMES: PIDE Library and Documentation Section
ADDRESS: P.O. Box 1091,
          Islamabad,
          PAKISTAN
          TEL: 812440-53 - TELEX: 5602 PIDE PK
CREATED: 1957   *HEAD:* Z. J. Naqvi, Acting Chief
SIZE OF STAFF: Professional: 7   Other: 11   Total: 18
TYPE OF SERVICE: National; public; non-profit
SYSTEMS & NETWORKS ATTACHED TO: Development Information Network on South Asia
          (DEVINSA)
WORKING LANGUAGE(S): English
SUBJECT COVERAGE: economics; sociology; social welfare; demography; development
          economics; Islamic economics; economic demography
GEOGRAPHICAL COVERAGE: Pakistan; developing countries, global
DATA BEING PROCESSED AND SIZE: 24,000 books; 8,000 research documents; 22,000
          periodical articles
DATA PROCESSING METHODS: partially computerized
STORAGE MEDIA: traditional shelving of publications; microfiches and microfilms
TYPE OF ACTIVITY: distribution of information; publication
PERIODICALS PUBLISHED: - Devindex Pakistan: Index to Pakistan Literature on Economic
          and Social Development, 1 p.a.
          - Current Periodical Literature: Documentation List, 52 p.a.
          - Library Bulletin of New Acquisitions, 12 p.a.
PUBLICATIONS: - Naqvi, Z. J., Analytical catalogue of research documents, 1984
          - Butt, I., List of doctoral dissertations and M.A. theses, 1984
          - Siddiqui, A. H., Agricultural credit in developing countries: a select
          bibliography, 1986
          - Naqvi, Z. J., Bibliographic aids (available in the PIDE library)
          - Naqvi, Z. J., Population and family planning studies: a catalogue of
          research documents available in the PIDE library, 1986
          - Naqvi, Z. J., Bibliography of IBRD/World Bank reports and documents
CLIENTELE: researchers
ACCESS TO SERVICE: open to researchers
TYPE & DESCRIPTION OF SERVICES PROVIDED: Provides library services, bibliographic an

literature searches, selective dissemination of information and photocopies.

82 - UNIVERSITY OF THE PUNJAB, SOCIAL SCIENCES RESEARCH CENTRE, LIBRARY

SYNONYMOUS NAMES: SSRC Library, Punjab
ADDRESS: New Campus,
Lahore,
PAKISTAN
TEL: 850826
CREATED: 1956   *HEAD:* Mr. M. Hussain, Director
SIZE OF STAFF: Professional: 9
TYPE OF SERVICE: international; public; non-profit
MATERIALS DESCRIBING THE SERVICE: - Social Sciences Research Centre, 1986, brochure
WORKING LANGUAGE(S): English
SUBJECT COVERAGE: social sciences; demography
GEOGRAPHICAL COVERAGE: Pakistan
DATA BEING PROCESSED AND SIZE: 7,000 books, research reports and periodicals
DATA PROCESSING METHODS: partially computerized
STORAGE MEDIA: traditional shelving of publications
TYPE OF ACTIVITY: data collection; data analysis; distribution of information; SSID
scientific and methodological activities; SSID training; publication
ACCESS TO SERVICE: services open to all users, some paid services
TYPE & DESCRIPTION OF SERVICES PROVIDED: Provides library services, quantitative data
searches, selective dissemination of information, photocopies and
translation of documents upon request.

83 - CENTRO DE ESTUDIOS LATINOAMERICANOS, CENTRO DE DOCUMENTACIÓN

SYNONYMOUS NAMES: CENDOC - CELA
PARENT ORGANIZATION: Centro de Estudios Latinoamericanos "Justo Arosemena"
ADDRESS: Apdo. 6-3093,
El Dorado,
PANAMA
TEL: 27-2136
CABLE: CELAPANAMA
HEAD: Mr. M. A. Gandásegui, Executive Secretary
SIZE OF STAFF: Professional: 1   Other: 4   Total: 5
TYPE OF SERVICE: international; private; non-profit
WORKING LANGUAGE(S): Spanish
SUBJECT COVERAGE: social sciences; political science; sociology; economics;
demography; history
GEOGRAPHICAL COVERAGE: Latin America
DATA BEING PROCESSED AND SIZE: 7,000 documentation items
DATA PROCESSING METHODS: manual
TYPE OF ACTIVITY: data collection; distribution of information; SSID scientific and
methodological activities; publication
PERIODICALS PUBLISHED:
- Boletín Bibliográfico

447

CLIENTELE: researchers, students
ACCESS TO SERVICE: open to specific categories of users, free of charge
TYPE & DESCRIPTION OF SERVICES PROVIDED: Offers library services and bibliographic
    searches of information; provides selective dissemination of information,
    microforms and translation of documents upon request.

584 - UNIVERSITY OF PAPUA NEW GUINEA, THE MICHAEL SOMARE LIBRARY

PARENT ORGANIZATION: University of Papua New Guinea
ADDRESS: P.O. Box 319,
    University, N.C.D.,
    PAPUA NEW GUINEA
    TELEX: NE 22366
CREATED: 1966   *HEAD:* F. Griffin, Chief Librarian
SIZE OF STAFF: Professional: 50   Other: 35   Total: 85
TYPE OF SERVICE: national; public; non-profit
WORKING LANGUAGE(S): English
SUBJECT COVERAGE: education; law; political science
GEOGRAPHICAL COVERAGE: Papua New Guinea
DATA BEING PROCESSED AND SIZE: 16,000 books per year
DATA PROCESSING METHODS: computerized
HARDWARE USED: PRIME 750
SOFTWARE USED: ADLIB
STORAGE MEDIA: traditional shelving of publications; fiches; tapes;
TYPE OF ACTIVITY: data collection; publication
PUBLICATIONS: - Butler, A., A New Guinea bibliography
    - Calvert, P. J., Research in teacher education
    - Griffin, A., Issues in leadership in the 1982 elections in Papua New
    Guinea
CLIENTELE: faculty, students, public at large
ACCESS TO SERVICE: services open to all users, free of charge
TYPE & DESCRIPTION OF SERVICES PROVIDED: Provides bibliographies, on-line searches
    and inter-library loan, and maintains the "Papua New Guinea Information
    Network".

585 - CENTRO PARAGUAYO DE DOCUMENTACIÓN SOCIAL

SYNONYMOUS NAMES: CPDS
PARENT ORGANIZATION: Centro Paraguayo de Estudios Sociológicos
ADDRESS: Eligio Ayala 973,
    Casilla de Correo 2157,
    Asunción,
    PARAGUAY
    TEL: 43-734
CREATED: 1969   *HEAD:* D. M. Rivarola, Director General
SIZE OF STAFF: Professional: 4   Other: 1   Total: 5
TYPE OF SERVICE: national; private; non-profit

SYSTEMS & NETWORKS ATTACHED TO: Red Latinoamericana de Información y Documentación en
Educación (REDUC) and Centro de Documentación del Cono Sur (CEDOCSUR)
MATERIALS DESCRIBING THE SERVICE: - 1964-1980 Centro Paraguayo de Estudios
Sociológicos, 1980
WORKING LANGUAGE(S): Spanish
SUBJECT COVERAGE: social sciences; history; linguistics; education; cultural
anthropology; sociology; economics; demography; statistics
GEOGRAPHICAL COVERAGE: Paraguay
DATA BEING PROCESSED AND SIZE: 15,000 books, articles, reports, etc.
DATA PROCESSING METHODS: manual
TYPE OF ACTIVITY: data collection; data analysis; publication
PERIODICALS PUBLISHED:
- Boletín del CPDS
- Documentación Paraguaya
- Documentos y Estudios Bibliográficos
- Resúmenes Analíticos en Educación
CLIENTELE: students, teachers, researchers, experts
ACCESS TO SERVICE: open to all users

686 - INVESTIGACIONES SOCIALES, EDUCACIÓN Y COMUNICACIONES, CENTRO DE DOCUMENTACIÓN

SYNONYMOUS NAMES: BASE-ISEC, CD;
Base Social Research, Education and Communication, Documentation Center
PARENT ORGANIZATION: Base, Investigaciones Sociales, Educación y Comunicaciones
(BASE-ISEC)
ADDRESS: Montevideo 822,
Casilla de Correo 1814,
Asunción,
PARAGUAY
TEL: (595 21) 45-081
CREATED: 1985   *HEAD:* H. G. De Rolón, Documentalist
SIZE OF STAFF: Professional: 2   Other: 1   Total: 3
TYPE OF SERVICE: national; private; non-profit
MATERIALS DESCRIBING THE SERVICE: - Cómo se utilizan los catálogos del Centro de
documentación, H. Rolón, 1986
WORKING LANGUAGE(S): Spanish
SUBJECT COVERAGE: social sciences; demography; education; political science;
anthropology; sociology
GEOGRAPHICAL COVERAGE: Paraguay
DATA BEING PROCESSED AND SIZE: 1,800 documentation items; 70 periodicals
DATA PROCESSING METHODS: computerized
HARDWARE USED: IBM PC AT
SOFTWARE USED: Micro-ISIS; DBase III; Wordstar 2000 Plus
STORAGE MEDIA: traditional shelving of publications, fiches
TYPE OF ACTIVITY: data collection; distribution of information; SSID training;
publication
PUBLICATIONS: - Accession list
- Catalogues
- Bibliographies
CLIENTELE: social researchers, technicians, attendants to promotion courses
ACCESS TO SERVICE: services open to specific categories of users, free of charge

Peru / Pérou / Perú

TYPE & DESCRIPTION OF SERVICES PROVIDED: Provides library services, bibliographic
      searches of information, selective dissemination of information, provision
      of photocopies and translation of documents upon request.

Peru / Pérou / Perú

587 - BANCO CENTRAL DE RESERVA DEL PERÚ, CENTRO DE INFORMACIÓN Y DOCUMENTACIÓN

ADDRESS: Jr. Miroquesada s/n,
         Apartado Postal 1958,
         Lima,
         PERU
         TEL: 276250
CREATED: 1946   HEAD: Ms. G. Capelli Castañeda,
SIZE OF STAFF: Professional: 6   Other: 14   Total: 20
TYPE OF SERVICE: international; public; non-profit
SYSTEMS & NETWORKS ATTACHED TO: RIALIDE (Red de Información de la Asociación
      Latinoamericana de Instituciones Financieras de Desarrollo); INFOPLAN
      (Sistema de Información para la Planificación en América Latina y el Caribe
MATERIALS DESCRIBING THE SERVICE: - Servicios del Centro de Información y
      Documentación
SUBJECT COVERAGE: economics; statistics
GEOGRAPHICAL COVERAGE: Peru
DATA BEING PROCESSED AND SIZE: 50,000 books and documents; 2,270 periodicals; 50
      theses
DATA PROCESSING METHODS: partially computerized
HARDWARE USED: IBM/PC/XT
SOFTWARE USED: MICRO-ISIS
PERIODICALS PUBLISHED:
      - Información Selectiva, Monografias
      - Información Selectiva, Artículos de Revistas
      - Actualización de contenidos de Publicaciones Periódicas
CLIENTELE: researchers (1,140 per month)
ACCESS TO SERVICE: services open to specific categories of users, free of charge
TYPE & DESCRIPTION OF SERVICES PROVIDED: Provides library services, bibliographic and
      literature abstract searches, selective dissemination of information,
      photocopies and translation of documents upon request.

588 - CENTRO DE INFORMACIÓN Y DOCUMENTACIÓN DEL BANCO DE LA NACIÓN

SYNONYMOUS NAMES: CIDBAN
ADDRESS: av. Javier Prado 2465,
         San Borja,
         Apartado 1835,
         Lima,
         PERU
         TEL: 362630
         CABLE: NACION BANK-LIMA
CREATED: 1986   HEAD: F. Green Zevallos, Chief
SIZE OF STAFF: Professional: 6   Other: 7   Total: 13

TYPE OF SERVICE: international; public; non-profit
SYSTEMS & NETWORKS ATTACHED TO: RIALIDE (Red de Información de la Asociación
       Latinoamericana de Instituciones Financieras para el Desarrollo, ABUSE
MATERIALS DESCRIBING THE SERVICE: - TRIPTICO (folleto explicativo)
WORKING LANGUAGE(S): Spanish; English
SUBJECT COVERAGE: administrative sciences; demography; economics; business
       management; socio-economic development; finance; regional planning
GEOGRAPHICAL COVERAGE: Peru; Latin America
DATA BEING PROCESSED AND SIZE: 3,000 books; 200 articles; 100 reports; 100 on-going
       research; 150 seminars; 50 courses
DATA PROCESSING METHODS: partially computerized; computerized
HARDWARE USED: PC BRAIN
SOFTWARE USED: MicroISIS; Wordstar; Lotus Panacea; DBase III
STORAGE MEDIA: fiches, discs
TYPE OF ACTIVITY: data collection; data analysis; distribution of information; SSID
       scientific and methodological activities; SSID training; publication
PERIODICALS PUBLISHED:
      - Alerta Informativa CIDBAN
      - Boletin Bibliografico
CLIENTELE: economists, lawyers, accountants, administrators (approx. 220 per month)
ACCESS TO SERVICE: services open to specific categories of users, free of charge
TYPE & DESCRIPTION OF SERVICES PROVIDED: Provides library services, bibliographic and
       literature abstract searches of information, selective dissemination of
       information and photocopies.

89 - CENTRO PERUANO DE ESTUDIOS SOCIALES, CENTRO DE DOCUMENTACIÓN AGRARIO

SYNONYMOUS NAMES: AGRODATA;
       CEPES, Centro de Documentación Agrario;
       Peruvian Center of Social Studies, Agrarian Documentation Center
PARENT ORGANIZATION: Grupo de Investigaciones Agrarias, Academia de Humanismo
       Cristiano
ADDRESS: Av. Salaverry 818,
       Lima 11,
       PERU
       TEL: 336610
CREATED: 1976   *HEAD:* Mr. F. Eguren Lopez,
SIZE OF STAFF: Professional: 2   Total: 2
TYPE OF SERVICE: private
WORKING LANGUAGE(S): Spanish
SUBJECT COVERAGE: social sciences; economics; political science; cultural
       anthropology; social welfare; sociology
GEOGRAPHICAL COVERAGE: Peru; Latin America
DATA BEING PROCESSED AND SIZE: 5.000 documentation items
DATA PROCESSING METHODS: computerized
SOFTWARE USED: MICRO ISIS
TYPE OF ACTIVITY: data collection; data analysis
ACCESS TO SERVICE: services open to specific categories of users
TYPE & DESCRIPTION OF SERVICES PROVIDED: Library services, searches of information
       and on-line services, provision of photocopies upon request.

590 - ESCUELA DE ADMINISTRACIÓN DE NEGOCIOS PARA GRADUADOS, CENTRO DE DOCUMENTACIÓN

SYNONYMOUS NAMES: CENDOC/ESAN
ADDRESS: Casilla Postal 1846,
        Lima 100,
        PERU
        TEL: 351760
        CABLE: ESAN
CREATED: 1964   *HEAD:* I. R. Olivera,
SIZE OF STAFF: Professional: 6   Other: 10   Total: 16
TYPE OF SERVICE: national; private; non-profit
SYSTEMS & NETWORKS ATTACHED TO: Agrupación para la Integración de la Información
        Socio Economica (ABIISE)
MATERIALS DESCRIBING THE SERVICE: - Centro de Documentación (CENDOC)
WORKING LANGUAGE(S): Spanish
SUBJECT COVERAGE: administrative sciences; economics; management; business
        administration
GEOGRAPHICAL COVERAGE: Latin America; North America; Europe
DATA BEING PROCESSED AND SIZE: 40,000 books; 600 periodicals; 6,000 documents; 40,00
        periodical articles; 10,000 research
DATA PROCESSING METHODS: manual
PERIODICALS PUBLISHED:
        - Catálogo de Publicaciones Periódicas, 1 p.a.
        - Información Selectiva del Centro de Documentación (CENDOC), 24 p.a.
CLIENTELE: executives and members of the business community
ACCESS TO SERVICE: services open to researchers, paid services
TYPE & DESCRIPTION OF SERVICES PROVIDED: Provides retrospective searches, question-
        answer service, selective dissemination of information (users profiles),
        current awareness, photocopying, loans and abstracts (specific subjects).

591 - INSTITUTO FRANCÉS DE ESTUDIOS ANDINOS, BIBLIOTECA

SYNONYMOUS NAMES: IFEA, Bibliothèque;
        Institut Français d'Etudes Andines, Bibliothèque
ADDRESS: Contralmirante Montero 141,
        Casilla 18.1217,
        Lima 18,
        PERU
        TEL: 476070
CREATED: 1948
SIZE OF STAFF: Professional: 2
TYPE OF SERVICE: national; public; non-profit
WORKING LANGUAGE(S): Spanish; French
SUBJECT COVERAGE: social sciences; geography; history; social anthropology; cultural
        anthropology
GEOGRAPHICAL COVERAGE: Bolivia; Colombia; Ecuador; Peru
DATA BEING PROCESSED AND SIZE: 35,000 books and periodicals; on-going research;
        seminars
DATA PROCESSING METHODS: partially computerized
HARDWARE USED: IBM PC/XT
SOFTWARE USED: MICROISIS

YPE OF ACTIVITY: distribution of information; publication
ERIODICALS PUBLISHED: - Travaux de l'IFEA
- Boletín del Instituto Francés de Estudios Andinos, 2 p.a.
CCESS TO SERVICE: services open to specific categories of users, free of charge
YPE & DESCRIPTION OF SERVICES PROVIDED: Provides library services, information
searches, microforms and photocopies.

92 - INSTITUTO NACIONAL DE ADMINISTRACIÓN, ESCUELA SUPERIOR DE ADMINISTRACIÓN PÚBLICA, BIBLIOTECA

YNONYMOUS NAMES: INAP/ESAP, Library;
National Institute of Public Administration, Higher School of Public
Administration, Library
DDRESS: Av 28 de Julio 878,
Miraflores,
Apartado Postal 18-0379,
Lima,
PERU
TEL: 46-0390
REATED: 1969   *HEAD:* Ms M. I. Cubas, Director
IZE OF STAFF: Professional: 3   Other: 2   Total: 5
YPE OF SERVICE: national; public
YSTEMS & NETWORKS ATTACHED TO: Red Latinoamericana de Documentación e Información en
Administración Pública
ATERIALS DESCRIBING THE SERVICE: - Servicios que ofrece la Biblioteca, 1985
ORKING LANGUAGE(S): Spanish
UBJECT COVERAGE: administrative sciences; economics; sociology; political science;
public administration
EOGRAPHICAL COVERAGE: Peru
ATA BEING PROCESSED AND SIZE: books, reports, on-going research
ATA PROCESSING METHODS: partially computerized
ARDWARE USED: JS-286/IBM Compatible AT
OFTWARE USED: CDS/Micro-ISIS
TORAGE MEDIA: traditional shelving of publications, fiches
YPE OF ACTIVITY: data collection; data analysis; distribution of information
ERIODICALS PUBLISHED:
- Boletín de Resúmenes
LIENTELE: researchers, students
CCESS TO SERVICE: services open to specific categories of users, free of charge
YPE & DESCRIPTION OF SERVICES PROVIDED: Provides library services, bibliographic,
literature abstract searches of information and photocopies.

93 - INSTITUTO NACIONAL DE PLANIFICACIÓN, CENTRO DE DOCUMENTACIÓN

YNONYMOUS NAMES: INP;
National Planning Institute, Documentation Centre
DDRESS: Calle Siete, 229,
Rinconada Baja,
La Molina,

Peru / Pérou / Perú

        Apartado 2027,
        Lima 100,
        PERU
        TEL: 371038 - TELEX: 21393 INAPLAN
CREATED: 1975   HEAD: Mr. H. Chávez Sánchez,
SIZE OF STAFF: Professional: 2   Other: 1   Total: 3
TYPE OF SERVICE: international; public; non-profit
SYSTEMS & NETWORKS ATTACHED TO: Sistema de Información para la Planificación
        (INFOPLAN)
WORKING LANGUAGE(S): Spanish; English
SUBJECT COVERAGE: social sciences; administrative sciences; demography; economics;
        statistics; law; political science; sociology; national planning
GEOGRAPHICAL COVERAGE: Peru
DATA BEING PROCESSED AND SIZE: books; articles; reports; on-going research; seminars
DATA PROCESSING METHODS: partially computerized
HARDWARE USED: IBM AT/XT
SOFTWARE USED: MICRO/ISIS
STORAGE MEDIA: traditional shelving of publications; fiches; diskettes
TYPE OF ACTIVITY: data collection; data analysis; SSID scientific and methodological
        activities; SSID training
CLIENTELE: researchers, post-graduate students
ACCESS TO SERVICE: services open to specific categories of users, free of charge
TYPE & DESCRIPTION OF SERVICES PROVIDED: Provides library services, bibliographic
        searches of information, photocopies and translation of documents upon
        request.

594 - UNIVERSIDAD DEL PACÍFICO, BIBLIOTECA-CENTRO DE DOCUMENTACIÓN E INFORMACIÓN

SYNONYMOUS NAMES: BUP-CENDI
ADDRESS: Av. Salaverry 2020,
        Apartado Postal 4683,
        Lima,
        PERU
        TEL: 712277 - TELEX: 25650 PE CP SHERA
CREATED: 1962   HEAD: Ms. M. C. Bonilla de Gaviria, Director-General
SIZE OF STAFF: Professional: 3   Other: 5   Total: 8
TYPE OF SERVICE: national; private; non-profit
WORKING LANGUAGE(S): Spanish
SUBJECT COVERAGE: social sciences; administrative sciences; economics; political
        science
DATA BEING PROCESSED AND SIZE: 25,000 books; 5,000 documents; 300 periodicals
DATA PROCESSING METHODS: manual
TYPE OF ACTIVITY: data analysis; distribution of information; publication
PERIODICALS PUBLISHED:
        - NOVUM, Boletín Bibliográfico
PUBLICATIONS: - Catálogo de tésis 1966, 1986
CLIENTELE: 1,500 students, 100 researchers, 200 graduates, 200 teachers p.a.
ACCESS TO SERVICE: services open to specific categories of users, free of charge
TYPE & DESCRIPTION OF SERVICES PROVIDED: Provides library services, bibliographic
        searches of information using own data bases, (THESIS and Pacific Universit
        Publications), selective dissemination of information and photocopies upon

454

request.

95 - UNIVERSIDAD FEMENINA DEL SAGRADO CORÁZON, BIBLIOTECA

YNONYMOUS NAMES: Femenina University of the Sacred Heart, Library
DDRESS: Av. de Los Frutales s/n ate.,
        Apartado 3604,
        Lima,
        PERU
        TEL: 36.46.41
REATED: 1962   *HEAD:* Ms. M. La Serna de Más, Head
IZE OF STAFF: Professional: 2   Other: 12   Total: 14
YPE OF SERVICE: private
ORKING LANGUAGE(S): Spanish; English; French
UBJECT COVERAGE: social sciences; education; geography; history; law; linguistics;
        philosophy; psychology; social anthropology; cultural anthropology;
        sociology; architecture; information science; communication
EOGRAPHICAL COVERAGE: Peru
ATA BEING PROCESSED AND SIZE: 30,000 documentation items
ATA PROCESSING METHODS: partially computerized
ARDWARE USED: IBM-PC-AT
OFTWARE USED: MICRO-ISIS
TORAGE MEDIA: fiches; discs
YPE OF ACTIVITY: data collection; distribution of information; publication
ERIODICALS PUBLISHED:
        - Boletin Bibliográfico
LIENTELE: graduate students and researchers
CCESS TO SERVICE: services open to specific categories of users
YPE & DESCRIPTION OF SERVICES PROVIDED: Provides library services, bibliographic
        information searches, selective dissemination of information, and
        photocopies.

96 - BOI INDUSTRY DOCUMENTATION SERVICE

ARENT ORGANIZATION: Department of Trade and Industry
DDRESS: Industry & Investments Bldg.,
        385 Sen. Gil J. Puyat Avenue,
        P.O. Box 676,
        Makati,
        Metro Manila,
        PHILIPPINES
        TEL: 818-1831 - TELEX: (742) 45555 BOI PM
        CABLE: INVESTBORD
REATED: 1968   *HEAD:* Miss M.-S. G. Elevera, Chief Librarian
IZE OF STAFF: Professional: 4   Other: 2   Total: 6
YPE OF SERVICE: public; non-profit
YSTEMS & NETWORKS ATTACHED TO: Philippine Industrial Information Network System
ORKING LANGUAGE(S): English

SUBJECT COVERAGE: statistics; economics; investments
GEOGRAPHICAL COVERAGE: Southeast Asia; Australia; USA; Europe; Japan
DATA BEING PROCESSED AND SIZE: books, pamphlets; government reports; conference
         proceedings; periodicals; serials; UN documents; feasibility studies;
         industry studies (30,000 overall total)
DATA PROCESSING METHODS: manual
STORAGE MEDIA: traditional shelving of publications
TYPE OF ACTIVITY: data collection; data analysis; distribution of information;
         publication
PUBLICATIONS: - Current trade and industrial information
         - Current literature service
CLIENTELE: business and industrial sectors experts, both public and private
ACCESS TO SERVICE: open to researchers, free of charge
TYPE & DESCRIPTION OF SERVICES PROVIDED: Provides retrospective bibliographic and
         literature searches, question-answer service, selective dissemination of
         information, current awareness service and loan services.

597 - CHILD AND YOUTH RESEARCH CENTER

SYNONYMOUS NAMES: CYRC
PARENT ORGANIZATION: Ministry of Education, Department of Education, Culture and
         Sports (MECS)
ADDRESS: 940 Quezon Avenue,
         Quezon City,
         PHILIPPINES
         TEL: 99-79-19
CREATED: 1963   *HEAD:* Ms. L. G. Palattao-Corpus, Director
SIZE OF STAFF: Professional: 56   Other: 24   Total: 80
TYPE OF SERVICE: national; public; non-profit
MATERIALS DESCRIBING THE SERVICE: - Child and Youth Research Center Brochure
WORKING LANGUAGE(S): English; Tagalog/Pilipino
SUBJECT COVERAGE: social sciences; demography; education; psychology; social
         anthropology; social anthropology; cultural anthropology; youth and child
         development; nutrition
GEOGRAPHICAL COVERAGE: global
DATA BEING PROCESSED AND SIZE: printed documents, seminars, training courses
DATA PROCESSING METHODS: manual; partially computerized
HARDWARE USED: Microcomputer
SOFTWARE USED: MBASIC; FORTRAN; WORDSTAR; STATPAK; SUPERCALC
STORAGE MEDIA: traditional shelving in the library publication and documentation
         section
TYPE OF ACTIVITY: data analysis; distribution of information; SSID scientific and
         methodological activities; publication
PERIODICALS PUBLISHED: - The Philippine Journal of Child-Youth Development
         - The Child-Youth Research Bulletin
PUBLICATIONS: - Catalogues of completed researches
         - Capsulized abstracts of researches (handbook)
         - Handouts of research abstracts (loose leaf form)
         - Series of research results
CLIENTELE: educators, psychologists, specialists and public interested in the child-
         youth development

ACCESS TO SERVICE: services open to all users, free of charge (some paid services)
TYPE & DESCRIPTION OF SERVICES PROVIDED: Provides library services and selective
        dissemination of information.

598 - NATIONAL COMMISSION ON THE ROLE OF FILIPINO WOMEN, CLEARINGHOUSE AND INFORMATION CENTER ON WOMEN

ADDRESS: 1145 J. P. Laurel Street,
        San Miguel,
        Manila,
        PHILIPPINES
        TEL: 841-5028; 741-7314 - TELEX: ITT 40404, Telex Box: 0893
CREATED: 1981   *HEAD:* E. P. Orate-Dumlao,
SIZE OF STAFF: Professional: 5   Other: 3   Total: 8
TYPE OF SERVICE: national; public; non-profit
MATERIALS DESCRIBING THE SERVICE: - Leaflet
WORKING LANGUAGE(S): English
SUBJECT COVERAGE: social sciences; women
GEOGRAPHICAL COVERAGE: Philippines; Asia; ASEAN countries
DATA PROCESSING METHODS: manual; computerized
HARDWARE USED: IBM PC XT
SOFTWARE USED: CDS Micro ISIS and SPSS
STORAGE MEDIA: traditional shelving of publications
TYPE OF ACTIVITY: data collection; data analysis; distribution of information;
        publication
CLIENTELE: law-makers, policy-makers, program planners and implementors, professional
        researchers from universities and private organizations (local and foreign)
ACCESS TO SERVICE: services open to all users, free of charge
TYPE & DESCRIPTION OF SERVICES PROVIDED: Provides library and referral services,
        bibliographic, literature abstract, and quantitative data searches of
        information using own data base, selective dissemination of information and
        photocopies.

599 - NATIONAL ECONOMIC AND DEVELOPMENT AUTHORITY, LIBRARY

SYNONYMOUS NAMES: NEDA Library
ADDRESS: NEDA sa Quezon City Bldg., EDSA,
        Quezon City,
        Metro Manila,
        PHILIPPINES
HEAD: S. Collas-Monsod, Director General
TYPE OF SERVICE: public; non-profit
MATERIALS DESCRIBING THE SERVICE: - The National Economic and Development Authority,
        1984
WORKING LANGUAGE(S): English
SUBJECT COVERAGE: economics; economic development
GEOGRAPHICAL COVERAGE: Philippines
DATA BEING PROCESSED AND SIZE: 16,000 books; 6,150 pamphlets; 370 microfiches; 125
        microfiches; 7,500 serials

Philippines / Philippines / Filipinas

DATA PROCESSING METHODS: partially computerized
HARDWARE USED: IBM PC-AT
SOFTWARE USED: DBase III
STORAGE MEDIA: traditional shelving of publications; microfiches; microfilms; discs
TYPE OF ACTIVITY: data collection; data analysis; distribution of information; SSID
        scientific and methodological activities; SSID training; publication
PERIODICALS PUBLISHED: - NEDA Statistical Yearbook, 1 p.a.
        - Journal of Philippine Development, 12 p.a.
        - Philippine Economic Indicator, 6 p.a.
        - Philippine Development Magazine, 6 p.a.
PUBLICATIONS: - Philippine medium-term plan
CLIENTELE: government officers; students; researchers
ACCESS TO SERVICE: services open to all users, free of charge
TYPE & DESCRIPTION OF SERVICES PROVIDED: Provides library services, quantitative data
        searches, selective dissemination of information and on-line services.

600 - PHILIPPINE SOCIAL SCIENCE COUNCIL, LIBRARY

SYNONYMOUS NAMES: PSSC Library
ADDRESS: P.O. Box 205,
        U.P. Post Office,
        Diliman,
        Quezon City, 3004,
        PHILIPPINES
        TEL: 922-9621
        CABLE: PHILSOCSI
CREATED: 1968   *HEAD:* Prof. R. F. Trinidad, Executive Director
SIZE OF STAFF: Professional: 8   Other: 13   Total: 21
TYPE OF SERVICE: national; private; non-profit
SYSTEMS & NETWORKS ATTACHED TO: APINESS (Asia-Pacific Information Network in the
        Social Sciences)
MATERIALS DESCRIBING THE SERVICE: - The Philippine Social Science Center (brochure)
        - PSSC social science information special issue
WORKING LANGUAGE(S): English
SUBJECT COVERAGE: social sciences
GEOGRAPHICAL COVERAGE: Philippines
DATA BEING PROCESSED AND SIZE: 1,400 books and monographs; 570 periodicals; 310
        theses; 144 dissertations
DATA PROCESSING METHODS: manual
STORAGE MEDIA: traditional shelving of publications
TYPE OF ACTIVITY: data collection; distribution of information; publication
PERIODICALS PUBLISHED:
        - PSSC Social Science Information, 4 p.a.
PUBLICATIONS: - Directory of social scientists in the Philippines
        - Bibliography of social science research in the Philippines
        - Abstracts of PSSC: funded research projects (1973-1978; 1980-1981)
CLIENTELE: faculty members, researchers, students
ACCESS TO SERVICE: services open to all users, free of charge
TYPE & DESCRIPTION OF SERVICES PROVIDED: Provides library services, bibliographic and
        literature searches and photocpies.

458

601 - POPULATION CENTER FOUNDATION, MANAGEMENT OF INFORMATION UNIT

SYNONYMOUS NAMES: PCF-MI
ADDRESS: P.O. Box 2065,
          Makati Commercial Center,
          Makati 3117, Metro Manila,
          PHILIPPINES
          TEL: 87-70-60
          CABLE: POPCENTER
CREATED: 1972   *HEAD:* Ms. M. S. Reyes, Head
SIZE OF STAFF: Total: 9
TYPE OF SERVICE: international; private; non-profit
SYSTEMS & NETWORKS ATTACHED TO: Philippine Population Information Network; ASEAM
          Population Information Network
WORKING LANGUAGE(S): English
SUBJECT COVERAGE: demography; mass communication; social sciences; social welfare;
          family planning; population; adolescent; women and development
GEOGRAPHICAL COVERAGE: Philippines; ASEAN countries
DATA BEING PROCESSED AND SIZE: 4,650 books; 400 periodicals; 2,550 reprints/area
          file; 4,300 titles of microfiches; magnetic tapes
HARDWARE USED: IBM PC
SOFTWARE USED: DBase III
STORAGE MEDIA: traditional shelving of publications; diskettes
TYPE OF ACTIVITY: data collection; data analysis; SSID training; publication
PERIODICALS PUBLISHED:
          - Kinabukasan (Annual ·Report)
          - PCF Media Service, 12 p.a.
          - Selective Dissemination of Information, 12 p.a.
          - Quarterly Acquisitions List
PUBLICATIONS: - Union catalog of population literature in Philippine libraries, 1987
          - PCF library research guide series
          - Selective dissemination of information: a publication of the PFC on
          population health and development, 1987
          - Philippine population literature: an annotated bibliography, 1987
CLIENTELE: population program professionals, researchers, policy makers, students and
          general public (35 users per day)
ACCESS TO SERVICE: open to all users, free of charge
TYPE & DESCRIPTION OF SERVICES PROVIDED: Provides library services, bibliographic,
          literature abstract and quantitative data searches, on-line services using
          own data base, selective dissemination of information, photocopies and
          production of union catalogues and annotated inventories.

602 - TECHNOLOGY AND LIVELIHOOD RESOURCE CENTER, TECHNOBANK PROGRAM

ADDRESS: TRC Building,
          Sen. Gil J. Puyat Avenue,
          Makati,
          Metro Manila,
          PHILIPPINES
          TEL: 818.79.44
          CABLE: TECHCENTER PHILIPPINES

Philippines / Philippines / Filipinas

CREATED: 1977   HEAD: M. Tariman, Head
SIZE OF STAFF: Professional: 9   Other: 6   Total: 15
TYPE OF SERVICE: national; public; non-profit
MATERIALS DESCRIBING THE SERVICE: - Technobank update
        - Technobank brochures
WORKING LANGUAGE(S): English; Tagalog/Pilipino
SUBJECT COVERAGE: demography; economics; information science; social sciences;
        statistics; appropriate technology for livelihood; labour; social policy;
        trade; industry; development
DATA BEING PROCESSED AND SIZE: 10,578 statistical materials, 340 textual materials
DATA PROCESSING METHODS: manual; computerized
HARDWARE USED: Univac 1100/10; telex machine
SOFTWARE USED: TRC-ISIS (Technology Resource Center-integrated set of information
        systems)
STORAGE MEDIA: traditional shelving of publications; microfiches; diskettes
TYPE OF ACTIVITY: data collection; data analysis; distribution of information
CLIENTELE: businessmen, inventors, researchers, scientists, students, marketers,
        engineers, educators, corporate planners, statisticians
ACCESS TO SERVICE: open to all users; both paid and free services
TYPE & DESCRIPTION OF SERVICES PROVIDED: Services provided to subscribers include:
        systems development, Technosearch service, National Technical Information
        Service (NTIS) and Development Planning Information Service.

603 - UNIVERSITY OF THE PHILIPPINES, ASIAN CENTER LIBRARY

ADDRESS: Diliman,
        Quezon City 3004,
        PHILIPPINES
        TEL: 961821
CREATED: 1957   HEAD: Mrs. V. V. Encarnacion, Head
SIZE OF STAFF: Professional: 3   Other: 6   Total: 9
TYPE OF SERVICE: national; public; non-profit
MATERIALS DESCRIBING THE SERVICE: - Asian Center Library handbook. Diliman, Quezon
        City Asian Center. University of the Philippines, 1987
WORKING LANGUAGE(S): English
SUBJECT COVERAGE: social sciences; demography; economics; education; geography;
        history; linguistics; philosophy; political science; social anthropology;
        sociology
GEOGRAPHICAL COVERAGE: Asia; Pacific area
DATA BEING PROCESSED AND SIZE: 28,000 books; 260 current periodicals; 5,400
        documents, articles, monographs; 3,000 nonprints
DATA PROCESSING METHODS: manual
TYPE OF ACTIVITY: data collection; data analysis; publication
PERIODICALS PUBLISHED:
        - Accessions List
PUBLICATIONS: - Asian information update series on: ASEAN, East Asia
        - Union catalogue of books on Asia in the Greater Manila Area
        - A Research guide to materials on the ASEAN
        - Thesis on Asia submitted to the Asian Center, University of the
        Philippines (1983-1986), a bibliography, 1987
CLIENTELE: students, faculty and government researchers (2,500 per month)

CCESS TO SERVICE: open to all users
YPE & DESCRIPTION OF SERVICES PROVIDED: Provides library services, bibliographic
       searches and dissemination of information.

04 - UNIVERSITY OF THE PHILIPPINES, INSTITUTE OF MASS COMMUNICATION

YNONYMOUS NAMES: UP-IMC
DDRESS: Plaridel Hall,
       Diliman,
       Quezon City,
       PHILIPPINES
       TEL: 993188
       CABLE: MASSCOMM, Manila
REATED: 1965   *HEAD:* Prof. G. R. Encanto, Dean
YSTEMS & NETWORKS ATTACHED TO: University of the Philippines System (UPS)
ORKING LANGUAGE(S): English; Tagalog/Pilipino
UBJECT COVERAGE: mass communication
ATA BEING PROCESSED AND SIZE: 8,250 books and documents; 126 periodicals; 600
       journal articles; on-going research; training courses
ATA PROCESSING METHODS: manual
YPE OF ACTIVITY: data collection; data analysis; distribution of information; SSID
       scientific and methodological activities; SSID training; publication
LIENTELE: students, professionals
CCESS TO SERVICE: services open to specific categories of users, free of charge;
       some paid services
YPE & DESCRIPTION OF SERVICES PROVIDED: Provides library services, selective
       dissemination of information and information on magnetic tapes.

05 - UNIVERSITY OF THE PHILIPPINES, SCHOOL OF ECONOMICS, LIBRARY

DDRESS: Diliman,
       Quezon City 3004,
       PHILIPPINES
       TEL: 989686
       CABLE: UPECON
REATED: 1965   *HEAD:* Miss R. G. Rosali, Librarian in Charge
IZE OF STAFF: Professional: 2   Other: 10   Total: 12
YPE OF SERVICE: national; public; non-profit
ATERIALS DESCRIBING THE SERVICE: - School of Economics catalogue of information
       - Handbook (mimeographed)
ORKING LANGUAGE(S): English
UBJECT COVERAGE: economics; demography; sociology; social sciences; international
       economics; labour economics; development economics; agricultural economics;
       population
EOGRAPHICAL COVERAGE: ASEAN countries
ATA BEING PROCESSED AND SIZE: 50,000 books, pamphlets, government documents,
       periodical articles (500 periodicals)
ATA PROCESSING METHODS: partially computerized
TORAGE MEDIA: traditional shelving of publications, microfiches, microfilms, slides

TYPE OF ACTIVITY: data collection; distribution of information; publication
PERIODICALS PUBLISHED:
    - Accessions List - Filipiniana
PUBLICATIONS: - Annotated bibliography on the Philippine economy
    - Theses bibliography
    - Contents page of journals
CLIENTELE: faculty, students, government researchers
ACCESS TO SERVICE: open to specific categories of users
TYPE & DESCRIPTION OF SERVICES PROVIDED: Provides library services, bibliographic
    searches, selective dissemination of information and photocopies.

606 - UNIVERSITY OF THE PHILIPPINES, SCHOOL OF URBAN AND REGIONAL PLANNING

SYNONYMOUS NAMES: SURP
ADDRESS: E. Jacinto Street,
    Diliman,
    Quezon City 3004,
    PHILIPPINES
    TEL: 97-16-37
    CABLE: SURP
CREATED: 1965   *HEAD:* A. M. Santiago, Dean
TYPE OF SERVICE: national; public
SYSTEMS & NETWORKS ATTACHED TO: University of the Philippines System
WORKING LANGUAGE(S): English
SUBJECT COVERAGE: administrative sciences; urban planning; regional planning
GEOGRAPHICAL COVERAGE: Philippines
DATA BEING PROCESSED AND SIZE: 10,600 books; 180 periodicals
DATA PROCESSING METHODS: partially computerized
HARDWARE USED: IBM PC
SOFTWARE USED: Wordstar; Framework II; Lotus 1,2,3
STORAGE MEDIA: discs
TYPE OF ACTIVITY: data collection; data analysis; distribution of information;
    publication
PERIODICALS PUBLISHED: - Philippine Planning Journal, 2 p.a.
    - New Acquisition List
CLIENTELE: students, faculty, researchers (100 per day)
ACCESS TO SERVICE: services open to specific categories of users
TYPE & DESCRIPTION OF SERVICES PROVIDED: Provides library services, bibliographic
    searches of information and selective dissemination of information.

607 - XAVIER UNIVERSITY, MINDANAO DEVELOPMENT STUDIES CENTER, LIBRARY

ADDRESS: P.O. Box 24,
    Cagayan de Oro City,
    PHILIPPINES
    TEL: 3742
    CABLE: XAVIER, CAGAYAN DE ORO CITY, PHILIPPINES
CREATED: 1986   *HEAD:* Dr. R. McAmis, Acting Director
TYPE OF SERVICE: national; private; non-profit

MATERIALS DESCRIBING THE SERVICE: - Brochure
WORKING LANGUAGE(S): English
SUBJECT COVERAGE: social sciences; development; peace; human rights
GEOGRAPHICAL COVERAGE: Southern Philippines, and especially Northern Mindanao
DATA BEING PROCESSED AND SIZE: studies; seminar reports
DATA PROCESSING METHODS: manual
TYPE OF ACTIVITY: data collection; data analysis; distribution of information; SSID
        scientific and methodological activities; SSID training
CLIENTELE: undergraduates, graduates, research students
ACCESS TO SERVICE: services open to all users, free of charge
TYPE & DESCRIPTION OF SERVICES PROVIDED: Provides library services, bibliographic,
        literature abstract and quantitative data searches of information.

Poland / Pologne / Polonia

508 - AKADEMIA EKONOMICZNA IM. KAROLA ACADIECKIEGO W KATOWICACH, BIBLIOTEKA GŁÓWNA

SYNONYMOUS NAMES: Karol Acadiecki Academy of Economics in Katowice, Main Library
ADDRESS: ul. Bogucicka 3,
        40-226 Katowice,
        POLAND
        TEL: 58.73.85
CREATED: 1937   *HEAD:* Mgr. A. Zielezińska, Director
SIZE OF STAFF: Professional: 26   Total: 26
TYPE OF SERVICE: public
MATERIALS DESCRIBING THE SERVICE: - Sulik, A. Akademia Ekonomiczna im. Karola
        Adamieckiego w Katowicach 1937-1987, 1987
SUBJECT COVERAGE: economics; administrative sciences; demography; sociology;
        statistics; urban planning
DATA BEING PROCESSED AND SIZE: 265,000 books; 1,030 periodicals
DATA PROCESSING METHODS: manual
STORAGE MEDIA: traditional shelving of publications
TYPE OF ACTIVITY: data analysis
PUBLICATIONS: - Zdaniewicz, H., Bibliografia publikacji pracowników naukowo-
        dydaktycznych Akademii Ekonomicznej im. Karola Adamieckiego w Katowicach za
        lata 1972-1974, 1973
        - Zielezińska, A., Bibliografia publikacji pracowników naukowo-dydaktycznych
        Wyzsrej Szkoły Ekonomicznej w Katowicach, 1937-1987
ACCESS TO SERVICE: services open to all users, free of charge
TYPE & DESCRIPTION OF SERVICES PROVIDED: Services available include library services
        and bibliographic searches of information.

509 - AKADEMIA EKONOMICZNA IM. OSKARA LANGEGO WE WROCŁAWIU, BIBLIOTEKA GŁÓWNA

SYNONYMOUS NAMES: AE WR;
        Oskar Lange Academy of Economics in Wrocław, Main Library
ADDRESS: ul. Komandorska 118/120,
        53-345 Wrocław,
        POLAND
        TEL: 67.23.59 - TELEX: 712427

CREATED: 1947   *HEAD:* Ms B. Sobala, Director
SIZE OF STAFF: Professional: 38   Other: 12   Total: 50
SYSTEMS & NETWORKS ATTACHED TO: System Informacji Naukowej, Technicznej i
        Organizacyjnej (SINTO)/System of Scientific, Technical and Organizational
        Information
MATERIALS DESCRIBING THE SERVICE: - Zagrajek, E.; Zmigrodzka, B., Biblioteka Główna
        1947-1982. Informator. Wrocław 1984/Main Library 1947-1982. Guide for
        readers. Wrocław, 1983
SUBJECT COVERAGE: economics; social sciences; computer science
DATA BEING PROCESSED AND SIZE: 275,430 books; 33,970 periodicals; 65 abstract
        journals; 120 microcopies; 2,000 microfiches; 600 manuscripts; 78
        audiovisual materials
DATA PROCESSING METHODS: partially computerized
HARDWARE USED: RIAD R-32
SOFTWARE USED: OS/MVT
STORAGE MEDIA: traditional shelving of publications; fiches; discs; microfiches;
        microfilms
TYPE OF ACTIVITY: data collection; publication
CLIENTELE: researchers, students
ACCESS TO SERVICE: open to all users free of charge
TYPE & DESCRIPTION OF SERVICES PROVIDED: Provides library services and bibliographi
        searches of information using "OZAGA" database through the Institute of
        Administration and Management. Also provides microfilms and photocopies.

610 - AKADEMIA EKONOMICZNA W KRAKOWIE, BIBLIOTEKA GŁÓWNA

SYNONYMOUS NAMES: AEK;
        Academy of Economics in Cracow, Library
ADDRESS: The Central Library,
        Academy of Economics,
        ul. Rakowicka 27,
        31-510 Cracow,
        POLAND
        TEL: 21.07.06 - TELEX: 0325414
CREATED: 1925   *HEAD:* Ms. M. Pęczaksja, Director
SIZE OF STAFF: Professional: 21   Other: 21   Total: 42
TYPE OF SERVICE: international; public; non-profit
SYSTEMS & NETWORKS ATTACHED TO: Centrum Informacji Naukowej, Technicznej i
        Ekonomicznej, Warszawa (CINTE)/National Center for Scientific, Technical a
        Economic Information (SINTO)
MATERIALS DESCRIBING THE SERVICE: - Informator Biblioteka Słowna AE w Krakowie, 198
WORKING LANGUAGE(S): Polish
SUBJECT COVERAGE: social sciences; economics; political science; sociology
DATA BEING PROCESSED AND SIZE: 228,400 books; 1,200 periodicals & abstract journals
        30,000 maps, atlases, audiovisual materials
DATA PROCESSING METHODS: manual
STORAGE MEDIA: traditional shelving of publications; fiches; microfiches
TYPE OF ACTIVITY: data collection; data analysis; distribution of information;
        publication
PUBLICATIONS: - Prace bibliograficzne: przeglad dorobku naukowego pracowników
        Akademii Ekonomicznej w Krakowie

- Wykaz nabytków zagranicznych: w wyborze
LIENTELE: students, institutions (3,000 p.a.)
ACCESS TO SERVICE: open to all users, free of charge
YPE & DESCRIPTION OF SERVICES PROVIDED: Provides library services, bibliographies,
        selective dissemination of information, list of documents for exchange,
        accession list of all foreign books, and bibliographic, literature and
        survey data searches in its own data base.

11 - AKADEMIA EKONOMICZNA W POZNANIU, BIBLIOTEKA GŁÓWNA

SYNONYMOUS NAMES: Academy of Economics in Poznan, Main Library
PARENT ORGANIZATION: Akademia Ekonomica w Poznaniu
ADDRESS: Marchliewskiego 146/150,
        60-967 Poznań,
        POLAND
        TEL: 524-15, 699-261 (ext. 10-65) - TELEX: 0413390
CREATED: 1926   *HEAD:* Dr. J. Sójka, Director
SIZE OF STAFF: Professional: 44   Other: 4   Total: 48
TYPE OF SERVICE: national; public; non-profit
MATERIALS DESCRIBING THE SERVICE: - Biblioteka Akademii Ekonomicznej w Poznaniu,
        informator, Poznań 1980
WORKING LANGUAGE(S): Polish; English; French; German; Russian; Italian
SUBJECT COVERAGE: social sciences
GEOGRAPHICAL COVERAGE: Poland
DATA BEING PROCESSED AND SIZE: 177,370 books; 32,510 periodicals; 85 abstract
        journals; microcopies; catalogues; bibliographical references of subjects of
        studies
DATA PROCESSING METHODS: manual; partially computerized
HARDWARE USED: ODRA 1305
STORAGE MEDIA: traditional shelving of publications; fiches; tapes; microfiches
TYPE OF ACTIVITY: publication; SSID scientific and methodological activities; SSID
        training; distribution of information
PERIODICALS PUBLISHED:
        - Wykaz Nabytków
        - Informacja Adresowana
CLIENTELE: researchers, students (approx. 3,000 p.a.)
ACCESS TO SERVICE: services open to all users, free of charge
TYPE & DESCRIPTION OF SERVICES PROVIDED: Provides library services, bibliographic and
        literature searches, microfilms and photocopies.

12 - AKADEMIA TEOLOGII KATOLICKIEJ, WARSZAWA, BIBLIOTEKA

SYNONYMOUS NAMES: Catholic Academy of Theology in Warsaw, Library
ADDRESS: ul. Dewajtis 3,
        01-653 Warsaw,
        POLAND
        TEL: 34.72.91
CREATED: 1954   *HEAD:* Mgr. A. Dubec, Director
SIZE OF STAFF: Professional: 7   Other: 5   Total: 12

Poland / Pologne / Polonia

TYPE OF SERVICE: international; national; public
SUBJECT COVERAGE: social sciences; geography; law; philosophy; psychology; religion
    theology; canon law
DATA BEING PROCESSED AND SIZE: 140,000 books; 2,411 periodicals; 600 microcopies;
    2,400 manuscripts
DATA PROCESSING METHODS: manual
STORAGE MEDIA: traditional shelving of publications
TYPE OF ACTIVITY: distribution of information; publication
ACCESS TO SERVICE: services open to all users, free of charge
TYPE & DESCRIPTION OF SERVICES PROVIDED: Provides library services and bibliographi
    searches of information using own data base and catalogues.

613 - AKADEMII NAUK SPOŁECZNYCH, OŚRODEK INFORMACJI NAUKOWEJ I BIBLIOTEKA

SYNONYMOUS NAMES: Academy of Social Sciences, Scientific Information Centre and
    Library
ADDRESS: ul. Bagatela 2,
    00-585 Warsaw,
    POLAND
    TEL: 284391
CREATED: 1950   *HEAD:* Mr. E. Król, Director of the Library
    E. Zaworski, Director of the Scientific Information Centre
SIZE OF STAFF: Professional: 35   Other: 5   Total: 40
SYSTEMS & NETWORKS ATTACHED TO: System of Scientific, Technical and Organizational
    Information (SINTO)
MATERIALS DESCRIBING THE SERVICE: - Eligiusz, L., Działalność Ośzodka Informacji
    Naukowej WSNS. Zeszyty Naukowe WSNS, 1977 no. 1
SUBJECT COVERAGE: social sciences; political science; philosophy; sociology;
    international labour movement; Marxist philosophy
DATA BEING PROCESSED AND SIZE: 170,000 books; 490 journals; 270,000 abstract cards
DATA PROCESSING METHODS: manual
STORAGE MEDIA: traditional shelving of publications; fiches
TYPE OF ACTIVITY: data collection; data analysis; publication
PERIODICALS PUBLISHED:
    - Biuletyn Informacyjny Ośrodka Informacji Naukowej ANS
PUBLICATIONS: - Wspołczesny miedzynarodowy ruch robotniczy. Materiały bibliograficz
    - Marksizm-Leninizm. Materiały bibliograficzne
    - Partie i systemy polityczne we wspołczesnym swiecie. Bibliografia
ACCESS TO SERVICE: open to all users, free of charge
TYPE & DESCRIPTION OF SERVICES PROVIDED: The Centre provides library services,
    bibliographic, literature and survey data searches and selective
    dissemination of information.

614 - CENTRAL EUROPEAN MASS COMMUNICATION RESEARCH DOCUMENTATION CENTRE

SYNONYMOUS NAMES: CECOM
PARENT ORGANIZATION: Press Research Centre
ADDRESS: Rynek Główny 23,
    31-008 Krakow,

POLAND
TEL: 22.06.44
REATED: 1974   *HEAD:* Prof. Dr. W. Pisarek, Director
IZE OF STAFF: Professional: 3   Other: 1   Total: 4
YPE OF SERVICE: international; Public
YSTEMS & NETWORKS ATTACHED TO: COMNET (International Network of Documentation
        Centres on Communication Research and Policies)
UBJECT COVERAGE: sociology; political science; mass communication
EOGRAPHICAL COVERAGE: Central and Eastern Europe
ATA BEING PROCESSED AND SIZE: books, articles (300 p.a.)
ATA PROCESSING METHODS: partially computerized
ARDWARE USED: IBM PC/XT
OFTWARE USED: DBase III
TORAGE MEDIA: traditional shelving of publications
YPE OF ACTIVITY: data collection; data analysis; publication
ERIODICALS PUBLISHED:
        - Mass Communication Research/Current Documentation, 2 p.a.
LIENTELE: media researchers, research centres, educators in journalism and mass
        communication (500 p.a.)
CCESS TO SERVICE: services open to specific categories of users, some paid services
YPE & DESCRIPTION OF SERVICES PROVIDED: Provides bibliographic and literature
        abstract searches, selective dissemination of information and photocopies
        (against payment).

15 - CENTRALNA BIBLIOTEKA STATYSTYCZNA

YNONYMOUS NAMES: CBS;
        Central Statistical Library
ARENT ORGANIZATION: Główny Urząd Statystyczny/Central Statistical Office
DDRESS: Aleja Niepodległości 208,
        00-925 Warsaw,
        POLAND
        TEL: 25.03.45; 25.73.97 - TELEX: 816059 cbs pl
REATED: 1918   *HEAD:* Mr. A. Jopkiewicz, Director
IZE OF STAFF: Total: 25
YPE OF SERVICE: national; public; non-profit
YSTEMS & NETWORKS ATTACHED TO: System of Scientific, Technical and Organizational
        Information (SINTO)
ATERIALS DESCRIBING THE SERVICE: - Informator o polskich bibliotekach
        ekonomicznych/Guide book of Polish economic libraries, 1987
ORKING LANGUAGE(S): Polish
UBJECT COVERAGE: demography; economics; statistics
EOGRAPHICAL COVERAGE: global
ATA BEING PROCESSED AND SIZE: 217,000 books; 91,000 periodicals
ATA PROCESSING METHODS: manual
TORAGE MEDIA: traditional shelving of publications
YPE OF ACTIVITY: data analysis; SSID training; publication
UBLICATIONS: - Bibliografia mydaconictu GUS
        - Bibliografia polskiego pis'miennictwa demograficinego
        - Bibligrafia polskiego pis'miennictwa statystycznego
LIENTELE: statistical offices, international organizations, libraries, other

institutions, individual users (485 users, p.a.)
ACCESS TO SERVICE: services open to all users, free of charge
TYPE & DESCRIPTION OF SERVICES PROVIDED: Provides library services, bibliographic,
    literature and survey and quantitative data searches, and photocopies.

616 - GŁÓWNA BIBLIOTEKA PRACY I ZABEZPIECZENIA SPOŁECZNEGO

SYNONYMOUS NAMES: GBP;
    Central Library of Labour and Social Security
PARENT ORGANIZATION: Ministry of Labour, Wages and Social Affairs
ADDRESS: ul. Mysia 2,
    00-496 Warsaw,
    POLAND
    TEL: 29-96-33
CREATED: 1974   HEAD: M. Kłossowska, Director
SIZE OF STAFF: Professional: 15   Other: 4
TYPE OF SERVICE: national; public; non-profit
SYSTEMS & NETWORKS ATTACHED TO: System Informacji Naukowej, Technicznej i
    Organizacyjnej/National System of the Scientific, Technical and
    Organizational Information (SINTO)
MATERIALS DESCRIBING THE SERVICE: - Guide for readers. Warsaw: Central Library of
    Labour and Social Security, 1987, 8 p.
SUBJECT COVERAGE: economics; social sciences; social welfare; labour; social securi
GEOGRAPHICAL COVERAGE: Poland
DATA BEING PROCESSED AND SIZE: 44,890 vol. of books; 13,200 vol. of periodicals;
    3,500 vol. of publications of the International Labour Office; 8,500
    documentation cards of the CMEA publications; 6,000 press-cuttings
DATA PROCESSING METHODS: manual
TYPE OF ACTIVITY: distribution of information; publication
PERIODICALS PUBLISHED: - Przeglad Dokumentacyjny/Documentation Review, 12 p.a. sinc
    1963
PUBLICATIONS: - Bibliografia ekonomicznych i społecznych zagadnień pracy/Bibliograp
    of economic and social problems of labour
    - Monothematic bibliographies
CLIENTELE: research workers, students, libraries, colleges, entreprises (around 3,0
    p.a.)
ACCESS TO SERVICE: services open to all users and to researchers particularly, free
    of charge
TYPE & DESCRIPTION OF SERVICES PROVIDED: Provides retrospective bibliographic
    searches, current awareness service, question-answer service, loan of
    documents, editing of reference works, exchanging of books and periodicals

617 - INSTYTUT FILOZOFII I SOCJOLOGII, OŚRODEK DOKUMENTACJI I INFORMACJI NAUKOWEJ, BIBLIOTEKA

SYNONYMOUS NAMES: IFiS/ODiIN;
    Institute of Philosophy and Sociology, Department of Documentation and
    Information Sciences, Library
PARENT ORGANIZATION: Polska Akademia Nauk/Polish Academy of Sciences

DDRESS: ul. Nowy Swiat 72,
00330 Warsaw,
POLAND
TEL: 26.71.81
REATED: 1956   *HEAD:* Prof. Dr. M. Kazimierz, Director
IZE OF STAFF: Total: 19
UBJECT COVERAGE: philosophy; sociology
ATA BEING PROCESSED AND SIZE: 140,000 books; 2,600 periodicals; 781 microcopies; 600
manuscripts
ATA PROCESSING METHODS: manual
TORAGE MEDIA: traditional shelving of publications
YPE OF ACTIVITY: data analysis; publication
ERIODICALS PUBLISHED:
- Acquisitions List
CCESS TO SERVICE: open to all users, free of charge
YPE & DESCRIPTION OF SERVICES PROVIDED: Provides library services, bibliographic,
literature and survey data searches.

18 - INSTYTUT GEOGRAFII I ZAGOSPODAROWANIA PRZESTRZENNEGO PAN

YNONYMOUS NAMES: Institute of Geography and Spatial Organization of the Polish
Academy of Sciences
ARENT ORGANIZATION: Polish Academy of Sciences
DDRESS: ul. Krakowskie Przedmiescie 30,
00-927 Warsaw,
POLAND
TEL: 261931 - TELEX: 81 79 35
EAD: Prof. Dr. P. Korcelli,
YPE OF SERVICE: international; public; non-profit
ORKING LANGUAGE(S): Polish
UBJECT COVERAGE: geography; social sciences; administrative sciences; demography;
economics; geography
EOGRAPHICAL COVERAGE: global
ATA BEING PROCESSED AND SIZE: books; articles; reports; on-going research; seminars
ATA PROCESSING METHODS: manual
ERIODICALS PUBLISHED: - Geographia Polonica
- Przeglad Geograficzny
- Prace Geograficzne
- Dokumentacja Geograficzna
CCESS TO SERVICE: services open to specific categories of users, some paid services
YPE & DESCRIPTION OF SERVICES PROVIDED: Provides library services and bibliographic
and quantitative data searches.

19 - INSTYTUT NAUK EKONOMICZNYCH PAN, BIBLIOTEKA

YNONYMOUS NAMES: Institute of Economics of the Polish Academy of Sciences, Library
ARENT ORGANIZATION: Polska Akademia Nauk
DDRESS: ul. Kniewskiego 1,
00-019 Warsaw,

POLAND
HEAD: Prof. J. Pajestka, Director
SIZE OF STAFF: Professional: 67   Other: 15   Total: 82
TYPE OF SERVICE: public; non-profit
WORKING LANGUAGE(S): Polish
SUBJECT COVERAGE: economics; social welfare
DATA BEING PROCESSED AND SIZE: books; articles; reports
DATA PROCESSING METHODS: partially computerized
TYPE OF ACTIVITY: data analysis; SSID scientific and methodological activities;
        publication
PERIODICALS PUBLISHED: - Studia Ekonomiczne. Serie. Wroclaw. Ossolineum.
        - Studia i Materiaty. Serie. Warszawa. Instytut Nauk Ekonomicznych PAN
CLIENTELE: scientists
ACCESS TO SERVICE: services open to all users, free of charge
TYPE & DESCRIPTION OF SERVICES PROVIDED: Provides library services, bibliographic a■
        literature abstract searches.

**620 - INSTYTUT PAŃSTWA I PRAWA POLSKIEJ AKADEMII NAUK, ZAKŁAD DOCUMENTACJI I
    INFORMACJI, BIBLIOTEKA**

SYNONYMOUS NAMES: The Institute of the State and Law of the Polish Academy of
        Sciences, Section of Documentation and Information, Library
PARENT ORGANIZATION: Polska Akademia Nauk/Polish Academy of Sciences
ADDRESS: Nowy Swiat 72,
        00-330 Warsaw,
        POLAND
        TEL: 26.52.31
CREATED: 1956   *HEAD:* Z. Nałecz, Chief
SIZE OF STAFF: Professional: 6   Other: 4   Total: 10
TYPE OF SERVICE: public; non-profit
WORKING LANGUAGE(S): Polish; French
SUBJECT COVERAGE: law; social sciences; administrative sciences; criminology;
        political science; social welfare
GEOGRAPHICAL COVERAGE: Eastern Europe; global
DATA BEING PROCESSED AND SIZE: 34,500 books; 800 periodicals; 67 microcopies; 2,000
        manuscripts
DATA PROCESSING METHODS: manual
STORAGE MEDIA: traditional shelving of publications; fiches
TYPE OF ACTIVITY: data collection; publication
PERIODICALS PUBLISHED: - Polska Bibliografia Prawnicza/Polish Juridical Bibliograph
        1 p.a.
ACCESS TO SERVICE: services open to all users, free of charge
TYPE & DESCRIPTION OF SERVICES PROVIDED: Provides library services, bibliographic,
        literature and survey data searches. Its data base "Polish Juridical
        Bibliography" consists of 22 vols. of Polish Juridical Bibliography, each
        of them offering 6,000 fiches.

21 - INSTYTUT PAŃSTWA I PRAWA POLSKIEJ AKADEMIII NAUK, CENTRUM DOKUMENTACJI INFORMACJI NAUKOWEJ O PRAWACH CZŁOWIEKA

YNONYMOUS NAMES: Institute of State and Law of the Polish Academy of Sciences, Human Rights Scientific Documentation and Information Centre
DDRESS: ul. Mielżyńskiego 27/29,
      61-725 Poznan,
      POLAND
      TEL: 520-260
REATED: 1981   *HEAD:* Dr. Z. Kedzia, Head
YSTEMS & NETWORKS ATTACHED TO: HURIDOCS (Human Rights Information and Documentation System)
UBJECT COVERAGE: human rights; law; administrative sciences; philosophy
ATA BEING PROCESSED AND SIZE: books; articles; documents; reports
YPE OF ACTIVITY: data collection; data analysis; distribution of information
ERIODICALS PUBLISHED:
    - Human rights. Documents
LIENTELE: scholars, teachers, parliamentarians, social movements representatives
CCESS TO SERVICE: open to all users
YPE & DESCRIPTION OF SERVICES PROVIDED: Provides library services, bibliographic and literature searches, selective dissemination of information, photocopies, and translations upon request.

22 - INSTYTUT ROZWOJU WSI I ROLNICTWA

YNONYMOUS NAMES: Institute of Rural and Agricultural Development
ARENT ORGANIZATION: Polska Akademia Nauk/Polish Academy of Sciences
DDRESS: Pałac Staszica,
      ul. Nowy Swiat 72,
      00-330 Warsaw,
      POLAND
      TEL: 26-94-36
REATED: 1971   *HEAD:* Prof. Dr. J. Okuniewski, Director
IZE OF STAFF: Professional: 42   Other: 24   Total: 66
ORKING LANGUAGE(S): Polish; Russian; English; German
UBJECT COVERAGE: social sciences; sociology; economics; rural sociology; ethnology; agricultural development
ATA BEING PROCESSED AND SIZE: 4,000 books; 1,000 periodicals; 200 manuscripts
ATA PROCESSING METHODS: partially computerized
TORAGE MEDIA: traditional shelving of publications; tapes
YPE OF ACTIVITY: data collection; SSID scientific and methodological activities; publication
ERIODICALS PUBLISHED: - Wieś i Rolnictwo/Countryside and Agriculture, 4 p.a. (with Russian and English summaries)
UBLICATIONS: - Problems of development of agriculture and countryside, (with Russian and English summaries)
YPE & DESCRIPTION OF SERVICES PROVIDED: Provides library services such as lending, international book exchange and interlibrary loans, bibliographic searches of information and selective dissemination of information.

Poland / Pologne / Polonia

623 - INSTYTUT ZACHODNI, BIBLIOTEKA

SYNONYMOUS NAMES: IZ;
        The Western Institute, Library
PARENT ORGANIZATION: Polska Academia Nauk/Polish Academy of Sciences
ADDRESS: Stary Rynek 78/79,
        61-772 Poznań,
        POLAND
        TEL: 527691 - TELEX: 0413420
CREATED: 1945   *HEAD:* Prof. Dr. A Czubiński, Director
SIZE OF STAFF: Professional: 6   Other: 2   Total: 8
SYSTEMS & NETWORKS ATTACHED TO: Sieć bibliotek Polskiej Akademii Nauk/Network of
        Libraries of the Polish Academy of Sciences
SUBJECT COVERAGE: history; political science; law; economics; sociology
DATA BEING PROCESSED AND SIZE: 54,730 books; 1,600 periodicals; 890 manuscripts
TYPE & DESCRIPTION OF SERVICES PROVIDED: Provides library services and bibliographic
        searches of information using own catalogues.

624 - OŚRODEK INFORMACJI NAUKOWEJ, POLSKIEJ AKADEMII NAUK, BIBLIOTEKA

SYNONYMOUS NAMES: OIN-PAN;
        Scientific Information Centre, Polish Academy of Sciences, Library;
        SIC-PAS
PARENT ORGANIZATION: Polska Akademia· Nauk (Polish Academy of Sciences)
ADDRESS: ul. Nowy Swiat 72,
        00-330 Warsaw,
        POLAND
        TEL: 26-84-10 - TELEX: 845414
CREATED: 1953   *HEAD:* Dr. A. Gromek, Acting Director
SIZE OF STAFF: Professional: 83   Other: 19   Total: 102
TYPE OF SERVICE: public; non-profit
SYSTEMS & NETWORKS ATTACHED TO: National System of Scientific, Technical and
        Organizational Information (SINTO)
MATERIALS DESCRIBING THE SERVICE: - Annual report of activities of the Polish Academy
        of Sciences
SUBJECT COVERAGE: social sciences; biology; science; political science; economics;
        sociology
GEOGRAPHICAL COVERAGE: Europe; USA
DATA BEING PROCESSED AND SIZE: 13,000 books; 540 periodicals; 8 abstract journals;
        213,000 microcopies
DATA PROCESSING METHODS: partially computerized
HARDWARE USED: IBM
SOFTWARE USED: AWIT
STORAGE MEDIA: traditional shelving of publications; tapes; microfiches
TYPE OF ACTIVITY: data analysis; publication; SSID scientific and methodological
        activities; SSID training
PERIODICALS PUBLISHED: - Zagadnienia Informacji Naukowej/Problems of Scientific
        Information
        - Przeglad Informacji o Naukoznawstwie/Review of Information on Science of
        Science
        - Przeglad Literatury Metodologicznej/Review of Methodological Literature

PUBLICATIONS: - Catalogue of microfilms
- Tugowski, B., Multilingual thesaurus in the science of science and scientific policy, 1984
ACCESS TO SERVICE: open to all users, some paid services
TYPE & DESCRIPTION OF SERVICES PROVIDED: Provides library services, bibliographic, literature and survey data searches using its own data base with 50,000 items in political science, economics and sociology. Also provides selective dissemination, microfilms and photocopies.

525 - POLSKA AMADEMIA NAUK, BIBLIOTEKA KÓRNICKA

SYNONYMOUS NAMES: Polish Academy of Sciences Kórnik, Library
PARENT ORGANIZATION: Polska Akademia Nauk
ADDRESS: Kórnik-Zamek, 62035,
 POLAND
 TEL: 170-081
CREATED: 1826   *HEAD:* Dr. J. Wislocki, Director
SIZE OF STAFF: Professional: 33   Other: 27   Total: 60
TYPE OF SERVICE: international; public; non-profit
MATERIALS DESCRIBING THE SERVICE: - Mezyński, A., Przewodnik po katalogach i informatorach Biblioteki Kórnickiej PAN /w: Pamietnik Biblioteki Kórnickiej, z.11, Kórnik 1974
- Chyczewska, A.; Weyman, S., Zamek Kórnicki. Muzeum i biblioteka. Ed. 4, Poznań 1973
- Pamietnik Biblioteki Kórnickekiej, z.1-20, Kórnik and others, 1929-1984
SUBJECT COVERAGE: social sciences; history; literature; culture; philosophy; political science; arts; sociology; linguistics; information science; science
GEOGRAPHICAL COVERAGE: global
DATA BEING PROCESSED AND SIZE: 281,700 books; periodicals; microcopies; manuscripts
DATA PROCESSING METHODS: manual
STORAGE MEDIA: traditional shelving of publications
TYPE OF ACTIVITY: publication
PERIODICALS PUBLISHED: - Pamiętnik Biblioteki Kórnickiej
PUBLICATIONS: - Various catalogues (in Polish)
CLIENTELE: scientists, students (1,050 p.a.)
ACCESS TO SERVICE: services open to all users, free of charge
TYPE & DESCRIPTION OF SERVICES PROVIDED: Provides library services, bibliographic searches of information, microfilms, microforms and photocopies.

526 - POLSKI INSTYTUT SPRAW MIĘDZYNARODOWYCH, ZAKŁAD INFORMACHI NAUKOWEJ I BIBLIOTEKA

SYNONYMOUS NAMES: Polish Institute of International Affairs, Department for Scientific Information and the Library
ADDRESS: ul. Warecka 1a,
 00-950 Warsaw,
 POLAND
 TEL: 27-28-26
CREATED: 1947   *HEAD:* L. Cyrzyk, Head

Poland / Pologne / Polonia

SIZE OF STAFF: Professional: 18   Other: 1   Total: 19
TYPE OF SERVICE: national; public; non-profit
WORKING LANGUAGE(S): Polish; English
SUBJECT COVERAGE: political science; history; law; economics; international relations
DATA BEING PROCESSED AND SIZE: 84,000 books; 250,000 articles; 3,500 microcopies
DATA PROCESSING METHODS: manual
STORAGE MEDIA: traditional shelving of publications
TYPE OF ACTIVITY: data collection; publication
PERIODICALS PUBLISHED:
        - Wykaz Nabytkow Biblioteki (accession list), 6 p.a.
CLIENTELE: around 6,000 readers p.a.
ACCESS TO SERVICE: Open to researchers and students, free of charge
TYPE & DESCRIPTION OF SERVICES PROVIDED: Provides library services and bibliographic
        data searches using its own catalogue including 300,000 bibliographical
        items.

627 - POZNAŃSKIEGO TOWARZTSTWA PRZYJACIOŁ NAUK, BIBLIOTEKA

SYNONYMOUS NAMES: PTPN/BIBL;
        Poznan Society of Friends of Arts and Sciences, Library
PARENT ORGANIZATION: Polska Akademia Nauk/Polish Academy of Sciences
ADDRESS: Mielzyński ego 27/29,
        61-725 Poznań,
        POLAND
        TEL: 5274-41
CREATED: 1857   HEAD: Dr. R. Marciniak, Assistant Professor
SIZE OF STAFF: Professional: 23   Total: 23
SYSTEMS & NETWORKS ATTACHED TO: National Network of ScOentific Libraries
SUBJECT COVERAGE: history; linguistics; literature; social sciences
DATA BEING PROCESSED AND SIZE: 126,000 books; 4,000 periodicals; 1,300 manuscripts
PERIODICALS PUBLISHED:
        - Accessions List, 1 p.a.
ACCESS TO SERVICE: services open to all users, free of charge
TYPE & DESCRIPTION OF SERVICES PROVIDED: Provides library services, bibliographic
        searches of information and photocopies.

**628 - SZKOŁA GŁÓWNA PLANOWANIA I STATYSTYKI, BIBLIOTEKA, CENTRALNA BIBLIOTEKA
        EKONOMICZNA**

SYNONYMOUS NAMES: Biblioteka SGPS;
        Central School of Planning and Statistics Library, Central Economic Library
ADDRESS: ul. Rakowiecka 22b,
        02-521 Warsaw,
        POLAND
        TEL: 49-50-13, 49-50-98 - TELEX: 816487 cbe pl
CREATED: 1906   HEAD: Dr. S. Wrzosek,
SIZE OF STAFF: Professional: 48   Other: 40   Total: 88
TYPE OF SERVICE: public; non-profit
SYSTEMS & NETWORKS ATTACHED TO: System of Scientific, Technical and Organizational

Information (SINTO)
MATERIALS DESCRIBING THE SERVICE: - Wrzosek, S.; Zabielska-Hella, A., Guidebook, 1972
    - Uniejewska, H., Biblioteka SGPS jako biblioteka centralna w dziedzinie
    nauk ekonomicznych, 1977
    - Zabielska-Helle, A., Działalność informacyjna Biblioteki Szkoły Głownej
    Planowania i Statystyki: zagadnienia informacji naukowej, 1980
SUBJECT COVERAGE: social sciences; economics
DATA BEING PROCESSED AND SIZE: 473,880 books; 16,325 periodicals; 1,880 microcopies;
    44,860 manuscripts; reports on on-going research
DATA PROCESSING METHODS: manual; partially computerized
HARDWARE USED: ODRA 1305
SOFTWARE USED: COBOL
STORAGE MEDIA: traditional shelving of publications; fiches; tapes; microfiches
TYPE OF ACTIVITY: data collection; publication
ACCESS TO SERVICE: services open to all users free of charge, some paid services
TYPE & DESCRIPTION OF SERVICES PROVIDED: Provides library services, selective
    dissemination of information, information on magnetic tapes, microfilms, and
    bibliographic, literature and survey data searches. The Centre has access to
    DIALOG and MISON - OIN PAN through the Center of Scientific Information of
    the Polish Academy of Sciences.

529 - UNIWERSYTET WARSZAWSKI, BIBLIOTEKA

SYNONYMOUS NAMES: BUW;
    The Warsaw University Library
ADDRESS: Krakowskie Przedmieście, 32,
    00-927 Warsaw,
    POLAND
    TEL: 26.41.55 - TELEX: buwar 817016
CREATED: 1817   *HEAD:* Dr. J. Krajewska, Director
SIZE OF STAFF: Professional: 430   Other: 48   Total: 478
TYPE OF SERVICE: international; public; non-profit
SYSTEMS & NETWORKS ATTACHED TO: National System for Scientific, Technical and
    Organizational Information/System Informacji Naukowej, Technicznej i
    Organizacyjnej (SINTO)
MATERIALS DESCRIBING THE SERVICE: - Biblioteka Uniwersytecka w Warszawie. Przewodnik
    Re. J. Krajeska Warszawa 1979 Wydawnictwa Uniwersytetu Warszawskiego 75
    s./Guide to the Warsaw University Library, 1979
WORKING LANGUAGE(S): Polish
SUBJECT COVERAGE: social sciences; humanities
GEOGRAPHICAL COVERAGE: global
DATA BEING PROCESSED AND SIZE: 3,880,980 vols. library holdings: books, periodicals,
    special materials as MSS, maps, atlases, prints, drawings, music prints,
    microforms
DATA PROCESSING METHODS: partially computerized
STORAGE MEDIA: traditional shelving of publications; fiches; tapes; microfiches
TYPE OF ACTIVITY: data collection; distribution of information; publication
PERIODICALS PUBLISHED: - Biennial List of Foreign Serials in Humanities and Social
    Sciences
    - List of New Foreign Acquisitions
PUBLICATIONS: - Current and retrospective bibliographies on the Warsaw University

- Catalogue of MSS of Warsaw University Library
- Catalogue of periodicals in Warsaw University Library
- Catalogue of microfilms in Warsaw University Library

CLIENTELE: academic staff, students, (55,935 readers registered in 1987)

ACCESS TO SERVICE: services open to all users, free of charge; some paid services (such as photocopies and microfilms)

TYPE & DESCRIPTION OF SERVICES PROVIDED: The Warsaw University Library is treated entirely as an information service. Since April 1979, has been functioning as "the First Central Social Science Research Library" in Poland. Provides library services, bibliographic searches of information, selective dissemination of information, provision of microfilms and photocopies. Also has access to other data bases such as BRIOLIS and Dialog through the British Institute in Warsaw.

630 - UNIWERSYTET WARSZAWSKI, POŁACZONE BIBLIOTEKI: INSTYTUTU FILOZOFII I SOCJOLOGII PAN ORAZ WYDZIAŁU FILOZOFII I SOCJOLOGII UW

SYNONYMOUS NAMES: Warsaw University, United Libraries of: Institute of Philosophy an Sociology of the Polish Academy of Sciences, Department of Social Sciences

ADDRESS: ul. Krakowskie Przedmieście 3,
00-047 Warsaw,
POLAND
TEL: 26-54-18

CREATED: 1952   *HEAD:* Mr. J. Siek, Head

SIZE OF STAFF: Professional: 18

TYPE OF SERVICE: national; public; non-profit

SYSTEMS & NETWORKS ATTACHED TO: SINTO, System Informacji Naukowej, Technicznej i Organizacyjnej

SUBJECT COVERAGE: social sciences; philosophy; political science; cultural anthropology; sociology

GEOGRAPHICAL COVERAGE: Poland

DATA BEING PROCESSED AND SIZE: 146,000 books with bibliographical and statistical data; 2,809 periodicals; 10,000 manuscripts, reports, microfilms, photographs

DATA PROCESSING METHODS: manual

PERIODICALS PUBLISHED:
- Current Bulletin of Recent Acquisitions, 4 p.a. since 1958

PUBLICATIONS: - Alphabetical and systematic catalogues for books
- Catalogue of periodicals
- Catalogue of special collections
- Catalogue of doctors' theses
- Catalogue of bibliographies preapred in the Library

CLIENTELE: academic researchers, students

ACCESS TO SERVICE: Open to all users, free of charge

TYPE & DESCRIPTION OF SERVICES PROVIDED: Library services, retrospective bibliographic searches, query answering service.

Puerto Rico / Porto Rico / Puerto Rico

31 - BIBLIOTECA REGIONAL DEL CARIBE

SYNONYMOUS NAMES: Caribbean Regional Library
ADDRESS: Box 21927,
        University Station,
        San Juan, PR 00931,
        PUERTO RICO
        TEL: 764-0000
CREATED: 1946   *HEAD:* A. Figuernoa, Librarian
SIZE OF STAFF: Professional: 2   Other: 4   Total: 6
TYPE OF SERVICE: international; public; non-profit
SUBJECT COVERAGE: social sciences; economics; history; political science; humanities
GEOGRAPHICAL COVERAGE: Caribbean area
DATA BEING PROCESSED AND SIZE: 159,000 books
DATA PROCESSING METHODS: manual
TYPE OF ACTIVITY: distribution of information
PERIODICALS PUBLISHED:
        - Current Caribbean Bibliography, irr.
CLIENTELE: researchers
ACCESS TO SERVICE: services open to all users, free of charge
TYPE & DESCRIPTION OF SERVICES PROVIDED: Provides library services, bibliographic
        searches of information and photocopies.

32 - CORTE SUPREMA, BIBLIOTECA DE DERECHO

SYNONYMOUS NAMES: Supreme Court, Law Library
ADDRESS: Box 2392,
        San Juan, PR 00903,
        PUERTO RICO
        TEL: 723-3863
CREATED: 1832   *HEAD:* Mr. R. Segarra, Director
SIZE OF STAFF: Professional: 5   Other: 12   Total: 17
TYPE OF SERVICE: national; public
WORKING LANGUAGE(S): Spanish; English
SUBJECT COVERAGE: law; civil law; common law
GEOGRAPHICAL COVERAGE: Puerto Rico; USA; Spain
DATA BEING PROCESSED AND SIZE: 80,525 books; 472 periodicals
DATA PROCESSING METHODS: manual
TYPE OF ACTIVITY: distribution of information
CLIENTELE: judges, lawyers, law students
ACCESS TO SERVICE: services open to specific categories of users, free of charge
TYPE & DESCRIPTION OF SERVICES PROVIDED: Provides library services, bibliographic
        searches of information, and photocopies.

633 - INTER-AMERICAN UNIVERSITY OF PUERTO RICO, DOMINGO TOLEDO ALAMO LIBRARY

ADDRESS: P.O. Box 8897,
Fernández Juncos Station,
Santurce, PR 00910,
PUERTO RICO
TEL: 727-1930

CREATED: 1961   HEAD: Mr. R. Sabater-Solá, Director
SIZE OF STAFF: Professional: 5   Other: 16   Total: 21
TYPE OF SERVICE: national; private; non-profit
SYSTEMS & NETWORKS ATTACHED TO: Inter-American University of Puerto Rico
MATERIALS DESCRIBING THE SERVICE: - Inter-American University School of Law catalog,
Santurce, P.R., 1986-87
WORKING LANGUAGE(S): Spanish; English
SUBJECT COVERAGE: law
GEOGRAPHICAL COVERAGE: Puerto Rico; USA; Spain; Latin America
DATA BEING PROCESSED AND SIZE: 126,940 books
DATA PROCESSING METHODS: computerized
HARDWARE USED: PCs and terminals
SOFTWARE USED: IBM / Dobis-Leuven; MEAD DATA CENTRAL - Lexis/Nexis
STORAGE MEDIA: traditional shelving of publications; fiches; tapes; discs
TYPE OF ACTIVITY: data collection; distribution of information; SSID scientific and
methodological activities
PERIODICALS PUBLISHED: - Revista Juridica de la Universidad Interamericana de Puerto
Rico
- Boletin Informativo - Biblioteca
PUBLICATIONS: - Inter-American University School of Law catalogue
CLIENTELE: law students, law professors
ACCESS TO SERVICE: services open to specific categories of users, free of charge
TYPE & DESCRIPTION OF SERVICES PROVIDED: Provides library services, bibliographic and
literature abstract searches, selective dissemination of information, and
photocopies. Also provides on-line services using own data base as well as
external data bases SOLINET and LEXIS/NEXIS.

634 - UNIVERSIDAD CATÓLICA DE PUERTO RICO, ESCUELA DE DERECHO, BIBLIOTECA DE DERECHO MONS. JUAN FREMIOT TORRES OLIVER

SYNONYMOUS NAMES: Catholic University of Puerto Rico, Law School, Mons. Juan Fremiot
Torres Oliver Law Library
ADDRESS: Ave. Las Americas,
Ponce, PR 00732,
PUERTO RICO
TEL: 844-4150

CREATED: 1961   HEAD: Ms. N. Padua, Director
SIZE OF STAFF: Professional: 5   Other: 8   Total: 13
TYPE OF SERVICE: private
SYSTEMS & NETWORKS ATTACHED TO: WESTLAW
MATERIALS DESCRIBING THE SERVICE: - Guia informativa de uso de la biblioteca
SUBJECT COVERAGE: law
GEOGRAPHICAL COVERAGE: southern region of Puerto Rico
DATA BEING PROCESSED AND SIZE: 24,950 books; 63,350 serials; 27,800 microforms;

12,880 periodicals
DATA PROCESSING METHODS: partially computerized
HARDWARE USED: IBM PC/AT, IBM PC/XT
SOFTWARE USED: Micro INMAGIC
STORAGE MEDIA: traditional shelving of publications; microforms; videocassettes
TYPE OF ACTIVITY: data collection; distribution of information; publication
PERIODICALS PUBLISHED:
     - Boletín Informativo (Nuevas Adquisiciones)
ACCESS TO SERVICE: services open to all users
TYPE & DESCRIPTION OF SERVICES PROVIDED: Provides library services, bibliographic
        information searches, photocopies, and on-line services using external data
        base "WESTLAW" available through TYMNET and TELENET.

835 - UNIVERSIDAD DE PUERTO RICO, COLEGIO UNIVERSITARIO DE CAYEY, BIBLIOTECA

SYNONYMOUS NAMES: University of Puerto Rico, University College of Cayey, Library
ADDRESS: Cayey,
      00633,
      PUERTO RICO
      TEL: 738-5651
CREATED: 1967   *HEAD:* Mr. D. González Vega, Public Services Director
SIZE OF STAFF: Professional: 8   Other: 20   Total: 28
TYPE OF SERVICE: public
MATERIALS DESCRIBING THE SERVICE: - Library resources manual
        - Library regulations
WORKING LANGUAGE(S): Spanish
SUBJECT COVERAGE: social sciences
GEOGRAPHICAL COVERAGE: Puerto Rico
DATA BEING PROCESSED AND SIZE: 84,000 books; 1,265 periodicals
DATA PROCESSING METHODS: manual
TYPE OF ACTIVITY: data collection; distribution of information; publication
CLIENTELE: students
ACCESS TO SERVICE: services open to all users, free of charge
TYPE & DESCRIPTION OF SERVICES PROVIDED: Provides library services, bibliographic
        searches of information and photocopies.

836 - UNIVERSIDAD DE PUERTO RICO, ESCUELA DE DERECHO, BIBLIOTECA

SYNONYMOUS NAMES: University of Puerto Rico, School of Law, Library
ADDRESS: Recinto Rio Piedras,
      Apartado L.,
      Rio Piedras,
      PUERTO RICO
      TEL: 764-0000
CREATED: 1913   *HEAD:* Mr. C. Delgado Cintrón, Director
SIZE OF STAFF: Professional: 10   Other: 32   Total: 42
TYPE OF SERVICE: national; public; non-profit
MATERIALS DESCRIBING THE SERVICE: - Guia del usuario
WORKING LANGUAGE(S): Spanish; English

SUBJECT COVERAGE: law
PERIODICALS PUBLISHED:
          - Boletín Bibliográfico
CLIENTELE: law students, law professors, general public
ACCESS TO SERVICE: services open to all users, free of charge
TYPE & DESCRIPTION OF SERVICES PROVIDED: Provides library services, bibliographic
          searches, selective dissemination of information, and photocopies. Also
          provides on-line services using external data bases LEXIS and NEXIS.

637 - UNIVERSIDAD DE PUERTO RICO SISTEMA DE BIBLIOTECAS, RÍO PIEDRAS CAMPUS

SYNONYMOUS NAMES: University of Puerto Rio, Rio Piedras Campus, Libraries System
ADDRESS: P.O.B. C, U.P.R. Sta.,
          Rio Piedras 00931,
          PUERTO RICO
          TEL: 385-9172
CREATED: 1903   *HEAD:* Mr. H. Muñoz Solá, Director
SIZE OF STAFF: Professional: 66   Other: 160   Total: 226
TYPE OF SERVICE: international; public; non-profit
WORKING LANGUAGE(S): Spanish
SUBJECT COVERAGE: social sciences
GEOGRAPHICAL COVERAGE: global
DATA BEING PROCESSED AND SIZE: 816,500 books; 33,000 articles
DATA PROCESSING METHODS: partially computerized
HARDWARE USED: IBM 4341
SOFTWARE USED: in-house system
STORAGE MEDIA: tapes; discs
TYPE OF ACTIVITY: data collection; distribution of information; publication
PERIODICALS PUBLISHED: - Anuario Bibliográfico Puertorriqueño
          - Boletines de Divulgación
          - Accession Lists
CLIENTELE: university professors, students
ACCESS TO SERVICE: services open to all users, free of charge
TYPE & DESCRIPTION OF SERVICES PROVIDED: Provides bibliographic searches, selective
          dissemination of information, microforms, photocopies, and on-line services
          using external data bases available through DIALOG.

**638 - UNIVERSIDAD INTERAMERICANA DE PUERTO RICO, INSTITUTO DE INVESTIGACIÓN, CENTRO
          DE DOCUMENTACIÓN DE LA MUJER**

SYNONYMOUS NAMES: Inter-American University of Puerto Rico, Research Institute,
          Documentation Centre on Women
ADDRESS: G.P.O. Box 3255,
          San Juan 00936,
          PUERTO RICO
          TEL: 766-1912
HEAD: Ms. E. Scalley, Director
TYPE OF SERVICE: non-profit
SUBJECT COVERAGE: social sciences; education; women

DATA PROCESSING METHODS: manual
STORAGE MEDIA: traditional shelving of publications
TYPE OF ACTIVITY: data collection
CLIENTELE: faculty, students, interested public, high-school students (200 p. month)
ACCESS TO SERVICE: services open to specific categories of users
TYPE & DESCRIPTION OF SERVICES PROVIDED: Provides library services, bibliographic and
       literature abstract searches of information, and on-line services.

Qatar

639 - UNIVERSITY OF QATAR DOCUMENTATION AND HUMANITIES RESEARCH CENTRE

ADDRESS: P.O. Box 2713,
       Doha,
       QATAR
       TEL: 86.76.30
CREATED: 1980   *HEAD:* Prof. Osman S. A. Ismail, Director
TYPE OF SERVICE: national; non-profit
SYSTEMS & NETWORKS ATTACHED TO: University of Qatar
SUBJECT COVERAGE: social sciences; demography; economics; geography; history;
       linguistics; social anthropology; cultural anthropology; sociology
GEOGRAPHICAL COVERAGE: Qatar; Arab countries in Arabian Gulf and Arabian Peninsula
TYPE OF ACTIVITY: data collection; data analysis; distribution of information; SSID
       scientific and methodological activities; SSID training; publication
ACCESS TO SERVICE: services open to specific categories of users, free of charge
TYPE & DESCRIPTION OF SERVICES PROVIDED: Provides library services, information
       searches, selective dissemination of information, and translation of
       documents upon request.

Romania / Roumanie / Rumania

640 - ACADEMIA DE ŞTIINŢE SOCIALE ŞI POLITICE, CENTRUL DE INFORMARE ŞI DOCUMENTARE

SYNONYMOUS NAMES: CIDSP
PARENT ORGANIZATION: Academia de Stiinte Sociale si Politice
ADDRESS: Str. Onestii,
       70119 Bucharest 6,
       ROMANIA
       TEL: 15.76.20
CREATED: 1970
SIZE OF STAFF: Total: 100
TYPE OF SERVICE: public; non-profit
SUBJECT COVERAGE: social sciences; political science
GEOGRAPHICAL COVERAGE: Romania; Europe; Eastern Europe
DATA PROCESSING METHODS: manual
TYPE OF ACTIVITY: data collection; publication
PERIODICALS PUBLISHED: - Revista de Referate si Recenzii
       - Romanian Scientific Abstracts
       - Buletin de Informare Stiintifica

641 - ACADEMIA DE ŞTIINŢE SOCIALE ŞI POLITICE, OFICIUL DE INFORMARE DOCUMENTARE IN STIINŢELE SOCIALE ŞI POLITICE

SYNONYMOUS NAMES: OIDSP;
       Academy of Social and Political Sciences, Office of Information and Documentation in Social and Political Sciences
PARENT ORGANIZATION: Academia de Ştiinţe Sociale şi Politice (ASSP)
ADDRESS: Str. Oneşti No.11, Sector 1,
       70119 Bucharest,
       ROMANIA
       TEL: 150847 - TELEX: 11939
CREATED: 1970   HEAD: Mr. V. Ipsilante, Director
TYPE OF SERVICE: national; public; non-profit
SYSTEMS & NETWORKS ATTACHED TO: INID
SUBJECT COVERAGE: social sciences; political science; history
GEOGRAPHICAL COVERAGE: global
DATA BEING PROCESSED AND SIZE: books, periodicals; bibliographical references
DATA PROCESSING METHODS: manual
PERIODICALS PUBLISHED: - Romanian Scientific Abstracts, 12 p.a. since 1973
CLIENTELE: researchers, teaching staff
ACCESS TO SERVICE: open to all users, free of charge
TYPE & DESCRIPTION OF SERVICES PROVIDED: Provides library services, bibliographical
       references, photocopies and syntheses.

642 - ACADEMIA DE ŞTIINTE SOCIALES ŞI POLITICE, OFICIUL DE INFORMARE-DOCUMENTARE

SYNONYMOUS NAMES: ASSP, Oficiul de Infomare-Documentare;
       Academy of Social and Political Science, Office for Documentary Informatio
ADDRESS: Str. Onesti nr. 9-11, Sector I,
       cod 79171,
       Bucarest,
       ROMANIA
       TEL: 147228
CREATED: 1971   HEAD: V. Ipsilante, Head
SIZE OF STAFF: Total: 14
TYPE OF SERVICE: international; public; non-profit
SUBJECT COVERAGE: social sciences
DATA BEING PROCESSED AND SIZE: books; periodicals; reports; on-going research
DATA PROCESSING METHODS: manual
PERIODICALS PUBLISHED: - Social and Political Sciences Abroad
       - Romania's History in International Historiography
       - New Books in Historical Sciences
PUBLICATIONS: - Newly discovered documents and archaeological information
       - Romanian scientific abstracts
       - Social and political sciences in Romania
CLIENTELE: researchers, teachers, students
ACCESS TO SERVICE: services open to specific categories of users, free of charge
TYPE & DESCRIPTION OF SERVICES PROVIDED: Provides library services, bibliographic a
       literature abstract searches of information, selective dissemination of
       information, information on magnetic tapes or discs and translation of
       documents upon request.

Rwanda

843 - INSTITUT AFRICAIN ET MAURICIEN DE STATISTIQUE ET D'ECONOMIE APPLIQUÉE

SYNONYMOUS NAMES: IAMSEA
ADDRESS: B.P. 1109,
     Kigali,
     RWANDA
CREATED: 1975   *HEAD:* Mr. I. Guira, Director
SIZE OF STAFF: Professional: 1
TYPE OF SERVICE: international; public; non-profit
MATERIALS DESCRIBING THE SERVICE: - Institut Africain et Mauricien de Statistique et
    d'Economie Appliquée (IAMSEA), 1985
WORKING LANGUAGE(S): French
SUBJECT COVERAGE: economics; statistics
GEOGRAPHICAL COVERAGE: Benin; Central African Republic; Cote d'Ivoire; Burkina-Faso;
    Niger; Rwanda; Senegal; Togo; Burundi; Comoros; Djibouti; Congo; Gabon;
    Madagascar; Mali; Mauritania; Zaire
DATA PROCESSING METHODS: computerized
HARDWARE USED: IBM-PC-XT
SOFTWARE USED: WORDSTAR, DBASE III PLUS, LOTUS I, II, III
STORAGE MEDIA: discs; diskettes
TYPE OF ACTIVITY: data analysis; data collection; distribution of information
PERIODICALS PUBLISHED:
    - Rapport d'Enquête, 1 p.a. since 1975
ACCESS TO SERVICE: services open to specific categories of users
TYPE & DESCRIPTION OF SERVICES PROVIDED: Provides library services, bibliographic,
    literature abstract, survey and quantitative data searches, as well as
    information on magnetic tapes.

Saudi Arabia / Arabie saoudite / Arabia Saudita

844 - KING SAUD UNIVERSITY, EDUCATIONAL RESEARCH CENTRE

ADDRESS: P.O. Box 2458,
    Riyadh 11451,
    SAUDI ARABIA
    TEL: 4674690 - TELEX: 201019 KSU SJ
CREATED: 1977   *HEAD:* Dr. O. A. Almofadda, Director
SIZE OF STAFF: Total: 10
TYPE OF SERVICE: international; public; non-profit
SYSTEMS & NETWORKS ATTACHED TO: King Abdulaziz City for Science and Technology
    (KACST); GULFNET
WORKING LANGUAGE(S): Arabic; English
SUBJECT COVERAGE: social sciences; education; psychology; sociology; cultural
    anthropology
GEOGRAPHICAL COVERAGE: Arab countries; global
DATA BEING PROCESSED AND SIZE: periodicals; reports; on-going research; seminars
DATA PROCESSING METHODS: computerized
HARDWARE USED: VMS/IBM
SOFTWARE USED: SAS, COBOL, FORTRAN, BASIC, SPSS-X, PASCAL, PLI, C, TSP, CAYLEY,
    SCRIPT, SIMSCRIPT, BMDP, SPSSC+

STORAGE MEDIA: traditional shelving of publications; microfiches, discs, tapes
TYPE OF ACTIVITY: data collection; data analysis; distribution of information; SSID
    scientific and methodological activities; publication
ACCESS TO SERVICE: services open to all users, free of charge
TYPE & DESCRIPTION OF SERVICES PROVIDED: Provide library services, bibliographic,
    literature abstracts, and quantitative data searches of information, and
    photocopies. Provides on-line services using external data bases accessed
    through KACST.

645 - MARKAZ AL-MAALOUMAT AL IHSAAIAH WA AL-TAWTHIQ AL-TARBAWI

SYNONYMOUS NAMES: Ministry of Education, Centre for Statistical Data and Educational
    Documentation (Data Center)
PARENT ORGANIZATION: Al-Tatweer al-Tarbawi, Wizarat al-M'Aref
ADDRESS: P.O. Box 2871,
    Riyadh 11461,
    SAUDI ARABIA
    TEL: 476-8831 RIYADH - TELEX: 405540 TATWIR
    CABLE: MALOMAT
CREATED: 1970   *HEAD:* Abdulaziz Ben Mohammad Ben Ghaith, Mudeer Markaz al-
    Maaloumat, Director of the Data Center
SIZE OF STAFF: Professional: 9   Other: 23   Total: 32
TYPE OF SERVICE: international; public; non-profit
MATERIALS DESCRIBING THE SERVICE: - Ministry of Education, Centre for Statistical
    Data and Educational Documentation, Manual on the services and the
    publications
WORKING LANGUAGE(S): Arabic; English
SUBJECT COVERAGE: social sciences; education; linguistics; philosophy; psychology;
    cultural anthropology; sociology; statistics
GEOGRAPHICAL COVERAGE: Saudi Arabia
DATA BEING PROCESSED AND SIZE: 4,500 documentation items p.a.
DATA PROCESSING METHODS: manual; partially computerized
STORAGE MEDIA: traditional shelving of publications, fiches, microfilms
TYPE OF ACTIVITY: data collection; data analysis; distribution of information; SSID
    scientific and methodological activities; publication
PERIODICALS PUBLISHED: - Ministry of Education: Educational Documentation, No. 20,
    p.a.
ACCESS TO SERVICE: services open to all users free of charge, with some paid servic
TYPE & DESCRIPTION OF SERVICES PROVIDED: Provides library services, bibliographic,
    literature abstract, survey and quantitative data searches of information,
    selective dissemination of information, microforms, photocopies, and
    translation of documents upon request.

646 - ARCHIVES CULTURELLES DU SÉNÉGAL

SYNONYMOUS NAMES: Cultural Archives of Senegal
ADDRESS: B.P. 11033,
    Dakar,

SENEGAL
TEL: 226.87
REATED: 1967 *HEAD:* Mr. S. N. Sar, Director
IZE OF STAFF: Professional: 12 Other: 2 Total: 14
YPE OF SERVICE: national; public; non-profit
YSTEMS & NETWORKS ATTACHED TO: Ministère de la Culture du Sénégal
ORKING LANGUAGE(S): French
UBJECT COVERAGE: social sciences; economics; history; linguistics; social
anthropology; cultural anthropology; sociology
EOGRAPHICAL COVERAGE: Senegal
ATA BEING PROCESSED AND SIZE: 970 magnetic tapes, 5,978 photographs, 4,376 colored
slides; 37 films
ATA PROCESSING METHODS: manual
YPE OF ACTIVITY: data collection; data analysis; distribution of information; SSID
scientific and methodological activities; publication
ERIODICALS PUBLISHED: - Oraliture
UBLICATIONS: - Catalogue des collections audio-visuelles No. 1 (1967-1968); No. 2
(1969); No. 3 (1.1. du 31/12/1970); No. 4 (1971-1972)
- Particularités ethniques du Sénégal-Dakar
- La Place de la femme dans les rites
- Répertoire culturel du Sénégal ACCT
- Organologie sénégalaise
- Réflexion sur la musique négro-africaine, 1975
LIENTELE: researchers, students, tourists
CCESS TO SERVICE: services open to all users, free of charge
YPE & DESCRIPTION OF SERVICES PROVIDED: Provides library services, searches of
information, selective dissemination of information and production of
information on magnetic tapes or discs.

47 - CENTRE DE RECHERCHES ET DE DOCUMENTATION DU SÉNÉGAL

YNONYMOUS NAMES: CRDS
DDRESS: B.P. 382,
Saint Louis,
SENEGAL.
TEL: 61.10.50
REATED: 1943 *HEAD:* Mr. A. H. Aidara, Director
IZE OF STAFF: Total: 16
YPE OF SERVICE: national; public; non-profit
ORKING LANGUAGE(S): French
UBJECT COVERAGE: social sciences; history
EOGRAPHICAL COVERAGE: Senegal; Western Africa
ATA PROCESSING METHODS: manual
YPE OF ACTIVITY: data collection; distribution of information; publication
LIENTELE: scholars, students, researchers, general public
CCESS TO SERVICE: services open to all users free of charge
YPE & DESCRIPTION OF SERVICES PROVIDED: Provides library services and searches of
information.

648 - CENTRE NATIONAL DE DOCUMENTATION SCIENTIFIQUE ET TECHNIQUE

SYNONYMOUS NAMES: CNDST;
        National Scientific and Technical Documentation Center
PARENT ORGANIZATION: Ministère du Plan et de la Coopération
ADDRESS: 61, bd. Pinet Laprade,
        B.P. 4010,
        Dakar,
        SENEGAL
CREATED: 1976   *HEAD:* Mr. O. Diop, Director
SIZE OF STAFF: Professional: 10   Other: 4   Total: 14
TYPE OF SERVICE: national; public; non-profit
SYSTEMS & NETWORKS ATTACHED TO: CARIS; INFOTERRA; RESADOC; ENERGIE
WORKING LANGUAGE(S): French
SUBJECT COVERAGE: economics; information science; law; social sciences; sociology
GEOGRAPHICAL COVERAGE: Senegal
DATA PROCESSING METHODS: computerized
SOFTWARE USED: CDS/ISIS
TYPE OF ACTIVITY: data collection; data analysis; distribution of information; SSID
        scientific and methodological activities; SSID training; publication
PUBLICATIONS: - Répertoires nationaux des organismes de documentation et
        d'information scientifique et technique, version 1 et 2
        - Index courants de documentation scientifique et technique, vol. 1 et 2
        - Caris, Sénégal
ACCESS TO SERVICE: services open to all users, free of charge
TYPE & DESCRIPTION OF SERVICES PROVIDED: Provides information searches of own data
        bases BIBLIO, CATOLPR and CARIS, selective dissemination of information an
        microforms.

649 - INSTITUT FONDAMENTAL D'AFRIQUE NOIRE - CHEIKH ANTA DIOP, BIBLIOTHÈQUE

SYNONYMOUS NAMES: IFAN - Ch. A. Diop, Bibliothèque
ADDRESS: B.P. 206,
        Dakar,
        SENEGAL
        TEL: 22.00.90
        CABLE: DIRIFAN, DAKAR
CREATED: 1938   *HEAD:* Mr. M. T. Diop, Librarian
SIZE OF STAFF: Professional: 5
TYPE OF SERVICE: national; public; non-profit
MATERIALS DESCRIBING THE SERVICE: - Institut Fondamental d'Afrique Noire Cheikh Ant
        Diop, 1987, Leaflet
WORKING LANGUAGE(S): French
SUBJECT COVERAGE: social sciences; natural sciences
GEOGRAPHICAL COVERAGE: Western Africa; Africa South of the Sahara
DATA BEING PROCESSED AND SIZE: 60,400 books; 7,250 brochures; 4,060 periodicals;
        1,600 microfilms; 2,600 maps; 32,000 photographs; 12,200 files of documen
TYPE OF ACTIVITY: data collection; data analysis; distribution of information;
        publication
PERIODICALS PUBLISHED: - Bulletin de l'IFAN. Série B, Sciences Humaines, 4 p.a.
        - Notes Africaines, 4 p.a.

UBLICATIONS: - Mémoires de l'IFAN
        - Initiations et études africaines
        - Catalogues et documents
LIENTELE: researchers, professors, students
CCESS TO SERVICE: open to all users
YPE & DESCRIPTION OF SERVICES PROVIDED: Provides library services, bibliographic
        researches of information and photocopies.

50 - UNIVERSITÉ DE DAKAR, FACULTÉ DES SCIENCES JURIDIQUES ET ECONOMIQUES, CENTRE DE RECHERCHES, D'ETUDES ET DE DOCUMENTATION SUR LES INSTITUTIONS ET LA LÉGISLATION AFRICAINE

YNONYMOUS NAMES: CREDILA
DDRESS: Dakar-Fann,
        SENEGAL
REATED: 1960   *HEAD:* Mr. I. Ndiaye, Director
IZE OF STAFF: Professional: 1   Total: 6
YPE OF SERVICE: public; non-profit
ORKING LANGUAGE(S): French
UBJECT COVERAGE: law; administrative sciences
EOGRAPHICAL COVERAGE: All French speaking Africa (except: Burundi, Rwanda, Zaire)
ATA BEING PROCESSED AND SIZE: bills and laws, decisions, decrees, legal texts
        published in the official gazettes of 15 African states, dissertations,
        journals dealing with African law
ATA PROCESSING METHODS: manual
TORAGE MEDIA: traditional shelving of publications
YPE OF ACTIVITY: data collection; data analysis; publication
ERIODICALS PUBLISHED: - Documentation Législative Africaine, 2 p.a.
LIENTELE: students, researchers, practitioners
CCESS TO SERVICE: open to specific categories of users, free of charge
YPE & DESCRIPTION OF SERVICES PROVIDED: Provides library and reference services.

51 - THE BRITISH COUNCIL, LIBRARY

DDRESS: 30 Napier Road,
        Singapore 1025,
        SINGAPORE (REPUBLIC)
        TEL: 473.1111 - TELEX: BRICO RS 20456
EAD: Ms. S. Aw, Librarian
IZE OF STAFF: Professional: 2   Other: 5   Total: 7
YPE OF SERVICE: public; non-profit
ATERIALS DESCRIBING THE SERVICE: - Library promotional brochure
ORKING LANGUAGE(S): English
UBJECT COVERAGE: social sciences; education; linguistics
EOGRAPHICAL COVERAGE: United Kingdom
ATA BEING PROCESSED AND SIZE: 17,000 documents; 3,000 audio-visual materials
ATA PROCESSING METHODS: manual
TORAGE MEDIA: traditional shelving of publications; microfiches

TYPE OF ACTIVITY: distribution of information
CLIENTELE: enquiries (400 per month); loans (3,000 per month)
ACCESS TO SERVICE: paid services open to all users
TYPE & DESCRIPTION OF SERVICES PROVIDED: Provides library services, bibliographic
      searches and photocopies.

652 - INSTITUTE OF SOUTHEAST ASIAN STUDIES LIBRARY

SYNONYMOUS NAMES: ISEAS Library
ADDRESS: Heng Mui Keng Terrace,
      Pasir Panjang,
      Singapore 0511,
      SINGAPORE (REPUBLIC)
      TEL: 7780955 - TELEX: RS 3708 ISEAS
      CABLE: ISEAS
CREATED: 1968   *HEAD:* Mrs. P. H. Lim, Librarian
SIZE OF STAFF: Professional: 4   Other: 12   Total: 16
TYPE OF SERVICE: national; public; non-profit
WORKING LANGUAGE(S): English
SUBJECT COVERAGE: social sciences; economics; political science; demography; social
      anthropology; cultural anthropology; sociology; history; education; law
GEOGRAPHICAL COVERAGE: Southeast Asia
DATA BEING PROCESSED AND SIZE: 67,200 books, bound periodicals and pamphlets (5,50
      p.a.); 105,500 microforms, 2,220 serials
DATA PROCESSING METHODS: manual
STORAGE MEDIA: traditional shelving of publications
TYPE OF ACTIVITY: data collection; data analysis; distribution of information;
      publication
PERIODICALS PUBLISHED:
      - Library Bulletin
PUBLICATIONS: - ASEAN: a bibliography, 1987
      - Lim, C. K., Habitat in Southeast Asia: a practical survey of folk
      architecture, 1987
      - Ong, C. S., Southeast Asian cultural heritage: images of traditional
      communities, 1986
      - Lim, P. H., Malay World of Southeast Asia: a select cultural bibliograp
      1986
CLIENTELE: researchers, teaching staff of universities, post-graduate students,
      public officials, diplomatic personnel
ACCESS TO SERVICE: services open to specific categories of users, free of charge
TYPE & DESCRIPTION OF SERVICES PROVIDED: Provides library services, retrospective
      bibliographic searches, query answering service, photocopies and microfor
      of documents.

653 - UNIVERSITY OF DURBAN-WESTVILLE, DOCUMENTATION CENTRE

SYNONYMOUS NAMES: UDW Documentation Centre
ADDRESS: Private Bag X54001,

Durban 4000,
SOUTH AFRICA
TEL: (031) 820.2350 - TELEX: 6.23228SA
CABLE: UDWEST
REATED: 1979   *HEAD:* Dr. C. G. Henning, Director
IZE OF STAFF: Professional: 2   Other: 2   Total: 4
YPE OF SERVICE: national; public; non-profit
ATERIALS DESCRIBING THE SERVICE: - Subject guide to materials accessioned at the
        Documentation Centre, University of Durban Westville, 1986, 16 p.
ORKING LANGUAGE(S): English
UBJECT COVERAGE: ethnic groups; Indian community history; social anthropology;
        cultural anthropology; demography; economics; education; political science;
        social welfare; sociology
EOGRAPHICAL COVERAGE: South Africa
ATA BEING PROCESSED AND SIZE: 115,000 documentation items (books, articles,
        newspapers, press cuttings, photographs, audio-visual, periodicals, reports)
ATA PROCESSING METHODS: partially computerized
TORAGE MEDIA: traditional shelving of publications, microfilms, microfiches
YPE OF ACTIVITY: data collection; publication
UBLICATIONS: - A General guide to materials on the Indians in South Africa, 1986
LIENTELE: students and researchers (30 per day)
CCESS TO SERVICE: services open to all users, free of charge
YPE & DESCRIPTION OF SERVICES PROVIDED: The Centre specializes on the Indian South
        African Community and provides library services and photocopies. Also
        provides cooperation in the preparation of exhibitions.

Spain / Espagne / España

54 - CENTRE D'INFORMACIÓ I DOCUMENTACIÓ INTERNACIONALS A BARCELONA

YNONYMOUS NAMES: CIDOB;
        International Information and Documentation Center in Barcelona
DDRESS: Elisabets, 12,
        08001 Barcelona,
        SPAIN
        TEL: 302.64.95 - TELEX: 99767 CIDOB-E
REATED: 1973   *HEAD:* Sr. J. Ribera Pinyol, Director
IZE OF STAFF: Professional: 4   Other: 3   Total: 7
YPE OF SERVICE: national; private; non-profit
ATERIALS DESCRIBING THE SERVICE: - Fundació CIDOB, brochure
ORKING LANGUAGE(S): Spanish; English; French
UBJECT COVERAGE: social sciences; international relations; peace; conflict;
        development
EOGRAPHICAL COVERAGE: developing countries; Latin America; Mediterranean area;
        Eastern Europe; Africa South of the Sahara
ATA BEING PROCESSED AND SIZE: 6,000 books; 110,000 articles; 620 periodicals; 3,500
        grey literature items; 2,000 reports; 7,000 manuscripts
ATA PROCESSING METHODS: computerized
ARDWARE USED: ALTOS-580; PC
OFTWARE USED: PAPYRUS; SMART
YPE OF ACTIVITY: data collection; data analysis; SSID scientific and methodological
        activities; publication

PERIODICALS PUBLISHED: - Revista CIDOB d'Afers Internacionals, 4 p.a.
- Dossier CIDOB-ROSA SENSAT (directed to teachers to help in the teaching international issues in schools)
- Dossier CIDOB (Information Bulletin), 18 p.a.
- Sobre Pau (Information and Bibliography), 18 p.a.
- Dossiers de Débate (compilation of documents and articles on specific issues)
- Dossiers d'Estudio
- DSI-CIDOB

ACCESS TO SERVICE: services open to all users, some paid services
TYPE & DESCRIPTION OF SERVICES PROVIDED: CIDOB maintains a research library specialized in international issues. It provides library services, bibliographic searches of information using its own data base, CIDOB, selective dissemination of information and photocopies.

655 - CENTRO DE DOCUMENTACIÓN ESPAÑOL DE LA COMUNICACIÓN

SYNONYMOUS NAMES: IBERCOMNET;
Spanish Mass Communication Documentation Centre
PARENT ORGANIZATION: Facultad de Ciencias de la Información
ADDRESS: Ciudad Universitaria s/n,
28040 Madrid,
SPAIN
TEL: 449-0300 - TELEX: 41793 UCINF
CREATED: 1980   HEAD: Mr. A. Garcia Gutierrez, Director
SIZE OF STAFF: Professional: 4   Other: 6   Total: 10
TYPE OF SERVICE: national; public; non-profit
SYSTEMS & NETWORKS ATTACHED TO: COMNET (Réseau des Centres de Documentation pour la Recherche et les Politiques de la Communication)
MATERIALS DESCRIBING THE SERVICE: - IBERCOMNET (brochure)
WORKING LANGUAGE(S): Spanish; Catalan, Galicien; Basque
SUBJECT COVERAGE: mass communication; sociology of communication; cross-cultural communication process; social sciences
GEOGRAPHICAL COVERAGE: Spain
DATA BEING PROCESSED AND SIZE: 17,000 books, articles, reports and Ph.D. theses
HARDWARE USED: IBM
SOFTWARE USED: Stairs; Docutex
STORAGE MEDIA: fiches; magnetic tapes
TYPE OF ACTIVITY: data collection; data analysis; SSID training
PERIODICALS PUBLISHED: - Spanish Mass Communication Bibliography (part of the annual periodical: "Documentación de las Ciencias de la Información")
- IBERCOMNET Newsletter
CLIENTELE: researchers, practitioners, students
ACCESS TO SERVICE: services open to specific categories of users, free of charge
TYPE & DESCRIPTION OF SERVICES PROVIDED: Provides on-line and bibliographic and literature abstract searches of information using own data base "BIES/PIC", computer listings and information on magnetic tapes or discs.

56 - GOBIERNO VASCO, DEPARTAMENTO DE PRESIDENCIA, INSTITUTO VASCO DE ADMINISTRACIÓN PÚBLICA, SERVICIO CENTRAL DE ARCHIVO, BIBLIOTECA Y DOCUMENTACIÓN

SYNONYMOUS NAMES: Basque Government, Department of Presidence, Basque Institute of
      Public Administration, Archive, Library and Documentation Central Service
ADDRESS: Duque de Wellington 2,
      01011 Vitoria-Gasteiz (Alava),
      SPAIN
      TEL: 24 60 00 - TELEX: 35 218 EUJK E - TELEFAX: 2/m (945) 243 095
CREATED: 1981   *HEAD:* Ms. M. Begoña Uriguen, Head
SIZE OF STAFF: Professional: 11   Other: 5   Total: 16
TYPE OF SERVICE: private; non-profit
MATERIALS DESCRIBING THE SERVICE: - Instituto Vasco de Administración Pública.
      Memoria de Actividades1986-1987, 1988
WORKING LANGUAGE(S): Spanish; Euskera
SUBJECT COVERAGE: administrative sciences; economics; public administration
GEOGRAPHICAL COVERAGE: Basque region, Spain
DATA BEING PROCESSED AND SIZE: 20,000 books; 300 periodicals; 75,000 microfiches
DATA PROCESSING METHODS: partially computerized
HARDWARE USED: BULL, DPS 7
SOFTWARE USED: MISTRAL V 5
TYPE OF ACTIVITY: data collection; data analysis; distribution of information; SSID
      training; publication
PERIODICALS PUBLISHED:
      - Boletín Bibliográfico
PUBLICATIONS: - Indice mensual del boletín oficial del Pais Vasco
ACCESS TO SERVICE: services open to specific categories of users
TYPE & DESCRIPTION OF SERVICES PROVIDED: Provides library services, selective
      dissemination of information, bibliographic and literature abstract searches
      of information, using own data bases: BOPV, JURICON, INFORPO, SEGUILEX,
      BIBLIO. Has also access to external data bases CELEX, LEDA, INDILEX and
      OUC..

57 - INSTITUTO DE COOPERACIÓN IBEROAMERICANA, BIBLIOTECA HISPÁNICA

SYNONYMOUS NAMES: Institute of Iberoamerican Cooperation, Hispanic Library
ADDRESS: Avenida de los Reyes Católicos, 4,
      Ciudad Universitaria,
      28040 Madrid,
      SPAIN
      TEL: 2440600
CREATED: 1945   *HEAD:* Mr. A. Cabello,
SIZE OF STAFF: Professional: 16   Other: 19   Total: 35
TYPE OF SERVICE: international; public; non-profit
SUBJECT COVERAGE: social sciences; economics; geography; history; political science;
      cultural anthropology; sociology
GEOGRAPHICAL COVERAGE: Latin America; Philippines
DATA BEING PROCESSED AND SIZE: 210,000 books; 8,500 periodicals
DATA PROCESSING METHODS: manual
PERIODICALS PUBLISHED:
      - Relación de Obras Incorporadas, 12 p.a.

CLIENTELE: researchers, students (35,000 p.a.)

ACCESS TO SERVICE: open to all users, free of charge

TYPE & DESCRIPTION OF SERVICES PROVIDED: Provides library services, photocopies an
bibliographical information.

658 - INSTITUTO DE INFORMACIÓN Y DOCUMENTACIÓN EN CIENCIAS SOCIALES Y HUMANIDADES

SYNONYMOUS NAMES: ISOC;
Institute for Information and Documentation in Social Sciences and
Humanities

PARENT ORGANIZATION: CENIDOC. Consejo Superior de Investigaciones Científicas,
Ministerio de Educación y Ciencia

ADDRESS: c/PINAR, 25 - 3a planta,
28006 Madrid,
SPAIN
TEL: 262.77.55

CREATED: 1975   *HEAD:* A. Roman, Director

SIZE OF STAFF: Professional: 17   Other: 26   Total: 43

TYPE OF SERVICE: national; public; non-profit

SYSTEMS & NETWORKS ATTACHED TO: Network of Automatized Scientific Information; Red
INCA

MATERIALS DESCRIBING THE SERVICE: - ISOC brochure

WORKING LANGUAGE(S): Spanish

SUBJECT COVERAGE: social sciences; humanities

GEOGRAPHICAL COVERAGE: Spain

DATA BEING PROCESSED AND SIZE: 1,500 books; 1,180 periodicals; 121 abstract journa

DATA PROCESSING METHODS: computerized

HARDWARE USED: UNIVAC 1100 and DIAL-UP Terminal

TYPE OF ACTIVITY: data analysis; publication; SSID scientific and methodological
activities; SSID training

PERIODICALS PUBLISHED: - Indice Español de Ciencias Sociales. Serie A: Psicología,
Ciencias de la Educación, 1 p.a.
- Indice Español de Ciencias Sociales. Serie B: Economía, Sociología,
Política, Urbanismo, 1 p.a.
- Indice Español de Ciencias Sociales. Serie C: Derecho, 1 p.a.
- Indice Español de Humanidades, 1 p.a.

PUBLICATIONS: - Serie A: psicología y ciencias de la educación
- Serie B: economía, sociología, ciencias políticas y urbanismo
- Serie C: derecho

ACCESS TO SERVICE: open to all users, paid services

TYPE & DESCRIPTION OF SERVICES PROVIDED: Provides query answering services,
bibliographic, literature and quantitative data searches of information,
selective dissemination of information, using its own data bases, URBISOC
ISOC-EC, ISOC-PS, ISOC-DE, ISOC-HU. Has also access to external data base
such as SDG, Telesystems QUESTEL, BELINDIS, CITERE, SPIDEL, DATA-STAR, ES,
QUEST, ORBI.

9 - INSTITUTO NACIONAL DE ADMINISTRACIÓN PÚBLICA, BIBLIOTECA

NONYMOUS NAMES: National Institute of Public Administration, Library
RENT ORGANIZATION: Ministerio para las Administraciones Públicas
DRESS: Plaza de San Diego s/n,
       Alcala de Henares,
       Madrid,
       SPAIN
       TEL: 8882200
EATED: 1958   *HEAD:* Mrs. F. Meroño Agüera, Director
ZE OF STAFF: Professional: 10   Other: 4   Total: 14
PE OF SERVICE: national; public; non-profit
TERIALS DESCRIBING THE SERVICE: - Puntos de Información cultural del Ministerio de
       Cultura (PIC)
       - Nueva guía de las Bibliotecas de Madrid, 1979
       - Directorio de Centros de Documentación y Bibliotecas especializadas
       (Ministerio de Educación y Ciencia), 1987
BJECT COVERAGE: administrative sciences; law; economics; political science;
       sociology; public administration
OGRAPHICAL COVERAGE: Spain
TA BEING PROCESSED AND SIZE: 45,000 books; 700 periodicals
TA PROCESSING METHODS: partially computerized
RDWARE USED: BULL Mini 6, mod. 53
FTWARE USED: JLB - Doc
PE OF ACTIVITY: data analysis; distribution of information; publication
RIODICALS PUBLISHED:
       - Boletin Informativo de la Biblioteca
IENTELE: public administration officials, researchers, specialists
CESS TO SERVICE: services open to specific categories of users, free of charge
PE & DESCRIPTION OF SERVICES PROVIDED: Provides library services, bibliographic
       searches and on-line services on own data bases "BIES-INAP (PIC)" and
       "INAP 1 (Biblioteca)", selective dissemination of information and
       information on magnetic tapes or discs. Microforms and photocopies are also
       available.

0 - INSTITUTO NACIONAL DE ESTADÍSTICA, SERVICIO DE DOCUMENTACIÓN Y BIBLIOTECA

NONYMOUS NAMES: INE
DRESS: Paseo de la Castellana 183,
       28046 Madrid,
       SPAIN
       TEL: 279.01.62
EATED: 1945   *HEAD:* Mr. J.-M. I. Serrano Sanchez, Head
ZE OF STAFF: Total: 16
PE OF SERVICE: national; private; non-profit
RKING LANGUAGE(S): Spanish
BJECT COVERAGE: demography; economics; statistics
OGRAPHICAL COVERAGE: Spain
TA BEING PROCESSED AND SIZE: 60,000 books; 700 periodicals; 10,000 documents
TA PROCESSING METHODS: manual
PE OF ACTIVITY: distribution of information

CLIENTELE: students, general public (5,000 p.a.)
ACCESS TO SERVICE: open to all users
TYPE & DESCRIPTION OF SERVICES PROVIDED: Provides library services, microforms and
        photocopies.

**661 - UNIVERSIDAD DE DEUSTO, INSTITUTO DE ESTUDIOS EUROPEOS, CENTRO DE DOCUMENTACIÓ
EUROPEA**

ADDRESS: Avda. de la Universidades 5,
        Apartado de Correos, 1,
        48080 Bilbao,
        SPAIN
        TEL: (94) 4.45.31.00
CREATED: 1981
TYPE OF SERVICE: private
SUBJECT COVERAGE: law; economics; history; international relations; international l
GEOGRAPHICAL COVERAGE: Europe
DATA BEING PROCESSED AND SIZE: publications and documents of the EEC; periodicals
TYPE OF ACTIVITY: data collection; distribution of information; publication
PERIODICALS PUBLISHED:
        - Boletín Bibliográfico
        - Folleto Informativo
CLIENTELE: jurists, economists, professors
TYPE & DESCRIPTION OF SERVICES PROVIDED: Provides library and reference services,
        interlibrary loans, retrospective searches and photocopies.

662 - BANDARANAIKE CENTRE FOR INTERNATIONAL STUDIES, LIBRARY

PARENT ORGANIZATION: SWRD Bandaranaike National Memorial Foundation
ADDRESS: Bandaranaike Memorial International Conference Hall,
        Bauddhaloka Mawatha,
        Colombo 7,
        SRI LANKA
        TEL: 598019/9113 - TELEX: 21494
        CABLE: INTHALL Colombo
CREATED: 1974   HEAD: Mr. R. G. B. Forbes, Director
SIZE OF STAFF: Professional: 4   Other: 3   Total: 7
TYPE OF SERVICE: private; non-profit
WORKING LANGUAGE(S): English; Singhalese
SUBJECT COVERAGE: social sciences; economics; law; political science; sociology;
        international affairs
GEOGRAPHICAL COVERAGE: global
DATA BEING PROCESSED AND SIZE: 6,000 books; journals; newspapers; dissertations;
        press-clippings
DATA PROCESSING METHODS: manual
STORAGE MEDIA: traditional shelving of publications
TYPE OF ACTIVITY: data collection; distribution of information
CLIENTELE: students, government officers, general public

CESS TO SERVICE: services open to all users
PE & DESCRIPTION OF SERVICES PROVIDED: Provides library services. The Centre is a
depository library of the United Nations and the European Economic
Community.

3 - DEVELOPMENT INFORMATION NETWORK ON SOUTH ASIA

NONYMOUS NAMES: DEVINSA
RENT ORGANIZATION: Committee on Studies for Cooperation in Development in South
Asia (CSCD)
DRESS: DEVINSA Coordinating Centre,
Marga Institute,
61 Isipathana Mawatha,
P.O. Box 601,
Colombo 5,
SRI LANKA
TEL: 585-186 - TELEX: 21642
MARGA
EATED: 1986   *HEAD:* Mrs. M. Nanayakkara, Project Leader
ZE OF STAFF: Professional: 5   Other: 4   Total: 9
PE OF SERVICE: international
TERIALS DESCRIBING THE SERVICE: - Report of the Project Workshop on Development of
a South Asian Information Network of Economic and Social Development,
Colombo 7-12 June, 1982, 38 p.
- Development Information Network on South Asia (DEVINSA) 1986, 8 p.
- Development of a South Asian Network on Social and Economic Development
(DEVINSA): report of the 1st technical policy meeting, 1986, 17 p.
- DEVINSA reference manual, 1986, 65 p. (Documents issued by Marga)
RKING LANGUAGE(S): English
BJECT COVERAGE: social sciences; development
OGRAPHICAL COVERAGE: South Asia
TA PROCESSING METHODS: computerized
RDWARE USED: IBM PC XT
FTWARE USED: INMAGIC
PE OF ACTIVITY: data collection; data analysis; distribution of information;
publication
BLICATIONS: - DEVINSA bibliography
- DEVINSA abstracts
IENTELE: social scientists
CESS TO SERVICE: services open to all users, some paid services
PE & DESCRIPTION OF SERVICES PROVIDED: Provides library services, bibliographic and
literature abstract searches of information, and photocopies.

4 - MARGA INSTITUTE, DOCUMENTATION CENTRE

DRESS: 61, Isipathana Mawatha,
P.O. Box 601,
Colombo 5,
SRI LANKA

TEL: 581514
CREATED: 1972   *HEAD:* Mrs. M. Nanayakkara, Chief
SIZE OF STAFF: Professional: 4   Other: 6   Total: 10
TYPE OF SERVICE: private; non-profit
SUBJECT COVERAGE: economics; social sciences
GEOGRAPHICAL COVERAGE: South Asia
DATA BEING PROCESSED AND SIZE: 16,000 books and reports including a special
        collection on Sri Lanka numbering more than 5,000; 350 periodicals;
        newspaper clippings; unpublished reports
DATA PROCESSING METHODS: partially computerized
HARDWARE USED: IBM PC/XT; IBM PC/AT
SOFTWARE USED: INMAGIC
STORAGE MEDIA: traditional shelving of publications
TYPE OF ACTIVITY: data collection; distribution of information
PERIODICALS PUBLISHED:
        - Current Awareness List
CLIENTELE: researchers, government officials, university professors
TYPE & DESCRIPTION OF SERVICES PROVIDED: Provides library services and bibliographic
        searches of information using its own data base.

665 - MINISTRY OF FINANCE AND PLANNING, CENTRE FOR DEVELOPMENT INFORMATION

SYNONYMOUS NAMES: CDI/NPD
PARENT ORGANIZATION: Ministry of Finance and Planning, National Planning Division
ADDRESS: Galle Face Secretariat,
        P.O. Box 1547,
        Colombo 01,
        SRI LANKA
        TEL: 549378 - TELEX: 21409 FINMIN CE
        CABLE: UNDEVPRO
CREATED: 1979   *HEAD:* Dr. L. S. Fernando, Director
SIZE OF STAFF: Professional: 6   Other: 6   Total: 12
TYPE OF SERVICE: national; non-profit
SYSTEMS & NETWORKS ATTACHED TO: DEVSIS (Development Science Information System, IDRC
        Canada); ASTINFO
MATERIALS DESCRIBING THE SERVICE: - Centre for Development Information, 1986, 8 p.
WORKING LANGUAGE(S): English
SUBJECT COVERAGE: social welfare; development planning; socio-economic development;
        social sciences
GEOGRAPHICAL COVERAGE: global; Sri Lanka
DATA BEING PROCESSED AND SIZE: 8,750 books; 1,000 reports, 105 periodical titles; 10
        microfiches
DATA PROCESSING METHODS: partially computerized
HARDWARE USED: IBM PC XT 52
SOFTWARE USED: DBase III
STORAGE MEDIA: traditional shelving of publications; microfiches
TYPE OF ACTIVITY: data collection; data analysis; distribution of information;
        publication
PERIODICALS PUBLISHED: - Guide to Current Periodical Literature on Economic and
        Social Development, 4 p.a.
        - Current Awarenesses Service, 12 p.a.

- Current Acquisitions, 4 p.a.
BLICATIONS: - UNIDEV/Union catalogue of economic and social development
publications in Sri Lanka libraries
- Bibliography of economic and social development in Sri Lanka 1975-1983
- Subject guide to current periodical literature in economic and social
development
- Register of recent on-going research in economic and social development in
Sri Lanka, 1986
- Acts of Sri Lanka 1980-1985, 1986
- Union list of economic and social development periodicals
- Public investment 1987-1991, 1987
LIENTELE: researchers, policy makers, planners
CCESS TO SERVICE: open to specific categories of users, free of charge
PE & DESCRIPTION OF SERVICES PROVIDED: Provides library services, interlibrary
loans, reference services, bibliographies, literature searches using its own
data base UNILIST. Also provides photocopies and selective dissemination of
information.

6 - NATIONAL LIBRARY OF SRI LANKA, SOCIAL SCIENCE DOCUMENTATION CENTRE

DDRESS: P.O. Box 1764,
Independence Avenue,
Colombo 07,
SRI LANKA
TEL: 598847
REATED: 1972
PE OF SERVICE: national; public; non-profit
STEMS & NETWORKS ATTACHED TO: APINESS (Asia Pacific Information Network in the
Social Sciences)
ORKING LANGUAGE(S): Sinhala; English; Tamil
BJECT COVERAGE: social sciences
EOGRAPHICAL COVERAGE: Sri Lanka; global
ATA BEING PROCESSED AND SIZE: 246,390 documentation items in the library
ATA PROCESSING METHODS: manual
TORAGE MEDIA: traditional shelving of publications; fiches; tapes
PE OF ACTIVITY: data collection; distribution of information; SSID scientific and
methodological activities; publication
ERIODICALS PUBLISHED:
- Library News, 4 p.a.
LIENTELE: research workers, university personnel, government departments and general
public
CCESS TO SERVICE: services open to all users, free of charge
PE & DESCRIPTION OF SERVICES PROVIDED: Provides library services, bibliographic and
quantitative data searches of information, selective dissemination of
information, and technical advisory services to libraries and library
authorities. Photocopying and translating facilities are also available.

667 - NATURAL RESOURCES, ENERGY AND SCIENCE AUTHORITY OF SRI LANKA

SYNONYMOUS NAMES: NARESA
ADDRESS: 47/5 Maitland Place,
Colombo 7,
SRI LANKA
CABLE: LAKSCIGNCG
CREATED: 1075   HEAD: Dr. R. P. Jayewardane, Director General
SIZE OF STAFF: Professional: 6   Other: 5   Total: 11
TYPE OF SERVICE: national; public; non-profit
SYSTEMS & NETWORKS ATTACHED TO: IDRC, SLSTINET
WORKING LANGUAGE(S): English
SUBJECT COVERAGE: social sciences; science
GEOGRAPHICAL COVERAGE: Sri Lanka; Asia
DATA BEING PROCESSED AND SIZE: books, journals, reports, articles
DATA PROCESSING METHODS: manual
STORAGE MEDIA: traditional shelving of publications; microfiches
TYPE OF ACTIVITY: data collection
PERIODICALS PUBLISHED:
          - Newsletter
          - Accession List
PUBLICATIONS: - Indexes
CLIENTELE: experts and researchers
ACCESS TO SERVICE: services open to all users, free of charge

668 - SRI LANKA INSTITUTE OF DEVELOPMENT ADMINISTRATION

SYNONYMOUS NAMES: SLIDA
PARENT ORGANIZATION: Ministry of Public Administration
ADDRESS: 28/10 Longdon Place,
Colombo 07,
SRI LANKA
TEL: 58218
CREATED: 1966   HEAD: V. T. Navaratne, Director
TYPE OF SERVICE: international; public; non-profit
WORKING LANGUAGE(S): English; Sinhalese
SUBJECT COVERAGE: administrative sciences; public administration
GEOGRAPHICAL COVERAGE: Sri Lanka
DATA BEING PROCESSED AND SIZE: 20,000 books; 100 periodicals
DATA PROCESSING METHODS: manual
TYPE OF ACTIVITY: distribution of information; SSID training; publication
ACCESS TO SERVICE: services open to specific categories of users, some paid services
TYPE & DESCRIPTION OF SERVICES PROVIDED: Provides library services, bibliographic
          searches, literature surveys, abstracts, photocopies and translation of
          documents upon request.

Sudan / Soudan / Sudán

669 - NATIONAL COUNCIL FOR RESEARCH, NATIONAL DOCUMENTATION CENTRE

ADDRESS: P.O. Box 2404,
          Khartoum,
          SUDAN
          TEL: 70776 - TELEX: 22342 ILMI SD
          CABLE: BOHUTH
CREATED: 1974   *HEAD:* Dr. C. Wesley Istasi, Director
SIZE OF STAFF: Professional: 3   Other: 5   Total: 8
TYPE OF SERVICE: national; public; non-profit
SYSTEMS & NETWORKS ATTACHED TO: INFOTERRA; PADIS
WORKING LANGUAGE(S): English; Arabic
SUBJECT COVERAGE: social sciences; administrative sciences; demography; economics;
          social anthropology
GEOGRAPHICAL COVERAGE: Sudan
DATA BEING PROCESSED AND SIZE: books; periodicals; reports
DATA PROCESSING METHODS: partially computerized
HARDWARE USED: IBM PC
SOFTWARE USED: CDS/ISIS
STORAGE MEDIA: traditional shelving of publications
TYPE OF ACTIVITY: data collection; data analysis; publication
PERIODICALS PUBLISHED: - Sudan Science Abstracts, 1 p.a.
PUBLICATIONS: - National register of current research, 1985
ACCESS TO SERVICE: services open to all users, free of charge
TYPE & DESCRIPTION OF SERVICES PROVIDED: Specializes in literature abstracting and
          indexing of research carried out in Sudan or published in Sudan. Also
          provides photocopies.

670 - NATIONAL DOCUMENTATION CENTRE

PARENT ORGANIZATION: National Council for Research
ADDRESS: P.O. Box 2404,
          Khartoum,
          SUDAN
          TEL: 70776 - TELEX: 22342 ILMI SD
          CABLE: BUHUTH
CREATED: 1974   *HEAD:* Dr. C. Wesley, Director
SIZE OF STAFF: Professional: 3   Other: 13   Total: 16
TYPE OF SERVICE: national; public; non-profit
SYSTEMS & NETWORKS ATTACHED TO: INFOTERRA; PADIS; UNISIST
WORKING LANGUAGE(S): Arabic; English
SUBJECT COVERAGE: social sciences; administrative sciences; demography; economics;
          social anthropology; cultural anthropology; sociology
GEOGRAPHICAL COVERAGE: Sudan
DATA PROCESSING METHODS: partially computerized
HARDWARE USED: IBM micro computer
SOFTWARE USED: CDS/ISIS
STORAGE MEDIA: traditional shelving of publications
TYPE OF ACTIVITY: distribution of information; publication

PERIODICALS PUBLISHED: - Sudan Science Abstracts
           - Library Accession Bulletin
PUBLICATIONS: - National register of current research
CLIENTELE: researchers
ACCESS TO SERVICE: services open to all users, free of charge
TYPE & DESCRIPTION OF SERVICES PROVIDED: Provides library services and literature
        abstract searches of information.

671 - SUDAN ACADEMY FOR ADMINISTRATIVE SCIENCES, INFORMATION SERVICE

SYNONYMOUS NAMES: SAAS
PARENT ORGANIZATION: Ministry of Labour and Social Security
ADDRESS: P.O. Box 2003,
        Khartoum,
        SUDAN
        TEL: 71391 - TELEX: 22876 ACAD SD
CREATED: 1980
SIZE OF STAFF: Professional: 52   Other: 50   Total: 102
TYPE OF SERVICE: national; public; non-profit
WORKING LANGUAGE(S): Arabic; English
SUBJECT COVERAGE: administrative sciences; economics; public administration;
        management; local government; development
GEOGRAPHICAL COVERAGE: Sudan
DATA BEING PROCESSED AND SIZE: reports; on-going research; seminars; training
        courses; consulting
DATA PROCESSING METHODS: manual
STORAGE MEDIA: traditional shelving of publications
TYPE OF ACTIVITY: data collection; SSID training
PERIODICALS PUBLISHED: - Majallat Al-Sudan lil Idarah wa al Tanmiyah, 1 p.a.
CLIENTELE: central and local government officials
ACCESS TO SERVICE: services open to specific categories of users, free of charge
TYPE & DESCRIPTION OF SERVICES PROVIDED: Provides library services.

**672 - UNIVERSITY OF KHARTOUM, FACULTY OF ECONOMIC AND SOCIAL STUDIES, DEVELOPMENT
STUDIES AND RESEARCH CENTRE**

SYNONYMOUS NAMES: DSRC
ADDRESS: P.O. Box 321,
        Khartoum,
        SUDAN
        TEL: 72012
CREATED: 1976   *HEAD:* Dr. K. O. Affan, Director
SIZE OF STAFF: Professional: 2   Other: 4   Total: 6
TYPE OF SERVICE: public; non-profit
WORKING LANGUAGE(S): Arabic; English
SUBJECT COVERAGE: economics; development
GEOGRAPHICAL COVERAGE: Sudan; developing countries
DATA BEING PROCESSED AND SIZE: 5,300 books; 20 periodicals
DATA PROCESSING METHODS: manual

TYPE OF ACTIVITY: SSID scientific and methodological activities
ACCESS TO SERVICE: services open to specific categories of users
TYPE & DESCRIPTION OF SERVICES PROVIDED: Provides library services, literature and
quantitative data searches.

Sweden / Suède / Suecia

573 - ARBETARRÖRELSENS ARKIV OCH BIBLIOTHEK

SYNONYMOUS NAMES: Swedish Labour Movement, Archives and Library
ADDRESS: Upplandsgatan 5,
Box 1124,
S-111 81 Stockholm,
SWEDEN
TEL: 08-241760
CREATED: 1902   *HEAD:* Mr. L. Wessman, Director
SIZE OF STAFF: Professional: 15
TYPE OF SERVICE: international; public; non-profit
WORKING LANGUAGE(S): Swedish
SUBJECT COVERAGE: economics; labour; history; political science; social welfare;
sociology
GEOGRAPHICAL COVERAGE: Sweden
PERIODICALS PUBLISHED: - Arbetarhistoria. Meddelande från Arbetarrörelsens arkiv och
bibliotek, 4 p.a.
CLIENTELE: scholars, students, general public (4,000 p.a.)
ACCESS TO SERVICE: services open to all users, free of charge
TYPE & DESCRIPTION OF SERVICES PROVIDED: Provides library services, bibliographic
searches of information, and photocopies.

574 - ARBETSLIVSCENTRUM, ARAMIS

SYNONYMOUS NAMES: The Swedish Center for Working Life, Department of Documentation,
Aramis
ADDRESS: Box 5606,
S-114 86 Stockholm,
SWEDEN
TEL: 08 790.95.00
CREATED: 1978   *HEAD:* Mr. G. Lingre, Information Manager
SIZE OF STAFF: Professional: 3   Other: 2   Total: 5
TYPE OF SERVICE: national; public; non-profit
WORKING LANGUAGE(S): Swedish; English; German; French
SUBJECT COVERAGE: working conditions; labour market; trade unions; workers
participation; ergonomics; organization of work; labour law; labour
relations; sex discrimination; employment policy
GEOGRAPHICAL COVERAGE: Sweden; Northern Europe; global
DATA BEING PROCESSED AND SIZE: books; reports; articles and various documents
DATA PROCESSING METHODS: computerized
HARDWARE USED: Siemen
SOFTWARE USED: Golem
STORAGE MEDIA: tapes and discs

TYPE OF ACTIVITY: data collection; data analysis
CLIENTELE: researchers, students and general public
ACCESS TO SERVICE: services open to all users, against payment
TYPE & DESCRIPTION OF SERVICES PROVIDED: Provides library services, literature
    abstract and bibliographic searches of information, selective dissemination
    of information and production of information on magnetic tapes and discs.
    On-line services using its own data bases, ALCDOK (Swedish and nordic
    literature on working life conditions) and ARBPROJ (Current research on
    working life and work environment in Sweden), as well as other data bases
    such as AMILIT, CISILO, DAISY, LABORDOC, LABORINF, MBLINE, NIOSHTIC, and
    SERIX.

675 - CENTRALFÖRBUNDET FÖR ALKOHOL- OCH NARKOTIKAUPPLYSNING, BIBLIOTEK OCH IOD-CENTRAL

SYNONYMOUS NAMES: Swedish Council for Information on Alcohol and Other Drugs, Library
    and I&D Centre
ADDRESS: Box 27302,
        S-10254 Stockholm,
        SWEDEN
        TEL: (08) 667-9720
HEAD: Ms. S. Valverius, Head
SIZE OF STAFF: Professional: 4
TYPE OF SERVICE: international; public; non-profit
SYSTEMS & NETWORKS ATTACHED TO: Datapak
MATERIALS DESCRIBING THE SERVICE: - Valverius. S., Information and documentation on
    alcohol and ather drugs of abuse in Sweden. Paper presented at the 187 SALIS
    symposium, November 2-6, 1987, Edmonton, Alberta, Canada
SUBJECT COVERAGE: social sciences; education; law; psychology; sociology; alcoholism;
    drug abuse
GEOGRAPHICAL COVERAGE: Northern Europe; global
DATA BEING PROCESSED AND SIZE: 145,000 volumes of books, reports, articles,
    conference proceedings, dissertations and journals
DATA PROCESSING METHODS: partially computerized
HARDWARE USED: AMDAHL (mainframe); COMPAQ (PC)
SOFTWARE USED: CDS/ISIS
STORAGE MEDIA: traditional shelving of publications; tapes; discs
TYPE OF ACTIVITY: data collection; distribution of information; SSID scientific and
    methodological activities; publication
PERIODICALS PUBLISHED: - "Alkohol och Narkotika. Svensk Litteratur, 1 p.a.
    - Acquisition List
PUBLICATIONS: - Drug abuse. Current research on alcohol and drug dependence
    - Alcohol, drugs and traffic safety. Current research literature.
CLIENTELE: researchers, practitioners, policy-makers, students, counsellors,
    librarians, lecturers
ACCESS TO SERVICE: services open to all users, free of charge
TYPE & DESCRIPTION OF SERVICES PROVIDED: Provides library services, bibliographic and
    literature abstract searches of information, magnetic tapes and photocopies.
    Also provides on-line services using own information system "DRUGAB"
    consisting of ALCONARC and NORDRUG data bases, as well as external data base
    DALCTRAF available through DALCTRAF.

76 - DAG HAMMARSKJÖLDBIBLIOTEKET

YNONYMOUS NAMES: Dag Hammarskjöld Library
ARENT ORGANIZATION: Uppsala Stadsbibliotek (Uppsala City Library)
DDRESS: P.O. Box 644,
S-751 27 Uppsala,
SWEDEN
TEL: (018) 116101
REATED: 1966   *HEAD:* Ms. N. Bergström, Librarian
IZE OF STAFF: Professional: 2   Other: 1   Total: 3
YPE OF SERVICE: international; public; non-profit
ORKING LANGUAGE(S): Swedish; English
UBJECT COVERAGE: economics; international law; political science
ATA BEING PROCESSED AND SIZE: U.N. documents and publications
CCESS TO SERVICE: open to all users, free of charge
YPE & DESCRIPTION OF SERVICES PROVIDED: United Nations depository library.

77 - ETNOGRAFISKA MUSEET, LIBRARY

YNONYMOUS NAMES: Ethnographical Museum of Sweden, Library
DDRESS: S-11527 Stockholm,
SWEDEN
TEL: (08) 670-560
REATED: 1935   *HEAD:* Ms. A. Murray, Librarian
IZE OF STAFF: Professional: 2
YPE OF SERVICE: international; public; non-profit
ORKING LANGUAGE(S): Swedish
UBJECT COVERAGE: social anthropology; cultural anthropology; ethnography
EOGRAPHICAL COVERAGE: global
ATA BEING PROCESSED AND SIZE: 20,000 books
ATA PROCESSING METHODS: manual
YPE OF ACTIVITY: distribution of information
CCESS TO SERVICE: open to all users
YPE & DESCRIPTION OF SERVICES PROVIDED: Provides library services.

78 - GÖTEBORGS UNIVERSITET, SPRÅKDATA

YNONYMOUS NAMES: Språkdata;
University of Göteborg, Språkdata
DDRESS: Renströmsgatan 6, plan F2,
412 98 Göteborg,
SWEDEN
TEL: (031) 634545
REATED: 1972   *HEAD:* Dr. M. Gellerstam, Director
ATERIALS DESCRIBING THE SERVICE: - Språkdata, Department of Computational
Linguistics, brochure
ORKING LANGUAGE(S): Swedish; English
UBJECT COVERAGE: linguistics; computer science
EOGRAPHICAL COVERAGE: Northern Europe

DATA PROCESSING METHODS: computerized
TYPE OF ACTIVITY: data collection; SSID training; SSID scientific and methodological
        activities; publication
PERIODICALS PUBLISHED: - Data Linguistica
PUBLICATIONS: - Swedish-Turkish dictionary
        - Swedish-Serbo-Croatian dictionary
        - Swedish Academy glossary, 1986
        - Swedish dictionary, 1986
CLIENTELE: students; professors; researchers
ACCESS TO SERVICE: open to all users
TYPE & DESCRIPTION OF SERVICES PROVIDED: Provides searches of information using own
        data base the "Language Bank" (comprising 30 million running words). Its
        "Lexical Database" is published as a monolingual Swedish dictionary, the
        Svensk Ordbok and the "TERMIN" project aims at storing in database form
        translations of Swedish social terminology.

679 - HANDELSHÖGSKOLANS BIBLIOTEK I STOCKHOLM

SYNONYMOUS NAMES: Stockholm School of Economics Library
ADDRESS: Box 6501,
        (Sveavägen 65),
        S-113 83 Stockholm,
        SWEDEN
        TEL: 089736 01 20 - TELEX: 16514
CREATED: 1909   *HEAD:* Mrs. E. Thomson-Roos, Head Librarian
SIZE OF STAFF: Professional: 19   Other: 2   Total: 21
TYPE OF SERVICE: international; public; non-profit
MATERIALS DESCRIBING THE SERVICE: - Stockholm School of Economics, the Library
WORKING LANGUAGE(S): Swedish
SUBJECT COVERAGE: economics; administrative sciences; law; statistics; geography
DATA PROCESSING METHODS: manual; computerized
TYPE OF ACTIVITY: data collection; distribution of information; publication
PERIODICALS PUBLISHED:
        - Ekonomisk Dokumentation
PUBLICATIONS: - List econ
CLIENTELE: students, researchers
ACCESS TO SERVICE: open to all users
TYPE & DESCRIPTION OF SERVICES PROVIDED: Provides library sciences, bibliographic
        searches of information, on-line services, information on magnetic tapes or
        discs, and photocopies upon request.

680 - NORDISKA AFRIKAINSTITUTETS BIBLIOTEK

SYNONYMOUS NAMES: Scandinavian Institute of African Studies, Library
ADDRESS: P.O. Box 1703,
        S-751 47 Uppsala,
        SWEDEN
        TEL: 018/155480
        CABLE: AFRICAN, Uppsala

CREATED: 1962   HEAD: Ms. B. Fahlander, Head Librarian
SIZE OF STAFF: Professional: 4   Other: 1   Total: 5
TYPE OF SERVICE: public; non-profit
WORKING LANGUAGE(S): English; French; Swedish
SUBJECT COVERAGE: social sciences; history; political science; economics; education
GEOGRAPHICAL COVERAGE: Africa
DATA BEING PROCESSED AND SIZE: 32,000 books; 700 periodicals; bibliographies;
        government publications; 200 microfilms
DATA PROCESSING METHODS: partially computerized
HARDWARE USED: PC
SOFTWARE USED: Revelation for Library Use
TYPE OF ACTIVITY: distribution of information; publication
PERIODICALS PUBLISHED: - Africana: Nordiska Afrikainstitutes Bibliotek
PUBLICATIONS: - Tidningar och tidskrifter i Nordiska Afrikainstitutets Bibliotek
        (Journals and Periodicals in the Library)
        - Subject catalogue of the Library
ACCESS TO SERVICE: services open to all users, free of charge
TYPE & DESCRIPTION OF SERVICES PROVIDED: Provides library services, bibliographic
        searches, on-line search of Dialog and Questel, selective dissemination of
        information and photocopies.

681 - RIKSDAGSBIBLIOTEKET

SYNONYMOUS NAMES: Library of the Swedish Parliament
PARENT ORGANIZATION: Riksdagens Förvaltningskontor
ADDRESS: 100 12 Stockholm,
        SWEDEN
        TEL: S-08-786.4000
CREATED: 1851   HEAD: B. Alexanderson, Head Librarian
SIZE OF STAFF: Professional: 23   Other: 6   Total: 29
SYSTEMS & NETWORKS ATTACHED TO: LIBRIS
SUBJECT COVERAGE: political science; administrative sciences; social sciences; law
DATA BEING PROCESSED AND SIZE: 600,000 vols. of books; 2,000 vols. of periodicals
DATA PROCESSING METHODS: manual; computerized
TYPE OF ACTIVITY: distribution of information
PUBLICATIONS: - Bibliographical handbook
        - Swedish government publications: bibliography
ACCESS TO SERVICE: services open to specific categories of users, free of charge
TYPE & DESCRIPTION OF SERVICES PROVIDED: Provides library services, bibliographic
        searches of information using catalogues and data bases of other services,
        i.e. LIBRIS, Rättsdata, and photocopies.

682 - STATENS PSYKOLOGISK-PEDAGOGISKA BIBLIOTEK

SYNONYMOUS NAMES: SPPB;
        The National Library for Psychology and Education
ADDRESS: P.O. Box 50063,
        S-104 05 Stockholm,
        SWEDEN

TEL: 8-151820
CREATED: 1885   *HEAD:* Mr. T. Lidman, Director
SIZE OF STAFF: Professional: 7   Other: 9   Total: 16
TYPE OF SERVICE: international; national; public; non-profit
SYSTEMS & NETWORKS ATTACHED TO: LIBRIS (Swedish Library Information System)
MATERIALS DESCRIBING THE SERVICE: - Hemborg, W., DOLDIS directory of on-line data
        bases produced in Sweden, Stockholm, DFI, 1983
WORKING LANGUAGE(S): Swedish; English
SUBJECT COVERAGE: education; psychology; behavioural sciences
DATA BEING PROCESSED AND SIZE: 245,000 documentation items; 2,000 manuscripts; 825
        periodicals
DATA PROCESSING METHODS: manual; partially computerized
SOFTWARE USED: 3RIP, POLYDOC, LIBRIS
STORAGE MEDIA: traditional shelving of publications; discs; microfiches; CD-ROM
TYPE OF ACTIVITY: data analysis; publication
PERIODICALS PUBLISHED: - Swedish Behavioural Sciences Research Reports, 1 p.a.
PUBLICATIONS: - National Bibliography of Psychology Swedish articles in periodicals
        - List of journals in SPPB
        - A Bibliography
        - List of journals in SPPB
ACCESS TO SERVICE: open to all users, some paid services
TYPE & DESCRIPTION OF SERVICES PROVIDED: Provides library services, interlibrary
        loans and bibliographic, literature abstract data searches on its own data
        base "SBS" (Swedish Behavioural Sciences) accessible through Medicin data
        and on the national data system LIBRIS (Library Information System). Also
        provides on-line services from other data bases such as ERIC, PsycInfo,
        PASCAL, FRANCIS, Social SciSearch and EUDISED, selective dissemination of
        information, and photocopies.

683 - STATISTISKA CENTRALBYRÅNS BIBLIOTEK

SYNONYMOUS NAMES: SCB;
        Statistics Sweden, Library
ADDRESS: S-11581 Stockholm,
        SWEDEN
        TEL: (46-8) 783-40-00 - TELEX: 15261 SWESTAT S
        SWESTAT
CREATED: 1858   *HEAD:* Mr. M. Lindmark, Chief Librarian
SIZE OF STAFF: Professional: 11   Other: 10   Total: 21
TYPE OF SERVICE: national; public; non-profit
WORKING LANGUAGE(S): Swedish
SUBJECT COVERAGE: social sciences; demography; education; social welfare; statistic
DATA BEING PROCESSED AND SIZE: 260,000 books, reports, serials and journals
DATA PROCESSING METHODS: manual
STORAGE MEDIA: traditional shelving of publications
TYPE OF ACTIVITY: distribution of information; publication
PERIODICALS PUBLISHED: - Statistik Från Enskilda Länder, 1 p.a.
        - Statistik Från Internationella Organ, 1 p.a.
        - Nyförvärv (Accessions List)
CLIENTELE: civil-service departments staff; governmental bodies, students, marketin
        researchers and the general public (5,600 p.a.)

ACCESS TO SERVICE: services open to all users, free of charge
TYPE & DESCRIPTION OF SERVICES PROVIDED: Provides library services, inter-library
        loans, simple reference questionnaires and photocopies. The Library has
        incorporated the Libraries of Socialstyrelsen (National Board of Health and
        Welfare) and Skolöverstyrelsen (National Board of Education).

684 - STOCKHOLMS UNIVERSITET, LATINAMERIKA-INSTITUTET, BIBLIOTEK

SYNONYMOUS NAMES: University of Stockholm, Institute of Latin American Studies,
        Library;
        LAIS, Library
ADDRESS: S-106 91 Stockholm,
        SWEDEN
        TEL: (46) 8.16.28.82 - TELEX: 8105199 UNIVERS
        CABLE: UNIVERSITY STOCKHOLM
CREATED: 1951   HEAD: Ms. B. Johansson, Librarian
SIZE OF STAFF: Professional: 4
TYPE OF SERVICE: national; public; non-profit
SYSTEMS & NETWORKS ATTACHED TO: NOSALF (Nordic Association for Research on Latin
        America, Stockholm); CEISAL (Consejo Europeo de Investigaciones Sociales
        sobre America Latina, Vienna); EADI (European Association of Development
        Research and Training Institutes, Tilburg); ASERCCA (Association for
        European Research on Central America and the Caribbean, Aix en Provence)
MATERIALS DESCRIBING THE SERVICE: - Informe de actividades, 1985/86
WORKING LANGUAGE(S): Swedish; Spanish; English
SUBJECT COVERAGE: social sciences; economics; geography; history; political science;
        social anthropology; cultural anthropology; sociology; international
        relations between Sweden and Latin America
GEOGRAPHICAL COVERAGE: Latin America; Central America
DATA BEING PROCESSED AND SIZE: 35,000 books, annual reports, conference proceedings,
        400 periodicals
DATA PROCESSING METHODS: partially computerized
TYPE OF ACTIVITY: data collection; data analysis; distribution of information; SSID
        scientific and methodological activities; publication
PERIODICALS PUBLISHED:
        - Latinoamericana
CLIENTELE: general public
ACCESS TO SERVICE: services open to all users, free of charge
TYPE & DESCRIPTION OF SERVICES PROVIDED: Provides library services, question-
        answering service, bibliographic searches of information using its own data
        base "Central America" and external data base LIBRIS. Also provides
        selective dissemination of information, information on magnetic tapes or
        discs and photocopies upon request.

685 - SVENSK SAMHÄLLSVETENSKAPLIG DATATJÄNST

SYNONYMOUS NAMES: SSD;
        Swedish Social Science Data Service
PARENT ORGANIZATION: Goteborg University

Sweden / Suède / Suecia

ADDRESS: Box 5048,
   S-402 21 Göteborg,
   SWEDEN
   TEL: (031) 20.54.00
CREATED: 1981   *HEAD:* Dr. L. Brantgärde, Director
SIZE OF STAFF: Professional: 6   Other: 4   Total: 10
TYPE OF SERVICE: international
SYSTEMS & NETWORKS ATTACHED TO: SUNET, GARN-BITNET through computing center of
   Göteborg University, contact organization for the Swedish national
   membership of ICPSR; member of IFDO and CESSDA
MATERIALS DESCRIBING THE SERVICE: - Swedish Social Science Data Service, European
   Political Data Newsletter no. 45, 1982
WORKING LANGUAGE(S): Swedish; English
SUBJECT COVERAGE: social sciences
GEOGRAPHICAL COVERAGE: Sweden; global
DATA BEING PROCESSED AND SIZE: research data files: 350 Swedish, 250 international
DATA PROCESSING METHODS: computerized
HARDWARE USED: PRIME 750, various PC/XT/AT
SOFTWARE USED: GIDO (ICPSR).
STORAGE MEDIA: tapes
TYPE OF ACTIVITY: publication
PERIODICALS PUBLISHED: - SSD-kontakt, 4 p.a.
PUBLICATIONS: - Svenska databaser I with English supplement, 1982
CLIENTELE: researchers
ACCESS TO SERVICE: open to specific category of users, free of charge
TYPE & DESCRIPTION OF SERVICES PROVIDED: Provides selective dissemination of
   information about factual data bases, archiving of data files produced in
   the process of Swedish academic research projects, information on magnetic
   tapes and microfilms.

686 - UMEÅ UNIVERSITET, DEMOGRAFISKA DATABASEN

SYNONYMOUS NAMES: Umeå University, Demographic Data Base
ADDRESS: Umeå University,
   S-901 87 Umeå,
   SWEDEN
   TEL: 090-16 5717
CREATED: 1978   *HEAD:* Mr. N. Häggström,
SIZE OF STAFF: Total: 60
TYPE OF SERVICE: national; public; non-profit
MATERIALS DESCRIBING THE SERVICE: - Databasen har till uppgift att..., introduktion
   till Demografiska Databasen, Haparanda-Umeå, 1982
   - History on data (booklet)
WORKING LANGUAGE(S): Swedish
SUBJECT COVERAGE: demography; history; geography
GEOGRAPHICAL COVERAGE: Sweden
DATA BEING PROCESSED AND SIZE: censuses, polls, surveys, church records
DATA PROCESSING METHODS: manual; computerized
HARDWARE USED: IBM 4361
SOFTWARE USED: Structured Query Language (SQL)
STORAGE MEDIA: tapes and discs

TYPE OF ACTIVITY: data collection; data analysis; publication
PERIODICALS PUBLISHED:
- Newsletter
PUBLICATIONS: - Tradition and transition, historical studies in microdemography and social change, 1982
- Time, space and man; essays on microdemography, 1979
- Lockridge, K., The Fertility transition in Sweden: a preliminary look at smaller geographic units, 1855-1890, 1984
CLIENTELE: researchers and university staff
ACCESS TO SERVICE: paid services open to specific categories of users
TYPE & DESCRIPTION OF SERVICES PROVIDED: Provides selective dissemination of information, magnetic tapes and advice on research material on the 19th century.

687 - UNIVERSITY OF GÖTEBORG, DEPARTMENT OF POLITICAL SCIENCE, NORDIC DOCUMENTATION CENTER FOR MASS COMMUNICATION RESEARCH

SYNONYMOUS NAMES: NORDICOM, Sweden
ADDRESS: Box 5048,
S-40221 Göteborg,
SWEDEN
CREATED: 1973   *HEAD:* Ms. U. Carlsson, Director
SIZE OF STAFF: Professional: 1   Other: 1   Total: 2
TYPE OF SERVICE: international; public; non-profit
SYSTEMS & NETWORKS ATTACHED TO: COMNET (International Network of Documentation Centres on Communication Research and Policies)
SUBJECT COVERAGE: mass communication; sociology of communication
GEOGRAPHICAL COVERAGE: Sweden; Denmark; Finland; Iceland; Norway
DATA BEING PROCESSED AND SIZE: 13,000 documents
DATA PROCESSING METHODS: computerized
STORAGE MEDIA: tapes
TYPE OF ACTIVITY: distribution of information; publication
PERIODICALS PUBLISHED: - Nordicom Bibliography of Nordic Mass Communication Literature, 1 p.a.
- Nordicom-NYH/Sverige, 4 p.a.
- Nordicom-Information, 4 p.a.
- Nordicom Review, 2 p.a.
ACCESS TO SERVICE: services open to all users, free of charge
TYPE & DESCRIPTION OF SERVICES PROVIDED: Provides bibliographic, literature abstract and survey data searches, selective dissemination of information. Also provides on-line searches using own data base "NCOM".

688 - BASLER MISSION, BIBLIOTHEK

SYNONYMOUS NAMES: Basler Mission, Library
PARENT ORGANIZATION: Evangelische Missionsgesellschaft in Basel
ADDRESS: Missionsstrasse 21,
CH-4003 Bale,

SWITZERLAND
TEL: (061) 25.33.99 - TELEX: 963315 KEM
CREATED: 1815   *HEAD:* Mr. M. C. Buess,
                Mr. P. Jenkins,
SIZE OF STAFF: Total: 2
TYPE OF SERVICE: international; public; private; non-profit
SYSTEMS & NETWORKS ATTACHED TO: Swiss Central Catalog (Swiss National Library)
MATERIALS DESCRIBING THE SERVICE: - Annual report of the Basel Mission (in German)
WORKING LANGUAGE(S): English; French; German
SUBJECT COVERAGE: social sciences; development; religion
GEOGRAPHICAL COVERAGE: Nigeria; Cameroon (United Republic); Indonesia; Ghana; India;
        Malaysia; Hong Kong
DATA BEING PROCESSED AND SIZE: 35,000 documentation items (books, periodicals, grey
        literature, microfiches, videos)
DATA PROCESSING METHODS: partially computerized
HARDWARE USED: IBM 36, Periphery Commodore (IBM compatible, AT)
SOFTWARE USED: Dbase III plus, OCLC-MARC, AACR-II Cataloging rules
TYPE OF ACTIVITY: data collection; SSID scientific and methodological activities;
        publication
PERIODICALS PUBLISHED:
        - Accessions List, 2 p.a.
CLIENTELE: 500 university staff, scholars, media (journalists); other libraries
ACCESS TO SERVICE: services open to all users free of charge; international service
        may be charged
TYPE & DESCRIPTION OF SERVICES PROVIDED: Provides library reference services,
        international interlibrary loans, bibliographic searches of information and
        photocopies upon request. Has an extensive archives department.

689 - CENTRE ASIATIQUE/IUHEI

SYNONYMOUS NAMES: Asian Centre/GIIS
PARENT ORGANIZATION: Institut Universitaire de Hautes Etudes Internationales
ADDRESS: 132 rue de Lausanne,
        P.O. Box 36,
        CH-1211 Geneva 21,
        SWITZERLAND
        TEL: (022) 328310 - TELEX: 412151 PAX CH
        CABLE: INSTONAL GENEVA
CREATED: 1971   *HEAD:* Prof. J. L. Maurer, Director
SIZE OF STAFF: Professional: 3   Other: 2   Total: 5
TYPE OF SERVICE: international; public; non-profit
MATERIALS DESCRIBING THE SERVICE: - The Asian Center, 1985, 15 p.a.
WORKING LANGUAGE(S): English; French
SUBJECT COVERAGE: social sciences; political science; economics; education;
        geography; history; social anthropology; contemporary Asian studies and
        research in the field of development economics and sociology
GEOGRAPHICAL COVERAGE: Asia
DATA BEING PROCESSED AND SIZE: 155 Asian periodicals; press bulletins; official
        reports
DATA PROCESSING METHODS: partially computerized
HARDWARE USED: DIGITAL RAINBOW

SOFTWARE USED: SYMPHONY LOTUS
TYPE OF ACTIVITY: data collection; data analysis; SSID scientific and methodological
      activities; publication
PUBLICATIONS: - Billeter, J.-F. et al., Asiatic societies: mutations and continuity,
      China. India, Indonesia, 1985
      - Maurer, J.-L., Agricultural modernization, economic development and social
      change, 1986
      - Régnier, P., Singapore and her regional environment, 1987
      - Deuchler, M., Modern Korea in historical perspective, 1987
      - Etienne, G., India's rural development, 1986
      - Billeter, J.-F., The System of the "classes status" in the Popular
      Republic of China, 1986
      - Centlivres, P., Peasantry and power in Afghanistan. From the end of the
      monarchy till the soviet intervention, 1985
      - Thien, T. T., "If" in History: Indonchina 1885-1985. Retrospective views
      of hundred years of history, 1986
CLIENTELE: students, teachers, researchers
ACCESS TO SERVICE: open to all users
TYPE & DESCRIPTION OF SERVICES PROVIDED: Provides library services, searches of
      information, selective dissemination of information and photocopies.

690 - DOKUMENTATIONSSTELLE FÜR WISSENSCHAFTSPOLITIK

SYNONYMOUS NAMES: Centre de Documentation de Politique de la Science;
      Documentation Centre for Science Policy
PARENT ORGANIZATION: Bundesamt für Bildung und Wissenschaft (Federal Office of
      Education and Science)
ADDRESS: Wildhainweg 9,
      Postfach 2732,
      CH-3001 Berne,
      SWITZERLAND
      TEL: 031/61 96 55 - TELEX: 912981 BBW CH - TELEFAX: 617854
CREATED: 1971   *HEAD:* Dr. R. Forclaz,
SIZE OF STAFF: Professional: 1   Other: 1   Total: 2
TYPE OF SERVICE: national; public; non-profit
SYSTEMS & NETWORKS ATTACHED TO: ABIM (Network of the Federal Administration)
SUBJECT COVERAGE: science policy; education; research policy
DATA BEING PROCESSED AND SIZE: 6,500 books; 381 periodicals
DATA PROCESSING METHODS: manual; computerized
HARDWARE USED: IBM PC AT
SOFTWARE USED: SWISSBASE
STORAGE MEDIA: traditional shelving of publications; microfiches
TYPE OF ACTIVITY: data collection; data analysis; distribution of information;
      publication
PERIODICALS PUBLISHED: - Wissenschaftspolitik (Politique de la Science)
CLIENTELE: scientists from the Federal Office of Education & Science, the Swiss
      Science Council, and from other federal offices (481 p.a.)
ACCESS TO SERVICE: services open to all users, free of charge
TYPE & DESCRIPTION OF SERVICES PROVIDED: Provides library services, bibliographic
      searches of information, and photocopies.

691 - HOCHSCHULE ST. GALLEN FÜR WIRTSCHAFTS- UND SOZIALWISSENSCHAFTEN, BIBLIOTHEK

SYNONYMOUS NAMES: University of St. Gallen for Business Administration, Economics a
    Social Sciences
ADDRESS: Dufourstrasse 50,
    CH-9000 St. Gallen,
    SWITZERLAND
    TEL: 071/302270 - TELEFAX: 0041/71/228355
CREATED: 1898   *HEAD:* Mr. X. Baumgartner, Head Librarian
SIZE OF STAFF: Professional: 9   Other: 9   Total: 18
TYPE OF SERVICE: public; non-profit
SUBJECT COVERAGE: administrative sciences; economics; social sciences; law;
    philosophy; political science; psychology; sociology
DATA BEING PROCESSED AND SIZE: 220,000 books and periodicals (9,000 p.a.)
DATA PROCESSING METHODS: manual; partially computerized
HARDWARE USED: IBM
SOFTWARE USED: Dobis/Libis
STORAGE MEDIA: traditional shelving of publications
TYPE OF ACTIVITY: distribution of information
CLIENTELE: students and faculty
ACCESS TO SERVICE: services open to specific categories of users
TYPE & DESCRIPTION OF SERVICES PROVIDED: Provides library services and photocopies.

**692 - INSTITUT UNIVERSITAIRE D'ETUDES DU DÉVELOPPEMENT, BIBLIOTHÈQUE ET CENTRE DE
    DOCUMENTATION**

SYNONYMOUS NAMES: IUED, Bibliothèque et Centre de Documentation;
    Institute of Development Studies, Library and Documentation Centre
ADDRESS: 24 rue Rothschild,
    1211 Geneva 21,
    SWITZERLAND
    TEL: (022) 31.59.40 - TELEX: 22810 IUED-CH
    CABLE: INSTIDEV GENEVA
CREATED: 1961   *HEAD:* Mr. R. Barbey, Head
SIZE OF STAFF: Professional: 4   Other: 2   Total: 6
TYPE OF SERVICE: public; non-profit
SYSTEMS & NETWORKS ATTACHED TO: IBISCUS (Système d'Information sur les Pays en
    Développement)
MATERIALS DESCRIBING THE SERVICE: - Institut Universitaire d'Etudes du Développemen
    (booklet)
    - Annual report
    - Guide de l'étudiant régulier/libre
WORKING LANGUAGE(S): French
SUBJECT COVERAGE: social sciences; economics; political science; social anthropolog
    cultural anthropology; sociology; demography; history; geography; educatic
    development
GEOGRAPHICAL COVERAGE: Africa; developing countries
DATA BEING PROCESSED AND SIZE: 33,000 books; 700 periodicals; 1,200 files
DATA PROCESSING METHODS: partially computerized
STORAGE MEDIA: traditional shelving of publications; fiches; microfiches
TYPE OF ACTIVITY: distribution of information; SSID scientific and methodological

activities; SSID training; publication
ERIODICALS PUBLISHED:
- New Acquisitions List, 24 p.a.
- Repertory of Periodicals, 1 p.a.
- List of Selected Articles, 4 p.a.
UBLICATIONS: - Suisse-Tiers monde: répertoire d'institutions
- Bibliographie Suisse-Tiers monde 1980-1985
- Guide de la documentation Suisse-Tiers monde
- Santé et développement: répertoire des principales institutions
LIENTELE: students, professors, researchers, libraries, institutions
CCESS TO SERVICE: services open to all users, free of charge
YPE & DESCRIPTION OF SERVICES PROVIDED: Provides library services, bibliographic, literature abstract searches of information on IBISCUS data base (accessed through GCAM), selective dissemination of information and photocopies.

93 - SCHWEIZERISCHES SOZIALARCHIV

YNONYMOUS NAMES: SSA;
Swiss Social Archives
ARENT ORGANIZATION: Bund, Kanton und Stadt Zürich
DDRESS: Stadelhoferstrasse 12,
8001 Zurich,
SWITZERLAND
TEL: (01) 251 76 44
REATED: 1906   *HEAD:* Dr. M. Tucek, Director
IZE OF STAFF: Professional: 2   Other: 9   Total: 11
YPE OF SERVICE: international; public; non-profit
ATERIALS DESCRIBING THE SERVICE: - Jahresberichte, 1 p.a.
UBJECT COVERAGE: social sciences; history; political science; social welfare; sociology; social history
EOGRAPHICAL COVERAGE: global
ATA BEING PROCESSED AND SIZE: 100,000 books; 4,200 periodicals; articles; manuscripts; pamphlets
ATA PROCESSING METHODS: manual
YPE OF ACTIVITY: data collection; publication
ERIODICALS PUBLISHED:
- Monatliche Züwachslisten (acquisition list), 12 p.a.
UBLICATIONS: - Occasional publications
LIENTELE: 20,000 visitors: Swiss and international interested persons, politicians, specialists of social problems
CCESS TO SERVICE: open to all users, free of charge
YPE & DESCRIPTION OF SERVICES PROVIDED: Provides library services, selective dissemination of information: standard profiles, retrospective bibliographic searches, photocopies and microforms of documents. The archives also include numerous often rare manuscripts of well-known personalities.

694 - SCHWEIZERISCHES WIRTSCHAFTSARCHIV

SYNONYMOUS NAMES: SWA;
>   Archives Economiques Suisses;
>   AES;
>   Swiss Economic Archives

PARENT ORGANIZATION: Offentliche Bibliothek der Universität Basel
ADDRESS: Kollegienhaus der Universität,
>   Petersgraben,
>   4051 Basel,
>   SWITZERLAND
>   TEL: (061) 25.44.99

CREATED: 1910   *HEAD:* Dr. H. U. Sulser, Director
SIZE OF STAFF: Professional: 1   Other: 9   Total: 10
TYPE OF SERVICE: national; public; non-profit
MATERIALS DESCRIBING THE SERVICE: - Zehntner, H., Gründung und Entwicklung des
>   schweizerischen Wirtschaftsarchivs in Basel, 1910-1960. Basel, 1960, 63 p.
>   - Annual report of the SWA

SUBJECT COVERAGE: social sciences; economics; administrative sciences; social
>   welfare; statistics; social policy; economic policy
GEOGRAPHICAL COVERAGE: Switzerland; Western Europe
DATA BEING PROCESSED AND SIZE: 422,000 books; 1,100 periodicals; 15,200 reports;
>   1,000,000 press clippings
DATA PROCESSING METHODS: manual
STORAGE MEDIA: traditional shelving of publications
TYPE OF ACTIVITY: data collection; publication
CLIENTELE: 10,500 users per year
ACCESS TO SERVICE: open to all users, free of charge
TYPE & DESCRIPTION OF SERVICES PROVIDED: Provides library services, photocopies of
>   documents, and retrospective bibliographic searches.

695 - SERVICE D'INFORMATION TIERS-MONDE

SYNONYMOUS NAMES: Informationsdienst.3. Welt;
>   i3m;
>   Service Ecole Tiers-Monde;
>   e3m;
>   Third World Information Service;
>   Third World School Service

ADDRESS: Chemin des Epinettes, 10,
>   CH-1007 Lausanne,
>   SWITZERLAND
>   TEL: (021) 27.43.53

CREATED: 1980   *HEAD:* Mr. M. Carera,
SIZE OF STAFF: Professional: 1   Other: 2   Total: 3
TYPE OF SERVICE: national; public; non-profit
MATERIALS DESCRIBING THE SERVICE: - Prospectus
WORKING LANGUAGE(S): French
SUBJECT COVERAGE: social sciences; demography; economics; education; geography;
>   political science; development
GEOGRAPHICAL COVERAGE: Switzerland; developing countries; Africa; Asia; Latin Amer

DATA BEING PROCESSED AND SIZE: 150 newspapers and periodicals; 10 statistical
     yearbooks; surveys
DATA PROCESSING METHODS: manual
TYPE OF ACTIVITY: data collection; distribution of information
PERIODICALS PUBLISHED:
     - Memento du Service d'Information Tiers-Monde, 12 p.a.
PUBLICATIONS: - Rencontres médias Nord-Sud, 1986
     - Femmes: une décennie pour s'entendre, 1986
CLIENTELE: teachers, students, journalists, voluntary-service overseas workers (800
     p.a.)
ACCESS TO SERVICE: services open to all users, free of charge
TYPE & DESCRIPTION OF SERVICES PROVIDED: Provides library services, searches of
     information and photocopies. Also provides press-clippings services (on a
     subscription basis). Other address: Monbijoustrasse 31, P.O. Box 1686, CH-
     3001 Bern.

Syrian Arab Republic / Rép. arabe syrienne / Rep. Arabe Siria

696 - OFFICE ARABE DE PRESSE ET DE DOCUMENTATION

SYNONYMOUS NAMES: OFA-Holding S.p.P.
ADDRESS: 67, Place Chahbandar,
     Damas,
     SYRIAN ARAB REPUBLIC
     TEL: (00963.11) 459.166 - TELEX: 411613 OFA SY
     CABLE: OFA
CREATED: 1964   *HEAD:* S. A. Darwich,
SIZE OF STAFF: Professional: 12   Other: 4   Total: 16
TYPE OF SERVICE: private; profit
MATERIALS DESCRIBING THE SERVICE: - EDINFO
     - Institut du Monde Arabe, Paris
WORKING LANGUAGE(S): French; English
SUBJECT COVERAGE: social sciences
GEOGRAPHICAL COVERAGE: Syrian Arab Republic; Arab countries
DATA BEING PROCESSED AND SIZE: books; periodicals; reports
DATA PROCESSING METHODS: partially computerized
HARDWARE USED: AMSTRAD 8512
STORAGE MEDIA: traditional shelving of publications; microfiches
TYPE OF ACTIVITY: data collection; distribution of information; publication
CLIENTELE: about 1,000 users
ACCESS TO SERVICE: paid service, open to specific categories of users
TYPE & DESCRIPTION OF SERVICES PROVIDED: Provides library services, literature
     abstract searches of information, selective dissemination of information,
     microforms, photocopies and translation of documents upon request.

Thailand / Thaïlande / Tailandia

697 - CHIANG MAI UNIVERSITY, SOCIAL RESEARCH INSTITUTE

SYNONYMOUS NAMES: CMU-SRI
ADDRESS:

Chiang Mai 50002,
THAILAND
TEL: (053) 211552
CREATED: 1964   *HEAD:* Prof. Dr. M. L. Bhansoon Ladavalya, Director
TYPE OF SERVICE: national; public; non-profit
MATERIALS DESCRIBING THE SERVICE: - Chiang Mai University, the Social Research
     Institute, 1985 Annual report, Chiang Mai, 1986
WORKING LANGUAGE(S): Thai; English
SUBJECT COVERAGE: social sciences
GEOGRAPHICAL COVERAGE: Northern Thailand
DATA BEING PROCESSED AND SIZE: 4,500 documentation items
DATA PROCESSING METHODS: manual
STORAGE MEDIA: traditional shelving of publications
TYPE OF ACTIVITY: data collection; data analysis; publication
CLIENTELE: general public
ACCESS TO SERVICE: services open to all users, free of charge
TYPE & DESCRIPTION OF SERVICES PROVIDED: Provides library services, bibliographic,
     literature abstract and quantitative data searchers, and selective
     dissemination of information.

698 - CHULALAONGKORN UNIVERSITY, INSTITUTE OF POPULATION STUDIES, ACADEMIC SERVICE DIVISION

ADDRESS: Bangkok 10500,
          THAILAND
          TEL: 252-0767; 251-1133-34
          CABLE: POPCHULA
CREATED: 1966   *HEAD:* Miss S. Vibulsresth,
SIZE OF STAFF: Professional: 2   Other: 2   Total: 4
TYPE OF SERVICE: national; public; non-profit
MATERIALS DESCRIBING THE SERVICE: - Institute of Population Studies, pamphlet
WORKING LANGUAGE(S): Thai
SUBJECT COVERAGE: demography; population
GEOGRAPHICAL COVERAGE: Southeast Asia
DATA BEING PROCESSED AND SIZE: 20,000 documentation items
DATA PROCESSING METHODS: manual
STORAGE MEDIA: traditional shelving of publications
TYPE OF ACTIVITY: distribution of information; publication
CLIENTELE: professors, researchers, students (2,500 p.a.)
ACCESS TO SERVICE: services open to all users, free of charge
TYPE & DESCRIPTION OF SERVICES PROVIDED: Provides library services and selective
     dissemination of information.

699 - CHULALONGKORN UNIVERSITY, ACADEMIC RESOURCE CENTER, THAILAND INFORMATION CENT

SYNONYMOUS NAMES: TIC
ADDRESS: Phaya Thai Rd.,
          Bangkok 10500,
          THAILAND

SELECTIVE INVENTORY OF DATA AND INFORMATION SERVICES
INVENTAIRE SELECTIF DES SERVICES D'INFORMATION

lease type or print, in English or French if possible/Prière de dactylographier ou d'écrire
n caractères d'imprimerie, en anglais ou en français si possible

. **Offical name of the Service & acronym**/Nom officiel du service et sigle:
   (50)

. **Name of parent organization (if applicable)**/Nom de l'organisation mère (s'il y a lieu):
   (59)

. **English translation of the official name of the service and of the parent organization**/
   Traduction en anglais du nom officiel du service et de l'organisation mère:
   (60)

. **Address**/Adresse:
   (84)

   Cable:
   Telephone: Telex: Telefax:

. **Date of establishment**/Date de création:

. **Name and functional title of present head of service**/Nom et titre fonctionnel du directeur
   actuel du service:
   (76)

. **Size of staff/Effectif:**
   (35)

| **Professionals/** | Others | |
Documentalistes, Bibliothécaires	Autres	Total

A. **STATUS & SCIENTIFIC FIELD of the SERVICE/**
   STRUCTURE & DOMAINE SCIENTIFIQUE du SERVIC
----

8. **Type of the service**/Type du service:
   (70)

   |____| International |____| Public |____| Profit-making/
                                                          But lucratif
   |____| National |____| Private/Privé |____| Non-profit making/
                                                          Sans but lucratif

9. **Attachment to a broader system or network**/Appartenance à un système ou réseau:
   (36)

                   |____| Yes/Oui |____| No/Non

   If yes, give complete name and acronym/Si oui, donnez-en le nom complet et le sigle:

10. **Publications describing the service. Give full bibliographic details**/Publications décrivant
    le service. Références bibliographiques complètes
    (37)
        Titles/Titres:

11. **Geographical coverage**/Zones géographiques couvertes:
    (82)

12. **Working language(s)**/Langue(s) de travail:
    (83)

13. **Main fields covered**/Principaux domaines d'étude. Mark in order of importance the
        appropriate box/Marquez par ordre d'importance la case appropriée:
        (81)
                |____| **Social sciences (General)**/Sciences sociales (en général)
                |____| **Administrative Sciences**/Sciences administratives
                |____| **Demography**/Démographie
                |____| **Economics**/Science économique
                |____| **Education**/Pédagogie
                |____| **Geography**/Géographie
                |____| **History**/Histoire
                |____| **Law**/Droit
                |____| **Linguistics**/Linguistique
                |____| **Philosophy**/Philosophie
                |____| **Political science**/Science politique
                |____| **Psychology**/Psychologie
                |____| **Social anthropology**/Anthropologie sociale
                |____| **Cultural anthropology**/Anthropologie culturelle
                |____| **Social welfare**/Action sociale
                |____| **Sociology**/Sociologie

        Specific subjects (Specify)/Domaines spécialisés (Précizez):

DATA COLLECTION / COLLECTE DES DONNEES

. **Categories of documents or data processed** (please detail). Approximate number
/Catégories de documents ou de données traitées (précisez). Nombre approximatif

(ex: books, periodicals, reports, on-going research, seminars, training courses, etc./livres, périodiques, rapports, recherches en cours, séminaires, cours, etc.) (38)	Total	p.a.

. **Data processing and retrieval**/Traitement et récupération de l'information
(74)

|____| **Manual (clerical)** |____| **Partially computerized/** |____| **Computerized/**
Manuel   Partiellement automatisé   Par ordinateur

If computerized, please indicate/Si par ordinateur, veuillez indiquer:

a) **hardware used**/matériel informatique utilisé:
(40)

b) **software used**/logiciel utilisé:
(41)

Storage-media/Stockage des données
(Traditional shelving of publications, fiches, tapes, discs, microfiches, etc./
Collection de publications sur rayonnages, fiches, bandes ou disques
magnétiques, micro-fiches, etc.)
(44)

. **Type of activity/**Type d'activité:
(71)

|____| **Data collection**/Collecte de données

|____| **Data analysis**/Analyse des données

|____| **Distribution of information (through library services, use of data bases, etc.)**/
Distribution d'information (service de bibliothèque, utilisation de bases de
données, etc.)

|____| **Scientific research and methodological activities in the field of SSID/**Activités
de recherche scientifique et méthodologique dans le domaine de l'information et la
documentation en sciences sociales

|____| **Training of SSID personnel**/Formation de personnel pour l'information et la documentation
en sciences sociales

|____| **Publication (printed products available**/Publication (produits disponibles)
ex. periodicals, yearbooks, accession lists, indexes, catalogues, etc./
Périodiques, annuaires, listes d'acquisitions, index, catalogues, etc.
Titles of periodicals/Titres des périodiques:
(62/68)

Titles of publications, catalogues/Titres des autres publications, catalogues, etc.
(93)

C: SERVICES PROVIDED / SERVICES OFFERTS
----

17. Nature and number of users/Type et nombre d'utilisateurs:
   (42)

----

18. Conditions of access to services/Conditions auxquelles les services sont offerts:
   (45)

   |____| **Services for internal users (members of the organization)**/Services
            à usage interne (réservés aux membres de l'organisation)
   |____| **Services open to specific categories of users, e.g. researchers**/Services
            offerts à des publics déterminés, par ex. chercheurs
   |____| **Services open to all users**/Services accessibles à tous
   |____| **Paid services**/Services payant
   |____| **Services free of charge (reimbursement of marginal costs)**/Service gratuit
            (remboursement des coûts marginaux)

----

19. Describe services provided and other characteristics of the Service, if any/Décrire les
   services offerts et le cas échéant toutes autres caractéristiques du service:
   (80)

   |____| **Library services**/Service de bibliothèque

   |____| **Search of information**/Recherche d'information

            |____| **Bibliographic**/Bibliographique
            |____| **Literature abstracts, surveys of literature, etc.**/Résumés analytiques
            |____| **Quantitative data**/Données quantitatives

   |____| **On-line services**/Services en ligne

            |____| **Own data bases**/Vos banques de données:
                     Name(s)/Nom(s):

            |____| **Data bases produced by other suppliers/**Banques de données produites
                     par d'autres:
                     Name(s)/Nom(s) | Accessed through/Accessible par
                                         |
                                         |
                                         |

   |____| **Selective dissemination of information**/Diffusion sélective d'information

   |____| **Production of information on magnetic tapes or discs**/Communication
            d'information sur bandes ou disques magnétiques

   |____| **Provision of microforms**/Provision de microformes

   |____| **Provision of photocopies**/Provision de photocopies

   |____| **Translation of documents upon request**/Traduction de documents sur demande

   |____| **Others (specify)**/Autres (précisez):

Name and functional title of respondant/
Nom et titre fonctionnel de la personne ayant rempli le questionnaire

TEL: 215-3616
REATED: 1972   *HEAD:* Mrs. K. Boon-Itt, Head
IZE OF STAFF: Professional: 8   Other: 4   Total: 12
YPE OF SERVICE: national; public; non-profit
ORKING LANGUAGE(S): Thai; English
UBJECT COVERAGE: social sciences
EOGRAPHICAL COVERAGE: Thailand; Southeast Asia
ATA BEING PROCESSED AND SIZE: 41,800 documentation items (research reports),
      monographs, surveys, articles, maps, theses and dissertations, speeches,
      conference proceedings
ATA PROCESSING METHODS: partially computerized
OFTWARE USED: Micro CDS/ISIS
TORAGE MEDIA: traditional shelving of publications; microfiches
YPE OF ACTIVITY: data collection; data analysis; distribution of information
LIENTELE: 300 university staff, graduate students, private scholars or researchers
      per month
CCESS TO SERVICE: open to all users, free of charge
YPE & DESCRIPTION OF SERVICES PROVIDED: Provides library services, bibliographic and
      literature abstract searches, on-line search of own data base "TIC Data
      Base", microforms and photocopies.

00 - CHULALONGKORN UNIVERSITY, INSTITUTE OF ASIAN STUDIES, LIBRARY

DDRESS: Bangkok 10500,
      THAILAND
      TEL: 251-5199, 251-9956
      CABLE: INSTASIA BANGKOK 10500
EAD: Prof.Dr. K. Theeravit, Director
YPE OF SERVICE: international; public; non-profit
ORKING LANGUAGE(S): Thai; English
UBJECT COVERAGE: social sciences; political science; sociology; economics;
      Indochinese problems
EOGRAPHICAL COVERAGE: Asia
ATA PROCESSING METHODS: partially computerized
OFTWARE USED: Wordstar, Lotus, CDS/ISIS
TORAGE MEDIA: traditional shelving of publications, discs
YPE OF ACTIVITY: data collection; data analysis; distribution of information; SSID
      scientific and methodological activities; publication
ERIODICALS PUBLISHED: - Asian Studies Information
LIENTELE: students, scholars, business community, government agencies
CCESS TO SERVICE: services open to all users, some paid services, some free of
      charge
YPE & DESCRIPTION OF SERVICES PROVIDED: Provides libary services, selective
      dissemination of information, information on magnetic tape, audio-visual aid
      programs, Asian studies training program and publications program.

**701 - MAHIDOL UNIVERSITY, INSTITUTE FOR POPULATION AND SOCIAL RESEARCH, DATA
COLLECTION AND PROCESSING UNIT**

ADDRESS: 25/25 Puthamonthol 4,
Nakornchaisi,
Nakornpathom 73170,
THAILAND
TEL: 4419521 - TELEX: 84770 UNIMAHI
CABLE: POPCENTER SALAYA 73170
CREATED: 1982   *HEAD:* Prof. U. Kanungsukkasem, Director
SIZE OF STAFF: Total: 3
TYPE OF SERVICE: national; public; non-profit
WORKING LANGUAGE(S): Thai; English
SUBJECT COVERAGE: demography; social sciences; administrative sciences; economics;
education; population
GEOGRAPHICAL COVERAGE: Thailand
DATA PROCESSING METHODS: computerized
HARDWARE USED: IBM microcomputer
SOFTWARE USED: DBase II, DBase III, SPSS/PC, SPSS
STORAGE MEDIA: diskettes, magnetic tapes
TYPE OF ACTIVITY: data analysis; distribution of information; SSID scientific and
methodological activities; publication
CLIENTELE: researchers, managers, planners, policy-makers
ACCESS TO SERVICE: services open to specific categories of users
TYPE & DESCRIPTION OF SERVICES PROVIDED: Provides bibliographic and quantitative data
searches, on-line services using own data base and selective dissemination
of information.

**702 - NATIONAL INSTITUTE OF DEVELOPMENT ADMINISTRATION, LIBRARY AND INFORMATION
CENTER**

SYNONYMOUS NAMES: NIDA, Library and Information Center
PARENT ORGANIZATION: National Institute of Development Administration
ADDRESS: Klong Chan,
Bangkapi,
Bangkok 10240,
THAILAND
TEL: 3775481
CABLE: NIDA BANGKOK
CREATED: 1970   *HEAD:* Prof. N. Berananda, Director
SIZE OF STAFF: Professional: 30   Other: 44   Total: 74
TYPE OF SERVICE: national; public; non-profit
WORKING LANGUAGE(S): Thai; English
SUBJECT COVERAGE: social sciences; administrative sciences; economics; political
science; demography; sociology; social anthropology; linguistics; cultural
anthropology
GEOGRAPHICAL COVERAGE: Thailand
DATA BEING PROCESSED AND SIZE: 148,000 volumes; 990 periodicals
DATA PROCESSING METHODS: partially computerized
HARDWARE USED: IBM PC/XT
SOFTWARE USED: CDS/ISIS

ORAGE MEDIA: fiches; tapes, discs, microfiches
YPE OF ACTIVITY: data collection; distribution of information; publication
ERIODICALS PUBLISHED:
    - NIDA Bulletin, 6 p.a.
UBLICATIONS: - Index to Thai periodicals
    - Index to Thai newspapers
    - Population: bibliography, 1981
    - Development information: an annotated bibliography
    - Doctoral dissertations on Thailand
    - Bibliography on economic and social development in Thailand
    - Bibliography of audio-visual materials in the NIDA Library and Information Center
    - Annotated bibliography of theses on public administration
LIENTELE: 150,000 users p.a.
CCESS TO SERVICE: open to all users, free of charge
YPE & DESCRIPTION OF SERVICES PROVIDED: Provides library services, information
    searches, selective dissemination of information, information on magnetic
    tapes, microforms and photocopies.

03 - NATIONAL RESEARCH COUNCIL, LIBRARY AND DOCUMENTARY SERVICE DIVISION

DDRESS: Phaholyothin Road,
    Bang Khen,
    Bangkok 10900,
    THAILAND
    TEL: 5791121-30 - TELEX: 82213 NARECOU TH
    CABLE: NRC
REATED: 1975   *HEAD:* Mr. S. Saenhorm, Director
IZE OF STAFF: Professional: 9   Other: 9   Total: 18
YPE OF SERVICE: national; public; non-profit
YSTEMS & NETWORKS ATTACHED TO: ASTINFO (Regional Network for the Exchange of
    Information and Experience in Science and Technology in Asia and the
    Pacific)
ORKING LANGUAGE(S): Thai; English
UBJECT COVERAGE: social sciences; administrative sciences; economics; education;
    geography; history; law; linguistics; philosophy; political science;
    psychology; sociology
EOGRAPHICAL COVERAGE: Thailand
ATA BEING PROCESSED AND SIZE: 38,000 books and documents; 308 periodicals
ATA PROCESSING METHODS: manual
YPE OF ACTIVITY: data collection; data analysis; distribution of information;
    publication
ERIODICALS PUBLISHED:
    - NRC Bulletin
LIENTELE: about 300 users per month
CCESS TO SERVICE: open to all users free of charge
YPE & DESCRIPTION OF SERVICES PROVIDED: Provides library services and
    bibliographies.

Thailand / Thaïlande / Tailandia

704 - OFFICE OF THE NATIONAL ECONOMIC AND SOCIAL DEVELOPMENT BOARD, DEVELOPMENT STUDIES AND INFORMATION DIVISION

ADDRESS: 962 Krung Kasem Road,
Bangkok,
THAILAND
TEL: 2824842
HEAD: Mr. S. Krusuansombat, Director
SIZE OF STAFF: Professional: 3
TYPE OF SERVICE: public
WORKING LANGUAGE(S): Thai; English
SUBJECT COVERAGE: social sciences; administrative sciences; demography; economics; education; geography; history; law; political science; development
DATA BEING PROCESSED AND SIZE: books (8,600 in Thai, 5,600 in English); periodicals (115 in Thai, 82 in English); 1,500 reports; pamphlets
DATA PROCESSING METHODS: manual
TYPE OF ACTIVITY: data collection; SSID scientific and methodological activities; publication
CLIENTELE: general public, civil servants, students, professors (18,000 p.a.)
ACCESS TO SERVICE: services open to all users, free of charge
TYPE & DESCRIPTION OF SERVICES PROVIDED: Provides library services.

705 - THAMMASAT UNIVERSITY, THAI KHADI RESEARCH INSTITUTE

ADDRESS: Bangkok 10200,
THAILAND
TEL: 223.01.95 - TELEX: 72432 TAMSAT TH
CREATED: 1975   *HEAD:* Dr. M. Krongkaew,
TYPE OF SERVICE: public; non-profit
SYSTEMS & NETWORKS ATTACHED TO: Thammasat University, T.U.
MATERIALS DESCRIBING THE SERVICE: - Brochure
WORKING LANGUAGE(S): Thai; English
SUBJECT COVERAGE: social sciences
GEOGRAPHICAL COVERAGE: Thailand
DATA BEING PROCESSED AND SIZE: books, periodicals, reports, on-going research, seminars, international conference
DATA PROCESSING METHODS: partially computerized
STORAGE MEDIA: traditional shelving of publications; tapes; discs
TYPE OF ACTIVITY: data analysis; distribution of information; publication
PERIODICALS PUBLISHED:
- Thai Studies Bulletin
CLIENTELE: academics, government public officers (10 per month)
ACCESS TO SERVICE: open to all users
TYPE & DESCRIPTION OF SERVICES PROVIDED: Provides library services, bibliographic a literature abstract searches, selective dissemination of information.

06 - TRIBAL RESEARCH INSTITUTE, LIBRARY

PARENT ORGANIZATION: Ministry of the Interior, Department of Public Welfare
ADDRESS:

> Huay Kaew Road,
> Chiang Mai Province 50002,
> THAILAND
> TEL: (053) 221933

CREATED: 1964
SIZE OF STAFF: Professional: 1   Other: 2   Total: 3
TYPE OF SERVICE: international; public; non-profit
SYSTEMS & NETWORKS ATTACHED TO: Thailand Information Centre
WORKING LANGUAGE(S): Thai
SUBJECT COVERAGE: social anthropology; cultural anthropology; social welfare;
> sociology; tribes
GEOGRAPHICAL COVERAGE: Thailand; global
DATA BEING PROCESSED AND SIZE: books, periodicals, reports
DATA PROCESSING METHODS: partially computerized
STORAGE MEDIA: traditional shelving of publications
TYPE OF ACTIVITY: data collection; distribution of information; publication
CLIENTELE: general public
ACCESS TO SERVICE: services open to all users, free of charge
TYPE & DESCRIPTION OF SERVICES PROVIDED: Provides library services, bibliographic
> searches, selective dissemination of information and photocopies.

07 - UNIVERSITÉ DE BENIN, UNITÉ DE RECHERCHE DÉMOGRAPHIQUE, CENTRE DE DOCUMENTATION

SYNONYMOUS NAMES: University of Benin, Demographic Research Unit, Documentation
> Centre
ADDRESS: B.P. 12971,
> Lomé,
> TOGO
> TEL: 21-17-21 - TELEX: UBETO 5258
CREATED: 1982   *HEAD:* Ms. A. Nomenyo, Documentalist
SIZE OF STAFF: Professional: 2   Other: 1   Total: 3
TYPE OF SERVICE: national; public; non-profit
SYSTEMS & NETWORKS ATTACHED TO: Population Information Network for Africa (POPIN-
> AFRICA)
MATERIALS DESCRIBING THE SERVICE: - Centre de Documentation (brochure); activités de
> l'URD
WORKING LANGUAGE(S): French
SUBJECT COVERAGE: demography; economics
GEOGRAPHICAL COVERAGE: Africa; Western Africa; Togo
DATA BEING PROCESSED AND SIZE: books, articles, reports (2,500 p.a.)
DATA PROCESSING METHODS: manual; computerized
HARDWARE USED: IBM-PC
SOFTWARE USED: CDS/ISIS
STORAGE MEDIA: traditional shelving of publications, fiches, magnetic discs
TYPE OF ACTIVITY: data collection; data analysis; distribution of information;
> publication

PERIODICALS PUBLISHED:
        - Liste d'Acquisitions
PUBLICATIONS: - Bibliographie démographique du Togo
        - Etudes togolaises de population
        - Population togolaise
CLIENTELE: researchers, teachers, students, experts (400 p.a.)
ACCESS TO SERVICE: services open to all users, free of charge
TYPE & DESCRIPTION OF SERVICES PROVIDED: Provides library services, bibliographic
        search and on-line services using database POPLINE, and selective
        dissemination of information.

708 - CARIBBEAN AGRICULTURAL RESEARCH AND DEVELOPMENT INSTITUTE, LITERATURE SERVICE

SYNONYMOUS NAMES: CARDI Literature Service
ADDRESS: U.W.I. Campus,
        St. Augustine,
        TRINIDAD AND TOBAGO
        TEL: 1.809.645.1205 - TELEX: 3000 POSTLX WG
        CABLE: CARDINST
CREATED: 1975
SIZE OF STAFF: Total: 3
TYPE OF SERVICE: international; public; non-profit
WORKING LANGUAGE(S): English
SUBJECT COVERAGE: economics; agricultural economics; agricultural development; rural
        development
GEOGRAPHICAL COVERAGE: Caribbean area; Europe; USA; Canada; Asia; Australia
DATA PROCESSING METHODS: partially computerized
HARDWARE USED: ICL Mainframe
SOFTWARE USED: Famulus
STORAGE MEDIA: traditional shelving of publications
TYPE OF ACTIVITY: distribution of information; publication
CLIENTELE: researchers, extension officers, farmers, students
ACCESS TO SERVICE: open to specific categories of users, free of charge
TYPE & DESCRIPTION OF SERVICES PROVIDED: Provides library services, bibliographic,
        literature abstract and quantitative data searches, on-line services using
        DIALOG, selective dissemination of information and photocopies.

709 - CIPRIANI LABOUR COLLEGE, LIBRARY

ADDRESS: Churchill Roosevelt Highway,
        Valsayn,
        TRINIDAD AND TOBAGO
        TEL: 662-5014
CREATED: 1966
SIZE OF STAFF: Professional: 1   Other: 3   Total: 4
TYPE OF SERVICE: private; non-profit
SUBJECT COVERAGE: administrative sciences; labour law; industrial relations;
        cooperatives

DATA BEING PROCESSED AND SIZE: 10,000 books, periodicals and reports
TYPE OF ACTIVITY: distribution of information; publication
ACCESS TO SERVICE: services open to specific categories of users, free of charge
TYPE & DESCRIPTION OF SERVICES PROVIDED: Provides bibliographies, information
        searches and photocopies.

710 - INDUSTRIAL COURT OF TRINIDAD AND TOBAGO, LIBRARY

ADDRESS: St. Vincent St. 26,
        P.O. Box 1289,
        Port-of-Spain,
        TRINIDAD AND TOBAGO
        TEL: 62-31304
CREATED: 1966   *HEAD:* Ms. S. Badree, Librarian
SIZE OF STAFF: Professional: 2   Other: 3   Total: 5
TYPE OF SERVICE: national; public
WORKING LANGUAGE(S): English
SUBJECT COVERAGE: administrative sciences; economics; law; political science; labour
        relations
GEOGRAPHICAL COVERAGE: Trinidad and Tobago
DATA BEING PROCESSED AND SIZE: books; reports; articles; court judgments
DATA PROCESSING METHODS: manual
TYPE OF ACTIVITY: distribution of information
CLIENTELE: lawyers, trade unionists, management-consultants, students, general public
ACCESS TO SERVICE: services open to all users, free of charge
TYPE & DESCRIPTION OF SERVICES PROVIDED: Provides library services, bibliographic
        searches of information, and photocopies.

Tunisia / Tunisie / Túnez

711 - CENTRE DE DOCUMENTATION NATIONALE

SYNONYMOUS NAMES: CDN;
        National Documentation Centre
PARENT ORGANIZATION: Ministère de l'Information
ADDRESS: Cité Montplaisir,
        B.P. 350,
        1002 Tunis Belvédère,
        TUNISIA
        TEL: 894 266 - TELEX 15458 TN
CREATED: 1957   *HEAD:* M. A. Daly, Director
SIZE OF STAFF: Professional: 21   Other: 50   Total: 71
TYPE OF SERVICE: national; public; non-profit
SYSTEMS & NETWORKS ATTACHED TO: CYCLADE-ARISNET
WORKING LANGUAGE(S): Arabic; French
SUBJECT COVERAGE: social sciences; political science; international problems;
        administrative sciences; history
GEOGRAPHICAL COVERAGE: global; Tunisia
DATA BEING PROCESSED AND SIZE: 10,700 books and monographs, 1,802 newspapers and
        periodicals, 5,500 clippings; audiovisual forms; 1,400 slides, 40,400

photographs, 2,189 microforms
DATA PROCESSING METHODS: partially computerized
HARDWARE USED: CII - HB, DPS 8; IBM 286
SOFTWARE USED: MISTRAL; CDS/ISIS
PERIODICALS PUBLISHED:
- Références Bibliographiques dans "Tunisie-actualités", 4 p.a.
- Liste d'acquisitions dans bulletin mensuel d'information, 12 p.a.
- Bulletin signalétique hebdomadaire "Trait-d'Union"
PUBLICATIONS: - Guide des services d'information en Tunisie, 1983
- Répertoire des périodiques tunisiens, 1987
CLIENTELE: journalists, researchers, students, teachers, others
ACCESS TO SERVICE: paid services open to all users, free of charge
TYPE & DESCRIPTION OF SERVICES PROVIDED: Library services, retrospective
bibliographic searches, current awareness service, provision of selective
dissemination of information, photographs, photocopies and documentary
dossiers. Has its own data bases: TANIT-CHRONO, TANIT-POLECO, TANIT-BIBLIO,
TANIT-BIO.

712 - INSTITUT D'ECONOMIE QUANTITATIVE, SERVICE DOCUMENTATION ET PUBLICATIONS

SYNONYMOUS NAMES: IEQ/DP
PARENT ORGANIZATION: Ministère du Plan
ADDRESS: Ministère du Plan,
27, rue du Liban,
1002 Tunis,
TUNISIA
TEL: 283 214
CABLE: 15117
CREATED: 1973   *HEAD:* Mr. M. Abbes, Head
SIZE OF STAFF: Professional: 3   Other: 2   Total: 5
TYPE OF SERVICE: national; public; non-profit
WORKING LANGUAGE(S): French
SUBJECT COVERAGE: social sciences; demography; economy; social economics; socio-
economic development; modelling; economic situation; economic system;
economic forecasting; social problems; public finance
GEOGRAPHICAL COVERAGE: Tunisia
DATA BEING PROCESSED AND SIZE: 5,000 books; 400 articles; reports; on-going research
seminars; magazines
DATA PROCESSING METHODS: partially computerized
HARDWARE USED: HP VECTRA
SOFTWARE USED: CDS/ISIS
STORAGE MEDIA: traditional shelving of publications; discs; fiches
TYPE OF ACTIVITY: data collection; data analysis; distribution of information; SSID
training; publication
PERIODICALS PUBLISHED: - Les Cahiers de l'IEQ
- Informations Bibliographiques
CLIENTELE: research personnel, students (100 p. month)
ACCESS TO SERVICE: services open to specific categories of users
TYPE & DESCRIPTION OF SERVICES PROVIDED: Provides library services, selective
dissemination of information, bibliographic, literature abstract and
quantitative data searches of information using own data base "BIBLOS" and

external data bases of the OECD. Photocopying and translation facilities are also available.

13 - AVRUPA TOPLULUKLARI KOMISYONU TURKIYE TEMSILCILIGI ANKARA

SYNONYMOUS NAMES: Representation of the Commission of the European Communities in Turkey
PARENT ORGANIZATION: Commission of the European Communities
ADDRESS: Kuleli Sokak No. 15,
          G.O.P. Ankara,
          TURKEY
          TEL: 1376840 - TELEX: 44320 atbe tr. - TELEFAX: (4) 137 79 40
          CABLE: 44320
CREATED: 1987   *HEAD:* J. van Rij, Head
SIZE OF STAFF: Professional: 1   Other: 9   Total: 10
TYPE OF SERVICE: international; public; non-profit
WORKING LANGUAGE(S): English; French; Turkish
SUBJECT COVERAGE: social sciences; demography; economics; political science; law
GEOGRAPHICAL COVERAGE: Europe; Mediterranean Area
DATA BEING PROCESSED AND SIZE: 7,000 books; 400 periodicals; surveys; research
          reports; leaflets; films; microforms
DATA PROCESSING METHODS: manual
STORAGE MEDIA: traditional shelving of publications, fiches
TYPE OF ACTIVITY: data collection; publication
PERIODICALS PUBLISHED:
          - EC News, 24 p.a.
PUBLICATIONS: - European textile industry, 1986 (in Turkish)
          - La Communauté des douze, bienvenue à l'Espagne et Portugal, 1986 (in Turkish)
          - Les Emmigrés dans les CE 1986 (in Turkish)
          - Institutions des CE, 1986 (in Turkish)
          - Dictionnaire des CE, 1984 (in Turkish)
          - What is Europe, 1982 (in Turkish)
          - Programme intégré méditerranéen, 1986 (in Turkish)
CLIENTELE: members of universities, government organizations, private firms and
          journalists
ACCESS TO SERVICE: open to all users, free of charge
TYPE & DESCRIPTION OF SERVICES PROVIDED: Provides library services, query answering
          services, photocopies and documents.

14 - DEVLET PLANLAMA TEŞKILATI, DOKUMANTASYON SERVISI

SYNONYMOUS NAMES: State Planning Organization, Documentation Service
ADDRESS: Bakanliklar,
          Ankara,
          TURKEY
          TEL: (4) 230.86.55 - TELEX: 44015 DEPT TR
CREATED: 1960   *HEAD:* A. Basak Kayiran, Chief Librarian

Turkey / Turquie / Turquia

SIZE OF STAFF: Professional: 5   Other: 5   Total: 10
TYPE OF SERVICE: national; public; non-profit
SUBJECT COVERAGE: economics; development planning; economic planning; social
     sciences; administrative sciences; demography; education; social welfare
GEOGRAPHICAL COVERAGE: Turkey
DATA BEING PROCESSED AND SIZE: books, periodicals, reports
DATA PROCESSING METHODS: manual; partially computerized
HARDWARE USED: VAX VT 220
TYPE OF ACTIVITY: data collection; data analysis; distribution of information;
     publication
PERIODICALS PUBLISHED:
     - Monthly Bulletin (Current Awareness Service)
PUBLICATIONS: - Bibliographies (Series)
CLIENTELE: researchers
ACCESS TO SERVICE: open to all users, free of charge
TYPE & DESCRIPTION OF SERVICES PROVIDED: Provides library services, documentation and
     press clippings, bibliographic and literature abstract searches, and
     photocopies.

715 - MILLI PRODÜKTIVITE MERKEZI EGITIM VE YAYIN ŞUBESI

SYNONYMOUS NAMES: MPM;
     National Productivity Centre, Department of Training and Publications
ADDRESS: Güvenevler,
     Gelibolu Sokak, 5,
     06420 Kavaklidere Ankara,
     TURKEY
     TEL: 286700 - TELEX: MIPM 46041
     CABLE: PRODUKTIVITE
CREATED: 1965   *HEAD:* Mrs. Z. Kuteş
SIZE OF STAFF: Professional: 6
TYPE OF SERVICE: national; public; non-profit
SUBJECT COVERAGE: economics; productivity
GEOGRAPHICAL COVERAGE: Turkey
DATA BEING PROCESSED AND SIZE: 10,000 books; 150 periodicals; reports; 70 films
DATA PROCESSING METHODS: manual
STORAGE MEDIA: traditional shelving of publications
TYPE OF ACTIVITY: distribution of information
PUBLICATIONS: - NPC Library Catalogue
CLIENTELE: research and administrative staff, managers and experts in different
     fields
ACCESS TO SERVICE: open to all users, free of charge
TYPE & DESCRIPTION OF SERVICES PROVIDED: Provides library services, provision of
     photocopies and microforms of documents.

716 - TÜRKIYE BILIMSEL VE TEKNIK DOKÜMANTASYON MERKEZI

SYNONYMOUS NAMES: TÜRDOK;
     The Turkish Scientific and Technical Documentation Centre

ARENT ORGANIZATION: Türkiye Bilimsel ve Teknik Araştirma Kurumu (TÜBITAK)/The
          Scientific and Technical Research Council of Turkey
DDRESS: Tunus Caddesi No. 33,
          Kavaklidere,
          Ankara,
          TURKEY
          TEL: 90.41.262770 - TELEX: 43186 BTAK TR
          CABLE: TÜBITAK-Ankara
REATED: 1966   *HEAD:* Mr. Z. Ebensoy, Director
IZE OF STAFF: Professional: 17   Other: 12   Total: 29
YPE OF SERVICE: national
ATERIALS DESCRIBING THE SERVICE: - TÜBES-Turkish Information Retrieval System,
          Ankara, 1987(brochure)
ORKING LANGUAGE(S): Turkish; English
UBJECT COVERAGE: social sciences
EOGRAPHICAL COVERAGE: global
ATA BEING PROCESSED AND SIZE: 12,000 books; 380 periodicals; 4,000 TÜBITAK
          publications; 10,000 theses
ATA PROCESSING METHODS: manual
YPE OF ACTIVITY: data collection; distribution of information
CCESS TO SERVICE: services open to all users, some paid services
YPE & DESCRIPTION OF SERVICES PROVIDED: Provides library services, bibliographic and
          literature abstract searches, on-line services using external data bases
          (Dialog, ESA/IRS, INFOLINE, BRS, Questel, SDC), microforms and photocopies.

Uganda / Ouganda / Uganda

17 - MAKERERE UNIVERSITY, MAKERERE INSTITUTE OF SOCIAL RESEARCH LIBRARY

YNONYMOUS NAMES: MISR Library
DDRESS: P.O. Box 16022,
          Wandegeya-Kampala,
          UGANDA
          TEL: 54582
          CABLE: MAKUNIKA, Kampala
REATED: 1948   *HEAD:* Mr. B. M. Kawesa, Librarian
IZE OF STAFF: Professional: 1   Other: 3   Total: 4
YPE OF SERVICE: international; public; non-profit
YSTEMS & NETWORKS ATTACHED TO: Makerere University Library Service
ORKING LANGUAGE(S): English
UBJECT COVERAGE: social sciences; administrative sciences; demography; economics;
          political science; social anthropology; cultural anthropology; social
          welfare; sociology; linguistics; psychology; economics of education
EOGRAPHICAL COVERAGE: Uganda; Eastern Africa
ATA BEING PROCESSED AND SIZE: 10,000 books; government publications; unpublished
          manuscripts and pamphlets; discussion papers; 300 periodicals
ATA PROCESSING METHODS: manual
TORAGE MEDIA: traditional shelving of publications
YPE OF ACTIVITY: distribution of information; publication
ERIODICALS PUBLISHED:
          - Policy Abstracts and Research Newsletter: a Journal of Policy
          Communication

- Accession List
PUBLICATIONS: - Makerere Institute of Social Research: institute publications
  - Economic development research papers (EDRP)
  - Rural development research papers (RDRP)
  - Mawazo: a publication of the faculties of arts and social sciences
CLIENTELE: students; researchers
ACCESS TO SERVICE: open to all users, free of charge
TYPE & DESCRIPTION OF SERVICES PROVIDED: Provides current awareness service, library
  services, bibliographic and literature abstract searches of information and
  photocopies.

718 - AKADEMIA NAUK UKRAINSKOI SSR, OTDEL NAUCHNOI INFORMATSII PO OBSHCHESTVENNYM NAUKAM

SYNONYMOUS NAMES: Onion an USSR;
  The Ukrainian Academy of Sciences, Department of Scientific Information in
  Social Sciences
ADDRESS: GSP ul. Kirova 4, Nauka,
  252001 Kiev,
  UKRAINIAN SSR
  TEL: 29-76-52
CREATED: 1977   *HEAD:* Dr. I. V. Valko, Head
SIZE OF STAFF: Professional: 14   Other: 5   Total: 19
SUBJECT COVERAGE: social sciences
TYPE OF ACTIVITY: publication

719 - BRITISH INSTITUTE OF MANAGEMENT, MANAGEMENT INFORMATION CENTRE

SYNONYMOUS NAMES: BIM/MIC
ADDRESS: Management House,
  Cottingham Road,
  Corby,
  Northants NN17 ITT,
  UNITED KINGDOM
  TEL: (0536) 204-222
CREATED: 1947   *HEAD:* R. Norton, Head of Information Services
SIZE OF STAFF: Professional: 11   Other: 6   Total: 17
TYPE OF SERVICE: national; private; non-profit
MATERIALS DESCRIBING THE SERVICE: - British Institute of Management, Information pac
WORKING LANGUAGE(S): English
SUBJECT COVERAGE: administrative sciences; management; marketing; local government;
  personnel management
GEOGRAPHICAL COVERAGE: global
DATA BEING PROCESSED AND SIZE: 60,000 books, pamphlets and related materials; 400
  periodicals
DATA PROCESSING METHODS: partially computerized
HARDWARE USED: ICL ME 29

SOFTWARE USED: Assassin
TYPE OF ACTIVITY: distribution of information; publication
PERIODICALS PUBLISHED: - MINT, 12 p.a.
             - Acquisitions Bulletin, 4 p.a.
             - Journals Holdings List, 2 p.a.
PUBLICATIONS: - Overseas management organizations
            - List of reading lists
CLIENTELE: managers, students
ACCESS TO SERVICE: open to all users, free of charge; paid services for extensive
        bibliographic searches
TYPE & DESCRIPTION OF SERVICES PROVIDED: Provides full library and information
        services, on-line retrieval service, current awareness service, research-
        and-report services, selective dissemination of information, press cuttings
        and photocopies.

720 - BRITISH LIBRARY, BUSINESS INFORMATION SERVICE

PARENT ORGANIZATION: British Library: Science Reference and Information Service
ADDRESS: 25, Southampton Buildings,
        London WC2A 1AW,
        UNITED KINGDOM
        TEL: (01) 323-7979 - TELEX: 266959 SCIREF G - TELEFAX: (01) 323-7495
CREATED: 1981   *HEAD:* Ms. S. Edwards, Head
SIZE OF STAFF: Professional: 6   Other: 8   Total: 14
TYPE OF SERVICE: international; public; profit; non-profit
MATERIALS DESCRIBING THE SERVICE: - Business Information: a guide to the reference
        resources of the British Library. 28 p.
        - Business Information Service, Leaflet
WORKING LANGUAGE(S): English
SUBJECT COVERAGE: economics; markets; trade
GEOGRAPHICAL COVERAGE: global, United Kingdom and trading partners, especially
        Western Europe
DATA BEING PROCESSED AND SIZE: 5,000 journals; 2,500 directories; 2,000 market
        research reports; trade literature from 20,000 companies
DATA PROCESSING METHODS: computerized
HARDWARE USED: IBM PC; BROMCOM MULTI-USER MICRO SYSTEM
SOFTWARE USED: Various
STORAGE MEDIA: traditional shelving of books; microfiches; periodicals
TYPE OF ACTIVITY: data collection; distribution of information; SSID training;
        publication
PERIODICALS PUBLISHED: - Directories held at the Science Reference & Information
        Service
        - Trade Directories in Journals
        - Market Research
PUBLICATIONS: - Company reports held at the Science Reference and Information Service
CLIENTELE: businessmen, information officers, librarians, market researchers,
        consultants (approx. 5,000)
ACCESS TO SERVICE: open to all users free of charge, some paid services
TYPE & DESCRIPTION OF SERVICES PROVIDED: Provides library services,
        market/company/product information searches, selective dissemination of
        information, magnetic tapes, microforms, photocopies, and translation of

documents upon request. Also provides on-line searches using own data base
"BISMARK", "BUSPER", "BISHOP", as well as numerous external data bases
accessed through DATASTAR, DIALOG, FINSBURY DATA SERVICES, PROFILE
INFORMATION, PERGAMON ORBIT INFOLINE and KOMPASS ONLINE.

721 - BRITISH LIBRARY OF POLITICAL AND ECONOMIC SCIENCE

SYNONYMOUS NAMES: BLPES
PARENT ORGANIZATION: London School of Economics and Political Science
ADDRESS: 10 Portugal Street,
           London WC2A 2HD,
           UNITED KINGDOM
           TEL: (01) 405-7686 - TELEX: 24655 BLPESG
CREATED: 1896   *HEAD:* C. J. Hunt, Librarian
SIZE OF STAFF: Professional: 34   Other: 46   Total: 80
TYPE OF SERVICE: national; public; non-profit
MATERIALS DESCRIBING THE SERVICE: - BLPES: Guide to the Library, annual
           - John, A.H., The British Library of Political and Economic Science: a bri
           history. London, LSE, 1971
           - Clarke, D. A., A new laboratory of sociological research: the British
           Library of Political and Economic Science, in Journal of Documentation, vc
           40, no. 2. June 1984 p. 152-157
SUBJECT COVERAGE: social sciences
GEOGRAPHICAL COVERAGE: global
DATA BEING PROCESSED AND SIZE: 3,000,000 items (books, periodicals, reports, films,
           microforms), of which 881,000 bound volumes
DATA PROCESSING METHODS: computerized
HARDWARE USED: GEAC 8000, IBM PCs
SOFTWARE USED: various standard software
STORAGE MEDIA: traditional shelving of publications; microforms
TYPE OF ACTIVITY: publication
PERIODICALS PUBLISHED:
           - Quarterly List of Russian and East European Accessions, since 1973
           - A London Bibliography of the Social Sciences, 1 p.a.
CLIENTELE: researchers
ACCESS TO SERVICE: open to specific categories of users, against payment; free of
           charge for academic researchers
TYPE & DESCRIPTION OF SERVICES PROVIDED: Provides library services and bibliograph
           searches of information. BLPES is a depository library for United States
           government publications, the publications of the UN and its specialized
           organizations, the European Communities, the Organization of American
           States, etc. Also provides microfilms and photocopies.

722 - CENTRE FOR MIDDLE EASTERN AND ISLAMIC STUDIES DOCUMENTATION UNIT

PARENT ORGANIZATION: Centre for Middle Eastern and Islamic Studies
ADDRESS: University of Durham,
           South End House,
           South Road,

Durham City DH1 3TG,
UNITED KINGDOM
TEL: (091) 374-2824 - TELEX: 537-351 DURLIB G.
CREATED: 1970   *HEAD:* R. Lawless,
SIZE OF STAFF: Professional: 2   Other: 2   Total: 4
TYPE OF SERVICE: national; public; non-profit
MATERIALS DESCRIBING THE SERVICE: - Information and activities, brochure
WORKING LANGUAGE(S): English; French; Arabic
SUBJECT COVERAGE: social sciences; demography; economics; statistics; socio-economic
        development; political development
GEOGRAPHICAL COVERAGE: Middle East; Islamic countries
DATA BEING PROCESSED AND SIZE: 150,000 documents, mainly government reports,
        statistics and publications of the main international organizations
DATA PROCESSING METHODS: partially computerized
HARDWARE USED: AMDAHL 470/V8
STORAGE MEDIA: traditional shelving of publications; microfiches; microfilms
TYPE OF ACTIVITY: data collection; publication; distribution of information
PERIODICALS PUBLISHED:
        - Additions and Accessions List, 12 p.a.
PUBLICATIONS: - COM Catalogue (cumulative catalogue of holdings on the computer
        produced on microfiches)
CLIENTELE: students, academic staff, experts
ACCESS TO SERVICE: open to all users; free of charge to all academic users;
        commercial users charged
TYPE & DESCRIPTION OF SERVICES PROVIDED: Its purpose is to monitor current economic,
        social and political developments in the region and to make available
        primary material relating to the modern Middle East. Provides bibliographic
        searches using its own computerized catalogue and photocopies upon request.

23 - CITY OF LONDON POLYTECHNIC, FAWCETT LIBRARY

ADDRESS: Calcutta House,
        Old Castle St.,
        London E1 7NT,
        UNITED KINGDOM
        TEL: (01) 283-1030, ext. 570
CREATED: 1926   *HEAD:* Ms. C. M. Ireland, Librarian
SIZE OF STAFF: Professional: 2   Other: 1   Total: 3
TYPE OF SERVICE: non-profit
MATERIALS DESCRIBING THE SERVICE: - Women's Studies International Forum, Vol. 10 no.
        3 (1987)
WORKING LANGUAGE(S): English
SUBJECT COVERAGE: social sciences; history; political science; womens studies;
        feminist studies
GEOGRAPHICAL COVERAGE: United Kingdom; Commonwealth
DATA BEING PROCESSED AND SIZE: 50,000 books, pamphlets, periodicals, archives
DATA PROCESSING METHODS: partially computerized
STORAGE MEDIA: traditional shelving of publications
CLIENTELE: academics (700 members p.a.)
ACCESS TO SERVICE: paid services open to all users
TYPE & DESCRIPTION OF SERVICES PROVIDED: Provides library services. Its data base

"Bibliofem" is based on computer-readable files of bibliographic
information and is available by subscription.

724 - COMMONWEALTH BUREAU OF AGRICULTURAL ECONOMICS

SYNONYMOUS NAMES: CBAE
PARENT ORGANIZATION: Commonwealth Agricultural Bureaux
ADDRESS: Dartington House,
        Little Clarendon Street,
        Oxford OX1 2HH,
        UNITED KINGDOM
        TEL: (0865) 59829 - TELEX: 847964
        CABLE: Comag, Slough
CREATED: 1964   *HEAD:* Dr. P. E. Stonham, Director
SIZE OF STAFF: Total: 14
TYPE OF SERVICE: international; non-profit
WORKING LANGUAGE(S): English
SUBJECT COVERAGE: economics; sociology; education; agricultural economics; rural
       sociology; agricultural development; rural development; rural planning;
       cooperative; leisure; tourism in rural areas; environment
GEOGRAPHICAL COVERAGE: global
DATA BEING PROCESSED AND SIZE: 12,000 documentation items p.a. (books, articles,
       reports, monographs, conference proceedings)
DATA PROCESSING METHODS: computerized
HARDWARE USED: Digital POPII
SOFTWARE USED: Formatext II
STORAGE MEDIA: magnetic tapes and discs
TYPE OF ACTIVITY: data collection; data analysis; publication; documentation
PERIODICALS PUBLISHED: - World Agricultural Economics and Rural Sociology Abstracts
       - Rural Development Abstracts
       - Rural Extension, Education and Training Abstracts
       - Leisure, Recreation and Tourism Abstracts
PUBLICATIONS: - Directory of information sources in agricultural economics and
       business
CLIENTELE: researchers and experts
ACCESS TO SERVICE: paid services (25.00 pounds plus 10p per reference for full
       abstracts; bibliographic details alone, cost 5p per reference)
TYPE & DESCRIPTION OF SERVICES PROVIDED: Provides hard-copy and on-line information
       by means of abstracts of relevant world literature covering all aspects of
       agricultural economics and rural sociology including a wide range of
       information on agricultural development, rural development, environmental
       policy, rural planning, rural extension and education, as well as all
       aspects of cooperatives, trade, leisure, recreation and tourism in rural
       areas and non-rural areas. Rural Development Abstracts are available on-l
       through Dialog, ESA/IRS or DIMDI, as the 2R subfile of the CAB Abstracts
       data base.

25 - ECONOMIC AND SOCIAL RESEARCH COUNCIL DATA ARCHIVE

SYNONYMOUS NAMES: ESRC Data Archive
ADDRESS: University of Essex,
Wivenhoe Park,
Colchester, Essex CO4 3SQ,
UNITED KINGDOM
TEL: (0206) 872103
CREATED: 1967   *HEAD:* Prof. H. Newby, Director
SIZE OF STAFF: Professional: 15   Other: 12   Total: 27
TYPE OF SERVICE: national; public; non-profit
SYSTEMS & NETWORKS ATTACHED TO: Member of IFDO (International Federation of Data
Organizations) and CESSDA (Committee of European Social Science Data
Archives)
MATERIALS DESCRIBING THE SERVICE: - Abbreviated guide
- Brochure
WORKING LANGUAGE(S): English
SUBJECT COVERAGE: social sciences; economics; geography; history; political science;
sociology social science surveys
GEOGRAPHICAL COVERAGE: United Kingdom; North America; Western Europe
DATA BEING PROCESSED AND SIZE: 2,220 data sets of machine readable data and non-
machine readable documentation of social science surveys, opinion polls and
aggregate statistics
DATA PROCESSING METHODS: manual; computerized
HARDWARE USED: DEC System 10; MICRO-VAX
SOFTWARE USED: own programmes
STORAGE MEDIA: tapes; optical discs
TYPE OF ACTIVITY: data collection; data analysis; distribution of information;
publication; SSID training; SSID scientific and methodological activities
PERIODICALS PUBLISHED:
- ESRC Data Archive Bulletin, 3 p.a.
PUBLICATIONS: - ESRC Data Archive catalogue, 2 vols., 1986
CLIENTELE: research workers, central and local government agencies, commercial bodies
ACCESS TO SERVICE: open to all users, against payment
TYPE & DESCRIPTION OF SERVICES PROVIDED: Provides library services, on-line searches,
computer readable data for secondary analysis on magnetic tapes or discs and
selective dissemination of information.

26 - EDICLINE ECONOMIC DOCUMENTATION AND INFORMATION CENTRE LTD.

SYNONYMOUS NAMES: NOMOS DATAPOOL/EDICLINE
ADDRESS: 2 Broyle Gate Cottages,
Ringmer BN8 5NA,
UNITED KINGDOM
TEL: 0273-813238
SYSTEMS & NETWORKS ATTACHED TO: EDIC Mail System (U.K); Euromail (G.F.R.)
SUBJECT COVERAGE: administrative sciences; economics; law
DATA PROCESSING METHODS: computerized
STORAGE MEDIA: tapes
TYPE OF ACTIVITY: distribution of information; publication
ACCESS TO SERVICE: services open to all users, against payment

TYPE & DESCRIPTION OF SERVICES PROVIDED: Provides library services, searches of information, information on magnetic tapes, translation of documents. On-line service provides access to various data bases produced by Edicline and NOMOS Datapool (Postfach 610, D-7570 Baden-Baden), including TIFA (7,000 citations on touristic-information facts and abstracts); SPEX (2,000 citations on social science experts); IVAG (3,200 citations on German-foreign organizations and foreign organizations in the Federal Republic of Germany and West Berlin); REX (2,000 citations on experts in law); WEX 2,0 citations on business science experts); CFA (1,550 citations on city facts and abstracts); IVIZ (3,500 citations on institutions for international co operation); BOWI (bibliographie zur öffentlichen Unternehmung und Verwaltung).

727 - GEO ABSTRACTS LTD.

ADDRESS: Regency House,
34 Duke Street,
Norwich NR3 3AP,
UNITED KINGDOM
TEL: (0603) 626-327 - TELEX: 975247 CHACOM G
CREATED: 1960   *HEAD:* Dr. J. Grijpma, Publishing Manager
SIZE OF STAFF: Professional: 12   Other: 7   Total: 19
TYPE OF SERVICE: international; profit
WORKING LANGUAGE(S): English
SUBJECT COVERAGE: geography; ecology; environment; international development; planning
GEOGRAPHICAL COVERAGE: global
DATA BEING PROCESSED AND SIZE: books; articles
TYPE OF ACTIVITY: data collection; distribution of information; publication
PERIODICALS PUBLISHED: - Geographical Abstracts
- International Development Abstracts
- Ecological Abstracts
TYPE & DESCRIPTION OF SERVICES PROVIDED: Abstracting service. Provides on-line services from own data base, GEOABS, containing 230,000 citations with abstracts.

728 - HOUSE OF COMMONS LIBRARY, PARLIAMENTARY ON-LINE INFORMATION SYSTEM

SYNONYMOUS NAMES: POLIS
ADDRESS: London SW1A OAA,
UNITED KINGDOM
TEL: 01-219.5714
CREATED: 1980   *HEAD:* Ms. J. Wainwright, Head, Computer & Technical Services
SIZE OF STAFF: Professional: 9   Other: 9   Total: 18
TYPE OF SERVICE: international; public; non-profit
SUBJECT COVERAGE: social sciences; administrative sciences; economics; education; law; political science; social welfare; parliamentary system
GEOGRAPHICAL COVERAGE: Europe
DATA BEING PROCESSED AND SIZE: parliamentary questions (40,000 p.a.), parliamentar

proceedings (20,000 p.a.), parliamentary publications (5,000 p.a.), European
Community regulations and documentation (5,000 p.a.), books and official
publications (5,000 p.a.)
TA PROCESSING METHODS: computerized
RDWARE USED: 2 X VAX 8200
FTWARE USED: BASIS
PE OF ACTIVITY: data collection; data analysis; distribution of information
RIODICALS PUBLISHED:
    - Weekly Information Bulletin
BLICATIONS: - House of Commons Library thesaurus
IENTELE: general public
CESS TO SERVICE: public information service by telephone and post open to the
    public free of charge. POLIS data base also used by 300 subscribers with
    payment
PE & DESCRIPTION OF SERVICES PROVIDED: Provides query-answering services,
    bibliographic, literature abstract and quantitative data searches of
    information using own data base "POLIS", and information on magnetic tapes
    or discs. Has also access to external data bases such as: World reporter,
    Textline, Lexis, Central Statistical Office through Datasolve, Finsbury Data
    Services and Mead Data Central.

9 - INSTITUTE FOR THE STUDY OF DRUG DEPENDENCE, LIBRARY AND INFORMATION SERVICE

DRESS: Hatton Place,
    Off St. Cross Street,
    London ECIN 8ND,
    UNITED KINGDOM
    TEL: 01-430.1991
EATED: 1968   *HEAD:* P. Defriez, Head
                      J. Witton, Head
ZE OF STAFF: Professional: 3   Other: 3   Total: 6
PE OF SERVICE: national; public; non-profit
RKING LANGUAGE(S): English
BJECT COVERAGE: behavioural sciences; drug abuse; drugs
OGRAPHICAL COVERAGE: global
TA BEING PROCESSED AND SIZE: 40,000 documentation items
TA PROCESSING METHODS: manual; partially computerized
RDWARE USED: IBM compatible
FTWARE USED: Microcairs
PE OF ACTIVITY: data collection; distribution of information; publication
RIODICALS PUBLISHED: - Press Digest, 12 p.a.
    - Drug Abstracts, 12 p.a.
    - Druglink
    - Drug Abuse Current Awareness Bulletin, 12 p.a.
IENTELE: students, professional workers, researchers and teachers (12,000 p.a.)
CESS TO SERVICE: open to all users free of charge (some paid services)
PE & DESCRIPTION OF SERVICES PROVIDED: Provides comprehensive library and
    information services on the non-medical use of drugs. Provision of
    photocopies upon request.

730 - INSTITUTE OF ADVANCED LEGAL STUDIES, LIBRARY

ADDRESS: Charles Clore House,
        17 Russell Square,
        London WC1B 5DR,
        UNITED KINGDOM
        TEL: 01-637.1731
HEAD: Miss M. Anderson,
SIZE OF STAFF: Professional: 6   Total: 16
TYPE OF SERVICE: national; public; non-profit
MATERIALS DESCRIBING THE SERVICE: - Institute of Advanced Legal Studies annual rep
WORKING LANGUAGE(S): English
SUBJECT COVERAGE: law
DATA BEING PROCESSED AND SIZE: 63,300 books and pamphlets; 111,400 serials (inclu
        2,400 periodicals)
TYPE OF ACTIVITY: data collection
PUBLICATIONS: - List of current legal research topics, 1986
CLIENTELE: 2,500 p.a.
TYPE & DESCRIPTION OF SERVICES PROVIDED: Provides library services, including inte
        library loans and photocopies. Also provides on-line searches on LEXIS a
        LAWTEL available on Prestel.

731 - INSTITUTE OF CONTEMPORARY HISTORY AND WIENER LIBRARY

ADDRESS: 4 Devonshire Street,
        London WIN 2BH,
        UNITED KINGDOM
        TEL: 01-636.7247
CREATED: 1933   *HEAD:* Prof. W. Z. Laqueur, Director
                  Prof. B. Krikler, Director
SIZE OF STAFF: Total: 15
TYPE OF SERVICE: private; non-profit
SUBJECT COVERAGE: history; political science; racial discrimination
GEOGRAPHICAL COVERAGE: Germany (Federal Republic); Middle East
DATA PROCESSING METHODS: manual
TYPE OF ACTIVITY: documentation; research promotion; publication
PERIODICALS PUBLISHED: - Wiener Library Bulletin
        - Journal of Contemporary History
PUBLICATIONS: - Wiener Library catalogue series
TYPE & DESCRIPTION OF SERVICES PROVIDED: Documentation center which aims at being
        leading source for the study of totalitarianism. Deals with racial
        discrimination and Jewish history. Provides library services and
        photocopies.

732 - INSTITUTE OF PERSONNEL MANAGEMENT, INFORMATION AND ADVISORY SERVICES

ADDRESS: IPM House,
        Camp Road,
        Wimbledon,

London SW19 4UW,
UNITED KINGDOM
TEL: (01) 946.9100 - TELEX: 947203 - TELEFAX: 879-1565
EATED: 1913   *HEAD:* D. Rockingham Gill, Assistant Director
ZE OF STAFF: Professional: 7   Other: 5   Total: 12
PE OF SERVICE: private; non-profit
TERIALS DESCRIBING THE SERVICE: - IPM information and advisory services (brochure)
RKING LANGUAGE(S): English
BJECT COVERAGE: administrative sciences; law; personnel management; labour
relations; manpower; psychology; surveys
OGRAPHICAL COVERAGE: United Kingdom; USA; Western Europe
TA BEING PROCESSED AND SIZE: 20,000 books; 18,000 articles; 200 training courses
TA PROCESSING METHODS: manual
PE OF ACTIVITY: data collection; data analysis; distribution of information;
publication
RIODICALS PUBLISHED:
- Information Note
BLICATIONS: - Bibliographies on library holdings (107 different topics covered)
IENTELE: 15,000 p.a.
CCESS TO SERVICE: for members and organizations subscribing to the IPM Company
Service plan
PE & DESCRIPTION OF SERVICES PROVIDED: Provides library services, bibliographic
searches of information on personnel management.

3 - LEARNED INFORMATION LTD.

DRESS: Woodside,
Hinskey Hill,
Oxford OX1 5AU,
UNITED KINGDOM
TEL: (0865) 730275 - TELEX: 837704 INFORM
EATED: 1979   *HEAD:* Mr. R. Bilbom, Managing Director
PE OF SERVICE: international; private; profit
STEMS & NETWORKS ATTACHED TO: Dialog Information Services; Pergamon Orbit Infoline
RKING LANGUAGE(S): English
BJECT COVERAGE: international affairs; social sciences; economics; education; law;
political science; international trade
OGRAPHICAL COVERAGE: Middle East
TA BEING PROCESSED AND SIZE: 50,000 books, articles, reports, on-going research,
seminars and training courses
TA PROCESSING METHODS: computerized
PE OF ACTIVITY: data collection
CCESS TO SERVICE: paid services open to all users
PE & DESCRIPTION OF SERVICES PROVIDED: Provides on-line services using own data
base "MIDEAST FILE" and information on magnetic tapes.

734 - LONDON RESEARCH CENTRE, RESEARCH LIBRARY

ADDRESS: Room 514, The County Hall,
        London SE1 7PB,
        UNITED KINGDOM
        TEL: (01) 633.7149 - FAX: 01-261.1710
HEAD: Mr. R. Golland, Head
SIZE OF STAFF: Professional: 15   Other: 9   Total: 24
TYPE OF SERVICE: international; public; profit
MATERIALS DESCRIBING THE SERVICE: - The Greater London Council Research Library-
        Computerized Information Services for local government, 1984
WORKING LANGUAGE(S): English
SUBJECT COVERAGE: administrative sciences; political science; social welfare; urban
        planning; regional planning; housing; social policy; transportation; local
        government; community relations; leisure; recreation policy; economic
        development; environmental conservation; public order
GEOGRAPHICAL COVERAGE: United Kingdom; Western Europe; North America; Australia
DATA BEING PROCESSED AND SIZE: 250,000 documents including research reports, journal
        articles, press cuttings, official reports, statistics, pressure group
        literature, books
DATA PROCESSING METHODS: partially computerized
HARDWARE USED: IBM Mainframe, Prime 2450 Mini, IBM PCs
SOFTWARE USED: ASSASSIN VI; ADLIB
STORAGE MEDIA: traditional shelving of publications; microfiches
TYPE OF ACTIVITY: distribution of information; publication
PERIODICALS PUBLISHED: - Urban Abstracts, 12 p.a.
        - HABS, 24 p.a.
ACCESS TO SERVICE: services open to specific categories of users against payment
TYPE & DESCRIPTION OF SERVICES PROVIDED: Provides inter-library loans and
        photocopies. Own on-line data bases ACOMPLINE and URBALINE, containing
        150,000 records of documents held by the Research Library, are available
        through Pergamon Orbit Infoline and ESA/IRS.

735 - NATIONAL CHILDREN'S BUREAU, INFORMATION AND LIBRARY SERVICE

SYNONYMOUS NAMES: NCB, Information and Library service
ADDRESS: 8 Wakley Street,
        Islington,
        London EC1V 7QE,
        UNITED KINGDOM
        TEL: 01-278.94.41
CREATED: 1963   *HEAD:* Hilliard, Information Officer and Librarian
SIZE OF STAFF: Professional: 3   Other: 2   Total: 5
TYPE OF SERVICE: national
WORKING LANGUAGE(S): English
SUBJECT COVERAGE: social welfare; psychology; education; child development; family
GEOGRAPHICAL COVERAGE: United Kingdom
DATA BEING PROCESSED AND SIZE: 10,000 items
DATA PROCESSING METHODS: manual
TYPE OF ACTIVITY: data collection; distribution of information; publication
PERIODICALS PUBLISHED:

- Accession List, 6 p.a.
- Highlights, 8 p.a.

JBLICATIONS: - 120 Bibliographies
CCESS TO SERVICE: services open to specific categories of users
YPE & DESCRIPTION OF SERVICES PROVIDED: Provides library services, selective
dissemination of information and photocopies.

36 - NATIONAL YOUTH BUREAU, INFORMATION SERVICES

YNONYMOUS NAMES: NYB, Information Services
DDRESS: 17-23 Albion Street,
Leicester LEI 6GD,
UNITED KINGDOM
TEL: 0533 471200 (6)
REATED: 1973   *HEAD:* Mr. J. Jeffries, Head
IZE OF STAFF: Professional: 28   Other: 31   Total: 59
YPE OF SERVICE: national; public; non-profit
ATERIALS DESCRIBING THE SERVICE: - Users guide to the National Youth Bureau, 1986
UBJECT COVERAGE: social welfare; youth
EOGRAPHICAL COVERAGE: United Kingdom
ATA BEING PROCESSED AND SIZE: 50,000 books, periodicals; films and microforms
ATA PROCESSING METHODS: partially computerized
ARDWARE USED: TANDON PCX 20 microcomputers (16)
OFTWARE USED: MICRO LIBRARY; DBase III+
YPE OF ACTIVITY: data collection; data analysis; distribution of information;
publication
ERIODICALS PUBLISHED: - Youth in Society, 11 p.a.
- Youth Service, 11 p.a.
JBLICATIONS: - Publications catalogue
LIENTELE: youth workers, social workers, teachers, career officers, community
workers
CCESS TO SERVICE: open to all users, free of charge
YPE & DESCRIPTION OF SERVICES PROVIDED: Provides query answering service,
retrospective bibliographic and literature abstracts searches, selective
dissemination of information and provision of photocopies.

37 - OVERSEAS DEVELOPMENT INSTITUTE LIBRARY

YNONYMOUS NAMES: ODI, Library
DDRESS: Regent's College,
Regent's Park,
Inner Circle,
London NW1 4NS,
UNITED KINGDOM
TEL: (01) 935-1644 - TELEX: 297371 quoting ODI H5673 - FAX: 01-935 5298
CABLE: PICODI, London NW1
REATED: 1960   *HEAD:* Ms. A. Siemsen, Head
IZE OF STAFF: Professional: 2   Total: 2
YPE OF SERVICE: private; non-profit

MATERIALS DESCRIBING THE SERVICE: - ODI annual report
- British Library Science Reference and Information Service; guide to Government Department and other libraries, 1986
WORKING LANGUAGE(S): English
SUBJECT COVERAGE: social sciences; administrative sciences; economics; geography; political science; social anthropology; cultural anthropology; developmen[t] aid; international finance; agricultural administration and extension; ru[ral] development; irrigation; pastoralism; social forestry
GEOGRAPHICAL COVERAGE: developing countries; developed countries only in relation their aid policies
DATA BEING PROCESSED AND SIZE: 17,000 books; 400 periodicals
DATA PROCESSING METHODS: computerized
HARDWARE USED: IBM AT and Tandon PCA
SOFTWARE USED: InMagic and Word Perfect
STORAGE MEDIA: traditional shelving of publications
TYPE OF ACTIVITY: data collection; distribution of information; publication
PERIODICALS PUBLISHED:
- Library Acquisition List
- List of Periodicals
- ODI Periodicals Reference Bulletin: Index to Development Literature, 6 p.a.
PUBLICATIONS: - Occasional subject bibliographies
CLIENTELE: researchers, consultants, journalists, students (circa 1,500 p.a.)
ACCESS TO SERVICE: services open to all users, free of charge
TYPE & DESCRIPTION OF SERVICES PROVIDED: Provides library services, bibliographic searches of information using own data base and selective dissemination o[f] information.

7.38 - THE PLANNING EXCHANGE

ADDRESS: 186 Bath Street,
Glasgow,
Scotland G2 4HG,
UNITED KINGDOM
TEL: (41) 332-8541
CREATED: 1973   *HEAD:* Mr. A. W. Burton, Director
SIZE OF STAFF: Professional: 14   Other: 16   Total: 30
TYPE OF SERVICE: international; private; non-profit
WORKING LANGUAGE(S): English
SUBJECT COVERAGE: administrative sciences; economics; geography; economic development; urban planning; regional planning; regional development; housing; local government
DATA BEING PROCESSED AND SIZE: 4,000 books; 200 journals; 8,000 semi-published research; 3,000 UK parliamentary and EEC publications
HARDWARE USED: DIGITAL PDP 11/23+
SOFTWARE USED: CUSTOM
STORAGE MEDIA: traditional shelving of publications
TYPE OF ACTIVITY: distribution of information; publication
PERIODICALS PUBLISHED:
- Information Bulletin
- Economic Development Digest

.

- Housing Information Digest
- Urban Development Information Service (UDIS)
- Local Economic Development Information Service (LEDIS)
- Planning and Development Digest
- Scottish Planning Appeal Decisions
- Scottish Planning Law and Practice

BLICATIONS: - Financial resources for economic development
IENTELE: public and private sector researchers and policy makers (500)
CESS TO SERVICE: paid services
PE & DESCRIPTION OF SERVICES PROVIDED: Provides library services, selective
dissemination of information, photocopies and information searches using own
data base "PLANEX" as well as external data bases (ACOMPLINE, CELEX)
available through ESA/IRS, PERGAMON ORBIT INFOLINE and EEC.

89 - ROYAL INSTITUTE OF INTERNATIONAL AFFAIRS, LIBRARY

NONYMOUS NAMES: RIIA, Library
DRESS: Chatham House,
10 St. James Square,
London SW1Y 4LE,
UNITED KINGDOM
TEL: (01) 930 2233 - Cable: AREOPAGUS London
REATED: 1920   *HEAD:* Mr. N. M. Gallimore, Librarian
IZE OF STAFF: Professional: 5   Other: 1   Total: 6
YPE OF SERVICE: national; private; non-profit
ATERIALS DESCRIBING THE SERVICE: - The Royal Institute of International Affairs.
Aims and activities (leaflet)
UBJECT COVERAGE: political science; social sciences; economics; statistics;
international affairs
EOGRAPHICAL COVERAGE: global
ATA BEING PROCESSED AND SIZE: 168,000 books and pamphlets, 650 journals
ATA PROCESSING METHODS: manual
ERIODICALS PUBLISHED: - International Affairs, 4 p.a.
- The World Today, 12 p.a.
UBLICATIONS: - Index to periodical articles in the Library of the Royal Institute of
International Affairs 1950-1964. Boston, Mass., G.K. Hall, 1965; 1st
supplement, 1965-1972, 1973; 2nd supplement, 1973-1978, 1979
- The Classified catalogue of the Library of the Royal Institute of
International Affairs, 1981
- Introduction to the microfiche edition of the classified catalogue of the
Library of the Royal Institute of International Affairs, 1981
LIENTELE: subscribing members, academics, researchers
CCESS TO SERVICE: open to specific categories of users for a quarterly fee
YPE & DESCRIPTION OF SERVICES PROVIDED: Provides library and information services.
Also enjoys depository status for United Nations publications and EEC
documents.

United Kingdom / Royaume-Uni / Reino Unido

740 - ROYAL INSTITUTE OF INTERNATIONAL AFFAIRS, PRESS LIBRARY

ADDRESS: Chatham House,
      10 St. James's Square,
      London SW1Y 4LE,
      UNITED KINGDOM
      TEL: (01) 839.3593
      CABLE: AREOPAGUS London
HEAD: Ms. S. J. Boyde, Press Librarian
SIZE OF STAFF: Professional: 5   Other: 1   Total: 6
TYPE OF SERVICE: national; private; non-profit
WORKING LANGUAGE(S): English; French; German; Italian; Russian
SUBJECT COVERAGE: political science; economics; geography; history; law;
      international relations; foreign policy
GEOGRAPHICAL COVERAGE: global
DATA BEING PROCESSED AND SIZE: 9 million press cuttings to which about 50,000 added
      annually
DATA PROCESSING METHODS: manual
STORAGE MEDIA: boxes of press cuttings from 1970 to date; microfilms of press
      cuttings, 1924-34
TYPE OF ACTIVITY: data collection; data analysis
CLIENTELE: subscribing members, elected members and researchers
ACCESS TO SERVICE: open to specific categories of users at a fee of 50 pounds p.a.
TYPE & DESCRIPTION OF SERVICES PROVIDED: Mainly concerned with international
      relations and military strategy. Provides library and information services

741 - UNIVERSITY OF BIRMINGHAM, ERGONOMICS INFORMATION ANALYSIS CENTRE

PARENT ORGANIZATION: University of Birmingham, Department of Engineering Production
ADDRESS: Department of Engineering Production,
      P.O. Box 363,
      Birmingham B15 2TT,
      UNITED KINGDOM
CREATED: 1968   *HEAD:* Dr. E. D. Megan,
SIZE OF STAFF: Professional: 2   Other: 2   Total: 4
TYPE OF SERVICE: international; public; non-profit
WORKING LANGUAGE(S): English
SUBJECT COVERAGE: psychology; ergonomics; human-computer interaction
GEOGRAPHICAL COVERAGE: global
DATA BEING PROCESSED AND SIZE: books, 350 periodicals, reports
DATA PROCESSING METHODS: manual; partially computerized
STORAGE MEDIA: traditional shelving of publications
PERIODICALS PUBLISHED: - Ergonomics Abstracts, 4 p.a. since 1969
CLIENTELE: academic, industrial
ACCESS TO SERVICE: open to all users, against payment
TYPE & DESCRIPTION OF SERVICES PROVIDED: Provides library services, query answering
      service, selective dissemination of information and photocopies.

42 - UNIVERSITY OF DUNDEE, EUROPEAN DOCUMENTATION CENTRE, LAW LIBRARY

ADDRESS: Perth Road,
Dundee DD1 4HN,
Scotland,
UNITED KINGDOM
TEL: (0382) 23181
CREATED: 1967   *HEAD:* Mr. D. R. Hart, Librarian
SIZE OF STAFF: Professional: 1   Other: 1   Total: 2
TYPE OF SERVICE: public
SYSTEMS & NETWORKS ATTACHED TO: European Documentation Centre Network
WORKING LANGUAGE(S): English
SUBJECT COVERAGE: European community law
GEOGRAPHICAL COVERAGE: United Kingdom
DATA BEING PROCESSED AND SIZE: official publications of the European Communities
DATA PROCESSING METHODS: manual
TYPE OF ACTIVITY: distribution of information
CLIENTELE: general public, university students
ACCESS TO SERVICE: services open to all users, free of charge
TYPE & DESCRIPTION OF SERVICES PROVIDED: Provides library services. Maintains EDCKEY,
a computer-readable bibliographic database.

43 - UNIVERSITY OF LEEDS, AFRICAN STUDIES UNIT

ADDRESS: Emmanuel Institute,
University of Leeds,
Leeds LS2 9JT,
UNITED KINGDOM
TEL: 431751
CREATED: 1964   *HEAD:* D. Beetham,
SIZE OF STAFF: Professional: 2
TYPE OF SERVICE: public; non-profit
WORKING LANGUAGE(S): English
SUBJECT COVERAGE: sociology; political science; demography; economics; statistics;
education; geography; history; linguistics; social anthropology; cultural
anthropology
GEOGRAPHICAL COVERAGE: Africa
DATA PROCESSING METHODS: manual
TYPE OF ACTIVITY: data collection; publication; conference-organization
PERIODICALS PUBLISHED:
- Leeds African Studies Bulletin, 2 p.a.
CLIENTELE: students and teachers
ACCESS TO SERVICE: open to all users
TYPE & DESCRIPTION OF SERVICES PROVIDED: Acts as a liaison between the various
departments of the university engaged in African studies.

744 - UNIVERSITY OF LONDON, INSTITUTE OF LATIN AMERICAN STUDIES, LIBRARY

ADDRESS: 31 Tavistock Square,
        London WC1H 9HA,
        UNITED KINGDOM
        TEL: 01 387.4055
CREATED: 1965   *HEAD:* Mrs. C. Travis, Librarian
SIZE OF STAFF: Professional: 4   Other: 1   Total: 5
TYPE OF SERVICE: national; public; non-profit
SYSTEMS & NETWORKS ATTACHED TO: British Library
MATERIALS DESCRIBING THE SERVICE: - Brochure
WORKING LANGUAGE(S): English
SUBJECT COVERAGE: social sciences; history; political science; sociology
GEOGRAPHICAL COVERAGE: Latin America
DATA BEING PROCESSED AND SIZE: 9,000 books; 500 periodicals (282 current titles)
DATA PROCESSING METHODS: manual
TYPE OF ACTIVITY: publication
PUBLICATIONS: - List of booksellers dealing with Latin American and the Caribbean,
        1987
        - Latin American studies in the universities of the United Kingdom, 1981
        - Theses in Latin American studies at British universities in progress and
        recently completed, 1984
        - Travis, C., Chile: guide to Latin American and West Indian census
        material: a bibliography and union list, 1982
ACCESS TO SERVICE: services open to specific categories of users, free of charge
TYPE & DESCRIPTION OF SERVICES PROVIDED: The Library contains bibliographic
        information on all subjects related to Latin American studies. Provides
        library reference services only, bibliographic searches of information usi
        their own catalogues including the British Union Catalogue of Latin Americ
        and photocopies.

745 - UNIVERSITY OF LONDON, INSTITUTE ON COMMONWEALTH STUDIES, LIBRARY

ADDRESS: 27-28 Russell Sq.,
        London WC1B 5DS,
        UNITED KINGDOM
        TEL: 01-580.5876
CREATED: 1949   *HEAD:* Mrs. P. Larby, Librarian
SIZE OF STAFF: Professional: 3   Other: 2   Total: 5
MATERIALS DESCRIBING THE SERVICE: - Larby, P. M., The Institute of Commonwealth
        Studies, London, Itinerario 1979 (2) pp. 56-58
        - Garside, K., Guide to the library resources of the University of London,
        U. of London, 1983 pp. 63-64
        - Hannam, H., SCOLMA directory of libraries and special collections on
        Africa. 4th ed. Zell, 1983 pp. 67-68
WORKING LANGUAGE(S): English
SUBJECT COVERAGE: social sciences; development
GEOGRAPHICAL COVERAGE: Commonwealth countries; Pakistan; South Africa
DATA BEING PROCESSED AND SIZE: 100,000 books; 8,000 periodicals abstract journals;
        3,052 microfiche & microfilm reels; 47 collections of manuscripts/archives
DATA PROCESSING METHODS: manual

ORAGE MEDIA: traditional shelving of publications; microforms
PE OF ACTIVITY: publication
RIODICALS PUBLISHED:
- Select List of Accessions, 4 p.a.
- Theses in Progress in Commonwealth Studies, 1 p.a.
CCESS TO SERVICE: services open to specific categories of users
PE & DESCRIPTION OF SERVICES PROVIDED: Provides library services, for reference only, and interlibrary loans within the country, publications on on-going research, list of documents for exchange, etc. Also provides bibliographic searches of information using own catalogues, and photocopies.

46 - UNIVERSITY OF LONDON, SCHOOL OF ORIENTAL AND AFRICAN STUDIES, LIBRARY

DDRESS: Malet Street,
London WC1E 7HU,
UNITED KINGDOM
TEL: (01) 637-23-88 - TELEX: 896616 SENDIT G (For attention: SOAS)
REATED: 1917   *HEAD:* Ms. B. Burton,
IZE OF STAFF: Professional: 15   Other: 30   Total: 45
YPE OF SERVICE: private; non-profit
ATERIALS DESCRIBING THE SERVICE: - Library guide. London: School of Oriental and African Studies Library, 1986
ORKING LANGUAGE(S): Western languages and the languages of Asia and Africa
UBJECT COVERAGE: social sciences
EOGRAPHICAL COVERAGE: Asia; Africa
ATA BEING PROCESSED AND SIZE: 2,767 manuscripts; 627,365 books and periodicals; 40,390 pamphlets; 1,465 sound recordings; 5,796 microforms; 45,750 maps; 41,000 slides
ATA PROCESSING METHODS: partially computerized
ARDWARE USED: GEAC Circulation System
TORAGE MEDIA: traditional shelving of publications; fiches; tapes; discs; microfiches
YPE OF ACTIVITY: distribution of information
ERIODICALS PUBLISHED:
- Montnly List of Titles added to the Catalogues
UBLICATIONS: - Library catalogue
LIENTELE: 2,475 external borrowers; 3,701 external reference members; 13 corporate members; 1,833 staff and students
CCESS TO SERVICE: paid services open to specific categories of users
YPE & DESCRIPTION OF SERVICES PROVIDED: Provides library services, microforms and photocopies.

47 - UNIVERSITY OF LONDON, SCHOOL OF SLAVONIC AND EAST EUROPEAN STUDIES, LIBRARY

YNONYMOUS NAMES: SSEES, Library
ARENT ORGANIZATION: University of London
DDRESS: Senate House,
Malet Street,
London WC17 7HU,

UNITED KINGDOM
TEL: (01) 637-49-34
CREATED: 1915   *HEAD:* Prof. M. A. Branch, Director
SIZE OF STAFF: Professional: 51   Other: 19   Total: 70
TYPE OF SERVICE: public
SYSTEMS & NETWORKS ATTACHED TO: Birmingham, Bristol, London, Oxford Consortium for
        Russian, Soviet and East European Studies
MATERIALS DESCRIBING THE SERVICE: - Guide to the library, 1986
WORKING LANGUAGE(S): Serbocroatian; Albanian; Russian; Georgian; Byelorussian;
        Ukrainian; Finnish; Estonian; Polish; German; Czech; Hungarian; Bulgarian;
        Rumanian; Slovak
SUBJECT COVERAGE: economics; education; history; geography; political science
GEOGRAPHICAL COVERAGE: USSR; Finland; Poland; Germany (Federal Republic); German
        Democratic Republic; Austria; Czechoslovakia; Hungary; Yugoslavia; Albania
        Romania; Bulgaria
DATA BEING PROCESSED AND SIZE: 270,000 books and periodicals; 100 manuscript
        collections
DATA PROCESSING METHODS: partially computerized
HARDWARE USED: two OCLC terminals; one IBM PLAT (with access to JANET)
SOFTWARE USED: Kermit
STORAGE MEDIA: traditional shelving of publications; discs; microfiches
TYPE OF ACTIVITY: data analysis; data collection; distribution of information; SSID
        scientific and methodological activities; SSID training; publication
PERIODICALS PUBLISHED: - Studies in Russia and Eastern Europe
        - Slavonic and East European Review
        - SSEES Occasional: Papers
CLIENTELE: students, library users
ACCESS TO SERVICE: services free of charge except for corporate use; a returnable
        deposit is required by library borrowers who are not teachers or registered
        students of the University of London
TYPE & DESCRIPTION OF SERVICES PROVIDED: Provides library services, bibliographic
        searches, microforms, photocopies (subject to copyright law). Also provides
        on-line services using external data, OCLC and JANET network.

748 - UNIVERSITY OF LONDON, WARBURG INSTITUTE, LIBRARY

ADDRESS: Woburn Square,
        London, WC1H OAB,
        UNITED KINGDOM
        TEL: 580.96.63
HEAD: W. F. Ryan, Librarian
SIZE OF STAFF: Total: 11
TYPE OF SERVICE: national; non-profit
WORKING LANGUAGE(S): English
SUBJECT COVERAGE: history; humanities; intercultural studies; classical civilization
GEOGRAPHICAL COVERAGE: Europe
DATA BEING PROCESSED AND SIZE: 5,400 books and reports; photographs
DATA PROCESSING METHODS: computerized
HARDWARE USED: Apple Laser Writer; Olivetti M24
TYPE OF ACTIVITY: data collection; data analysis; distribution of information;
        publication

PERIODICALS PUBLISHED: ·- Journal of the Warburg Institute
         - Annual Report of the Warburg Institute
PUBLICATIONS: - Studies of the Warburg Institute (series)
CLIENTELE: academic staff, postgraduate students (8,000 p.a.)
ACCESS TO SERVICE: open to specific categories of users
TYPE & DESCRIPTION OF SERVICES PROVIDED: Provides library services, question-
         answering service, assistance to researchers.

**749 - UNIVERSITY OF MANCHESTER, INSTITUTE FOR DEVELOPMENT POLICY AND MANAGEMENT,
       LIBRARY**

SYNONYMOUS NAMES: IDPM, Library
ADDRESS: Crawford House,
         Precinct Centre,
         Oxford Rd.,
         Manchester M13 9QS,
         UNITED KINGDOM
         TEL: 061-275-2802
CREATED: 1958   *HEAD:* Ms. F. Sullivan, Librarian
SIZE OF STAFF: Professional: 1   Other: 1   Total: 2
TYPE OF SERVICE: non-profit
MATERIALS DESCRIBING THE SERVICE: - Annual brochure and prospectus
WORKING LANGUAGE(S): English
SUBJECT COVERAGE: social sciences; administrative sciences; demography; economics;
         education; political science; psychology; social anthropology; cultural
         anthropology; social welfare; sociology; development
GEOGRAPHICAL COVERAGE: developing countries
DATA BEING PROCESSED AND SIZE: 11,000 books; 120 periodicals; 2,000 reports
HARDWARE USED: IBM PC compatible with 20 meg. hard disk
SOFTWARE USED: DBase III Plus
STORAGE MEDIA: traditional shelving of publications
TYPE OF ACTIVITY: distribution of information; publication
PERIODICALS PUBLISHED:
         - Accessions List
         - Contents Pages of Journals
CLIENTELE: 300 current borrowers (200 internal, 100 external)
ACCESS TO SERVICE: services open to all users, free of charge
TYPE & DESCRIPTION OF SERVICES PROVIDED: Provides library services, photocopies, and
         bibliographic, literature abstract and survey searches.

750 - UNIVERSITY OF SUSSEX, INSTITUTE OF DEVELOPMENT STUDIES, LIBRARY

SYNONYMOUS NAMES: IDS Library
ADDRESS: Andrew Cohen Building,
         Falmer,
         Brighton BN1 9RE,
         UNITED KINGDOM
         TEL: (0273) 678263/606261 - TELEX: 877997 IDS BTNG
         CABLE: Development Brighton

CREATED: 1966
SIZE OF STAFF: Professional: 8   Other: 12   Total: 20
TYPE OF SERVICE: national; private; non-profit
MATERIALS DESCRIBING THE SERVICE: - Guide to the library, Gorman, G. E., 1976
          - Annual report
SUBJECT COVERAGE: economics; sociology; political science; social welfare;
          administrative sciences; demography; development
GEOGRAPHICAL COVERAGE: Developing countries
DATA BEING PROCESSED AND SIZE: 180,000 books; 10,000 periodicals; 150 abstract
          journals; 2,000 microcopies
DATA PROCESSING METHODS: partially computerized
HARDWARE USED: Hewlett Packard HP 3000
SOFTWARE USED: MINISIS
STORAGE MEDIA: traditional shelving of publications
TYPE OF ACTIVITY: publication
PUBLICATIONS: - Gorman, G. E.; Downey, J. A., Bibliographic control of official
          publications at IDS, 1982
CLIENTELE: researchers, students, policy-makers, government and international agency
          personnel
ACCESS TO SERVICE: services open to all users, free of charge in most cases
TYPE & DESCRIPTION OF SERVICES PROVIDED: Mainly concerned with third world
          development studies. Provides library services, bibliographic searches of
          information using own card catalogues. Also provides on-line searches and
          photocopies.

751 - UNIVERSITY OF WARWICK, LIBRARY

ADDRESS: Gibbet Hill Road,
          Coventry CVA 7AL,
          UNITED KINGDOM
          TEL: (0203) 523523 - TELEX: 31406
CREATED: 1963   HEAD: P. E. Tucker, Librarian
SIZE OF STAFF: Professional: 25   Other: 69   Total: 94
TYPE OF SERVICE: public; non-profit
SYSTEMS & NETWORKS ATTACHED TO: Birmingham Cooperative Library Mechanisation Project
WORKING LANGUAGE(S): English
SUBJECT COVERAGE: social sciences; labour relations; labour history
GEOGRAPHICAL COVERAGE: Western Europe; North America; South America; global
DATA PROCESSING METHODS: partially computerized
HARDWARE USED: Data General MV 4000
SOFTWARE USED: own
CLIENTELE: academic staff; students (12,000)
ACCESS TO SERVICE: services open to specific categories of users, free of charge
TYPE & DESCRIPTION OF SERVICES PROVIDED: Provides library services, bibliographic and
          quantitative data searches, photocopies, dissemination of information. Also
          provides on-line searches of information using own data bases and external
          data bases.

Uruguay

752 - BIBLIOTECA DEL PODER LEGISLATIVO

SYNONYMOUS NAMES: Library of the Legislative Power
ADDRESS: Palacio Legislativo,
      Montevideo,
      URUGUAY
      TEL: 208937
CREATED: 1929   *HEAD:* Mr. H. A. Mazzeo, Director
SIZE OF STAFF: Professional: 12   Other: 123   Total: 135
TYPE OF SERVICE: national; public; non-profit
WORKING LANGUAGE(S): Spanish; English; French; Portuguese
SUBJECT COVERAGE: law; administrative sciences; economics; history; political science
GEOGRAPHICAL COVERAGE: Uruguay
DATA BEING PROCESSED AND SIZE: books, articles, reports, references
DATA PROCESSING METHODS: manual
STORAGE MEDIA: traditional shelving of publications, fiches, microfilms
TYPE OF ACTIVITY: distribution of information; publication
PERIODICALS PUBLISHED:
      - Boletín Bibliográfico
      - Fichas Analíticas de Artículos de Publicaciones Periódicas
PUBLICATIONS: - Bibliografía Uruguay
CLIENTELE: senators and deputies of the country, students, researchers
ACCESS TO SERVICE: services open to all users, free of charge
TYPE & DESCRIPTION OF SERVICES PROVIDED: Provides library services, bibliographic
      searches of information, on-line services, selective dissemination of
      information, photocopies, translation of documents upon request, depositary
      of legal documentation emanating from national publications.

753 - CENTRO DE INFORMACIÓN, INVESTIGACIÓN Y DOCUMENTACIÓN DEL URUGUAY

SYNONYMOUS NAMES: CIIDU-SERCOM
ADDRESS: 18 de Julio 1377/Primer Piso,
      Montevideo,
      URUGUAY
      TEL: 903434
CREATED: 1984   *HEAD:* Mr. V. Bjorgan,
SIZE OF STAFF: Professional: 1   Other: 4   Total: 5
TYPE OF SERVICE: private; non-profit
SYSTEMS & NETWORKS ATTACHED TO: Electronic mail service EIES (through TELENET)
MATERIALS DESCRIBING THE SERVICE: - SERCOM, las otras voces
WORKING LANGUAGE(S): Spanish
SUBJECT COVERAGE: social sciences; social welfare; sociology; communication;
      education
GEOGRAPHICAL COVERAGE: Uruguay; South America
DATA BEING PROCESSED AND SIZE: books, periodicals, reports, seminars and on-line
      information (2,000 references)
DATA PROCESSING METHODS: manual; partially computerized
HARDWARE USED: IBM-XT
SOFTWARE USED: UNIX

STORAGE MEDIA: traditional shelving of publications
TYPE OF ACTIVITY: data collection; data analysis; SSID scientific and methodological
    activities; SSID training; distribution of information; publication
CLIENTELE: NGOs, students and researchers, decision-makers, grass roots movements
ACCESS TO SERVICE: open to a specific category of users, free of charge
TYPE & DESCRIPTION OF SERVICES PROVIDED: Provides library services, bibliographic
    searches of information, literature abstracts and surveys, on-line services
    using its own data base SERCOM. Has access through TELENET to IBASE of
    Brazil Data Base. Also provides selective dissemination of information and
    photocopies.

754 - CENTRO DE INFORMACIONES Y ESTUDIOS DEL URUGUAY, CENTRO DE DOCUMENTACIÓN

SYNONYMOUS NAMES: CIESU Centro de Documentación;
    Information and Studies Centre of Uruguay, Documentation Centre
ADDRESS: Calle Juan Paullier 1174,
    Casilla de Correo 10587,
    Montevideo,
    URUGUAY
    TEL: 403866
    CABLE: CIESUMONT
CREATED: 1979   *HEAD:* Ms. M. Sabelli de Louzao, Librarian
SIZE OF STAFF: Professional: 2   Total: 2
TYPE OF SERVICE: national; private; non-profit
SUBJECT COVERAGE: sociology; social sciences; demography
GEOGRAPHICAL COVERAGE: Uruguay; Latin America
DATA BEING PROCESSED AND SIZE: 15,000 books; 120 journals; 70 serials
DATA PROCESSING METHODS: manual
STORAGE MEDIA: traditional shelving of publications, fiches
TYPE OF ACTIVITY: data collection; data analysis; publication
PUBLICATIONS: - Serie bibliográfica: No. 1. Bibliografía sobre empleo
    - Serie bibliográfica: No. 2. Indice de revistas existentes en el bibliotec
    - Serie bibliográfica: No. 3. Lista de bibliografías: bibliografía de
    bibliografías existentes en la biblioteca CIESU
    - Serie bibliográfica: No. 4. Indice de las publicaciones del CIESU
CLIENTELE: 100 researchers, students
ACCESS TO SERVICE: services open to specific categories of users, free of charge
TYPE & DESCRIPTION OF SERVICES PROVIDED: Provides library services, bibliographies,
    surveys, documentation projects.

755 - JUNTA DE VECINOS DE MONTEVIDEO, BIBLIOTECA "JOSÉ ARTIGAS"

ADDRESS: 25 de Mayo 609,
    Montevideo,
    URUGUAY
    TEL: 961808
CREATED: 1962   *HEAD:* Ms. E. Duarte de Bogadjián, Director
SIZE OF STAFF: Professional: 3   Other: 4   Total: 7
TYPE OF SERVICE: national; public; non-profit

MATERIALS DESCRIBING THE SERVICE: - Bibliotecas del Uruguay, 1978
 - Directorio de Servicios de Información y Documentación en el Uruguay, 1983
SUBJECT COVERAGE: social sciences; public administration; local government; law;
 economics; history; political science
GEOGRAPHICAL COVERAGE: Montevideo, Uruguay
DATA BEING PROCESSED AND SIZE: 10,500 books; 135 periodicals; maps
DATA PROCESSING METHODS: manual
STORAGE MEDIA: traditional shelving of publications, fiches
TYPE OF ACTIVITY: data collection; data analysis; distribution of information;
 publication
PERIODICALS PUBLISHED:
 - Boletín Biblioteca 'José Artigas'
 - Lista de Canje
PUBLICATIONS: - Estudio de la ISBD
 - Repertorio nacional de siglas
CLIENTELE: executives; researchers; civil servants
TYPE & DESCRIPTION OF SERVICES PROVIDED: Provides library services, inter-library
 loans, exchange of publications, bibliographic search of information,
 selective dissemination of information, consulting on legal issues and
 photocopies.

56 - UNIVERSIDAD DE LA REPÚBLICA, ESCUELA UNIVERSITARIA DE PSICOLOGÍA, BIBLIOTECA

SYNONYMOUS NAMES: EUP, Biblioteca
ADDRESS: Mercedes 1737,
 Montevideo,
 URUGUAY
 TEL: 4.26.29
CREATED: 1975   *HEAD:* Dr. Scherzer,
SIZE OF STAFF: Professional: 3
TYPE OF SERVICE: public; non-profit
WORKING LANGUAGE(S): Spanish; English
SUBJECT COVERAGE: psychology; social anthropology; philosophy; social sciences
DATA BEING PROCESSED AND SIZE: 3,250 books; 500 articles; 75 seminars; 60 periodicals
DATA PROCESSING METHODS: manual
TYPE OF ACTIVITY: data collection; distribution of information; publication
PERIODICALS PUBLISHED:
 - Boletín Bibliografico
 - Accession List
CLIENTELE: 150 teachers, 2,000 students, 1,000 psychologists p.a.
ACCESS TO SERVICE: services open to all users, free of charge
TYPE & DESCRIPTION OF SERVICES PROVIDED: Provides library services, bibliographic and
 literature abstract searches of information, selective dissemination of
 information and photocopies.

**57 - UNIVERSIDAD DE LA REPÚBLICA, FACULTAD DE CIENCIAS ECONÓMICAS Y DE
 ADMINISTRACIÓN, INSTITUTO DE ADMINISTRACIÓN, BIBLIOTECA**

SYNONYMOUS NAMES: University of the Republic, School of Economic and Administrative

Sciences, Institute of Administration, Library
ADDRESS: Avenida Gonzalo Ramírez 1926,
Montevideo,
URUGUAY
TEL: 40.46.34
CREATED: 1966
TYPE OF SERVICE: national; public; non-profit
WORKING LANGUAGE(S): Spanish
SUBJECT COVERAGE: administrative sciences; business administration; small business; public administration; public enterprises
GEOGRAPHICAL COVERAGE: Uruguay
DATA PROCESSING METHODS: computerized
HARDWARE USED: IBM XT
SOFTWARE USED: Lotus, Dbase III, Wordstar
STORAGE MEDIA: discs
TYPE OF ACTIVITY: data collection; data analysis; SSID scientific and methodological activities
CLIENTELE: private enterprises, professors and students
ACCESS TO SERVICE: services open to specific categories of users
TYPE & DESCRIPTION OF SERVICES PROVIDED: Provides library services, bibliographic searches of information, selective dissemination of information, production of information on magnetic tapes and discs and has its own data base.

758 - UNIVERSIDAD DE LA REPÚBLICA, FACULTAD DE DERECHO Y CIENCIAS SOCIALES, DEPARTAMENTO DE DOCUMENTACIÓN Y BIBLIOTECA

SYNONYMOUS NAMES: University of the Republic, Faculty of Social Sciences and Law, Library and Documentation Department
ADDRESS: Av. 18 de Julio 1824 1er Piso, entre Tristán Narvaja y Eduardo Acevedo, Montevideo,
URUGUAY
TEL: 4.38.09
CREATED: 1892   *HEAD:* Ms. R. Ortiz de Balbis, Director
SIZE OF STAFF: Professional: 25   Other: 7   Total: 32
TYPE OF SERVICE: national; public; non-profit
SYSTEMS & NETWORKS ATTACHED TO: SICTUR (Servicio de Información Científica y Técnica de la Universidad de la República)
WORKING LANGUAGE(S): Spanish
SUBJECT COVERAGE: law; social sciences; administrative sciences; economics; political science; social anthropology; sociology
GEOGRAPHICAL COVERAGE: global; France; Spain; Italy; United Kingdom; USA; Latin America
DATA BEING PROCESSED AND SIZE: 450,000 books and periodicals
DATA PROCESSING METHODS: manual; computerized
HARDWARE USED: AT 18 MHZ 80 M
SOFTWARE USED: MICRO/ISIS
STORAGE MEDIA: traditional shelving of publications, fiches, microfiches
TYPE OF ACTIVITY: data collection; data analysis; distribution of information; publication
PERIODICALS PUBLISHED: - Revista de la Facultad de Derecho y Ciencias Sociales
- Cuadernos de la Facultad de Derecho y Ciencias Sociales

- Lista de Adquisiciones
- Boletín Bibliográfico

CLIENTELE: lawyers, notaries, procurers, magistrates, sociologists, translators, teachers, students, researchers

ACCESS TO SERVICE: services open to all users, free of charge

TYPE & DESCRIPTION OF SERVICES PROVIDED: Provides library services, bibliographies and photocopies.

759 - ABI/INFORM

PARENT ORGANIZATION: Data Courier, Inc.

ADDRESS: 620 South Fifth Street,
Louisville,
Kentucky 40202-2297,
U. S. A.
TEL: (502) 582-4111 - TELEX: 204235

CREATED: 1971   *HEAD:* Ms. B. B. Hawkwood, Managing Editor

SIZE OF STAFF: Professional: 10   Other: 30   Total: 40

TYPE OF SERVICE: international; public; profit

MATERIALS DESCRIBING THE SERVICE: - Why use ABI
- Business and Management Information Services (corporate brochure)

WORKING LANGUAGE(S): English; (all non-English articles are translated; original language documents available)

SUBJECT COVERAGE: economics; finance; management; business law; marketing

GEOGRAPHICAL COVERAGE: global

DATA BEING PROCESSED AND SIZE: 650 periodicals

DATA PROCESSING METHODS: computerized

TYPE OF ACTIVITY: data collection

PUBLICATIONS: - The Complete journals list of ABI/INFORM
- Search INFORM

CLIENTELE: users worldwide in major corporations, governments and academic institutions

ACCESS TO SERVICE: paid services

TYPE & DESCRIPTION OF SERVICES PROVIDED: Data base (290,000 citations with abstracts) providing worldwide coverage of periodical literature, monthly tape service and document delivery services. Data base is available on-line through DIALOG, SSDC, BRS, VU/TEXT, ESA/IRS, Data-Star, Mead Data Central, ITT and HRIN.

760 - ACADEMY OF EDUCATIONAL DEVELOPMENT, CLEARINGHOUSE ON DEVELOPMENT COMMUNICATION

ADDRESS: 1255 23rd Street NW,
Suite 400,
Washington, D.C. 20037,
U. S. A.
TEL: (202) 862-1900 - TELEX: 197601 ACADED WSH

CREATED: 1972   *HEAD:* Ms. J. Brace, Director

SIZE OF STAFF: Professional: 3   Other: 2   Total: 5

TYPE OF SERVICE: international; private; non-profit
WORKING LANGUAGE(S): English
SUBJECT COVERAGE: education; social welfare; social anthropology; communication;
       development; agriculture; nutrition; population; health
GEOGRAPHICAL COVERAGE: global, principally developing countries
DATA BEING PROCESSED AND SIZE: books; 300 newsletters; 100 journals
DATA PROCESSING METHODS: partially computerized
HARDWARE USED: Leading Edge Computer System; Epson Printer
SOFTWARE USED: XYWrite Software; R-Base 5000
STORAGE MEDIA: traditional shelving of publications
TYPE OF ACTIVITY: data collection; distribution of information; publication
PERIODICALS PUBLISHED: - DCR: Development Communication Report, 4 p.a.
       - Bulletin
PUBLICATIONS: - Beyond the flipchart: three decades of development communication,
       1985
       - Thesaurus of development communication, 1981
CLIENTELE: 6,000
ACCESS TO SERVICE: open to all users, free of charge
TYPE & DESCRIPTION OF SERVICES PROVIDED: The Clearinghouse publishes case studies of
       development projects throughout the world that use communication
       technologies in agriculture, education, nutrition, population, health and
       integrated development. Provides bibliographic, literature abstract and
       quantitative data searches, selective dissemination of information,
       photocopies, audiovisual materials such as films, videotapes and slidetapes

761 - AGENCY FOR INTERNATIONAL DEVELOPMENT, CENTER FOR DEVELOPMENT INFORMATION AND EVALUATION

SYNONYMOUS NAMES: AID/CDIE
PARENT ORGANIZATION: US Government
ADDRESS: Document and Information Handling Facility,
       7222 47th Str., Suite 100,
       Chevy Chase,
       Maryland 20815,
       U. S. A.
       TEL: (301) 951-7191 - TELEX: 3730100 LTSCORP
CREATED: 1981
TYPE OF SERVICE: international; public
WORKING LANGUAGE(S): English
SUBJECT COVERAGE: economics; development; evaluation
DATA BEING PROCESSED AND SIZE: 45,000 documention items
HARDWARE USED: HP 3000/48
SOFTWARE USED: MINISIS
STORAGE MEDIA: fiches; tapes; discs
TYPE OF ACTIVITY: data collection; distribution of information; SSID training
PERIODICALS PUBLISHED: - AID Research and Development Abstracts, 4 p.a.
ACCESS TO SERVICE: services open to all users against payment
TYPE & DESCRIPTION OF SERVICES PROVIDED: Its Computerized Development Information
       System "DIS" provides online access to citations of over 45,000 documents
       for more than 6,000 projects. Documents are available on microfiche and in
       paper copy. Its library provides specialized services including reference

assistance, document citations, inter-library loan and technical data base searches.

762 - ALICE LLOYD COLLEGE, APPALACHIAN ORAL HISTORY PROJECT

ADDRESS: Pippa Passes,
Kentucky 41844,
U. S. A.
TEL: (606) 368-2101
CREATED: 1972   *HEAD:* Ms. K. R. Martin, Director
SIZE OF STAFF: Professional: 1   Other: 2   Total: 3
TYPE OF SERVICE: national; private; non-profit
MATERIALS DESCRIBING THE SERVICE: - printed notice
WORKING LANGUAGE(S): English
SUBJECT COVERAGE: history; social anthropology; cultural anthropology
GEOGRAPHICAL COVERAGE: USA and Eastern Kentucky
DATA BEING PROCESSED AND SIZE: books, periodicals; 2,000 recorded oral history
interviews, 500 transcripts, 5,000 photographs, films, video tapes
DATA PROCESSING METHODS: manual
STORAGE MEDIA: tapes; transcripts
TYPE OF ACTIVITY: data collection; publication
PUBLICATIONS: - Union catalog
- Time WAS, collection of photographs
- Mountain memories, student publication
CLIENTELE: authors, researchers, teachers, students
ACCESS TO SERVICE: open to all users, free of charge
TYPE & DESCRIPTION OF SERVICES PROVIDED: Library services. Provides selective
dissemination of information and photocopies upon request.

763 - AMERICAN ECONOMIC ASSOCIATION, ECONOMIC LITERATURE INDEX

ADDRESS: P.O. Box 7320,
Oakland Station,
Pittsburgh,
Pennsylvania 15213,
U. S. A.
TEL: (412) 621-2291
CREATED: 1983
TYPE OF SERVICE: non-profit
MATERIALS DESCRIBING THE SERVICE: - Ekwurzel, D.; Saffran, B., Online information
retrieval for economists: the economic literature index, 1985
WORKING LANGUAGE(S): English
SUBJECT COVERAGE: economics; economic history and theory; economic systemseconomic
development
GEOGRAPHICAL COVERAGE: global
DATA BEING PROCESSED AND SIZE: 1,500 books; 285 journals
DATA PROCESSING METHODS: computerized
ACCESS TO SERVICE: paid services
TYPE & DESCRIPTION OF SERVICES PROVIDED: Provides bibliographic searches and on-line

searches using own data base "Economic Literature Index" available through Dialog.

764 - AMERICAN INSTITUTE FOR ECONOMIC RESEARCH, HARWOOD LIBRARY

ADDRESS: Division St.,
      Great Barrington,
      MA 01230,
      U. S. A.
      TEL: (413) 528-1216
CREATED: 1933   *HEAD:* Ms. L. Tucker, Librarian
SIZE OF STAFF: Professional: 4
TYPE OF SERVICE: non-profit
MATERIALS DESCRIBING THE SERVICE: - AIER after 50 years
SUBJECT COVERAGE: economics; economic history; economic systems; economic
      development; business organizations; finance; investment
DATA BEING PROCESSED AND SIZE: 10,000 books; 70 periodicals
PERIODICALS PUBLISHED:
      - Research Report, 24 p.a.
      - Economic Education Bulletin, 12 p.a.
TYPE & DESCRIPTION OF SERVICES PROVIDED: Provides library services and interlibrary
      loans.

765 - AMERICAN PSYCHOLOGICAL ASSOCIATION, ARTHUR W. MELTON LIBRARY

ADDRESS: 1200 17th Street, NW,
      Washington, D.C. 20036,
      U. S. A.
CREATED: 1978   *HEAD:* Mr. R. A. Sample, Head Librarian
SIZE OF STAFF: Professional: 2   Total: 2
TYPE OF SERVICE: private; non-profit
SUBJECT COVERAGE: psychology; social sciences; education; social welfare
ACCESS TO SERVICE: services open to specific categories of users
TYPE & DESCRIPTION OF SERVICES PROVIDED: Provides library services and selective
      dissemination of information.

766 - BALCH INSTITUTE FOR ETHNIC STUDIES, LIBRARY

ADDRESS: 18 S. 7th St.,
      Philadelphia,
      PA 19106,
      U. S. A.
      TEL: (215) 925-8090
CREATED: 1971   *HEAD:* Mr. J. R. Anderson, Library Director
SIZE OF STAFF: Professional: 7   Other: 2   Total: 9
TYPE OF SERVICE: national; private; non-profit
SYSTEMS & NETWORKS ATTACHED TO: OCLC (Online Computer Library Consortium)

WORKING LANGUAGE(S): English
SUBJECT COVERAGE: demography; history; cultural anthropology; ethnic groups; history of immigration to Canada and USA; American and Canadian ethnic studies
GEOGRAPHICAL COVERAGE: North America
DATA BEING PROCESSED AND SIZE: 60,000 vol.; 12,000 photographs; 2,500 linear feet of manuscripts; 6,000 reels of microfilms; articles, conference papers and audio recordings
DATA PROCESSING METHODS: computerized
SOFTWARE USED: OCLC system
STORAGE MEDIA: traditional shelving of publications; microfilms
TYPE OF ACTIVITY: distribution of information; publication
PERIODICALS PUBLISHED:
- New Dimensions, 2 p.a.
PUBLICATIONS: - Studies on American immigration history and ethnic life
- Exhibition Catalogs
CLIENTELE: 2,100 users p.a.
ACCESS TO SERVICE: services open to all users, free of charge
TYPE & DESCRIPTION OF SERVICES PROVIDED: Provides library services.

767 - BRIGHAM YOUNG UNIVERSITY, SOCIAL SCIENCE DIVISION LIBRARY

ADDRESS: Provo,
Utah 84602,
U. S. A.
TEL: (801) 378-3809
CREATED: 1875   *HEAD:* Mr. M. E. Wiggins, Librarian
SIZE OF STAFF: Professional: 3   Other: 4   Total: 7
TYPE OF SERVICE: private
SUBJECT COVERAGE: social sciences; economics; education; political science; psychology; cultural anthropology; social welfare; sociology
DATA BEING PROCESSED AND SIZE: government documents, maps
DATA PROCESSING METHODS: partially computerized
HARDWARE USED: IBM
SOFTWARE USED: NOTIS, CD RM Services for ERIC, Wilsonline
TYPE OF ACTIVITY: distribution of information
CLIENTELE: faculty, students, community guests
ACCESS TO SERVICE: open to all users
TYPE & DESCRIPTION OF SERVICES PROVIDED: Provides library services, inter-library loans, on-line services using its own data base as well as others such as: DIALOG, SDC, BRS information technologies, Mead Data Central Reference Service and OCLC. Photocopying facilities are also available.

768 - BROOKINGS INSTITUTION, SOCIAL SCIENCE COMPUTATION CENTRE AND LIBRARY

SYNONYMOUS NAMES: B I
ADDRESS: 1775 Massachusetts Avenue, N.W.,
Washington, D.C. 20036,
U. S. A.
TEL: (202) 797-6000

CABLE: BROOKINST WASHINGTON
HEAD: Mr. J. P. Fennell, Director Social Science Computation Center
Mrs. L. P. Walker, Librarian
SIZE OF STAFF: Professional: 86   Other: 171   Total: 257
TYPE OF SERVICE: national; private; non-profit
MATERIALS DESCRIBING THE SERVICE: - Brookings Institution Annual report
WORKING LANGUAGE(S): English
SUBJECT COVERAGE: social sciences; economics; political science
GEOGRAPHICAL COVERAGE: global
DATA BEING PROCESSED AND SIZE: 80,000 volumes; 700 periodicals; pamphlets; governmen
documents; selective United Nations collection
DATA PROCESSING METHODS: computerized
HARDWARE USED: VAX
SOFTWARE USED: Mass 11
TYPE OF ACTIVITY: data collection; data analysis; distribution of information;
publication
PERIODICALS PUBLISHED: - Brookings Review, 4 p.a.
- Brookings Papers on Economic Activity, 2 p.a.
ACCESS TO SERVICE: services open to specific categories of users against payment
TYPE & DESCRIPTION OF SERVICES PROVIDED: Provides library services, inter-library
loans and selective dissemination of information. A program of on-line dat
base bibliographic searching broadens and facilitates research
opportunities. The Social Science Computation Center provides computing an
related services to organizations engaged in social science research and
public administration, and the Federal government.

769 - CALIFORNIA INSTITUTE OF INTERNATIONAL STUDIES, WORLD AFFAIRS REPORT

SYNONYMOUS NAMES: CIIS/WAR
ADDRESS: 766 Santa Ynez,
Stanford,
CA 94305,
U. S. A.
TEL: (415) 322-2026
HEAD: Mr. R. Hilton,
SIZE OF STAFF: Professional: 4
TYPE OF SERVICE: international; non-profit
SYSTEMS & NETWORKS ATTACHED TO: DIALOG
SUBJECT COVERAGE: political science
GEOGRAPHICAL COVERAGE: global
DATA BEING PROCESSED AND SIZE: books; articles; reports; on-going research
DATA PROCESSING METHODS: computerized
HARDWARE USED: IBM PC Diablo
SOFTWARE USED: Word perfect
STORAGE MEDIA: tapes; microfiches
TYPE OF ACTIVITY: data collection; data analysis; distribution of information; SSID
training; publication
PERIODICALS PUBLISHED: - World Affairs Report, 4 p.a.
CLIENTELE: researchers, government officials, teachers
TYPE & DESCRIPTION OF SERVICES PROVIDED: Provides on-line services using own data
base "World Affairs Report" containing more than 10,000 records, updated

monthly and available through Dialog. It analyzes the Soviet version of
world developments based on Soviet and non-Soviet sources.

70 - CALIFORNIA STATE LAW LIBRARY

ADDRESS: Library and Courts Building,
        P.O. Box 942837,
        Sacramento,
        California 94237-0001,
        U. S. A.
        TEL: (916) 445-8833
CREATED: 1850   *HEAD:* M. Hoppes, Law Librarian
SIZE OF STAFF: Professional: 5   Other: 8   Total: 13
TYPE OF SERVICE: national; public; non-profit
WORKING LANGUAGE(S): English
SUBJECT COVERAGE: law
GEOGRAPHICAL COVERAGE: California, USA
DATA BEING PROCESSED AND SIZE: 161,000 books; 700 serials and periodicals;
        microcards, microfiches, 643 reels of microfilms
DATA PROCESSING METHODS: partially computerized
TYPE OF ACTIVITY: distribution of information; publication
PERIODICALS PUBLISHED: - California County Law Library Basic List, 1 p.a.
PUBLICATIONS: - California county law library directory
ACCESS TO SERVICE: open to all users, free of charge
TYPE & DESCRIPTION OF SERVICES PROVIDED: Provides library services and photocopies.

71 - CASE WESTERN RESERVE UNIVERSITY, APPLIED SOCIAL SCIENCES LIBRARY

ADDRESS: School of Applied Social Sciences,
        2035 Abington Rd.,
        Cleveland,
        OH 44106,
        U. S. A.
        TEL: (216) 368-2302
CREATED: 1916   *HEAD:* Mr. A. S. Biagianti, Director
SIZE OF STAFF: Professional: 1   Other: 2   Total: 3
TYPE OF SERVICE: private; non-profit
SYSTEMS & NETWORKS ATTACHED TO: OCLC, Inc.; Association for Library Information
        (AFLI); Cleveland Area Metropolitan Library System (CAMLS)
WORKING LANGUAGE(S): English
SUBJECT COVERAGE: social welfare; social work; poverty; alcoholism; juvenile
        delinquency; old age; children; minority groups; community development;
        social psychology; mental health
DATA BEING PROCESSED AND SIZE: 18,500 books; 1,200 bound periodicals; 7,000 pamphlets
        and monographs; 158 microforms; 201 AV programs; 288 current journals and
        other serials
DATA PROCESSING METHODS: partially computerized
TYPE OF ACTIVITY: distribution of information
CLIENTELE: students, faculty

ACCESS TO SERVICE: services open to all users for reference use only, paid services
        for interlibrary loans
TYPE & DESCRIPTION OF SERVICES PROVIDED: Provides library services, photocopies, and
        on-line services using own data base "Geac Library Information System", as
        well as external data bases, OCLC, DIALOG and BITNET (electronic mail
        service).

772 - CATALYST INFORMATION CENTER

ADDRESS: 250 Park Avenue South,
        New York,
        N.Y. 10003-1459,
        U. S. A.
        TEL: (212) 777-8900
HEAD: Ms. S. O. Crocker, Director
SIZE OF STAFF: Professional: 2   Other: 2   Total: 4
TYPE OF SERVICE: national; non-profit
SUBJECT COVERAGE: demography; working women; labour; employment
GEOGRAPHICAL COVERAGE: USA
DATA BEING PROCESSED AND SIZE: 4,000 books; periodicals
DATA PROCESSING METHODS: partially computerized
HARDWARE USED: Hewlett Packard
TYPE OF ACTIVITY: data collection; data analysis; distribution of information;
        publication
CLIENTELE: corporations
ACCESS TO SERVICE: services open to specific categories of users
TYPE & DESCRIPTION OF SERVICES PROVIDED: Provides bibliographic, literature abstract
        survey and quantitative data searches. Also provides on-line searches using
        own data base "Catalyst Resources on the Workforce and Women" (available
        on BRS) as well as external data bases (BRS, Dialog).

773 - CENTER FOR MIGRATION STUDIES OF NEW YORK, LIBRARY ARCHIVES

SYNONYMOUS NAMES: CMS, Library Archives
ADDRESS: 209 Flagg Place,
        Staten Island,
        New York 10304-1148,
        U. S. A.
        TEL: (212) 351-8800
CREATED: 1964   HEAD: Ms. D. Zimmerman,
SIZE OF STAFF: Professional: 3   Other: 1   Total: 4
TYPE OF SERVICE: non-profit
MATERIALS DESCRIBING THE SERVICE: - The City University of New York (CUNY)
SUBJECT COVERAGE: demography; sociology; economics; history; political science; law;
        migration; refugees; ethnic groups
GEOGRAPHICAL COVERAGE: global
DATA PROCESSING METHODS: partially computerized
TYPE OF ACTIVITY: data collection; data analysis; distribution of information; SSID
        scientific and methodological activities; publication

UBLICATIONS: - CMS authority list of subject heading for migration
- Refugees; holdings of the CMS Library/Archives, 1987
LIENTELE: researchers, students (300 p.a.)
CCESS TO SERVICE: services free of charge
YPE & DESCRIPTION OF SERVICES PROVIDED: Provides library services, bibliographic and
literature abstracts searches of information, and microfilms.

74 - CITYCORP DATABASE SERVICES

DDRESS: P.O. Box 966,
New York,
NY 10268,
U. S. A.
TEL: (212) 968-6919
REATED: 1968   *HEAD:* J. Su,
IZE OF STAFF: Professional: 5   Other: 5   Total: 10
YPE OF SERVICE: national; private; profit
UBJECT COVERAGE: economics; statistics; finance
EOGRAPHICAL COVERAGE: USA
ATA BEING PROCESSED AND SIZE: Data bases (5,000 time series from 1947 to present, US
Government and statistical agencies and proprietary sources economic data),
foreign exchange and interest rates database
ATA PROCESSING METHODS: computerized
ARDWARE USED: IBM PC disketts, various mainframes; 370, PUP 20 and others
OFTWARE USED: various PC statistical packages and various programs such as Troll,
SAS, SAGE etc.
YPE OF ACTIVITY: data collection; distribution of information; publication
UBLICATIONS: - Citibank economic database directory, 1986
LIENTELE: government, universities, industry, banks, statisticians, economists
CCESS TO SERVICE: open to all users, against payment
YPE & DESCRIPTION OF SERVICES PROVIDED: Services include on-line services using its
own economic data bases: Citibase and Citibase Weekly, and production of
information on magnetic tapes.

75 - CLEARINGHOUSE ON CHILD ABUSE AND NEGLECT INFORMATION

ARENT ORGANIZATION: National Center on Child Abuse and Neglect
DDRESS: P.O. Box 1182,
Washington, DC 20013,
U. S. A.
TEL: (703) 821-8955
EAD: Ms. A. P. Cowan, Project Director
IZE OF STAFF: Professional: 5   Other: 2   Total: 7
YPE OF SERVICE: national
ORKING LANGUAGE(S): English
UBJECT COVERAGE: social sciences; social welfare; children; child abuse and neglect
EOGRAPHICAL COVERAGE: USA
ATA BEING PROCESSED AND SIZE: 8700 documents; 3,600 state law; 3,400 programs; 83
on-going research projects; 550 audiovisuals

561

DATA PROCESSING METHODS: computerized
STORAGE MEDIA: traditional shelving of publications (in reading room)
TYPE OF ACTIVITY: data collection; distribution of information; publication
CLIENTELE: professionals and concerned citizens (10,000 p.a.)
ACCESS TO SERVICE: services open to all users, free of charge, some services against
        payment
TYPE & DESCRIPTION OF SERVICES PROVIDED: Provides bibliographic and literature
        abstract searches of information, on-line services using own data base
        "Child Abuse and Neglect" (DIALOG File 64), and photocopies upon request.

776 - COLUMBIA UNIVERSITY, CENTER FOR THE SOCIAL SCIENCES, DATA ARCHIVE RESEARCH AND TRAINING SERVICES

SYNONYMOUS NAMES: DARTS
ADDRESS: 420 West 118 Street,
        814 International Affairs Building,
        New York,
        New York 10027,
        U. S. A.
        TEL: (212) 280.3038
CREATED: 1976   *HEAD:* W. Bourne, Coordinator
SIZE OF STAFF: Total: 3
TYPE OF SERVICE: national; private; non-profit
SYSTEMS & NETWORKS ATTACHED TO: Inter-University Consortium for Political and Social
        Research (ICPSR); IBM-based Network at New York City Universities (BITNET)
MATERIALS DESCRIBING THE SERVICE: - Brochure
WORKING LANGUAGE(S): English
SUBJECT COVERAGE: social sciences; surveys; community; consumer; elites; political
        behaviour; political attitudes; government; politics; crime; minorities;
        race relations; socialization; students; youth; international organizations
        conflict; aggression; violence
GEOGRAPHICAL COVERAGE: USA
DATA BEING PROCESSED AND SIZE: 500 datasets
DATA PROCESSING METHODS: computerized
HARDWARE USED: IBM-4341, Dec-20, VAX 8700
SOFTWARE USED: SPSSX, SAS, FORTRAN, SIR
STORAGE MEDIA: tapes and disks
TYPE OF ACTIVITY: data analysis; publication
CLIENTELE: students, faculty and research associates
ACCESS TO SERVICE: free of charge to university affiliates
TYPE & DESCRIPTION OF SERVICES PROVIDED: Provides data services and census data
        service, consulting in statistical program use and training in computer
        techniques for members of the Columbia community engaged in quantitative
        research.

777 - COLUMBIA UNIVERSITY, COLLEGE OF PHYSICIANS AND SURGEONS, CENTER FOR POPULATION AND FAMILY HEALTH, LIBRARY/INFORMATION PROGRAM

SYNONYMOUS NAMES: CPFH, Library Information Program

ADDRESS: 60 Haven Avenue,
   New York,
   N. Y. 10032,
   U. S. A.
   TEL: (212) 305-6960 - TELEX: 971913 POPFAMHLTH
   CABLE: Pophealth, New York
CREATED: 1968 *HEAD:* Dr. S. K. Pasquariella, Head Librarian
SIZE OF STAFF: Professional: 4 Other: 4 Total: 8
TYPE OF SERVICE: international; non-profit
SYSTEMS & NETWORKS ATTACHED TO: One of 4 contributors to the POPLINE (Population
   information on line) data base. The library/information program is also a
   member of POPIN
WORKING LANGUAGE(S): English
SUBJECT COVERAGE: demography; social welfare; population; statistics; family
   planning; health; fertility
GEOGRAPHICAL COVERAGE: global
DATA BEING PROCESSED AND SIZE: 25,000 documents including journal articles,
   monographs, conference papers, government and technical reports, unpublished
   papers
DATA PROCESSING METHODS: computerized
SOFTWARE USED: Elhill
STORAGE MEDIA: traditional shelving of publications; files; films
TYPE OF ACTIVITY: distribution of information; publication
PERIODICALS PUBLISHED:
   - POPLINE Brochure
PUBLICATIONS: - POPLINE thesaurus
CLIENTELE: 5-6,000 computer searches provided p.a.; services provided to students,
   visitors and others (mail correspondence)
ACCESS TO SERVICE: services free of charge for requests from developing countries or
   users affiliated with international agencies
TYPE & DESCRIPTION OF SERVICES PROVIDED: The Center's on-line data base POPLINE
   (POPulation information onLINE) containing 150,000 records provides
   bibliographic citations and abstracts of worldwide literature on population
   and family planning including research in human fertility, statistics and
   related health law and policy issues. It is available through the MEDLARS
   system of the United States National Library of Medicine (NLM). Also
   provides selective dissemination of information, information on magnetic
   tape, photocopies and consults the National Library of Medicine's data base
   MEDLINE.

778 - CONGRESSIONAL INFORMATION SERVICE, INC.

SYNONYMOUS NAMES: CIS
PARENT ORGANIZATION: Elsevier-NDU nv
ADDRESS: 4520 East-West Highway, Suite 800,
   Bethesda,
   Maryland 20814-3389,
   U. S. A.
   TEL: 301-654.1550
CREATED: 1969 *HEAD:* Mr. P. P. Massa,
SIZE OF STAFF: Professional: 126 Other: 118

TYPE OF SERVICE: international; private; profit
WORKING LANGUAGE(S): English
SUBJECT COVERAGE: social sciences; statistics
GEOGRAPHICAL COVERAGE: USA; municipal, state and national; Global
DATA BEING PROCESSED AND SIZE: government documents, statistical reports and articles
DATA PROCESSING METHODS: computerized
HARDWARE USED: IBM 4341
SOFTWARE USED: SAMANTHA
TYPE OF ACTIVITY: publication
PUBLICATIONS: - CIS federal register index
             - American statistics index and microfiche
             - Statistical reference index and microfiche
             - Index to international statistics and microfiche
             - CIS 1986-1987 catalog
             - CIS/index and microfiche
CLIENTELE: libraries, attorneys, government officials, scholars, other researchers
ACCESS TO SERVICE: paid services
TYPE & DESCRIPTION OF SERVICES PROVIDED: Provides on-line data base and comprehensive
         access to congressional committee publications; provides complete citations
         and reproductions of official publications; access to statistics; detailed
         indexing of rules, proposed rules, notices and presidential documents.

**779 - CORNELL UNIVERSITY, CORNELL INSTITUTE FOR SOCIAL AND ECONOMIC RESEARCH, DATA
SERVICE**

SYNONYMOUS NAMES: CISER
ADDRESS: 323 Uris Hall,
         Ithaca,
         New York 14853,
         U. S. A.
         TEL: (607) 255-4801
CREATED: 1981   HEAD: Ms. A. Gray, Data Archivist
SIZE OF STAFF: Professional: 3   Other: 4   Total: 7
TYPE OF SERVICE: international; public; non-profit
WORKING LANGUAGE(S): English
SUBJECT COVERAGE: social sciences; demography; economics; statistics; socio-economic
         indicators
GEOGRAPHICAL COVERAGE: global
DATA PROCESSING METHODS: computerized
HARDWARE USED: IM 4381, IBM 3090, IBM-PC
SOFTWARE USED: SAS, SPSS-X, DbaseIII+
STORAGE MEDIA: magnetic tapes; discs
TYPE OF ACTIVITY: data analysis; distribution of information; publication
PUBLICATIONS: - Holdings of machine readable data files
             - New York data files
CLIENTELE: faculty and students, business, government officials
TYPE & DESCRIPTION OF SERVICES PROVIDED: Provides library services and on-line
         services using own data base OASIS (Online Archive Statistical Information
         System). Also provides information on magnetic tapes and photocopies as well
         as support to researchers in locating, acquiring, and using data resources.

780 - DATA RESOURCES

SYNONYMOUS NAMES: DRI
PARENT ORGANIZATION: Standard and Poor's, McGraw-Hill
ADDRESS: Data Products Division,
      1750 K Street NW, 9th Floor,
      Washington, DC 20006,
      U. S. A.
      TEL: (202) 663-7720 - TELEX: 440480 DRI WASHDC
CREATED: 1968   *HEAD:* Ms. M. Disario, Vice-President
SIZE OF STAFF: Professional: 600   Other: 150   Total: 750
TYPE OF SERVICE: international; profit
MATERIALS DESCRIBING THE SERVICE: - DRI data bases
SUBJECT COVERAGE: economics; international economics; finance; industry; energy;
      statistics
GEOGRAPHICAL COVERAGE: global
DATA PROCESSING METHODS: computerized
SOFTWARE USED: PC-Gateway
TYPE OF ACTIVITY: data collection; data analysis; distribution of information;
      publication
PUBLICATIONS: - DRI data catalog
ACCESS TO SERVICE: paid services
TYPE & DESCRIPTION OF SERVICES PROVIDED: Maintains 125 historical and forecast data
      bases which are accessible by personal computer, timesharing, or directly
      from mainframe to mainframe.

781 - THE DATACENTER

ADDRESS: 464 19th Street,
      Oakland,
      California 94612,
      U. S. A.
      TEL: (415) 835-4692
CREATED: 1977   *HEAD:* F. Goff, President
SIZE OF STAFF: Professional: 9   Other: 2   Total: 11
TYPE OF SERVICE: international; private; non-profit
WORKING LANGUAGE(S): English
SUBJECT COVERAGE: history; economics; social welfare
GEOGRAPHICAL COVERAGE: North America; Latin America
DATA BEING PROCESSED AND SIZE: 7,000 files; 400 periodicals
DATA PROCESSING METHODS: manual; partially computerized
HARDWARE USED: CP/M & MS-DOS systems
SOFTWARE USED: dBase II
STORAGE MEDIA: Traditional shelving of publications, micro-fiches, disks
TYPE OF ACTIVITY: data collection; distribution of information; publication
PUBLICATIONS: - Information services Latin America
        - Central America monitor
        - Corporate responsibility monitor
        - Plant shutdown monitor
        - Director of plant shutdowns
        - Neo-conservative monitor

CLIENTELE: Students, journalists, academics, community activists, lawyers, business•
(2,000 p.a.)
ACCESS TO SERVICE: Services open to all users against payment
TYPE & DESCRIPTION OF SERVICES PROVIDED: Provides searches of information, on-line
services and photocopies.

782 - EAST-WEST CENTER, INSTITUTE OF CULTURE AND COMMUNICATION, RESOURCES MATERIALS COLLECTION

ADDRESS: John A. Burns Hall, Room 4063,
Honolulu,
HI 96848,
U. S. A.
TEL: (808) 944-7335 - TELEX: 989171
CABLE: EASSWESCEM HI VIA WUW
CREATED: 1971   *HEAD:* Mr. S. Konoshima, Research Information Specialist
SIZE OF STAFF: Professional: 3   Other: 2   Total: 5
TYPE OF SERVICE: international; public; non-profit
WORKING LANGUAGE(S): English
SUBJECT COVERAGE: sociology of communication; communication and socio-economic
development; mass media; culture; international relations; cross-cultural
communication process; social sciences
GEOGRAPHICAL COVERAGE: Asia; Pacific Area
DATA BEING PROCESSED AND SIZE: 15,000 books; 550 periodicals; 10,000 documents
(conference papers, research reports, seminar/training materials
DATA PROCESSING METHODS: partially computerized
HARDWARE USED: C. ITOH CIE 680/150; IBM 3081
SOFTWARE USED: ADABAS modified; ADVANCE
STORAGE MEDIA: traditional shelving of publications; fiches; tapes
TYPE OF ACTIVITY: data collection; distribution of information; SSID training;
publication
PERIODICALS PUBLISHED:
- Accessions List
PUBLICATIONS: - Bibliograhies
CLIENTELE: researchers, students, professionals
ACCESS TO SERVICE: open to all users
TYPE & DESCRIPTION OF SERVICES PROVIDED: Provides library srevices, biblicgraphic a•
literature abstract searches of information, on-line services using its ow•
data bases. Also provides selective dissemination of information and
photocopies.

783 - EDUCATIONAL RESOURCES INFORMATION CENTER CLEARINGHOUSE FOR SOCIAL STUDIES/SOCIAL SCIENCE EDUCATION

SYNONYMOUS NAMES: ERIC/ChESS
ADDRESS: Social Studies Development Centre,
120 Smith Research Centre,
2805 East 10th Street,
Bloomington,

Indiana 47405,
U.·S. A.
TEL: (812) 335-3838
CREATED: 1970   *HEAD:* Dr. J. J. Patrick, Director
SIZE OF STAFF: Professional: 5   Other: 9   Total: 14
TYPE OF SERVICE: public; non-profit
MATERIALS DESCRIBING THE SERVICE: - ERIC/ChESS, 1986, leaflet
        - A Pocket guide to ERIC, leaflet
WORKING LANGUAGE(S): English
SUBJECT COVERAGE: social sciences; education; economics; geography; history;
        political science; social psychology; sociology; anthropology; comparative
        education; ethnic groups
GEOGRAPHICAL COVERAGE: global
DATA BEING PROCESSED AND SIZE: 5,000 social studies resources
DATA PROCESSING METHODS: manual; computerized
HARDWARE USED: IBM PC XT
SOFTWARE USED: WORD STAR; DBASE III plus database management system; LOTUS 1-2-3
STORAGE MEDIA: microfiche collection, ERIC on compact disc (CD-ROM)
TYPE OF ACTIVITY: data collection; data analysis; SSID training; publication
PERIODICALS PUBLISHED:
        - Keeping UP, News Bulletin, 2 p.a.
PUBLICATIONS: - Digests
        - Reference sheets
CLIENTELE: education community (researchers, policy makers, administrators, teachers,
        parents)
ACCESS TO SERVICE: services open to all users, some services against payment
TYPE & DESCRIPTION OF SERVICES PROVIDED: ERIC/ChESS is one of the 16 subject-
        specialized clearing-houses in the system. Provides library services,
        question-answering services (more than 100,000 inquiries from users),
        searches of information using its own data base ERIC which can be searched
        on-line by computer via all three of the major vendors of on-line retrieval
        service: DIALOG Information Services, SDC (System Development Corporation)
        and BRS (Bibliographic Retrieval Services). Also provides selective
        dissemination of information available on magnetic tapes or microfiches
        (200,000) against payment. Translation of documents and provision of
        photocopies can also be obtained upon request.

784 - EUROPEAN COMMUNITY INFORMATION SERVICE, LIBRARY

PARENT ORGANIZATION: Delegation of the Commission of the European Communities, Office
        of Press and Public Affairs
ADDRESS: 2100 M St., N.W., Suite 707,
        Washington, DC 20037,
        U. S. A.
        TEL: (202) 862-9500 - TELEX: 64215 EURCOM UW
CREATED: 1954   *HEAD:* Ms. B. Sloan, Head of Public Inquiries
SIZE OF STAFF: Professional: 3   Other: 2   Total: 5
TYPE OF SERVICE: international
SYSTEMS & NETWORKS ATTACHED TO: Commission of the European Communities (CEC)
WORKING LANGUAGE(S): English
SUBJECT COVERAGE: demography; law; economics; European Communities

GEOGRAPHICAL COVERAGE: Western Europe
DATA BEING PROCESSED AND SIZE: legislative documents, periodicals, newsletters, pre
        releases, reports and monographs of the EC and about the EC
DATA PROCESSING METHODS: manual; partially computerized
HARDWARE USED: Siemens
SOFTWARE USED: Mistral and others
TYPE OF ACTIVITY: distribution of information; publication
PUBLICATIONS: - A Selective guide to the European Community
CLIENTELE: business sector (50%), academic (40%), government (5%), general public
        (5%); (around 1,300 users per month)
ACCESS TO SERVICE: open to all users
TYPE & DESCRIPTION OF SERVICES PROVIDED: Provides bibliographic and quantitative da
        searches, selective dissemination of information, microforms and
        photocopies.

785 - FLORIDA JOINT LEGISLATIVE MANAGEMENT COMMITTEE, DIVISION OF LEGISLATIVE LIBRA
SERVICES

ADDRESS: Room 701,
        Capitol Building,
        Tallahassee,
        Florida 32399-1400,
        U. S. A.
        TEL: (904) 488-2812
CREATED: 1949   HEAD: Mr. B. G. Baker, Director
SIZE OF STAFF: Professional: 3   Other: 3   Total: 6
TYPE OF SERVICE: national; public; non-profit
MATERIALS DESCRIBING THE SERVICE: - The Florida Legislative Library: functions,
        scope, procedures, 1981
WORKING LANGUAGE(S): English
SUBJECT COVERAGE: social sciences; political science; law
GEOGRAPHICAL COVERAGE: USA
DATA BEING PROCESSED AND SIZE: 35,000 books and reports; 3,400 microforms; 400
        periodicals; 165 vertical files
DATA PROCESSING METHODS: partially computerized
HARDWARE USED: IBM PC
SOFTWARE USED: Card Datalog from DTI Data Trek
STORAGE MEDIA: traditional shelving of publications, microfiches and microfilms
TYPE OF ACTIVITY: distribution of information
PUBLICATIONS: - The Summary of general legislation
CLIENTELE: legislators, legislative staff, civil servants, students and general
        public
ACCESS TO SERVICE: open to all users
TYPE & DESCRIPTION OF SERVICES PROVIDED: Provides library services, query answering
        service, selective dissemination of information and photocopies. Has acces
        to data base LEXIS/NEXI'S through Mead Data Central.

786 - GEORGIA STATE UNIVERSITY, CENTER FOR PUBLIC AND URBAN RESEARCH

SYNONYMOUS NAMES: CPUR
ADDRESS: University Plaza,
　　　　Atlanta,
　　　　Georgia 30303-3091,
　　　　U. S. A.
CREATED: 1976　　*HEAD:* Dr. J. D. Hutcheson, Director
SIZE OF STAFF:　　Total: 2
TYPE OF SERVICE: national; public; non-profit
WORKING LANGUAGE(S): English
SUBJECT COVERAGE: political science; social sciences; public policy; evaluation;
　　　　public opinion
GEOGRAPHICAL COVERAGE: State of Georgia, USA
DATA BEING PROCESSED AND SIZE: 10,000 documentation items
DATA PROCESSING METHODS: computerized
HARDWARE USED: UNIVAC 90/80
SOFTWARE USED: SPSS
TYPE OF ACTIVITY: data collection; data analysis; publication
CLIENTELE: faculty members, students
ACCESS TO SERVICE: open to specific categories of users, free of charge
TYPE & DESCRIPTION OF SERVICES PROVIDED: Its collection includes 75 survey data sets,
　　　　census data and special studies.

787 - GIANNINI FOUNDATION OF AGRICULTURE ECONOMICS, LIBRARY

PARENT ORGANIZATION: University of California at Berkeley
ADDRESS: 248 Giannini Hall,
　　　　Berkeley,
　　　　California 94720,
　　　　U. S. A.
　　　　TEL: (415) 642 71 21
CREATED: 1930　　*HEAD:* Ms. G. Dote, Librarian
SIZE OF STAFF: Professional: 1　　Other: 2　　Total: 3
TYPE OF SERVICE: public; non-profit
WORKING LANGUAGE(S): English
SUBJECT COVERAGE: agricultural economics; sociology; social anthropology; resources
　　　　economics; economic development; rural sociology
GEOGRAPHICAL COVERAGE: California, Western USA; global
DATA BEING PROCESSED AND SIZE: books; articles; reports; government documents;
　　　　conference papers; symposium papers (2,000 p.a.)
DATA PROCESSING METHODS: partially computerized
TYPE OF ACTIVITY: distribution of information; publication
PERIODICALS PUBLISHED:
　　　　- Materials added to the Giannini Foundation Library, 10 p.a.
PUBLICATIONS: - Economic research of interest to agriculture
CLIENTELE: faculty and graduate students, general public, business consultants,
　　　　economists
ACCESS TO SERVICE: services open to specific categories of users, free of charge
TYPE & DESCRIPTION OF SERVICES PROVIDED: Provides library services, bibliographic,
　　　　literature abstract and survey searches, selective dissemination of

information. Photocopies are charged. Also provides on-line services using
own data base "Ingres Database Management System".

788 - GLOBAL INFORMATION NETWORK

PARENT ORGANIZATION: Council on International and Public Affairs
ADDRESS: 777 United Nations Plaza,
New York,
N.Y. 10017,
U. S. A.
TEL: (212) 286-0123
CREATED: 1986   *HEAD:* Mr. D. Dion, Managing Editor
SIZE OF STAFF: Professional: 2   Other: 2   Total: 4
TYPE OF SERVICE: national; public; non-profit
SYSTEMS & NETWORKS ATTACHED TO: Inter Press Service (IPS)
WORKING LANGUAGE(S): English
SUBJECT COVERAGE: social sciences; demography; economics; political science; social
welfare
GEOGRAPHICAL COVERAGE: USA
DATA BEING PROCESSED AND SIZE: 10-18 articles daily
DATA PROCESSING METHODS: computerized
HARDWARE USED: PC's, modems
SOFTWARE USED: word processor, communications
STORAGE MEDIA: disks
TYPE OF ACTIVITY: distribution of information; publication
PERIODICALS PUBLISHED:
- Global Information Network Report
CLIENTELE: media, non-profit organizations, educational institutions, businesses
ACCESS TO SERVICE: paid services open to all users
TYPE & DESCRIPTION OF SERVICES PROVIDED: Provides on-line searches using own data
base "IPS-USA", available online through Dialcom, Inc. and Nexis. Also
provides selective dissemination of information, magnetic tapes and
photocopies.

789 - HARVARD UNIVERSITY, CENTER FOR POPULATION STUDIES LIBRARY

ADDRESS: 665 Huntington Avenue,
Boston, MA 02115,
U. S. A.
TEL: (617) 732-1234
CREATED: 1965   *HEAD:* Ms. E. E. Sonntag, Librarian
SIZE OF STAFF: Professional: 1   Other: 1   Total: 2
TYPE OF SERVICE: non-profit
WORKING LANGUAGE(S): English
SUBJECT COVERAGE: demography; population
GEOGRAPHICAL COVERAGE: global
DATA BEING PROCESSED AND SIZE: 22,000 books; articles; 235 periodicals; reports; on-
going research; seminars; training courses
DATA PROCESSING METHODS: partially computerized

TYPE OF ACTIVITY: distribution of information; publication
PUBLICATIONS: - Harvard University Center for Population Studies discussion papers
CLIENTELE: researchers, faculty, students
ACCESS TO SERVICE: open to all users
TYPE & DESCRIPTION OF SERVICES PROVIDED: Provides library services, interlibrary
loans, bibliographic and literature abstract searchers, selective
dissemination of information, and photocopies. Also provides on-line
services using external data bases available through MEDLARS, DIALOG and
BRS.

790 - HARVARD UNIVERSITY, TOZZER LIBRARY

ADDRESS: 21 Divinity Avenue,
Cambridge,
Massachusetts 02138,
U. S. A.
TEL: (617) 495.2253
CREATED: 1979   *HEAD:* Ms. S. Williams, Acting Librarian
SIZE OF STAFF: Professional: 4   Other: 12   Total: 16
TYPE OF SERVICE: international; private; non-profit
SYSTEMS & NETWORKS ATTACHED TO: OCLC
MATERIALS DESCRIBING THE SERVICE: - "Tozzer Library", Harvard University, brochure
WORKING LANGUAGE(S): English; European languages
SUBJECT COVERAGE: social anthropology; cultural anthropology; linguistics
GEOGRAPHICAL COVERAGE: global
DATA BEING PROCESSED AND SIZE: 166,570 books; 1,950 serials; microfilms and reports
DATA PROCESSING METHODS: partially computerized
HARDWARE USED: ZENITH, TELEX, IBM, M300
SOFTWARE USED: CUSTOM, OCLC
TYPE OF ACTIVITY: distribution of information; publication
PERIODICALS PUBLISHED:
- Anthropological Literature, an Index to Periodical Articles and Essays, 4
p.a. since 1979
CLIENTELE: faculty researchers, teachers and students (460 per week)
ACCESS TO SERVICE: open to specific categories of users
TYPE & DESCRIPTION OF SERVICES PROVIDED: Provides library services, bibliographic
searches of information, on-line services from its own data base, provision
of microforms and photocopies.

791 - HAWAII STATE, LEGISLATIVE REFERENCE BUREAU, LIBRARY

SYNONYMOUS NAMES: LRB Library
ADDRESS: State Capitol - Room 005,
Honolulu,
HI 96813,
U. S. A.
TEL: (808) 548 78 53
CREATED: 1943   *HEAD:* Ms. F. Enos, Head Research Librarian
SIZE OF STAFF: Professional: 3   Other: 2   Total: 5

TYPE OF SERVICE: public
WORKING LANGUAGE(S): English
SUBJECT COVERAGE: law; administrative sciences; economics; education; history;
    political science; social welfare
DATA BEING PROCESSED AND SIZE: 50,000 State and Federal Government documents; 17,00
    other monographs (personal, corporate authorship); 250 periodicals
DATA PROCESSING METHODS: computerized
HARDWARE USED: IBM 3277, 3278 (terminals linked to a IBM 3090 mainframe)
SOFTWARE USED: IBM AIMS, STAIRS
STORAGE MEDIA: traditional shelving of publications
TYPE OF ACTIVITY: data collection; distribution of information; publication
ACCESS TO SERVICE: services open to all users free of charge
TYPE & DESCRIPTION OF SERVICES PROVIDED: Provides library services, interlibrary
    loans, bibliographic searches using its own data bases. Also provides
    photocopies upon request.

**792 - INDIANA UNIVERSITY, GRADUATE SCHOOL OF BUSINESS, INDIANA BUSINESS RESEARCH
CENTER, ECONOMIC DEVELOPMENT INFORMATION NETWORK**

SYNONYMOUS NAMES: IBRC/EDIN
ADDRESS: Bloomington,
    Indiana 47405,
    U. S. A.
    TEL: (812) 335-5507
CREATED: 1925   *HEAD:* Mr. M. J. Marcus, Director
SIZE OF STAFF: Professional: 6   Other: 30   Total: 36
TYPE OF SERVICE: national; public; non-profit
SUBJECT COVERAGE: demography; economics; economic development
GEOGRAPHICAL COVERAGE: Indiana and the Great Lakes region, USA
DATA PROCESSING METHODS: computerized
TYPE OF ACTIVITY: data collection; data analysis; distribution of information;
    publication
PERIODICALS PUBLISHED: - Indiana Business Review, 6 p.a.
PUBLICATIONS: - Indiana factbook
ACCESS TO SERVICE: open to all users free of charge, some paid services
TYPE & DESCRIPTION OF SERVICES PROVIDED: Provides on-line services from its econom
    and demographic data bases. "STATIS: the statistical information system"
    and "BASIS: the business activities and services information system".

793 - INSTITUTE FOR SCIENTIFIC INFORMATION

SYNONYMOUS NAMES: ISI
ADDRESS: 3501 Market Street,
    Philadelphia,
    Pennsylvania 19104,
    U. S. A.
    TEL: (215) 386-0100 - TELEX: 84-5305
    CABLE: SCINFO
CREATED: 1960   *HEAD:* Mr. E. Garfield, President

SIZE OF STAFF: Total: 625
TYPE OF SERVICE: national; private; profit
WORKING LANGUAGE(S): English
SUBJECT COVERAGE: social sciences; humanities; science
GEOGRAPHICAL COVERAGE: global
DATA BEING PROCESSED AND SIZE: 1,400 social science journals; 1,300 arts and
         humanities journals; 3,100 science journals containing information relevant
         to the social sciences or arts and humanities
DATA PROCESSING METHODS: computerized
TYPE OF ACTIVITY: data collection; publication
PERIODICALS PUBLISHED: - Arts and Humanities Citation Index, 3 p.a. including annual
         cumulation
         - ASCA (An individualized, computer produced alerting services), 52 p.a.
         - ASCATOPICS, 52 p.a.
         - Current Contents, 52 p.a.
         - Index to Social Sciences and Humanities Proceedings, 4 p.a. and cumulated
         annually
         - Social Sciences Citation Index, 2 p.a. and cumulated annually
         - Current Contents Address Directory - Social.Sciences/Art and Humanities, 1
         p.a.
         - SSCI Journal Citation Reports, 1 p.a.
CLIENTELE: research scientists, librarians, engineers, clinicians, teachers, graduate
         students, R&D administrators, and editors of journals and books
ACCESS TO SERVICE: open to all users, on a subscription basis
TYPE & DESCRIPTION OF SERVICES PROVIDED: Provides the following data bases and
         services in the social sciences: Social SciSearch (containing 1.5 million
         citations corresponding to the printed Social Sciences Citation Index),
         available online through DIALOG, BRS and DIMDI; Arts and Humanities Search
         (containing 600,000 citations corresponding to the printed Arts and
         Humanities Citation Index) accessible online through BRS; selective
         dissemination of information; production of information on magnetic tapes or
         discs; photocopies, and genuine article document delivery service.

94 - THE JOHNS HOPKINS UNIVERSITY, POPULATION INFORMATION PROGRAM

ADDRESS: 624 North Broadway,
         Baltimore,
         Maryland 21205,
         U. S. A.
         TEL: (301) 955.8200 - TELEX: 240430 JHUPCS UR
         CABLE: POPINFORM
CREATED: 1972   HEAD: Dr. P. T. Piotrow, Director
SIZE OF STAFF: Professional: 12   Other: 19   Total: 31
TYPE OF SERVICE: international; private; non-profit
SYSTEMS & NETWORKS ATTACHED TO: POPLINE (Population Information On-Line) is part of
         the U.S. National Library of Medicine MEDLARS system, Management Section
         (MMS), Bethesda
MATERIALS DESCRIBING THE SERVICE: - POPLINE brochure
WORKING LANGUAGE(S): English
SUBJECT COVERAGE: demography; statistics; population; health; family planning
GEOGRAPHICAL COVERAGE: global

DATA BEING PROCESSED AND SIZE: 150,000 journal articles, monographs, technical
        reports and unpublished literature (10,000 p.a.)
DATA PROCESSING METHODS: computerized
HARDWARE USED: Host is located at the U.S. National Library of Medicine
STORAGE MEDIA: traditional shelving of publications
TYPE OF ACTIVITY: data collection; SSID training; publication
PERIODICALS PUBLISHED:
        - Population report, 5 p.a. in English with translations in French,
        Portuguese and Spanish. Selected issues in Arabic, Turkish, and bahasa
        Indonesia
CLIENTELE: POPLINE: 2,000 potential users; population reports - 80,000 subscribers
ACCESS TO SERVICE: paid services open to all users; population reports, POPLINE
        searching services and most document reproductions are free to organizatic
        and individuals in developing countries
TYPE & DESCRIPTION OF SERVICES PROVIDED: Contributes bibliographic data to the
        POPLINE data base maintained by the Center for Population and Family Healt
        (CPFH) Library, and provides current awareness (SDI) and retrospective
        searches of POPLINE (on-line access to population literature). Also provi
        reproduction of documents.

795 - THE KINSEY INSTITUTE FOR RESEARCH IN SEX, GENDER, AND REPRODUCTION, INFORMAT
        SERVICE

PARENT ORGANIZATION: Affiliated with the Indiana University
ADDRESS: Morrison Hall 313,
        Indiana University,
        Bloomington,
        Indiana 47405,
        U. S. A.
        TEL: (812) 335-7686
CREATED: 1970   *HEAD:* Ms. J. Scherer Brewer, Information Services Officer
                        Ms G. Pershing, Head
SIZE OF STAFF: Professional: 1   Other: 3   Total: 4
TYPE OF SERVICE: international; private; non-profit
MATERIALS DESCRIBING THE SERVICE: - The Kinsey Institute for Research (brochure)
WORKING LANGUAGE(S): English
SUBJECT COVERAGE: social sciences; sexual behaviour; sex and gender
GEOGRAPHICAL COVERAGE: global
DATA BEING PROCESSED AND SIZE: books; journals; reprints; audio-tapes; video-tapes;
        films; photographs; slides; phono-recordings
DATA PROCESSING METHODS: partially computerized
SOFTWARE USED: ACROBAT
STORAGE MEDIA: traditional shelving of publications
TYPE OF ACTIVITY: data collection; data analysis; distribution of information;
        publication
PERIODICALS PUBLISHED:
        - The Kinsey Report
CLIENTELE: students, researchers, clinicians, legal authorities, educators, media
        representatives (1700 p.a.)
ACCESS TO SERVICE: open to all users, free of charge, some paid services
TYPE & DESCRIPTION OF SERVICES PROVIDED: On-site use of the research collections is

available to qualified researchers with demonstrable research needs. The
information service responds to requests for bibliographies, special
bibliographic, literature and quantitative data searches.

96 - LIBRARY OF CONGRESS, LAW LIBRARY

ADDRESS: 101 Independence Avenue, S. E.,
      Washington, D. C. 20540,
      U. S. A.
      TEL: (202) 287-5065
CREATED: 1832   *HEAD:* Mr. C. W. Kenyon, Law Librarian
SIZE OF STAFF: Professional: 63   Other: 38   Total: 101
TYPE OF SERVICE: national; public; non-profit
MATERIALS DESCRIBING THE SERVICE: - Services of the Law Library of the Library of
      Congress. Nov. 1981, 8 p.
SUBJECT COVERAGE: law; linguistics
GEOGRAPHICAL COVERAGE: global
DATA BEING PROCESSED AND SIZE: 1,900,000 volumes; 36,000 microfilm reels; 430,000
      microfiche pieces
DATA PROCESSING METHODS: partially computerized
HARDWARE USED: IBM 3033 AP MVS
SOFTWARE USED: ATS, BIBSYS, SCORPIO
STORAGE MEDIA: traditional shelving of publications; computerized compact book
      shelves electro-mechanically powered; and microform storage cabinets
TYPE OF ACTIVITY: data collection; data analysis; publication
PERIODICALS PUBLISHED:
      - Index to Latin American Legislation
PUBLICATIONS: - Papademetriou, T., Marriage and maritial property under the new Greek
      family law, 1985
      - Finkelman, P., Slavery in the courtroom, 1985
      - Sung Yoon Cho, The Constitution of the Democratic People's Republic of
      Korea, 1986
      - Gonzales, A. E., Dominican Republic: divorce law, 1986
      - Employee invention laws in various European countries, 1986
      - Buzescu, P., Foreign investments and taxation in foreign enterprises and
      persons in Romania, 1986
      - Tao-tai Hsia; Johnson, C. A., Law making in the People's Republic of
      China: terms, procedures, hierarchy and interpretation, 1986
      - The American constitution: its global heritage, 1987
      - The Constitution of the United States of America in various foreign
      languages
      - Sipkov, I., Legal assistance within the socialist Commonwealth of the East
      European countries, 1987
      - The Press law in Hungary, 1987
CLIENTELE: members and committees of the U.S. Congress; U.S. Government agencies;
      educational institutions; foreign diplomatic corps; international
      organizations, etc.
ACCESS TO SERVICE: open to all users, free of charge
TYPE & DESCRIPTION OF SERVICES PROVIDED: Provides foreign law research and reference
      service, inter-library loans and photocopies. Has several Divisions:
      American-British Law, European Law, Hispanic Law, Far Eastern Law, Near

Eastern Law and African Law.

797 - LOUISIANA STATE UNIVERSITY, LAW LIBRARY

PARENT ORGANIZATION: Louisiana State University
ADDRESS: Baton Rouge,
　　　　　Louisiana 70803-1010,
　　　　　U. S. A.
　　　　　TEL: (504) 388-8802
HEAD: Ms. R. Millican, Acting Director
SIZE OF STAFF: Professional: 10　　Other: 14　　Total: 24
TYPE OF SERVICE: private
WORKING LANGUAGE(S): English
SUBJECT COVERAGE: law
DATA BEING PROCESSED AND SIZE: 300,000 books
ACCESS TO SERVICE: services open to specific categories of users
TYPE & DESCRIPTION OF SERVICES PROVIDED: Provides library services and photocopies
　　　　　Also provides on-line services using external data bases WESTLAW, LEXIS and
　　　　　DIALOG.

798 - MEAD DATA CENTRAL, INC.

SYNONYMOUS NAMES: MDC
PARENT ORGANIZATION: Mead Corporation
ADDRESS: P. O. Box 933,
　　　　　9393 Springboro Pike,
　　　　　Dayton,
　　　　　Ohio 45401,
　　　　　U. S. A.
　　　　　TEL: (513) 865-6800
CREATED: 1970　　　*HEAD:* Mr. J. W. Simpson, President
SIZE OF STAFF:　　　Total: 1858
TYPE OF SERVICE: international; public; profit
WORKING LANGUAGE(S): English
SUBJECT COVERAGE: law; economics; medical sciences
GEOGRAPHICAL COVERAGE: USA; United Kingdom; Canada; France; global
DATA BEING PROCESSED AND SIZE: articles (over 15 million); reports
DATA PROCESSING METHODS: computerized
TYPE OF ACTIVITY: distribution of information
CLIENTELE: over 200,000 users worldwide
ACCESS TO SERVICE: paid services
TYPE & DESCRIPTION OF SERVICES PROVIDED: Provides an on-line 24 hour service
　　　　　providing searches on own data bases "LEXIS(R)" (full-text legal
　　　　　information retrieval), "NEXIS(R)" (news and business information
　　　　　retrieval), "EXCHANGE(TM) (financial information and investment research
　　　　　retrieval), and "MEDIS(R) (full-text medical information retrieval). The
　　　　　data bases are accessed through MeadNet via Telenet, Tymnet and other
　　　　　communications networks.

9 - MERRIAM CENTER LIBRARY

NONYMOUS NAMES: Charles E. Merriam Center for Public Administration
DRESS: 1313 East 60th Street,
    Chicago,
    Illinois 60637,
    U. S. A.
    TEL: (312) 947-2160
EATED: 1932   *HEAD:* Director P. Coatsworth,
ZE OF STAFF: Professional: 2   Other: 5   Total: 7
PE OF SERVICE: national; public; non-profit
RKING LANGUAGE(S): English
BJECT COVERAGE: administrative sciences; public administration; planning; urban
    planning; regional planning
OGRAPHICAL COVERAGE: USA; Canada; Australia
TA BEING PROCESSED AND SIZE: books, periodicals; conference reports; training
    courses
TA PROCESSING METHODS: partially computerized
RDWARE USED: Apple Macintosh
FTWARE USED: Microsoft Word; Microsoft File; Apple Macwrite; Apple Macpaint,
    Software Ventures Microphone, Kermit
ORAGE MEDIA: traditional shelving of publications
PE OF ACTIVITY: data collection; publication
RIODICALS PUBLISHED:
    - Recent Publications on Governmental Problems, 24 p.a.
    - RPGP Cumulation, 1 p.a.
    - Council of Planning Librarians Bibliography Series, 24 p.a.
IENTELE: 1000 subscribers to its periodical
CESS TO SERVICE: open to all users, paid services
PE & DESCRIPTION OF SERVICES PROVIDED: Honors interlibrary loan requests, provides
    both manual and on-line bibliographic search services via DIALOG and OCLC
    through COMPOSERVE. Also provides photocopies upon request.

0 - MICHIGAN STATE UNIVERSITY, AFRICANA LIBRARY

RENT ORGANIZATION: Michigan State University Libraries
DRESS: Michigan State Universities,
    East Lansing,
    Michigan 48824-1048,
    U. S. A.
    TEL: (517) 355-2366
EATED: 1964   *HEAD:* Mrs. O. Ezera, Head
ZE OF STAFF: Professional: 2   Other: 5   Total: 7
PE OF SERVICE: national; public; non-profit
RKING LANGUAGE(S): English; French
BJECT COVERAGE: social sciences
OGRAPHICAL COVERAGE: Africa
TA BEING PROCESSED AND SIZE: 102,000 books; 26,000 pamphlets; 3,100 periodicals;
    6,600 maps; 32,100 titles of microforms; 800 audio-tapes
TA PROCESSING METHODS: manual; partially computerized
TWARE USED: CLSI, OCLC, INNOVAC

STORAGE MEDIA: traditional shelving of publications; audio-tapes; microfilms;
microfiches
TYPE OF ACTIVITY: distribution of information
PUBLICATIONS: - de Benko, E., Research sources for African studies
- Lauer, J., A Guide to Africana materials
- Shu, A. C., Modern Chinese authors: a list of pseudonyms
- Ezera, A., Women in Africa: a selection of resources since 1975
CLIENTELE: students and researchers
ACCESS TO SERVICE: open to all users, free of charge
TYPE & DESCRIPTION OF SERVICES PROVIDED: Provides library services, current awarene
service and bibliographic advisory service.

801 - MICHIGAN STATE UNIVERSITY, SAHEL DOCUMENTATION CENTER

SYNONYMOUS NAMES: SDC
PARENT ORGANIZATION: Africana Library of the Michigan State University
ADDRESS: Michigan State University Libraries,
East Lansing,
Michigan 48824-1048,
U. S. A.
CREATED: 1976   HEAD: Mr. L. Dorsey, Librarian
SIZE OF STAFF: Professional: 1   Other: 2   Total: 3
TYPE OF SERVICE: national; public
SYSTEMS & NETWORKS ATTACHED TO: Réseau Sahélien d'Information et de Documentation
Scientifiques et Techniques (RESADOC)
WORKING LANGUAGE(S): English; French
SUBJECT COVERAGE: social sciences; economics; social anthropology; cultural
anthropology; geography; socio-economic development; agricultural economic
GEOGRAPHICAL COVERAGE: Senegal; Mali; Burkina-Faso; Niger; Mauritania; Chad; Gambia
Cape Verde; Sahel
DATA BEING PROCESSED AND SIZE: 10,500 books, articles, documents, research reports,
theses
DATA PROCESSING METHODS: manual
STORAGE MEDIA: traditional shelving of publications; microfiches
TYPE OF ACTIVITY: data Collection; publication
CLIENTELE: students, scholars, researchers
ACCESS TO SERVICE: open to all users, free of charge
TYPE & DESCRIPTION OF SERVICES PROVIDED: Collects, describes, organizes and
disseminates information about publications and documents dealing with
various aspects of socio-economic development in Sahel and agricultural
economics.

802 - MODERN LANGUAGE ASSOCIATION OF AMERICA

SYNONYMOUS NAMES: MLA
ADDRESS: 10 Astor Place,
New York,
NY 10003-6981,
U. S. A.

TEL: (212) 475-9500
EATED: 1883   *HEAD:* Dr. P. Franklin, Executive Director
ZE OF STAFF: Total: 85
PE OF SERVICE: national; private; non-profit
TERIALS DESCRIBING THE SERVICE: - MLA on-line (leaflet)
BJECT COVERAGE: linguistics; languages; literature; education; social sciences
OGRAPHICAL COVERAGE: global
TA BEING PROCESSED AND SIZE: books, articles, dissertations
TA PROCESSING METHODS: computerized
ORAGE MEDIA: traditional shelving of publications; discs
PE OF ACTIVITY: data collection; data analysis; distribution of information;
     publication
RIODICALS PUBLISHED: - PMLA
     - MLA International Bibliography, 1 p.a.
BLICATIONS: - Helping students write well, 1986
     - Convergences. Transactions in reading and writing, 1986
     - Wallace, M. E. (ed.), Part-time academic employment in the humanities,
     1984
     - Connolly, P.; Vilardi, T. (ed.), New methods in college writing programs,
     1987
     - Directory of Master's programs in foreign languages, literature and
     linguistics, 1987
     - Nelson, C.; Seccombe, M., British newspapers and periodicals 1641-1700,
     1987
     - Orange, L. e., English, the preprofessional major, 1986
     - Mackesy, E. M., MLA directory of periodicals 1988-1989, 1988
CESS TO SERVICE: open to all users
PE & DESCRIPTION OF SERVICES PROVIDED: Provides bibliographic searches, on-line
     services using own data base MLA, including 677,000 citations and available
     through DIALOG.

3 - MONTEREY INSTITUTE OF INTERNATIONAL STUDIES, WILLIAM TELL COLEMAN LIBRARY

DRESS: 425 Van Buren Street,
     Box 1978,
     Monterey,
     CA 93940,
     U. S. A.
     TEL: 408 647-4133
EATED: 1955   *HEAD:* Mr. K. Brehmer, Library Director
ZE OF STAFF: Professional: 3   Other: 7   Total: 10
PE OF SERVICE: international; private; non-profit
TERIALS DESCRIBING THE SERVICE: - Monterey Institute of International Studies
     (College catalog)
BJECT COVERAGE: social sciences; administrative sciences; economics; education;
     history; linguistics; political science; international policy studies;
     international management; language and humanities
OGRAPHICAL COVERAGE: global
TA BEING PROCESSED AND SIZE: books; journals; international documents
TA PROCESSING METHODS: computerized
RDWARE USED: MOTOROLA CPV; WYSF terminals

SOFTWARE USED: INNOPAC; INNOVACQ
STORAGE MEDIA: traditional shelving of publications; microfiches; microfilms
TYPE OF ACTIVITY: distribution of information; SSID scientific and methodological
        activities
PERIODICALS PUBLISHED:
        - Accession Lists
        - Directory of Periodicals. 2 p.a.
CLIENTELE: students, researchers, faculty, general public
ACCESS TO SERVICE: open to all users
TYPE & DESCRIPTION OF SERVICES PROVIDED: Provides library services, bibliographic,
        literature and quantitative data searches of information with on-line
        services, selective dissemination of information, and photocopies upon
        request. Has access to external data base MANX, through DIALOG and ORBIT.

804 - NATIONAL ANTHROPOLOGICAL ARCHIVES

PARENT ORGANIZATION: Smithsonian Institution
ADDRESS: Smithsonian Institution,
        Washington, D.C. 20560,
        U. S. A.
        TEL: (202) 357-1986
CREATED: 1879   *HEAD:* Mr. J. R. Glenn,
SIZE OF STAFF: Professional: 4   Other: 6   Total: 10
TYPE OF SERVICE: national; public; non-profit
MATERIALS DESCRIBING THE SERVICE: - The National Anthropological Archives, 4 p.
        brochure
WORKING LANGUAGE(S): English
SUBJECT COVERAGE: linguistics; history; social anthropology; cultural anthropology
GEOGRAPHICAL COVERAGE: global, but largely North American
DATA BEING PROCESSED AND SIZE: 40,000 private papers; official records and historic
        manuscripts; 350,000 photographs
DATA PROCESSING METHODS: manual; partially computerized
HARDWARE USED: GEAC 8000 .
SOFTWARE USED: GEAC Library Information System 11.0
STORAGE MEDIA: archival inventories, registers and special lists
PUBLICATIONS: - Catalogue of manuscripts at the National Anthropological Archives,
        Boston, Mass., G.K. Hall, 1975
        - Viola, H. J., North American indians: photographs from the National
        Anthropological Archives, Chicago, University Press, 1974 (microfiche)
CLIENTELE: scholarly researchers, general public (4,000 p.a.)
ACCESS TO SERVICE: open to all users, free of charge
TYPE & DESCRIPTION OF SERVICES PROVIDED: Archival services, provision of photograph
        and copies, general guidance for searches.

805 - NATIONAL ASSOCIATION OF SOCIAL WORKERS, SOCIAL WORK RESEARCH AND ABSTRACTS

PARENT ORGANIZATION: National Association of Social Workers
ADDRESS: 7981 Eastern Avenue,
        Silver Spring,

MD 20910,
U. S. A.
TEL: (301) 565-0333
ATED: 1965   *HEAD:* Ms. A. H. Payne, Managing Editor
ZE OF STAFF: Professional: 2   Other: 2   Total: 4
PE OF SERVICE: national; private; non-profit
BJECT COVERAGE: social welfare; social work
OGRAPHICAL COVERAGE: USA
TA BEING PROCESSED AND SIZE: 300 professional journals
TA PROCESSING METHODS: computerized
PE OF ACTIVITY: publication
RIODICALS PUBLISHED: - Social Work Research and Abstracts, 4 p.a.
IENTELE: students, social workers, researchers
CESS TO SERVICE: paid services
PE & DESCRIPTION OF SERVICES PROVIDED: Provides bibliographic and literature
    abstract searches from its own data base "Social Work Abstracts" including
    13,000 entries and accessible on-line via BRS Information Technologies.

- NATIONAL CENTER FOR COMPUTER CRIME DATA

RESS: 2700 N. Cahuenga Blvd., Suite 2113,
    Los Angeles,
    CA 90068,
    U. S. A.
    TEL: (213) 874-8233
ATED: 1980   *HEAD:* J. Bloombbecker, Director
E OF STAFF: Professional: 2   Total: 2
PE OF SERVICE: international; private; non-profit
JECT COVERAGE: law; social sciences; social welfare; sociology; computer crime;
    and the social implications of computing
GRAPHICAL COVERAGE: global
A PROCESSING METHODS: computerized
DWARE USED: PC
TWARE USED: word processing, database, spreadsheet, graphics
RAGE MEDIA: discs
E OF ACTIVITY: data analysis; data collection; distribution of information; SSID
    scientific and methodological activities
IODICALS PUBLISHED:
    - Conscience in computing, 4 p.a.
LICATIONS: - Computer crime law reporter
    - Introduction to computer crime
ENTELE: security professionals, media, academics, law enforcement personnel
ESS TO SERVICE: services open to all users, some paid services
E & DESCRIPTION OF SERVICES PROVIDED: Provides library services and photocopies.

- NATIONAL COUNCIL ON FAMILY RELATIONS, FAMILY RESOURCES DATABASE

ONYMOUS NAMES: FRD
RESS: 1910 West Country Road B., Suite 147,

St. Paul,
Minnesota 55113,
U. S. A.
TEL: (612) 633-6933
CREATED: 1981   *HEAD:* Dr. M. D. Ralebipi, Director
SIZE OF STAFF: Professional: 3   Other: 9   Total: 12
TYPE OF SERVICE: international; public; non-profit
MATERIALS DESCRIBING THE SERVICE: - Brochures and indexing manuals
WORKING LANGUAGE(S): English
SUBJECT COVERAGE: social sciences; sociology; social welfare; family; family
        planning; parents; children; marriage; divorce; social service
DATA BEING PROCESSED AND SIZE: 100,000 records (570-1,000 p.m.); bibliographic data
        plus abstracts and descriptors; journal articles; books; reports; audio-
        visuals; periodicals; newsletters
DATA PROCESSING METHODS: computerized
HARDWARE USED: 3B2 ATET computer system
SOFTWARE USED: Informix
STORAGE MEDIA: tapes, discs, microfiches
TYPE OF ACTIVITY: data collection; distribution of information
PERIODICALS PUBLISHED: - The Inventory of Marriage and Family Literature, 1 p.a.
PUBLICATIONS: - The Family Resources Database series of publications
        - Teenage pregnancy: an anotated bibliography
CLIENTELE: librarians, educators, researchers, social workers, students, etc.
ACCESS TO SERVICE: paid services for searches
TYPE & DESCRIPTION OF SERVICES PROVIDED: Provides library services, bibliographic a
        literature abstract searches. Identifies, processes and disseminates
        information relevant to the family, family planning, parents and children,
        social services to families, marriage and divorce. The On-Line Family
        Resource Data Base is vended by Bibliographic Retrieval Services, Inc.
        (BRS), Dialog Information Services and by Executive Telecom Systems Inc.
        (ETSI).

808 - NEW SCHOOL FOR SOCIAL RESEARCH, RAYMOND FOGELMAN LIBRARY

ADDRESS: 65 Fifth Avenue,
        New York,
        N.Y. 10003,
        U. S. A.
CREATED: 1941   *HEAD:* Ms. K. A. Cassell, Librarian
SIZE OF STAFF: Professional: 4   Other: 8   Total: 12
TYPE OF SERVICE: non-profit
SYSTEMS & NETWORKS ATTACHED TO: Research Library Assocation of South Manhattan
WORKING LANGUAGE(S): English
SUBJECT COVERAGE: social sciences; economics; philosophy; political science;
        psychology; social anthropology; cultural anthropology; sociology
GEOGRAPHICAL COVERAGE: New York, USA
DATA BEING PROCESSED AND SIZE: 140,000 books; 670 periodicals
DATA PROCESSING METHODS: partially computerized
HARDWARE USED: GEAC 9000 mainframe
TYPE OF ACTIVITY: data collection; data analysis; distribution of information
CLIENTELE: university students and faculty

CCESS TO SERVICE: services open to specific categories of users
YPE & DESCRIPTION OF SERVICES PROVIDED: Provides library services, interlibrary
loans, searches of information, on-line services, microforms and
photocopies.

09 - NEW YORK STATE EDUCATION DEPARTMENT, LAW/SOCIAL SCIENCE REFERENCE SERVICE

DDRESS: Cultural Education Center,
Empire State Plaza,
Albany,
New York 12230,
U. S. A.
REATED: 1818   *HEAD:* Ms. S. Legendre, Acting State Law Librarian
IZE OF STAFF: Professional: 8   Other: 4   Total: 12
YPE OF SERVICE: national; public; non-profit
YSTEMS & NETWORKS ATTACHED TO: OCLC
ORKING LANGUAGE(S): English
UBJECT COVERAGE: administrative sciences; education; law; political science;
statistics
EOGRAPHICAL COVERAGE: New York State, USA
ATA BEING PROCESSED AND SIZE: 650,000 books; 9,000 periodicals; 50,000 documents
ATA PROCESSING METHODS: computerized
ARDWARE USED: Burroughs
OFTWARE USED: own software
TORAGE MEDIA: discs
ERIODICALS PUBLISHED:
- Annual Report
UBLICATIONS: - Bibliographies on special collections
CCESS TO SERVICE: open to all users, free of charge
YPE & DESCRIPTION OF SERVICES PROVIDED: Provides interlibrary loans, research on
legislative intent and photocopies.

10 - NEW YORK UNIVERSITY, ELMER HOLMES BABST LIBRARY, TAMIMENT LIBRARY

DDRESS: 70 Washington Square, S.,
New York,
N. Y. 10012,
U. S. A.
TEL: (212) 998-2630
REATED: 1906   *HEAD:* Ms. D. Swanson, Head Librarian
IZE OF STAFF: Professional: 4   Other: 3   Total: 7
YPE OF SERVICE: public; non-profit
YSTEMS & NETWORKS ATTACHED TO: RLIN: Research Librarian Group
ORKING LANGUAGE(S): English
UBJECT COVERAGE: social sciences; labour and trade unions; social history;
socialism; communism; radicalism
ATA BEING PROCESSED AND SIZE: 53,000 books; microfilms; microfiches; manuscripts
YPE OF ACTIVITY: distribution of information
LIENTELE: 3,000 users p.a.

ACCESS TO SERVICE: open to all users
TYPE & DESCRIPTION OF SERVICES PROVIDED: provides library services, inter-library
        loans and photocopies.

811 - NNSR MACHINE READABLE BRANCH, SPECIAL ARCHIVES DIVISION

SYNONYMOUS NAMES: NNSR
ADDRESS: Washington, D.C. 20408,
        U. S. A.
        TEL: (202) 523-3267
CREATED: 1969   *HEAD:* Dr. E. W. Hedlin, Branch Chief
SIZE OF STAFF: Professional: 9   Other: 4   Total: 13
TYPE OF SERVICE: national; public; non-profit
MATERIALS DESCRIBING THE SERVICE: - Computer data bulletin, spring 1981
WORKING LANGUAGE(S): English
SUBJECT COVERAGE: social sciences; demography; economics; education; history
GEOGRAPHICAL COVERAGE: global
DATA BEING PROCESSED AND SIZE: 360 series containing over 3,000 data sheets; 3,100
        reels
DATA PROCESSING METHODS: computerized
HARDWARE USED: IBM 360 and 370
SOFTWARE USED: own in standard programming language
STORAGE MEDIA: magnetic tapes; microfiches
TYPE OF ACTIVITY: distribution of information
CLIENTELE: social scientists, private corporations, government agencies, research
        institutions, general public
ACCESS TO SERVICE: open to all users (some files restricted), against payment
TYPE & DESCRIPTION OF SERVICES PROVIDED: Provides tape copies, tape extracts and
        printed extracts.

812 - NORTH CAROLINA STATE UNIVERSITY, COLLEGE OF HUMANITIES AND SOCIAL SCIENCES, NATIONAL COLLEGIATE SOFTWARE CLEARINGHOUSE

ADDRESS: NCSU Box 8101,
        Raleigh,
        NC 27695,
        U. S. A.
        TEL: (919) 737-3067
CREATED: 1983   *HEAD:* Mr. G. D. Garson, Director
SIZE OF STAFF: Professional: 5   Other: 3   Total: 8
TYPE OF SERVICE: international
SYSTEMS & NETWORKS ATTACHED TO: ScholarNet (online international network)
WORKING LANGUAGE(S): English
SUBJECT COVERAGE: computer science aspects of social sciences
GEOGRAPHICAL COVERAGE: USA; global
DATA BEING PROCESSED AND SIZE: 200 computer products for social sciences, including
        12 datasets
HARDWARE USED: Apple II, IBM mainframe
SOFTWARE USED: NCSU software

TORAGE MEDIA: disks
YPE OF ACTIVITY: data collection; data analysis; distribution of information; SSID
    scientific and methodological activities; SSID training; publication
ERIODICALS PUBLISHED: - Social Science Computer Review, from 1988
UBLICATIONS: - NCSC Catalog
LIENTELE: university faculties (2,000)
CCESS TO SERVICE: paid services open to all users
YPE & DESCRIPTION OF SERVICES PROVIDED: Provides selective dissemination of
    information and magnetic tapes, as well as social science computer programs.
    Also provides on-line searches using own data bases "Teaching Datasets for
    Social Sciences" and "ScholarNet" as well as external data bases (US.
    Census).

13 - NORTHERN ILLINOIS UNIVERSITY, CLEARINGHOUSE FOR SOCIOLOGICAL LITERATURE

DDRESS: Department of Sociology,
    Dekalb,
    Illinois 60 115,
    U. S. A.
    TEL: (815) 753-1194
REATED: 1965   HEAD: Mr. H. O. Engelmann, Director and Editor
YPE OF SERVICE: international; private; non-profit
UBJECT COVERAGE: social sciences; sociology
EOGRAPHICAL COVERAGE: USA; North America
ATA BEING PROCESSED AND SIZE: books, articles, data collections submitted by workers
    in the field
ATA PROCESSING METHODS: manual
CCESS TO SERVICE: open to all users free of charge (reimboursement of marginal
    costs)
YPE & DESCRIPTION OF SERVICES PROVIDED: Provides full printout copies of deposits
    concerned with sociology and related social science disciplines.

14 - NORTHWESTERN UNIVERSITY, INTERNATIONAL COMPARATIVE POLITICAL PARTIES PROJECT

DDRESS: Department of Political Science,
    Scott Hall,
    601 University Place,
    Evanston,
    Illinois 60208,
    U. S. A.
    TEL: (312) 491-2634
REATED: 1967   HEAD: Prof. K. Janda, Director
IZE OF STAFF: Professional: 1   Other: 1   Total: 2
YPE OF SERVICE: international; public; non-profit
ORKING LANGUAGE(S): English
UBJECT COVERAGE: political science; political parties
EOGRAPHICAL COVERAGE: global
ATA BEING PROCESSED AND SIZE: Computer-readable quantitative data on 158 political
    parties in 53 countries across the world, primarily during 1950 to 1952;

from 3,500 documents of all types: books, articles, newspapers, party
publications, letters, statistical reports
DATA PROCESSING METHODS: computerized
HARDWARE USED: CDC CYBER, Eastman Kodak MIRACODE
SOFTWARE USED: RIQS system and SPSS
STORAGE MEDIA: computer tapes and 16mm microfilms
TYPE OF ACTIVITY: data collection; data analysis; publication
PUBLICATIONS: - Janda, K., Managing qualitative information and quantitative data on
political parties, social science information studies, 1982
- Janda, K., Political parties: a cross-national survey, New York, 1980
- Janda, K., Comparative political parties data, 1950-1962, 1980
CLIENTELE: mostly scholars at universities in the U.S., Canada and Europe. 35
institutions have the quantitative data
ACCESS TO SERVICE: services open to all users free of charge
TYPE & DESCRIPTION OF SERVICES PROVIDED: Provides information on magnetic tapes,
literature and quantitative data searches.

815 - POPULATION REFERENCE BUREAU, DECISION DEMOGRAPHICS

ADDRESS: Suite 800,
777 14th Street, N. W.,
Washington, D.C. 20005,
U. S. A.
TEL: (202) 639-8641
CREATED: 1983   *HEAD:* Ms. D. Dowdell, Technical Information Specialist
SIZE OF STAFF: Professional: 2   Other: 1   Total: 3
TYPE OF SERVICE: profit
SUBJECT COVERAGE: demography; statistics; population
DATA BEING PROCESSED AND SIZE: 10,000 p.a. books; 460 p.a. periodicals; 1,000
reports; censuses
TYPE OF ACTIVITY: data collection; data analysis; publication
PERIODICALS PUBLISHED:
- Population Bulletin
- Population Today
- World Population Data Sheet
PUBLICATIONS: - Population trends and public policy
CLIENTELE: students, demographers, journalists, experts (5,000 p.a.)
ACCESS TO SERVICE: services open to all users; paid services for data base searching
TYPE & DESCRIPTION OF SERVICES PROVIDED: Offers interlibrary loans and reference
services, projections and analyses for individual clients seeking
professional interpretation of population trends, and data base searches on
POPLINE and Population Bibliography. Formerly known as: Population Reference
Bureau, Inc..

816 - PREDICASTS

ADDRESS: 11001 Cedar Ave.,
Cleveland,
Ohio 44106,

U. S. A.
TEL: (216) 795-3000 - TELEX: 985.604
REATED: 1960   *HEAD:* Mr. R. M. Harris, President
TYPE OF SERVICE: international; private; profit
MATERIALS DESCRIBING THE SERVICE: - Brochure
WORKING LANGUAGE(S): English
SUBJECT COVERAGE: economics; business information; marketing industry
GEOGRAPHICAL COVERAGE: global
DATA BEING PROCESSED AND SIZE: 2,500 serials and all other types of documents
DATA PROCESSING METHODS: computerized
HARDWARE USED: Tandem
SOFTWARE USED: Misc
STORAGE MEDIA: traditional shelving of publications, fiches, tapes, discs and
        microfiches
TYPE OF ACTIVITY: data collection; publication
PERIODICALS PUBLISHED: - Update Current Awareness Newsletter Series (marketing,
        technology, planning, chemical industry, updates)
        - Defense Markets and Technology, 12 p.a.
        - Promt, 12 p.a.
        - F & S Index Service, 12 p.a.
        - Source Directory, 1 p.a.
PUBLICATIONS: - Predicasts basebook
        - Market reports
CLIENTELE: public and academic libraries, special libraries in all industry sectors,
        management consulting firms, government agencies
ACCESS TO SERVICE: paid services by contract or subscription, open to all users
TYPE & DESCRIPTION OF SERVICES PROVIDED: Suppliers of business, economic and
        technical information and research including marketing information,
        producing a full range of services which include: retrospective
        dissemination of information, current awareness, abstract, index and
        statistical services, delivery services, magnetic tape sales and selective
        photocopies. Provides printed products and on-line data retrieval using
        vendor systems Dialog, Datastar, BRS and Finsbury Data Services. Data bases
        relevant to the social sciences include: PST Business and Industry News, PST
        F & S Indexes, PTS Forecasts, PTS Time Series. European office: Predicasts,
        First Floor, Central Court, 1B Knollrise, Orpington, Kent BR6 0JA, United
        Kingdom.

617 - PRINCETON UNIVERSITY, OFFICE OF POPULATION RESEARCH

ADDRESS: 21 Prospect Avenue,
        Princeton,
        New Jersey 08540,
        U. S. A.
        TEL: (609) 452-4949
CREATED: 1935   *HEAD:* Mr. R. Hankinson, Editor
SIZE OF STAFF: Professional: 4   Other: 2   Total: 6
TYPE OF SERVICE: non-profit
SYSTEMS & NETWORKS ATTACHED TO: POPLINE; National Library of Medicine, Bethesda,
        Maryland
WORKING LANGUAGE(S): English

SUBJECT COVERAGE: demography; statistics; population
GEOGRAPHICAL COVERAGE: global
DATA BEING PROCESSED AND SIZE: yearly 4,000 books, articles, working papers, theses, reports, conference proceedings
DATA PROCESSING METHODS: computerized
HARDWARE USED: IBM 30/81
SOFTWARE USED: SPIRES
STORAGE MEDIA: traditional shelving of publications and tapes
TYPE OF ACTIVITY: publication
PERIODICALS PUBLISHED:
   - Population Index, 4 p.a.
CLIENTELE: 4,700
ACCESS TO SERVICE: paid services open to all users
TYPE & DESCRIPTION OF SERVICES PROVIDED: Apart from the journal Population Index, online services are available through POPLINE at the National Library of Medicine.

818 - PSYCHOLOGICAL ABSTRACTS INFORMATION SERVICES

SYNONYMOUS NAMES: PsycINFO
PARENT ORGANIZATION: American Psychological Association
ADDRESS: 1400 N. Uhle Street,
          Arlington, Virginia 22201,
          U. S. A.
          TEL: (703) 247-7719
CREATED: 1969   *HEAD:* Mrs. L. Granick, Director
SIZE OF STAFF: Professional: 57   Other: 23   Total: 80
TYPE OF SERVICE: International; private; non-profit
SYSTEMS & NETWORKS ATTACHED TO: Major information retrieval networks: DIALOG, BRS, DIMDI, DATA-STAR, Tsukuba
MATERIALS DESCRIBING THE SERVICE: - PsycINFO user manual, American Psychological Association, 1987 (143 p.)
WORKING LANGUAGE(S): English
SUBJECT COVERAGE: psychology; social sciences; education; sociology
GEOGRAPHICAL COVERAGE: global
DATA BEING PROCESSED AND SIZE: 560,000 documentation items including periodicals, reports and dissertations
DATA PROCESSING METHODS: computerized
STORAGE MEDIA: tapes; CD-ROM discs
TYPE OF ACTIVITY: data collection; publication
PERIODICALS PUBLISHED: - Psychological Abstracts, 12 p.a.
          - PsycSCAN: Clinical Psychology, 4 p.a.
          - PsycSCAN: Developmental Psychology, 4 p.a.
          - PsycSCAN: Applied Psychology, 4 p.a.
          - PsycSCAN: Learning Disorders and Mental Retardation (LD/MR), 4 p.a.
          - PsycSCAN: Psychoanalysis
          - PsycSCAN: Applied Experimental and Engineering Psychology
PUBLICATIONS: - Thesaurus of psychological index terms, 5th edition, 1988
          - PsycINFO restrospective-mental retardation. An abstracted bibliography 1971-1980
          - PsycINFO retrospective-learning and communication disorders. An abstracte

bibliography 1971-1980
CLIENTELE: all major libraries, departments of higher education in psychology,
        international community of researchers in social sciences
ACCESS TO SERVICE: paid services open to all users
TYPE & DESCRIPTION OF SERVICES PROVIDED: PsycINFO and PsyALERT online databases
        provide a variety of services and publications available by subscription
        (including bibliographic searches and information on magnetic tapes).
        PsycLIT provides access to the literature from 1974 through the current
        quarter on 2 compact discs and is available by subscription. PASAR provides
        individually prepared bibliographies from data base searches. Other services
        include user aids, seminars, workshops and exhibits.

819 - PUBLIC AFFAIRS INFORMATION SERVICE, INC.

SYNONYMOUS NAMES: PAIS
ADDRESS: 11 West 40th Street,
        New York,
        N. Y. 10018-2693,
        U. S. A.
        TEL: (212) 736-6629
CREATED: 1914   HEAD: Ms. B. M. Preschel, Executive Director
SIZE OF STAFF: Professional: 9   Other: 7   Total: 16
TYPE OF SERVICE: international; non-profit
MATERIALS DESCRIBING THE SERVICE: - Public Affairs Information Source (PAIS) in:
        Encyclopedia of Information Systems and Services, Gale, Michigan, 1987
WORKING LANGUAGE(S): English
SUBJECT COVERAGE: social sciences; economics; political science; administrative
        sciences; public policy; international relations; labour; sociology;
        demography
GEOGRAPHICAL COVERAGE: global
DATA BEING PROCESSED AND SIZE: 187,000 periodical articles (18,000 p.a.); 85,000
        monographs including government publications (8,000 p.a.)
DATA PROCESSING METHODS: computerized
HARDWARE USED: IBM
SOFTWARE USED: New York Public Library, Library Information and Online Network
        Systems software
STORAGE MEDIA: traditional shelving of publications; tapes
TYPE OF ACTIVITY: publication
PERIODICALS PUBLISHED:
        - PAIS Bulletin, 12 p.a.
        - PAIS Foreign Language Index, 4 p.a.
PUBLICATIONS: - PAIS subject headings
        - PAIS selection policy and periodical list
CLIENTELE: 3,500 college and university libraries, public libraries, government
        libraries, special libraries
ACCESS TO SERVICE: open to all users
TYPE & DESCRIPTION OF SERVICES PROVIDED: Services offered include bibliographic
        searches, selective dissemination of information and production of
        information on discs. Provides bibliographic indexes covering material
        published world-wide in English, French, German, Italian, Portuguese and
        Spanish. Its data base, PAIS International, is available through Dialog, BRS

and Data-Star and on CD-ROM.

820 - RADCLIFFE COLLEGE, ARTHUR AND ELIZABETH SCHLESINGER LIBRARY ON THE HISTORY OF WOMEN IN AMERICA

ADDRESS: 10 Garden Street,
          Cambridge,
          MA. 02138,
          U. S. A.
          TEL: (617) 495-8647
CREATED: 1943   *HEAD:* Ms. P. King, Director
SIZE OF STAFF: Professional: 8   Other: 6   Total: 14
TYPE OF SERVICE: public; non-profit
SYSTEMS & NETWORKS ATTACHED TO: OCLC, Inc.; RLIN (Research Libraries Group, Inc.);
          HOLLIS (Harvard On-line Library Information System)
MATERIALS DESCRIBING THE SERVICE: - Fortieth anniversary report, 1981-1983
WORKING LANGUAGE(S): English
SUBJECT COVERAGE: history; women's history; women's studies
GEOGRAPHICAL COVERAGE: USA
DATA BEING PROCESSED AND SIZE: 30,000 books; 450 periodicals; 700 major manuscript
          collections
DATA PROCESSING METHODS: partially computerized
HARDWARE USED: IBM-PC, IBM-XT
SOFTWARE USED: Note Bene, Word Star, DBase III Plus, software for bibliographic
          utilities (OCLC, RLIN, HOLLIS)
STORAGE MEDIA: traditional shelving of publications; temperature and humidity-
          controlled vaults for manuscripts; microforms; tapes
TYPE OF ACTIVITY: distribution of information
PERIODICALS PUBLISHED:
          - Newsletter, 1 p.a.
PUBLICATIONS: - The Manuscript inventories and the catalogs of manuscripts, books a
          periodicals, 10 vols., 1984
CLIENTELE: undergraduate and graduate students, professors and the general public
ACCESS TO SERVICE: open to all users
TYPE & DESCRIPTION OF SERVICES PROVIDED: Provides library services, microforms and
          photocopies.

821 - THE RESEARCH LIBRARIES, THE NEW YORK PUBLIC LIBRARY, ECONOMIC AND PUBLIC AFFAIRS DIVISION

ADDRESS: 5th Ave. & 42nd Street,
          New York,
          N. Y. 10018,
          U. S. A.
          TEL: (212) 930-0750
CREATED: 1911   *HEAD:* Mr. J. V. Ganly, Chief
SIZE OF STAFF: Professional: 15   Other: 17   Total: 32
TYPE OF SERVICE: national; public; non-profit
SYSTEMS & NETWORKS ATTACHED TO: Research Libraries Group, Inc.

WORKING LANGUAGE(S): English
SUBJECT COVERAGE: economics; social sciences; demography; political science; sociology
GEOGRAPHICAL COVERAGE: global
DATA BEING PROCESSED AND SIZE: 1,500,000 volumes; 1,000,000 microforms; 11,000 current serials
DATA PROCESSING METHODS: partially computerized
STORAGE MEDIA: traditional shelving of publications; microforms
TYPE OF ACTIVITY: data collection; publication
PUBLICATIONS: - Guide to the research collections of the New York Public Library, Chicago, American Library Association, 1975, 336 p.
CLIENTELE: business, college and university students, faculty, government officers, general public (400-500 readers a day)
ACCESS TO SERVICE: services open to all users, free of charge
TYPE & DESCRIPTION OF SERVICES PROVIDED: Provides bibliographic and reference service to the public and resources for research in depth, on-line bibliographic search using their data base CATNYP, and photocopies.

822 - THE ROCKEFELLER UNIVERSITY, ROCKEFELLER ARCHIVE CENTER

ADDRESS: Hillcrest,
          Pocantico Hills,
          North Tarrytown,
          New York 10591-1598,
          U. S. A.
          TEL: (914) 631 4505
CREATED: 1975   HEAD: D. H. Stapleton, Director
SIZE OF STAFF: Professional: 10   Other: 6   Total: 16
TYPE OF SERVICE: national; private; non-profit
SYSTEMS & NETWORKS ATTACHED TO: Research Libraries Information Network (RLIN)
MATERIALS DESCRIBING THE SERVICE: - Rockefeller Archive Center, brochure
WORKING LANGUAGE(S): English
SUBJECT COVERAGE: social sciences; history; education; social sciences; demography; economics; political science; psychology; social welfare; sociology; specific subjects covered by the collections include agriculture; economic development; international relations; labour; medical sciences; population; religion
GEOGRAPHICAL COVERAGE: global
DATA BEING PROCESSED AND SIZE: 40 million documents from institutions and individuals; films; photographs
DATA PROCESSING METHODS: manual
TYPE OF ACTIVITY: distribution of information; publication
PERIODICALS PUBLISHED:
          - Annual Newsletter
PUBLICATIONS: - Open collections, 1983
          - Photograph collections in the Rockefeller Archive Center, 1986
          - A Survey of manuscript sources for the history of nursing and nursing education in the Rockefeller Archive Center, 1987, 62 p.
          - A Survey of manuscript sources for the history of psychiatry and related areas in the Rockefeller Archive Center, 1985, 107 p.
          - A Survey of sources for the history of labour and industrial relations in

the Rockefeller Archive Center, 1986, 41 p.
- Source guide in the history of agriculture in the Rockefeller Archive
Center, 1987
- List of folder titles for each collection
- Index

CLIENTELE: researchers and qualified students (around 150 p.a.)

ACCESS TO SERVICE: open to specific categories of users, free of charge

TYPE & DESCRIPTION OF SERVICES PROVIDED: Provides library services, on-line service
using its own data base on RLIN (Research Library Information Network) and
photocopies upon request.

823 - RUTGERS - THE STATE UNIVERSITY, CENTER FOR URBAN POLICY RESEARCH, LIBRARY

ADDRESS: P.O. Box 489,
Kilmer Area, Bldg. 4051,
New Brunswick,
New Jersey 08903,
U. S. A.
TEL: (201) 932-3136

HEAD: Mr. E. E. Duensing,

TYPE OF SERVICE: non-profit

SUBJECT COVERAGE: social sciences; demography; economics; urban planning; regional
planning; urbanization

GEOGRAPHICAL COVERAGE: North America

DATA BEING PROCESSED AND SIZE: 5,000 books; 6,000 other catalogued items; 175
periodicals

ACCESS TO SERVICE: open to all users

TYPE & DESCRIPTION OF SERVICES PROVIDED: Provides library and reference services and
inter-library loans.

824 - RUTGERS UNIVERSITY, CRIMINAL JUSTICE-NCCD COLLECTION

ADDRESS: 115 Washington Street,
Newark,
New Jersey 07102,
U. S. A.
TEL: (201) 648-5522

CREATED: 1961   *HEAD:* Mrs. P. Schultze, Librarian

SIZE OF STAFF: Professional: 1   Other: 1

TYPE OF SERVICE: international; private; public; non-profit

SYSTEMS & NETWORKS ATTACHED TO: Rutgers University Libraries

WORKING LANGUAGE(S): English

SUBJECT COVERAGE: criminology; sociology; criminal justice

GEOGRAPHICAL COVERAGE: global

DATA BEING PROCESSED AND SIZE: 9,000 books, 40,000 reports, 205 periodicals; studies
clippings and pictures

DATA PROCESSING METHODS: manual; partially computerized

TYPE OF ACTIVITY: distribution of information; publication

PERIODICALS PUBLISHED: - Criminal Justice Abstracts, 4 p.a. since 1970

PUBLICATIONS: - All abstracts and non-copyrighted documents available on microfiche
CLIENTELE: criminal justice students and practitioners
ACCESS TO SERVICE: open to all users, free of charge, except for literature searches
TYPE & DESCRIPTION OF SERVICES PROVIDED: Provides library services, bibliographic and
        literature abstract searches, query answering service and provision of
        photocopies.

825 - SCHOMBURG CENTER FOR RESEARCH IN BLACK CULTURE

PARENT ORGANIZATION: New York Public Library
ADDRESS: 515 Lenox Avenue,
        New York,
        N.Y. 10037,
        U. S. A.
        TEL: (212) 862-4000
CREATED: 1925   *HEAD:* Mr. H. Dodson, Chief
SIZE OF STAFF: Professional: 20   Other: 40   Total: 60
TYPE OF SERVICE: national; public; non-profit
SYSTEMS & NETWORKS ATTACHED TO: Research Libraries Group (RLG); New York State Inter-
        Library Loan (NYSILL)
WORKING LANGUAGE(S): English
SUBJECT COVERAGE: history; social anthropology; cultural anthropology; culture;
        social sciences; black culture
GEOGRAPHICAL COVERAGE: global
DATA BEING PROCESSED AND SIZE: 100,000 books; periodicals; tapes; photographs; audio-
        visual materials; prints; art and artifacts; clippings; microfiches
DATA PROCESSING METHODS: partially computerized
PERIODICALS PUBLISHED: - The Schomburg Center Journal
PUBLICATIONS: - Index of selected, current black periodicals
        - Catalogues of major exhibitions
CLIENTELE: students, scholars, general public (50,000 readers p.a.)
ACCESS TO SERVICE: open to all users, over the age of 18, free of charge
TYPE & DESCRIPTION OF SERVICES PROVIDED: Provides reference services and photocopies.

826 - SOCIOLOGICAL ABSTRACTS, INC., DATABASE SERVICES

ADDRESS: P.O. Box 22206,
        San Diego,
        California 92122,
        U. S. A.
        TEL: (619) 565-6603
MATERIALS DESCRIBING THE SERVICE: - SA user's reference manual, 1983
WORKING LANGUAGE(S): English
SUBJECT COVERAGE: sociology; social work; law; linguistics; behavioural sciences
DATA BEING PROCESSED AND SIZE: bibliogr. references of articles, proceedings, theses
TYPE OF ACTIVITY: distribution of information; SSID training
PERIODICALS PUBLISHED:
        - Note Us
PUBLICATIONS: - Thesaurus of sociological indexing terms

TYPE & DESCRIPTION OF SERVICES PROVIDED: On-line searches through BRS, Data-Star, Dialog and GIDC. Also provides an on-line thesaurus and CD-ROM information products (sociofile).

827 - STANFORD UNIVERSITY, THE HOOVER INSTITUTION ON WAR, REVOLUTION AND PEACE, LIBRARY AND ARCHIVES

ADDRESS: Stanford,
California 94305-6010,
U. S. A.
TEL: (415) 497-2058
CREATED: 1919   *HEAD:* Mr. C. Palm, Associate Director
SIZE OF STAFF: Professional: 33   Other: 61   Total: 94
TYPE OF SERVICE: national; private; non-profit
SYSTEMS & NETWORKS ATTACHED TO: Research Libraries Group (RLG); Research Libraries Information Network (RLIN)
MATERIALS DESCRIBING THE SERVICE: - Guide to the Hoover Institution Archives, 1980
- The Library of the Hoover Institution on War, Revolution and Peace, 1985
WORKING LANGUAGE(S): English
SUBJECT COVERAGE: history; political science; economics; social sciences; demography socio-political change; economic change
GEOGRAPHICAL COVERAGE: global
DATA BEING PROCESSED AND SIZE: 1.6 million books; 3,500 periodicals; 4,500 archival collections
DATA PROCESSING METHODS: partially computerized
TYPE OF ACTIVITY: data collection; publication
PUBLICATIONS: - Dwyer, J. (ed.), Russia, the Soviet Union, and Eastern Europe: a survey of holdings at the Hoover Institution, 1980
- Moussavi, F., Guide to the Hanna collection at the Hoover Institution, 1982
- Leadenham, C. A., Guide to the Hoover Institution Archives relating to Imperial Russia, the Russian revolutions and civil war, and the first emigration, 1986
- Myers, R. H., Guide to the primary western language sources for Asian studies in the Stanford University libraries, 1986
CLIENTELE: 1,200 students, professors, historians and independent researchers
ACCESS TO SERVICE: open to all users, free of charge
TYPE & DESCRIPTION OF SERVICES PROVIDED: Provides library services and professional reference services.

828 - STATE UNIVERSITY OF NEW YORK AT ALBANY, GRADUATE LIBRARY FOR PUBLIC AFFAIRS AN POLICY

ADDRESS: Hawley Library,
1400 Washington Ave.,
Albany,
NY 12222,
U. S. A.
CREATED: 1979   *HEAD:* Ms. J. Gavryck, Acting Head

SIZE OF STAFF: Professional: 7   Other: 5   Total: 12
TYPE OF SERVICE: public; non-profit
SYSTEMS & NETWORKS ATTACHED TO: Suny Albany Libraries, GLPP
SUBJECT COVERAGE: administrative sciences; economics; law; political science; social
        welfare; criminal law; public administration
DATA BEING PROCESSED AND SIZE: 75,000 books; 9,000 reference books; 1,700
        periodicals; 88,591 microfiche titles; 2,377 microfilm titles
TYPE OF ACTIVITY: distribution of information
CLIENTELE: students, faculty, researchers
ACCESS TO SERVICE: services open to all users free of charge
TYPE & DESCRIPTION OF SERVICES PROVIDED: Provides library services with on-line
        service using own data base "Online Catalog". Has also access to all
        relevant data bases through BRS, DIALOG, WESTLAW, VUTEXT, WILSONLINE.
        Provides microforms and photocopies upon request.

29 - TULANE UNIVERSITY OF LOUISIANA, LATIN AMERICAN LIBRARY

ADDRESS: University Libraries,
        Howard Tilton Memorial Library,
        New Orleans,
        LA 70118,
        U. S. A.
        TEL: (504) 865-5681
CREATED: 1924   *HEAD:* Mr. T. Niehaus, Director
SIZE OF STAFF: Professional: 1   Other: 6   Total: 7
TYPE OF SERVICE: national; public; non-profit
SYSTEMS & NETWORKS ATTACHED TO: OCLC, Columbus Ohio
WORKING LANGUAGE(S): Spanish; English; Portuguese; French
SUBJECT COVERAGE: social sciences; demography; economics; education; history;
        political science; social anthropology; cultural anthropology
GEOGRAPHICAL COVERAGE: Mexico; Central America; South America; Spanish and French
        Caribbean area
DATA BEING PROCESSED AND SIZE: 200,000 books, journals, newspapers; 100,000
        manuscripts
DATA PROCESSING METHODS: manual
STORAGE MEDIA: traditional shelving of publications; microfilms and microfiches
TYPE OF ACTIVITY: data collection; distribution of information
PUBLICATIONS: - Catalogue of the Latin American Library of the Tulane University
        Library, Boston, Mass-Hall, 1970, 9 vol.; 1st supplement, 1973, 2 vol.; 2nd
        supplement, 1975, 2 vol.; 3rd supplement, 1977, 2 vol.
        - Olivera, R., comp., A bibliography of Latin American theses and
        dissertations, Tulane University, 1979. ca. 100 pp.
        - Kupper, M. comp., A bibliography of contemporary art in Latin America:
        books, articles and exhibition catalogues in the Tulane University Library,
        1950-1980, 1983, 110 p.
CLIENTELE: faculty and students of Tulane University, visiting scholars from US,
        Latin America and Europe
ACCESS TO SERVICE: open to all users, free of charge
TYPE & DESCRIPTION OF SERVICES PROVIDED: Provides library services, query answering
        service, microforms and photocopies.

830 - UNIVERSITY OF ALABAMA, COLLEGE OF COMMERCE AND BUSINESS ADMINISTRATION, CENT** FOR BUSINESS AND ECONOMIC RESEARCH

SYNONYMOUS NAMES: CBER, University of Alabama
ADDRESS: P.O. Box AK,
      Tuscaloosa,
      AL 35487,
      U. S. A.
      TEL: (205) 348-6191
CREATED: 1930   *HEAD:* Dr. C. E. Ferguson, Director
SIZE OF STAFF: Professional: 10   Other: 5   Total: 15
TYPE OF SERVICE: public
WORKING LANGUAGE(S): English
SUBJECT COVERAGE: demography; economics; surveys; models; forecasts, population;
      housing
GEOGRAPHICAL COVERAGE: Alabama, Southeast United States, USA
DATA BEING PROCESSED AND SIZE: machine-readable data holdings
DATA PROCESSING METHODS: partially computerized
HARDWARE USED: IBM PC or IBM compatible
SOFTWARE USED: AREMOS, IAS
STORAGE MEDIA: traditional shelving of publications; fiches; tapes; discs;
      microfiches
TYPE OF ACTIVITY: data collection; data analysis; distribution of information;
      publication
PERIODICALS PUBLISHED:
      - Alabama Business
      - Economic Abstract of Alabama
      - Alabama Economic Outlook
      - ASDC News
TYPE & DESCRIPTION OF SERVICES PROVIDED: Provides library services, supplies
      demographic and socio-economic data.

831 - UNIVERSITY OF CALIFORNIA, BERKELEY, INSTITUTE OF GOVERNMENTAL STUDIES, LIBRAR**

SYNONYMOUS NAMES: IGS Library
ADDRESS: 109 Moses Hall,
      Berkeley,
      California 94720,
      U. S. A.
      TEL: (415) 642-5659
CREATED: 1919   *HEAD:* Mr. J. Leister, Head Librarian
SIZE OF STAFF: Professional: 4   Other: 6   Total: 10
TYPE OF SERVICE: public
SYSTEMS & NETWORKS ATTACHED TO: OCLC
MATERIALS DESCRIBING THE SERVICE: - Institute of Governmental Studies, biennial
      report 1985-87
WORKING LANGUAGE(S): English
SUBJECT COVERAGE: social sciences; administrative sciences; political science; publ**
      policy; socio-economic planning; state; local government; elections;
      housing; urban planning
GEOGRAPHICAL COVERAGE: USA

U.S.A. / Etats-Unis d'Amérique / Estados Unidos de América

ATA BEING PROCESSED AND SIZE: collection of ephemeral and non-trade publications
including 393,000 pamphlets and documents from federal, state and local
governments; 1,970 periodicals
ATA PROCESSING METHODS: partially computerized
YPE OF ACTIVITY: data collection; data analysis; distribution of information;
publication
ERIODICALS PUBLISHED:
- Accessions List, 12 p.a.
- Contents at IGS, 12 p.a.
UBLICATIONS: - Nathan, H., Critical choices in interviews: conduct, use and research
role, 1986
- Belzer, D.; Kroli, C., New jobs for the timber region: economic
diversification for Northern California, 1986
- Wilms, W. W., Reshaping job training for economic productivity, 1986
- Occasional bibliographies (series)
LIENTELE: university community and the general public
CCESS TO SERVICE: services open to all users, free of charge
YPE & DESCRIPTION OF SERVICES PROVIDED: Provides in-depth reference and information
services, interlibrary loans, bibliographic and literature abstract searches
of information and photocopies. Holdings are available on-line through OCLC.
Also provides on-line services through DIALOG. Is a depository for
California local documents.

**32 - UNIVERSITY OF CALIFORNIA, PUBLIC POLICY RESEARCH ORGANIZATION, DATA MANAGEMENT
AND ANALYSIS**

DDRESS: 310 Social Ecology Building,
Irvine,
California 92717,
U. S. A.
TEL: (714) 856-7098
REATED: 1966   *HEAD:* Dr. D. Dunkle, Director
IZE OF STAFF: Professional: 2   Other: 2   Total: 4
YPE OF SERVICE: public
ORKING LANGUAGE(S): English
UBJECT COVERAGE: social sciences; administrative sciences
EOGRAPHICAL COVERAGE: California, USA
ATA PROCESSING METHODS: computerized
ARDWARE USED: UBN 4341 (VM/CMS), IBM PC-XT's
OFTWARE USED: SPSS-X, SAS, SCA, CART
TORAGE MEDIA: magnetic tapes; floppy disks
YPE OF ACTIVITY: data collection; data analysis; SSID training
CCESS TO SERVICE: services open to specific categories of users
YPE & DESCRIPTION OF SERVICES PROVIDED: Provides assistance with research design,
data collection, computer support, data management and data analysis. Also
provides information on floppy disks and magnetic tapes.

833 - UNIVERSITY OF CALIFORNIA, STATE DATA PROGRAM

ADDRESS: Survey Research Center,
        2538 Channing Way,
        Berkeley,
        94720 California,
        U. S. A.
        TEL: (415) 642-6571
CREATED: 1968   *HEAD:* Mr. R. Wolfinger,
SIZE OF STAFF: Professional: 4   Other: 2   Total: 6
TYPE OF SERVICE: national; public; non-profit
MATERIALS DESCRIBING THE SERVICE: - State data program guide and catalogue, annual
SUBJECT COVERAGE: demography; economics; history; political science; sociology;
        criminology; social sciences; health status; surveys
GEOGRAPHICAL COVERAGE: USA
DATA BEING PROCESSED AND SIZE: data bases: 800 files of social surveys, 200 of publi
        opinion polls, 100 of census data, 80 of administrative data
DATA PROCESSING METHODS: computerized
HARDWARE USED: IBM 3090, VAX and various microcomputers
SOFTWARE USED: SPSS, SAS and others
TYPE OF ACTIVITY: data analysis; distribution of information; SSID scientific and
        methodological activities
CLIENTELE: all users, especially government services, students
ACCESS TO SERVICE: open to all users, against payment
TYPE & DESCRIPTION OF SERVICES PROVIDED: Provides library services, quantitative da
        searches of information, information on magnetic tapes or discs and
        photocopies.

834 - UNIVERSITY OF CHICAGO, FAR EASTERN LIBRARY

ADDRESS: Chicago,
        Illinois 60637-1502,
        U. S. A.
        TEL: (312) 702-8432 - TELEX: 282131
CREATED: 1936   *HEAD:* Dr Tai-loi Ma, Curator
SIZE OF STAFF: Professional: 7   Other: 11   Total: 18
TYPE OF SERVICE: national; private; non-profit
SYSTEMS & NETWORKS ATTACHED TO: Research Libraries Group (RLG)
WORKING LANGUAGE(S): English; Chinese; Japanese; Korean
SUBJECT COVERAGE: social sciences; economics; humanities; geography; history;
        linguistics; political science
GEOGRAPHICAL COVERAGE: China (People's Republic); Japan; Taiwan; Hong Kong; Korea
        (Republic)
DATA BEING PROCESSED AND SIZE: 412,000 books
DATA PROCESSING METHODS: manual; partially computerized
TYPE OF ACTIVITY: distribution of information
PUBLICATIONS: - Hall, G. K. and al., Catalogue of the Far Eastern Library, Universi
        of Chicago. Boston: 1973, 18 vols., 1st supplement 1981, 12 vols.
        - Far Eastern serials, 1977
        - Daisaku Ikeda collection of Japanese religion and culture, 1977
        - Japanese newspapers, 1983

CLIENTELE: academic researchers, teaching faculties, students
ACCESS TO SERVICE: Open to specific categories of users, free of charge
TYPE & DESCRIPTION OF SERVICES PROVIDED: Provides library services. Uses RLIN for
        cataloging.

**35 - UNIVERSITY OF CHICAGO, NATIONAL OPINION RESEARCH CENTER, PAUL B. SHEATSLEY
        LIBRARY**

SYNONYMOUS NAMES: NORC, Library
ADDRESS: 1155 E. 60th Street,
        Chicago,
        Illinois 60637,
        U. S. A.
        TEL: (312) 702-1213
CREATED: 1941   *HEAD:* Mr. P. Bova, Librarian
SIZE OF STAFF: Professional: 1   Other: 2   Total: 3
TYPE OF SERVICE: national; public; non-profit
SYSTEMS & NETWORKS ATTACHED TO: Chicago Library System
MATERIALS DESCRIBING THE SERVICE: - The NORC Library as information center and data
        archive, IASSIST Quarterly, vol.II, no. 2, 1978
WORKING LANGUAGE(S): English
SUBJECT COVERAGE: political science; social sciences; sociology; demography;
        economics; education; public opinion; survey resarch; methodology
GEOGRAPHICAL COVERAGE: USA
DATA BEING PROCESSED AND SIZE: books and periodicals; results of polls and surveys;
        data from NORC surveys
DATA PROCESSING METHODS: partially computerized
HARDWARE USED: Corona PC
SOFTWARE USED: Word Perfect, Plan Perfect
STORAGE MEDIA: traditional shelving of publications
TYPE OF ACTIVITY: distribution of information
PERIODICALS PUBLISHED:
        - NORC Reporter, newsletter
CLIENTELE: scholars, general public
ACCESS TO SERVICE: services open to all users, free of charge
TYPE & DESCRIPTION OF SERVICES PROVIDED: Provides library services, bibliographic
        searches of information on Dialog and Wilsonline databases and production of
        information on magnetic tapes (NORC MRDF).

**36 - UNIVERSITY OF CINCINNATI, INSTITUTE FOR POLICY RESEARCH, SOUTHWEST OHIO
        REGIONAL DATA CENTER**

SYNONYMOUS NAMES: UC/IPR/SORDC
ADDRESS: Mail Location 132,
        Cincinnati,
        Ohio 45221,
        U. S. A.
        TEL: (513) 475-5028
CREATED: 1980   *HEAD:* Mr. S. R. Howe, Director

SIZE OF STAFF: Professional: 1   Total: 1
TYPE OF SERVICE: national; public; non-profit
SYSTEMS & NETWORKS ATTACHED TO: Inter-University Consortium for Political and Soci
        Research (ICPSR); State Data Center System at the U.S. Census Bureau; Bur
        of Economic Analysis User Group
WORKING LANGUAGE(S): English
SUBJECT COVERAGE: social sciences; demography; economics
GEOGRAPHICAL COVERAGE: primarily Ohio, Kentucky and Indiana, USA
DATA BEING PROCESSED AND SIZE: computerized census data files (approx. 2,500 data
        sets on 325 high-density types)
DATA PROCESSING METHODS: computerized
HARDWARE USED: Amdahl 5880/Amdahl 470/V6, IBM compatible micros
SOFTWARE USED: primarily SAS but some SPSS-X and OSIRIS
STORAGE MEDIA: magnetic tapes
TYPE OF ACTIVITY: data collection; data analysis
CLIENTELE: students and faculty members, general public
ACCESS TO SERVICE: paid services for analytic products
TYPE & DESCRIPTION OF SERVICES PROVIDED: Provides query-answering services, comput
        print-outs, computer-generated graphics, analytic services, photocopies,
        information on magnetic tapes.

**837 - UNIVERSITY OF CONNECTICUT, INSTITUTE FOR SOCIAL INQUIRY, ROPER CENTER FOR
        PUBLIC OPINION RESEARCH**

ADDRESS: University of Connecticut,
        P.O. Box 440,
        Storrs,
        Connecticut 06268-0440,
        U. S. A.
        TEL: (203) 486-4440
CREATED: 1968   *HEAD:* Dr. E. C. Ladd, Executive Director
SIZE OF STAFF: Professional: 20   Other: 10   Total: 30
TYPE OF SERVICE: international; public; non-profit
WORKING LANGUAGE(S): English
SUBJECT COVERAGE: social sciences; sociology; economics; political science; survey
GEOGRAPHICAL COVERAGE: global
DATA BEING PROCESSED AND SIZE: public-opinion survey data; graduate training in
        survey research; yearly seminar for journalists
DATA PROCESSING METHODS: partially computerized
HARDWARE USED: IBM Mainframe 3090
SOFTWARE USED: SPIRES, SAS, SPSS, BMDP and locally developed software
STORAGE MEDIA: traditional shelving of publications; tapes; discs; microfilms
TYPE OF ACTIVITY: data collection; data analysis; distribution of information;
        publication; SSID training
PERIODICALS PUBLISHED:
        - Dataset News, irr.
        - Opinion Roundup
        - Accession Lists
CLIENTELE: opinion researchers, experts, public policy makers, journalists,
        educators, business analysts
ACCESS TO SERVICE: open to all users against payment

PE & DESCRIPTION OF SERVICES PROVIDED: Specializes in location, retrieval and
analysis of public-opinion information stored on computer tapes and disks.
Archives contain thousands of individual surveys dating from 1936 to the
present from 70 countries. Provides library services, quantitative data
searches of information, on-line services using its own data base POLL.
Provision of photocopies upon request.

**B - UNIVERSITY OF FLORIDA, COLLEGE OF BUSINESS ADMINISTRATION, BUREAU OF ECONOMIC
AND BUSINESS RESEARCH**

NONYMOUS NAMES: BEBR
DRESS: 221 Matherly Hall,
Gainesville,
FL 32611,
U. S. A.
TEL: (904) 392-0171
EATED: 1942   *HEAD:* Dr. J. W. Milliman, Director
ZE OF STAFF: Professional: 14
PE OF SERVICE: national; public; non-profit
RKING LANGUAGE(S): English
BJECT COVERAGE: social sciences; demography; economics; socio-economic indicators
OGRAPHICAL COVERAGE: Florida, USA
TA BEING PROCESSED AND SIZE: computer readable data
TA PROCESSING METHODS: computerized
RDWARE USED: IBM mainframe and PCs; Apple MacIntosh PCs
FTWARE USED: Troll; SAS; Desktop Publishing; Lotus 1,2,3; Excel Spreadsheet; DBase
III
ORAGE MEDIA: traditional shelving of publications; microfiches; diskettes; tapes
PE OF ACTIVITY: data collection; data analysis; distribution of information, SSID
research and methodological activities, publication
RIODICALS PUBLISHED: - Florida Statistical Abstract, 1 p.a.
- Florida Estimates of Population, 1 p.a.
- Population Studies, 4 p.a.
- The Florida Outlook, 4 p.a.
- Economic Leaflet, 12 p.a.
- Florida Consumer Data Service, 9 p.a.
BLICATIONS: - 1980 census handbook: Florida countries
- Microcomputers and economic analysis: spread sheet templates for local
government, 1987
- BEBR country profiles (series)
- Mc Coy, C. B.; Gonzalez, D. H., Cuban immigration analyzed
IENTELE: 20 requests p. day
CESS TO SERVICE: paid services, some free of charge
PE & DESCRIPTION OF SERVICES PROVIDED: Provides bibliographic searches of
information on its own data base "BEBR", selective dissemination of
information, information on magnetic tapes, microforms and photocopies.

839 - UNIVERSITY OF GEORGIA, SCHOOL OF LAW, LAW LIBRARY

ADDRESS: Athens,
         Georgia 30602,
         U. S. A.
         TEL: (404) 542-1922
CREATED: 1869
SIZE OF STAFF: Professional: 9   Other: 10   Total: 19
TYPE OF SERVICE: international; public
MATERIALS DESCRIBING THE SERVICE: - The University of Georgia Law Library reader's
         guide
WORKING LANGUAGE(S): English
SUBJECT COVERAGE: law; international law; legal history
GEOGRAPHICAL COVERAGE: USA
DATA BEING PROCESSED AND SIZE: 325,000 books
DATA PROCESSING METHODS: manual
TYPE OF ACTIVITY: distribution of information
ACCESS TO SERVICE: open to all users
TYPE & DESCRIPTION OF SERVICES PROVIDED: Provides library services and on-line
         services using external data bases LEXIS and WESTLAW.

840 - UNIVERSITY OF IDAHO, SOCIAL SCIENCES LIBRARY

PARENT ORGANIZATION: University of Idaho Library
ADDRESS: Moscow,
         Idaho 83843,
         U. S. A.
         TEL: (208) 885-6344
CREATED: 1955   *HEAD:* Mr. D. W. Baird, Social Science Librarian
SIZE OF STAFF: Professional: 3   Other: 2   Total: 5
TYPE OF SERVICE: public
SYSTEMS & NETWORKS ATTACHED TO: Western Library Network (WLN)
WORKING LANGUAGE(S): English
SUBJECT COVERAGE: history; education; political science; social sciences;
         administrative sciences; demography; economics; geography; social
         anthropology; cultural anthropology; sociology
GEOGRAPHICAL COVERAGE: USA
DATA BEING PROCESSED AND SIZE: 156,000 books; periodicals; articles; 430,000
         government documents (US & international)
DATA PROCESSING METHODS: partially computerized
HARDWARE USED: IBM
SOFTWARE USED: MS-DOS
STORAGE MEDIA: traditional shelving of publications; microfiches; magnetic tapes; C
         ROM
TYPE OF ACTIVITY: distribution of information
CLIENTELE: students and general public (approximately 50,000 users p.a.)
ACCESS TO SERVICE: services open to all users, free of charge
TYPE & DESCRIPTION OF SERVICES PROVIDED: Provides library services, literature
         abstract searches of information and photocopies. Also provides on-line
         searches using DIALOG data bases ERIC, SocioFile and Dissert. Abstracts
         available through CD-ROM dial-up.

1 - UNIVERSITY OF ILLINOIS AT URBANA-CHAMPAIGN, EDUCATION AND SOCIAL SCIENCE LIBRARY

ADDRESS: 100 Main Library,
1408 West Gregory Drive,
Urbana,
Illinois 61801,
U. S. A.
TEL: (217) 333-2305
HEAD: Ms. S. Klingberg, Head
SIZE OF STAFF: Professional: 5   Other: 9   Total: 14
TYPE OF SERVICE: public; national
SYSTEMS & NETWORKS ATTACHED TO: OCLC
MATERIALS DESCRIBING THE SERVICE: - Guides to services
WORKING LANGUAGE(S): English
SUBJECT COVERAGE: social sciences; administrative sciences; demography; education; political science; psychology; social anthropology; cultural anthropology; social welfare; sociology; arms control collection
DATA BEING PROCESSED AND SIZE: 131,000 books and bound periodical volumes; 2,250 journal and serial titles
DATA PROCESSING METHODS: computerized
HARDWARE USED: IBM terminals
SOFTWARE USED: WLN (Circulation System, Automated Catalog) and Silver Platter (ERIC, PsycLIT)
STORAGE MEDIA: traditional shelving of publications
TYPE OF ACTIVITY: distribution of information
CLIENTELE: students, faculty
ACCESS TO SERVICE: services open to specific categories of users
TYPE & DESCRIPTION OF SERVICES PROVIDED: Provides library services, interlibrary loans and on-line searches using external data bases.

2 - UNIVERSITY OF ILLINOIS, INSTITUTE OF LABOR AND INDUSTRIAL RELATIONS LIBRARY

ADDRESS: 504 East Amory Street,
Champaign,
Illinois 61820,
U. S. A.
TEL: (217) 333-2380
CREATED: 1947   *HEAD:* Ms. K. Chaplan, Librarian
SIZE OF STAFF: Professional: 1   Other: 2   Total: 3
TYPE OF SERVICE: public
SYSTEMS & NETWORKS ATTACHED TO: Illinois Library Network (ILLINET); Online Computer Library Center (OCLC)
MATERIALS DESCRIBING THE SERVICE: - Goldber, E. D., Problems and resources of research in American labor history, 1971
WORKING LANGUAGE(S): English
SUBJECT COVERAGE: administrative sciences; economics; labour relations; labour economics; labour law; trade unions; human resources management
GEOGRAPHICAL COVERAGE: Illinois, USA; Western Europe; Asia; Latin America
DATA BEING PROCESSED AND SIZE: 11,502 books; 457 serials; 27,969 pamphlets; 3,300 microforms; 62 audio tapes

603

DATA PROCESSING METHODS: computerized
SOFTWARE USED: LCS, WLN
TYPE OF ACTIVITY: distribution of information; publication
PERIODICALS PUBLISHED: - ILIR Library Selected Recent Acquisitions
PUBLICATIONS: - CIRL exchange bibliographies
CLIENTELE: faculty, students, university staff, unions, business firms
ACCESS TO SERVICE: services open to all users, free of charge
TYPE & DESCRIPTION OF SERVICES PROVIDED: Provides library services, bibliographic
    searches of information, on-line services using own data base "Online
    Catalog" and external data bases through BRS, DIALOG and ORBIT. Also
    provides microforms and photocopies.

843 - UNIVERSITY OF IOWA, IOWA SOCIAL SCIENCE INSTITUTE

SYNONYMOUS NAMES: ISSI
ADDRESS: 345 Schaeffer Hall,
    University of Iowa,
    Iowa City, Iowa 52242,
    U. S. A.
CREATED: 1969   *HEAD:* Mr. A. Miller,
SIZE OF STAFF:
TYPE OF SERVICE: national; public; non-profit
SUBJECT COVERAGE: social sciences
GEOGRAPHICAL COVERAGE: global
DATA BEING PROCESSED AND SIZE: data bases: 200 survey data, 100 aggregate data, U.S
    census data, 20 historical census data
DATA PROCESSING METHODS: computerized
HARDWARE USED: IBM 3330
SOFTWARE USED: SPSSX, OSIRIS, SAS, IBM Utilities
TYPE OF ACTIVITY: data collection; data analysis; distribution of information; SSID
    scientific and methodological activities; SSID training
CLIENTELE: students, teachers, research workers
ACCESS TO SERVICE: open to all users, free of charge
TYPE & DESCRIPTION OF SERVICES PROVIDED: Provision of information for secondary
    analysis and data on magnetic tapes.

844 - UNIVERSITY OF MASSACHUSETTS, LABOR RELATIONS AND RESEARCH CENTER, LIBRARY

SYNONYMOUS NAMES: LRRC Library
ADDRESS: 125 Draper Hall,
    Amherst,
    Massachusetts 01003,
    U. S. A.
    TEL: (413) 545-2884
TYPE OF SERVICE: national; public; non-profit
SYSTEMS & NETWORKS ATTACHED TO: Commonwealth of Massachusetts
MATERIALS DESCRIBING THE SERVICE: - LRRC brochure
    - University of Massachusetts Graduate School catalogue
WORKING LANGUAGE(S): English

BJECT COVERAGE: labour relations
OGRAPHICAL COVERAGE: Massachusetts and New England; USA; global
TA BEING PROCESSED AND SIZE: 5,000 books; 10,000 documents; 400 periodicals
PE OF ACTIVITY: distribution of information; publication
RIODICALS PUBLISHED: - Labour Center Review
CESS TO SERVICE: open to specific categories of users, free of charge, some paid
    services
PE & DESCRIPTION OF SERVICES PROVIDED: Provides library services, inter-library
    loans, bibliographic and literature abstract searches of information,
    selective dissemination of information and photocopies.

5 - UNIVERSITY OF MICHIGAN, CENTER FOR RESEARCH ON ECONOMIC DEVELOPMENT, LIBRARY

NONYMOUS NAMES: CRED, Library
DRESS: Lorch Hall,
    Ann Arbor,
    Michigan 48109-1220,
    U. S. A.
    TEL: (313) 764-9490 - TELEX: 432-0815
    CABLE: CREDMICH, Ann Arbor, Michigan
EATED: 1961
PE OF SERVICE: national; public; non-profit
TERIALS DESCRIBING THE SERVICE: - CRED (brochure)
RKING LANGUAGE(S): French; English
BJECT COVERAGE: economics; social sciences; economic development
OGRAPHICAL COVERAGE: Africa and Middle East; also South Asia; France; Central
    America; South America; developing countries
TA PROCESSING METHODS: manual; computerized
RDWARE USED: IBM
ORAGE MEDIA: diskettes
PE OF ACTIVITY: data collection; data analysis; distribution of information; SSID
    scientific and methodological activities; SSID training; publication
RIODICALS PUBLISHED:
    - CREDITS - The newsletter of the Center for Research on Economic
    Development
BLICATIONS: - Project reports(series)
    - Discussion papers (series)
    - Special publications (series)
IENTELE: 400 users approx.
CESS TO SERVICE: services open to specific categories of users, free of charge
PE & DESCRIPTION OF SERVICES PROVIDED: Provides library services and publication
    exchange arrangements.

6 - UNIVERSITY OF MICHIGAN, INSTITUTE FOR SOCIAL RESEARCH, INTER-UNIVERSITY
CONSORTIUM FOR POLITICAL AND SOCIAL RESEARCH

NONYMOUS NAMES: ICPSR
DRESS: P.O. Box 1248,
    Ann Arbor,

Michigan 48106,
U. S. A.
TEL: (313) 764-2570
CABLE: ICPSR

CREATED: 1962   *HEAD:* J. M. Clubb, Executive Director

SIZE OF STAFF: Professional: 13

TYPE OF SERVICE: international; public; non-profit

MATERIALS DESCRIBING THE SERVICE: - Guide to resources and services, Inter-Universi
        Consortium for Political and Social Research; Ann Arbor, Michigan, Institu
        for Social Research, annual

WORKING LANGUAGE(S): English

SUBJECT COVERAGE: political science; social sciences; demography; education; public
        opinion; surveys

GEOGRAPHICAL COVERAGE: global

DATA BEING PROCESSED AND SIZE: 1,500 data collections (censuses, statistical survey
        polls, social surveys, research studies); 1,400 printed code books

DATA PROCESSING METHODS: computerized

HARDWARE USED: PRIME 9955 super minicomputer, IBM 3090 mainframe, and IBM, Zenith a
        MacIntosh microcomputers

SOFTWARE USED: SPIRES, Oracle, SPSS, OSIRIS III and IV

STORAGE MEDIA: large system magnetic disk drives and microsystem disk drives;
        magnetic tapes; floppy disks, microfiches

TYPE OF ACTIVITY: data collection; data analysis; distribution of information; SSID
        training; publication

PERIODICALS PUBLISHED:
        - ICPSR Bulletin
        - CJAIN Newsletter
        - NACDA Newsletter

PUBLICATIONS: - ICPSR Summer program in quantitative methods
        - ICPSR annual report

CLIENTELE: faculty, students, researchers, marketing consultants and managers from
        corporate and entrepreneurial environments

ACCESS TO SERVICE: services open to specific categories of users

TYPE & DESCRIPTION OF SERVICES PROVIDED: Provides information on magnetic tapes or
        discs. Relevant data bases available for searches and ordering include:
        ICPSR Guide, ICPSR Variables, ICPSR ROLLCALLS and SMIS (Survey Methodology
        Information System).

847 - UNIVERSITY OF MINNESOTA, DRUG INFORMATION SERVICES

ADDRESS: 3-106 Health Sciences Center, Unit F,
        308 Harvard Street, S.E.,
        Minneapolis,
        Minnesota 55455,
        U. S. A.
        TEL: (612) 624-6492

CREATED: 1968   *HEAD:* Ms. Martha Joy, Director

SIZE OF STAFF: Professional: 3   Other: 1   Total: 4

TYPE OF SERVICE: public

SYSTEMS & NETWORKS ATTACHED TO: University of Minnesota, College of Pharmacy

WORKING LANGUAGE(S): English

SUBJECT COVERAGE: social sciences; psychology; sociology; social research on
        alcoholism and drug abuse
GEOGRAPHICAL COVERAGE: USA; global
DATA BEING PROCESSED AND SIZE: 24,000 books and documents; 80 periodicals
DATA PROCESSING METHODS: computerized
HARDWARE USED: IBM XT
SOFTWARE USED: WORDSTAR, CROSSTALK
TYPE OF ACTIVITY: distribution of information
PERIODICALS PUBLISHED:
        - DIS Update
PUBLICATIONS: - Thesaurus for the Druginfo Database
CLIENTELE: students, researchers, health professionals. chemical-dependency treatment
        personnel; (1,600 p.a. + over 3,000 database users)
ACCESS TO SERVICE: paid services open to all users
TYPE & DESCRIPTION OF SERVICES PROVIDED: Provides library services, interlibrary
        loans bibliographic and literature abstract searches, selective
        dissemination of information, magnetic tapes and photocopies. Also provides
        on-line services using own data base "DRUGINFO" as well as external data
        bases MEDLINE, HEALTH, PSYCINFO, ERIC, IPAD available through NLM and BRS.

848 - UNIVERSITY OF NEW HAMPSHIRE, STATE AND REGIONAL INDICATORS ARCHIVE

SYNONYMOUS NAMES: SRIA
ADDRESS: 128 Horton Social Science Center,
        Durham,
        NH 03824,
        U. S. A.
        TEL: (603) 862-1888
CREATED: 1979   HEAD: M. A. Straus, Director
SIZE OF STAFF: Professional: 2
TYPE OF SERVICE: non-profit
SYSTEMS & NETWORKS ATTACHED TO: University of New Hampshire
WORKING LANGUAGE(S): English
SUBJECT COVERAGE: social sciences; socio-economic indicators; economy; political
        system
GEOGRAPHICAL COVERAGE: USA
DATA BEING PROCESSED AND SIZE: machine-readeable data for 14,000 variables
DATA PROCESSING METHODS: computerized
HARDWARE USED: VAX; IBM-PC
SOFTWARE USED: SPSS-X; SPSS-PC
STORAGE MEDIA: tapes, discs
TYPE OF ACTIVITY: data collection; data analysis; distribution of information; SSID
        scientific and methodological activities; publication
PUBLICATIONS: - Subject Index
CLIENTELE: researchers
ACCESS TO SERVICE: paid services, open to all users
TYPE & DESCRIPTION OF SERVICES PROVIDED: Provides information on magnetic tapes,
        diskettes or printouts.

849 - UNIVERSITY OF NORTH CAROLINA AT CHAPEL HILL, THE CENTER FOR EARLY ADOLESCENCE, INFORMATION SERVICES DIVISION

ADDRESS: Carr Mill Mall, Suite 223,
Carrboro,
North Carolina 27510,
U. S. A.
TEL: (919) 966-1148
CREATED: 1978   *HEAD:* Ms. S. Rosenzweig, Director
SIZE OF STAFF: Professional: 2   Other: 2   Total: 4
TYPE OF SERVICE: national; non-profit
WORKING LANGUAGE(S): English
SUBJECT COVERAGE: education; psychology; young adolescents; child development; schoo
DATA BEING PROCESSED AND SIZE: books, periodicals, program materials (approx. 10,000
documents processed)
DATA PROCESSING METHODS: partially computerized
HARDWARE USED: IBM/PC
SOFTWARE USED: PROCITE
STORAGE MEDIA: traditional shelving of publications
TYPE OF ACTIVITY: distribution of information; publication
PERIODICALS PUBLISHED:
    - Common Focus
    - List of publications
PUBLICATIONS: - Rosenzweig, S.; Dunleavy, K., Early adolescence: a resource
directory, 1987
    - Rosenzweig, S.; Mineiro, B., Families with young adolescents: a resource
list, 1987
    - Rosenzweig, S., Resources for youth workers and program planners, 1986
CLIENTELE: 2,200 requests and 200 visitors p.a.
ACCESS TO SERVICE: services open to all users, free of charge
TYPE & DESCRIPTION OF SERVICES PROVIDED: Provides library services, query answering
service, bibliographic, literature abstract and quantitative data searches
of information, resource lists, selective dissemination of information and
photocopies.

850 - UNIVERSITY OF NORTH CAROLINA, INSTITUTE FOR RESEARCH IN SOCIAL SCIENCE, SOCIAL SCIENCE DATA LIBRARY

SYNONYMOUS NAMES: SSDL
ADDRESS: Room 10 Manning Hall,
Chapel Hill,
NC 27514,
U. S. A.
TEL: (919) 966-3346
CREATED: 1969   *HEAD:* Ms. D. McDuffeer, Director
SIZE OF STAFF: Professional: 3
TYPE OF SERVICE: national; public; non-profit
MATERIALS DESCRIBING THE SERVICE: - Data for dissemination, 2nd ed., January 1977, 5
p.
SUBJECT COVERAGE: social sciences; political science; economics; psychology;
sociology; public opinion; surveys

GEOGRAPHICAL COVERAGE: USA; Canada; Western Europe
DATA BEING PROCESSED AND SIZE: 1,500 machine readable data sets (censuses,
        statistical surveys, polls), social surveys, by-products of: economic
        activities, administrative processes, research studies and others
DATA PROCESSING METHODS: computerized
HARDWARE USED: IBM 360/75 or IBM 370/165 operating under MVT-HASP
SOFTWARE USED: SPSS, SAS, BMD-P, etc.
TYPE OF ACTIVITY: distribution of information
ACCESS TO SERVICE: open to all users, against payment
TYPE & DESCRIPTION OF SERVICES PROVIDED: Serves as the Louis Harris Data Center, a
        depository for Harris public opinion polls and surveys and maintains the
        Harris Question Retrieval System. Also provides consulting services.

851 - UNIVERSITY OF PITTSBURGH, ECONOMICS LIBRARY

ADDRESS: 4P56 Forbes Quadrangle,
        Pittsburgh,
        PA 15260,
        U. S. A.
        TEL: (412) 624-4492
HEAD: Ms. P. A. Suozzi, Head, Forbes Quadrangle Libraries
SIZE OF STAFF: Professional: 2   Other: 3   Total: 5
TYPE OF SERVICE: non-profit
WORKING LANGUAGE(S): English
SUBJECT COVERAGE: economics; demography; international trade; finance; statistics
DATA BEING PROCESSED AND SIZE: 19,600 books; 325 periodicals; 6,320 working papers;
        160 doctoral dissertations
DATA PROCESSING METHODS: partially computerized
TYPE OF ACTIVITY: distribution of information
PERIODICALS PUBLISHED:
        - Economics Books: Current Selections, 4 p.a.
        - Acquisitions Letter, 6 p.a.
CLIENTELE: scholarly researchers, students, general public
ACCESS TO SERVICE: open to all users
TYPE & DESCRIPTION OF SERVICES PROVIDED: Provides library services and interlibrary
        loans. Has access to DIALOG, OCLC, VU-TEXT external data bases and performs
        searches on a fee basis.

852 - UNIVERSITY OF PITTSBURGH, NASA INDUSTRIAL APPLICATIONS CENTER

ADDRESS: William Pitt Union, 8th Floor,
        Pittsburgh,
        PA 15260,
        U. S. A.
        TEL: (412) 648-7000
CREATED: 1963   HEAD: Mr. P. A. McWilliams, Executive Director
SIZE OF STAFF: Professional: 21   Other: 4   Total: 25
TYPE OF SERVICE: international; public; non-profit
SYSTEMS & NETWORKS ATTACHED TO: National Aerospace Administration - NASA

WORKING LANGUAGE(S): English
SUBJECT COVERAGE: political science; foreign policy; international relations; public
        administration; social sciences
GEOGRAPHICAL COVERAGE: global
DATA BEING PROCESSED AND SIZE: 30,000 journal articles
DATA PROCESSING METHODS: computerized
HARDWARE USED: VA 4
TYPE OF ACTIVITY: data analysis; data collection; distribution of information; SSID
        scientific and methodological activities; SSID training; publication
PUBLICATIONS: - Political science thesaurus
ACCESS TO SERVICE: paid services open to all users
TYPE & DESCRIPTION OF SERVICES PROVIDED: Provides library services, bibliographic,
        literature abstracts, and quantitative data searches, selective
        dissemination of information, information on magnetic tapes, microforms and
        translation of documents upon request. Also provides on-line services using
        own data base "US Political Science Documents" as well as external data
        bases.

853 - UNIVERSITY OF PITTSBURGH, SOCIAL SCIENCE COMPUTER RESEARCH INSTITUTE

SYNONYMOUS NAMES: SSCRI
ADDRESS: 2RO3 Forbes Quad,
        Pittsburgh,
        PA 15260,
        U. S. A.
        TEL: (412) 648-7380
CREATED: 1967   HEAD: Mr. P. S. Sidel, Director
SIZE OF STAFF: Professional: 4   Other: 3   Total: 7
TYPE OF SERVICE: national; public; non-profit
WORKING LANGUAGE(S): English
SUBJECT COVERAGE: social sciences; demography; economics; geography; history;
        political science; social anthropology; cultural anthropology; social
        welfare; sociology
GEOGRAPHICAL COVERAGE: USA
DATA BEING PROCESSED AND SIZE: machine-readable data
HARDWARE USED: DEC VAX/VMS
SOFTWARE USED: SYSTEM 1032 and other retrieval programs
STORAGE MEDIA: magnetic tapes
TYPE OF ACTIVITY: data collection; data analysis
PERIODICALS PUBLISHED:
        - SSCRI Notes, (occasional publication)
CLIENTELE: faculty and students
ACCESS TO SERVICE: free of charge, some paid services
TYPE & DESCRIPTION OF SERVICES PROVIDED: Data library providing quantitative data
        searches of information and assistance in the use of computer facilities fo
        research and teaching.

54 - UNIVERSITY OF SOUTH DAKOTA, SCHOOL OF BUSINESS, BUSINESS RESEARCH BUREAU

DDRESS: 414 E. Clark Street,
Vermillion,
South Dakota 57069-2390,
U. S. A.
TEL: (605) 677-5287
REATED: 1937   *HEAD:* Mr. D. Lewis, Director
IZE OF STAFF: Professional: 8   Other: 11   Total: 19
YPE OF SERVICE: national; public; non-profit
ORKING LANGUAGE(S): English
UBJECT COVERAGE: economics; economic development; econometrics; models; trade;
education; population; housing
EOGRAPHICAL COVERAGE: USA
ATA BEING PROCESSED AND SIZE: machine-readable census data
ATA PROCESSING METHODS: computerized
ARDWARE USED: AT & T
OFTWARE USED: Lotus 1,2,3
YPE OF ACTIVITY: data collection; distribution of information; SSID scientific and
methodological activities; publication
ERIODICALS PUBLISHED:
- South Dakota Business Review
- Data Supplement, 6 p.a.
UBLICATIONS: - South Dakota population projections 1985-2005
LIENTELE: businesses, government agencies, experts, researchers, educators (1,500
p.a.)
CCESS TO SERVICE: services open to all users, free of charge, some paid services
YPE & DESCRIPTION OF SERVICES PROVIDED: Provides quantitative data searches,
selective dissemination of information, photocopies and publications upon
request. The various divisions of the Business Research Bureau include: the
State Data Center, the Small Business Development Center, the Procurement
Assistance Program and the South Dakota International Trade Center which are
able to offer applied research, generally in the form of surveys, as well as
maintain data bases on a contractual basis to various organizations.

**55 - UNIVERSITY OF TENNESSEE, KNOXVILLE, COLLEGE OF BUSINESS ADMINISTRATION, CENTER
FOR BUSINESS AND ECONOMIC RESEARCH**

DDRESS: 100 Glocker Building,
Knoxville,
TN 37996-4170,
U. S. A.
TEL: (615) 974-5441
EAD: Dr. D. A. Hake, Director
IZE OF STAFF: Professional: 23   Other: 12   Total: 35
YPE OF SERVICE: public; non-profit
UBJECT COVERAGE: economics; demography; statistics; economic forecasting; finance
EOGRAPHICAL COVERAGE: USA, mainly Tennessee
ATA BEING PROCESSED AND SIZE: machine-readable holdings, statistical abstracts and
census data
OFTWARE USED: DBase, Lotus 1-2-3, Displaywrite 3, Nodler

STORAGE MEDIA: traditional shelving of publications
TYPE OF ACTIVITY: data collection; data analysis; distribution of information; SSID
    scientific and methodological activities; SSID training; publication
PERIODICALS PUBLISHED: - Tennessee Statistical Abstract, 1 p.a.
CLIENTELE: general public
ACCESS TO SERVICE: open to all users
TYPE & DESCRIPTION OF SERVICES PROVIDED: Offers inquiry-answering services, searches
    of information and selective dissemination of information.

856 - UNIVERSITY OF TEXAS AT AUSTIN, LINGUISTICS RESEARCH CENTER

ADDRESS: Box 7247,
    University Station,
    Austin,
    TX 78713-7247,
    U. S. A.
    TEL: (512) 471-4566
HEAD: Dr. W. P. Lehmann, Director
SIZE OF STAFF: Professional: 14   Other: 4   Total: 18
TYPE OF SERVICE: international; public; non-profit
SYSTEMS & NETWORKS ATTACHED TO: Siemens, AG
WORKING LANGUAGE(S): English; German; Spanish
SUBJECT COVERAGE: linguistics; computer science; computer translation, natural
    language processing, proto Indo-European
DATA BEING PROCESSED AND SIZE: technical reports; quarterly and annual progress
    reports
DATA PROCESSING METHODS: manual; partially computerized
STORAGE MEDIA: traditional shelving of publications; computerized archiving; tapes;
    microfiches
TYPE OF ACTIVITY: data analysis; SSID scientific and methodological activities;
    publication
ACCESS TO SERVICE: services open to specific categories of users
TYPE & DESCRIPTION OF SERVICES PROVIDED: Provides photocopies. Has developed the
    METAL system for machine translation. Assists scholars in the humanities an
    other disciplines with automated text processing. Has also developed
    programs for computerized teaching.

857 - UNIVERSITY OF WISCONSIN, MADISON, CENTER FOR DEMOGRAPHY AND ECOLOGY, LIBRARY

ADDRESS: 4412 Social Science Bldg.,
    1480 Observatory Drive,
    Madison, WI 53706,
    U. S. A.
    TEL: (608) 262-2182
CREATED: 1968   *HEAD:* Ms. R. Sandor, Director
SIZE OF STAFF: Professional: 1   Other: 3   Total: 4
TYPE OF SERVICE: public
SYSTEMS & NETWORKS ATTACHED TO: Association for Population/Family Planning Libraries
    and Information Centers - International (APLIC-I)

WORKING LANGUAGE(S): English
SUBJECT COVERAGE: demography; statistics; methodology; fertility; mortality;
          migration; manpower; urban-rural census
GEOGRAPHICAL COVERAGE: global
DATA BEING PROCESSED AND SIZE: 10,000 monographs; 250 periodicals
DATA PROCESSING METHODS: manual; partially computerized
HARDWARE USED: IBM-XT
SOFTWARE USED: PC-File
STORAGE MEDIA: traditional shelving of publications; microforms
TYPE OF ACTIVITY: distribution of information
PERIODICALS PUBLISHED:
          - Montly Selected Acquisition List
PUBLICATIONS: - A Bibliographic guide to working paper series held by the Library
          - Periodical holdings of the Library, Center for Demography and Ecology
          - Serial holdings of the Library, Center for Demography and Ecology
CLIENTELE: faculty, students, local and state governments, demography researchers and
          information specialists, general public
ACCESS TO SERVICE: services open to all users, free of charge, some paid services
TYPE & DESCRIPTION OF SERVICES PROVIDED: Provides library services, bibliographic and
          literature abstract searches of information, and photocopies. Also provides
          on-line services using own data bases "PERIODICAL HOLDINGS" and "SERIAL
          HOLDINGS", as well as external data base NETWORK LIBRARY SERVICE (NLS)
          available through DIAL-UP.

858 - UNIVERSITY OF WISCONSIN-MADISON, DATA AND PROGRAM LIBRARY SERIVCE

SYNONYMOUS NAMES: DPLS
ADDRESS: 3313, Social Sciences Building,
          1180 Observatory Drive,
          Madison, Wisconsin 53706,
          U. S. A.
CREATED: 1966   *HEAD:* L. Guy,
SIZE OF STAFF: Professional: 2
TYPE OF SERVICE: national; public; non-profit
MATERIALS DESCRIBING THE SERVICE: - Directory of the machine-readable holdings of the
          Data and Program Library Service, April 1978 (Introduction of Directory of
          the machine readable and program holdings of the Data and Program Library
          Service, Madison, University of Wisconsin-Madison, 1983, 219 p.)
SUBJECT COVERAGE: political science; sociology; economics; history; demography;
          social sciences
GEOGRAPHICAL COVERAGE: global
DATA BEING PROCESSED AND SIZE: data bases (numeric machine-readable data files)
DATA PROCESSING METHODS: computerized
HARDWARE USED: IBM, UNIVAC, VAX
SOFTWARE USED: statistical and data management
TYPE OF ACTIVITY: distribution of information; SSID training
PERIODICALS PUBLISHED:
          - Data sets
CLIENTELE: social sciences research and instructional community
ACCESS TO SERVICE: services open to all users, against payment
TYPE & DESCRIPTION OF SERVICES PROVIDED: Provides library services and data for

secondary analysis.

859 - URBAN INSTITUTE LIBRARY

ADDRESS: 2100 M Street, N.W.,
        Washington, D. C. 20037,
        U. S. A.
        TEL: (202) 857.8688
CREATED: 1968   *HEAD:* C. A. Motta, Director
SIZE OF STAFF: Professional: 2   Other: 3   Total: 5
TYPE OF SERVICE: national; private; non-profit
MATERIALS DESCRIBING THE SERVICE: - Library services
WORKING LANGUAGE(S): English
SUBJECT COVERAGE: social sciences; economics; statistics; demography
GEOGRAPHICAL COVERAGE: USA
DATA BEING PROCESSED AND SIZE: 28,000 books and documents; 650 journals, 4,500 reel
        of microfilm
DATA PROCESSING METHODS: partially computerized
HARDWARE USED: DEC VAX computer for U.I. publications
SOFTWARE USED: OCLC for cataloging + ILL
TYPE OF ACTIVITY: data collection; distribution of information; publication
PERIODICALS PUBLISHED:
        - Bimonthly Acquisitions List
PUBLICATIONS: - New Urban Institute Research Papers
CLIENTELE: 1,550 visitors per month
ACCESS TO SERVICE: services open to specific categories of users against payment
TYPE & DESCRIPTION OF SERVICES PROVIDED: Provides library services, selective
        dissemination of information, inter-library loans with on-line services on
        data base "Urban Institute Publications". Bibliographic and literature
        abstracts searching are also available against payment. Has access to on-
        line data bases of DIALOG, BRS, Wilson Line and VU-TEXT. Also distributes
        Urban Institute research and working papers and provides photocopies of
        journal articles with charge.

860 - U.S. DEPARTMENT OF COMMERCE, BUREAU OF THE CENSUS, LIBRARY

ADDRESS: Federal Building no. 3,
        Suitland, MD 20233,
        U. S. A.
        TEL: (301) 763-5040
CREATED: 1952   *HEAD:* E. Chapman,
SIZE OF STAFF: Professional: 5   Other: 12   Total: 17
TYPE OF SERVICE: national
SYSTEMS & NETWORKS ATTACHED TO: OCLC Computer Network
SUBJECT COVERAGE: demography; economics; statistics
GEOGRAPHICAL COVERAGE: global; USA
DATA BEING PROCESSED AND SIZE: 127,200 books; 3,400 periodicals; 11,500 microfiches
        and other archives
DATA PROCESSING METHODS: computerized

PERIODICALS PUBLISHED:
- Library Notes, 12 p.a.
PUBLICATIONS: - Catalogues of the Bureau of the Census Library, 20 vols. 1979
ACCESS TO SERVICE: open to specific categories of users
TYPE & DESCRIPTION OF SERVICES PROVIDED: Provides library services, provision of
photocopies and selective dissemination of information.

861 - U.S. DEPARTMENT OF HEALTH AND HUMAN SERVICES, PROJECT SHARE

PARENT ORGANIZATION: U.S. Department of Health and Human Services
ADDRESS: P.O. Box 2309,
Rockville,
Maryland 20852,
U. S. A.
TEL: (301) 251-5170
CREATED: 1975   *HEAD:* Ms. R. E. Lewis, Program Manager
SIZE OF STAFF: Total: 14
TYPE OF SERVICE: national; public
SYSTEMS & NETWORKS ATTACHED TO: Part of the U.S. Human Services Network
WORKING LANGUAGE(S): English
SUBJECT COVERAGE: administrative sciences; social welfare; social planning; health
GEOGRAPHICAL COVERAGE: USA
DATA BEING PROCESSED AND SIZE: 10,000 books, periodicals, reports, theses
DATA PROCESSING METHODS: computerized
HARDWARE USED: IBM 3330, 4341
SOFTWARE USED: ASPENSEARCH, NOMAD
STORAGE MEDIA: microfiche; tapes
TYPE OF ACTIVITY: data collection; distribution of information; publication
PERIODICALS PUBLISHED: - Journal of Human Services Abstracts, 4 p.a.
- Human Services Bibliographies, 5 p.a.
- Sharing Newsletter, 6 p.a.
PUBLICATIONS: - Human services monographs (series)
CLIENTELE: 10,000 government employees, public interest groups, universities
ACCESS TO SERVICE: paid services open to all users
TYPE & DESCRIPTION OF SERVICES PROVIDED: Provides reference and referral services.
Maintains a computer readable data base of documents abstracts (11,000
items) from which on-line searches are provided.

862 - U.S. DEPARTMENT OF HOUSING AND URBAN DEVELOPMENT, HUD USER

ADDRESS: P.O. Box 280,
Germantown,
Maryland 20874-0280,
U. S. A.
TEL: (301) 251-5154
CREATED: 1978   *HEAD:* Mr. M. Shea, Project Director
SIZE OF STAFF: Professional: 4   Other: 5   Total: 9
TYPE OF SERVICE: national; public; non-profit
SYSTEMS & NETWORKS ATTACHED TO: BRS Search/Service

U.S.A. / Etats-Unis d'Amérique / Estados Unidos de América

MATERIALS DESCRIBING THE SERVICE: - HUD USER (brochure)
SUBJECT COVERAGE: demography; economics; social welfare; housing; urban development
GEOGRAPHICAL COVERAGE: USA; global
DATA BEING PROCESSED AND SIZE: books; articles; reports; case studies; bibliographie
        (5,500)
DATA PROCESSING METHODS: computerized
SOFTWARE USED: BRS Search
STORAGE MEDIA: files, fiches; tapes
TYPE OF ACTIVITY: distribution of information; publication
PERIODICALS PUBLISHED: - Recent Research Results, 12 p.a.
CLIENTELE: 10,000 users p.a.
ACCESS TO SERVICE: services open to all users, free of charge (some paid services)
TYPE & DESCRIPTION OF SERVICES PROVIDED: Provides library services, bibliographic a
        literature abstract searchs of information and on-line services using its
        own data bases "HUD USER Online", containing 4,000 citations with
        abstracts. Also provides selective dissemination of information, informatic
        on microforms, photocopies, blueprints and audiovisuals.

863 - U.S. DEPARTMENT OF LABOR, BUREAU OF LABOR STATISTICS

SYNONYMOUS NAMES: BLS
ADDRESS: 441 G. St., N.W.,
        Washington, D.C. 20212,
        U. S. A.
        TEL: (202) 523-1221
CREATED: 1884   *HEAD:* Mrs. J. L. Norwood, Commissioner
SIZE OF STAFF: Total: 2,500
TYPE OF SERVICE: public
SYSTEMS & NETWORKS ATTACHED TO: U.S. Department of Labor (DOL)
MATERIALS DESCRIBING THE SERVICE: - Major programs: Bureau of Labor Statistics, 198
SUBJECT COVERAGE: labour economics; labour; prices; employment; unemployment;
        economic growth; productivity; wages; collective bargaining; statistics;
        socio-economic indicators
GEOGRAPHICAL COVERAGE: USA
DATA BEING PROCESSED AND SIZE: publications; statistical data; special surveys and
        tabulations; machine-readable data files
DATA PROCESSING METHODS: computerized
HARDWARE USED: IBM System 370
SOFTWARE USED: Table Producing Language; X-11 & X11 ARIMA for seasonal adjustment o
        data
STORAGE MEDIA: traditional shelving of publications; fiches; tapes; discs;
        microfiches
TYPE OF ACTIVITY: data collection; data analysis; distribution of information;
        publication
PERIODICALS PUBLISHED: - CPI Detailed Report, 1 p.a.
        - Current Wage Developments, 1 p.a.
        - Employment and Earnings, 1 p.a.
        - Monthly Labor Review, 12 p.a.
        - Occupational Outlook Quarterly, 4 p.a.
        - Producer Price Indexes, 12 p.a.
PUBLICATIONS: - Goldberg, J. P.; Moye, W. T., The First hundred years of the Bureau

of Labor Statistics 1884-1984
- Handbook of labor statistics, 1985
CLIENTELE: economists; social scientists; researchers; managers and policy-makers
ACCESS TO SERVICE: open to all users
TYPE & DESCRIPTION OF SERVICES PROVIDED: Its main data base "Labor Statistics"
includes 180,000 time series. The Bureau provides information it produces
through its publications, periodicals and also news releases which are
available upon request without charge on specific subjects. An electronic
news release service enables access to selected news releases. Reports on
BLS programs are available without charge. Information is also available on
microfiche, diskettes and magnetic tapes. The Bureau also prepares special
surveys and tabulations, makes software available, and provides consultative
services.

864 - WAYNE STATE UNIVERSITY, WALTER P. REUTHER LIBRARY OF LABOR AND URBAN AFFAIRS

ADDRESS: 5401 Cass Avenue,
Detroit,
Michigan 48202,
U. S. A.
TEL: (313) 577-4003
CREATED: 1960   *HEAD:* Mr. P. P. Mason, Director
SIZE OF STAFF: Professional: 11   Other: 10   Total: 21
TYPE OF SERVICE: international; public; non-profit
MATERIALS DESCRIBING THE SERVICE: - Pflug, W.W. (ed.), A guide to the archives of
labor history and urban affairs, Wayne State University Press, 1974
SUBJECT COVERAGE: history; social sciences; social welfare; sociology; social
history; labour history
GEOGRAPHICAL COVERAGE: USA; Canada
DATA BEING PROCESSED AND SIZE: 20,000 books; 750,000 photographs; 2,500 audio-tapes;
500 newspapers; 95,000,000 archives and manuscripts
DATA PROCESSING METHODS: partially computerized
HARDWARE USED: IBM
STORAGE MEDIA: discs; microfilms
TYPE OF ACTIVITY: data analysis; publication
PERIODICALS PUBLISHED:
- Newsletter
PUBLICATIONS: - Indexes
CLIENTELE: students, researchers, writers, labour union officers and members (1,200
p.a.)
ACCESS TO SERVICE: open to specific categories of users, free of charge
TYPE & DESCRIPTION OF SERVICES PROVIDED: Provides library services and photocopies.

865 - THE H. W. WILSON COMPANY, WILSONLINE

ADDRESS: 950 University Avenue,
Bronx,
NY 10452,
U. S. A.

TEL: (212) 588-8400

CREATED: 1984   *HEAD:* Mr. J. Regazzi, Director

TYPE OF SERVICE: international

MATERIALS DESCRIBING THE SERVICE: - New data bases and system enhancements:
Wilsonline retrieval system, brochure
- Wilsonline quick reference guide
- Wilsonline information system

WORKING LANGUAGE(S): English

SUBJECT COVERAGE: social sciences; anthropology; economics; ethnic groups; geography;
international relations; law; criminology; public administration; political
science; psychology; social work; sociology; urban development

GEOGRAPHICAL COVERAGE: USA

DATA BEING PROCESSED AND SIZE: English language periodicals

DATA PROCESSING METHODS: computerized

HARDWARE USED: IBM; Hitachi and Philips CD Rom drive

SOFTWARE USED: own

TYPE OF ACTIVITY: data collection; distribution of information; SSID training;
publication

PERIODICALS PUBLISHED: - Social Sciences Index, 4 p.a.
- Wilson Library Bulletin

CLIENTELE: academic and secondary school librarians, special librarians, students,
researchers

ACCESS TO SERVICE: paid services open to all users

TYPE & DESCRIPTION OF SERVICES PROVIDED: On-line retrieval system providing
bibliographic data from its 26 specialized data bases including Humanities
Index, Index to Legal Periodicals and Social Sciences Index. Wilsonline is
also available through OCLC link and telebase's EasyNet; Wilsondisc is a CD
ROM retrieval system offering the ability to search its databases on
separate compact discs as well as on-line accession a subscription basis;
Wilsearch is a personal computer software package designed for direct
position access to the Wilsonline databases; and Wilsonline workstation is
package providing all of the hardware needed.

866 - YALE UNIVERSITY, HUMAN RELATIONS AREA FILES

SYNONYMOUS NAMES: HRAF

ADDRESS: P.O. Box 2054 Yale Station,
New Haven,
Connecticut 06520,
U. S. A.

TEL: (203) 777.2334

CREATED: 1949   *HEAD:* M. E. Ember,

SIZE OF STAFF: Professional: 11   Other: 10   Total: 21

TYPE OF SERVICE: private; non-profit

MATERIALS DESCRIBING THE SERVICE: - Nature and use of the HRAF files: a research and
teaching guide

WORKING LANGUAGE(S): English

SUBJECT COVERAGE: social sciences; behavioural sciences; ethnology; social
anthropology; cultural anthropology; culture; ethnography; cross-cultural
analysis; ethnic groups

GEOGRAPHICAL COVERAGE: global

DATA BEING PROCESSED AND SIZE: books, articles, unpublished manuscripts, cultural
        files of organized ethnographic information of over 330 ethnic groups
DATA PROCESSING METHODS: partially computerized; computerized
HARDWARE USED: PC
STORAGE MEDIA: microfiches; floppy disks
TYPE OF ACTIVITY: data collection; conference-organization; publication
PERIODICALS PUBLISHED: - Behavior Science Research
        - Annual Report
CLIENTELE: researchers, university teachers, students, members of academic
        institutions and libraries
ACCESS TO SERVICE: services open to specific categories of users
TYPE & DESCRIPTION OF SERVICES PROVIDED: Data archive providing computerized
        retrieval services, computerized analytical bibliographies, data analysis,
        microfiches, photocopies, computer disks. Its aim is to make available
        primary research materials relevant to the human sciences covering selected
        cultures or societies representing all major areas of the world.

67 - YOUNG MEN'S CHRISTIAN ASSOCIATIONS OF THE UNITED STATES OF AMERICA, HISTORICAL LIBRARY

SYNONYMOUS NAMES: YMCA Historical Library
ADDRESS: 6400 Shafer Ct.,
        Rosemont,
        Illinois 60018,
        U. S. A.
CREATED: 1877   *HEAD:* Mr. R. C. Goff, Director
SIZE OF STAFF: Professional: 1   Other: 1   Total: 2
TYPE OF SERVICE: national; public; non-profit
SUBJECT COVERAGE: history; religion; social groups; social work; youth
GEOGRAPHICAL COVERAGE: USA
DATA BEING PROCESSED AND SIZE: 6,000 books; 35 periodicals; 20,000 printed documents
DATA PROCESSING METHODS: manual
STORAGE MEDIA: traditional shelving of publications; microfilms
CLIENTELE: researchers
ACCESS TO SERVICE: open to specific categories of users, free of charge
TYPE & DESCRIPTION OF SERVICES PROVIDED: Provides query answering service,
        interlibrary loans and photocopies.

U.S.S.R. / U.R.S.S. / U.R.S.S.

68 - AKADEMIA NAUK KAZAKHSKOI SSR, OTDEL NAUCHNOI INFORMATSII PO OBSHCHESTVENNYM NAUKAM

SYNONYMOUS NAMES: ONION AN Kaz. SSR;
        The Academy of Sciences of the Kazakh SSR, Section of Scientific Information
PARENT ORGANIZATION: Prezidium Akademii nauk Kazakhskoi SSR/Presidium of the Academy
        of Sciences of the Kazakh SSR
ADDRESS: ul. Shevchenko 28,
        480021, Alma-Ata 21,
        Kazakh SSR,

U. S. S. R.
TEL: 69-12-98; 69-11-22
CREATED: 1977   *HEAD:* Dr. A. N. Batishevna, Head
SIZE OF STAFF: Professional: 20   Other: -   Total: 20
SYSTEMS & NETWORKS ATTACHED TO: State System of Scientific-Technological Informatic
    (GSNTI)
SUBJECT COVERAGE: social sciences
DATA PROCESSING METHODS: manual
TYPE OF ACTIVITY: data collection; data analysis; publication; SSID scientific and
    methodological activities
ACCESS TO SERVICE: services open to specific categories of users, free of charge
TYPE & DESCRIPTION OF SERVICES PROVIDED: Provides bibliographic, literature and
    survey data searches, selective dissemination of information and translat'
    of documents.

**869 - AKADEMIA NAUK KIRGIZSKOI SSR, SEKTOR NAUCHNOI INFORMATSII PO OBSHCHESTVENNYM
NAUKAM**

SYNONYMOUS NAMES: The Academy of Sciences of the Kirgiz SSR, Institute of Scientif'
    Information in Social Sciences
PARENT ORGANIZATION: The USSR Academy of Sciences, Institute of Scientific
    Information in Social Sciences
ADDRESS: Leninski prospect 265-a,
    720071 Frunze,
    Kirgizskoi SSR,
    U. S. S. R.
    TEL: 25.53.84
CREATED: 1976   *HEAD:* S. A. Amanov, Head
SIZE OF STAFF: Professional: 5   Other: 1   Total: 6
TYPE OF SERVICE: national; public; non-profit
SYSTEMS & NETWORKS ATTACHED TO: State System of Scientific-Technological Informatic
    (GSNTI)
WORKING LANGUAGE(S): Russian/Kirgiz
SUBJECT COVERAGE: social sciences; economics; history; law; linguistics; literature
    philosophy; psychology; science
GEOGRAPHICAL COVERAGE: The Kirgiz SSR; USSR
DATA BEING PROCESSED AND SIZE: abstract surveys and collections of abstracts
DATA PROCESSING METHODS: manual
STORAGE MEDIA: traditional shelving of publications
TYPE OF ACTIVITY: data collection; distribution of information; publication
CLIENTELE: researchers
ACCESS TO SERVICE: open to all users
TYPE & DESCRIPTION OF SERVICES PROVIDED: Provides library services, selective
    dissemination of information, bibliographic, literature and survey data
    searches of information on INION AN USSR and translation of documents upon
    request.

570 - AKADEMIJA NAUK SSSR, INSTITUT NAUCHNOI INFORMATSII PO OBSHCHESTVENNYM NAUKAM

SYNONYMOUS NAMES: INION AN SSSR;
Institute of Scientific Information in the Social Sciences of the Academy of Sciences of the USSR
PARENT ORGANIZATION: Akademija Nauk SSSR/The USSR Academy of Sciences
ADDRESS: ul. Krasikova 28/45,
117418 Moscow,
U. S. S. R.
TEL: 128-89-30
CREATED: 1969   *HEAD:* V. A. Vinogradov, Director
SIZE OF STAFF: Professional: 1114   Other: 242
TYPE OF SERVICE: national; public; non-profit
SYSTEMS & NETWORKS ATTACHED TO: Central body of the social science scientific
information subsystem of the State System of the USSR Scientific-
Technological Information, (GSNTI); Member of MISON
MATERIALS DESCRIBING THE SERVICE: - Obshchestvennye nauki i informacia, Vinogradov,
V. A., 1978, 263 p.
SUBJECT COVERAGE: social sciences; administrative sciences; demography; economics;
history; law; linguistics; philosophy; political science; social
anthropology; cultural anthropology; social welfare; sociology
GEOGRAPHICAL COVERAGE: global
DATA BEING PROCESSED AND SIZE: 12,000,000 documentation units: books, brochures,
periodicals, fiches, films
DATA PROCESSING METHODS: manual; partially computerized
HARDWARE USED: Hewlett-Packard 3000; EC-1055 M
SOFTWARE USED: MINISIS; ISIS
STORAGE MEDIA: traditional shelving of publications; fiches; tapes; discs;
microfiches
TYPE OF ACTIVITY: data collection; data analysis; distribution of information; SSID
scientific and methodological activities; SSID training; publication
PERIODICALS PUBLISHED: - Novaja inostrannaja literatura po obscestvennym naukam.
Ekonomika
- Novaja inostrannaja literatura po obscestvennym naukam. Filosofija i
sociologija
- Novaja inostrannaja literatura po obscestvennym naukam. Istorija.
Arheologija. Etnografija
- Novaja sovetskaja i inostrannaja literatura po obscestvennym naukam.
Narodnaja Respublika Bolgarija
- Novaja sovetskaja i inostrannaja literatura po obscestvennym naukam.
Cehoslovackaja Socialisticeskaja Respublika
- Novaja sovetskaja i inostrannaja literatura po obscestvennym naukam.
Germanskaja Demokraticeskaja Respublika
- Novaja sovetskaja i inostrannaja literatura po obscestvennym naukam.
Socialisticeskaja Federativnaja Respublika Jugoslavija
- Novaja sovetskaja i inostrannaja literatura po obscestvennym naukam.
Evropejskie socialisticeskie strany. Obscie problemy
- Novaja sovetskaja i inostrannaja literatura po obscestvennym naukam.
Problemy Slavjanovedenija i Bakkanistiki
- Novaja sovetskaja i inostrannaja literatura po obscestvennym naukam.
Pol'skaja Narodnaja Respublika
- Novaja sovetskaja i inostrannaja literatura po obscestvennym naukam.
Socialisticeskaja Respublika Rumynija

621

- Novaja sovetskaja i inostrannaja literatura po obscestvennym naukam.
Bliznij i srednij vostok. Afrika
- Novaja sovetskaja i inostrannaja literatura po obscestvennym naukam.
Juznaja i Jugo-vostocnaja Azija. Dal'nij Vostok
- Novaja sovetskaja i inostrannaja literatura po obscestvennym naukam.
Strany Azii i Afrikii. Obscie problemy
- Novaja sovetskaja i inostrannaja literatura po obscestvennym naukam.
Vengerskaja narodnaja respublika
- Novaja sovetskaja literatura po obscestvennym naukam. Èkonomika
- Novaja sovetskaja literatura po obscestvennym naukam. Filosofskie nauki
- Novaja sovetskaja literatura po obscestvennym naukam. Istorija,
arheologija, etnografija
PUBLICATIONS: - Abstract journals: Obscestvennye nauki v SSSR (7 series),
Obscestvennye nauki za rubezom (9 series)
- Abstract collections, scientific-analytical surveys, retrospective and
occasional bibliographies
- Vinogradov, V. A., The Contribution of information activities into the
development of international cooperation among social scientists, 1985
CLIENTELE: scientific workers, teachers in higher education institutions,
postgraduate students
ACCESS TO SERVICE: services open to specific categories of users, free of charge
TYPE & DESCRIPTION OF SERVICES PROVIDED: Provides library services, photocopies and
microforms, selective dissemination of information, elaboration of
information systems, methodological guidance, searches of information usir
its own data base "Biblio, Bibnew, Person" including 750,000 bibliographic
and factual items. Also has access to other data bases through VNIIPAS,
Moscow and "Radio Vienna".

871 - GOSUDARSTVENNAJA ORDENA LENINA BIBLIOTEKA SSSR IMENI V.I. LENINA

SYNONYMOUS NAMES: GBL;
V. I. Lenin State Library of the USSR
PARENT ORGANIZATION: Ministry of Culture of the USSR
ADDRESS: Moscow 101000,
Prospect Kalinina 3,
U. S. S. R.
TEL: 202-40-56 - TELEX: 7167 Wg bibl su
CREATED: 1862   *HEAD:* Dr. N. S. Kartasov, Director
SIZE OF STAFF: Professional: 2502   Other: 782
TYPE OF SERVICE: national; public; non-profit
SYSTEMS & NETWORKS ATTACHED TO: All-Union Scientific and Methodical Centre for the
Country Libraries (except scientific and technical ones); one of the Centre
of the State Automated System of Scientific and Technical Information
(GSNTI); and of the Automated Centres System of Scientifc and Technical
Information (in cooperation with All-Union Book Chamber, VINITI AN SSSR,
State Public Scientific and Technical Library, INION AN SSSR
SUBJECT COVERAGE: social sciences
GEOGRAPHICAL COVERAGE: global
DATA BEING PROCESSED AND SIZE: 28,216,000 books, periodicals and serials; newspaper
DATA PROCESSING METHODS: manual; computerized
HARDWARE USED: various computers

SOFTWARE USED: own systems
CLIENTELE: general public
ACCESS TO SERVICE: open to all users, free of charge
TYPE & DESCRIPTION OF SERVICES PROVIDED: Provides library services, photocopies and
microfilms, query answering service bibliographical references,
bibliographic searches, selective dissemination of information and
compilation of documentary syntheses.

672 - GOSUDARSTVENNAYA PUBLICHNAYA ISTORICHESKAYA BIBLIOTEKA MINISTERSTVA KULTURY RSFSR

SYNONYMOUS NAMES: RSFSR/GPIB;
State Public Historical Library of the Ministry of Culture of the RSFSR
PARENT ORGANIZATION: Ministerstvo Kultury RSFSR/Ministry of Culture of the RSFSR
ADDRESS: Starosadsky per., 9,
101000 Moscow,
U. S. S. R.
TEL: 925-48-31 - TELEX: 112062 "ILLIADA"
CREATED: 1939   *HEAD:* L. M. Maslova, Head of Reference/Bibliographic Dept.
SIZE OF STAFF: Professional: 12   Total: 12
SUBJECT COVERAGE: history; education; information science; political science
DATA BEING PROCESSED AND SIZE: 1,903,500 books; 1,128,950 periodicals; 15,130
microcopies; 9,800 manuscripts
DATA PROCESSING METHODS: manual
STORAGE MEDIA: traditional shelving of publications; tapes
TYPE OF ACTIVITY: publication; SSID scientific and methodological activities
ACCESS TO SERVICE: services free of charge
TYPE & DESCRIPTION OF SERVICES PROVIDED: Provides library services and bibliographic
searches of information.

673 - TSENTR NAUCHNOI INFORMATSII PO OBSHCHESTVENNYM NAUKAM AKADEMII NAUK ARMYANSKOI SSR

SYNONYMOUS NAMES: TsNION;
Centre of Scientific Information in Social Sciences of the Academy of
Sciences of the Armenian SSR
PARENT ORGANIZATION: Akademia Nauk Armyanskoi SSR/Academy of Sciences of the Armenian
SSR
ADDRESS: ul. Marshala Bagramyana, 24d,
Erevan, 375019,
Armenian SSR,
U. S. S. R.
TEL: 52.93.11
CREATED: 1970   *HEAD:* B. K. Akopovich, Head
SIZE OF STAFF: Professional: 31   Other: 16   Total: 47
SYSTEMS & NETWORKS ATTACHED TO: State System of Scientific-Technological Information
(GSNTI)
WORKING LANGUAGE(S): Russian; Armenian
SUBJECT COVERAGE: social sciences

DATA BEING PROCESSED AND SIZE: 5,000 books; 17,000 serials; 32 newspapers
DATA PROCESSING METHODS: manual
TYPE OF ACTIVITY: data collection; publication
ACCESS TO SERVICE: services open to all users; free of charge
TYPE & DESCRIPTION OF SERVICES PROVIDED: Library service is only for interlibrary
loans within the country. Provides bibliographic, literature and survey da
searches, selective dissemination of information and translation of
documents.

874 - TSENTR NAUCHNOI INFORMATSII PO OBSHCHESTVENNYM NAUKAM AKADEMII NAUK AZERBAIJANSKOI SSR

SYNONYMOUS NAMES: TsNION AN Azerb. SSR;
Centre of Scientific Information in Social Sciences of the Academy of
Sciences of the Azerbaijan Soviet Socialist Republic
PARENT ORGANIZATION: Akademia Nauk Azerbaijanskoi SSR/Academy of Sciences of the
Azerbaijan SSR
ADDRESS: Prospect Narimanova 31,
Akademgorodok,
370143, Baku,
Azerbaijan SSR,
U. S. S. R.
TEL: 387020, 394082
CREATED: 1971   *HEAD:* A. G. A. O. Zargarov, Head
SIZE OF STAFF: Professional: 31   Other: 15   Total: 46
SYSTEMS & NETWORKS ATTACHED TO: State System of Scientific-Technological Informatic
(GSNTI)
SUBJECT COVERAGE: social sciences
DATA BEING PROCESSED AND SIZE: 1,800 books; 10,860 serials; 350 articles; 6,550
newspapers; 2,300 bibliographical references
DATA PROCESSING METHODS: manual
STORAGE MEDIA: traditional shelving of publications
TYPE OF ACTIVITY: data collection; data analysis; publication; SSID scientific and
methodological activities; SSID training
ACCESS TO SERVICE: services open to all users, free of charge
TYPE & DESCRIPTION OF SERVICES PROVIDED: Provides bibliographic, literature and
survey data searches, selective dissemination of information and translat
of documents upon request.

875 - TSENTR NAUCHNOI INFORMATSII PO OBSHCHESTVENNYM NAUKAM AKADEMII NAUK ESTONSKO] SSR

SYNONYMOUS NAMES: TsNION AN ESSR;
Centre of Scientific Information in Social Sciences of the Estonian Acade
of Sciences
PARENT ORGANIZATION: Akademia Nauk Estonskoi SSR/The Estonian Academy of Sciences
ADDRESS: Prospect Estonia, 7,
Tallin,
200101, Estonian SSR,

U. S. S. R.
TEL: 448-416; 605-159
REATED: 1976   *HEAD:* L. I. Apananski, Head
IZE OF STAFF: Professional: 7   Other: 12   Total: 19
YSTEMS & NETWORKS ATTACHED TO: State Network of Automated Centers of Scientific
      Information in Social Sciences (SATSNION, a subdivision of the State System
      of Scientific Technological Information -GSNTI)
UBJECT COVERAGE: social sciences
ATA BEING PROCESSED AND SIZE: 700 periodicals; 4,350 abstract journals
ATA PROCESSING METHODS: computerized
ARDWARE USED: computer EC-1052; Terminals: EC-8001; VDT-52130, DZM-180
OFTWARE USED: POISK-4, AISIS, KAMA
TORAGE MEDIA: traditional shelving of publications; tapes; discs; microfiches
YPE OF ACTIVITY: data collection; data analysis; publication; SSID scientific and
      methodological activities
CCESS TO SERVICE: services open to specific categories of users, free of charge
YPE & DESCRIPTION OF SERVICES PROVIDED: Provides library services, bibliographic,
      literature and survey data searches. On-line services through the Institute
      of Cybernetics of the Estonian Academy of Sciences, ESSR, Tallin, 21; Has
      access to the data base of the Institute of Scientific Information in Social
      Sciences of the USSR Academy of Sciences, Moscow, Krasikova, 22/21 (INION).
      Services also available include selective dissemination of information,
      information on magnetic tapes, photocopies and translation of documents upon
      request.

6 - TSENTR NAUCHNOI INFORMATSII PO OBSHCHESTVENNYM NAUKAM AKADEMII NAUK GRUZINSKOI
      SSR

NONYMOUS NAMES: Centre of Scientific Information in Social Sciences of the Georgian
      Academy of Sciences
RENT ORGANIZATION: Akademia Nauk Gruzinskoi SSR/Academy of Sciences of the Georgian
      SSR
DRESS: ul. Paliashvili 87,
      Tbilisi 380062,
      Georgian SSR,
      U. S. S. R.
      TEL: 22.41.04
EATED: 1970   *HEAD:* N. I. Kikvadze, Director
ZE OF STAFF: Professional: 107   Other: 25   Total: 132
STEMS & NETWORKS ATTACHED TO: State System of Scientific-Technological Information
      (GSNTI)
TERIALS DESCRIBING THE SERVICE: - Problems of effectiveness of information work.
      Papers of the II MISON Scientific Conference, Tallin, 22-24 November, 1982.-
      M., 1983, p. 335-342
BJECT COVERAGE: social sciences; history; linguistics; economy; archaeology
TA BEING PROCESSED AND SIZE: 130,000 books; 12,000 periodicals; 370 abstract
      journals; 2,000 microcopies; 120 manuscripts
TA PROCESSING METHODS: partially computerized
RDWARE USED: EC 1040 computer, terminal AP4
FTWARE USED: ISIS-4; DIPS (Doc. Inf. Retrieval Syst.); FIPS (Factogr. Inf. Retr.
      Syst.)

STORAGE MEDIA: traditional shelving of publications; tapes; discs
TYPE OF ACTIVITY: data collection; data analysis; publication; SSID scientific and
     methodological activities
ACCESS TO SERVICE: services open to specific categories of users, free of charge
TYPE & DESCRIPTION OF SERVICES PROVIDED: The Centre has 2 data bases: the Republica■
     Automated Retrieval System in Documentation consisting of 9,000
     bibliographic items covering history, arts, literary criticism, linguistic■
     and economy while the Factographic Information Retrieval System consists o■
     1,000 factographical items covering archaeology. Provides library services
     bibliographical, literature and survey data searches, selective
     dissemination of information, information on magnetic tapes and translatio■
     of documents.

877 - TSENTR NAUCHNOI INFORMATSII PO OBSHCHESTVENNYM NAUKAM AKADEMII NAUK LATVIISKO■ SSR

SYNONYMOUS NAMES: TsNION;
     Centre of Scientific Information in Social Sciences of the Academy of
     Sciences of the Latvian SSR
PARENT ORGANIZATION: Institut Economiki Akademii Nauk Latviiskoi SSR/Institute of
     Economics of the Academy of Sciences of the Latvian SSR
ADDRESS: Ulitsa Turgeneva 19,
     Riga 226524,
     Latvian SSR,
     U. S. S. R.
     TEL: 226979
CREATED: 1979   HEAD: A. J. Berzins, Chief
SIZE OF STAFF: Professional: 16
TYPE OF SERVICE: national; public; non-profit
SYSTEMS & NETWORKS ATTACHED TO: State System of Scientific-Technological Informatio■
     (GSNTI)
WORKING LANGUAGE(S): Latvian; Russian
SUBJECT COVERAGE: social sciences; humanities
GEOGRAPHICAL COVERAGE: USSR; Latvian SSR
DATA BEING PROCESSED AND SIZE: 250 books p.a.; 1,500 articles p.a.; 10 grey
     literature p.a.
DATA PROCESSING METHODS: partially computerized
HARDWARE USED: SM-4, SM-1420, APD-2M, ACPU, VDT-52100-C
SOFTWARE USED: operational system DIAMS-3 and a complex of applied programmes in
     language MUMPS
STORAGE MEDIA: traditional shelving of publications; tapes; magnetic discs; fiches■
     microfiches
TYPE OF ACTIVITY: data collection; data analysis; distribution of information; SSI■
     scientific and methodological activities; SSID training; publication
PUBLICATIONS: - Ozola, A.; Romm, R., Referativnaya informacia o publicatsiyach
     obshchestvovedov soyuznych respublic 1979-1981. Izvestiya Akademii Nauk
     Latviiskoi SSR, 1982, No. 8, p. 130-133
     - Grandovska, S., Formirovanie respublicanskoi avtomatizirovannoi bazy
     dannykh po obshchestvennym naukam. Izvestiya Akademii Latviyskoi SSR, 198■
     No. 11, p. 134-137
     - Berzins, A.; Khysamutdinov, V., Osnovnaya Kontseptsia razrabotki tipovo■

avtomatizirovannoi informatsionnoi sistemi po obshchestvennim naukam.
Izvestiya Akademii Nauk Latviiskoi SSR, 1985, No.I, p. 101-103
- Sotsialnoje razvitije sela, 1975-1985: informatsionnij ukazatel
publikatsij avtorov pribaltiki, Riga, 1987, 71 p.

IENTELE: researchers, university professors and instructors, students
CESS TO SERVICE: services open to specific categories of users, free of charge
PE & DESCRIPTION OF SERVICES PROVIDED: Provides bibliographic, literature and
survey data searches of information, selective dissemination of information,
information on magnetic tapes and microfilms. Has access to INION's data
bases and to foreign data bases. Created its own data base "Lettonica I"
(annotated bibliographical descriptions of the publications of Latvian SSR
in social sciences).

8 - TSENTR NAUCHNOI INFORMATSII PO OBSHCHESTVENNYM NAUKAM PRI OTDELENII OBSHCHESTVENNYKH NAUK AKADEMII NAUK LITOVSKOI SSR

NONYMOUS NAMES: TsNION;
    Centre of Scientific Information in Social Sciences of the Academy of
    Sciences of the Lithuanian SSR;
    SICSS
RENT ORGANIZATION: Akademia Nauk Litovskoi SSR/Academy of Sciences of the
    Lithuanian SSR
DRESS: ul. Michurina, 1/46,
    232600 Vilnius,
    Lithuanian SSR,
    U. S. S. R.
    TEL: 732443
EATED: 1971   *HEAD:* A. B. Balsys, Head
ZE OF STAFF: Professional: 15   Other: 2   Total: 17
STEMS & NETWORKS ATTACHED TO: State System of Scientific-Technological Information
    (GSNTI)
BJECT COVERAGE: social sciences; religion
TA PROCESSING METHODS: manual; partially computerized
PE OF ACTIVITY: data collection; data analysis; publication
CESS TO SERVICE: services open to specific categories of users, free of charge
PE & DESCRIPTION OF SERVICES PROVIDED: Provides abstract journals, periodicals,
    bibliographic, literature and survey data searches, selective dissemination
    of information and translation of documents. Also deals with studies on
    scientific atheism and religion.

9 - TSENTR NAUCHNOI INFORMATSII PO OBSHCHESTVENNYM NAUKAM PRI PRESIDIUME AKADEMII NAUK UZBEKSKOI SSR

NONYMOUS NAMES: TsNION AN Uz. SSR;
    Center of Scientific Information in Social Sciences at the Presidium of the
    Academy of Sciences of the Uzbek SSR
RENT ORGANIZATION: Akademia Nauk Uzbekskoi SSR/Academy of Sciences of the Uzbek SSR
DRESS: Prospect Gor'kogo 81,
    700170 Tashkent-170,

Uzbek SSR,
U. S. S. R.
TEL: 62-56-51
CREATED: 1969   *HEAD:* R. R. Turgunovich, Head
SIZE OF STAFF: Professional: 8   Other: 4   Total: 12
SYSTEMS & NETWORKS ATTACHED TO: State System of Scientific-Technological Informatio
        (GSNTI)
WORKING LANGUAGE(S): Russian
SUBJECT COVERAGE: history; information science
DATA BEING PROCESSED AND SIZE: books; 116 periodicals; 16 abstract journals
DATA PROCESSING METHODS: manual
TYPE OF ACTIVITY: data collection; publication
PUBLICATIONS: - Mukhammad Ibn Musa, Al-Khorezmi i ego vklad v razvitie mirovoi nauk
        Bibliographic index - Tashkent: Fan, 1982
        - Khorezmi v zarubejnoi nauchnoi literature: abstract collection - Tashken
        Fan, 1983
ACCESS TO SERVICE: services open to specific categories of users, free of charge
TYPE & DESCRIPTION OF SERVICES PROVIDED: Provides library services, bibliographic,
        literature abstracts, data survey, searches of information, selective
        dissemination of information and translation of documents upon request.

880 - VSESOJUZNAJA GOSUDARSTVENNAJA BIBLIOTEKA INOSTRANNOJ LITERATURY

SYNONYMOUS NAMES: VGBIL;
        All-Union State Library of Foreign Literature
PARENT ORGANIZATION: USSR Ministry of Culture
ADDRESS: ul. Uljanovskaja 1,
        Moscow 109189,
        U. S. S. R.
        TEL: 297 28 39 - TELEX: Stacii 7234 SU
        CABLE: Moscow 240 Stacii
CREATED: 1922   *HEAD:* Ms N. Igumnova, Director
SIZE OF STAFF: Professional: 500   Other: 100   Total: 600
TYPE OF SERVICE: international; public; non-profit
SUBJECT COVERAGE: social sciences; humanities; education; history; linguistics;
        philosophy; political science
GEOGRAPHICAL COVERAGE: global
DATA BEING PROCESSED AND SIZE: books and articles in foreign languages (1,900,000
        books; 2,674,000 periodicals)
DATA PROCESSING METHODS: manual
TYPE OF ACTIVITY: data collection; data analysis; distribution of information;
        publication
PUBLICATIONS: - Bibliographies and other reference publications
CLIENTELE: institutions, general public
ACCESS TO SERVICE: open to all users, free of charge
TYPE & DESCRIPTION OF SERVICES PROVIDED: Provides library services, photocopies and
        microforms, bibliographic searches, bibliographic references, selective
        dissemination of information, compilation of documentary syntheses and
        translations upon request.

Venezuela

1 - CENTRO DE INFORMACIÓN, DOCUMENTACIÓN Y ANALISIS LATINOAMERICANO

NONYMOUS NAMES: CIDAL;
    Centre for Latin American Information, Documentation and Analysis
DRESS: Apartado Los Ruices 70442,
    Caracas 1071,
    VENEZUELA
    CABLE: CIDI-CARACAS
EATED: 1971   *HEAD:* Mr. J. A. Barbeito Precedo, President
                    Mr. G. A. J. Hudon, Director General
ZE OF STAFF: Professional: 5   Other: 11   Total: 16
PE OF SERVICE: international; private; non-profit
RKING LANGUAGE(S): Spanish; English; French; Portuguese
BJECT COVERAGE: social sciences
OGRAPHICAL COVERAGE: Latin America
TA PROCESSING METHODS: computerized
PE & DESCRIPTION OF SERVICES PROVIDED: Provides library services and data for
    secondary analysis.

2 - CENTRO DE INVESTIGACIONES EN CIENCIAS SOCIALES, DEPARTAMENTO DE INFORMACIÓN PARA EL DESARROLLO SOCIAL

NONYMOUS NAMES: CISOR-DIDES;
    Center for Social Science Research, Information Department for Social
    Development
DRESS: Apdo 5894,
    Caracas 1010-A,
    VENEZUELA
    TEL: 562.70.97
EATED: 1975   *HEAD:* Ms. M. Parra,
ZE OF STAFF: Professional: 3   Other: 3   Total: 6
PE OF SERVICE: national; private; non-profit
STEMS & NETWORKS ATTACHED TO: REDINSE, SINACITI
TERIALS DESCRIBING THE SERVICE: - CISOR, Centros de información en organizaciones
    de desarrollo social, 1987
RKING LANGUAGE(S): Spanish
BJECT COVERAGE: social sciences; social welfare; demography; anthropology;
    sociology; social psychology; human resources; socio-economic development;
    economic planning; statistics
OGRAPHICAL COVERAGE: Venezuela
TA BEING PROCESSED AND SIZE: 6,000 books; 150 journals; 250 bulletins; reports;
    theses; 15,000 microfiches
TA PROCESSING METHODS: partially computerized
RDWARE USED: Epson Equity I + II, III
TWARE USED: Micro CDS/ISIS
ORAGE MEDIA: traditional shelving of publications, microfiches; magnetic disks
PE OF ACTIVITY: data collection; data analysis; distribution of information; SSID
    scientific and methodological activities; SSID training
BLICATIONS: - Tesauro SINTAB para la referencia a los cuadros de las estadísticas

nacionales, 1982
CLIENTELE: researchers, students
ACCESS TO SERVICE: open to specific categories of users, free of charge
TYPE & DESCRIPTION OF SERVICES PROVIDED: Provides library services, photocopies and
bibliographies, documentary searches, question-answering service,
information on magnetic tapes or discs and microforms. Has developed two
documentation systems "SINTAB" for the tabulation of national statistics
(50,000 statistical tables) and "SINDOC" for literature references, and a
project for the establishment of social welfare information centres.

883 - FUNDACIÓN PARA EL DESARROLLO DE LA COMUNIDAD Y FOMENTO MUNICIPAL, CENTRO DE DOCUMENTACIÓN E INFORMACIÓN SOBRE AREAS MARGINALES Y MUNICIPALISMO

SYNONYMOUS NAMES: CEDISAM;
Foundation for Community Development and Municipal Improvement, Centre for
Documentation and Information for Squatter Settlements and Municipal Affai
ADDRESS: Final Av. Abraham Lincoln,
Chacaito,
Apartado 50218,
Caracas 1050,
VENEZUELA
TEL: 712323
CREATED: 1975   HEAD: L. Alvarez de Perez,
SIZE OF STAFF: Professional: 3   Other: 2   Total: 5
TYPE OF SERVICE: national; non-profit
SYSTEMS & NETWORKS ATTACHED TO: REDINSE (Red de Documentación e Información
Socioeconómica)
WORKING LANGUAGE(S): Spanish
SUBJECT COVERAGE: social sciences; education; social welfare; community development
GEOGRAPHICAL COVERAGE: America; Europe
DATA BEING PROCESSED AND SIZE: 11,000 books; 7,000 documents
DATA PROCESSING METHODS: manual
STORAGE MEDIA: traditional shelving of publications; fiches
TYPE OF ACTIVITY: data analysis; distribution of information; publication
PERIODICALS PUBLISHED:
- Boletín Nuevas Adquisiciones
PUBLICATIONS: - Bibliografías especializadas
- Noticiario
- Catálogo de publicaciones periódicas
CLIENTELE: researchers, professionals, university students
ACCESS TO SERVICE: services open to all users, free of charge
TYPE & DESCRIPTION OF SERVICES PROVIDED: Provides library services, bibliographic
searches of information, photocopies and translation of documents upon
request.

884 - INSTITUTO DE ESTUDIOS SUPERIORES DE ADMINISTRACIÓN, BIBLIOTECA LORENZO MENDO

SYNONYMOUS NAMES: IESA Biblioteca
ADDRESS: Apartado de Correos 1640,

Caracas 1010-A,
VENEZUELA
TEL: 52.87.12 - TELEX: 28381 IESA VC
CABLE: IESAVEN
REATED: 1968   *HEAD:* Ms. A. Curiel, Head
IZE OF STAFF: Professional: 4   Other: 9   Total: 13
YPE OF SERVICE: national; public; non-profit
YSTEMS & NETWORKS ATTACHED TO: REDINSE (Red de Información Socio-Económica)
ATERIALS DESCRIBING THE SERVICE: - Manual de la biblioteca, Caracas, 1985, 22 p.
UBJECT COVERAGE: social sciences; economics; administrative sciences; political
    science
EOGRAPHICAL COVERAGE: global
ATA BEING PROCESSED AND SIZE: 24,000 books; 6,000 theses, documents and leaflets;
    2,000 articles
ATA PROCESSING METHODS: manual; partially computerized
ARDWARE USED: Micro-Epson, Equity 1
OFTWARE USED: Micro-Isis
TORAGE MEDIA: traditional shelving of publications
YPE OF ACTIVITY: distribution of information; SSID training
ERIODICALS PUBLISHED:
    - Lista de Canje, irr.
    - Lista de Publicaciones Ingresadas a la Biblioteca IESA, 12 p.a.
    - Boletín Bibliográfico, irr.
UBLICATIONS: - Catálogo de publicaciones periódicas
    - Catálogo colectivo de publicaciones periódicas, Caracas, CONICIT, 1978
    - Bibliografía sobre inflación, Caracas, Redinse, 2 vol., 1977-1978
    - Occasional bibliographies
LIENTELE: students, teachers, researchers
CCESS TO SERVICE: open to specific categories of users, free of charge, some
    services against payment
YPE & DESCRIPTION OF SERVICES PROVIDED: Provides library services, query answering
    service, current awareness service, bibliographic and quantitative searches
    of information, selective dissemination of information, photocopies, and
    loan of documents.

85 - UNIVERSIDAD CENTRAL DE VENEZUELA, CENTRO DE ESTUDIOS DEL DESARROLLO, BIBLIOTECA

YNONYMOUS NAMES: CENDES Biblioteca
DDRESS: Av. Neveri, Edif. Asovac,
    Colinas de Bello Monte,
    Apdo. 6622,
    Caracas,
    VENEZUELA
    TEL: 752.38.62
REATED: 1961   *HEAD:* Ms. M. E. Quintero, Coordinator
IZE OF STAFF: Total: 5
YPE OF SERVICE: international; public; non-profit
YSTEMS & NETWORKS ATTACHED TO: Red Socio-Económica, Conicit, Venezuela
UBJECT COVERAGE: social sciences; economics; education; political science; planning;
    theory
ATA BEING PROCESSED AND SIZE: 14,000 books, articles, reports, on-going research,

seminars and courses

DATA PROCESSING METHODS: partially computerized

TYPE OF ACTIVITY: data collection; data analysis; distribution of information; SSID training

PERIODICALS PUBLISHED: - Cuadernos del CENDES, 3 p.a.

CLIENTELE: researchers, professors, students

ACCESS TO SERVICE: services open to specific categories of users, against payment

TYPE & DESCRIPTION OF SERVICES PROVIDED: Provides library services, bibliographic searches, on-line services, selective dissemination of information and photocopies.

886 - VIEN KINH TE THE GIOI, PHONG THONG TIN TU LIEU

SYNONYMOUS NAMES: Institute of World Economy, Information and Documentation Section

ADDRESS: 27 Tran Xuan Soan,
Hanoi,
VIET-NAM (SOCIALIST REPUBLIC)
TEL: 54773

CREATED: 1980   *HEAD:* Mr. Ta Kim Ngoc, Head

SIZE OF STAFF: Professional: 10

TYPE OF SERVICE: public; non-profit

WORKING LANGUAGE(S): Vietnamese; English; Russian

SUBJECT COVERAGE: economics

GEOGRAPHICAL COVERAGE: Asia; Africa; Latin America; Europe; North America

TYPE OF ACTIVITY: data collection; distribution of information; publication

PERIODICALS PUBLISHED: - World Economics Problems, 2 p.a.

CLIENTELE: economic researchers

ACCESS TO SERVICE: services open to all users

TYPE & DESCRIPTION OF SERVICES PROVIDED: Provides library services, selective dissemination of information, bibliographic, literature abstract and quantitative data searches of information.

887 - CENTER ZA PROUCEVANJE SODELOVANJA Z DEZELAMI V RAZVOJU, SPECIALNA KNJIZBUCA/DOKUMENTACIJSKO-INFORMACIJSKA SLUZBA

SYNONYMOUS NAMES: CPSDVR;
Research Centre for Cooperation with Developing Countries, Special Library/Documentation-Information Service;
RCCDC, Special Library/Documentation-Information Service

ADDRESS: Kardeljeva ploscad 1,
61000 Ljubljana,
YUGOSLAVIA
TEL: (38-61) 347-597 - TELEX: 32139 Yu JCS za DVR
CABLE: CENTER ZA DVR

CREATED: 1967   *HEAD:* Ms. T. Kovse, Head Librarian
Mr. M. Verbic, Head of Documentation-Information Service

SIZE OF STAFF: Professional: 4   Other: 1   Total: 5

YPE OF SERVICE: national; public; non-profit

YSTEMS & NETWORKS ATTACHED TO: Central Library of Economics, Faculty of Edvard
        Kardel, Ljubljana

ORKING LANGUAGE(S): English; French; Serbocroatian; Slovenian

UBJECT COVERAGE: social sciences; demography; economics; law; political science;
        transnational corporations; women; human rights; economic cooperation among
        developing countres; trade

EOGRAPHICAL COVERAGE: developing countries

ATA BEING PROCESSED AND SIZE: 11,000 books; 400 periodicals; reports; studies;
        conference papers; reference books

ATA PROCESSING METHODS: partially computerized

ARDWARE USED: IBM PC 30 mb Hard Disk

OFTWARE USED: Micro-ISIS

TORAGE MEDIA: traditional shelving of publications

YPE OF ACTIVITY: data collection; distribution of information; publication

ERIODICALS PUBLISHED: - Development & South-South Cooperation, 2 p.a.
        - News on Developing Countries, 48 p.a.
        - Chinese Perspectives. 2 p.a.
        - Accessions List, 6 p.a.

UBLICATIONS: - Bibliography on economic cooperation and integration among developing
        countries, 1984
        - South-South cooperation: a select, annotated bibliography 1961-1986, 1986
        - Decisions and recommendations on South-South cooperation, 1981-1986, 1986

LIENTELE: academic community, researchers, students, professors, managers,
        businessmen, journalists, professional departments, other libraries (100
        p.a.)

CCESS TO SERVICE: services open to all users free of charge; paid services for
        enterprises

YPE & DESCRIPTION OF SERVICES PROVIDED: Provides library services, selective
        dissemination of information, bibliographic, literature abstract and
        quantitative data searches of information using its own data base "LEGAL
        DATABASE". Also provides translation of documents and photocopies upon
        request.

88 - INSTITUT EKONOMSKIH NAUKA BIBLIOTEKA

YNONYMOUS NAMES: Institute of Economic Sciences Library

DDRESS: Zmaj Jovina 12,
        P.O. Box 611,
        11001 Belgrade,
        YUGOSLAVIA
        TEL: 622.357

REATED: 1958   HEAD: Ms. L. Martinović, Head

IZE OF STAFF: Professional: 2

YPE OF SERVICE: national; public; non-profit

ATERIALS DESCRIBING THE SERVICE: - Institute of Economic Sciences, 1958-1983. 25
        years of scientific works, 1983

ORKING LANGUAGE(S): serbocroatian; English

UBJECT COVERAGE: economics; demography; education; political science; sociology;
        social sciences; information system; theory; research and development

EOGRAPHICAL COVERAGE: Yugoslavia; global

DATA BEING PROCESSED AND SIZE: 22,100 books; 220 periodicals; 605 reports; on-going
        research
DATA PROCESSING METHODS: partially computerized
HARDWARE USED: PC Olivetti M24
SOFTWARE USED: CDS/ISIS
STORAGE MEDIA: traditional shelving of publications; PC diskettes; tapes; hard disc
TYPE OF ACTIVITY: data collection; data analysis; distribution of information;
        publication
PERIODICALS PUBLISHED:
        - Library Acquisitions List
PUBLICATIONS: - List of periodicals
CLIENTELE: researchers, students, libraries, institutes, faculties, firms
ACCESS TO SERVICE: services open to all users, free of charge
TYPE & DESCRIPTION OF SERVICES PROVIDED: Provides library services, bibliographic a
        literature abstract searches of information and photocopies. Also provides
        on-line services using external data bases, DIALOG, DATA-START, ISA/IRS
        through Pergamon INFOLINE, ECHO and EURONET DIANE.

**889 - INSTITUT ZA MEDJUNARODNU POLITIKU I PRIVREDU, CENTAR ZA NAUCNU INFORMACIJU I
        DOKUMENTACIJU, BEOGRAD**

SYNONYMOUS NAMES: Institute of International Politics and Economics, Information an
        Documentation Centre, Belgrade
ADDRESS: Makedonska 25,
        P.O. Box 750,
        11000 Belgrade,
        YUGOSLAVIA
        TEL: 325-611
        CABLE: INSTINTPOL
CREATED: 1947   *HEAD:* Dr. G. Milosavljević, Director
SIZE OF STAFF: Professional: 8   Other: 1   Total: 9
TYPE OF SERVICE: national; public; non-profit
MATERIALS DESCRIBING THE SERVICE: - printed notice
SUBJECT COVERAGE: political science; international relations; law
GEOGRAPHICAL COVERAGE: global
DATA BEING PROCESSED AND SIZE: 264,000 books, 34 abstracts, 1010 periodicals
DATA PROCESSING METHODS: manual
CLIENTELE: researchers, students, civil servants
ACCESS TO SERVICE: open to all users, free of charge
TYPE & DESCRIPTION OF SERVICES PROVIDED: Provides library services, retrospective
        bibliographic searches, provision of documentary dossiers, photocopies and
        microforms.

**890 - INTERNATIONAL CENTRE FOR PUBLIC ENTERPRISES IN DEVELOPING COUNTRIES,
        INFORMATION AND LIBRARY SERVICE**

SYNONYMOUS NAMES: ICPE Information and Library Service
ADDRESS: Titova 104,
        P.O. Box 92,

61109 Ljubljana,
YUGOSLAVIA
TEL: (061) 346-361 - TELEX: 31400 yu icpe
CABLE: INTERCENT, Ljubljana
CREATED: 1987   *HEAD:* Ms. P. Zdravka, Head
SIZE OF STAFF: Professional: 3   Other: 1   Total: 4
TYPE OF SERVICE: international; non-profit
MATERIALS DESCRIBING THE SERVICE: - Annual report
WORKING LANGUAGE(S): English
SUBJECT COVERAGE: administrative sciences; economics; public enterprise; management
        development; public administration; workers' self-management; technology
        transfer; working women; marketing
GEOGRAPHICAL COVERAGE: developing countries
DATA BEING PROCESSED AND SIZE: 11,000 books; 450 periodicals; 3,000 articles
DATA PROCESSING METHODS: computerized
HARDWARE USED: Microcomputer IBM XT with 40 MB hard disk and streamer
SOFTWARE USED: CDS/ISIS; DBase III; IV + V; Wordstar; Lotus 123
STORAGE MEDIA: traditional shelving of publications; microfiches
TYPE OF ACTIVITY: distribution of information; SSID training; publication
PERIODICALS PUBLISHED:
        - Accession List
        - Awareness List
PUBLICATIONS: - ICPE bibliography 1971-1982; 1982-1984; 1985-1986
        - Public enterprises in developing countries, vol. I; vol. II
        - Occasional thematic bibliographies
CLIENTELE: researchers, administrators, managers, politicians, experts, faculty,
        students (500 p.a.)
ACCESS TO SERVICE: services open to specific categories of users, free of charge
TYPE & DESCRIPTION OF SERVICES PROVIDED: Provides library services, bibliographic and
        literature abstract searches of information, selective dissemination of
        information and photocopies.

891 - REFERALNI CENTAR ZA NAUCNE INFORMACIJE

SYNONYMOUS NAMES: R C;
        Referral Center for Scientific Informations
PARENT ORGANIZATION: Narodna i Univerzitetska Biblioteka BIH
ADDRESS: Obala vojvode Stepe 42,
        P.O. Box pob 337,
        71000 Sarajevo,
        YUGOSLAVIA
        TEL: 071/537-398
CREATED: 1976   *HEAD:* O. Kravić, Head
SIZE OF STAFF: Other: 6
TYPE OF SERVICE: national; public; non-profit
WORKING LANGUAGE(S): Serbocroatian
SUBJECT COVERAGE: social sciences; political science; economics; sociology;
        education; history; law; linguistics; mass communication; psychology;
        statistics; science; technology
GEOGRAPHICAL COVERAGE: Yugoslavia
DATA BEING PROCESSED AND SIZE: 3,545 research projects; 5,000 foreign serial

publications; 1,450 doctoral dissertations; etc.
DATA PROCESSING METHODS: partially computerized
HARDWARE USED: Honeywell 6/20
STORAGE MEDIA: discs
TYPE OF ACTIVITY: data collection; data analysis; distribution of information;
    publication
CLIENTELE: researchers, students
ACCESS TO SERVICE: services open to all users, free of charge
TYPE & DESCRIPTION OF SERVICES PROVIDED: Provides retrospective bibliographic
    searches, and question-answering service using its own data base.

892 - UNIVERZA EDVARDA KARDELJA V LJUBLJANI, OSREDNJA DRUZBOSLOVNA KNJIZNICA JOZETA GORICARJA, SPECIALIZIRANI INDOC CENTER ZA DRUZBOSLOVJE

SYNONYMOUS NAMES: University Edvarda Kardelja, Central Library for Social Sciences
    Jozeta Goricar, Specialized Information Centre for Social Sciences
ADDRESS: Kardeljeva Ploscad 5,
    Ljubljana,
    YUGOSLAVIA
    TEL: 061 341.461
CREATED: 1978   *HEAD:* M. Ambrozic, Head
SIZE OF STAFF: Total: 4
TYPE OF SERVICE: national; public; non-profit
WORKING LANGUAGE(S): Slovene; English
SUBJECT COVERAGE: social sciences; education; political science; social anthropology
    sociology; communication
DATA BEING PROCESSED AND SIZE: 142,000 books and research reports; 410 periodicals
DATA PROCESSING METHODS: computerized
HARDWARE USED: DEC-1092 (Central computer), ISKRA-DELTA Terminals, ATARI-St p. comp.
SOFTWARE USED: IBIS and ST-EVE (for personal computers ATARI-ST)
STORAGE MEDIA: tapes; discs
TYPE OF ACTIVITY: data collection; distribution of information; SSID scientific and
    methodological activities; publication
CLIENTELE: students, university professors, research workers and others
ACCESS TO SERVICE: services open to all users, free of charge
TYPE & DESCRIPTION OF SERVICES PROVIDED: Provides library services, bibliographic
    searches of information using its own data bases containing 60,000
    bibliographical records, selective dissemination of information and
    photocopies.

Zaire / Zaïre / Zaire

893 - UNIVERSITÉ DE KINSHASA, CENTRE INTERDISCIPLINAIRE D'ETUDES ET DE DOCUMENTATION POLITIQUES, SERVICE DE DOCUMENTATION ET DES PUBLICATIONS

SYNONYMOUS NAMES: CIEDOP
ADDRESS: B.P. 867 Kinshasa XI,
    ZAIRE
    TEL: 30123 Ext. 241 - TELEX: 242 Kinshasa XI
CREATED: 1976

SIZE OF STAFF: Professional: 16   Other: 2   Total: 18
TYPE OF SERVICE: national; public; non-profit
SUBJECT COVERAGE: administrative sciences; economics; history; law; political
        science; social sciences; sociology
GEOGRAPHICAL COVERAGE: global
DATA BEING PROCESSED AND SIZE: Official documents (colonial and post colonial Zaire,
        Africa and other countries); periodicals, documents of UAO and UNO
DATA PROCESSING METHODS: manual
CLIENTELE: researchers, students
ACCESS TO SERVICE: services open to all users, free of charge
TYPE & DESCRIPTION OF SERVICES PROVIDED: Provides library services, bibliographic
        searches and loan of documents.

894 - UNITED NATIONS INSTITUTE FOR NAMIBIA, INFORMATION AND DOCUMENTATION DIVISION

SYNONYMOUS NAMES: UNIN/IDD
ADDRESS: P.O. Box 33811,
        Lusaka,
        ZAMBIA
        TEL: 216468 - TELEX: ZA 41960
        CABLE: UNATIONS, Lusaka
CREATED: 1980   HEAD: Mrs. C. O. Kisiedu, Assistant Director and Head of Division
SIZE OF STAFF: Professional: 5   Other: 12   Total: 17
TYPE OF SERVICE: international; public; non-profit
MATERIALS DESCRIBING THE SERVICE: - UNIN in brief 1985 (brochure)
WORKING LANGUAGE(S): English
SUBJECT COVERAGE: administrative sciences; social sciences
GEOGRAPHICAL COVERAGE: Namibia; Southern Africa
DATA BEING PROCESSED AND SIZE: books (1,200 p.a.); serials (50 p.a.); articles (500
        p.a.); reports
DATA PROCESSING METHODS: manual; partially computerized
STORAGE MEDIA: traditional shelving of publications; microfiches; discs
TYPE OF ACTIVITY: data collection; data analysis; distribution of information;
        publication
PERIODICALS PUBLISHED: - Namibia Abstracts, 4 p.a.
        - UNIN News: A Bi-monthly News Service
        - Library Accessions Bulletin, 4 p.a.
        - News about Namibia
PUBLICATIONS: - A Descriptive list of United Nations reference documents on Namibia
        (1946-1978), 1979
        - Texts of United Nations Resolutions on Namibia (1946-1978). Part I:
        General Assembly. Part II: Security Council and Economic and Social Council,
        1979
        - Namibia: facts and figures
CLIENTELE: students, bona fide researchers on Namibia: 600 users
ACCESS TO SERVICE: services open to specific categories of users, free of charge
TYPE & DESCRIPTION OF SERVICES PROVIDED: Provides library services, profiles (for
        researchers), bibliographic searches, inter-library loans, limited
        reproduction of documents, documentation services, statistical compilations,
        in-service training programme and production of demonstration material and

Zambia / Zambie / Zambia

audio-visual aids for teaching purposes.

A

Abbes, M.; Head *712*
Abdel Kader, S.; Interim Coordinator
  269
Abdulaziz Ben Mohammad Ben Ghaith,
  Mudeer Markaz al-Maaloumat;
  Director of the Data Center *645*
Abrous, A.; Chief *72*
Affan, K. O.; Director *672*
Agoston, M.; Director General *392*
Agrawal, S. P.; Director *435*
Agüero de Franco, A. M.; Librarian *91*
Ahmad Khan, A. *434*
Aidara, A. H.; Director *647*
Aigbede, E.; Head *154*
Ainsworth, S. *518*
Akinsete, J. O.; Assistant Chief
  Librarian *568*
Akisanya, J. A.; Institute Librarian
  570
Akopovich, B. K.; Head *873*
Alain, J.-M.; Director *197*
Alexanderson, B.; Head Librarian *681*
Almada de Ascencio, M.; Director *528*
Almeida Chaves, L.; Head Librarian *163*
Almofadda, O. A.; Director *644*
Alvarez de Perez, L. *883*
Amanov, S. A.; Head *869*
Ambrozic, M.; Head *892*
Anda Vela, F.; Coordinator *527*
Anderson, J. R.; Library Director *766*
Anderson, M. *730*
Andrade Lleras, G.; Director *500*
Andreotti, M. E.; Librarian *81*
Andresen, I. H.; Head Librarian *575*
Angel, M.; Head *205*
Apananski, L. I.; Head *875*
Arencibia Huidobro, Y.; Librarian *75*
Arguedas, C.; Head *38*
Arnaud, R.; Head *326*
Arsac, P.; Director *337*
Arteaga, M.; Head Librarian *275*
Asante, S. K. B.; Director *67*
Asif, D.; Acting Executive
  Chairman/Librarian *454*
Augustinho, V.; Director *165*
Auliel de Villa, A. *114*
Aw, S.; Librarian *651*

B

Babini, D.; Director *100*
Badree, S.; Librarian *710*
Bahri, A.; Chief, Population Division
  74
Baird, D. W.; Social Science Librarian
  840
Baker, B. G.; Director *785*
Balázs-Veredy, K.; Director-General *391*
Ballon, R. J. *493*
Balsinhas Covas, F.; Head *47*
Balsys, A. B.; Head *878*
Bamba, Z.; Coordinator p.i. *512*
Banjo, A. O.; Director *569*
Banovski, K. T.; Director *174*
Bantgheva, T.; Senior Research
  Associate *168*
Barbeito Precedo, J. A.; President *881*
Barbey, R.; Head *692*
Barcala de Moyano, G. G.; Head
  Librarian *89*
Baretje, R.; Director *304*
Barragan Rojas, M.; Coordinator *533*
Barrett, A.; Chief Librarian *471*
Barrett, W. F. *28*
Barrington, O.; Library Officer *182*
Barry, F.; Head *291*
Basak Kayiran, A.; Chief Librarian *714*
Báthory, J.; Head *382*
Batishevna, A. N.; Head *868*
Battistelli, F.; Secretary-General *462*
Bauer, H.; Director *132*
Baumgartner, X.; Head Librarian *691*
Beccaria, L. A. *103*
Becker-Moelands, M. A.; Director *552*
Beetham, D. *743*
Begoña Uriguen, M.; Head *656*
Beier, F.-K.; Managing Director *361*
Bentabet, F. *87*
Benzine, D. E.; Director *59*
Berananda, N.; Director *702*
van Berckel, M.; Research, Information,
  Documentation Officer *554*
Berg, K.; Librarian *62*
Bergström, N.; Librarian *676*
Berzins, A. J.; Chief *877*
Beza, J.; Chief Librarian *23*
Bezan, F.; Head *245*
Bhansoon Ladavalya, M. L.; Director *697*
Bhardwaj, S. R. C.; Director *438*
Bhatia, S. C.; Librarian *422*
Biagianti, A. S.; Director *771*

Bilbom, R.; Managing Director 733
Biswas, S. C.; Director 430
Bjorgan, V. 753
Bjorkman, J. W.; Director 395
Blanc Renard, N.; Head Librarian 217
Bloombbecker, J.; Director 806
Böhm, G. 223
Bong, E.; Programme Specialist 8
Bonilla de Gaviria, M. C.; Director-
    General 594
Boon-Itt, K.; Head 699
Bordcosh, R. C.; Chief 73
Borgogno, E.; Chief of Library 102
Boulet, D. 322
Boullet, A.; Head 314
Bourne, W.; Coordinator 776
Bova, P.; Librarian 835
Boyde, S. J.; Press Librarian 740
Boyko, E. 184
Brace, J.; Director 760
Branch, M. A.; Director 747
Brandeis, R. C.; Chief Librarian 207
Brantgärde, L.; Director 685
Brehmer, K.; Library Director 803
Brekke, K.; Head 578
Broms, H.; Chief Librarian 280
Buess, M. C. 688
Burda, M.; Director 320
Burian, F. J. 31
Burshtyn, H.; Director 185
Burton, A. W.; Director 738
Burton, B. 746
Busch, B. J.; Area Coordinator 202

C

Cabello, A. 657
Cabutey-Adodoadji, E.; Librarian 373
Cáceres, V. 215
Cagnoli, R. V.; Director 96
Capelli Castañeda, G. 587
Capelli, F.; Prof. 465
Carera, M. 695
Carlsson, U.; Director 687
Cassell, K. A.; Librarian 808
Castillo Lopez, V.; Director 378
Cerný, A.; Library 244
Chakrabarti, R.; Director 436
Chaplan, K.; Librarian 842
Chapman, E. 860
Charpin, J.-M.; Director 296
Chaudenson, R.; Director 316
Chávez Sánchez, H. 593
Chevalier, B.; Chief of the Division
    323
Chevrier, Y. 303
Chevrolet, H.; Head Librarian 36
Chikkamallaiah; Librarian 411

Chitre, V. S.; Director 406
Churchill, E.; Head 60
Ciurlizza Mellon, A.; Chief 9
Clausen, N. S.; Director 263
Clavo, H.; Director 111
Clifford, M.; Head of Library 580
Clubb, J. M.; Executive Director 846
Coatsworth, P. 799
Coenen, W. H.; Director 539
Cohen-Naar, C.; Director 297
Collas-Monsod, S.; Director General 59
Conçalves de Araugo, J.; Director 159
Copans, J.; Director 501
Coquand, P.; Head of Documentation
    Centre 27
Cosse, G.; Director 98
Cotta Schoenberg, M.; Chief Librarian
    259
Courbis, R.; Director 336
Cowan, A. P.; Project Director 775
Crocker, S. O.; Director 772
Csahók, I.; Director 384
Cubas, M. I.; Director 592
Cuisenier, J.; Conservateur en Chef 28
Cummins, N. P.; Chief 30
Curiel, A.; Head 884
Cyrzyk, L.; Head 626
Czubiński, A; Director 623

D

Da Fonseca Ferreira, A.; Director 88
Dabezies, B.; Head 22
Daly, M. A.; Director 711
Dandekar, R. N.; Honorary Secretary 39
Daneri de Correa, A. C. 115
Dannemann, W.; Director, Bureau of
    Statistics 52
Darkowska-Nidzgorski, O.; Responsable de
    la Bibliothèque 292
D'Arras d'Haudrecy, L.; Librarian 151
Darshan, J. 65
Darwich, S. A. 696
Dassetto, F.; Coordinator 150
Datta, A.; Director 157
Davis, M.; Head 118
Dawe, P. S. J.; Director 43
De Abreu Neto, J. V. 161
De Boischevalier, B.; Documentalist 29
De González, I.; Head 377
De Guchteneire, P. F. A.; Director 558
De Lange, H.; Director, Studies and
    Documentation Service 149
De Pivetta, N. J.; Director 97
De Rolón, H. G.; Documentalist 586
De Saedeleer, G.; Head Librarian 143
Deák, J.; General Director 383
Defriez, P.; Head 729

Dehennin, W.; Librarian 37
Delgado Cintrón, C.; Director 636
Delgado Hurtado de Mendoza, R.; Head 523
Delp, L. 347
Deokattey, S.; Documentalist 442
Devaud, E.; Secretary General 306
Díaz, E.; Head 92
Dion, D.; Managing Editor 788
Diop, M. T.; Librarian 649
Diop, O.; Director 648
Disario, M.; Vice-President 780
Dix, W.; Principal 117
Dloutý, E. 252
Dodson, H.; Chief 825
Dorsey, L.; Librarian 801
Dote, G.; Librarian 787
Dowdell, D.; Technical Information Specialist 815
Draghi, S.; Director 461
Duarte de Bogadjián, E.; Director 755
Dubec, A.; Director 612
Dubois, J.; Director 329
Duensing, E. E. 823
Dumaine, C.; Head 311
Dumont, F.; President 189
Dunkle, D.; Director 832
Duparc, C.; Head of the Documentation Service 296
Duport, Cl.; Librarian 321
Dyrud, J. 140

E

Ebensoy, Z.; Director 716
Echavarría, A. L. S.; Director 237
Eddy, K.; Director 563
Edwards, S.; Head 720
Eguren Lopez, F. 589
Eladio Proaño, L. 266
Elevera, M.-S. G.; Chief Librarian 596
Ellis, G.; Director 195
Elvalide Seye, C.; Head 177
Ember, M. E. 866
Encanto, G. R.; Dean 604
Encarnacion, V. V.; Head 603
Endara, S. 267
Engelmann, H. O.; Director and Editor 813
Enos, F.; Head Research Librarian 791
Estevez Guzman, A.; Coordinator 530
Etchevers, P.; Chief Librarian 220
Evangelista, C.; Director 21
Evenhuis, E.; Librarian 554
Everts, P. P.; Director 543
Evmenov, L. F.; Head 178
Van Eyndhoven, J.; Principal Information Services Officer 63

Ezera, O.; Head 800

F

Fahlander, B.; Head Librarian 680
Fameli, M.; Director 463
Fassi-Fihri, A. 534
Feldbrugge, F. J. M. 555
Feldheim, P.; President 146
Felvinczi, T.; Head 387
Fennell, J. P.; Director Social Science Computation Center 768
Ferguson, C. E.; Director 830
Fernandes, W.; Director 417
Fernando, L. S.; Director 665
Ferrer Andrade, M.G.; Coordinator 531
Figuernoa, A.; Librarian 631
Filio Moreno, A.; Head 517
Filleul, M.; Information & Communication Director 286
Finney, D.; Director 54
Finney, D. J. 546
Fischer, E. J.; Director 545
Flory, M. 302
Földi, T.; Head 386
Forbes, R. G. B.; Director 662
Forclaz, R. 690
Forero de Moreno, I.; Head 229
Fortin, J.; Director, Information Division 187
Foster, J.: Head of Division 204
Franco, L. M.; Chief 235
Franklin, P.; Executive Director 802
Freudenstein, R.; Director 362
Fukuo, T.; Librarian 497

G

Galan; General Delegate 325
Galinski, C.; Director 46
Gallimore, N. M.; Librarian 739
Gandásegui, M. A.; Executive Secretary 583
Ganly, J. V.; Chief 821
Garcia Acosta, A.; Director 107
Garcia Acosta, A.; Library Coordinator 106
Garcia, E.; Librarian 156
Garcia Gutierrez, A.; Director 655
Garcia Ortiz, I.; Librarian 522
Garcia, S.; Coordinator 186
Garfield, E.; President 793
Garson, G. D.; Director 812
van Garsse, Y. 142
Garza, G.; Director 515
Gaskell, E.; Head 25
Gavryck, J.; Acting Head 828
vanGeel, H. J. C.; Librarian 541

Gehrke, U.; Head of Department   349
Gellerstam, M.; Director   678
Gerbeau, H.; Director   295
Ghaffar, A. S. A.   268
Ghosh, A. K.; Librarian   403
Giacaman, M.; Head Librarian   214
Giles-Peters, L.; Coordinator   124
Glenn, J. R.   804
Gober, L.   393
Goff, F.; President   781
Goff, R. C.; Director   867
Goldrian, G.; Head   355
Golland, R.; Head   734
Gomez, M.-L. E.; Director   108
Gomez Villa, O. F.; Executive Director
      227
Gonçalves, M. I.; Director   535
González Vega, D.; Public Services
      Director   635
Gopalakrishnan, N. K.; Chief, Library &
      Documentation   423
Gourd, F.; Head   318
Gowtham, M. S.; Senior Documentation
      Officer   432
Goyal, M. M.; Librarian   429
Granick, L.; Director   818
Graulich, P.   152
Gray, A.; Data Archivist   779
Green, A.; Chief, Library and Population
      Information Services Unit   77
Green Zevallos, F.; Chief   588
Greene, R.; Director   196
Griffin, F.; Chief Librarian   584
Griffon, M.; Director   327
Grijpma, J.; Publishing Manager   727
Gromek, A.; Acting Director   624
Guerrero, A. C.; Director   11
Guignard, M.; Délégué général   287
Guira, I.; Director   643
Gupta, S. R.; Chief   409
Gutman, P.; Director   95
Guy, L.   858

H

Haellquist, K. R.; Head   61
Hagen Andersen, K.; Head of Library   571
Häggström, N.   686
Hake, D. A.; Director   855
Hanamura, N.; Chief   481
Hankinson, R.; Editor   817
Hansen, C. K.; Secretary   261
Haque, S.; Chief Librarian   136
Harju-Khadr, M.-L.; Librarian   282
Harris, R. M.; President   816
Hart, D. R.; Librarian   742
van Hartevelt, J. H. W.; Head   548
Hasenbalg, C. A.   158

Hastings, P. K.   64
Havlik, P.; Database Administrator   134
Hawkwood, B. B.; Managing Editor   759
Hayward, J.; Director   566
Hedlin, E. W.; Branch Chief   811
Heerma van Voss, A. J.   551
Heidemann, E.; Director   366
Heiniger; Librarian   181
Helseth, A.; Librarian   572
Henao Jaramillo, A.; Director   234
Henning, C. G.; Director   653
Henrichs, N.; Head   365
Henrichsen, B.; Director   574
Henrichsen, B.; Executive Director   576
Hentgen, C; Responsable de l'Informatio
      et de l'Education au Développement
      308
Hermansen, D.; Librarian   577
Hermosilla-Palma, E.   218
Hernández Acosta, S.; Director   520
d'Hertefelt, M.; Head of Department   14
Hidekazu, E.; Director   477
Hien, T.; Director   176
Hilliard; Information Officer and
      Librarian   735
Hilton, R.   769
Hohnholz, J.; Director   359
Hoppes, M.; Law Librarian   770
Hossain, M.; Director General   138
How, A.   10
· Howe, S. R.; Director   836
Huck, B. J.; Head   350
Hudon, G. A. J.; Director General   881
Huizer, G.   547
Humayn Kabir, Md.; Director   139
Hunke, H.; Secretary General   45
Hunt, C. J.; Librarian   721
Husmann, R.   341
Hussain, M.; Director   582
Huszár, H.; Director General   388
Hutcheson, J. D.; Director   786
Hvidt, K.; Head   257

I

Ibañez, M. E.; Director   526
Igumnova, N.; Director   880
Iibuchi, Y.   485
Ipsilante, V.; Director   641
Ipsilante, V.; Head   642
Ireland, C. M.; Librarian   723
Isaza, V. G.; Librarian   19
Ishii, Y.; Director   487
Iskra, V.; Director   171
Ismail, Osman S. A.; Director   639
Ito, T.; Director   478

ministrative law
INDIA *416*
ministrative sciences
ARGENTINA *11, 90, 92, 101, 104,*
  105, 111, 112, 113
AUSTRALIA *119*
AUSTRIA *129, 130, 132*
BANGLADESH *138*
BELGIUM *25, 47, 142, 143, 151, 153*
BERLIN (WEST) *371*
BOLIVIA *155*
BRAZIL *160, 161, 163*
BULGARIA *168, 169, 174*
CANADA *188, 195, 197, 198*
CHILE *216, 217, 224*
COLOMBIA *19, 83, 226, 228, 232,*
  234
CZECHOSLOVAKIA *254, 255*
DENMARK *257, 258, 259*
EL SALVADOR *274, 275*
ETHIOPIA *59*
FINLAND *279, 280*
FRANCE *29, 290, 295, 311, 312,*
  313, 318, 320, 326
GERMANY (FEDERAL REPUBLIC) *349,*
  353, 360
GHANA *373*
HUNGARY *388, 391, 392, 393*
INDIA *394, 402, 407, 411, 412,*
  414, 423, 428, 429, 434, 437,
  446
INDONESIA *454*
IRELAND *35*
ISRAEL *460*
ITALY *467, 468*
JAPAN *66, 478, 491, 497, 499*
KENYA *503*
KOREA (REPUBLIC) *505*
MEXICO *516, 524, 525, 533*
MOROCCO *4*
NETHERLANDS *36, 557*
NIGERIA *568*
PERU *588, 590, 592, 593, 594*
PHILIPPINES *606*
POLAND *608, 618, 620, 621*
SENEGAL *2, 650*
SPAIN *656, 659*
SRI LANKA *668*
SUDAN *669, 670, 671*
SWEDEN *679, 681*

SWITZERLAND *48, 691, 694*
THAILAND *701, 702, 703, 704*
TRINIDAD AND TOBAGO *32, 709, 710*
TUNISIA *57, 711*
TURKEY *714*
U. S. A. *67, 70, 791, 799, 803,*
  809, 819, 828, 831, 832, 840,
  841, 842, 861
U. S. S. R. *870*
UGANDA *717*
UNITED KINGDOM *719, 726, 728, 732,*
  734, 737, 738, 749, 750
URUGUAY *752, 757, 758*
VENEZUELA *884*
YUGOSLAVIA *890*
ZAIRE *893*
ZAMBIA *894*
Adolescent
FRANCE *14*
PHILIPPINES *601*
U. S. A. *849*
Adult education
CHILE *222*
CZECHOSLOVAKIA *33*
Aggression
U. S. A. *776*
Agricultural development
FRANCE *331*
MADAGASCAR *508*
NETHERLANDS *542*
POLAND *622*
THAILAND *30*
TRINIDAD AND TOBAGO *708*
UNITED KINGDOM *724*
Agricultural economics
FRANCE *322, 331*
HUNGARY *389*
INDIA *418*
PHILIPPINES *605*
TRINIDAD AND TOBAGO *708*
U. S. A. *787, 801*
UNITED KINGDOM *724*
Agricultural policy
FRANCE *331*
SWITZERLAND *51*
Agriculture
ARGENTINA *90, 108*
AUSTRALIA *128*
BANGLADESH *15, 136*
BOLIVIA *155*
BRAZIL *165*
CAMEROON (UNITED REPUBLIC) *180*
COTE D'IVOIRE *241*
FIJI *278*
FRANCE *331*
IRAQ *73*
IRELAND *456*
ITALY *39, 466*

Z

Zaire *643*